KU-624-706

FUNDAMENTALS OF MANAGEMENT:

A Framework for Excellence

Fundamentals of Management:

A Framework for Excellence

Donald S. Miller
EMPORIA STATE UNIVERSITY

Stephen E. Catt
EMPORIA STATE UNIVERSITY

James R. Carlson
MANATEE COMMUNITY COLLEGE

WEST PUBLISHING COMPANY
MINNEAPOLIS/ST. PAUL NEW YORK SAN FRANCISCO LOS ANGELES

■ Production Credits

Cover Image   ©Romilly Lockyer/The Image Bank
Chapter Opening Art and Text Design   Roslyn M. Stendahl, Dapper Design
Copyedit   Mary George
Figure Illustrations   Nancy Wirsig McClure, Hand-to-Mouse Arts
Photo Research   Beaura K. Ringrose
Composition   Parkwood Composition
Index   Bernice Eisen

■ WEST'S COMMITMENT TO THE ENVIRONMENT

In 1906, West Publishing Company began recycling materials left over from the production of books. This began a tradition of efficient and responsible use of resources. Today, 100% of our legal bound volumes are printed on acid-free, recycled paper consisting of 50% new paper pulp and 50% paper that has undergone a de-inking process. We also use vegetable-based inks to print all of our books. West recycles nearly 22,650,000 pounds of scrap paper annually—the equivalent of 187,500 trees. Since the 1960s, West has devised ways to capture and recycle waste inks, solvents, oils, and vapors created in the printing process. We also recycle plastics of all kinds, wood, glass, corrugated cardboard, and batteries, and have eliminated the use of polystyrene book packaging. We at West are proud of the longevity and the scope of our commitment to the environment.

West pocket parts and advance sheets are printed on recyclable paper and can be collected and recycled with newspapers. Staples do not have to be removed. Bound volumes can be recycled after removing the cover.

Production, Prepress, Printing and Binding by West Publishing Company.

British Library Cataloguing-in-Publication Data. A catalogue record for this book is available from the British Library.

COPYRIGHT ©1996   By WEST PUBLISHING COMPANY
610 Opperman Drive
P.O. Box 64526
St. Paul, MN 55164-0526

All rights reserved

Printed in the United States of America

03 02 01 00 99 98 97 96   8 7 6 5 4 3 2 1 0

Library of Congress Cataloging-in-Publication Data

Miller, Donald S. (Donald Stanley), 1942–
    Fundamentals of management : a framework for excellence / Donald
S. Miller, Stephen E. Catt, James Carlson.
        p.   cm.
    Includes bibliographical references and index.
    ISBN 0-314-06231-9 (hard : alk. paper). — ISBN 0-314-06230-0
(soft : alk. paper)
    1. Management.   I. Catt, Stephen E.   II. Carlson, James.
III. Title.
HD31.M4377   1996
658—dc20

95-30795
CIP

DEDICATION

To Linda and Mabel, for their patience, encouragement, and assistance—DSM

To my mother, Virginia Mae Catt—SEC

To Val, for her encouragement and support—JRC

Brief Contents

Contents

PART II   *FUNCTIONS OF MANAGEMENT   141*

CHAPTER *6*

Organizing   176

CHAPTER 7
**Staffing and
Training**   210

CHAPTER 8

Leading   246

CHAPTER *9*
Controlling   282

To the Instructor

■ Why a New Management Text?

Just as the business world has become more complex and challenging, so has the job of preparing today's students to be the managers of tomorrow. The American Assembly of Collegiate Schools of Business acknowledges this challenge and has provided guidelines to encourage the development of curriculum in all business disciplines. As a result, many business schools are evaluating how they have traditionally taught the first course in management. We believe textbooks should be a partner in this educational evolution. Unfortunately, today's principles of management texts have grown to be overreaching and rigid in their presentation and format. Recently, there has been a backlash against this group of texts and shorter, less encyclopedic texts have been produced. These texts tend to take a very broadbrush approach to the subject, attempting to address all of the topics included in the bigger texts without their depth of coverage.

In *Fundamentals of Management: A Framework for Excellence,* we have produced an instructional package that offers a clear alternative to either of these two approaches. We want students to leave the course fully grounded in the fundamentals of management. To accomplish this, we worked backward, in a sense. We asked ourselves, "What core concepts are absolutely necessary for management students to master to prepare them for their later studies as well as their careers?" From that brainstorming session came the first 13 chapters of this text. They contain in-depth coverage of what we believe should be included in the first course in the study of management. However, we wanted to offer instructors the flexibility of adding to the core concepts those topics that fit the structure and tenor of their curriculum. Chapters 14–20 are therefore available from a database; any or all of these seven chapters can be produced for class, according to the individual instructor's needs.

The price of textbooks has risen as instructional packages have become more complex. *Fundamentals of Management* is available in three formats: hardback, paperback, and loose-leaf. The last format offers a flexibility and price that should meet the needs of both instructors and students.

You have in your hands a unique instructional package—one with a solid framework from which to build a course plan to meet the needs of students. We hope you are as excited about the concept as we are. As you delve into the text, feel free to share any feedback or suggestions you may have with us or your West representative. Your suggestions will ensure continuous improvement of the text for future management students.

Donald S. Miller   *Stephen E. Catt*   *James R. Carlson*

Preface

As we approach the year 2000, increased complexity, rapid change, and greater customer expectations will characterize the business world. Thus, the job of a manager will involve attainment of goals in a highly challenging business environment. We have designed *Fundamentals of Management: A Framework for Excellence* to include traditional management concepts and also to accommodate the growing interest in the field of business management in product and service quality, teamwork, globalism, empowerment, and human-resource issues. In addition, we have highlighted the importance of communication skills as an essential aspect of successful management.

Our main goal is to provide comprehensive treatment of contemporary management topics, which are discussed from a practical perspective with abundant use of examples to illustrate key points. In this way, we provide a framework on which to build an understanding of the evolving field of management. *Fundamentals of Management* enables students to gain essential insights about management and to understand and learn to apply their knowledge of management issues in real-world situations.

■ *Organization of the Text*

Based on our framework design, the text contains four parts: "An Overview of Management," "Functions of Management," "The Managerial Environment," and "Managerial Challenges."

■ Part One identifies the nature of management and its role in the workplace, describes philosophies of management, introduces the role of communication in the management process, and explains managerial decision making.

■ Part Two presents a comprehensive treatment of management functions. This approach provides students with a solid understanding of managerial duties and responsibilities before they are introduced to the more extensive discussions of the managerial environment and managerial challenges.

■ Part Three examines several topics that managers must understand to succeed in the ever-changing world of business. These topics include motivating job performance, social responsibilities and ethics, international management, and production/operations management.

■ Part Four looks at the challenges encountered by modern managers. Topics discussed in this last part, which is available in a flexible module format, include working with groups, managing change and conflict, employee-management relations, promoting job satisfaction and productivity, human-resource issues, current trends in management, and preparing for management careers.

■ Special Features

With its emphasis on presentation of contemporary coverage, *Fundamentals of Management* incorporates a number of special features to enhance its usefulness for both instructors and students.

■ *Integrated Communication Theme*   Communication is recognized as a topic of importance to managers. From presidents to supervisors, managers frequently indicate that problems related to ineffective communication create difficulties for them. In addition to a chapter on communication (Chapter 3), coverage of this topic is integrated into chapters throughout the book.

■ *Remember to Communicate Boxes*   These boxed sections highlight key points and help students retain a focus on communication considerations.

■ *Creative Module Format*   We recognize that instructors wish to have discretion in selecting content for classroom presentation. Consequently, Chapters 14–20 are available in a creatively designed module format. This approach offers instructors flexibility in choosing chapters according to individual preferences.

■ *Learning Objectives*   Most management texts include a list of learning objectives and make no further references to them, but this text explores each objective and repeats it in the Looking Back section.

■ *Looking Back*   In each chapter, this section repeats the learning objectives and briefly summarizes each of them.

■ *Real-World Applications*   Each chapter opens with an introductory discussion of a real-world application related to a key concept presented in the chapter. This feature provides a relevant illustration of why the content to be studied is important.

■ *Consider This*   All chapters include boxed sections with thought-provoking questions. Instructors can use the questions in these boxes to stimulate class discussions or as homework exercises.

■ *Think About It*   Every chapter contains a list of relevant points to consider. This feature emphasizes practical applications of the content and provides a method to reinforce the value of reading the chapter assignments.

■ *A Perspective on Quality*   Quality awareness is essential for success in today's business environment, and this topic is integrated throughout the text. In addition, all chapters feature boxes to emphasize the importance of quality to managers.

■ *Global View*   The interesting and informative material contained in these boxes helps students to recognize the pervasiveness of the growing globalization of business. These features show students how the management concepts they are learning are applied in other countries or how management issues are handled differently.

■ *Critical Thinking Incidents*   Every chapter features several critical-thinking case exercises. These incidents focus on realistic situations, promote insight into management issues, and give students opportunities to develop problem-solving capabilities. To formulate answers, students are challenged to think critically and apply their reasoning skills.

■ Supplements

A comprehensive package of user-friendly supplements accompanies the book. These materials are designed to assist instructors and to help students reinforce what they learn about management in this text.

■ **Instructor's Resource Manual** The authors have prepared a comprehensive Instructor's Resource Manual to serve the needs of instructors. For each chapter of the book, the manual includes an overview, teaching objectives, an outline, a list of key terms, a detailed chapter summary (including teaching hints and additional suggested readings), answers to review and discussion questions, and answers to Critical Thinking Incidents.

■ **Computerized Test Bank** Prepared by Jon Kalinowski of Mankato State University, the test bank includes an extensive variety of true-or-false, multiple-choice, and fill-in-the-blank questions. The multiple-choice questions are keyed as to difficulty level, are classified by type of question (recall, comprehension, or application), and are referenced to the applicable page(s) in the text.

■ **Study Guide** The Study Guide is available in both English and Spanish. Written by Harold C. Babson of Columbus State Community College and Murray S. Brunton of Central Ohio Technical College, the guide features an innovative arrangement of chapter outlines that corresponds to the learning objectives for each chapter in the text. The format also includes, on a chapter-by-chapter basis, key study questions, chapter overviews, objective questions keyed to learning objectives, and a review of important terms. In addition, the Study Guide incorporates creative concept applications, skill-practice exercises, and individual and group case assessments.

■ **Transparency Acetates** These color acetates highlight major concepts presented in the text. For easy usage, they are coordinated to accompany the textbook presentation and are available to adopters. Transparency masters are also available.

■ **Video Cases** These cases bring an extra dimension of interest to classroom instruction. They are designed to reinforce the concepts presented in the text and to give students opportunities to apply their knowledge to resolve practical, real-world business problems.

■ **Simulation Software** The Complete Manager simulation software walks the student through multiple managerial situations encountered in business. It can be used in group or individual instruction.

■ Acknowledgments

Many individuals, including managers and employees from numerous organizations, have provided ideas and suggestions that we have incorporated into the text. In addition, we give special thanks to the following reviewers for their advice, comments, and recommendations.

David Aiken
Hocking Technical College

Robert J. Ash
Rancho Santiago College

Hal Babson
Columbus State Community College

Lorraine P. Bassette
Prince George Community College

James H. Brewster
University of Central Oklahoma

Duane C. Brickner
South Mountain Community College

Charles Burney
San Jacinto College-South

Roosevelt D. Butler
Trenton State College

David W. E. Cabell
McNeese State University

Pamela Chandler
University of Mary Hardin-Baylor

Ronald J. Collins
West Virginia State College

Noble Deckard
University of Mary Hardin-Baylor

Richard J. Dick
Missouri Western State College

Max E. Douglas
Indiana State University

C. S. Everett
Des Moines Area Community College

Arthur K. Fisher
Pittsburg State University

Dana T. Fogg
University of Tampa

Kathleen Ganley
Robert Morris College

Andrea Goehner
Catawba Valley Community College

Matthew Gross
Moraine Valley Community College

Edward Hamburg
Gloucester County College

Donald E. Harris
Oakton Community College

Paul Hegele
Elgin Community College

Sandy Jeanquart-Barone
Murray State University

Julius Kantor
Bauder College

George Kelley
Eric Community College

G. Scott King
Sinclair Community College

James M. Lahiff
University of Georgia

K. A. Mach
Irvine Valley Community College

Irving Mason
Herkimer County Community College

Carl J. Meskimen
Sinclair Community College

Peter J. Moutsatson
Montcalm Community College

Anthony Murphy
Hillsborough Community College

Stephanie Newport
Creighton University

John E. Pearson
Dabney S. Lancaster Community College

Donald Pettit
Suffolk Community College

Clifford C. Phifer
Tennessee Technical University

Allayne B. Pizzolatto
Nicholls State College

Joseph Platts
Miami-Dade Community College

Sandra Powell
Weber State College

Nick Sarantakes
Austin Community College

Tom Shaughnessy
Illinois Central College

Dawn Sheffler
Central Michigan University

Jane E. Siebler
Oregon State University

Nancy Smith
Vernon Regional Junior College

Shari Tarnutzer
Utah State College

Anthony Urbaniak
Northern State University

Philip Van Auken
Baylor University

Kitty Wilkinson
Southwest Missouri State University

Bob E. Wooten
Lamar University

We extend our sincere appreciation to the members of our West Publishing team, who are professionals in every sense of the word: John Szilagyi, acquiring editor; Susan Smart, developmental editor; Mary Verrill, production editor; and Ann Hillstrom, promotion manager. Linda Miller deserves special recognition for her excellent work in typing the Instructor's Resource Manual.

Donald S. Miller   *Stephen E. Catt*   *James R. Carlson*

PART ONE

AN OVERVIEW OF MANAGEMENT

CHAPTER 1
Management and the Workplace

An introductory overview of management's role and the management process is presented. The chapter discusses each level of management and identifies key management concerns. The importance of effective communication and quality in the work environment and of growing globalization in the marketplace is emphasized.

CHAPTER 2
Philosophies of Management

This chapter describes how the field of modern management has evolved since the Industrial Revolution. A primary focus is on the wealth of knowledge to be learned from our management predecessors.

CHAPTER 3
The Role of Communication

The importance of communication to managers is emphasized. In addition to describing the communication process, this chapter discusses how to develop listening skills. Various communication techniques and patterns are explained.

CHAPTER 4
Decision Making

This chapter emphasizes the role of managers as decision makers and identifies the steps in the decision-making process. The topic of creativity is introduced, and suggestions for encouraging creativity in the workplace are presented. The emerging use of information technology is also discussed.

CHAPTER **1**

MANAGEMENT AND
THE WORKPLACE

■ LEARNING OBJECTIVES

To assist you in understanding the chapter content, each chapter of this text will include learning objectives. The purpose of this chapter is to help you to comprehend the nature of management and to recognize characteristics of today's workplace. This chapter also provides a foundation for the study of topics in greater detail in subsequent chapters. The learning objectives for this chapter are to:

- Explain the nature of management.
- Identify functions included in the management process.
- Differentiate among the levels of management.
- Describe the importance of communication in the workplace.
- Discuss the various managerial roles.
- Specify four types of managerial skills.
- Identify key management concerns.
- Recognize the forces that influence the business environment.
- Discuss the characteristics of an increasingly diverse workplace.

■ CHAPTER OUTLINE

THE REAL WORLD   *The Rags-to-Riches Story of Wal-Mart*

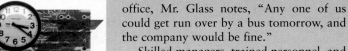

From its humble beginning in Arkansas during the early 1960s, Wal-Mart grew to become the nation's leading retailer in the United States. By 1993, some 2500 stores were generating more than $67 billion in sales and $2 billion in profits. Financial analysts project that the company's sales will increase at a rate of 18 percent for each remaining year in the 1990s. *Fortune*'s corporate reputations survey has consistently cited Wal-Mart among the top general merchandisers due to the quality of its management.

At Wal-Mart, there is no showy display of corporate greatness. The Bentonville, Arkansas, headquarters is identified simply as the "home office," and its executive offices overlook a parking lot. Top managers spend much of their time traveling to stores and talking with employees. Company identification badges contain only photos and first names. David Glass, President and Chief Executive Officer, succeeded the legendary founder Sam Walton. The philosophy of Glass evidences the culture of the firm. "We have no superstars," Glass states. "We have average people operating in an environment that encourages everyone to perform way above average." Company managers practice "servant leadership," which stresses providing workers with the necessary support (including merchandise to sell, information, and encouragement) to satisfy customer needs and then giving them the opportunity to get results.

What factors have contributed to the phenomenal growth and success of Wal-Mart? The firm practices proven business strategies and demonstrates a sensitivity to its customers. Stores feature an abundant variety of merchandise, instant exchanges or refunds without hassles, convenient shopping hours, ample customer parking, greeters stationed at entrances, and low prices. This approach enables the company to be fiercely competitive, especially during economic downturns when many customers focus on getting the best values for their shopping dollars. At each store, managers of various departments are expected to function as if they were operating their own businesses. In reference to executives at the home office, Mr. Glass notes, "Any one of us could get run over by a bus tomorrow, and the company would be fine."

Skilled managers, trained personnel, and concern for customers are hallmarks of the Wal-Mart success story. In the years ahead, it will be interesting to observe the company's progress as it expands to establish new outlets within the United States and also grows internationally. Wal-Mart's regard for human resources is noteworthy. According to Glass, "Our grass-roots philosophy is that the best ideas come from people on the firing line."

Wal-Mart became the world's largest retailer by operating stores, supercenters, and warehouse membership clubs. Efficient and innovative management practices contribute to the firm's impressive success in a very competitive market.

ADAPTED FROM: "How Companies Rank in 42 Industries," *Fortune* (February 7, 1994), p. 92; "Leaders of the Most Admired," *Fortune* (January 29, 1990), p. 46; Ellen Neuborne, "Wal-Mart Wins with Folksy Approach," *USA Today* (December 12, 1990), pp. 1–2B; Bill Saporito, "And the Winner Is Still . . . Wal-Mart," *Fortune* (May 2, 1994), pp. 62–65, 68, 70.

AN OVERVIEW OF MANAGEMENT

You have experienced the results of managerial actions.

Each day, you view management in action. When you visit a grocery store, eat at a restaurant, or shop for clothing, you come into contact with employees and frequently with their managers. You have the opportunity to observe well-managed firms and, at times, may wonder whether some businesses *really* are managed at all. You form opinions about management and share them with others. You may buy at a particular store because your satisfaction is guaranteed and you face no hassles when you return merchandise. Another store may have lower prices but also may be staffed with sales clerks who have little, if any, knowledge about the products available for sale. Although you may not think about it, management determines return-and-allowance policies, pricing decisions, and skill requirements for sales personnel.

Management is both an art and a science. In this text, you will learn about different philosophies of management and the factors that influence decision-making practices. Although studying about management will enhance your ability to be a good manager, it does not guarantee your success. Managerial success depends on a combination of knowledge, experience, and, most important, an understanding of human behavior. This chapter presents an overview of management, describes managerial roles and skills, and discusses key management concerns. It also provides you with insights into the characteristics of today's workplace.

WHAT IS MANAGEMENT?

What is management?

Management involves the effective use of human, equipment, and information resources to achieve objectives, which include making a profit, meeting customer needs, and expanding the firm's market share. Employees seek job satisfaction, opportunities for advancement, adequate working conditions, and equitable salaries. Therefore, management faces complex challenges that may often necessitate compromises. For example, to increase profits, it may be necessary to raise prices; however, higher prices can result in fewer sales. Significant declines in sales can cause layoffs, reduced work hours, or lower salaries.

In every firm, management is a critical element. Peter F. Drucker, a noted management expert, considered management to be "a multipurpose organ that manages a business *and* manages managers *and* manages workers and work."[1] Even though the management of a small hardware store is much different than the management of a giant corporation, its importance cannot be underestimated. Richard L. Daft defines management as, "the attainment of organizational goals . . . through planning, organizing, leading, and controlling organizational resources."[2] How well each of these activities is performed is the real measure of managerial success.

Why do formal organizations exist?

Formal organizations, which are an inherent part of our everyday lives, are necessary for several reasons.[3] They serve society, enable objectives to be reached, help to preserve knowledge, and provide jobs. We depend on police and fire departments and the military to protect us against disastrous and feared events. Without formal organizations, products used in everyday life would not exist. In addition, formal organizations provide a way to preserve the records of our society's achievements and help us attain a standard of living that would otherwise not be possible.

■ *The Management Process*

What are the functions of management?

The management process consists of five functions that assist the firm in reaching its objectives. Figure 1–1 shows these functions: planning, organizing, staffing, leading, and controlling. Even though these functions are carried out by all managers, the time allocated to them varies considerably. As shown in Figure 1–2, planning and organizing consume most of upper management's time; lower-level management devotes the most time to leading and controlling.

Later chapters will focus on specific details about each management function. For now, you should strive to understand the terminology and gain an overview of the interrelationships among the five management functions.

■ **Planning** relates to setting goals, formulating policies, and establishing procedures.

■ **Organizing** is grouping tasks and assigning authority.

■ **Staffing** is concerned with the recruitment, selection, and training of personnel.

■ **Leading** involves the provision of instructions and guidance to employees.

■ **Controlling** focuses on determining if actions conform to expectations. The controlling function includes setting standards, reviewing work performance, and correcting deviations.

Figure 1–3 illustrates activities related to the various functions of management.

A firm's success depends on how well the five functions of management are performed. Although textbook presentations usually discuss each of these functions in a separate chapter, they are interrelated. Assume your employer plans to introduce a new product, complete the development of a production plan, and organize work activities for each department. Everything will not necessarily proceed as scheduled. Controls might be flawed, allowing product defects to occur; workers may not be sufficiently skilled; or managers might give inaccurate directions.

Review Figure 1–3, and notice the final enumerated item for each function. Regardless of how much thought and effort go into an activity, a lack of or

Outcomes depend on how well functions are performed.

■ **FIGURE 1–2** Comparison of Time Spent in Performing Functions by Upper Management and First-Line Managers

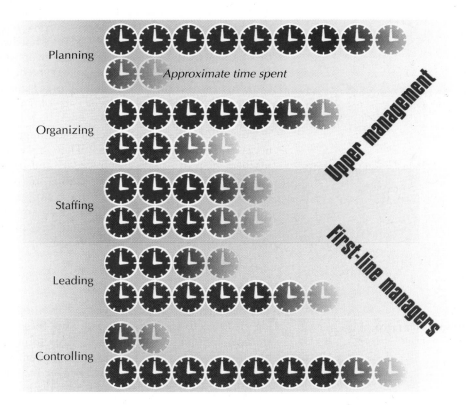

■ **FIGURE 1–3**   The Five Functions of Management

Planning

1. Perform self-audit; determine the present status of the organization.

2. Survey the environment.

3. Set objectives.

4. Forecast future situation.

5. State actions and resource needs.

6. Evaluate proposed actions.

7. Revise and adjust the plan in light of control results and changing conditions.

8. Communicate throughout the planning process.

Controlling

1. Establish standards.

2. Monitor results and compare to standards.

3. Correct deviations.

4. Revise and adjust control methods in light of control results and changing conditions.

5. Communicate throughout the control process.

Organizing

1. Identify and define work to be performed.

2. Break work into duties.

3. Group duties into positions.

4. Define position requirements.

5. Group positions into manageable and properly related units.

6. Assign work to be performed, accountability, and extent of authority.

7. Revise and adjust the organizational structure in light of control results and changing conditions.

8. Communicate throughout the organizing process.

Staffing

1. Determine human resource needs.

2. Recruit potential employees.

3. Select from the recruits.

4. Train and develop the human resources.

5. Revise and adjust the quantity and quality of the human resources in light of control results and changing conditions.

6. Communicate throughout the staffing process.

Leading

1. Communicate and explain objectives to subordinates.

2. Assign performance standards.

3. Coach and guide subordinates to meet performance standards.

4. Reward subordinates based on performance.

5. Praise and censure fairly.

6. Provide a motivating environment by communicating the changing situation and its requirements.

7. Revise and adjust the methods of leadership in light of control results and changing conditions.

8. Communicate throughout the leadership process.

SOURCE: Leslie W. Rue and Lloyd L. Byars, *Management: Skills and Application,* 6th ed. (Homewood, IL: Richard D. Irwin, 1992), p. 7. © 1992 Richard D. Irwin, Inc. All rights reserved. Reprinted with permission.

poor communication hinders accomplishment. Furthermore, carelessness creates undesired complications. To illustrate, *The Wall Street Journal's* Chicago news bureau inadvertently received a facsimile transmission of a top-secret document that outlined a corporate acquisition plan proposed by a Minnesota-based company. How did such an event happen? Apparently the *Journal's* fax number is quite similar to the number of the intended receiver, a major stock-holder, and a new employee entered the wrong number.[4]

■ *Managers: Who Are They?*

A manager has diverse responsibilities.

A **manager** guides the activities of others in order to reach organizational goals. The responsibilities of managers are diverse and include formulating plans, making decisions, appraising job performances, and developing teamwork. In practice, managers are different things to different people. To subordinates, they are bosses; to customers, they are ultimately responsible for product quality and satisfaction. You are probably aware that managers spend vast amounts of time dealing with other people's problems. Unfortunately, problems must be dealt with as soon as they occur and are frequently quite unpredictable.

> Thus, managerial work is hectic and fragmented and requires the ability to shift continually from person to person, from one subject or problem to another. It is almost the diametric opposite of the studied, analytical, persisting work pattern of the professional who expects and demands closure: the time to do a careful and complete job that will provide pride of authorship.[5]

How are managers chosen?

As a rule, managers are chosen because of demonstrated job capabilities. Supervisors, or first-line managers, are selected because of their records as employees, and the process continues on up the managerial hierarchy. Managers acquire experiences at each management level that prepare them to handle increasingly greater responsibilities at the next level. Technical competence, by itself, cannot assure managerial success because the essence of a manager's work is to accomplish tasks through other employees. An analysis comparing a sample of 50 company presidents to a college graduate normative group revealed that the presidents tended to be "more dynamic and more assertive and seemed to have more positive attitudes toward other people."[6] Of course, the results of one survey are not conclusive, but the main point is that capable managers demonstrate excellent human relations skills.

Managers wear many hats. They must be prepared to respond to a wide variety of circumstances which often involve unexpected events or problems.

Managers are "responders." People who want to have control of their work lives are not apt to like managing, which involves numerous pressure circumstances.[7] Deadlines, crises, commitments to failing courses of action, and accidents are among the concerns that require a manager's attention. To meet such challenges, managers must have the temperament, judgment, and insight to provide remedies and avoid further complications. It is inappropriate to conclude that workers always work and managers always manage. At times, managers must willingly "pitch in" to do whatever needs to be done. For example, a line manager of a convenience store, or even its owner, may have to "cover" a shift because an employee is absent. Whenever strikes occur, managers are expected to perform a variety of nonmanagerial duties.

■ Levels of Management

Many differences are apparent among firms. They vary in terms of sales revenues, organizational structure, number of employees, and types of goods produced or services performed. For example, Richard L. Gelb is Chairman and Chief Executive Officer of Bristol-Meyers Squibb, a corporation that consists of four core businesses and employs a worldwide sales force of almost 14,000 people. In another example, Chrysler has several major divisions and many employees, but the entire management and staff of a local retailer may consist of fewer than ten persons. Figure 1–4 shows the three levels of management and representative job titles for each level.

TOP MANAGEMENT   **Top management** has the overall responsibility for a firm's activities. Top managers are referred to by such titles as chief executive officer, president, and senior vice president. At this level, major duties include setting goals, developing policies, and formulating strategies. Much of a top manager's time is spent attending meetings with other top- and middle-level executives and dealing with groups and individuals outside the firm: major customers, the external community, and regulatory or government agencies.

At times, superhuman traits are ascribed to outstanding corporate leaders. Yet all of them possess considerable foresight and energy, as well as human frailties. Thomas Watson, Sr., who built IBM into a firm known throughout the world, is widely proclaimed to be one of history's great corporate leaders. Peter F. Drucker observes

> He had a vision—he *was*. But unlike most seers, Watson *acted* on his vision. . . . Without Watson and his vision, the computer would have emerged as a "tool" rather than as a "technology." . . . Watson was a generous leader but a demanding boss and not one bit permissive. But he demanded the right things: dedication and performance to high standards. He was irascible, vain, opinionated, a publicity hound, and an incorrigible name-dropper.[8]

MIDDLE MANAGERS   **Middle managers** convert policies and strategies set forth by top management into specific operational guidelines for implementation by first-line managers. Sometimes called "managers of managers," representative job titles for a middle-management position include division, plant, or operations manager.

Following years of growth, the number of middle managers started to decline during the 1980s. Mergers, reorganizations, and pressures to reduce

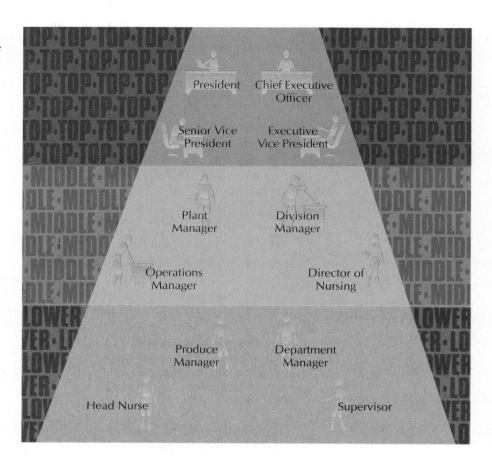

costs have contributed to the erosion of these positions. To illustrate, the Santa
Fe Railway had slightly over 32,000 employees and 14 divisions in 1981; by the
end of the decade, it employed 18,000 workers and had six divisions. During
the 1990s, announced cutbacks included nearly 15,000 employees at McDonnell Douglas, slightly over 10,000 workers at AT&T, and 8000 people at Digital Equipment Corporation.[9]

FIRST-LINE MANAGERS   Foreperson, crew chief, and supervisor are typical job
titles for **first-line managers,** who comprise the lowest level of management and
have direct contact with nonmanagerial personnel. **Supervisors** are "people in
the middle": they must respond to the concerns of their workers and also represent management's views to them. Compared to other managers, the supervisory sphere of responsibility is more restricted to include a certain shift or a particular department.

Supervisors are managers.

However, the importance of first-line managers should not be underestimated. Effective supervision is vital to a firm's success. Supervisors must be
skilled at understanding human behavior and applying management principles.
They are leaders who must demonstrate initiative, be flexible, and serve as role
models to subordinates. Supervisors must make judgments about such factors
as appearance, temperament, sensitivity to concerns, credibility, and knowledge
on a daily basis.[10]

1. Which function of the management process is most important?
2. How are people selected for managerial positions?
3. What level of management is most responsible for attaining organizational objectives?

■ *The Importance of Communication*

Communication is a vital concern.

Communication is the sharing of meaning between senders and receivers of messages. Although computer technology has increased the speed of data transmission, the value of excellent written, spoken, and nonverbal communication still remains. According to studies of executive communication, telephone calls and meetings were favored methods of communicating.[11] Henry Mitzberg notes that "brevity, fragmentation, and verbal communication characterize the work of managers."[12] At any managerial level, attention given to improving communication minimizes waste, conserves time, and promotes positive employee relations. A multiyear survey of 561 managers who participated in supervisory seminars identified many types of interpersonal problems, but "almost all of them related to either the [middle] manager's interference in the supervisor's job or to the perceived inability of the manager to communicate effectively with the supervisor."[13]

Thomas J. Peters and Robert H. Waterman, Jr., authors of *In Search of Excellence,* describe several attributes of communication in excellent companies.[14] Corporate communication tends to be informal and intense. It is given physical supports: blackboards are everywhere, and tables are arranged to encourage innovative interaction among employees. At Bechtel, for example, a portion of time is set aside for project managers to experiment with new ideas and concepts. Finally, the environment of these firms is characterized by informal checks as methods of control.

It is important for customers, employees, and the public to perceive a business or corporation in a positive light. In performing managerial roles, managers initiate and maintain relationships with many people and groups.

REMEMBER TO COMMUNICATE

Assumptions Can Be Misleading

The sharing of meaning is a key aspect of communication. Assumptions about the clarity of meaning can be misleading. The following examples show what happens if communication is vague.

Most states have departments of corrections to handle prison systems. In the early 1950s, the American Prison Association, a major professional group, revised its name and is now known as the American Correctional Association.

Do people understand what departments of corrections actually do? Apparently, confusion does exist. Some persons believe these agencies correct birth certificates, Social Security numbers, driver's licenses, housing-code violations, and even walkways clogged with plants. Two illustrations demonstrate the extent of these misunderstandings.

■ A deputy director of corrections spoke at his daughter's career day at school. He asked students what a department of corrections does. One student responded, "You fix snowmobiles."

■ In one state, the telephone directory indicates that the department of corrections is housed in the Stevens T. Mason building, named to honor the state's first governor. Some upset callers demanded to speak with Mr. Mason.

These examples indicate how functions of departments of correction are misunderstood. Similarly, a lack of understanding affects many aspects of business operations and relations with customers, employees, or the public. A failure to communicate complicates situations, causes frustrations, contributes to inappropriate responses, and needlessly consumes time. Therefore, managers must not overlook the importance of communication, which, if neglected, can create numerous problematic consequences.

ADAPTED FROM: John Bussey, "If This Story Needs Fixing, Don't Call Us—Just Call THEM," *The Wall Street Journal* (April 4, 1988), p. 1.

What are the five Ws of communication?

The five Ws of communication—who, what, when, where, and why—are important to all managers. Too often, managers assume workers can read their minds; consequently, needless mistakes and anxieties occur. For instance, you, as the manager, tell a subordinate, "Review the projects, select the most important one, and complete it as soon as possible." You have a perfectly clear understanding of what you want your employee to do. However, the subordinate may have another view as to which project is most important and may attach an entirely different interpretation of the word "soon." Remember, communication is a two-way process; it involves *both* the senders and the receivers of the messages.

REALITIES OF MANAGEMENT

Managers are busy people.

Based on the formal authority given to them, managers perform several roles. Henry Mintzberg's classification of these roles will be discussed in the following section. A firm's success depends on how well managerial roles are fulfilled. Managers must also apply communication, people, technical, and conceptual skills. In a short span of time, they make decisions about any variety of major and minor issues, discuss concerns of mutual interest with subordinates or colleagues, respond to customer requests, meet with representatives of organized labor, and review sales information.

■ *Managerial Roles*

Mintzberg identifies three managerial roles.

According to Mintzberg's widely accepted description, managers play interpersonal, informational, and decisional roles.[15] Figure 1–5 shows the representative duties associated with each of these managerial roles.

INTERPERSONAL ROLES   As you might expect, managers must interact with many people. Basically, they assume three primary **interpersonal roles.** In the **figurehead role,** managers represent the firm, division, or work unit at ceremonial functions. For instance, a president often "cuts the ribbon" at the grand opening of a major corporate facility, or a plant manager presents a gold watch to an employee who is retiring after many years of service. Although this role does not consume a lot of time, it is expected by subordinates and the public.

■ **FIGURE 1–5**
Managerial Roles

ADAPTED FROM: Henry Mintzberg, "The Manager's Job: Folklore and Fact," Eliza G. C. Collins, ed., *Executive Success: Making It in Management* (New York: Wiley, 1983), p. 421.

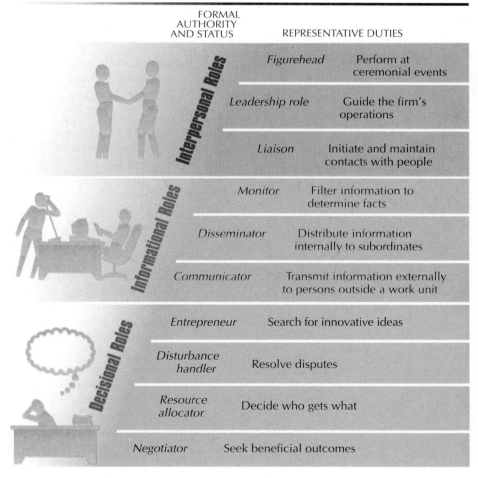

	FORMAL AUTHORITY AND STATUS	REPRESENTATIVE DUTIES
Interpersonal Roles	Figurehead	Perform at ceremonial events
	Leadership role	Guide the firm's operations
	Liaison	Initiate and maintain contacts with people
Informational Roles	Monitor	Filter information to determine facts
	Disseminator	Distribute information internally to subordinates
	Communicator	Transmit information externally to persons outside a work unit
Decisional Roles	Entrepreneur	Search for innovative ideas
	Disturbance handler	Resolve disputes
	Resource allocator	Decide who gets what
	Negotiator	Seek beneficial outcomes

In the **leadership role**—the most commonly recognized managerial role—managers are responsible for the operations of the firm, selection of personnel, training and development activities, and motivation of employees. As **liaisons,** managers initiate and maintain contacts with many persons inside and outside the firm. Executives cultivate relations with legislators and major customers; supervisors have contacts with local professional groups and other colleagues. Ideally, liaison relationships can enhance the firm's image and serve as a way to obtain advice and locate possible customers.

Information provides a basis for actions.

INFORMATIONAL ROLES Information is a key ingredient in influencing managerial actions. Mintzberg's study concluded that "chief executives spent 40 percent of their contact time on activities devoted exclusively to the transmission of information."[16] A multitude of information, both accurate and inaccurate, abounds in a company's internal and external environments.

Managers assume three types of **informational roles.** In the role of a **monitor,** managers filter information to glean pertinent facts. Also, they act as **disseminators,** telling some or all of what they learn to others. Finally, as a **communicator,** a manager selects information and transmits it to persons who are not direct subordinates. When IBM encountered difficulties and announced a major decline in sales, the general manager of its mainframe computer operations publicly acknowledged prior inaccurate market assessments and communicated the importance of seeking new markets for mainframe technology.

DECISIONAL ROLES Managers also assume four types of **decisional roles.** In the role of **entrepreneur,** managers respond to changes and seek new ways of doing things. When Alfred P. Sloan, Jr., a legendary leader at General Motors, assumed control of the company, a group of key executives headed units that had been their own companies a few years earlier.

> Everyone before Sloan had seen the problem as one of personalities, to be solved through a struggle for power from which one man would emerge victorious. Sloan saw it as a constitutional problem to be solved through a new structure—decentralization—which balances local autonomy in operations with central control of direction and policy.[17]

As **disturbance handlers,** managers respond to pressures they do not voluntarily initiate. A top executive has to explain the company's position on the alleged contamination of products or to respond to union threats of a strike. For example, many corporate leaders experienced opposition to business transactions in South Africa because of apartheid. Supervisors must resolve unexpected disputes among subordinates and may have to determine how to staff positions with fewer employees than desirable.

Managers make decisions.

As **resource allocators,** managers decide how resources are distributed within a firm. A key aspect of this role involves approving requests for equipment and personnel. The importance of allocating time is overlooked by some managers. Yet time is probably the most important resource at their disposal.[18]

Finally, managers are **negotiators.** They strive to attain outcomes that are advantageous for the firm. The negotiator seeks the best terms in a union contract or the most profit on a sales transaction. The ability to negotiate skillfully has a major impact on a firm's bottom line. Wise managers envision both the short-run and long-run consequences of negotiations. After becoming the chair-

Managers must serve customer needs. Mike Wright, CEO of Super Valu, Inc., recognizes the importance of meeting and exceeding customer expectations.

man of the Chrysler Corporation, Lee Iacocca averted the collapse of the firm by reducing its staff, gaining wage concessions, and securing finances, thereby initiating a turnaround that made the company competitive again.

■ *Managerial Skills*

There are four types of managerial skills.

Managers encounter a steady stream of challenges, and it is difficult, if not impossible, to satisfy all of the expectations placed on them. Communication, people, technical, and conceptual skills are quite relevant.

COMMUNICATION SKILLS   Throughout the text, the importance of **communication skills,** which stress the sharing of meaning, will be emphasized. During the past decade, significant advancements in the speed and processing of information transfer have occurred: cellular telephones; fax machines; and portable, laptop computers. Most agree, however, that the skillful application of communication skills by managers has not kept pace with the development of communication technology. In the 1960s, Peter F. Drucker commented, "Communications, by and large, are just as poor today as they were 20 or 30 years ago when we first became aware of the need for, or lack of, adequate communications in the modern organization."[19] Three decades later, Drucker's observation still has merit.

PEOPLE SKILLS   **People skills** involve abilities to lead, motivate, and understand the feelings and behaviors of others. Perhaps you have heard someone comment, "She really has people sense." The comment implies that this person demonstrates a respect for other people, a willingness to consider their views, and a receptive attitude toward their concerns. Those who possess people skills choose words carefully so they do not offend their listeners. To deny a request, it is easy to say, "No, your request is absurd." However, it is quite likely that this response will create hostile relations. It would be better to say, "I'm really sorry, but I cannot approve your request."

TECHNICAL SKILLS **Technical skills** relate to knowledge about the actual jobs that subordinates do. Supervisors must have considerable technical knowledge in order to give first-hand instructions to employees or correct their mistakes. Upper management needs to understand why certain equipment or resources are necessary. For example, a plant manager does not need to be a computer expert, but if he or she does not have a grasp of the rationale for computer usage, the firm is apt to be at a competitive disadvantage.

CONCEPTUAL SKILLS **Conceptual skills** involve the ability to consider abstract relationships. They help managers to formulate strategic plans and grasp the implications of change. Mike Wright, Chief Executive Officer of Super Valu stores, applies conceptual thinking and focuses decisions on concerns of his customers. In his Cub Food stores, customers select products from crated merchandise and sack their own groceries. However, by pushing a button located at the end of each aisle, they can learn the location of any item that they cannot find.[20] Even though solutions do not appear to be readily available, managers who possess conceptual abilities can envision how the "pieces fit."

CONSIDER THIS

1. How can managers learn to become better communicators?

2. Which managerial role is the most challenging one for managers to perform?

3. In the next decade, which managerial skill will be the most important for job success?

■ *Key Management Concerns*

Any list of management concerns is endless and includes both major and minor issues. Several of these concerns will be discussed here to increase your awareness of the challenges that today's managers encounter.

It is necessary for companies to produce valued goods or services and remain profitable. During the early 1990s, the number of bankrupt organizations grew considerably and caused much loss of employment. Efforts to increase employee job satisfaction and to retain well-trained, capable personnel have helped to avoid costly employee absenteeism and turnover. Today, quality is a major concern; inferior work, defective products, and excessive warranty claims translate into lost customers and high costs.

Are you efficient *and* effective?

EFFICIENCY AND EFFECTIVENESS Some people confuse the meanings of these two words. **Efficiency** implies proper performance of a task. **Effectiveness** refers to the initial selection of an appropriate task.

Assume it is a Monday. Your boss asks you to submit a budget request for new equipment and gives you a deadline of tomorrow night. You also need to complete appraisal forms for your subordinates by Friday. Which tasks will you do first? If you are effective, you will get started on the budget request. If you have never developed a budget and fail to ask relevant questions or review procedures before you begin, then you will be inefficient and will waste a consid-

A PERSPECTIVE ON QUALITY

Characteristics of Successful Managers

Although it is difficult to be "everything to everybody," successful managers possess a mix of capabilities. They must balance the need to meet company goals with their employees' desires for job satisfaction. Successful managers

- *Practice effective communication.* Managers offer guidance and issue directions; they also seek opinions, listen to others, and provide feedback. Skill in communicating is commonly regarded as a major managerial asset.

- *Use time wisely.* Time exists in a limited quantity. To accomplish tasks, managers must recognize the demands placed on them and schedule available time in order to maximize productive results.

- *Apply decision skills.* Capable decision makers use available information to weigh alternatives and identify opinions before they reach an ultimate decision.

- *Demonstrate positive attitudes.* According to an old adage, "Enthusiasm is contagious." Successful managers encourage subordinates to develop "can do" attitudes.

- *Are flexible.* Managers have many responsibilities and must adapt to a variety of circumstances. Within a short period of time, they may be called on to handle a customer complaint, discipline a worker, or conduct a meeting.

- *Provide leadership and a sense of direction for employees.* Successful managers make sure that personnel understand company objectives and know their job duties.

- *Value learning.* The business environment is constantly changing due to technological advancements, competitor reactions, and new products or services. Outstanding managers recognize the need to learn and apply new knowledge.

- *Emphasize the importance of quality.* Managers know that service or product quality is a priority consideration that is vital to organizational success in a competitive marketplace.

- *Appreciate workers as company assets.* The successful manager values workforce diversity and recognizes the role of human resources as an important organizational asset.

erable amount of time on trial-and-error solutions. As this example illustrates, you can be effective without being efficient.

In practice, some managers get bogged down in the details of their jobs and overlook the importance of their leadership roles. It is essential not to lose sight of organizational objectives, since they are crucial to job success. Pause and ask yourself, "Am I doing the *right* things?" If so, your efforts are focused in the correct direction and desired outcomes are more likely to occur. Then ask yourself, "Am I doing these things *properly?*" An affirmative response indicates your time is probably being allocated correctly.

The ability to be effective and efficient is often hindered by poor communication and inadequate work habits. Some people conclude telephone conversations only to discover they neglected to note time, place, or date information. This can easily be avoided by simply repeating relevant facts to the other party as a double-check before hanging up. Too frequently, inordinate amounts of time are lost because information is misplaced or not filed properly.

It is important to promote job satisfaction.

JOB SATISFACTION   A feeling of enjoyment or contentment toward a job is called **job satisfaction.** Managers do influence the amount of job satisfaction their subordinates experience. According to one study, high job satisfaction is associated with managers who practice good listening skills, demonstrate empathy, evidence emotional control, and accept criticism.[21] Inequity of rewards, failure to recognize employee efforts, or the perception of unreasonable work demands can ultimately lead to poor attitudes and loss of job interest among subordinates.

In the short run, managers may not be able to alter job designs or revise established procedures. However, they can be receptive to employee views, explain the reasons for existing organizational policies, and, whenever feasible, initiate recommendations for change. These practices demonstrate concern for employees and often serve to remedy small problems before they become major issues.

How is job satisfaction increased?

Other factors also promote job satisfaction. Employees like to do meaningful work that gives them the opportunity to apply their skills and talents. They prefer to have some flexibility in deciding how jobs are done. Pleasant working conditions, availability of needed tools or equipment, and provision of adequate training promote job contentment. Employees respond to a workplace atmosphere in which helpful attitudes prevail among colleagues. When this occurs, advice and positive criticism can be exchanged without fear of "losing face" or the perception of being a less-than-capable worker.

To encourage commitment, some companies have instituted no-layoff policies, which benefit both employees and employers. Employees have the assurance of job security and potential opportunities for career growth within the firm. Companies are more likely to keep managerial talent, retain the services of trained workers, and develop greater corporate loyalty. Hallmark Cards practices the redeployment of personnel; Federal Express reduces overtime to offset losses; and Lincoln Electric guarantees employment after three years of

Modern technology and effective communication are important concerns to managers. Productivity gains and quality improvements are closely related to business success. Here, a representative works at the 24-hour-per-day customer telephone center at Florida Power and Light Corp., a winner of the Deming Prize for Quality.

service. However, economic downturns can affect employment practices. In the early 1990s, the Digital Equipment Corporation was faced with the decision to make layoffs for the first time in the history of the company.[22]

PRODUCTIVITY   A measure of output per worker is called **productivity**. Compared to the previous two decades, American productivity grew more slowly in the 1980s. Yet the United States still leads other nations in terms of per-worker output today. By the late 1980s, however, the percentage of expenses allocated to research and development in this country began to lag behind Japan, West Germany, Britain, and France.[23] Much attention is now focused on the ability of American firms to be competitive in the next decade.

How can managers stimulate productivity? In addition to applying advanced technology, employees are sources for ideas and suggestions. Sometimes, efforts to reduce costs and increase profits erroneously neglect the human dimension.

> We are, in fact, discovering that "production" neither begins nor ends in the factory. Thus, the latest models of economic production extend the process both upstream and downstream—forward into aftercare or "support" for the product even after it is sold. . . . Similarly it [the company] may extend the definition backward to include such functions as training of the employee, provision of day care, and other services.[24]

Productivity does not just happen.

The concept of productivity must be understood and recognized throughout a firm. Progress requires demonstrated actions, not mere lip service, on behalf of all personnel. Ways to increase productivity include

- Evaluate job performance and do not accept shoddy work.
- Promote an efficient work environment and ensure that training practices are adequate. Recommendations for job restructuring can be an alternative to wasted time.
- Select personnel on the basis of job competency.
- Recognize employee contributions and reward outstanding performance. Excellent work is often taken for granted, until capable employees leave or assume duties with other departments of the firm.
- Understand objectives so that work efforts can be properly directed toward attaining them.
- Examine communication practices. Ineffective communication creates confusion and wastes time.[25]

All personnel affect productivity.

It is important for each worker to realize that his or her job performance directly contributes to organizational productivity. Suggestion systems, quality circles (periodic meetings to identify solutions to job problems), and rewards for cost-saving ideas represent sincere efforts to enhance productivity. Firms cannot disregard problems that are caused by needless mistakes in the workplace.

> Today, in most American industrial companies, making sure things are done right and fixing things that are wrong consumes 15 to 30 cents of every sales dollar. The figure is about 35 cents of every dollar in the typical service organization.[26]

There is no substitute for quality.

QUALITY   Forty years ago, Japanese products were not characterized as defect-free, dependable, or durable. Impressive progress has taken place, and the

A PERSPECTIVE ON QUALITY

Ten Commandments of Quality

1. There is no such thing as acceptable quality. It can always get better.
2. From the corner office to the shop floor, quality is everybody's business.
3. Keep your ears open. Some of the best ideas will come from the most unexpected sources.
4. Develop a detailed implementation plan. Talking about quality isn't enough.
5. Help departments work together. The territorial imperative is your biggest obstacle.
6. Analyze jobs to identify their elements and set quality standards for each step.
7. Take control of your process. You must know why something goes wrong.
8. Be patient. Don't expect gains to show up next quarter.
9. Make extraordinary efforts in unusual situations. Customers will remember those best.
10. Think beyond cutting costs. The benefits of improved quality should reach every part of the organization.

SOURCE: Joel Dreyfuss, "Victories in the Quality Crusade," *Fortune* (October 10, 1988), p. 84. © 1988 Time Inc. All rights reserved.

image of these products has changed. In a recent two-year period, defects per 100 Japanese cars sold in America declined by nearly 8 percent.[27] **Quality** implies an anticipated level of excellence or superiority. Quality is evidenced by reputations for excellence, positive organizational images, and feelings of pride on behalf of managers and workers.

W. Edwards Deming, who introduced quality control to the Japanese, was a well-known advocate of quality. His principles include emphasis on teamwork, training, and continued efforts to produce improved goods and services. Deming criticized American management techniques and observed, "We are all born with intrinsic motivation, self-esteem, dignity, and eagerness to learn. Our present system of management crushes all that out."[28]

An emphasis on quality has been quite beneficial for some firms. Florida Power and Light, America's first competitor for the esteemed Deming Prize, spent nearly $2.5 million to improve the company's reliability and productivity. These improvements contributed to increased profits of more than $13 million.[29] In a six-year period following emphasis on quality, defect-free supplies to Xerox Corporation increased by more than 7 percent.[30] At Centerior Energy, improved communication between managers and employees is an essential component of the total quality approach, which also underscores the role of quality in serving customers.

> High-quality performance is the surest way to succeed in an unforgiving marketplace. Increased sales, greater market share, and higher profits will follow when a corporation provides quality products and services at reasonable prices.[31]

By providing high-quality goods and services, a firm enhances its reputation, encourages repeat business, and maintains a competitive advantage in the marketplace.

UNDERSTANDING THE WORKPLACE

The workplace is changing.

Managers oversee a sequence of activities in which materials, information, or skills (inputs) are used to produce goods and services (outputs). Technological, economic, societal, and political forces influence the flexibility to manage. Also, managers must recognize the impact of internal departments or units (such as marketing, accounting/finance, personnel, and purchasing) on operations. In addition, actions by competitors frequently require managers to revise company plans and alter business strategies. Finally, managers will be faced with an increasingly diverse labor force in terms of age, gender, ethnicity, and education.

■ *The Business Environment*

How managers respond to events varies according to the circumstances. A firm with the desperate need to reduce expenses encounters a different challenge than a company that has just signed a lengthy, profitable contract to produce at its maximum level. Of necessity, managers must recognize the implications of forces in the business environment and be prepared to respond to them. Let's examine several of these environmental forces.

Technological advances are amazing.

TECHNOLOGICAL FORCES   Within a relatively short span of time, computers, dry copiers, and fax machines have altered the way in which people do things. In one minute, the Cray-2 supercomputer does the work that is accomplished by a personal computer in three weeks. Typists no longer use carbon paper to make duplicate copies of documents. Dry copiers can rapidly make multiple copies of papers and even produce them in color. A few years ago, many people had not even heard of fax machines; now millions of transmissions are faxed each day. By contrast, many businesses depend on toll-free 800 numbers to sell products, answer customer questions, and handle complaints.

Managers should respond to such **technological forces** in the business environment by thoughtfully considering and carefully analyzing the available technology. A company's commitment to adopt new technology may necessitate remodeling or rearranging facilities, increasing training costs, or facing higher maintenance fees. Various questions merit consideration: Is the investment worthwhile? How soon will the technology become obsolete? Does the purchase or lease affect the company's competitive position? If technological breakdowns occur, what alternatives are available?

Economic forces impact on the operating capabilities of a business.

ECONOMIC FORCES   Land, labor, and capital are used to produce goods and services. **Economic forces** (such as inflation or recession), interest rates, supply-and-demand factors, wage rates, and prices influence a firm's operating capability. Business decisions often involve much uncertainty, and managers may have a minimum amount of time available to them to make choices.

Consider the plight of an independent convenience-store operator who faces intense price competition from chains in an environment of volatile wholesale gasoline costs. The operator serves one locality. Therefore, profits and losses cannot be spread over a number of geographic locations. Several critical questions emerge. What will the next truckload of gasoline cost? Should the retail price be set below cost with an expectation of increased in-store sales (pop, cigarettes, candy, or other convenience items)? To maintain a desired profit margin, should the retail price of gasoline include the customary markup? If so, will customer traffic decline significantly?

SOCIETAL FORCES   Behavior is governed by society's values, beliefs, and traditions. Our heritage emphasizes the merit of hard work, honesty, and respect for individual rights. A concern for civil rights dominated the 1960s; the Watergate scandal and political ethics were major topics in the 1970s. In the view of many people, materialism was a major theme of the 1980s. While predicting the future is an inexact art, author Tom Wolfe says, "We are leaving the period of money fervor that was the eighties and entering a period of moral fever."[32]

Societal forces affect customer buying patterns and lifestyles. It has become commonplace to see men casually wearing baseball caps (even inside of buildings) and earrings. The use of credit cards has swelled; the Discover card is now competitive with Visa, MasterCard, and American Express. Alcohol and drug problems have emerged as a national concern. In turn, business and industry have assumed a more active role in reducing substance abuse in the workplace. The use of drug testing as an employment practice has generated much controversy.

POLITICAL FORCES   Federal, state, and local governments pass legislation stipulating what actions are deemed appropriate or unacceptable. Every business must comply with the laws established by these **political forces,** which can benefit as well as hinder a firm's interests. For example, federal legislation permitting a yearly tax deduction of up to $2000 for individual retirement accounts was a boon to the financial services industry. Several years later, the law was revised to restrict tax deductibility according to income levels. This action reduced commissions and fees earned on money flowing into IRA accounts. Government initiatives forced the breakup of corporate giant American Telephone and Telegraph (AT&T), deregulated the commercial airlines, and required the automobile industry to become more safety-conscious.

The hostility between the United States and Iraq illustrates how political forces affect businesses. Stock and commodity exchanges had to consider what to do in the event of war. To deploy personnel for Operation Desert Storm, employees who served as military reservists had to be called to active duty. The normal activities of firms doing business in the Persian Gulf region were disrupted, and international business travel declined.

Managers cannot neglect the realities of the political environment. To further self-interests, some organizations employ lobbyists who present their views to legislators. Top managers may negotiate with municipal governments for tax-break incentives. Supervisors must be sure health and safety laws are observed in the work environment and must comply with laws governing employment practices, especially ones dealing with antidiscrimination in the workplace.

INTERNAL FORCES   Each department or subunit of a firm has specific responsibilities. Personnel departments are involved with recruiting, keeping employee records, and administering professional development programs. Marketing departments focus on advertising and product promotion. Purchasing units process orders for materials and supplies.

Society has expectations.

The political environment cannot be ignored.

The departments or subunits of a firm have different perspectives.

To attain organizational objectives, the efforts of various departments and subunits need to be coordinated, and the importance of cooperation must be emphasized. For example, the interests of sales and credit personnel can conflict and create friction. The objective for salespeople is to generate sales, but the credit staff is most concerned about the collection of accounts.

At times, **internal forces** may challenge corporate goals, and management may need to deal with employees whose personal interests do not coincide with the attainment of organizational objectives. Priorities often require a greater allocation of money or human resources to one department than to others. When this occurs, justification and clear explanations help to preserve cooperative attitudes among organizational subunits. Excellent communication and human relations skills can prevent interdepartmental misunderstandings and retain the support of other managers who realize a decision is not in the best interests of their own departments.

■ *Growing Globalization*

The trend toward increasingly greater globalization is of major importance to managers. Modern technology enables information to be communicated instantly among far-flung locations. Today's managers have almost instant access to information on sales, revenues, and other marketplace factors. It is not unusual for a product to be manufactured in the United States, assembled in Mexico, and sold in Europe. Jamaican-based workers process airline reservations from American customers. Insurance policies sold in the United States are reviewed for accuracy by Metropolitan Life personnel in Ireland.

By the mid-1990s, U.S. multinationals had 6.7 million foreign employees and Americans had invested some $450 billion in equipment and facilities located in other countries.[33] Britain, Germany, and Japan are the largest direct foreign investors in the United States. **Multinational corporations** do business in more than one country. Such household names as Exxon, IBM, General Motors, and Dow Chemical are among the largest of these companies. Royal Dutch Shell, Pillsbury, Toyota, and Nestle are examples of well-known, foreign-owned multinationals.

Globalization poses numerous challenges for U.S. managers who frequently encounter unfamiliar laws, cultures, political regimes, and languages. Yet if the managers of a firm are flexible and willing to learn, they will have opportunities to develop rewarding personal as well as professional international business relationships.

As you study this text, you will gain insights into management from an international perspective. Why are more and more firms becoming interested in doing business on a global basis? According to a survey of 433 chief executive officers from three continents, the top-ranked reason for going global was to increase corporate revenues. Other major reasons were to increase profitability and lower business expenses. Over one-half of the CEOs expected to expand into new foreign markets within 12 months of the survey.[34]

Serving customers is an important incentive to the growth of multinational corporations.

> Today, however, the pressure for globalization is driven not so much by diversification or competition as by the needs and preferences of customers. . . . Managing effectively in this new, borderless environment . . . means paying attention to delivering value to customers. . . . Before everything else, comes the need to see your customers clearly.[35]

GLOBAL VIEW

How to Succeed in the Global Marketplace—Some Dos and Don'ts

The most successful global firms provide competitively priced quality products and services to meet needs of their customers. These firms must retain a global perspective and simultaneously know how various local marketplaces operate. For example, Gucci handbags, a top-of-the-line fashion item, are marketed in a somewhat similar manner throughout the world. Yet Japanese doctors do not respond positively to the American practice of using a sales force to market pharmaceutical products.

Savvy global firms make it difficult for potential competitors to gain a foothold against them. They seek to establish advantages that cannot be easily replicated and demonstrate strengths in such areas as production, finance, or marketing that dissuade rivals. Caterpillar, a well-known builder of construction equipment, strives for economies in the design of its products and makes large investments in capital. Its capital spending is more than three times greater than Komatsu, a leading Japanese competitor.

The Volkswagon Vanagon was originally developed in Germany to transport eggs but eventually was sold all over the world. In the United States, the company name also became widely recognized with its "Beetle" automobile.

In 1991, Volkswagon, a transnational automobile manufacturer, held the largest share of the European automobile market. Known for its "Beetle," the company expanded operations to include vans, which originated from a suggestion to build a vehicle that could be used for transporting eggs. To make profits and provide continued employment for German citizens, Volkswagon needs to market its product successfully outside the country. The company emphasizes the importance of specialty markets. Once the major automobile importer in the United States, Volkswagon lost its U.S. market share for various reasons, including an emphasis on style at the expense of stressing superb engineering and a failure to mesh American and German operations.

Unilever, a British and Dutch consumer products firm, stresses the importance of flexibility as well as a need to balance "a common corporate culture" with a high degree of decentralization. The company faces the difficult task of developing uniform standards for widely separated units but recognizes the role of generally accepted standards for dealing with labor, government, and socially related concerns. Floris A. Maljers, Cochair and Chief Executive Officer of Unilever, stresses that management in an informal multinational network not "lose its sense of urgency." He believes managers should not become complacent and underestimate the serious nature of their role expectations.

ADAPTED FROM: Bernard Avishai, "A European Platform for Global Competition," *Harvard Business Review* **69** (July/August 1991): 103–106, 108–10; James F. Bolt, "Global Competitors: Some Criteria for Success," *Business Horizons* **31** (January/February 1988): 34–36; Floris A. Maljers, "Inside Unilever: The Evolving Transnational Company," *Harvard Business Review* **70** (September/October 1992): 50–51; and Kenichi Ohmae, "Managing in a Borderless World," *Harvard Business Review* **68** (May/June 1989): 156, 159.

■ Diversity and the Workplace

Changes in the demographics of America's workplace include an aging labor force, greater cultural diversity, and more female and minority employees. Compared to the previous two decades, a higher percentage of U.S. workers have completed high school and college in the 1990s. Let's examine these changes to help you better understand the nature of today's workers.

The labor force is getting older.

THE AGING LABOR FORCE   During the past decade, the percentages of employed persons between the ages of 20 and 24 and the ages of 45 and 64 have declined. However, there has been a 6-percent rate of growth for workers in the 25-to-44 age category.[36] Between the mid-1980s and the year 2000, the U.S. population under the age of 65 is expected to grow by 10 percent. Yet the growth rate for the 65-to-84 age group is projected to be over 22 percent.[37]

Although older workers are sometimes victims of negative stereotypes, they possess many positive characteristics.

> For the most part, they are healthier, can expect to live longer with better health care, have more vitality, and are enjoying the benefit of significant medical advances. They are also committed to the work ethic and are trained to find considerable fulfillment from their jobs and their companies.[38]

Greater numbers of women are working.

WOMEN AND MINORITIES   Women account for 45 percent of the American labor force. Consistently greater numbers of women have been employed over the past 30 years. The percentage of female managers has shown considerable growth.[39] However, relatively few women hold top positions in major corporations today. A recent survey indicated that fewer than 3 percent of senior-level managers are female.[40] More and more women are electing career choices outside of the traditionally female fields of education, nursing, and secretarial work.

Women have encountered various employment-related barriers, such as the absence of female "networking" opportunities, the need for training or credentials not directly related to job duties, and the focus on departmental seniority systems.[41] Women also are victims of myths concerning their managerial abilities, including allegations that they cannot handle job pressures, lack aggressiveness, and do not make career commitments. In a recent survey of 722 female executives, participants indicated that men underestimated the value of their experience, treated them differently, and excluded them from social activities.[42]

By the year 2000, minorities and immigrants are expected to hold 26 percent of all jobs in the American workplace. Although the percentage of white female workers is projected to increase by 2 percent during this time frame, the percentage of employed white males is expected to decline from 51 to 45 percent.[43] At the turn of the century, the United States will have a more culturally diverse labor force.

African Americans represent the largest minority group.

African Americans make up approximately 12 percent of the population, the largest minority group in the United States. Compared to whites, African Americans are underrepresented in managerial and professional occupations. Less than 5 percent of all African Americans are doctors, lawyers, or dentists. Traditional areas of African American employment include licensed practical nursing, social work, and law enforcement.[44] In the past, very few African Americans have held senior executive positions in the largest U.S. firms. However, greater numbers of African Americans are expected to enter the ranks of top management by the end of the 1990s.[45]

The percentage of Hispanic workers will almost double by the year 2000. Despite this accelerated employment rate, the majority of Hispanics will probably have lower-paying jobs and higher rates of unemployment than whites. Asians, about 3 percent of the U.S. population, will represent a larger proportion of the work force by the turn of the century. Compared to other minority groups, Asians are unlikely to be at an economic disadvantage, however, because great value is placed on education in their culture.

EDUCATION   Workplace demands for knowledge-based job skills assure a growing emphasis on training and education as the 1990s draw to a close.[46] Each year, businesses continue to spend greater amounts of money to train workers, to prepare them to use more sophisticated equipment resources, and to increase their decision-making capabilities.

Even though workers are better educated today than ever before, managers are concerned about the abilities needed in the workplace in the near future. Increasing levels of conceptual and applied skills will be required to function successfully in more complex business environments. There is danger of a growing gap between the skills demanded by employers and those possessed by job applicants.

> The Hudson Institute . . . confirms the growing complexity of most jobs. By the year 2000, it says, below-average skills will be good enough for only 27 percent of jobs created between 1985 and then, compared with 40 percent of the jobs existing in the mid-1980s. And 41 percent of the new jobs will require average-or-better skill levels, up from 24 percent. . . .[47]

From a global view, the world's labor force is becoming more highly educated—a trend that has tremendous implications for businesses. As workers encounter fewer restrictions to movement among countries, managers will become increasingly exposed to a growing worldwide labor market. Service-sector growth will attract labor to the United States and Germany. Countries such as Argentina and the Philippines are expected to export labor because the rising levels of education in these countries will exceed the numbers of available jobs there. Compared to more than 90-percent school attendance in the United States, France, and Australia, less than 50 percent of the young people between 13 and 17 years old currently go to high school in India, Brazil, and Thailand. Yet developing nations represent an enormous potential as future sources of educated human resources.[48]

THINK ABOUT IT

1. Many subordinates envy the higher salaries and benefits earned by managers. Yet they may not fully understand the burden of managerial responsibilities.

2. Despite their best efforts, it is difficult for managers to be everything to everybody. Until you have to do it yourself, a manager's job may appear to be relatively easy.

3. Managers must be adept at handling other people's problems.

4. Although communication skills are frequently discussed, communication does not receive the emphasis as a management technique that it deserves. Consider the magnitude of problems caused by lack of or poor communication.

5. An excellent employee does not necessarily make a capable manager. Doing tasks yourself is not the same as trying to get others to do them.

6. Managers learn from experiences. However, there is a difference between a decade of experience and one year of experience repeated ten times.

7. Employee contentment does not always directly translate into greater productivity.

8. To obtain desired outcomes, a positive attitude is important. Notice how subordinates respond to positively oriented managers, compared to managers who generally react negatively.

LOOKING BACK

Each chapter concludes with a restatement of chapter objectives, including a brief summary of the content presented. To help you learn, it is important to take time to review these major concepts. Now that you have read Chapter 1, briefly review some of the highlights.

Explain the nature of management.

Management is both an art and a science. It involves using human, equipment, and information resources to achieve business objectives, which include making a profit, meeting customer needs, and expanding the firm's market share. Through managers, formal organizations serve society's needs, attain objectives, preserve knowledge, and provide employment for citizens.

Identify functions included in the management process.

The management process consists of five functions. Planning relates to setting goals, formulating policies, and establishing procedures. Organizing is grouping tasks and assigning authority. Leading involves providing instructions and guidance to employees. Staffing is concerned with the recruitment, selection, and placement of personnel. Controlling focuses on determining if actions conform to expectations.

Differentiate among the levels of management.

Top management has the overall responsibility for a firm's activities. Top managers are frequently called chief executive officers, presidents, or senior vice presidents. Middle managers convert the policies and strategies set forth by top management into guidelines for implementation by first-line managers, or supervisors. Typical job titles for a middle-management position include division, plant, or operations manager. Produce manager and head nurse are representative job titles for the lowest level of managers.

Describe the importance of communication in the workplace.

Communication serves to share meaning between senders and receivers of messages. It is through communication that information is transmitted. Attention to improving communication minimizes waste, conserves time, and promotes positive relations. By focusing on the who, what, when, where, and why aspects of messages, managers are more likely to convey accurate messages and are less apt to experience frustration when communicating with subordinates.

Discuss the various managerial roles.

Managers assume interpersonal, informational, and decisional roles. In the interpersonal role, they serve as figureheads, leaders, and liaisons. Information is a key factor influencing managerial actions. As monitors, managers filter information to identify pertinent facts. They also disseminate some or all of what they learn to others and, as communicators, transmit selected information to persons who are not direct subordinates. In decisional roles, managers act as entrepreneurs, disturbance handlers, resource allocators, and negotiators.

Specify four types of managerial skills.

Communication skills stress the sharing of meaning. People skills involve the abilities to lead, motivate, and understand the feelings and behaviors of others. Technical skills relate to knowledge about actual jobs. Conceptual skills involve an ability to consider abstract relationships.

Identify key management concerns.

Managers are concerned about efficiency and effectiveness. Other management concerns include promoting employee job satisfaction, increasing productivity, and maintaining quality. It is important for all personnel in a firm to understand the concept of productivity, since each worker's job performance directly contributes to it. Quality is evidenced by reputations for excellence, positive organizational images, and feelings of pride.

Recognize the forces that influence the business environment.

The business environment is impacted by technological, economic, societal, and political forces. Computers, dry copiers, and fax machines illustrate technological advances. Economic conditions influence a firm's operating capabilities. Behavior is governed by society's values, beliefs, and traditions. All businesses are affected by the political process because they must comply with laws passed by government units.

Discuss the characteristics of an increasingly diverse workplace.

America's labor force is aging. Greater numbers of women are employed outside the home. By the year 2000, minorities and immigrants are expected to hold slightly over one-fourth of all jobs in the American workplace. Workers are better educated. Increasingly larger numbers of employed persons are high-school graduates, and more of them are earning college degrees.

KEY TERMS

communication
communication skills
communicator
conceptual skills
controlling
decisional role
disseminator
disturbance handler
economic forces
effectiveness
efficiency
entrepreneur
figurehead role

first-line manager
informational role
internal forces
interpersonal role
job satisfaction
leadership role
leading
liaison
management
manager
middle manager
monitor
multinational corporation

negotiator	resource allocator
organizing	societal forces
people skills	staffing
planning	supervisor
political forces	technical skills
productivity	technological forces
quality	top management

REVIEW AND DISCUSSION QUESTIONS

1. What are the five functions of the management process?

2. How do the job responsibilities of workers differ from those of managers?

3. Why should all personnel understand the concept of productivity?

4. In what ways will the labor force change during the remainder of the 1990s?

5. Which type of skill is most important to managerial success: communication, technical, or conceptual skill?

6. What is the difference between the job responsibilities of middle managers and those of first-line managers (supervisors)?

7. Differentiate among the interpersonal, informational, and decisional roles of managers.

8. How can managers increase employee job satisfaction?

9. What can managers do to emphasize the importance of product or service quality?

10. How can a person determine if he or she is interested in becoming a manager?

CRITICAL THINKING INCIDENT 1.1

Why Me?

Jane, Joe, and Herb are employed by Modern Electric, a relatively small heating and air-conditioning firm that serves a growing number of commercial customers. They work together as a team; however, because of their knowledge and experience, no person has been designated to be manager of the group. The types of jobs at Modern Electric include a need to dismantle existing equipment, install ducts, rearrange interior facilities, and repair malfunctioning units.

When the group arrives at a work site, all three employees must discuss who is going to do what. Generally, Herb and Jane defer to Joe, who always selects the easiest job.

Herb volunteers to do the mundane tasks so he will encounter few, if any, difficulties doing his job. Jane is left with the most undesirable jobs, which require more effort and often present more problems. To make matters worse for Jane, Herb and Joe criticize her work and blame her when things do go wrong.

Jane has become increasingly frustrated. Last week, she told John Hollander, the owner of the company, about her feelings. She asked him to hire another person to work with the team and insisted that the new employee be designated the manager of the group. John was not receptive to Jane's suggestion. He indicated the company could not afford to pay an additional salary and stressed the unfairness of giving a new employee any managerial authority. John emphasized that veteran workers should be able to work together cooperatively. He encouraged Jane to be more assertive and to express her views to Herb and Joe.

After some thought, Jane has decided against this approach. Jane thinks that such an action will only make things worse and will give Herb and Joe the impression that she is just a complainer, especially since she is the only female in the group. Jane has considered working for another company, but comparable positions are scarce. In addition, she and her husband, Arthur, just recently purchased their "dream home." With Arthur's career to consider, quitting does not appear to be a feasible alternative for Jane.

Discussion Questions

1. Discuss John Hollander's perspective of management.

2. To what extent has Jane contributed to the difficulties she encounters with Herb and Joe?

3. Should Jane be more assertive and express her views to Herb and Joe? Explain your response.

4. Should Jane place greater emphasis on job satisfaction and less importance on family and financial considerations? Explain your response.

5. Assuming that John changes his mind, should a member of the group be designated as the manager? Explain your response.

CRITICAL THINKING INCIDENT 1.2

I'm the Chief

For the past 15 years, Carl Abrams served as Director of Training for Frontier Incorporated. His duties included doing needs assessments, developing training programs, presenting instructional sessions, and performing evaluations. Carl was highly regarded for his job skills as well as his ability as a presenter. His presentations were enthusiastic and always received high ratings from trainees. Carl earned progressively greater salary increases and was considered to be one of Frontier's most valued employees.

Several months ago, Carl submitted his resignation to form his own firm, Learning Consultants. The company specializes in conducting seminars and workshops on relevant business topics. Another service involves counseling executives who want to develop, restructure, or otherwise improve their own training departments.

As sources of business, Carl counted on business acquaintances. He mass mailed brochures to potential customers and installed an 800 telephone line in a small, rented office. To keep costs to a minimum, Caroline, Carl's wife, is the only salaried employee. Training personnel are hired on an as-needed basis and are paid a fee plus expenses for services rendered.

Events have not progressed as anticipated, however. Carl intended to serve potential customers in a six-state midwestern region, but most of his clients are firms located on either coast. Travel has consumed more time than expected—one day in New York, two days in San Francisco, then to Philadelphia, and so on. In addition, hiring trainers on an as-needed basis is problematic in itself. It has been hard to locate capable people, and too many customer complaints have been received about poorly presented programs.

Response to promotional brochures has been better than anticipated. Yesterday, Helen Jones, a prospective customer, asked Carl, "Your program on employee motivation looks good, but we will need at least eight sessions spread out over a month at each of our regional locations. Can Learning Consultants guarantee this type of arrangement?"

To add to Carl's challenges, Caroline believes her abilities are underutilized. Last evening, she informed Carl that she wants to be a seminar leader and conduct seminars on how to deal with your boss and how to be a better secretary. While these topics are relevant, Caroline has no prior instructional experience, has never held a job outside the home, and handles her personal affairs in a rather disorganized way. Carl is unconvinced about her ability to conduct training sessions for fee-paying audiences.

Carl ponders the situation. Indeed, operating his own firm has become quite eventful. He thinks to himself, "Why did I ever leave the 'comfortable surroundings' of Frontier? I had it made—an excellent reputation, regular salary increases, and certainly a lot fewer headaches. Is it really worthwhile to be the chief?"

Discussion Questions

1. How do the managerial responsibilities at Learning Consultants differ from those at Frontier Incorporated?

2. Why is Carl experiencing difficulties with his managerial role at Learning Consultants?

3. Is Carl an effective manager? Explain your response.

CRITICAL THINKING INCIDENT 1.3

Who Gets What?

Marvin Pearson is the administrator of the Newberg County Medical Center, which is located in a suburb of Kansas City. The medical center was built a decade ago to provide quality health care and strives to keep its equipment up-to-date with advances in medical technology.

Also, the center is committed to serving all people who need hospital care. In many cases, however, reimbursement from insurers does not fully compensate for services rendered to patients. A growing number of patients are not able to pay for hospital services. Although the center's patient load has increased, its revenues have not grown as rapidly as predicted.

There is a pressing need for several major hospital expenditures. The surgical unit needs extensive renovation, and a piece of expensive equipment is necessary to update the capability of the radiology unit. Joan Congrove, the controller, has repeatedly expressed concern about upgrading the computerized systems used for accounting and issuing patient statements. This morning, Sally Conrad, Director of Nursing, threatened to resign. She told Marvin, "I don't think nursing is getting a fair share of the resources. We've gotten too little for too long. We need additional nurses, and our salaries are already lower than other hospitals in the area."

The hospital board knows about these problems but has instructed Marvin to operate the facility on a profitable basis. Board members believe that funds for new or improved equipment, remodeling, and salary increases need to be generated without incurring additional debt. In their view, Marvin should strive to introduce cost-cutting measures to achieve additional revenues; they have given him the flexibility to determine how greater efficiency is to be attained. Marvin thinks that the only way for the center to show a profit is to reduce specialized services in the psychiatric unit and to eliminate the recently introduced medical-assistance program for substance abusers.

Marvin contemplates what course of action to take. Although he is concerned about providing the best patient care possible, he also knows that sufficient funds are simply not available to do this. Marvin tells his assistant, "Proportional budget reductions will not work too well because everybody will get less than is really needed. But if the expensive equipment is purchased, it will consume a significant amount of money. How do I decide who gets what?"

Discussion Questions

1. Is Marvin's dilemma unique to hospital administrators? Explain your response.

2. What can Marvin do to gain the staff's support for his ultimate decision and to retain the cooperation of all hospital employees?

3. How should Marvin respond to the board's point of view?

4. Because she has threatened to resign, should Sally's request be given a top priority? Explain your response.

NOTES

1. Peter F. Drucker, *The Practice of Management* (New York: Harper & Row, 1954), p. 17.

2. Richard L. Daft, *Management* (Chicago: Dryden, 1988), p. 5.

3. James A. F. Stoner and R. Edward Freeman, *Management,* 4th ed. (Englewood Cliffs, NJ: Prentice-Hall, 1989), pp. 5–6.

4. Alex Kotlowitz, "Believe Us: This Isn't the Way We Break Most of Our Stories," *The Wall Street Journal* (December 19, 1988), p. B1.

5. Leonard R. Sayles, *Leadership: Managing in Real Organizations,* 2d ed. (New York: McGraw-Hill, 1989), pp. 16–17.

6. William P. Sullivan, "Have You Got What It Takes to Get to the Top?," *Management Review* 72 (April 1983): 9.

7. Morgan W. McCall, Jr., and Robert E. Kaplan, *Whatever It Takes: The Realities of Managerial Decision Making,* 2d ed. (Englewood Cliffs, NJ: Prentice-Hall, 1990), pp. 49–53.

8. Peter F. Drucker, *The Frontiers of Management* (New York: Truman Talley Books/E. P. Dutton, 1986), pp. 277, 285.

9. "Corporate Cutbacks," *USA Today* (November 28, 1990), p. 1B.

10. Stephen E. Catt and Donald S. Miller, *Supervision: Working with People,* 2d ed. (Homewood, IL: Richard D. Irwin, 1991), p. 3.

11. Eliza G. C. Collins, ed., *Executive Success: Making It*

in *Management* (New York: Wiley, 1983), pp. 418–19.

12. Ibid., p. 420.

13. Buck Joseph, "How Middle Managers Err as Supervisors," *Supervisory Management* **29** (November 1984): 9.

14. Thomas J. Peters and Robert H. Waterman, Jr., *In Search of Excellence* (New York: Warner Books, 1984), pp. 218–23.

15. Collins, *Executive Success*, pp. 421–28.

16. Ibid., p. 424.

17. Peter F. Drucker, *The Effective Executive* (New York: Harper & Row, 1967), pp. 120–21.

18. Collins, *Executive Success*, p. 427.

19. Drucker, *The Effective Executive*, p. 65.

20. "Mike Wright Has Service in the Bag," *Fortune* (June 4, 1990), p. 62.

21. S. J. Motowidlo, "Does Job Satisfaction Lead to Consideration and Personal Sensitivity?," *Academy of Management Journal* **27** (December 1984): 914.

22. Mary Lord, "Where You Can't Get Fired," *Fortune* (January 14, 1991), p. 48.

23. Stuart Gannes, "The Good News about U.S. R & D," *Fortune* (February 1, 1988), p. 49.

24. Alvin Toffler, "Powershift," *Newsweek* (October 15, 1990), p. 87.

25. Catt and Miller, *Supervision*, p. 7.

26. Robert W. Goddard, "In Quest of Quality," *Management World* **17** (May/June 1988): 19.

27. Robert Neff, "Now Japan Is Getting Jumpy about Quality," *Business Week* (March 5, 1990), p. 41.

28. "Deming's Demons," *The Wall Street Journal Reports* (June 4, 1990), p. R39.

29. Andrea Gabor, "The Leading Light of Quality," *U.S. News & World Report* (November 25, 1988), p. 54.

30. Jeremy Main, "How to Win the Baldridge Award," *Fortune* (April 23, 1990), p. 104.

31. *Centerior Energy, Third Quarter Report*, Cleveland, Ohio (1990), p. 1.

32. "The Most Fascinating Ideas for 1991," *Fortune* (January 14, 1991), p. 43.

33. Brian O'Reilly, "Your New Global Work Force," *Fortune* (December 14, 1992), pp. 58, 62.

34. George Anders, "Going Global: Vision versus Reality," *The Wall Street Journal* (September 22, 1989), p. R21.

35. Kenichi Ohmae, "Managing in a Borderless World," *Harvard Business Review* **68** (May/June 1989): 161.

36. *Handbook of Labor Statistics*, U.S. Department of Labor, Bureau of Labor Statistics (Washington, DC: U.S. Government Printing Office, August 1989), p. 64.

37. Kathleen Glynn, "Providing for Our Aging Society," *Personnel Administrator* **33** (November 1988): 56.

38. David Bywaters, "Business Should Look to Older Employees as Work Force Shrinks," *Wichita Business Journal* (May 8, 1989), p. 25.

39. Joel Dreyfuss, "Get Ready for the New Work Force," *Fortune* (April 23, 1990), p. 168.

40. Tom Lester, "A Woman's Place . . ." *Management Today* **20** (April 1993): 46.

41. "Barriers Trip Women in the Workplace," *USA Today* (December 12, 1985), p. 1A.

42. Helen Reagan, "Top Women Executives Find Path to Power Is Strewn with Hurdles," *The Wall Street Journal* (October 25, 1984), pp. 35, 37.

43. Dreyfuss, "Get Ready for the New Work Force," pp. 165, 180.

44. "Facts and Figures," *Black Enterprise* **16** (August 1986): 27.

45. Larry Reibstein, "Many Hurdles, Old and New, Keep Black Managers Out of Top Jobs," *The Wall Street Journal* (July 10, 1986), p. 25.

46. Dean Elmuti, "Managing Diversity in the Workplace: An Immense Challenge for Both Managers and Workers," *Industrial Management* **35** (July/August 1993): 21.

47. Alecia Swasy and Carol Hymowitz, "The Workplace Revolution," *The Wall Street Journal* (February 9, 1990), p. R6.

48. William B. Johnston, "Global Work Force 2000," *Harvard Business Review* **69** (March/April 1991): 116, 121.

▪ SUGGESTED READINGS

Argyris, Chris. "Good Communication That Blocks Learning." *Harvard Business Review* **72** (July/August 1994): 77–95.

Boker, Stephen, and others. "Mini-Nationals Are Making Maximum Impact." *Business Week* (September 9, 1993), pp. 66–69.

Byrne, John A. "The Horizontal Corporation." *Business Week* (December 20, 1993), pp. 77–81.

Gouillart, Francis J., and Frederick D. Sturdivant. "Spend a Day in the Life of Your Customers." *Harvard Business Review* **72** (January/February 1994): 117–25.

Kaeter, Margaret. "The Age of the Specialized Generalist." *Training* **30** (December 1992): 48–53.

Miles, Carrie A., and Jean M. McCloskey. "People, Key to Productivity." *HR Magazine* **38** (February 1993): 40–45.

Overman, Stephanie. "Success Comes from Accepting Challenges." *HR Magazine* **38** (October 1993): 60–62, 64, 66.

Rossett, Allison, and Terry Bickham. "Diversity Training: Hope, Faith, and Cynicism." *Training* **31** (January 1994): 41–46.

Sandwith, Paul. "Building Quality into Communications." *Training and Development* **48** (January 1994): 55–58.

Stewart, Thomas A. "Welcome to the Revolution." *Fortune* (December 13, 1993), pp. 66–68, 70, 72, 76, 80.

CHAPTER *2*

PHILOSOPHIES OF MANAGEMENT

■ LEARNING OBJECTIVES

The purpose of this chapter is to help you see how the "modern" field of management has evolved since the start of the Industrial Revolution. Although the historical aspects of this development may be interesting, it is what we can learn from our management predecessors that is the primary focus of this chapter. The learning objectives for this chapter are to:

- Understand the changes that have caused businesses to develop new management techniques.
- Appreciate and understand how many of the early management principles are still valid in today's business world.
- Comprehend the main points and emphases of the early classical approaches to management.
- Appreciate what the early developers of management thought were trying to accomplish.
- Identify the contributions the behavioral approach has made to the field of management.
- Comprehend some of the current ideas in management thought.

■ CHAPTER OUTLINE

There once was a time when the label "Made in Japan" did not mean much. Times have definitely changed. Today, items like automobiles made in Japan are valuable commodities. Why the change? It may be because Japanese managers have looked closely at all the management styles of the past, and they have managed to keep most of the "good" and throw away most of the "bad."

The NUMMI Plant in Fremont, California, is a prime example. In 1982, Toyota, the largest Japanese automaker, and General Motors (GM) joined together under one roof to make cars for the United States market. Since 1982, the Japanese have been manufacturing Toyota Corollas, while General Motors has been manufacturing GEO Prisms. By 1995, both models were still being produced on the same assembly line.

Representatives of General Motors (left) and Toyota symbolically reopen the NUMMI plant.

The plant was named NUMMI for New United Motor Manufacturing, Inc. The new company settled in an old GM plant that had been closed down in February 1982 due to severe labor problems and poor profits. The NUMMI plant hired back 2000 previous employees, but the Japanese took over the managerial positions. This joint venture not only changed the automaking industry but literally changed America's thinking about management techniques and production outcomes. Utilizing the same plant and workers, the Japanese turned the NUMMI plant into a profitable and harmonious place to work.

The Japanese did not "reinvent the wheel" in terms of their management techniques at NUMMI. They borrowed from the old management styles and made some of their own modifications. This management approach is not only noticeable in the NUMMI plant but in virtually all North American-Japanese automobile plants today.

In these companies, we see examples of the classical management approach, which stresses the scientific analyses of job tasks to increase efficiency. Japanese managers increased speed on their assembly lines by training and utilizing teams whose members work in many capacities as production-line workers. The managers do time studies, as in the classical approach, but let the workers be responsible for keeping the production line going. In addition, managers stress communication constantly, and the results reflect considerable success. By the end of 1992, Japanese automakers, which produced no cars or trucks in the United States ten years ago, had assembled 1.4 million automobiles on the American mainland. Much of this success can be attributed to *Kaizen*, which means constant improvement in

—Continued

A LOOK AT THE EVOLUTION OF MANAGEMENT: WHAT CAN WE LEARN FROM IT?

The field of management has gone through many changes as it has evolved over the years and will continue to evolve in the future. Many "Japanese-style" management techniques at North American-Japanese plants seem "new" to a lot of current managers. As the Real World opening case points out, however, many of today's so-called modern management techniques are really just different applications of management principles that were developed a long time ago. Thus, it is very important to know how the field of management has evolved in order to understand the management principles of today.

A look at the evolution of management clearly indicates that the field has gone through a number of major changes, each of which was necessary at a efficiency, productivity, and the quality of the finished product.

An example of the behavioral approach at these North American-Japanese companies is participative decision making. The workers are trained in several areas on the production line, such as finding defects and repairing machines. They are free to rotate on the jobs on the line whenever they feel the need. When a defect comes up on the line, they must decide if they can fix it without shutting down the line. If the problem is significant, they have the authority to stop the entire assembly line.

The management science approach is very visible in these North American-Japanese plants. Computers constantly monitor changes, and robots can be seen welding, moving parts from place to place, or doing a myriad of other tedious jobs that the workers prefer not to do. Thus, employees are relieved from the most laborious tasks and extreme boredom on the job.

The teamwork or systems approach to management is also very evident at North American-Japanese companies. They have a relatively flat, or decentralized, organizational structure built around work teams that have been given a great deal of freedom and authority. Problem-solving groups and new product-development teams stress communication and teamwork. Management and production workers have common parking lots and cafeterias, common uniforms, name tags with first names only, and open offices to create team building. The results show that absenteeism at the NUMMI plant has gone from 20 percent, when General Motors ran the plant, to 3 percent today. Employee grievances and turnover have also been greatly reduced.

The contingency approach allows management techniques to vary according to specific circumstances. Thus,

planning becomes a big component in management training. A good example is the planning and decision making that goes into hiring practices at almost all North American-Japanese plants. They hire mostly young, inexperienced workers for the assembly lines. The interview process is planned carefully; candidates must pass through a series of tests and interviews that can take up to 24 hours. Most of these workers have never been members of a union and are not partial to them. These young, stable workers, in turn, keep down health-care and pension costs. This allows these plants to pay wages of $18.00+ per hour, offer employee benefits comparable to those in unionized plants, and still maintain a cost advantage.

This Japanese style of management has gotten the attention of the "Big Three" American automobile manufacturers: General Motors, Ford, and Chrysler. These companies are beginning to adopt some of the Japanese styles of management and production methods in their own plants, in many cases with considerable success.

SOURCES: John Daly, "When West Meets East," *McClean's* (April 15, 1991), pp. 48–49; Howard Gleckman, Zachary Schiller, and James B. Treece, "Toyota Retooled," *Business Week* (April 4, 1994), pp. 54–57; Gary Katzenstein, "Japanese Management Style," *Working Women* (February 1991): 49–101; Powell Niland, "U.S.-Japanese Joint Venture: New United Motor Manufacturing, Inc. (NUMMI)," *Planning Review* 17 (January/February 1989): 40–45; "Linda McColgan of NUMMI," *Automative/OEM News* (September 12, 1991), p. 32A1; Robert R. Rehder, "Japanese Transplants: A New Model for Detroit," *Business Horizons* 31 (January/February 1988): 52–61; Alex Taylor III, "U.S. Cars Come Back," *Fortune* (November 16, 1992), p. 52.

particular point in time. Today, the business world is changing faster than ever before. If you, as one of today's managers, do not adapt and change to meet these new circumstances, you are sure to be left behind by more progressive foreign and domestic business managers who are changing to meet these new challenges.

Figure 2–1 illustrates a brief breakdown of the major approaches or schools of management thought and their approximate time periods of major influence. Most if not all of these management approaches are still valid today. The really astute manager takes the best points from all of them and combines them into a management approach that fits his or her particular situation and style. This chapter is designed to assist you, as a manager, in developing a management style that will incorporate the best practices of the early management styles and also help you avoid their negative aspects.

MANAGEMENT APPROACH	APPROXIMATE MAIN TIME PERIOD OF INFLUENCE IN THE FIELD	MAJOR EMPHASIS
Earliest historical management	Biblical times up to the Industrial Revolution	Basic organizational division of labor
Classical management/ administrative management/ scientific management	Early 1900s	Development of basic "principles of management" and the scientific analysis of job tasks for maximum efficiency
Behavioral management	1930s	Recognition of the importance of high employee morale and humanitarian treatment of employees
Management science approach	1950s	The use of quantitative analysis to help managers make more rational decisions
Systems management	1960s	Organizations made up of a group of interrelated systems that are required to work together as one unified system
Contingency management	1970s	Various management organizations and management styles, dictated by individual circumstances
Japanese management	1980s	Participative decision making and problem solving; team approach
Innovative management	1980s to present	Constant innovation; emphasis on quality and service; information-based organizations (IBOs)

EARLY HISTORICAL MANAGEMENT PRACTICES

Management is as old as mankind.

While the *field* of modern management has only been truly studied and formalized since the advent of the Industrial Revolution, some forms of management and organization have been around since mankind first walked on the earth.[1] In a cave in southern France, paintings on the walls illustrate a successful hunting expedition. These pictures clearly show a division of labor and even a simplified chain of command. Although this breakdown of duties was probably rather informal, you can be sure that these prehistoric hunters all knew who the "boss" was and who would be giving the orders.

As civilization advanced, so did the field of management. All we have to do to see how quickly management techniques evolved is to look at the Egyptian pyramids or the Great Wall of China. We can only imagine the tremendous amount of planning, organizing, staffing, leading, and controlling that must have been required to accomplish these two great feats.

Finally, as we look far back in history, we find that many current management terms and principles were originally devised by early civilizations. For instance, scholars believe that the Greeks taught us participative management and that the Romans taught us geographical organization.[2] Nevertheless, not much significance was attributed to management practices until the Industrial Revolution began, when it became necessary to manage many people at the same time under the same roof. One common thread that continuously improved in various ways as the field of management evolved, however, was the need to communicate better to the people in the organization and to the people affected by the organization.

CLASSICAL MANAGEMENT

Classical management is a broad term used to encompass two schools of thought called *scientific management* and *administrative management*. These two approaches developed at approximately the same time, at the beginning of the Industrial Revolution.

Prior to the Industrial Revolution, most products were produced by "craftsmen" who worked in their homes. Products such as rifles, shoes, and furniture were made, one at a time, in what was commonly termed **cottage industries**. These products were then either sold or traded for products or services that the craftsmen desired. This form of production was obviously not very efficient. Most people were basically self-employed, either as a craftsman or as a farmer, and there really wasn't a great need for management as we know it today. In fact, the only groups that were employing formal management principles at all were the military and the Roman Catholic Church.[3]

All of this changed with the advent of the Industrial Revolution. Starting in approximately 1860, the use of machines to replace and/or supplement human power, the introduction of production with mass-produced, interchangeable parts, and the specialization of labor all created the need to assemble large numbers of craftsmen together under one roof so that large numbers of products could be produced at one time. Of course, mass production forced factory owners to institute "management principles" to prevent total chaos in the workplace.[4] Early forms of these management principles were modeled after

The "cottage" industry produced quality but not much quantity.

Child labor in the United States was common during the Industrial Revolution. Children were routinely used for menial jobs such as keeping the spindles full in this Georgia cotton mill.

The Industrial Revolution and mass production forced business owners to be more organized.

one style of management that was extremely autocratic and regimented, and communication traveled only in one direction—downward.

As time went by, a need to improve efficiency and productivity caused owners and managers to sit down and try to develop management principles and practices that would do just that. Thus, the classical approach to management was developed. The classical management school consisted of the administrative branch and the scientific management branch. Both of these schools of thought were developed together at approximately the same time, in early 1900.

■ Scientific Management

Scientific management is best represented by the works of Frederick W. Taylor, Frank and Lillian Gilbreth, and Henry Gantt. **Scientific management** attempted to apply scientific principles to job tasks in order to make workers as efficient as possible. Concern here was solely for increased productivity and not for the welfare of the worker.

FREDERICK W. TAYLOR   Frederick W. Taylor is easily the most prestigious name in this field. In fact, he is commonly known as "the father of scientific management" for his many contributions. Taylor was an engineer by trade, and he was accustomed to dealing with precise methods of operation. What Taylor observed, in his experiences at the Midvale Steel Company and later at the Bethlehem Steel Company, was an imprecise structure for both workers and management. Laborers purposely worked at a slow pace, and management simply didn't realize there were better ways for workers to perform their tasks.

Taylor decided that the scientific method of careful analysis and experimentalism could be applied to work tasks. He tried to find the "one best way" to perform each task in order to make it as efficient as possible. Many of Taylor's ideas were almost radically new, but the results spoke for themselves. Basically, **principles of Taylor's scientific management** consisted of the four basic steps outlined in Figure 2–2.

Taylor's principles of scientific management were applied most notably in what was probably his best-known experiment, which dealt with improving the efficiency of workers who were loading pig iron (steel slabs) into railroad cars.[5] The average man picked up a 92-pound "pig" of iron from the storage area and carried it into a railroad car. The average productivity for each worker was 12.5 tons of pig iron per day. By applying his scientific principles, Taylor analyzed the job and felt strongly that productivity could be significantly increased.

Taylor scientifically analyzed each element of the job: how the men picked up the pig iron, how they carried it, how they walked, how they set it down, and so on. Taylor then very carefully selected his own man for the job. He trained him in the proper techniques of how to carry and load the pig iron. Taylor also offered the worker piece-rate compensation to help motivate him to be more productive. This form of "differential pay system" was particularly unique at that time. Finally, Taylor assumed the planning and organizing duties to allow the worker to concentrate strictly on loading the pig iron. The results were very impressive: productivity increased almost four times to 48 tons per day, and the worker's salary rose from $1.15 to $1.85 per hour.[6]

Taylor firmly believed that his scientific principles could be applied to a wide variety of jobs, thereby producing benefits for management in the form of higher productivity and profits and benefits for workers in the form of higher

■ **FIGURE 2–2**   Frederick W. Taylor's Principles of Scientific Management

SOURCE: Frederick W. Taylor, *The Principles of Scientific Management* (New York: Harper, 1911), pp. 36–37.

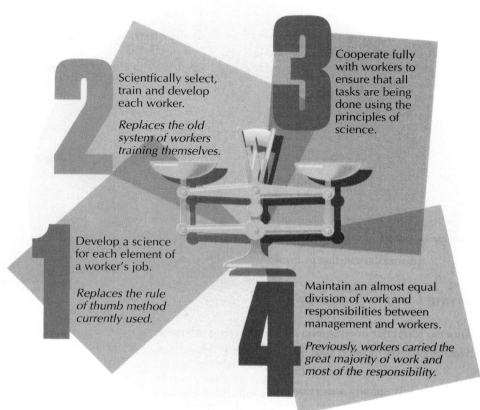

Develop a science for each element of a worker's job.

Replaces the rule of thumb method currently used.

Scientifically select, train and develop each worker.

Replaces the old system of workers training themselves.

Cooperate fully with workers to ensure that all tasks are being done using the principles of science.

Maintain an almost equal division of work and responsibilities between management and workers.

Previously, workers carried the great majority of work and most of the responsibility.

Both workers and management benefit from Taylor's scientific principles.

wages. Many of Taylor's management techniques are still valid today. Through training, Taylor did improve communications between managers and workers, although communications were still very poor in comparison with today's standards.

Time and motion studies are still utilized today.

FRANK AND LILLIAN GILBRETH   Following in Taylor's footsteps, Frank and Lillian Gilbreth, a husband and wife team, did extensive studies utilizing time and motion techniques to improve efficiency in the workplace. Frank Gilbreth was a building contractor prior to entering the field of scientific management, and he applied time and motion techniques to bricklaying. By carefully studying the hand and body motions of bricklayers with the assistance of a movie camera, he was able to reduce the number of these motions from 18 to five. Training the workers in this more efficient method increased hourly output from 120 to 350 bricks per hour.[7]

Together, the Gilbreths studied many different jobs and identified 17 basic hand motions, which they termed **Therbligs** ("Gilbreth" spelled backward, transposing the "t" and "h"). These Therbligs could be used to study the hand motions on any job.

It should be noted that Lillian Gilbreth was not just "assisting" her husband in their scientific studies. Lillian received a Ph.D. degree in psychology from Brown University. Her dissertation was "The Psychology of Encouragement," which was later published as a book. Lillian was more concerned with the workers' welfare than most scientific managers at that time. Thus, she made

Frank and Lillian Gilbreth with 11 of their 12 children outside of their home in Nantucket Island, Massachusetts. Their contributions to the field of management are still being applied today in many industries, from bricklaying to surgery.

some early contributions to the field of personnel management.[8] After Frank's death in 1924, Lillian carried on their work and eventually became a professor of management at Purdue University. Lillian was known as the "first lady of management" until her death in 1972.[9]

One additional interesting aspect of this Gilbreth team centered on how they raised their 12 children. They ran their household just like a business. Children "bid" for jobs, work flows were charted, budgets were developed, and control systems were put in place. The book and movie, *Cheaper by the Dozen*, was based on the Gilbreths' actual family routines.

HENRY GANTT   Henry Gantt was a very close follower of Frederick Taylor's scientific management principles and a contributor in his own right. Gantt worked directly with Taylor and understood his principles extremely well. Gantt is undoubtedly remembered most for his **Gantt chart**—a graphically illustrated bar chart showing schedules of specific activities. Two bars are superimposed above calendar days or hours of a day, so progress toward completion dates and times can be easily assessed on a daily or hourly basis. A sample Gantt chart appears in Figure 2–3.

However, Henry Gantt contributed much more to the field of scientific management than his scheduling chart. Gantt was one of the first management consultants to be concerned with the welfare of subordinates. He advocated a participative form of leadership. He stressed teaching subordinates as much as possible about all aspects of their jobs so they could be as productive as possible. In fact, Gantt's views on training and employee development are the fundamental concepts used in industry today. Gantt's emphasis on communication was truly remarkable for this period. For the first time, upward communication became evident as workers were encouraged to ask questions if they did not understand their jobs. Workers were even encouraged to voice new ideas and suggestions.

Finally, Gantt was one of the earliest management pioneers to advocate paying workers a good wage. In Gantt's time, industry paid workers the lowest

Gantt charts are commonly used today in a large variety of ways.

Many of Gantt's ideas were far ahead of his time.

SOURCE: Reprinted, by permission
of the publisher, from *Gantt on Management* by Alex W. Rathe, ed., ©
1961 AMACOM, a division of
American Management Association.
All rights reserved.

■ FIGURE 2–3 Gantt Chart
for Construction of a House

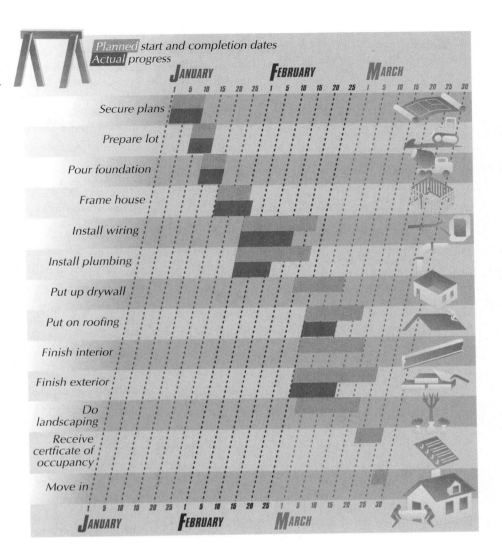

possible wages. Gantt strongly believed that if management paid good workers a higher wage, those workers would give the firm back more than enough increased productivity to offset the wage increase and also would increase the quality of their work. Gantt also believed that many workers were attracted to unions because they were paid extremely low wages and because ingenuity and efficiency were not recognized by management.[10] These points have certainly been proven very well in today's successful businesses.

■ *Administrative Management*

Administrative management centered on how the organization should be organized and what practices an effective manager should follow. The two main contributors to this school of thought were Henri Fayol and Max Weber.

HENRI FAYOL Henri Fayol was trained as a mining engineer in France, and he first developed his management principles at about the same time Frederick W. Taylor was developing his scientific management approach. However, Fayol's

Fayol's main elements of management are very similar to today's management functions.

writing did not reach the United States until 1925. Fayol's five main elements of management—planning, organizing, command, coordination, and control—are very similar to the management functions we use today. Fayol also was the first person to stress the universality of management principles, or the fact that these principles apply to all types of businesses—small or large, public or private.

In addition to these five basic management elements, he also developed Fayol's 14 **principles of management**, which are illustrated in Figure 2–4. For the first time, the need to communicate clearly from the top to the bottom of the organization was definitely stressed. Notice how many of Fayol's principles are valid even today.

■ **FIGURE 2–4**   Henri Fayol's 14 Principles of Management

ADAPTED FROM: Henri Fayol, *Industrial and General Management*, Trans. J. A. Conbrough (General International Management Institute, 1930).

1. *Division of work:* Specialization of work tasks by individuals is the most efficient way to divide work.

2. *Authority:* Managers must have the authority to command workers, but they must also be responsible for results produced.

3. *Discipline:* Discipline must be maintained at all times, but the truly effective leader knows that this is best achieved through good communication of the company's rules and regulations and not constant threats and punishment.

4. *Unity of command:* Any worker should only receive orders from one supervisor.

5. *Unity of direction:* Every part of the organization should be operating under one plan and one manager, so that objectives are achieved.

6. *Subordination of individual interests to the general interests:* The interests of the organization must take precedence over individual interests.

7. *Renumeration:* Workers should be paid a fair wage in relation to their contribution to the firm.

8. *Centralization:* Whether to centralize decision making at the top or decentralize decision making down to the lower levels depends on the organization and the circumstances in which the organization is operating. The proper amount of centralization needs to be determined for each situation.

9. *Scalar chain:* A chain of authority exists from the very top to the lowest level of management. It is the responsibility of the first-line managers to keep top management informed as to their activities. This chain then is also the communication chain as well as the authority chain.

10. *Order:* Both people and materials should be in the right place at the right time.

11. *Equity:* Managers should treat all employees in a similar fair and kind manner.

12. *Stability of tenure of personnel:* It is always more desirable to have well-trained employees than to recruit new employees because turnover and training costs are high, and errors increase. Stable firms with low turnover are more profitable. Managers need to plan in order to always have replacement personnel available.

13. *Initiative:* Allowing employees the chance to carry out new tasks without close supervision will create a great deal of effort.

14. *Esprit de corps:* Unity and harmony should always be promoted by management personnel.

MAX WEBER   German sociologist Max Weber, Fayol's counterpart, was concerned with organizational structure through the use of different types of authority.[11] Weber defined three basic types of authority: *traditional*, or authority resulting from respect of the person and position; *charismatic*, or authority from the dramatic appeal of the manager; and *legal*, or authority from the rules and regulations established by top management.

Weber attempted to describe what he felt was a "model" organizational structure. His model utilized all three types of authority and contained a very clear hierarchy, specialization of labor, and numerous rules and regulations. Weber referred to his model organizational structure as a **bureaucracy**.

Today, of course, this term has nothing but negative connotations and is usually associated with government "red tape" and inefficiency. Weber's original concept, however, was really a model of efficiency in which every worker had specific tasks and areas of responsibility. Extensive rules and regulations were in place so that workers knew exactly what was expected of them and how to handle various situations. The "right" person, was selected based on experience and ability, and each person was trained to perform their job tasks more efficiently.

Unfortunately, Weber's bureaucracy was a very impersonal structure and relied heavily on written communication to maintain order. Obviously this approach, in its purest sense, would not work in today's organizations. However, Weber's basic themes are heavily incorporated in the structures of most medium and large organizations.

■ *Concluding Thoughts on the Classical Management Approach*

As you look back at the two schools of classical management, it becomes very clear that what these men and women did was quite remarkable. For the first time, the field of management was truly studied and developed in a formal sense. For the first time, principles were developed to try to create harmony and efficiency out of chaos and inefficiency. For the first time, workers were selected, trained, and motivated to try to increase productivity as much as possible. Finally, for the first time, the need to communicate clearly and effectively was at least partially addressed. Many of the classical principles are still very valid and useful in today's business setting.

CONSIDER THIS

1. How different from Fayol's management principles are the five basic management functions utilized today?

2. What is wrong with taking a purely scientific approach toward managing a company, such as a manufacturing firm?

3. How do some of the principles advanced by Henry Gantt compare with modern management principles?

Unfortunately the classical management approach did have its negative side. Although scientific managers like Taylor and the Gilbreths did increase efficiency tremendously through effective job design, they only considered the worker as a tool: something that could be manipulated so production would

John D. Rockefeller (1839–1937), founded Standard Oil in Cleveland, Ohio, in 1870. He expanded the company into a virtual U.S. oil monopoly that lasted into the 1930s. A typical Standard Oil station in 1911 provided many services to motorists, a brand new market at the time.

increase. Only Gantt and, later, Lillian Gilbreth had any concern for the welfare of the workers themselves.

In fact, this negative aspect was even recognized while the scientific management approach was employed. In 1914, Edward Cadbury wrote the first case against scientific management when he stated two principal objections. His first objection was the "task idea," or the idea that human beings were to be treated as "inanimate things." Cadbury's second objection was to the hostility of proponents of the scientific management approach toward trade unions. He believed trade unions were beneficial to the relationship between management and employees.[12]

Thanks in part to Cadbury's efforts, the awareness of lack of concern for the worker and the desire to improve conditions in the workplace contributed to

REMEMBER TO COMMUNICATE

Communication: The Missing Link

Although the classical approach did advance the field of management considerably, one of its most glaring faults was the poor communication systems. For the most part, communication went in only one direction—downward. Employees were to listen and obey. Orders were given in harsh, strict terms; there was little or no discussion allowed. In fact, in Weber's bureaucracy management, employee relationships were purposely designed to be very impersonal. Most communications were in the form of numerous written rules, regulations, policies, and procedures. Is it any wonder that workers raced to join trade unions and demanded the right to be heard?

the development of the behavioral school of management, which began to evolve in the early 1930s.

For example, the "task idea" was vividly illustrated in some of the rules and regulations created for an office staff in Lichfield, Staffordshire, England in 1852. These rules were considered "new" at that time:

1. Workday hours were reduced to the hours of 7:00 A.M. to 6:00 P.M.

2. Since the hours were "greatly" reduced, partaking of food for lunch was scheduled from 11:30 A.M. to noon, but at no time during this period would work stop.

3. All workers were expected to furnish their own pens.

4. Each worker was asked to bring four pounds of coal each day for heat when the weather was cold.

5. Daily prayers were required at the start of each day.

6. The use of tobacco, wine, or other spirits was strictly forbidden.

7. No talking was allowed during working hours.

8. No one was allowed to leave the room without permission from the office manager.

Finally, since these new rules created near utopian conditions, a great rise in output was expected from all personnel.

THE BEHAVIORAL SCHOOL OF MANAGEMENT

As time went by, two things were becoming increasingly clear. First, the proponents of scientific management theory had studied and experimented with just about every job factor imaginable. Thus, it was becoming more and more difficult to find ways to improve worker productivity further. Second, worker resentment was definitely growing over the ever-increasing specialization of work tasks and the inhumane way in which managers dealt with employees. Both of these factors were starting to make managers think more about the welfare of their employees. The real breakthrough, however, came out of the Hawthorne studies through what could be termed an accidental finding.

■ *The Hawthorne Studies*

The Hawthorne studies were scientific studies that produced surprising results.

The **Hawthorne studies** were conducted at Western Electric's Hawthorne plant near Chicago, Illinois, from 1924 to 1932. The studies started out as a scientific analysis by Western Electric industrial engineers on the effects of lighting on productivity.[13] Two groups of workers in the relay-assembly test room were selected. The groups were approximately equal in their current production standards.

In one group, the control group, nothing was changed and only production was monitored. For the second group, the experimental group, lighting levels were periodically altered and production outputs were monitored for changes. As lighting levels were increased, production increased. As the industrial engineers increased the lighting even more, production increased even more.

Then to really test the theory that more lighting results in higher productivity, the engineers started to slowly lower the level of lighting in the experimental group's room. Much to their surprise, productivity didn't fall. In fact, it continued to rise until the lighting was reduced to the equivalent of full moonlight. This outcome totally baffled the engineers. Even more inexplicable, however, was the fact that all the time that the productivity of the experimental group was increasing as lighting levels increased, the productivity of the control group was also rising—and nothing was being altered in that group's room.

The length of the Hawthorne studies is very impressive.

THE HAWTHORNE EFFECT Finally, in 1927, Western Electric asked Elton Mayo, a Harvard professor, and his associates to come to the Hawthorne plant to assist with the studies. For the next five years, Mayo and his associates studied the following elements: changes in productivity brought on by changes in working hours on both a daily and a weekly basis, changes in the length of coffee breaks, temperature control, wage incentives, and supervision practices.[14] The results truly surprised the researchers. In almost every case, notable productivity increases were observed no matter what changes were made.

When researchers questioned the workers, they found that the worker productivity had increased not because of changes in work environment but because of social issues such as feeling special because they were part of an important study. Workers in both groups had been separated from the rest of the workers in the room; they had also enjoyed how their new supervisors treated them and communicated with them on a daily basis. These new causes of changes in worker productivity have become known as the **Hawthorne Effect,** which is the name given to changes that result from some factor other than the factors being manipulated in a research study.[15]

The Hawthorne Effect is the name given to changes caused by new or unknown factors.

A SECOND FINDING Another major finding to come out of the Hawthorne studies occurred when Mayo and his associates examined the effects of piece-rate incentives in a group setting. The study took place in Western Electric's Bank Wiring Room, where men in small, well-established work groups assembled telephone terminal banks. The incentive plan was set up so that everyone in the group would get more money if the group produced more terminals. The researchers thought that this would lead to increased production, but—much to their surprise—the productivity changed very little.

The Hawthorne studies produced one of the earliest findings on the power of group norms.

Workers who did try to increase production were pressured by the group to slow down and maintain group norms. Researchers came to the conclusion that groups themselves establish production norms and that this standard is very difficult to change, even with monetary incentives. This finding has been verified in many modern businesses today and illustrates one of the potential problems of managing an established work group.

A NEW VIEW OF MANAGING PEOPLE In conclusion, the Hawthorne studies lead to a whole new view of managing people. Through the relay-assembly, test-room experiments, we learned that treating workers better and being concerned for them increases their morale and their productivity. At the conclusion of the Hawthorne studies, many managers started believing that the new key to increased productivity was simply to increase employee morale. These studies also shed new light on the role that group social pressure plays in productivity rates. For the first time, managers became aware that group production norms are set informally by the group itself and that sometimes the only way to change these norms is to change the makeup of the work group. Thus, the theory of **behavioral management** was born.

Does higher morale always mean higher productivity?

The Hawthorne studies have come under fire in the years since their inception. On further analysis of the data, critics have tried to show that several other factors could have caused output levels to increase. Among these factors may have been the on-going Great Depression or even the personalities of the workers selected for the experiments.[16]

Whatever caused the increases in productivity, these studies did make managers start to think differently. The studies also show that, even today, the following suggestions appear to be valid.

1. Individual work behavior is rarely a pure consequence of simple cause-and-effect relationships; instead, it is determined by a complex set of factors.

2. The internal group develops its own norms that mediate between the needs of individuals and the work setting.

3. The social structure of these groups is influenced by job-related symbols of prestige and power.

4. Management must listen to the personal context of employee attitudes to understand the unique needs and satisfactions of individuals. Good communication is essential to good employee morale and high productivity.

5. Awareness of employee sentiments and employee participation in decision making can reduce resistance to change.

6. The workplace must be seen as a social system and not merely as a production system.[17]

■ *Other Contributors to Behavioral Management Theory*

MARY PARKER FOLLETT Another major contributor to the behavioral school of management thought was Mary Parker Follett. Follett was a social worker by trade. Although she never worked in a factory, her contributions to the field of management have been profound.

Mary Parker Follett was one of the first people to study group interaction.

Follett's main premise was that managers needed to cultivate group interaction, since it allowed the group to generate far better ideas than could ever be produced by individual group members alone. Follett's emphasis on intergroup communication is heavily stressed today.

Follett also provided the field of management with a new way of handling interpersonal conflicts. She believed in an "integrative process," whereby the two parties in a conflict could jointly work out a solution that was acceptable to both of them.[18] Follett felt that managers who tried to force solutions on employees were doomed to fail, since a conflict can be truly resolved only if the solution is acceptable to both parties. This "negotiated" form of conflict resolution is also considered one of the best ways to end conflicts today.

CHARLES A. BARNARD Charles A. Barnard was another major contributor who believed in some very radical ideas for his time. As president of the New Jersey Bell Telephone Company, he saw first-hand that the effectiveness of an organization relied on good interaction and cooperation between everyone concerned. In his text, *The Functions of the Executive,* which has become a management classic, Barnard stressed the need for management to elicit the cooperation of its workers to achieve organizational objectives.[19] The way to obtain employee cooperation, he noted, was by communicating effectively and creating an atmosphere of harmony in the workplace. Barnard was the first person to realize the true importance of communication to management.

Barnard was also the first person to challenge the traditional view of authority between management and its employees. The traditional view held that managers, due to the power of their position, had the right to expect employees to always accept their commands. However, Barnard argued that "position power" was not the source of true authority. Barnard believed that a manager only had authority over an employee as long as the employee was willing to accept that command. This view that employees control real authority was very controversial for its time and may help to explain why so many employees today are "blowing the whistle" on employers who ask them to do illegal or unethical acts.

■ *Conclusions about the Behavioral Management Approach*

In classical management theory, managers viewed workers primarily as nothing more than tools that could be manipulated and controlled in order to increase productivity and profits. New ways to increase productivity, however, became harder and harder to identify using this method. Then researchers stumbled onto the Hawthorne Effect: productivity increased, not because of the factors being studied, such as changes in the amount of light, but because of something entirely different—management's concern for the workers.

Behavioral managers believed that through better human relations, morale would improve and therefore productivity would increase. In other words, happy workers are productive workers. Although there is some truth to this statement, we now know that real productivity results from several factors in addition to morale. Human relations play a role in the management of all firms. However, this role does vary, depending on a number of other factors that will be discussed in subsequent chapters.

CONSIDER THIS

1. Why did the worker's productivity in the control group of the Hawthorne studies increase when nothing in the workplace environment was altered?

2. Why didn't the workers in the Bank Wiring Room experiment increase production when economic incentives were provided?

3. Does raising morale through better treatment of workers always raise the level of production?

Management Science: The Quantitative Approach

Computers have greatly expanded the use of the quantitative approach to management.

The **management science** or **quantitative approach** to management utilizes mathematical models, simulations, statistical trend analysis, linear programming, and a whole series of computer programs for inventory control, production schedules, and even "what-if" analysis. Application of any and all of these computer-assisted devices increases a manager's ability to make logical decisions. For instance, some of the more common quantitative approaches to management include the following.

1. Utilizing mathematical models to ascertain cost-revenue projections and breakeven analyses. These models force managers to "look at the numbers" to see how potentially profitable a decision may be.

2. Statistical trend analysis is often used in forecasting sales, costs, markets, and the economy. By carefully studying past trends, some logical projections about the future can be made.

3. Simulations have been found to be very helpful in determining the impact of different marketing approaches. For instance, the different outcomes of an advertising promotional campaign can be at least partially determined by using different media mixes.

4. Linear programming is used extensively in allocating scarce resources. This mathematical model is used extensively in businesses today.

5. Production schedules like Program Evaluation and Review Tech (PERT) and Critical Path Method (CPM) are used extensively in construction and production. These programs help managers to determine final completion dates and possible bottlenecks in productivity.

6. Inventory control programs like Just-In-Time (JIT) help to keep inventory costs at a minimum. Firms that utilize this program only carry approximately one day's inventory and receive shipments from suppliers daily.

7. Computer-spreadsheet "what-if" programs allow managers to view possible outcomes by changing key variables.

Several of these approaches will be explained more fully in Chapters 9 and 13.

Today's managers are using the management science approach to assist them in making tough decisions that involve many variables and have many possible outcomes. Although this approach can give a manager some very valuable information, rarely will managers be able to strictly rely on the numbers and not temper their decisions with intuition and other qualitative factors.

There are some limitations to the management science approach.

Systems Management

Systems management attempts to look at an organization as a set of independent but interrelated subsystems that must operate in harmony or the results for the whole organization will be disastrous. Good communication between all parts of the organization and critical external forces is very crucial.

■ *Open versus Closed Systems*

David Katz and Robert L. Kahn describe a typical business organization as utilizing an **open system** when it communicates with and reacts to outside environmental forces and adjusts accordingly.

An organization that does not communicate or react to its environment is said to be operating in a **closed system** and normally will have a very limited life.[20] For example, your automobile consists of several subsystems that must all work together properly or your car will not run very well—in fact, maybe not at all. Your automobile has a fuel system, an electrical system, and a cooling system. If any one of these systems is not working properly, the "whole" car will not run very well. You also must react to outside environmental changes, such as falling temperatures when you drive north in winter. Eventually, you will need to add antifreeze to your cooling system; if you don't, the whole engine will overheat as your cooling system freezes and stops working.

■ *Coordinating the Whole Organization*

Why wouldn't all of the parts of a business naturally work together?

Similarly, organizations must make sure that all of their subsystems are working efficiently and in harmony with one another; if they are not, the whole organization will falter. Although this sounds feasible, in reality many times it is not.

A LOOK AT A TYPICAL BUSINESS ORGANIZATION   Let's look at a typical business organization that is manufacturing shoes for men and women. The organization first must gather inputs in the form of labor, materials, machinery, and so on. The firm then must transform them into products—in this case, shoes that become outputs to consumers. If this organization takes a closed-system approach and fails to determine what kind and styles of shoes consumers want before it begins to manufacture them, it will fail miserably. As illustrated in Figure 2–5, many external environmental factors can and do affect the organi-

■ **FIGURE 2–5**   Systems Management

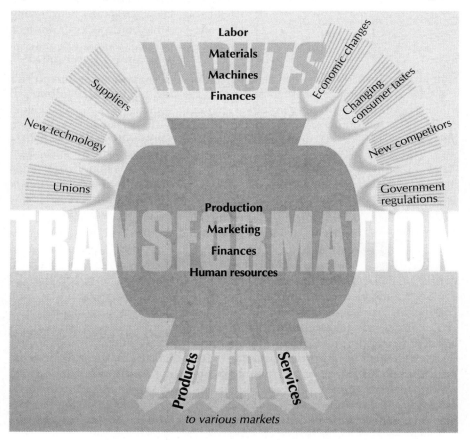

zation as a whole and, in particular, some of the firm's subunits. It is through constant monitoring of and communication with its environment that a firm receives feedback and adjusts accordingly.

Next, management must be sure that the independent departments or subunits are working together for the good of the whole organization. This doesn't always happen. Many times, the basic objectives of various subunits or departments can be almost diametrically opposed, and communication between departments is often very poor. For instance, in the previous shoe-manufacturing example, the production department's main objective may be to produce shoes as efficiently and cheaply as possible. The best way to do this is to manufacture only one very simple style of shoe. Of course, the marketing department's goal is just the opposite: to have a hundred different shoe styles and colors available to appeal to every market.

In this case, management must be sure everyone understands that only by working together can the firm as a whole be profitable and survive. Good communication is the key element here. Every worker and every department must be able to conceptualize that what they do has an impact on every other department in the firm.

> The systems approach stresses that all of the independent subunits of a firm should work together.

ORGANIZATIONAL TECHNIQUES Business organizations today must operate as open systems. In order to adjust to changes in the business environment quickly, management must constantly communicate with every person inside the firm and with those outside who are relevant to the organization. No longer can the top management of an organization take a closed-system approach, as Henry Ford did when he made his infamous statement about the colors consumers could choose from when buying a Model T Ford. He said, "They can have any color they want, so long as it is black."

A number of different organizational techniques can be used to get all of the subunits working together for the good of the whole organization. First and foremost, establishing an excellent communication system is a must. Every

> Businesses today *must* use open systems to succeed.

Henry Ford sits behind the steering wheel of his 1912 Model T Ford automobile. His assembly-line techniques of mass production were the forerunners for modern assembly lines and revolutionized how products were manufactured worldwide. Unfortunately, his "closed system" approach to marketing was a real gift to his competitors.

Good communication is essential for all organizations.

individual in the organization must completely understand what the organization is trying to do and how he or she fits into the achievement of its objectives. Also, the use of joint management/labor planning sessions can be of considerable help in getting all of the parts of an organization to pull in the same direction. Finally, utilizing a planning system in which all relevant departments plan strategies and solve problems jointly can eliminate a lot of setbacks later on and improve communication among the different departments.

The "whole" can be greater than the sum of the parts. The best management style depends on a number of variables.

If the systems approach is employed properly, an organization can also receive a **synergy effect**, in which the outcomes from all subsystems working together are greater than the outcome would have been if each subsystem had worked separately. For example, a manufacturer will normally produce more shoes if employees work together collectively and specialize in given tasks than if each worker tries to produce an entire shoe alone.

CONTINGENCY MANAGEMENT

The theory underlying **contingency management** simply states that the proper way to manage any area of an organization depends on a number of different situational variables. When we look back at the classical managers and even the behavioral managers, we see a group of people who were trying to find the truly "one best way" to manage people. Many times, through research and experimentation, they honestly thought they had found the answer—only to see it begin to be questioned when circumstances changed. Also, one organization might experience tremendous success when it applied a certain management technique, but another firm would try the same approach and fail.

The best management style depends on a number of variables.

When the contingency approach is applied, the manager considers a number of variables before selecting a management approach. Unfortunately, the choice of which variables to consider is very debatable, and even the total number of variables cannot be definitely determined. However, most managers agree that the following variables should be considered when attempting to implement various management techniques.

1. *Stability of the External Environment.* A firm that operates in a rapidly changing environment normally needs to be very flexible, decentralized in its decision making, participative in its problem solving, and extremely effective in its communication. Very stable environments, such as the one in which public utility companies operate, do not necessarily require this type of an organization.

2. *Complexity of Tasks.* This factor affects the span of control, or the number of workers a manager can supervise, as well as the basic management leadership style to be used. For example, the manager of an assembly line on which highly specialized tasks are performed would employ a much different management style than the manager of a research and development department that utilizes self-managed work teams.

3. *Skill and Proficiency Level of the Worker.* The manager of a group of college professors or surgeons in a hospital, all of whom are very well-trained and technically competent, obviously must employ a different management style than a manager who supervises unskilled workers.

4. *Degree of Participation Desired.* Although a participative management style is very popular, it probably would not be very effective if the work

force had very little interest in or knowledge of the topic that was being discussed.

5. *Amount of Risk and Uncertainty.* Leadership styles need to be modified as the amount of risk and uncertainty change. If risk is high, but outcomes are certain, then a more autocratic approach is appropriate. However, if outcomes are uncertain or risk is low, a more participative style is appropriate.

6. *Management-Employee Relations.* Different styles of leadership, motivation, and decision making are necessary to encourage employees to trust, cooperate, and get involved. Communication plays a key role in all of these styles.

7. *Size of the Organization.* Many times, what works for a small sole proprietorship fails as the firm grows and/or adds additional firms.

The way in which a manager applies the basic management principles changes as situational factors change. Assessing what management style to use is not a one-time decision but an on-going one that managers need to evaluate periodically.

All firms need to change their management styles as their situations change.

CONSIDER THIS

1. What are the main forms of quantitative information being used in the business world today to assist managers in decision making?

2. Why can't managers rely only on numerical data or statistics when they make decisions?

3. What are the main factors that can influence the style of management that should be used in a given situation?

A RECENT MANAGEMENT TREND—JAPANESE MANAGEMENT

Many books and articles have been written on the subject of **Japanese management.** Some experts feel it is, without a doubt, the best way to manage employees; others are quick to point out its negative aspects and failures. Whatever opinion you currently hold of Japanese management, one thing is clear: Japanese management methods and techniques radically influenced the thinking of American management during the decade of the 1980s.

After World War II, the Japanese rebuilt their industrial base and adopted virtually all of the management principles promoted by W. Edwards Deming. Deming's emphasis on quality was ignored by the United States during the 1950s but was eagerly accepted by the Japanese.[21] The use of mathematically defined flow processes and check sheets, teamwork, and constant improvement fit the Japanese culture perfectly. In a very short time, the rest of the world was trying to catch up with the Japanese. Deming's 14 points, which are discussed in Chapter 13, are now being followed by many American companies. Although many American and Japanese firms have successfully implemented Japanese management principles, some problem areas still need to be worked out, as illustrated in the following Global View. There have been so many variations of it that Japanese management is a difficult term to define, both in

GLOBAL VIEW

The Global Arena

Japanese management practices have worked well for Japanese firms in Japan, but in some cases, substantial problems have arisen when Japanese firms have tried to implement these practices in their firms located in the United States. The problems occur primarily in white-collar jobs, not in factory jobs. These white-collar American workers complain that communication problems and cultural differences frustrate them continually.

Communication problems result primarily from differences in translations and how thoughts are expressed. The Japanese use standard phrases that tend to be "polite" and are composed of more "surface"-type thoughts. Most Americans attach deeper meanings to these phrases and tend to take them literally. For example, if a Japanese manager is asked to meet a request that will be very difficult and perhaps impossible, he or she will usually answer with a phrase like "I'll try" instead of explaining that the odds of getting the request fulfilled are very poor.

Cultural differences have also caused many problems. Japanese-managed companies award promotions very slowly, and only about 20 percent of the American-based Japanese firms have American CEOs. As a result, many of America's top managers do not even apply for employment with a Japanese firm, and the turnover of Americans working for Japanese firms is increasing.

Cultural differences have also caused some American firms to discard various techniques that they had adopted from Japanese management. For instance, General Electric, which had instituted quality circles, recently dropped them, citing that they were too rigid and restrictive. Although Japanese workers are very structured, some American workers have difficulty staying focused on small, specific problems. So General Electric replaced the quality circles with "Work-out"—a town-hall type of atmosphere in which entirely new radical ideas for improvement in product quality are promoted. This free-wheeling atmosphere has been found to produce much better ideas and results for General Electric.

Even in Japan, some of the main aspects of Japanese management appear to be changing. The Japanese "baby boomers" are now in their forties, and there definitely are not enough managerial positions for all of them. Labor costs continue to rise, and Japanese firms are desperately looking for ways to trim them. Both of these factors point to the possible end of the "lifetime employment" concept that has so readily permeated Japan for several decades.

ADAPTED FROM: Jim Impoco, Betsy Streisand, and Susan Dentzer, "The Great Divide," *U.S. News & World Report* (July 6, 1992), pp. 52–54; Amal Kumar Naj "Shifting Gears," *The Wall Street Journal* (May 7, 1993); Mauricio Lorence, "Assignment USA: Japanese Solution," *Sales & Marketing Management* (October 1992): 60–66; Karen Lowry Miller, "Land of the Rising Jobless," *International Business* (January 11, 1993), p. 47.

In Japan, morning exercises are commonly done before the start of each work day. In addition to getting workers "ready to work," they also help create team spirit.

Japan and in the United States. Basically, however, Japanese management generally includes the following points:

- Morning physical exercise for all employees
- Managers and workers given the same company uniforms to wear
- Morning pep talks by supervisors
- High value placed on company loyalty; loyalty as a condition of employment
- Bonuses paid for extraordinary performance
- Vague job classifications; for example, Honda lumps all of its employees together as "automobile assembly workers"
- Full implementation of problem-solving teams and zero defect movements
- One dining room or cafeteria for managers and workers alike (a marked improvement in the quality of food from the workers' point of view)
- No direct orders given to workers; lots of lateral communication; bottom-up, consensus-type decision making
- Overtime expected of all workers (at the option of management)
- The just-in-time (JIT) system of inventory control in place and used
- No layoffs to the greatest extent possible; abandonment by management of direct labor costs as a variable expense
- Lawyers and lawsuits not tolerated within the enterprise
- Drinks after work with fellow employees to build company loyalty and to allow gripes to be aired harmlessly
- Company outings and retreats for all members of each employee's family.[22]

In Japan, most companies exhibit these characteristics, but Japanese-owned plants in the United States usually differ slightly. One of the more popular versions used in the United States has been coined **Theory Z**. Theory Z was popularized in the early 1980s by Professor William G. Ouchi, who tried to take the best management styles and techniques from successful U.S. firms and combine them with the best aspects of Japanese management.[23] These points are summarized in Figure 2–6.

Theory Z is really a combination of American and Japanese management principles.

■ FIGURE 2–6 Theory Z

	Japanese	Theory Z	American
Employment duration	Lifetime	Long-term; layoffs avoided	Short-term
Evaluation and promotion	Slow	Relatively slow	Rapid
Control mechanisms	Implicit	Informal, implicit	Explicit
Decision making	Collective	Shared	Individual
Career paths	Non-specialized	Non-specialized; job rotation	Specialized
Responsibility	Collective	Shared	Individual
Values	Development of a family environment	Family environment heavily promoted	Concern for each person

SOURCE: William G. Ouchi, *Theory Z* (Reading, MA: Addison-Wesley), p. 58. © 1981 by Addison-Wesley Publishing Company, Inc. Reprinted with permission of the publisher.

Modern management theory applies
a lot of the historical techniques.

Ouchi points out that Theory Z makes allowances for cultural differences between Japanese and American workers but still capitalizes on the strengths of both management systems. Theory Z, for instance, does not utilize the Japanese principles of morning exercises or no layoffs. However, Theory Z does include a more participative style of decision making, an extremely high amount of communication, increased job rotation, less-specialized career paths, and a much stronger emphasis on teamwork and good employer-employee relationships. Some Japanese firms in the United States that have adopted this more moderate form of Japanese management with good success are the YKK Zipper Plant in Macon, Georgia; the Kawasaki Motorcycle Factory in Lincoln, Nebraska; and the Fujitsu Computer Disk Drive Plant in Hillsboro, Oregon.[24] American firms that have successfully adopted Theory Z are Hewlett-Packard, Proctor & Gamble, and IBM Corporation.[25]

When we look at the actual components of Japanese management or Theory Z management, we can see that they rely heavily on many points from several other management approaches. The emphasis on efficiency and quality is right out of the scientific school of management thought. The constant striving for teamwork and participative decision making is derived from the behavioral school of management. Also, the use of a lot of job rotation and less specialized career paths fits nicely into the systems approach to management.

Whatever version of Japanese management a firm considers adopting, one thing appears to be quite certain. Increases in productivity, morale, and profits have been found in many firms that have adopted this style of management, which is why many American firms are moving in this direction. Some of the main ways in which the Japanese have been able to increase product quality are explained in the following Perspective on Quality.

INNOVATIVE MANAGEMENT

Two of the most recent contemporary management researchers and consultants are Thomas J. Peters and Robert H. Waterman, Jr. They first hit the management scene when they coauthored the best-selling book *In Search of Excellence* in 1982. Since that time, both authors have written additional books in which they explain the techniques of **innovative management** used by some of the most successful American firms. The characteristics of several of the excellent U.S. companies they have studied include the following.

- Successful firms must have good information systems and the flexibility to act on them. Information-based organizations (IBOs)—a current management trend—completely rely on information systems in their decision-making processes.

- These firms get things done, no matter what obstacles are present. A successful firm is not afraid to make a decision in a reasonable amount of time.

- These companies know their customers. They listen to customer feedback on a constant basis and use this information to produce new products.

- These firms actively encourage new ideas and realize that there are going to be errors and failures. A lack of failures, in fact, indicates that management has been afraid to take chances on bold new ideas or products.

- The rank-and-file employees are treated with respect; management realizes that they are the producers of its products or services. Teamwork and

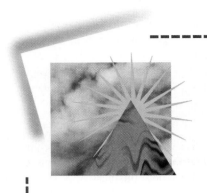

A PERSPECTIVE ON QUALITY

How the Japanese Maintain High Product Quality

John E. Rehfeld has worked for the past ten years for two very large Japanese firms who have plants in the United States. As vice president and general manager of Toshiba America and as president of Seiko Instruments USA, Rehfeld has learned much about how the Japanese have been able to attain their current levels of product quality. Basically, Rehfeld feels the following seven management directives contribute to the high-quality levels of Japanese productivity.

1. Stick to what you do best and try very hard not to get sidetracked. Japanese management stays very focused on the core business functions of the firm and only rarely takes on new outside opportunities.

2. Study the process as well as the results. *Kaizen,* which means "continuous improvement"—improving the entire process to see how results can be improved—is constant.

3. Quantify everything. Although some things are difficult to quantify, numbers do force a manager to make estimates and compare alternatives even when exact figures are not available.

4. Encourage people to buy into decisions. If everyone is involved in a decision to improve product quality, then there is commitment as well as agreement among the decision makers. Participative decision making produces results.

5. Get to know the whole person at work and outside work. The Japanese have a taboo against discussing business affairs during after-work social occasions. By getting to know people on a personal level, Japanese managers start to build a relationship of trust.

6. Fix the problem rather than look for someone to blame. When a problem arises, a Japanese manager is much more concerned with finding a way to solve that problem than with finding a scapegoat to blame for it.

7. Establish close relationships with customers. Customer visits on a regular basis are part of *everyone's* job duties and are even built into the managerial bonus plans of Japanese firms.[26]

Although Japanese companies do not have a corner on product quality, they lead in many areas. If American-made products are to remain competitive with Japanese products, then U.S. managers must learn to utilize the best underlying techniques of Japanese management.

trust are essential to success. Management by walking around (MBWA) facilitates communication and problem solving.

■ Company values are communicated to and accepted by all employees. Management demonstrates these values through actions as well as words.

■ A successful firm stays in the business that it knows well. Management can be innovative and spontaneous but should lead from its strengths—its particular core skills or competencies.

■ Top management is kept to a minimum, and the organizational structure is clear and simple. Flexibility and the ability to change very quickly are in place, and functional barriers are routinely bypassed as everyone interacts freely.

Dealing with a faster rate of change may be the biggest challenge facing today's managers.

■ Decentralized decision making is done as much as possible, but a few critical areas are still centralized at the top. The successful organization stresses self control and establishes critical control points.

■ The successful firm is able to "see" itself in the true context of the changing world. It is becoming increasingly difficult for management to even anticipate what changes should be made to "stay on top."

■ Managers must keep a balance between their home and business lives.[27]

Both Peters and Waterman now see "change" as the single biggest factor that management must deal with in the future. The ever-increasing rate of change is forcing managers to constantly be on the lookout for new business opportunities and threats. With the advent of the European Economic Council and the international move toward world marketing, changes are now going to take place even faster.[28]

Peters states that one way for a firm to stay on top is to establish new basics, such as world-class quality and service, enhanced responsiveness through greatly increased flexibility and continuous short-cycle innovation, and the creation of additional markets for both new and mature products and services. To accomplish these objectives, management must maintain constant, on-going communication with its customers, suppliers, and employees. These **information-based organizations (IBOs)** base all pertinent decisions on the massive amounts of information collected. The success of this innovative management technique is clearly illustrated in the following example.

In 1990, Southland Corporation, an American firm which owned 7-Eleven convenience stores in Japan, was deeply in debt and on the verge of bankruptcy. In stepped Ito-Yokado, Japan's most profitable retailer. It purchased 70 percent of the U.S. company in Japan and immediately made some significant management changes—customer focus being number one. The 7-Eleven stores in Japan now track customer preferences constantly, and clerks even key in the sex and approximate age of customers. Product inventories contain up to 3000 different items, and 70 percent are replaced annually.

The president of 7-Eleven in Japan meets with 20 store managers three times a week to sample store products. There are also over 200 "testers," who check products in the stores at random on a continuous basis. Customer convenience is highly stressed—not only in the products the stores carry, but also in the convenient services they provide. Customers can make photocopies, pay utility and insurance bills, send faxes, and develop film. The results show a marked improvement in both sales and profits.[29]

Although not all management researchers agree with the observations of Peters and Waterman, their basic management points are derived from the performances of firms that have had excellent records for a number of years and that are, for the most part, still doing rather well.

The field of management has gone through a tremendous number of changes and will continue to change. The truly successful managers of tomorrow will almost certainly borrow from their predecessors and continue to adopt and change as the need arises.

THINK ABOUT IT

1. Modern management is really a relatively new field that has only been studied professionally since the Industrial Revolution.

2. Although it is easy to criticize early managers for their lack of concern for workers, it should be remembered that their only managerial models were the military and the Catholic Church, both of which were managed very autocratically.

3. Many early principles of management are remarkably similar to the modern-day principles.

4. The scientific analysis of individual job tasks is still an important idea for present-day managers to consider in pursuing maximum efficiency.

5. Even though women were rare in management positions in the early 1900s, Mary Parker Follett and Lillian Gilbreth made very significant contributions to the development of the field that are still of use today.

6. Probably the single most important factor that early managers neglected was to establish a good two-way communication system.

7. The behavioral school of management, which evolved out of the Hawthorne studies, was really an accidental finding that previous industrial researchers totally overlooked.

8. The use of quantitative techniques and computers has improved managerial decision making, but managers must be sure that the data are solid and the results are interpreted correctly.

9. Every organization must make sure that systems and subsystems are working together or the efficiency of the entire organization is sure to suffer.

10. The rate of change is definitely increasing. With the advent of the European Economic Council (EEC) and other global economic agreements, the need to adapt and change may increase even faster.

11. Both Japanese management and the newer, innovative U.S. management methods illustrate the importance of constant quality, flexibility, and communication with employees and customers.

Carefully review the learning objectives listed at the beginning of this chapter. Note that each of these objectives answers or illustrates a major point worth remembering.

Understand the changes that have caused businesses to develop new management techniques.

Although primitive forms of management have been around since the beginning of humankind, it took the Industrial Revolution to motivate business owners to attempt to develop the most efficient management techniques possible. Once factories began to be constructed, managers were forced to deal with masses of people, materials, and equipment. This new work environment presented problems that management had never encountered before.

Appreciate and understand how many of the early management principles are still valid in today's business world.

Even though many of the earliest management techniques had their drawbacks, virtually all of them were designed to increase worker efficiency and productivity. Task efficiency, organizational rules, policies and procedures, and good human relations are certainly as valid in the work environment today as they were then.

Comprehend the main points and emphases of the early classical approaches to management.

Keep in mind that the early classical management approach had two areas of concentration: administrative management and scientific management. The administrative school of thought focused on the entire organization and how it should be set up. Basic principles of management were developed, as were rules, regulations, and procedures. The scientific school of thought concentrated on making individual job tasks as efficient as possible.

Appreciate what the early developers of management thought were trying to accomplish.

The key terms here are increased efficiency, competitive advantage, and increased profits. Like today's managers, the early developers of management thought were constantly trying to find ways to cut costs and increase productivity.

Identify the contributions the behavioral approach has made to the field of management.

The human relations movement, which evolved out of the Hawthorne studies, not only further increased worker efficiency but also resulted in the much more humane treatment of employees. For the first time, the behavioral school of management thought acknowledged that managers had to treat their employees humanely in order to motivate them to perform at levels that even came close to their potential abilities.

Comprehend some of the current ideas in management thought.

Contingency management, which means changing the management style to fit the situation, is certainly a valid management technique. The use of quantitative or mathematical techniques, when properly applied, has definitely helped managers to improve their decision-making abilities.

Japanese management principles and Theory Z management, an Americanized version, are close to the state of the art today. The use of participative management techniques, profit-sharing incentives, and a strong emphasis on teamwork have all worked very effectively.

Finally, with the advent of world competition, the need for management to be flexible, innovative, and extremely adaptive to market changes is very important. Good customer service and an ever-increasing quest for quality are both essential attributes if a firm is going to remain competitive in today's world markets.

 # KEY TERMS

administrative management	contingency management
behaviorial management	cottage industry
bureaucracy	Fayol's 14 principles of management
classical management	Gantt chart
closed system	Hawthorne Effect

Hawthorne studies
information-based organizations
    (IBOs)
innovative management
Japanese management
management science (quantitative)
    approach
open system

scientific management
synergy effect
systems management
Taylor's principles of scientific
    management
Theory Z
Therbligs

REVIEW AND DISCUSSION QUESTIONS

1. What was the main problem with Max Weber's bureaucracy?

2. What were the main criticisms of Frederick W. Taylor's scientific management approach?

3. What primary contribution to the field of management did Frank and Lillian Gilbreth make?

4. What area did Mary Parker Follett feel should be of critical concern to managers?

5. How can managers ensure that all of the systems and subsystems of an organization are working together?

6. How does Japanese management differ from Theory Z management?

7. What are the main management techniques that Thomas J. Peters and Robert H. Waterman, Jr., feel a firm must utilize to stay out in front competitively in today's world markets?

CRITICAL THINKING INCIDENT 2.1

The American Steel Corporation Faces Bankruptcy

The American Steel Corporation is on the verge of filing for bankruptcy due to increasing costs and sales lost to foreign competitors. At one time during the 1950s and 1960s, American Steel was quite profitable. During the 1970s, however, things began to change; throughout the 1980s the company either lost money each year or made a very small profit. In the 1990s, the situation has really become critical: two consecutive years of large losses—and all indicators point to another very large loss next year.

American Steel points to a number of things that appear to be part of the problem.

■ First, management-labor relations have deteriorated to the point where strikes are common, turnover is very high, and the number of employee grievances is skyrocketing. All of these problems have caused productivity to decline and costs to rise.

■ Second, the quality of the steel varies too much. The company has updated equipment and technology that can produce steel of excellent quality, but this only happens about 60 percent of the time.

■ Third, delivery schedules are regularly missed due to a variety of reasons, most of them employee-related.

Management has tried to fix these problems by increasing the number of supervisors and quality control inspectors. Although this decision has helped slightly, the increased costs of hiring these additional people are higher than the gains in productivity or quality.

In a final attempt to solve these problems, management recently asked the employees to fill out a survey that asked for their solutions to these problems. Many employees answered the survey very negatively with such statements as, "Why should I work at solving these problems? After all,

"What's in it for me?" However, a few employees had some really good ideas.

One employee wrote, "Have each department check the quality of the steel as it flows from one department to the next. This way quality is checked constantly instead of just at the end of the line." Another employee suggested that some form of incentive system be implemented to increase quality or productivity.

One employee stated he was shocked that the survey asked for the employees' help. He went on to state that in the 16 years he had worked there, this was the first time the company had ever asked him for his ideas. He concluded the survey by giving the company two excellent ideas to reduce production costs immediately.

American Steel is now wondering what to do next to continue to solve their problems. The management has turned to you, the management consultant, and asked for your answers to the following questions.

Discussion Questions

1. What school of management thought most closely corresponds to the business philosophy practiced at American Steel prior to the company surveys?

2. What specific areas does American Steel obviously have to change if it is going to turn its problems around?

3. What specific ideas do you recommend they implement to be more competitive?

 # CRITICAL THINKING INCIDENT 2.2

Who Is Right?

Harry Morgan was the assistant general manager of the Ocala Inn. Everyone liked Harry; he was one of the easiest-going guys you ever met. If you had a problem, Harry's door was always open, and he generally gave you whatever you wanted if he could.

Harry had one problem, however. He just couldn't seem to relate to the general manager, Bud Carraway. Bud was a good general manager who had been in the field for almost 30 years. Bud knew what it was like to "come up through the ranks"; he had started as a busboy when times were really tough. Bud was a very assertive leader who did not mind showing you who was BOSS whenever the opportunity arose. Although the inn stayed on budget and all the reports were in on time, there was constant tension in the air and stress was high for all of the employees.

Harry was not looking forward to this Monday's staff meeting; once again, he would have to try and persuade Bud to lighten the work schedules of the new employees. Currently, new employees were expected to work the eleven-to-seven shift, with duty every weekend and most holidays. This continued until newer workers were hired, at which time these more senior employees could change their schedules and improve their hours. The real problem was that the time between openings was so long that the new employees were quitting before they ever got off their first work schedules.

Harry opened the meeting by telling the latest joke, which everyone laughed at but Bud. Finally, Bud said to Harry, "Morgan, is that all you have to do is tell jokes all day?"

Harry simply answered, "No, sir," and dropped it right there. Harry thought to himself, "That guy has the personality of a gorilla."

Bud opened the floor for problems, and Harry reluctantly raised his hand. Bud responded, "Morgan, go ahead."

Harry said, "Mr. Carraway, I would like to suggest again that the work schedule for beginning employees be changed to allow them every other weekend off. We are just losing too many people the way it is now."

Bud responded, "Morgan, if I have told you once, I have told you a hundred times that this work schedule is permanent! If those cry babies cannot take the hours, then who needs them? Besides, this way we will find out who really wants to work in this field. This is the schedule I came up under, and it is the schedule they are going to come up under—and that is final! Are there any other items to discuss?"

No one wanted to bring anything else up, as a noticeable silence swept through the room. "Boy, that guy's tough to work with," Harry thought to himself. "I just do not seem to be able to relate to him."

Discussion Questions

1. Which type of management thought represents Bud Carraway's perspective?

2. What kind of problems do you foresee the Ocala Inn having because of Bud's management style?

3. If you were the new the owner of the Ocala Inn, what changes would you make to increase its efficiency and profits? Why?

Whom Do I Answer To?

Mrs. Johnson was a registered nurse who recently accepted a position as Training and Development Coordinator at the Memorial Head Injury Rehabilitation Hospital on the east coast.

Memorial Rehab had a behavioral unit and an active rehab unit. The bed capacity was 70 (50 active; 20 behavioral). The hospital had one Director of Nursing (DON), Mrs. Marshall, who was 45 years old and had worked there for 15 years. Mrs. Marshall had two assistant DONs. Mrs. Carey was Assistant DON for the active rehab unit. She liked being in charge but rarely left her office or communicated with her staff. Mrs. Doe was the assistant DON for the behavioral unit. She was very new, had little experience with handling behavioral patients and staff, and generally did not say much to either group.

At Memorial Rehab, the behavioral unit and the active rehab unit did not act as one unit. They operated as two separate units, and there was obvious competition for funds and staff between them.

The Medical Director, Dr. Carson, was 65 years old and in poor health. He had been the medical director for 11 years. He would come into the hospital at 9:00 A.M. and would dictate answers to his correspondence. He would make sporadic rounds, rarely to the behavioral unit, and leave for lunch promptly at noon. Only a couple days a week would he return after lunch. Then he would check in with the nurses; if all was fine, he would leave. He felt that he had a "professional" staff and the nurses really did not need him to tell them how to do their jobs.

After Mrs. Johnson had worked at the hospital for three months, Dr. Carson died of a heart attack. Dr. Owens became the new Medical Director. He came on board with a very energetic manner and made complete daily rounds in the active rehab and the behavioral units. He spent a lot of time talking to patients, nurses, aides, and therapists. He was not at all pleased with the level of patient care and general efficiency of the hospital.

After being there one month, Dr. Owens met with Mrs. Marshall and the assistants. He criticized the unprofessional attitude of several of the nurses. He noted that many of them left for a cigarette or a cup of coffee whenever they felt like it. He also noted that patients would put their lights on for the nursing staff and sometimes would have to wait 20–30 minutes for a nurse. All three of the DONs resented his remarks and disliked Dr. Owens' new "autocratic style."

One month later, Dr. Owens noted that nothing seemed to have changed. He called Mrs. Johnson into his office and requested that she work on coordinating the behavioral unit and the active rehab unit into one department so personnel could interchange as needed. He requested that she report directly to him about any problems or required changes.

Mrs. Johnson understood the rift between Dr. Owens and Mrs. Marshall and the correct protocol to use, so she decided to discuss the situation with Mrs. Marshall. Mrs. Marshall told her to report directly to her daily. Mrs. Johnson was not sure how to handle Dr. Owen's request, so she decided to report to Mrs. Marshall instead of to Dr. Owens.

Mrs. Marshall reported that both Mrs. Casey and Mrs. Doe were valuable employees and that whatever Mrs. Johnson did should be worked out with them. Mrs. Johnson then went to Mrs. Casey and to Mrs. Doe. They were not happy to see her, and they told her that they felt the situation was fine except for the need for more nurses and orderlies. They noted that morale was down—mostly because of "the way Dr. Owens orders everyone around"—and that the higher absenteeism among staff members was due to their dislike for Dr. Owens.

When Mrs. Johnson began to observe the staffs on the behavioral unit and on the active rehab unit, she noted the following.

- Staff from the active rehab unit would take coffee breaks that extended well over the 15-minute allotment.

- Staff from the active rehab unit never went to relieve staff on the behavioral unit, even when it was extremely short of nurses.

- Communication between the units was almost nonexistent.

- Morale on both units was very poor.

- Several members of the staff were poorly trained in proper medical procedures; when asked what their job duties were, many were not sure.

Mrs. Johnson discussed all of her findings with Mrs. Marshall, who became very defensive and refused to discuss the major issues at all. Mrs. Marshall noted that things were fine before Dr. Owens came, and she did not see why they needed to be changed now.

Shortly thereafter, Mrs. Marshall went on vacation for three weeks. Dr. Owens put Mrs. Johnson in charge as acting DON and requested that she "clean up the mess."

Mrs. Johnson immediately called a meeting of all nurses and aides. She handed each of them a detailed job description denoting exactly what was expected of them, along with rules and regulations for coffee and cigarette breaks. She insisted that the active rehab and behavioral units begin working together, sharing personnel and responsibilities when one unit was short. Weekly meetings were held to discuss problems and solutions, and several changes resulted from these meetings.

By the end of the three-week period, the amount and quality of patient care appeared to have improved. Most of the staff noted that they felt more comfortable because they knew what to do and that they appreciated being allowed to help solve problems. Dr. Owens approached Mrs. Johnson on the last day of the three-week period and praised her for the "good job" she had done, noting that many patients had said that their care had improved considerably.

The following Monday, Mrs. Marshall returned from her vacation. At 9:30 A.M., Mrs. Johnson was called into Mrs. Marshall's office. Mrs. Marshall noted that both Mrs. Carey and Mrs. Doe were close to handing in their resignations because they were so unhappy with her changes. Mrs. Marshall told Mrs. Johnson that she could not afford to lose either of these people and requested that Mrs. Johnson not interfere further in the operations of the active rehab unit or the behavioral unit. Mrs. Marshall also told Mrs. Johnson that she should return to her job as Training and Develop-

ment Coordinator and leave the operation of the hospital to the nurses in charge.

Mrs. Johnson left the meeting feeling confused and angry. She knew that Dr. Owens would continue to expect her to coordinate the two units. She also knew that Mrs. Carey and Mrs. Doe would probably revert to the old ways of doing things, which would cause all of the old problems to reappear. She felt angry that all her work in the past three weeks was about to "go down the drain," and she frankly did not know what to do about it.

Discussion Questions

1. What management approach is the top management at Memorial Rehab primarily using?

2. What systems approach would you recommend be implemented to get the two units to work together?

3. What kind of management approach do you think is needed here to increase efficiency and improve employee morale?

NOTES

1. David S. Brown, "Management: How and Where It Originated," *The Bureaucrat* **16** (Fall 1987): 28–30.

2. Ibid.

3. Daniel Wren, *The Evolution of Management Thought* (New York: Ronald Press, 1972).

4. Ibid.

5. Frederick W. Taylor, *The Principles of Scientific Management* (New York: Harper, 1911), pp. 36–37.

6. Ibid.

7. Claude S. George, Jr., *History of Management Thought* (Englewood Cliffs, NJ: Prentice-Hall, 1968), pp. 96–98.

8. Lillian M. Gilbreth, *The Psychology of Management* (New York: Sturgis and Walton, 1914; revised by MacMillan, 1921).

9. "Dr. Lillian Gilbreth," editorial, *Fortune* (September 1935).

10. Peter B. Peterson, "Training and Development: The Views of Henri L. Gantt (1861–1919)," *SAM Advanced Management Journal* **52** (Winter 1987): 20–23.

11. Max Weber, *The Protestant Ethic and the Spirit of Capitalism,* trans. Tolcott Parsons (New York: Scribner, 1958).

12. Michael Rowlinson, "The Early Application of Scientific Management by Cadbury," *Business History* **30** (October 1988): 380–93.

13. C. E. Snow, "A Discussion of the Relation of Illumination Intensity to Productive Efficiency," and George C. Holman, "Fatigue of Workers: Its Relation to Industrial Pro-

duction." Both from *Technical Engineering News* (November 3, 1927).

14. Snow, "The Relation of Illumination Intensity to Productive Efficiency."

15. Holman, "Fatigue of Workers."

16. Stephen R. G. Jones, "Worker Interdependence and Output: The Hawthorne Studies Reevaluated," *American Sociological Review* **55** (April 1990): 176–89.

17. Jeff Sonnenfeld, "Clarifying Critical Confusion in the Hawthorne Hysteria," *American Psychologist* **37** (December 1982): 1397–99.

18. Henry G. Metcalf and Lyndall Urwick, *Dynamic Administration: The Collected Papers of M. P. F.* (New York: Harper & Row, 1940), pp. 32–37.

19. Chester A. Barnard, *Functions of the Executive* (Cambridge, MA: Harvard University Press, 1938).

20. D. Katz and R. L. Kahn, *The Psychology of Organizations,* 2nd. ed. (New York: Wiley, 1978).

21. Kerry Rottenberger and Richard Kern, "The Upside-down Deming Principle," *Sales & Marketing Management* **143** (June 1992): 39–44.

22. Chalmers Johnson, "Japanese-Style Management in America," *Journal of Management* **12** (Winter 1986).

23. William G. Ouchi, *Theory Z—How American Business Can Meet the Japanese Challenge* (Reading, MA: Addison-Wesley, 1981).

24. Johnson, "Japanese-Style Management in America."

25. Ouchi, *Theory Z.*

26. John E. Rehfeld, "What Working for Japanese Com-

pany Taught Me," *Harvard Business Review* **68** (November/December 1990): 167–76.

27. Thomas J. Peters and Robert H. Waterman, Jr., *In Search of Excellence* (New York: Harper & Row, 1982), pp. 13–16; Thomas J. Peters and Nancy Austin, *A Passion for Excellence* (New York: Harper & Row, 1985); Thomas J. Peters, *Thriving on Chaos: Handbook for a Management Revolution* (New York: Harper & Row, 1987); Robert H.

Waterman, Jr., *The Renewal Factor* (New York: Bantam, 1987).

28. Michael Johnson, "Change or Die," *International Management* (April 1988): 46–48.

29. Karen Lowry Miller, "Listening to Shoppers' Voices," *Business Week*, Bonus Issue on Reinventing America (1992).

■ SUGGESTED READINGS

Coccari, Ronald L. "How Quantitative Business Techniques Are Being Used." *Business Horizons* **32** (July/August 1989): 70–74.

Eisman, Regina. "When Cultures Clash." *Incentive* **13** (May 1991): 65–70.

Fallows, James. "Looking at the Sun." *The Atlantic Monthly* (November 1993), pp. 69–100.

Forbes, Daniel. "The Lessons of NUMMI." *Business Month* (June 1987): 34–37.

Hyatt, Joshua. "Ideas at Work." *INC.* (May 1991), pp. 59–66.

Johnson, H. Thomas. "Managing Costs versus Managing Activities—Which Strategy Works?" *Financial Executive* **6** (January/February 1990): 32–41.

Katzenstein, Gary. "Japanese Management Style." *Working Woman* **16** (February 1991): 49–101.

Laver, Ross. "The Future of the Car." *Maclean's* (April 15, 1991), pp. 42–45.

Newman, Richard G., and Anthony K. Rhee. "A Case Study of NUMMI and Its Suppliers." *Journal of Purchasing and Materials Management* **26** (Fall 1990): 15–20.

Ouchi, William G., and Raymond L. Price. "Hierarchies, Clans, and Theory Z: A New Perspective on Organization Development." *Organizational Dynamics* (Spring 1993): 62–70.

Peters, Tom. "Beating the Great Blight of Dullness." *Forbes* (September 13, 1993), pp. 178–80.

Peters, Tom. "Let the Talk Show Begin." *Forbes* (June 7, 1993), pp. 127–28.

Peters, Tom. "Let Us Celebrate Bold Botches." *Forbes* (October 25, 1993), pp. 166–68.

Rock, Charles P., and Mark A. Klinedinst. "Worker-Managed Firms, Democratic Principles, and the Evolution of Financial Relations." *Journal of Economic Issues* **26** (June 1992): 605–13.

Sandeman, Hugh. "The U.S. Management Evolution." *World Press Review* (March 1985), pp. 27–28.

Schlender, Brenton R. "Japan Hits the Wall." *Fortune* (November 1, 1993), pp. 129–34.

Taylor, Alex, III. "The Dangers of Running Too Lean." *Fortune* (June 14, 1993), p. 113.

Thornton, Emily. "Japan's Struggle to Be Creative." *Fortune* (April 19, 1993), pp. 129–34.

Tosi, Henry L., and Stephen J. Carroll. *Management: Contingencies, Structure, and Process.* Chicago,: St. Clair Press, 1976.

Withers, Pam Miller. "The Smarter Way to Make Decisions." *Working Woman* **15** (March 1990): 31–33.

CHAPTER *3*

THE ROLE OF
COMMUNICATION

■ LEARNING OBJECTIVES

Problems caused by poor interpersonal communication plague both large and small companies. However, managers who are skilled at effective communication can spare their companies many of the difficulties associated with miscommunication that less skilled managers experience. The following objectives will help you learn how to communicate effectively as a manager. The learning objectives for this chapter are to:

- Explain the communication process.
- Identify strategies for avoiding miscommunication that results from inferences.
- Identify the functions of nonverbal messages.
- Explain the difference between hearing and listening.
- Distinguish between downward, upward, and horizontal communication.
- Identify ways to deal with the grapevine.

■ CHAPTER OUTLINE

The last time the U.S. Army decided to acquire restyled helmets for U.S. soldiers, few problems were expected. After all, the helmets had not been radically redesigned, and their purpose remained simple—to protect heads! However, even the purchase of new helmets became a problem for the Army.

During 4½ years, the Army purchased 461,000 new-styled helmets. Within that time period, the helmets were tested and even taken into battle during the 1983 U.S.-led invasion of Grenada. However, the Army suddenly shocked the manufacturer, Gentex Corporation, by pro-

The Gentex Corporation experienced a major problem in its attempt to manufacture a restyled helmet for the U.S. Army. The problem occurred as a result of poor communication regarding interpretation of the word "layer."

nouncing the helmets unacceptable. The culprit in this mess was poor communication. Apparently, the specifications for the helmet were interpreted differently by the manufacturer and the Army. One thing everyone involved in the dispute agrees on is that the contract called for the helmets to contain 19 layers of Kevlar material. Kevlar stops bullets and is used to make bulletproof vests. Due to the manufacturing process used by Gentex, the top and bottom layers were solid sheets of Kevlar. However, the middle 17 layers were comprised of smaller pieces of Kevlar stitched together to reduce costs. The Army says it wanted all the layers to be solid.

The key question in this communication problem is, "What is a layer?" According to Gentex, its contract with the Army does not specify that each layer must be made with one seamless piece of Kevlar. As a result, Gentex interprets the word "layer" to mean either a solid or stitched sheet of material. The Army interprets the same word to mean *only* a solid sheet of material. The helmets, as manufactured, passed all the Army's tests. However, the consequences of this communication problem were incredible. Gentex had to lay off 200 workers, and the company suffered losses of tens of millions of dollars. Furthermore, one Army official noted that the mess had produced a situation in which 18 lawyers were on each side of the table. Needless to say, poor communication can be very expensive!

ADAPTED FROM: Tim Carrington, "Pentagon's Dispute with Army Helmet Supplier Shows Pervasiveness of Its Procurement Problem," *The Wall Street Journal* (December 13, 1985), p. 50.

TO MANAGE, YOU MUST COMMUNICATE

On the job, there are many instances in which a manager must demonstrate good communication skills.

The functions of management cannot be fulfilled if managers lack the ability to communicate. The situations in which managers must communicate well are endless. For example, as a manager you will need to provide employees with directions and guidance on how they should perform certain job duties. You also will need to collaborate with other managers. In addition, you will be expected to interact with customers. Throughout these activities, your boss will observe how well you communicate with others.

In one study, a comparison was made of the job-performance evaluations received by employees who were considered to be either good or poor communicators. Those individuals in the study who were judged to be good communicators received high job-performance evaluations. However, those employees who were considered poor communicators received low overall job-performance evaluations. The findings of this study indicate that communication competency on the job is a reliable predictor of overall performance evaluations.[1] Clearly, managers who are good communicators are likely to be perceived as doing a better overall job than managers who are poor communicators.

WHAT IS COMMUNICATION?

Communication is more than just sending and receiving messages.

Simply stated, **communication** is the sharing of meaning between the sender and the receiver of a message. If the receiver of your message understands exactly what you mean, then you have communicated very well. However, miscommunication results when the receiver misunderstands what you mean. An example of miscommunication between a manager and an employee is illustrated in Figure 3–1.

As another example, a manager for one company was responsible for purchasing a large machine to fabricate sheet metal. The machine had to be custom made. Due to a communication mistake made by the manager, the machine was manufactured incorrectly. The faulty design rendered the machine worthless and cost the manager's company $40,000. The company immediately saw a need to train its managers to avoid miscommunication problems with others.

THE COMMUNICATION PROCESS

The first step in learning how to communicate more effectively as a manager is to understand how the communication process works. Specifically, the **communication process** involves the sending and receiving of messages for the purpose of sharing meaning.

The model in Figure 3–2 illustrates the different aspects of the communication process. The person on the left in the model represents the sender, who

■ **FIGURE 3–1** Example of Miscommunication

SOURCE: Stephen E. Catt and Donald S. Miller, *Supervision: Working with People*, 2d ed. (Homewood, IL: Richard D. Irwin, 1991), p. 198. Reprinted by permission.

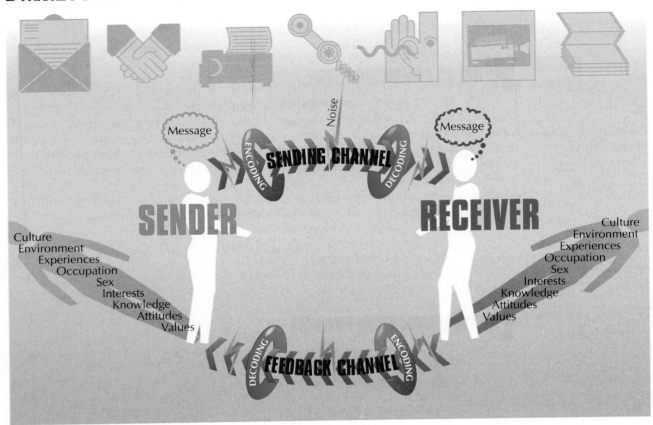

ADAPTED FROM: Rudolph F. Verderber and Kathleen S. Verderber, *Inter-Act: Using Interpersonal Communication Skills,* 6th ed. (Belmont, CA: Wadsworth, 1992), p. 21. Used with permission of Wadsworth Publishing Company.

initiates the communicative interchange. For example, when you wish to express a thought, you must create a message. Messages may occur in verbal or nonverbal form. Putting an idea or thought into message form is called **encoding**. The thoughts or feelings you want to share are influenced and shaped by your total field of experience. Specific factors representing your field of experience include values, culture, environment, experiences, occupation, sex, interests, knowledge, and attitudes.[2] The section in the model that connects the two people represents the channels through which messages are conveyed.

After your message reaches the receiver, represented by the person on the right in Figure 3–2, it is decoded. Specifically, **decoding** is interpreting a message. As the sender, you should do your best to make it easy for the receiver to interpret your message correctly. For example, use words and terminology with which the other person is familiar. A manager may impress others with a sophisticated vocabulary, but if the receivers of the message are unfamiliar with the jargon, poor communication will result. The meaning we attach to a message is based on our experiences. Therefore, the receiver will decode your message based on his or her total field of experience. To respond, the receiver creates a message (encoding) and sends it back through the feedback channel to you. The ability of the sender and the receiver to share meaning can be hindered by noise. As a result, key aspects of the communication process include *participants*, *messages*, *channels*, *noise*, and *feedback*.

■ Participants

The meaning we attach to a message is based on our experiences.

People differ in their backgrounds. Furthermore, different backgrounds provide individuals with different experiences, and we interpret statements and events based on our experiences. The following example demonstrates how differences in experiences can affect perceptions.

Administrators at a university decided to implement summer hours from May to August. During this period, the university's business hours were changed from 8:00 A.M. through 5:00 P.M. to 7:30 A.M. through 4:00 P.M. on weekdays. Only a half-hour lunch break was provided for university employees during summer hours. University administrators thought summer hours were appropriate because offices would be cool in the mornings and few people were on campus to use university services after 4:00 P.M. Therefore, from the administrators' perspective, summer hours were a great idea.

However, many university employees with young children hated the summer hours. As several of them explained, "Getting children up one-half hour earlier for day care in the summer is an almost impossible task." Other employees complained that the shortened lunch break made their jobs more stressful. These individuals viewed summer hours from a different perspective than the administrators did.

■ Messages

You are *always* sending messages. For example, your physical appearance sends messages to others about your age, height, weight, and so on. When you are angry or happy, your facial expressions probably signal the emotion you are

Our life experiences influence how we interpret what others say and do. Although managers and employees work together, their jobs and difficulties will differ, and thus so will the ways they view and respond to work situations. Face-to-face communication is the best way for managers and employees to understand each other's perspectives.

experiencing. Furthermore, the words you speak and the letters you send to others are also examples of messages that you may send as a manager.

However, although you can send a message, you cannot send meaning. That is, others can receive your messages, but they cannot receive the meaning you intend. Instead, others must give meaning to your messages. *The extent to which the receiver of your message gives the same meaning to it as you intended, is the degree to which communication has occurred.*

The messages you send do not carry meaning.

■ *Channels*

In the communication process, a **communication channel** represents both the path of a message and the means by which the message is transmitted. A message conveyed by a sender to a receiver travels in the direction of the receiver. A feedback message conveyed by a receiver to a sender travels in the opposite direction.

Managers communicate through many channels. Common channels include light and sound. However, people can use any of their five senses to communicate. Communication channels for managers often include face-to-face discussions, memorandums, and telephone calls.

■ *Noise*

When two people are attempting to communicate with each other, **noise** represents any interference with the message that hinders the sharing of meaning. In actuality, three types of noise can impede the communication process: *environmental*, *psychological*, and *semantic*.

ENVIRONMENTAL NOISE　All of the surrounding sights and sounds that distract people who are attempting to communicate with each other are known as **environmental noise**. Clothing style, a loud car horn, the conversation of others, and the color of a room represent distractions that hinder communication.

PSYCHOLOGICAL NOISE　The thoughts and feelings that hinder communication while we interact with others are referred to as **psychological noise**. Daydreaming is a classic example of this type of noise. Psychological noise can act as a distraction, causing your mind to wander while you attempt to listen to others. Biases or prejudices that lead to closed-mindedness are also examples of psychological noise.

Stereotypes we may have about others can hinder our ability to communicate with them.

SEMANTIC NOISE　Alternative meanings for a message that hinder communication because they are different from the meaning intended by the sender represent **semantic noise**. For example, "dorms" at colleges are now often referred to as "residence halls" by school administrators. Actually, some administrators are offended when a person naively refers to student housing as a "dorm." This offense is due to semantic noise; no disrespect was intended, but the administrator interpreted the reference negatively. As another example, innocent use of the term "stewardess" instead of "flight attendant" in the airline industry may anger female employees due to semantic noise. Jargon and ambiguous terms that cause confusion are also forms of semantic noise.

Different types of noise, such as from this moving work station, can interfere with efforts to communicate on the job. A lot of environmental noise with busy people in motion, for example, is very distracting. In addition, psychological noise and semantic noise can hinder efforts to communicate with others.

Managers need to be aware of the importance of semantics in communication. **Semantics** involves the study of meaning. In reality, words do not have meaning. Instead, we give meaning to words. For example, if a manager instructs a new employee to submit sales reports "biweekly," how often are these reports to be done? Are the reports due twice a week or once every two weeks? The fact that the word "biweekly" can be assigned different meanings by the manager and the employee creates a potential communication problem. As a manager, you should be aware of the impact of semantics in your interactions with others. A good way to avoid problems with meanings is to give and request feedback.

Receivers may give different meanings to our words than we expected.

■ *Feedback*

Any type of response to a message represents a form of **feedback**. The feedback you receive as a manager will give you an idea of how well you have communicated with others. For example, an employee's response to a suggestion you make may clearly indicate to you that miscommunication has occurred. On the other hand, even without saying a word, an employee's actions can provide feedback that your instructions have been interpreted correctly. Feedback helps managers to become aware of and deal with communication problems as they are developing.

INFERENCES CAUSE MISCOMMUNICATION

Making inferences is a common cause of miscommunication by managers. An **inference** can be defined as the act or process of drawing a conclusion about something unknown based on facts or indications. Unlike a fact, which can be proven to be true, an inference is a guess that seems correct. The act of inferring works as follows. A manager gains information, perhaps by observing something, hearing comments from others, or reading certain material. The manager then analyzes the information and makes an educated guess from it. The conclusion or inference that results may be correct or incorrect.

Inferences may be wrong and cause problems.

THINK ABOUT IT

The following exercise helps to demonstrate how making inferences can lead to miscommunication. At this time, read the instructions and complete the exercise.

Instructions

Read the following short story. All the information in the story is accurate. After reading the story, you will find seven statements. The symbols "T, F, ?" follow each statement. If you think a statement is true, based on the information in the story, circle T. If you think a statement is false, circle F. If you are not sure whether a statement is true or false, circle ?. Circle only one symbol at the end of each statement. Feel free to refer back to the story when responding to the statements.

The Story

A prisoner was being fed when suddenly a man appeared with a gun to help free him. The convict made a run for it and escaped. The highway patrol immediately set up roadblocks around the area.

Statements about the Story

1. A man with a gun appeared as the convict was being fed.	T	F	?
2. The man who appeared did not have a gun.	T	F	?
3. The man who escaped was a convict.	T	F	?
4. The man who appeared with a gun helped the convict escape.	T	F	?
5. The highway patrol set up roadblocks to help capture the convict.	T	F	?
6. Roadblocks were set up around the area.	T	F	?
7. The following events occurred. A prisoner was eating dinner when a man with a gun suddenly appeared. An escape was made, and the highway patrol set up roadblocks.	T	F	?

The correct answers are discussed in the next Think About It. Any incorrect answers you made while completing the exercise are probably due to *inferences*. The inferences managers make on the job can lead to miscommunication that is very damaging.[3]

SOURCE: Stephen E. Catt and Donald S. Miller, *Supervision: Working with People,* 2d ed. (Homewood, IL: Richard D. Irwin, 1991), pp. 195–96. Used by permission.

■ *How Inferences Can Cause Miscommunication*

The inferences you make while interacting with others on the job can lead you to incorrectly interpret their statements. Miscommunication then results. For example, Carol, a manager for a large company, was asked to speak for 30 minutes regarding her company's expansion plans during a luncheon meeting for the local Chamber of Commerce. Carol agreed to speak and asked what time she should arrive for the meeting. She was instructed to be there at noon.

Our inferences seem safe because they make sense to us.

Carol *inferred* that she would begin speaking at noon. Based on that inference, Carol scheduled a 1:00 P.M. meeting in her office with an important client. Unfortunately, when Carol arrived at the luncheon meeting to give her presentation, she learned that she was not scheduled to speak until the lunch was over at 12:30 P.M. Carol quickly realized that she could not speak at 12:30 and make her 1:00 meeting. Carol's inference caused miscommunication and put her in a difficult situation.

THINK ABOUT IT

Answers to the "Story" Exercise

To see how you did on the exercise you completed, compare your responses to the statements about the story with the answers below.

1. ? You do not know if the "prisoner" and the "convict" are the same person. For example, a civilian could be held prisoner by an escaped convict. The prisoner and the convict may or may not be the same person; you simply do not know, and that is why ? is the correct answer. To conclude otherwise would be to make an inference.

2. F The story clearly states that the man who appeared had a gun.

3. ? You do not know that the convict was a man. The story does not say whether the convict was a man or a woman, so ? is the correct answer.

4. ? You do not know that the man who appeared actually helped the convict escape. This does not make the statement false; it just makes it uncertain. To say that the man helped the convict escape, you would also have to infer that the prisoner and the convict are one and the same, which is not certain.

5. ? The story does not say why the highway patrol set up roadblocks; you are uncertain as to the reason.

6. T The story specifically states that roadblocks were set up around the area.

7. ? You do not know what meal the prisoner was eating. Maybe the meal was breakfast. Due to the uncertainty, ? is the correct answer.

SOURCE: Stephen E. Catt and Donald S. Miller, *Supervision: Working with People,* 2d ed. (Homewood, IL: Richard D. Irwin, 1991), pp. 195–96. Used by permission.

■ *Strategies for Avoiding Miscommunication Due to Inferences*

Managers naturally make inferences when they communicate with others. However, by practicing the following strategies, miscommunication that results from making false inferences can be avoided.[4]

BE AWARE OF YOUR IMPORTANT INFERENCES To keep your important inferences from causing communication problems, you should be aware of them. Too often we treat inferences as facts, which camouflages their existence. Therefore, the first step in avoiding miscommunication that can result from making inferences is to realize when you are making an important inference. In the Chamber of Commerce luncheon example, Carol acted on her inference as if it were a fact.

As a manager, you cannot know or observe everything that goes on. In addition, you are not expected to spend a great deal of time reflecting on every inference you make. However, you need to distinguish between what you know and

Just because an inference appears to be correct, that does not make it a fact.

A PERSPECTIVE ON QUALITY
Communication Is the Key in TQM

Making a shift to total quality management (TQM) involves more than just tinkering with a few items. Even before an attempt is made to implement new quality procedures, a significant shift in thinking is often necessary. Furthermore, everyone needs to work together.

Effective communication is necessary to coordinate a quality process. As a matter of fact, research by the American Productivity and Quality Center (APQC) shows that companies experiencing success with TQM programs have inevitably assigned a major role to communication. "They always include communication as a critical link to employees, suppliers, customers, shareholders and the media. Communication is one of the things that must be present in order to achieve a successful quality process," says APQC vice president Charlotte Scroggins.

Steve Stewart, another member of APQC, adds, "Communication is at the heart of the quality effort." Furthermore, communication between managers and employees about a quality initiative should begin well before the quality process is underway. Otherwise, managers run the risk that company employees will simply perceive the quality program as just another fad. To make sure the message on quality gets out, some companies have one or more individuals who are specifically responsible for communicating with employees about the quality programs being implemented. In short, communication is the lubricant necessary to make the TQM machine operate smoothly.

ADAPTED FROM: Jane Easter Bahls, "Managing for Total Quality," *Public Relations Journal* **48** (April 1992): 16–20.

what you are inferring.[5] Remaining alert to important inferences you make allows you to isolate and examine them. As a result, you will be less likely to treat key inferences as facts, which may cause miscommunication.

LABEL YOUR IMPORTANT INFERENCES   When you label your inferences, you let the other person know what you are inferring. As a result, the other person can tell you if your inferences are incorrect. Going back to our earlier example, Carol should have labeled her inference by saying, "I'm inferring that I start speaking at noon when I arrive for the meeting." The Chamber of Commerce representative would then have explained that Carol's presentation was not supposed to start until later. Thus, the confusion could have been addressed before a problem developed.

CONSIDER THIS

1. The term "communication" is misunderstood and misused by many managers. As discussed earlier, communication can be defined as the sharing of meaning. How is the term "communication" misused in the following statement? "The communication was communicated, but no communication occurred."

2. We interpret statements and actions based on our field of experience. Why, then, is there a natural tendency for communication problems to occur between employees and executives in organizations?

3. Think of an inference you made that caused a communication problem. In looking back at the situation, what should you have done to avoid the communication problem?

NONVERBAL COMMUNICATION

Managers send and receive many nonverbal messages on the job each day. Interestingly, according to one estimate, 93 percent of a message's impact is influenced by nonverbal behavior, which leaves only 7 percent accounted for by word selection.[6] As a result, managers should be aware of important aspects of nonverbal communication and how it works.

■ *Nonverbal Communication Defined*

Each day, you send many different types of messages to others.

When interacting with others, **nonverbal communication** is communication made in ways other than through spoken words. There are many ways in which managers can communicate without using spoken words. For example, without saying a word, a manager's facial expressions can indicate satisfaction or confusion. Gestures can add clarification to what is said, and eye movements may indicate anxiety.

Although much can be learned from the nonverbal messages we receive on the job, caution must be exercised in interpreting these messages. We have no standard nonverbal dictionaries to rely on to define nonverbal behaviors. However, you are *always* sending nonverbal messages on the job, and understanding how to make effective use of nonverbal communication can enhance your performance as a manager.

■ *Functions of Nonverbal Messages*

Research into nonverbal communication has revealed that nonverbal messages serve several functions. Consider how the following functions influence the way managers communicate on the job.

The way you say something can be just as important as the words you select.

TO ACCENT AND COMPLEMENT   A valuable function of nonverbal messages is that they can be used to emphasize, highlight, and reinforce parts of our verbal messages. Sometimes, as the old saying goes, "It is not what you say, but how you say it" that is important. Your tone of voice, for example, can emphasize that a certain goal has a high priority. The determined look on your face highlights that you expect the goal to be accomplished. Rolling up your shirt sleeves reinforces that work is to begin immediately to accomplish the goal.

TO REPEAT   Nonverbal messages can also repeat or restate the meaning we intend by our verbal messages. For example, in explaining where new equipment should be placed, a manager might use hand signals in addition to verbal instructions.

TO CONTRADICT   In some situations, nonverbal messages may appear to contradict verbal messages. For example, suppose you congratulate an employee

The nonverbal messages we send on the job have a significant influence on how others view us. You should be aware of your nonverbal behaviors, such as frowns or arm-crossing, and how nonverbal actions are likely to be interpreted by others at work. Remember, you are always sending nonverbal messages.

on an award she received. However, your tone of voice lacks enthusiasm and your facial expression fails to show excitement. Which will the employee believe—your verbal or nonverbal messages? Experts say that when such a contradiction occurs, we tend to believe the nonverbal messages. As a result, the employee will likely conclude that your congratulation is insincere.

TO REGULATE If you nod your head in agreement while another person speaks, you are encouraging that person to continue. Furthermore, in a conversation with others, your facial expression may provide an immediate indication that a topic introduced by one individual is inappropriate for discussion at that point. While conducting a meeting, a manager may use a gesture to signal which person should speak next. In all of these situations, nonverbal messages act to regulate conversations.

Facial expressions by themselves can be very expressive, even when no words are spoken.

TO SUBSTITUTE In some situations, nonverbal messages can be used to take the place of verbal messages. On a noisy construction site, for example, a sales representative can indicate to a customer where certain rooms will be built by using only hand gestures. Without saying a word, your eyes can indicate surprise.

As mentioned earlier, managers must exercise caution when interpreting nonverbal messages. Especially when managing a culturally diverse workforce, managers can experience communication problems if they assume nonverbal messages have standard, universal meanings. For example, in the United States, nodding the head indicates agreement; in other cultures in different countries, nodding indicates disagreement.[7] Suggestions regarding how to communicate better with foreign-born employees are contained in Figure 3–3.

■ Nonverbal Communication Can Motivate

Many managers overlook the fact that their nonverbal behavior can act as an important motivational tool. Subtle aspects in the way in which a manager interacts with employees can influence their level of motivation.[8] For example, if a manager shows an interest in employees and what they are doing, this behavior probably will have a positive effect on their level of motivation. On the job, when you interact with employees, "desirable nonverbal cues are those that express warmth, respect, concern, equality, and willingness to listen."[9]

As a manager, you must consider the nonverbal messages you send on the job. For instance, managers find that quality-improvement programs that look good on paper can be sabotaged by poor nonverbal communication. To illustrate, Richard Green, who is a quality-improvement consultant with Philip Crosby Associates, Inc., of Winter Park, FL, explains that managers make a mistake when they only issue a memorandum proclaiming their commitment to quality. Instead of the memo, managers should express and display their commitment to quality through face-to-face interactions with employees. According to Green, the nonverbal message this approach sends to employees is, "I care about your involvement, and I'm serious about improving quality."[10]

The nonverbal messages a manager sends on the job can influence the interest subordinates take in their work.

■ **FIGURE 3–3** How Managers Can Communicate Better with Foreign-Born Employees

ADAPTED FROM: Charlene Marmer Solomon, "Managing Today's Immigrants," *Personnel Journal* **72** (February 1993): 62.

When attempting to communicate with employees for whom English is a second language:

- Phrase your sentences carefully and precisely.
- Do not shout.
- Speak slowly and distinctly.
- Avoid jargon.
- Emphasize key words.
- Use visual aids.
- Use nonverbal messages cautiously.
- Watch your tone of voice.
- Use familiar words.
- Check for understanding.
- Do not cover too much information at one time.

To determine how well you are understood:

- Watch for nonverbal signs that indicate confusion.
- Notice a lack of questions.
- Have the listener paraphrase what you have said.
- Notice how instructions are followed.
- Invite questions in private.
- Distinguish between "Yes, I hear your question" and "Yes, I understand."
- Be alert to a positive response to a negative question.

A negative nonverbal message, unfortunately, can send the opposite signal (see Figure 3–4). A cost-control program, for example, at one company was so successful that top management held a party for its employees. The executives arrived in rented limousines! This excessive expense sent a message that led employees to believe top management was not really serious about reducing costs. As a result, employee morale declined and the cost-control program began to experience setbacks.[11]

Too often, managers are unaware of the negative nonverbal messages they send to employees. Although they are unintentional, these messages may be interpreted as demonstrations of coolness, aloofness, disinterest, and/or disrespect. Needless to say, when employees are left with such impressions, their levels of motivation are likely to decrease. On the other hand, if a manager's nonverbal messages indicate support for employees and satisfaction with their performances, employees' levels of motivation are likely to increase. Your efforts, for example, to maintain good eye contact, use a pleasant tone of voice, show enthusiasm, and acknowledge others with a smile will be noticed and appreciated by employees.

Managers need to consider whether their nonverbal behavior is interpreted positively or negatively by subordinates.

■ **FIGURE 3–4**   Common Nonverbal Cues That Produce Negative Reactions

NONVERBAL CUE	SIGNAL RECEIVED	REACTION FROM RECEIVER
Manager looks away when talking to the employee	I do not have this person's undivided attention	My supervisor is too busy to listen to my problem or simply does not care.
Failure to acknowledge greeting from fellow employee.	This person is unfriendly.	This person is unapproachable.
Ominous glaring (i.e., the evil eye).	I am angry.	Reciprocal anger, fear, or avoidance depending on who is sending the signal in the organization.
Rolling of the eyes.	I am not being taken seriously.	This person thinks he or she is smarter or better than I am.
Deep sighing.	Disgust or displeasure.	My opinions do not count. I must be stupid or boring to this person.
Heavy breathing (sometimes accompanied by hand waving).	Anger or heavy stress.	Avoid this person at all costs.
Eye contact not maintained when communicating.	Suspicion and/or uncertainty.	What does this person have to hide?
Manager crosses arms and leans away.	Apathy and closed-mindedness.	This person already has made up his or her mind; my opinions are not important.
Manager peers over glasses.	Skepticism or distrust.	He or she does not believe what I am saying.
Continues to read a report when employee is speaking.	Lack of interest.	My opinions are not important enough to get the supervisor's undivided attention.

SOURCE: G. Michael Barton, "Communication: Manage Words Effectively," *Personnel Journal* 69 (January 1990): 36. Copyright © January 1990. Reprinted with the permission of *Personnel Journal*, Costa Mesa, CA; all rights reserved.

LISTENING

To manage effectively, you need to receive information that will assist you in accomplishing goals. Much of that information comes to you in verbal form, and for that reason, you must be skilled at listening. **Listening** is paying attention to what the speaker says and giving meaning to what you have heard. Interestingly, as shown in Figure 3–5, about 53 percent of our communication time is spent listening. However, research indicates that many listeners remember only about *25 percent* of the information they hear.[12] Fortunately, listening is a skill that managers can improve upon by practicing specific listening techniques.

Listening requires you to give meaning to what you have heard.

■ *Hearing versus Listening*

Poor listeners often view hearing and listening as the same, but there is a difference between these two activities. Hearing is automatic; you have little control over your ability to hear. However, *listening* only occurs when you make an effort to pay attention to what a speaker says and give meaning to what you have heard. Therefore, listening requires mental effort beyond just hearing.

■ *Listening Is Good Business*

When managing the work of others, mistakes in listening can be expensive. For example, it is estimated that with more than 100 million employees in the United States, a $10 error by each worker as a result of poor listening would total in excess in 1 billion dollars.[13]

Large numbers of organizations are incorporating listening training as part of their employee-development programs to enhance employee performance on the job. For example, one large manufacturing company in New York state planned to introduce a new computer system that would influence the work performed by many employees in two divisions. One week before installation of the new computer system, 204 employees in Division B participated in a 15-hour program in listening training. None of the 187 employees in Division A received any listening training.

Interestingly, "the employees who received the listening training program performed at significantly higher levels with the new technology than employ-

■ FIGURE 3–5 Percentage of Time Spent in Communication Activities

ADAPTED FROM: Larry Barker, Karen Gladney, Renee Edwards, Frances Holley, and Connie Gaines, "An Investigation of Proportional Time Spent in Various Communication Activities by College Students," *Journal of Applied Communications Research* 8 (November 1980): 101–109.

16% Speaking 53% Listening 17% Reading 14% Writing

ees who did not receive training."[14] The employees needed to be able to listen well to the information and directions given them about the new computer system in order to operate it properly. The benefits of improved listening were demonstrated by the superior performance of those employees who had received listening training.

■ *Strategies for Comprehensive Listening*

One area of listening training that is appropriate for managers is in *comprehensive* listening. When you listen for the purpose of understanding and remembering the information contained in a verbal message, you are engaging in **comprehensive listening.**[15] Managers face many situations on the job that require them to engage in comprehensive listening. The following strategies are designed to enhance a manager's skill in comprehensive listening.

ASK QUESTIONS TO ENHANCE UNDERSTANDING   It is a good idea to ask questions if you are confused by a speaker's statements or if you are uncertain about whether your interpretation is accurate. Suppose an employee says, "From now on, any long-overdue account will be subject to more aggressive collection procedures." As a manager, it would be wise for you to ask, "How many days delinquent does an account have to be before you consider it to be long overdue?" and "What are the aggressive collection procedures you plan to use?" The answers to these questions will help you decide whether the employee's actions are appropriate.

CONFIRM YOUR UNDERSTANDING   Especially when the consequences of a misunderstanding are high, you want to confirm your understanding of the speaker's statements. For example, you might say, "I want to make sure I understand you correctly. You believe our marketing approach is not working because _____. Is that right?" This technique will shed light on any miscommunication.

MAXIMIZE YOUR EXCESS THOUGHT TIME   In general, listeners think at a rate of about 500 words per minute, but the typical speaker talks at a rate of about 125–150 words per minute.[16] As a result, we mentally process words almost four times as fast as people normally talk. This gap between thinking speed and speaking rate, which gives you time to think about various things while listening, is called **excess thought time.**

Your listening effectiveness will be hindered if you use your excess thought time to think about things that are unrelated to the speaker's comments. Mental detours of this type can cause you to fall behind in listening to the speaker. To avoid this problem, use the excess thought time to review what has been said. During this review, think of relevant questions to ask or comments to make. As a result, you will stay in tune with the speaker.

LISTEN FOR THE SPEAKER'S MAIN IDEA   While listening, it is important to identify and remember the speaker's main idea. Suppose, for example, an employee contacts you and says, "The insurance company has offered to pay 80 percent of the cost of repairing the damaged warehouse." The employee then goes on to explain in detail how the insurance company arrived at the 80 percent amount.

Listeners seldom remember all of a lengthy verbal message. However, in passing the information on to your boss, you want to make sure you retain the employee's main idea that 80 percent of the damage is covered. Listening will be less effective if you remember other parts of the message at the expense of the speaker's main idea.

LISTEN FOR SUPPORTING DETAILS   In addition to listening for the main idea, it is also important to listen for details that *support* the speaker's main idea.[17] **Supporting details** confirm the speaker's main idea. For example, an employee may explain, "I have determined that we can cut our insurance costs by 40 percent. All we have to do is make the following three changes." Of course, you want to remember the employee's main idea that insurance costs can be cut by 40 percent. However, the three changes the employee identifies represent supporting details that confirm the main idea. They are also important to remember, but they are secondary in importance to the main idea.

Remembering key words can help you recall lengthy messages.

LISTEN FOR KEY WORDS   Specific words that aid you in remembering parts of what a speaker says are called **key words**.[18] Another manager, for example, may contact you and say, "Instead of owning our photocopiers, we should consider leasing. With a lease, our maintenance costs would be lower. Also, the new copiers have such features as a built-in stapler and the ability to copy on both sides. In addition, we will get a new replacement copier every two years if we lease. I'm not sure it makes sense to own photocopiers for several years when we can lease them."

The manager's main idea is that the company should consider leasing photocopiers. Three key words—*maintenance, features,* and *replacement*—will help you remember much of what the speaker said. For example, by remembering the word *"maintenance,"* you probably will recall that a lease results in lower costs for maintenance. The same principle applies to the other key words.

Taking notes can help a listener to remember what a speaker has said.

TAKE NOTES   If you have an opportunity to take notes, the stress associated with trying to remember much of the speaker's message is reduced. For example, taking notes during telephone conversations is often appropriate and can help you remember at a later date what was discussed. In meetings, others may be flattered to know that you are interested enough in what they are saying to take notes.

FORMAL COMMUNICATION PATHS

Organizations have both formal and informal communication networks. **Formal communication** can be defined as communication between individuals in the organization about formal, work-related matters. Formal communication paths are dictated by the organizational hierarchy or by job function.[19]

In the boardroom, as in the classroom, your willingness and ability to take good notes can be of great help to you. The extra effort to take notes as a listener pays off when you must remember key information later. Taking notes conveys to others that the information is important to you.

Furthermore, formal communication generally occurs along downward, upward, and horizontal paths.

DOWNWARD COMMUNICATION

Specifically, **downward communication** refers to the flow of messages from managers to employees. As a manager, any time you send messages to employees, you are utilizing downward communication. Typical examples include explanations of procedures, policies, and practices; feedback on performance; and statements of company missions and goals.[20] The general rule is that good downward communication should include information that

Employees are kept informed through downward communication.

- Is needed by employees
- Is wanted by employees
- Is accurate
- Flows quickly to employees
- Is provided by the employees' supervisor (the preferred source)

Too often, unfortunately, managers fail to keep employees informed about important information that is relevant to the employees and to the work they do. For example, the owners of a graphic arts company discovered that morale problems among employees could be attributed to inadequate downward communication about business objectives, priorities, and results.[21] Furthermore, when managers provide employees with limited and inaccurate information, the end result is often mistrust and a demoralizing atmosphere.[22] As a matter of fact, "each time, purposely or inadvertently, that someone leaves people hanging on something that is important to them, their acceptance of their leadership has, in some small way, been diminished."[23]

Subordinates are likely to distrust a manager who withholds important information from them.

Robert J. Keith, former president and board chairman of Pillsbury, cautions that outdated attitudes toward downward communication hinder organizations. For example, managers should not rely exclusively on a third party, like a union representative, to convey important information to employees. In addition to keeping union representatives informed, managers should talk directly to employees to make sure they get the information they need.

Employees are interested in learning how their work fits in with the company's goals. Therefore, managers should show employees how important their work is to the company and how it impacts on the work of others. Furthermore, the view by some that communication may be fine but it takes too much time represents a backward and harmful attitude. The position that it is best for managers not to tell employees any more than they must is also inappropriate. According to Keith, good downward communication is a management accountability equal in priority to quality and cost control.[24]

CONSIDER THIS

1. People have an invisible bubble around them that represents their personal space. How does it make you feel when people invade your personal space by standing too close to you?

2. It has been said, "To be a good listener, you must accept the speaker as he or she is." What does this statement mean to you?

3. It is often claimed that information is power. How does this assertion explain why some managers withhold important information from employees?

■ *Downward Communication Skills*

There is much more to downward communication than just giving orders to employees. New managers are often unaware of the things they should do to enhance their effectiveness in downward communication. Experienced managers have found that the following recommendations concerning downward communication are important to good management.

It is not uncommon for subordinates to be confused about the goals of a company.

ACQUAINT EMPLOYEES WITH COMPANY GOALS   You cannot expect employees to work together to accomplish company goals if there is confusion concerning what those goals are. Managers should not take it for granted that employees are automatically aware of the company's goals. In one manufacturing company, for example, a management consultant asked employees what the company's goals were. Regarding quality production, most employees said management's goal was four or fewer flaws per item manufactured. Top management was stunned by this news. Customers, according to top management, wanted zero flaws per item they purchased and that was the goal set by the company. This misperception of the goal explained part of the problem the company was having in continuous quality improvement.

EXPLAIN COMPANY POLICIES AND PRACTICES   You cannot expect employees to follow company policies and practices if they are unfamiliar with them. Managers need to disseminate that information to employees through downward communication. Managers who ignore this responsibility share a large part of the blame for violations that occur.

EXPLAIN WHY SPECIFIC RULES EXIST   Managers must make sure that company rules are followed. However, it is much easier to gain compliance for some rules when employees see the value and the need for them. Especially for new employees, managers should explain why important rules have been established.

EXPLAIN THE IMPORTANCE OF WORKERS' JOBS   Too often, managers assume employees realize that their jobs are important to the company. However, employees do not always understand how their work relates to the operation of the organization. Employees who feel appreciated and see that what they are doing is important will be motivated to do their work well. Part of a manager's job is to explain to employees the importance of their work, especially in jobs where it may not be readily apparent.

Let employees know that the work they perform is appreciated.

PASS ON RELEVANT INFORMATION   As a manager, you will receive information that is relevant to your employees and should be shared with them. It is your job to make sure this information is passed on to your employees. In many cases, the quality of their performances will be hindered if you delay in sharing part or all of the relevant information. Your employees count on you. Make sure that important information is passed on to them.

CLEARLY STATE DOWNWARD MESSAGES   Engaging in downward communication is of little value if the information passed downward is confusing and leads to miscommunication. In some cases, the consequences of miscommunication resulting from a vague message may be worse than if no attempt is made to share the information. As a manager, you need to make sure that the messages you send downward are phrased in a way that enables them to be easily understood and interpreted correctly.

Messages sent downward need to be stated clearly.

PROVIDE FEEDBACK ON PERFORMANCE   Managers who are reluctant to provide feedback on performance are taking unnecessary risks. Those employees who are performing well may incorrectly interpret your lack of feedback as an indication that you are dissatisfied with their job performance. Conversely, in the absence of feedback from you, poor performers may conclude that you are actually satisfied with the quality of their work.

Consider the following guidelines when providing feedback to employees. Feedback is most effective when it occurs within interpersonal relationships among people who trust and care about one another.[25] Your feedback should concern an issue the employee can do something about or control. Focus on a few issues at a time; do not overwhelm employees with a long list of items. Limit your comments to what is factual and has been observed. For example, do not say, "Your report is incomplete." Instead, state that, "Your report was supposed to contain the results from ten inspections, but you only included data from four inspections." Lastly, change in organizations is inevitable, and informed employees adjust to change more readily.[26]

Feedback that helps employees improve is valued by them.

UPWARD COMMUNICATION

The value of upward communication is becoming more recognized.

In organizations, **upward communication** refers to the flow of messages from employees to managers. Upward communication has much to offer organizations. As a matter of fact, the Opinion Research Corporation indicates that

GLOBAL VIEW

The International Marketplace

Any U.S. company that attempts to enter international markets can expect to face communication problems. The most obvious problem is dealing with foreign languages. This challenge, however, is not overcome simply by learning appropriate foreign languages. For example, if you wish to do business in Japan, it has been said that you will never really learn the language —that is, as a Westerner, no matter how hard you try, the nuances and impressions certain words have on the Japanese mind will escape you. One international organization doing business in China described itself as an "old friend" of China in marketing materials distributed there. Unfortunately, the Chinese character used in the firm's literature to convey "old" was interpreted by native Chinese readers as "bygone," "used," or "former." Needless to say, the firm had not intended to leave the Chinese people with the impression that it was a has-been.

There are many communication challenges associated with doing business in another country such as dealing with different foreign languages. Understanding the traditions and values inherent in foreign cultures is also critical.

Beyond difficulties created by different languages, the traditions and values inherent in foreign cultures create obstacles to the globalization efforts of U.S. organizations. Consider the plight of one U.S. firm that offered free graduate education to new college recruits from the Netherlands. Dutch candidates were amused because in their country graduate education is already paid for by the government. Such parochialism in dealing with potential candidates from the Netherlands damaged the firm's image in that country.

Cultural inclinations toward monochronic-time values (focusing on completing one task at a time) versus polychronic-time values (attempting several tasks at the same time) can also affect how behaviors are interpreted. For example, in interactions between a monochronic North American and a polychronic Latin American, there can be disagreement over how important it is to be on time for a scheduled meeting. These differences in the values associated with timeliness can influence how prompt people are in arriving for scheduled activities. Unless the cultural influences on behaviors that lead to people being late are understood, misinterpretations of this behavior will persist. Lacking the understanding to interpret cross-cultural behaviors correctly can be a major source of miscommunication.

ADAPTED FROM: Rene White, "Beyond Berlitz: How to Penetrate Foreign Markets through Effective Communication," *Public Relations Quarterly* **31** (Summer 1986): 12–16; Nancy J. Adler and Susan Bartholomew, "Managing Globally Competent People," *Academy of Management Executive* **6** (August 1992): 52–65; Allen C. Bluedorn, Carol Felker Kaufman, and Paul M. Lane, "How Many Things Do You Like to Do at Once? An Introduction to Monochronic and Polychronic Time," *Academy of Management Executive* **6** (November 1992): 17–26.

"management appears to be taking upward communication from employees more seriously today and acting upon it."[27]

■ Facilitating Upward Communication

The ideas, suggestions, and comments from employees through upward communication can benefit organizations in many ways. As a manager, you should encourage this upward flow of information. How can you promote appropriate upward communication? The following suggestions are designed to help you in this regard.[28]

For upward communication to occur, it must be encouraged.

SHOW A POSITIVE ATTITUDE   If you want to receive upward communication, you must demonstrate that interest to employees. At work, employees will look for cues from you which indicate that you want them to keep you informed of important work-related matters. To get upward communication started, managers have to make the first effort by showing an interest in the ideas of employees.

INDICATE THE INFORMATION DESIRED   Help employees understand what types of upward communication are most beneficial. For example, explain that you cannot know everything that is going on and that you want them to let you know about any work-related problems they may be experiencing or any assistance they need. Indicate that you are also interested in their suggestions for improvements. Furthermore, encourage them to tell you about their achievements and to what extent changes in the organization have been successful.

LISTEN TO WHAT EMPLOYEES SAY   If your request for upward communication is not sincere, employees probably will sense this and fail to participate. To show that you are sincere, listen carefully when employees contact you with their concerns or suggestions. Ask questions to clarify and encourage them to elaborate. Also, make sure your facial expressions and other nonverbal messages confirm your interest in what they have to say.

BE OPEN-MINDED   Employees do not expect you to agree with all of the comments or suggestions they express through upward communication. However, they do want you to be open-minded when you consider new ideas. If employees are to make the effort to communicate upward, they must believe that their ideas will be given fair consideration. Also, they need to know that you are willing to make changes when valid reasons for doing so are provided. If you demonstrate an unwillingness to make changes, upward communication will be minimal.

Subordinates expect a response to their upward communication.

RESPOND   It is natural for employees to be interested in your reaction to their suggestions and comments. As a matter of fact, they feel you have an obligation to respond to them. If you agree or disagree with the upward communication you receive from employees, say so. Also, give reasons to justify your reactions. Failure to respond to upward communication will probably decrease or stop it.

ESTABLISH A MECHANISM FOR UPWARD COMMUNICATION   Managers cannot expect upward communication to occur on its own. Instead, they must make an effort to encourage it. Several methods are available to help funnel upward communication to managers. Common techniques include suggestion boxes, question-and-answer sessions, and procedures for employees to voice their concerns and ideas anonymously.

A PERSPECTIVE ON QUALITY

Sensing Sessions at Haworth, Inc.

Dick Haworth, president of Haworth, Inc., wants employees of the company to feel like they are part of the corporate team. As a result, employees of this Holland, Michigan-based office-furniture manufacturer are called "members." Haworth also wants all of its 4000 employees in Michigan to have an opportunity to express any concerns and suggestions for company improvement directly to top management. To accomplish this goal and further its total quality management (TQM) effort, Haworth has implemented "sensing sessions" for employees at all levels in the company.

A sensing session promotes upward communication and a continuous improvement process by asking employees to share their views on important company issues. The sessions can focus on broad topics or on a specific problem the company wants to address. In either case, employees are given an opportunity to indicate what is working and what is not working when offering suggestions for improvement.

At Haworth, the sensing session process begins with a survey of employees. The survey provides top management with feedback from employees regarding critical issues facing the company. Executives at Haworth focus on issues of highest concern to employees and use the sensing sessions to get more input from them. Participants in the sessions come from different levels and various departments to provide company-wide input. Two facilitators, one from management, are present during the sessions to assist. The managers selected as facilitators must be viewed as effective listeners. In addition, they receive formal training in how to function effectively as a facilitator.

One survey at Haworth, for example, resulted in the scheduling of 23 sensing sessions involving 250 employees. These sessions produced approximately 240 pages of documentation. From this information, management developed action plans for dealing with critical issues facing the company. Conducting employee surveys but not responding to them is a mistake some companies make that executives at Haworth are determined to avoid. Therefore, Haworth action plans are shared and discussed with employees in the company.

Through sensing sessions at Haworth, officers in the company get to hear concerns that others have. The whole process is driven by senior managers; they want the sensing sessions and are willing to commit their personal time to make the process work. Employees at Haworth indicate that they like having an opportunity to speak directly to officers in the company. For officers at Haworth, the sensing sessions have provided a more comprehensive perspective concerning important issues facing the company.

The sensing sessions, therefore, have enabled employees and management at Haworth to collaborate in making important improvements. Have the sensing sessions improved communication and cooperation at the company? The answer is an unequivocal "Yes!"

ADAPTED FROM: Jennifer J. Laabs, "Interactive Sessions Further TQM Effort," *Personnel Journal* **73** (March 1994): 22–28.

One way to encourage upward communication is to conduct an employee attitude survey. By completing such a survey, employees provide upward communication ranging from their feelings about job duties and working conditions to training and personnel policies. When analyzing the results of the survey as a manager, you should do two things. First, continue to implement procedures and practices that the survey indicates are working well. Second, promote an open dialogue with employees on how to improve problem areas identified by the survey. It is wise to translate these problem areas into action statements. If, for example, improvements are needed in training, a possible action statement would be, "Change the training program to include opportunities for employees to practice communication skills through role playing."[29]

A good way to determine how to improve a job is to talk to the person performing the job.

At Chrysler, upward communication played an important role in helping the company develop its new small car, the Neon. Robert Marcell, the person in charge of developing the Neon, knew that the new car needed to meet high standards for quality in order to be successful. To help him determine how to build the Neon with few defects, Marcell asked a group of 90 Chrysler automobile workers for ideas on how the car should be assembled. The workers offered over 4000 valuable suggestions for changing the production process Chrysler engineers had developed. As United Auto Workers quality coordinator Bob Dunlavy explains, "Engineers are great, but they've never built a car."[30] The engineers liked the suggestions offered by the Chrysler automobile workers.

HORIZONTAL COMMUNICATION

In the formal communication system, **horizontal communication** refers to the lateral exchange of messages among people on the same level of authority. When two managers communicate directly with each other, for example, they are engaging in horizontal communication. This type of communication permits the direct sharing of ideas and coordination of activities between the two managers. Without horizontal communication, their messages would have to detour around the organizational chart to reach one another. Such a detour is inefficient and time consuming.

■ Uses of Horizontal Communication

Horizontal communication is an efficient way for many individuals to communicate in organizations.

Managers can accomplish much through the use of horizontal communication. Some of the information you require to do your job well as a manager will need to come from your peers in the organization. Therefore, if you contact these individuals directly, you will gain the needed information faster than you will if you wait for it to arrive in other ways. In addition, you may need to coordinate the efforts of your department with those of another department. As a result, you should contact the manager of the other department to begin the coordination. Producing high-quality products and services often requires that departments in companies cooperate with one another. Without appropriate horizontal communication to promote this cooperation, needless errors and rework will inevitably result.[31]

Another valuable use of horizontal communication is to facilitate problem solving. For example, as a manager, you may need the help of one or more other managers to solve a problem your work unit is experiencing. If you meet together with the other managers, the collective wisdom of the group can be harnessed to solve the problem.

Managers may need to schedule appropriate horizontal communication.

In some cases, you may realize that horizontal communication among some of your employees should exist, but it has not occurred. As a result, you should schedule a meeting of these employees so the appropriate horizontal communication actually occurs. In the meeting, emphasize the importance of working together to achieve common goals.

■ *Diagonal Communication*

Diagonal communication actually includes aspects of both horizontal and vertical (downward and upward) communication. Specifically, **diagonal communication** involves the flow of information among people at different levels and involved in different functions in the organization. For example, diagonal communication occurs when a production supervisor communicates directly with the vice president for engineering in a company. These two individuals are in different areas and at different levels of authority within the company's organizational structure.

A FOCUS ON QUALITY IN COMMUNICATION

Figure 3–6 illustrates the differences among downward, upward, and horizontal communication paths. Effective use of the different forms of formal communication is necessary for the successful implementation of quality management programs in organizations. Thus, there needs to be a fostering of communication across departments and between the planners of total quality management programs and the employees responsible for making the plans work.[32]

One way to develop the type of effective communication needed to promote continuous quality improvement is to develop a "customer focus" within the company. At Texas Instruments, for example, employees are informed that, "Everyone has a customer, internal or external, whose expectations must be met."[33] This principle of customer focus necessitates that employees be informed as to how the work they perform relates to the work performed by others and to the quality of the finished product. As a result, discussion increases between employees and departments regarding what is expected and how quality can be improved.

A focus on quality requires that employees know how their work relates to the finished product.

■ **FIGURE 3–6** Formal Communication Paths

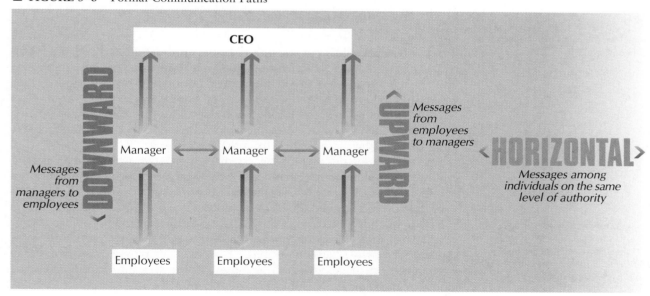

Managers in companies that have won the Malcolm Baldrige National Quality Award indicate that it is important to communicate that each employee must contribute to total quality.[34] These companies encourage upward communication as a way to keep creative ideas flowing from employees to executives who can coordinate the implementation of these ideas. To maintain a quality-focused corporate culture, managers in these award-winning companies emphasize that it is necessary to have frequent, honest, and open communication with all employees.[35]

THE GRAPEVINE

In organizations, the **grapevine** represents the informal communication system or the unofficial flow of information about people and events. Information that is not official or required by job conditions, company rules, or procedures is considered grapevine information.[36] A manager who is upset with the company grapevine cannot banish it. As a matter of fact, psychologists view an organization as psychologically sick if its employees are so uninterested in their work that they do not engage in "shop talk." However, grapevine activity is likely to increase beyond its normal level when

The grapevine will always exist.

- Formal communication channels restrict the flow of important information.
- Information the employees want to know is withheld from them.
- Employees feel insecure about the future of their jobs or how they will be affected by organizational change.[37]

When one or more of these conditions exist, employees probably will turn to the grapevine to get answers to their questions. The more the formal communication system fails to meet the information needs of employees, the greater the activity of the grapevine will be.

■ *Dealing with the Grapevine*

Grapevine messages may be incorrect or incomplete.

Interestingly, most of the stories carried by the grapevine are incomplete in detail.[38] Furthermore, even when most of the information in the stories is correct, the parts that are incorrect or missing frequently are very important. As a result, employees prefer to get job-related information from their manager, whom they believe to be knowledgeable and honest. For example, a survey of 10,000 General Electric employees found that those who received information from immediate supervisors were much more satisfied with their jobs than were those who got their information from the grapevine.[39]

The findings of this survey suggest that an effective way for managers to influence grapevine activity is to establish a climate of open communication with employees. To accomplish this goal as a manager, you first should keep your employees informed. If they get important job-related information from you, they will not need to go to the grapevine for the information. Then engage in behaviors that will signal to your employees that they can feel comfortable contacting you to discuss work-related issues. If employees view you as an approachable manager, they will be more likely to seek information from you than the grapevine.

If employees view their manager as a person with whom they can exchange important information, there will be less reason for them to use the grapevine.

SUMMARIZE IMPORTANT DECISIONS   On the job, managers often must discuss important issues with others. After you, as a manager, explain the relevant aspects of an issue, do not assume everyone has the same understanding of the conclusions that have been reached. Summarize what you believe has been determined and agreed to in the discussion. If misunderstandings exist, they will surface at this point.

LIMIT MESSAGES TO THOSE THAT ARE NECESSARY   Communication overload occurs when too many messages are sent to employees in organizations. When employees receive more messages than they can effectively deal with, they often ignore some of the messages. Needless to say, if one of the messages that goes unattended is important, a serious problem can develop. As a manager, avoid creating communication overload by limiting the messages you send to only those messages that are necessary.

The timing of a message can influence its impact.

TIME MESSAGES PROPERLY   It has been said that timing is everything in business, and timing certainly can influence the impact of a message. For example, information that is important to employees should be provided quickly by managers. Furthermore, poor performance by an employee should be discussed soon after a manager becomes aware of the problem. In general, as a manager, make sure the timing of your messages enhances the chance that they will accomplish their purpose.

GIVE AND SEEK FEEDBACK   By providing feedback, managers help employees set goals and accomplish them in an effective manner. As a result, employees are more motivated and find greater satisfaction in their work.[42] If an employee makes a mistake, you, as the manager, should explain what is wrong and how the employee can improve the situation. Regarding messages you receive, clarify the important points in them. Likewise, seek feedback from employees regarding important directions you give to make sure your subordinates understand what needs to be done.

THINK ABOUT IT

1. Managers who think that communication automatically occurs once their messages are received leave themselves vulnerable to a lot of miscommunication.

2. When you become a manager, make sure you get feedback on how well important tasks are being performed.

3. Before you make key decisions, consider the important inferences you may be making and the problems they could cause.

4. Managers' actions often speak louder than their words.

5. Managers hear with their ears, but they listen with their minds.

6. It has been said that effective managers know how to ask the right questions.

7. As a manager, if you do not respond to upward communication from employees, you will lose a source of valuable information.

8. Managers cannot eliminate the grapevine.

LOOKING BACK

Now that you have studied the concept of communication and techniques for effective communication, it is appropriate to review the objectives stated at the beginning of this chapter and to summarize highlights for each of them.

Explain the communication process.

The communication process involves sending and receiving messages for the purpose of sharing meaning. The sender encodes a thought into message form. The receiver decodes the message. This encoding and decoding process is influenced by the sender's and the receiver's fields of experience. The sending, receiving, and interpreting of messages may be hindered by various forms of noise.

Identify strategies for avoiding miscommunication that results from inferences.

First, be aware of the important inferences you make. You cannot deal with your inferences if you are not aware of them. Second, label the important inferences you make.

Identify the functions of nonverbal messages.

Research into nonverbal communication has revealed that nonverbal messages serve several functions. Specifically, nonverbal messages can accent and complement, repeat, contradict, regulate, or substitute for verbal messages.

Explain the difference between hearing and listening.

Hearing is automatic; you have little control over your ability to hear. However, listening only occurs when you make an effort to pay attention to what a speaker says and give meaning to what you have heard. Therefore, listening requires mental effort beyond just hearing.

Distinguish between downward, upward, and horizontal communication.

Downward communication refers to the flow of messages from managers to employees. Upward communication represents the flow of messages from employees to managers. Horizontal communication is the lateral exchange of messages among people at the same level of authority.

Identify ways to deal with the grapevine.

Managers can minimize grapevine activity by developing a climate of open communication with their employees. In doing so, they should keep their employees informed. Also, managers should engage in behaviors that lead employees to view them as approachable people.

KEY TERMS

communication	downward communication
communication channel	encoding
communication process	environmental noise
comprehensive listening	excess thought time
decoding	feedback
diagonal communication	formal communication

grapevine
horizontal communication
inference
key word
listening
noise
nonverbal communication

psychological noise
rumor
semantic noise
semantics
supporting detail
upward communication

REVIEW AND DISCUSSION QUESTIONS

1. In addition to sending and receiving a message, what else is needed for communication to occur?

2. How does the communication process work?

3. We give meaning to messages based on what?

4. How can inferences cause miscommunication?

5. Why are managers often unaware of important inferences they make when interacting with others?

6. Why are so many communication problems associated with nonverbal messages?

7. How can you use your excess thought time to enhance your listening effectiveness?

8. As a manager, how can you facilitate good upward communication?

9. How should management respond to a false rumor that is harming the organization?

CRITICAL THINKING INCIDENT 3.1

A Troubled Bank

The Metropolitan Bank of Elmdale wanted to improve its overall efficiency. The bank hired consultant Mark Fletcher to review its operations. During his study of the bank, Mark learned of the following incidents.

■ Top management at the bank decided that a good way to improve overall efficiency was to introduce competition among department managers. Specifically, valuable prizes were to be awarded each quarter to the manager and employees of the most productive department. One morning a customer asked a bank receptionist which person he should talk to about applying for a loan to purchase a local business. The receptionist mistakenly directed him to talk to Mr. Arnold, manager of the retail loan department, which makes loans to customers who wish to purchase automobiles, furniture, home appliances, and so on.

During the discussion, Mr. Arnold quickly determined that a mistake had been made and that the customer needed a commercial loan, which he could not make. The customer should have been transferred to the commercial loan department, but Mr. Arnold knew that sending new business to another department would hurt his department's chances of winning the productivity competition. Therefore, Mr. Arnold informed the customer that he could not make him a commercial loan but that the bank across the street would be glad to do so. Shaking his head in disbelief, the customer walked out of the Metropolitan Bank and headed to the bank across the street.

■ In the marketing department, manager Sharon Howell learned from a subordinate that the training department planned to inform bank tellers about a new free-checking account the bank was to introduce soon. Sharon liked the idea of developing a marketing campaign around the theme of free-checking accounts, and she began to think of different ways to promote the idea. Once Sharon put together a basic marketing strategy, she assigned two employees to develop her strategy further.

After the employees had done a considerable amount of work, Sharon took the marketing plans to her superior, Carol. The following conversation occurred between them.

Sharon: I want to show you the general marketing plan my department has developed to promote free checking.

Carol: We are not trying to promote free checking.

Sharon: I was told that the training department will incorporate information on free checking in the teller training program.

Carol: Who in the training department told you that?

Sharon: Well, someone there told one of my employees, who told me.

Carol: There are no plans for a new free-checking account. You've wasted your time.

■ Every Wednesday morning, Carol and other managers at the bank are expected to attend a meeting held by the bank president. However, Carol received a memo from the bank president indicating that the next meeting would be held on Tuesday, a day early, at the regular time.

On Monday, the day before the rescheduled meeting, Carol asked one of her employees to check with the president's secretary to reconfirm that the staff meeting was tomorrow. However, the secretary was unaware that the regular meeting date had been changed. As a result, in responding to the employee's inquiry, the secretary said, "Since tomorrow is Tuesday, it is not a meeting day." The employee told Carol, "The president's secretary said there is no meeting tomorrow." Carol told Jeff, another manager, that the president's meeting for tomorrow had been canceled. In actuality, the meeting was held the next day, and both Carol and Jeff were not present. Their absences angered the bank president.

Discussion Questions

1. Was it a good idea for top management to introduce the award system to promote competition among departments? Explain.

2. What mistake did Sharon make in acting on the information she received from the employee concerning the free-checking account? Explain.

3. What mistake did Jeff make in dealing with the information he received from Carol? Explain.

4. What suggestions do you believe Mark Fletcher should make to the bank?

CRITICAL THINKING INCIDENT 3.2

Quality Is Job 4

Harvey Mayes is the plant manager for Sleek Craft, a manufacturer of aluminum boats used for fishing and water skiing. In recent years, major changes have been occurring in the recreational boating industry. For one thing, boating customers are demanding higher-quality products from boat manufacturers. Companies that fail to produce higher-quality products risk losing their market share to competitors. A large decline in sales will probably put them out of business.

The public opinion polling firm of Kingston and Associates (K&A) routinely surveys consumer attitudes regarding various products. In a recent survey by K&A of consumers' experiences and views associated with various brands of aluminum boats, Sleek Craft boats received low scores on quality.

When Harvey first saw the results of the K&A survey, he dismissed them with little consideration. According to Harvey, "Consumers don't know how our boats are manufactured. They can't see the hidden quality that exists." Harvey does not see a need for a quality-improvement effort at Sleek Craft because he believes adequate quality exists in the company's products. Furthermore, as Harvey explains, "Our dealers fix any problems customers call to their attention."

In examining Harvey's management style, it becomes obvious that he assumes all the employees know what their jobs entail and what should be done to make any needed improvements in quality. As a result, Harvey does not spend much time discussing the employees' jobs with them. The other day a friend of Harvey asked him how he knew whether the work performed by his employees was of high quality. "If they do their job well, the quality will be there," Harvey responded.

Harvey regrets that it is difficult for him to find time to be a hands-on, detail-oriented manager. He expects each of his employees to do a self analysis in order to identify and assess his or her strengths and weaknesses. Harvey does not like change, and he does not make many changes in the way he manages.

Interestingly, many employees at Sleek Craft do have ideas about changes that could be made to improve product quality. However, they are not sure management is especially interested in hearing their ideas. When employees made suggestions for improvements in the past, they saw little evidence of any follow-up by management.

Harvey scoffs at the idea that employees may be reluctant to approach him with suggestions. As Harvey explains, "My employees know I am interested in their thoughts on how quality might be improved; I do appreciate their input. As a matter of fact, when employees make a suggestion, I don't intervene. I let them run with it to make the needed change."

However, Harvey concedes that he does not always provide employees with a lot of feedback to keep change moving in the right direction. Harvey's general view is that if employees do not hear much from him regarding the changes they are making, that is a good sign to them that things are going fine. Furthermore, Harvey sees total quality as an outcome rather than a process. According to Harvey, "You either have quality, or you don't."

Discussion Questions

1. What communication mistakes is Harvey making?
2. What should Harvey do differently to improve his performance as a manager?
3. What is your assessment of Harvey's view that quality is an outcome rather than a process?

CRITICAL THINKING INCIDENT 3.3

A Slow Perk

The Brew-Right Company has prospered for years, due in part to the worldwide popularity of its high-quality products used in brewing espresso and cappuccino. The company now wishes to produce a line of traditional drip-coffeemaker products.

Brew-Right has a large bureaucracy with many different departments. Each department has its own culture, norms, and procedures for getting things done. Through downward communication, top management instructed the engineering department to start designing a coffeemaker for the company to manufacture and market. In addition, the marketing department was instructed to begin developing a strategy to promote this new product.

Upon receiving the request to develop the new machine, two senior engineers, Alice and Ernesto, have the following conversation.

Alice: I'm glad the company has decided to develop a coffeemaker for commercial use in restaurants. It is a joy to work on a task like this one, where quality is the main focus and the cost of the product is secondary in importance.

Ernesto: How many different models of the coffeemaker are we supposed to design?

Alice: For now, just one.

There is some rivalry between the engineering department and the marketing department in the company. Members of the engineering department are convinced that the company's products sell well mainly because they are engineered in a superior way. On the other hand, members of the marketing department believe their efforts are more responsible for the company's success. The confidence of two experienced members of the marketing department is evident in the following conversation about the new product.

Jason: We finally got top management to produce the new product we have wanted to market for years—a coffeemaker for use at home.

Lindsay: The home-use market for coffeemakers is huge. With our marketing expertise, the biggest problem will be to fill all the orders we get.

Jason: There is another problem, too. The budget for our department will need to be increased. We have a lot of good ideas for marketing this new product, and it will take money to implement them.

Although the engineering and marketing departments have been notified of top management's decision to produce drip coffeemakers, lower-level employees in the company have not been informed of the decision. The company grapevine, however, is very active; before long, many of the employees learn about the company's plans. As speculation about the new product travels through the grapevine, company employees share reactions about it with each other. The following conversation between two employees is representative of grapevine reaction to the new product.

John: From what I hear, it looks like we will get a new coffeemaker to assemble.

Lisa: I heard it would be a commercial model.

John: That's strange. I was told it would be for home use. In either case, I hope they don't try to design every part from scratch, as they have done with other products in the past. For example, does it make sense for us to have so many different types of on–off switches?

Lisa: Maybe you should make that suggestion.

John: I'll wait until they ask for my ideas, which may be a long time.

Top management expects it to take several months for various departments to complete their work on the new product. At that point, these efforts will be merged together to produce, distribute, and market the new project. Any problems that surface then will be taken care of so the new product will be a success.

Discussion Questions

1. What communication problems is the company experiencing?

2. What problems can you predict will occur with the process the company is using to develop the new product?

3. What should the company do differently in developing the new product?

Notes

1. Joseph N. Scudder and Patricia J. Guinan, "Communication Competencies as Discriminators of Superiors' Ratings for Employee Performance," *Journal of Business Communication* **26** (Summer 1989): 224.

2. Rudolph F. Verderber and Kathleen S. Verderber, *Inter-Act: Using Interpersonal Communication Skills,* 6th ed. (Belmont, CA: Wadsworth, 1992), p. 21.

3. William V. Haney, *Communication and Interpersonal Relations: Text and Cases,* 5th ed. (Homewood, IL: Richard D. Irwin, 1986), pp. 213–23.

4. Ibid., p. 223.

5. Ibid., p. 226.

6. A. Mehrabian, *Silent Messages: Implicit Communication of Emotions and Attitudes,* 2d ed. (Belmont, CA: Wadsworth, 1981), p. 77.

7. Loretta A. Malandro and Larry Barker, *Nonverbal Communication* (Reading, MA: Addison-Wesley, 1983), p. 7.

8. Norman Hill, "Staff Members Do Better When You Set High Standards," *Association Management* **9** (February 1977): 75–77.

9. John E. Baird, Jr., and Gretchen K. Weiting, "Nonverbal Communication Can Be a Motivational Tool," *Personnel Journal* **58** (September 1979): 608.

10. "Poor Communication: Quality Saboteur," *Training* (October 1992): 14.

11. Ibid.

12. Lyman K. Steil, Larry L. Barker, and Kittie W. Watson, *Effective Listening: Key to Your Success* (Reading, MA: Addison-Wesley, 1983), p. 51.

13. Sperry advertisement, *The Wall Street Journal* (March 11, 1980), p. 17.

14. Michael J. Papa and Ethel C. Glenn, "Listening Ability and Performance with New Technology: A Case Study," *Journal of Business Communication* **25** (Fall 1988): 6.

15. Andrew W. Wolvin and Carolyn Coakley, *Listening* (Dubuque, IA: Wm. C. Brown, 1982), p. 85.

16. Ibid., p. 88.

17. Ibid., p. 92.

18. Florence I. Wolff, Nadine C. Marsnik, William S. Tracey, and Ralph G. Nichols, *Perceptive Listening* (New York: Holt, Rinehart & Winston, 1983), p. 161.

19. Gerald M. Goldhaber, *Organizational Communication,* 6th ed. (Dubuque, IA: Wm. C. Brown, 1993), p. 155.

20. Daniel Katz and Robert L. Kahn, *The Social Psychology of Organizations,* 2d ed. (New York: John Wiley, 1978), p. 440.

21. Hubbartt and Associates, "New Year's Resolution: Improve Employee Communications," *Supervision* **51** (January 1990); 26.

22. G. Michael Barton, "Communication: Manage Words Effectively," *Personnel Journal* **69** (January 1990): 32.

23. Ted Pollock, "Sharpening Your Communications," *Supervision* **51** (May 1990): 24.

24. Louis I. Gelfand, "Communicate through Your Supervisors," *Harvard Business Review* **48** (November/December 1970): 102.

25. Robert A. O'Hare and Michael P. O'Hare, "Feedback: The Key to Error-Free Performance," *Supervisory Management* **35** (January 1990): 5.

26. Barton, "Communication: Manage Words Effectively," p. 32.

27. "Relying on Bottom-to-Top Communications," *Employee Benefit Plan Review* **41** (October 1986): 30.

28. Earl Planty and William Machaver, "Upward Communications: A Project in Executive Development," *Personnel* **28** (January 1952): 304–17.

29. J. E. Osborne, "Surveying Employee Attitudes," *Supervisory Management* **37** (December 1992): 5.

30. David Woodruff and Karen Lowry Miller, "Chrysler's Neon," *Business Week* (May 3, 1993), p. 122.

31. "Poor Communication: Quality Saboteur," p. 16.

32. R. Krishnan, A. B. (Rami) Shani, R. M. Grant, and R. Baer, "In Search of Quality Improvement: Problems of Design and Implementation," *Academy of Management Executive* **7** (November 1993): 13–14.

33. Ibid., p. 14.

34. Richard Blackburn and Benson Rosen, "Total Quality and Human Resources Management: Lessons Learned from Baldridge Award-Winning Companies," *Academy of Management Executive* **7** (August 1993): 50.

35. Ibid., p. 52.

36. Keith Davis, "The Care and Cultivation of the Corporate Grapevine," *Dun's Review* **102** (July 1973): 47.

37. John W. Newstrom, Robert E. Monczka, and William E. Reif, "Perceptions of the Grapevine: Its Value and Influence," *Journal of Business Communication* **11** (Spring 1974): 12.

38. Davis, "The Care and Cultivation of the Corporate Grapevine," p. 47.

39. "GE Campaigns to Boost Execs' Job Satisfaction," *World of Work Report* **9** (March 1984): 1–2.

40. Davis, "The Care and Cultivation of the Corporate Grapevine," p. 47.

41. Mortimer R. Feinberg, "The Barriers of Communication," *Restaurant Business* **83** (May 1984): 104.

42. O'Hare and O'Hare, "Feedback: The Key to Error-Free Performance," p. 5.

 ## SUGGESTED READINGS

Baher, Connie. "How to Avoid Communication Clashes." *HR Focus* **71** (April 1994): 3.

Dreyer, R. S. "What It Takes to Be a Leader—Today!" *Supervision* **55** (May 1994): 22–23.

Hull, William W. "Beating the Grapevine to the Punch." *Supervision* **55** (August 1994): 17–19.

Johnson, J. David, William A. Donohue, Charles K. Atkin, and Sally Johnson. "Differences between Formal and Informal Communication Channels." *Journal of Business Communication* **31** (April 1994): 111–22.

Knippen, Jay T., and Thad B. Green. "How the Manager Can Use Active Listening." *Public Personnel Management* **23** (Summer 1994): 357–59.

Knoll, Ann. "10 Tips for Effective Employee Communication." *HR Focus* **71** (March 1994): 24.

Leonard, Bill. "Communication Is Key to Employee Benefits Program." *HR Magazine* **39** (January 1994): 58–59.

Maznevski, Martha L. "Understanding Our Differences: Performance in Decision-Making Groups with Diverse Members." *Human Relations* **47** (May 1994): 531–52.

Trumfio, Ginger. "More than Words." *Sales & Marketing Management* **146** (April 1994): 55.

Weiss, W. H. "Handling Communication Problems." *Supervision* **55** (March 1994): 17–19.

CHAPTER 4

DECISION MAKING

■ LEARNING OBJECTIVES

Decision making is a major managerial responsibility. In the workplace, today's decisions will have a significant impact on tomorrow's results. Knowledge of the decision-making process will guide you in weighing the pros and cons of alternative choices. You will also learn about creativity and information systems. The learning objectives for this chapter are to:

- Understand the behavioral aspects of decision making.
- Identify steps in the decision-making process.
- Describe the conditions of certainty, risk, and uncertainty.
- Explain the approaches to group decision making.
- Discuss the role of creativity in the workplace.
- Provide an overview of business information systems.

■ CHAPTER OUTLINE

Throughout history, oil-well firefighters never had to confront a challenge as great as the fires started by Saddam Hussein's military during the Persian Gulf War. Over 500 oil wells, approximately 70 percent of the producing wells in Kuwait, were set ablaze. During April of 1991, 3–6 million barrels—between $54 and $126 million in oil revenues—were lost each day.

In addition, the country faced environmental pollution and potential health damage from hydrogen sulfide and hydrocarbons. Based on his experience as a traveler in Kuwait, Mortimer B. Zuckerman, editor-in-chief of *U.S. News & World Report,* observed

> Nothing in my experience compared to the eerie environment of the Burgan oil fields, the second largest in the world. Though it was high noon, darkness had descended. . . . It was like the anteroom of hell; day became night. Temperatures were 20 degrees cooler than in places where the sky was clear.

Think about the challenges encountered by decision makers representing the Kuwaiti government and fire-fighting companies. Prior to the Persian Gulf War, only five fires had ever burned at the same time in an oil field. In the entire world, there are few skilled oil-well firefighters and a handful of companies to employ them. Considerable training is required to learn necessary firefighting skills, and learning the business takes time. In Kuwait, additional problems emerged. The Iraqis took much oil-well equipment with them and were careful to place explosives where the greatest amount of damage could be done. There were differences of opinion regarding the quality of the replacement equipment. According to one view, the decision as to where to get the new equipment was based on how soon it could be delivered rather than on its quality.

Despite much uncertainty, decisions needed to be made. Extinguishing fires was only one aspect of the problem. Beneath the ground, the delicate balance of water, natural gas, and oil were altered. Efforts to stop fires and repair wells were hampered by undiscovered land mines and possible booby traps. Furthermore, water was not readily available, which necessitated drilling new water wells or using pipes to transport water into the area.

Decision making is not an easy task, especially when decision makers must deal with a large number of variables and uncertain outcomes. When information is available, it may be unreliable. Estimates are often unrealistic. For example, early estimates on the amount of time required to put out the oil-well fires proved to be inaccurate. The work was completed in a much shorter period of time than originally anticipated.

ADAPTED FROM: Tony Horwitz and Ken Wells, "Texas Meets Kuwait as Top Firefighters Reach Blazing Wells," *The Wall Street Journal* (March 27, 1991): A1; Allanna Sullivan, "Estimates Cut on Putting Out Kuwait Oil Fires," *The Wall Street Journal* (April 17, 1991): A2; Allanna Sullivan, "Even after Fires Die, Kuwait's Oil Fields Will Never Be the Same," *The Wall Street Journal* (April 26, 1991): A1, A6; John Schneidawind, "U.S. Exports Ready Assault on Rig Blazes," *USA Today* (February 26, 1991): 1–2B; Rae Tyson and Sam V. Meddis, "Kuwait Blazes Compared to Agent Orange," *USA Today* (March 15–17, 1991): 2A; James Cox, "Emirate Looks to Restarting Production," *USA Today* (April 24, 1991): 1–2B; Mortimer B. Zuckerman, "When It's Dark at High Noon," *U.S. News & World Report* **110** (April 1, 1991): 46.

After the Persian Gulf War, oil-well firefighters were challenged to make crucial decisions in order to extinguish oil-well fires of a magnitude never previously encountered.

THE ROLE OF DECISION MAKING

What is decision making?

Decision making is the process of choosing among various courses of action. For example, a manufacturer might follow the much-publicized Japanese approach and decide to automate operations. However, Federal-Mogul, an auto parts maker, has chosen to avoid the time needed to adjust sophisticated machinery in order to reduce maintenance costs. Instead of complex equipment, the company uses assembly sections that are manually interchanged to accommodate the various types and sizes of items being produced.[1]

Consider the challenge caused by declining sales at an automobile dealership. The problem may be caused by layoffs at a major employer, by increasing interest rates to purchasers, or by noncompetitive pricing. Alternative courses of action must be developed and evaluated: establish a broader geographic market; seek interest rate breaks from lenders; reduce profit margins to stimulate sales. Finally, a decision, which may include one or a combination of these alternatives, needs to be reached.

Decision makers can choose to do nothing. This choice, which at times is worth considering, is a decision. Ultimately, the need to make a decision may not be necessary. For example, a manager may be considering two prospective employees and may spend much time worrying about which person to select. While the manager contemplates the decision, one of the candidates accepts another job offer. The manager has lost much time fretting about a decision that is now beyond his or her control.

■ *Teamwork in Decision Making*

Increasingly, self-directed work teams are involved in the decision-making process. Generally, teams strive to attain the most opportune results to serve customer needs and, in turn, attain company objectives. Members seek to identify problems, discuss alternatives, and implement recommended solutions.

At Martin Marietta's recently acquired GE/Aerospace unit, a group called "Work Out" was instrumental in acquiring a military contract. The team worked together to accomplish tasks, regardless of job titles and individual job responsibilities. In four days, the team finished an assignment that would normally take 10–12 weeks to complete. Another team was able to improve

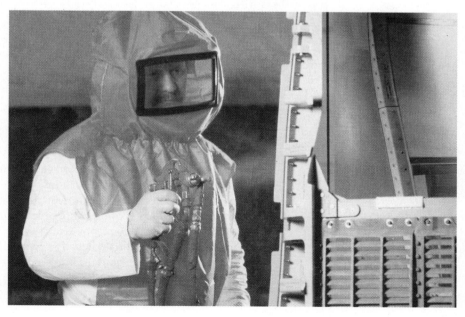

Decisions to use modern equipment and provide necessary training help firms increase productivity, serve customers, and remain competitive. Firms are consistently challenged to install up-to-date equipment. This man is spray-painting MA-25 heat protectorant on the interior of a jet engine thrust reverser at Martin Marietta Corporation.

inventory control, reorganize material flow, and coordinate operations with suppliers to significantly reduce manufacturing and material cycles.[2]

■ What Is a Good Decision?

Good decisions do not just happen.

What is a good decision? The answer is not as simple as you might expect. Assume a firm's decision to increase productivity involves adding state-of-the-art equipment and giving operators the most up-to-date training available. If the objective is to increase output, then this decision is an optimal choice. However, it may not be possible to sell all of the products produced by the new equipment, which would lead to employee layoffs and idle machines. To complicate matters, the firm might need to increase prices to cover the added expenses of the new equipment. As a result, the company could cease to be competitive—a concern to be avoided. Returning to the question, we can conclude that a good decision recognizes the best interests of an organization and its personnel.

■ The Search for Quality

The search for quality is an essential aspect of decision making. To remain competitive and retain customers, managers must continually strive to make better decisions. Employee participation instills a sense of commitment to chosen courses of action.

The late W. Edwards Deming, a well-known quality expert, emphasized the importance of breaking down barriers among different departments and maintaining lines of communication with suppliers. Managers who make arbitrary decisions, such as setting a standard without consulting those who will actually be doing the work, risk losing the willingness of their employees to go the "extra mile" to assure quality job performance.

BEHAVIORAL ASPECTS OF DECISION MAKING

Decisions are made and implemented by people who possess different outlooks, motives, and expectations. Most of us consider ourselves to be rational decision makers. However, we often encounter limitations, especially when dealing with complex problems that have many variables. We possess limited amounts of energy, become frustrated by challenging obstacles, and often lack the desired amount of information on which to act.

■ Prior Decisions

Managers learn from experience.

According to an old adage, "Experience keeps a dear school." Capable managers gain insights from prior decisions.

The impact of decisions on human resources is a necessary consideration. For instance, installation of new, upgraded equipment not only may reduce the number of defective products but also may alleviate the frustrations of workers who will no longer need to do costly rework. Remember, the concept of quality improvement stresses gaining knowledge from experiences and recognizing the importance of job-performance excellence as a key to attaining managerial objectives.

■ Attitudes and Opinions

Attitudes and opinions influence behaviors. If a problem is considered to be important, it probably will receive a lot of attention. If an attitude of indifference prevails, a necessary decision can easily be put off or even avoided.

As an example of attitude influencing behavior, many people share the opinion that the word "new" automatically means an absence of problems. Consequently, they buy new equipment without expecting to encounter difficulties with it. In practice, newness and availability of guarantees do not necessarily imply freedom from breakdowns.

■ Knowledge

Knowledge is a key factor in decision making. Decision makers attempt to learn as much as possible about issues and use this information to further corporate interests.

As an example, Sears used its knowledge of the business environment to radically restructure operations. Once the nation's largest retailer, Sears found itself ranked third behind Kmart and Wal-Mart in 1993. Traditionally known as a retailer, Sears had evolved into a giant conglomerate that included insurance, financial service, and real estate businesses.

The firm's management assessed business conditions and decided to spin-off the Dean Witter Reynolds brokerage unit, offer some ownership of Allstate Insurance to the public, and sell the Coldwell Banker residential real estate subsidiary. Consequently, Sears substantially reduced its debt and committed itself to becoming more dominant in the retail industry.

■ Emotions

Emotions (anger, happiness, sadness, and frustration) affect decision-making perspectives. "In a curious way, any attempts to remove the emotional element from one's deliberations is a denial of reality. Sound judgments are made with the full awareness that feelings such as pride, prejudice, and vanity are always subconsciously at play."[3]

A worker stressed by a heavy workload may be overly concerned about getting tasks finished and decide to take shortcuts that actually create additional work and wasted time. If frustrated and pressed for an immediate response by a subordinate, a manager might reply, "Just do whatever you want." Granting such permission gives some employees too much discretion. They may make too many inappropriate decisions.

■ Intuition

Intuition can provide guidance in decision making.

Some persons spot trends and draw relevant implications from data to a greater extent than others do. Many intuitive decisions cannot be justified by accumulated information. Nevertheless, intuition cannot be disregarded, as it can influence choices.

> The need to understand and use intuition exists because few strategic business decisions have the benefit of complete, accurate, and timely information. It would be easier to manage if we lived in a world that was totally quantifiable and predictable. As long as corporations exist in a world of rapid and unprecedented change, intuition will play a significant role in decision-making processes.[4]

■ Current Circumstances

Prevailing circumstances influence decisions. When fewer customers are served, sales revenue declines. In response to this set of circumstances, a fast-food retailer may decide to run a promotion featuring a coupon for a "buy one, get one free" special. The purpose of the sale is to bring customers into the business, even though the incentive decreases profit on the featured special.

When responding to market realities, seemingly good decisions can have negative results. Ford's Edsel automobile, developed during the 1950s at a cost of $250 million, was the result of extensive research and had a distinctive appearance. In the first year of sales, $10 million was budgeted for advertising; yet the Edsel was produced for only two years. Several circumstances adversely affected the Edsel: an impending recession, growing interest in smaller automobiles, and a confusing pricing system.[5]

■ Communication Practices

Finally, the growing globalization of markets has forced managers to balance differences in behavioral and communication practices. The failure to recognize informal cultural expectations can create unnecessary obstacles to the decision-making process. Some examples of how cultural differences can affect business decisions follow.

- ■ In some Asian cultures, a smile and a nod of approval signify politeness, not necessarily agreement.
- ■ The need to "save face" and avoid embarrassment is especially important to Orientals.
- ■ In many cultures, personal friends and acquaintances influence decisions to a greater extent than they do in America.
- ■ Written contracts, which formalize decisions in American businesses, have lesser meaning in the Middle East.
- ■ When meeting to make decisions, Americans tend to be direct and to the point. However, informal talk characteristically precedes business discussions in Mexican and other cultures.

Managers as Decision Makers

Decision making can be hectic.

Managers are often portrayed as calm, rational individuals who focus on logical analyses and apply systematic techniques to get results. Although many decisions are reached in this manner, decision making can be a chaotic experience: reacting to emotional outbursts, hurrying to meet deadlines, and pressing to gain acceptance for a point view. Leonard R. Sayles, an authority on leadership, observes

> Thus, managerial work is hectic and fragmented and requires the ability to shift continually from person to person, from one subject or problem to another. It is almost the diametric opposite of the studied, analytical, persisting work pattern of the professional who expects and demands closure: the time to do a careful and complete job that will provide pride of authorship.[6]

In this section, you will learn about managers as decision makers. Successful decision making requires a commitment to choices. Capable decision makers seek explanations for faulty decisions and practice good communication techniques. Managers respond to different decision circumstances. Some decisions are repetitive in nature; others occur less frequently. Guidelines are available to help managers make sound decisions.

Commitment to a course of action is often a key aspect of managerial success. In practice, however, managers can become committed to ineffective strategies for several reasons.[7] Actual participation in the decision-making process increases commitment to choices. Accountability for results, public awareness of actions, and a belief that inadequate performance corresponds to inability can cause adherence to inopportune alternatives. Managers must continually assess the merits of their decisions and recognize that organizational concerns should not be sacrificed for self-interest.

■ *How to Avoid Faulty Decisions*

Decisions can be wrong.

Why do managers make faulty decisions? They do so as a result of a number of factors, including their personality characteristics, biases or prejudices, faulty assumptions, and failure to solicit the involvement of the right people.[8] No manager always makes correct decisions. A focus on priorities and an ability to work cooperatively with people who have dissimilar backgrounds are valuable attributes of a good decision maker.

Capable managers combine foresight and understanding with the selection of employees who possess the job skills required to complete specific assignments. Also, effective **delegation,** or granting the authority to do a task to a subordinate, helps managers to avoid making poor decisions. Delegating a task to a skilled worker is likely to result in fewer mistakes than assigning that task to a new trainee.

Effective communication alleviates problems.

Clear explanations reduce misunderstandings, unnecessary anxieties, and wasted time. For example, assume the commission rate for salespeople is lowered but that management agrees to provide more training and secretarial assistance in return. If the reasons for this decision are not stated by management or accepted as legitimate by the sales staff, job satisfaction and morale will deteriorate. If the soundness of a managerial decision is questioned, then communication of the explanation for the decision by management becomes especially relevant.

Managers need to recognize the amount of time and effort that can reasonably be given to any problem situation. For example, to trace who leaked company information to *The Wall Street Journal,* the management of Procter & Gamble asked authorities to search mountains of telephone records and determine which employees tried to contact a reporter. Later, P&G managers concluded they had created a problem that was greater than the one they were investigating.[9]

■ *Programmed and Nonprogrammed Decisions*

Decisions that are routine and repetitive in nature are called **programmed decisions.** Examples include ordering replacement inventory, filing information about credit applications, and filling orders at a warehouse. Programmed decisions are structured and generally require little thought. As such, responsibility for them can be shifted to the lowest level of the managerial chain of command.

The importance of programmed decisions should not be underestimated. Consider this example: Each day, banks open doors in the morning and lock them at the close of business. One afternoon a customer arrives just as an employee is locking the door and is told, "You're too late. Can't you see the hours posted on the window?" Although the message is clearly communicated by the employee, it can easily be perceived as being rude and too abrupt. Subsequently, the customer, who could have substantial sums of money on deposit with this bank, may decide to do business with another bank.

Nonprogrammed decisions are nonrepetitive in nature and include nonroutine choices. Because these decisions can be somewhat subjective and often are not clearly defined, they generally fall within the purview of top management.

Since the late 1980s, businesses have encountered economic pressures to be more competitive and as a consequence have had to make more nonprogrammed decisions. As a result, greater numbers of personnel have been terminated as managers attempt to economize and operations are automated. Shell Oil has reduced its work force by up to 4000 people; Citicorp has cut 10,000 jobs; and Digital Equipment has announced job reductions for 9000 employees.[10]

Also, nonprogrammed decisions can be caused by unusual life-threatening situations. An example is Johnson & Johnson's immediate decision to withdraw Tylenol, primarily from the Chicago market in 1982, because potassium cyanide had been deliberately inserted into a few of the capsules. Another example is Jack In the Box restaurants changing their cooking procedures (for example, allowing meat to cook at a higher temperature for a longer period of time) following meat contamination in the Seattle area in 1993 that resulted in the illness of many patrons and even death.

■ Decision Guidelines

It is good advice to think before acting.

Hindsight is an optimal predictor for correct decisions. However, decisions must be future-oriented and often involve sifting through a multitude of data to form conclusions. Occasionally, decisions consume too much time, resulting in lost opportunity. On the other hand, hasty decisions may fail to take relevant facts into consideration. The following guidelines for managerial decision making are useful.

■ Base decisions on reliable and accurate information. Refer to secondary sources (government documents, periodicals, and trade journals) before doing primary research.

■ Review decisions as situations necessitate. Be flexible; avoid commitment to only one course of action.

■ Devote attention to relevant problems and issues. Too much concentration on relatively minor concerns or unimportant details is likely to be counterproductive.

■ Consider the assumptions on which decisions are formulated. If assumptions are incorrect, any number of complexities can occur.

■ Prepare to defend decisions and justify the rationales used to make them. Have facts and supporting data readily available.

■ Recognize the importance of effective communication. It is unlikely that people will react positively and be committed to decisions that are not understood. Contemplate the reactions of customers, employees, and colleagues who are affected by decisions.

■ Develop accurate methods of assessment to assure that quality standards are met.

■ Determine if a decision establishes any unanticipated precedents.

Next, we will examine the five-step decision-making process. Even though each step will be discussed separately, you should not overlook the comprehensive nature of the entire process. Complications at any step can cause breakdowns that hinder the likelihood of attaining effective and desirable managerial solutions.

THE DECISION-MAKING PROCESS

Decision making involves five steps.

The rational decision-making process gives managers a framework for structuring decision choices. Figure 4–1 illustrates the five steps in this process: identify the problem, develop and evaluate alternatives, select the best alternative, implement the alternative, and follow up. Decision making can be difficult due to pressures from colleagues, bosses, and subordinates. Also, personal factors, such as a desire to establish a good reputation or project a positive self image, can influence decision choices.

Concern for quality is a relevant aspect of all decisions. Likewise, a failure to focus on productivity is an invitation to ultimate loss of competitiveness. When making a decision, it is essential to consider potential results *before* initiating action. Otherwise, unanticipated consequences will occur too frequently. Effective communication alleviates complications that can arise from incorrect assumptions, misunderstandings, or inaccurate information. Communication concerns should be recognized at each step of the decision-making process.

■ **FIGURE 4–1**   The Decision-Making Process

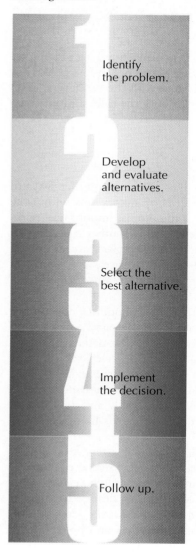

Identify the problem.

Develop and evaluate alternatives.

Select the best alternative.

Implement the decision.

Follow up.

■ Identify the Problem

The first step in the decision-making process is critical; an unidentified problem cannot be solved. Careful analysis distinguishes between a problem and the symptoms of a problem. Efforts directed toward alleviating symptoms are not likely to resolve the problem. For example, a manager notices an increase in accidents and immediately concludes that the problem is inadequate training. Yet the real difficulty may be the job tasks performed; they are so repetitive and boring that employees do not concentrate on doing them.

How is a problem identified? Several questions provide useful guidance.

■ Who must contend with the problem?
■ What evidence exists that there is a problem?
■ Where does the problem happen?
■ When does the problem happen?
■ How much does the problem affect company costs?[11]

Identification enables decision makers to gain a comprehensive understanding of the problem by carefully considering who, what, where, when, and how much. At this step, it is important to list as many factors as possible. Efforts directed toward encouraging decision makers to *think* are not likely to be wasted.

Perspectives influence how potential problems are considered; various people may view them differently. Let's assume that returns are running quite high on lumber sold to contractors. Sales personnel consider the difficulty to be low

Discussion and analysis are keys to correctly identifying problems. It is advantageous for several decision makers to combine their knowledge and skills while problem solving.

Views about problems can differ.

product quality. According to the purchasing department, however, the lumber is of sufficient quality to meet needs and is as good as top-of-the-line grades but costs less because price concessions were negotiated with the producers. Who is right? Probably there are merits to the views of both the sales and purchasing departments.

■ *Develop and Evaluate Alternatives*

After the problem is identified, the decision maker needs to consider ways to resolve it. It is important to generate several ideas or suggestions within the amount of available time. Some decisions are of the utmost importance: selection of a new corporate president, possible merger with another company, or proposed entry into the competitive international marketplace are examples. Others are relatively minor: type of color schemes for office suites, kinds of refreshments to serve at a reception, or number of athletic teams to sponsor in the community recreation league.

Decision makers are not free to choose alternatives without any constraints. Potential limiting factors include compliance with laws, company policies, budget controls, time restrictions, and ethical concerns. Checks to determine if laws are being obeyed can save unexpected litigation costs. Directives from decision makers specify acceptable actions. After two executives were suspended for allegations of improper trading, Howard Clark, Chief Executive Officer at Shearson, wrote to employees and said, "We will act quickly and decisively to ensure that we continually meet the highest ethical standards in all aspects of our business."[12]

Evaluation is a necessity.

The evaluation of alternatives requires foresight and consistency of purpose. After considering the merits of each alternative, the decision maker chooses the best alternative. Common selection criteria include feasibility; compatibility with policies, rules, or guidelines; and likelihood of getting desired results.

Feasibility considers cost, time, and human resource factors. Consider the following example. The owner of a clothing store explores an opportunity to serve the needs of college students and contemplates opening a specialty store near the local university. Although this choice will increase revenues, the merchant thinks the additional overhead will be too great. In addition, a new store will place greater demands on managerial time and necessitate hiring more personnel. Therefore, the manager must evaluate the pros of serving another market sector and compare them against the offsetting concerns.

Policies and guidelines should not be overlooked.

Company policies and guidelines provide standards against which policymakers evaluate decisions. If a decision benefits the firm but violates regulations, it should not be implemented. When pressured by subordinates, superiors, colleagues, or others, managers should rely on company regulations to justify whether a decision can or cannot be made. If the decision maker feels an exception to the rules is necessary, it should be requested; perhaps approval can be granted. Difficulties arise when decisions are made with full knowledge that company policies or guidelines are being violated.

A manager should evaluate an alternative decision on the basis of whether its implementation will produce the desired results. A seemingly good decision does not guarantee a preferred outcome. For example, accumulating a stock of designer jeans to sell is a good decision only as long as this item remains popular. When its popularity diminishes, revenues resulting from a seemingly correct decision will decline. Therefore, it is important to determine if a decision is really worthwhile.

■ Select the Best Alternative

This step involves making the actual decision. Perhaps the best alternative or combination of alternatives is clearly evident; if so, then the choice is easy. At times, however, it may not be possible to choose the best alternative. For example, a job may be offered to a next-best candidate because the top-ranked candidate turned it down. When this type of situation occurs, it pays to exercise caution and be certain that desired qualities are not sacrificed for the expediency of finalizing the decision-making process.

If a gap exists between the expected and desired outcomes, the following conditions must exist before decision makers will exert initiative.

"Gaps" can be reduced.

- ■ The gap must be considered significant.
- ■ Motivation must be present to reduce the gap.
- ■ A belief must exist that the gap can be reduced.[13]

High levels of motivation and enthusiasm do not guarantee good outcomes. Decision makers do not deliberately seek adverse choices. Yet events can change and alter the appropriateness of a chosen alternative.

■ Implement the Alternative

Do not underestimate the importance of implementation.

The implementation of alternatives should not be taken for granted. Some decisions are more easily implemented than others. A decision to lower qualifications for a bonus is likely to be eagerly anticipated and implemented without much debate. However, a decision requiring a major change of job-duty assignments as a result of layoffs would be much more difficult to implement.

Successful introduction of decisions requires clear-cut explanations and possibly revised operational procedures. For example, Sears divided its merchandising group into "power formats" to strengthen its competitiveness and establish a way to measure the profitability of each merchandise category.[14] The decision was quite a departure from regular practices and may ultimately involve setting some "formats" up as stores by themselves, such as Home Life furniture stores.

It is especially difficult for managers to implement decisions that will have negative implications for human resources. Communication plays an important role. Explaining rationales, practicing fairness, and being considerate of human feelings all enhance the possibility that such decisions will be successfully implemented.

Even though a decision is quite unfavorable, it may be necessary and may serve as a prelude to later success. In the 1980s, Exxon reduced employment, cut refinery capacity, and closed service stations. The company focused on automating refineries and improving high-volume service stations. During the 1990s, Exxon experienced a considerable increase in the volume of its products sold at stations.[15]

■ Follow Up

Things do not always work out as expected.

Events do not always unfold as intended. A decision may prove to be untimely or even totally wrong. Follow-up activities serve as checks to determine if changes are necessary. They can range from a brief note or informal conversation to a very detailed formal report. Through communication, knowledge is gained that serves as a basis for subsequent actions. A key consideration is not to take expected outcomes for granted. Wise decision makers are prepared and ready to revise decisions whenever necessary.

When the completion of a task depends on personnel who are unaccustomed to their roles, follow up is especially important. Russia, a part of the former Soviet Union, has sought to implement a western-style economic system and western management techniques. A decision to transform Zaria, a collective farm near Moscow, illustrates some of the complexities faced by managers.[16] In this case,

■ Pensioners claimed the land was inappropriately taken from them and became dissatisfied that repairs were not made.

■ The director decided to adopt a new method of breeding cattle only to encounter resistance to lost jobs and longer work hours.

■ At a potato-growing operation, local farmers decided not to plant the crop and quit. Additional farmers were hired, and they also decided not to work.

Even though the director, who was ultimately replaced, faced a difficult managerial task, early efforts to follow up decisions that were made and to solicit input from subordinates might have led to a better understanding of potential complications and even to a rethinking of the decisions that were made.

CONSIDER THIS

1. What is the most important step in the decision-making process?

2. When should managers change their decisions?

3. How can managers improve their decision-making skills?

THE DECISION ENVIRONMENT

Decision making can be complex.

According to an old adage, few things are certain except death and taxes. Generally, managers do not have all of the information they need to make decisions. Available information may be too unreliable or inaccurate. The decision environment can be relatively stable or quite unpredictable. Capable managers do not always develop winning strategies, but initial complexities can often be overcome. Sam Walton, who founded Wal-Mart stores, opened his first store, a Ben Franklin, in Newport, Arkansas. Although successful, the store was ultimately sold to the landlord's son because the landlord did not want to renew Walton's lease. When Wal-Mart's eighteenth store was opened in Newport, the Ben Franklin store closed its doors.[17]

International politics and regulations governing business practices among nations complicate the global business environment.[18] Some countries follow a protectionist policy; their primary objective is to protect national interests. Other countries are willing to open up markets but only when sought-after concessions are granted.

Gaining approval for overseas routes is a classic example of the challenges encountered in the global marketplace. In 1993, Air France successfully blocked greater access of U.S. airlines to Paris and persuaded the French government to seek a more restrictive agreement with the United States. Germany, Australia, and Japan have also attempted to curtail expansion of U.S. airlines. International air traffic is governed by a huge number of bilateral contracts among nations. The basis for these pacts is the prevailing practice that international markets are not open to outsiders unless specific permission is granted. From a practical perspective, the strength of U.S. carriers, which have withstood deregulation and major competitive challenges, is perceived as a threat by international airlines, many of which are considerably less efficient and have higher operating costs.

The rules and regulations within different countries can complicate the operations of airlines flying international routes. Doing business in a complex environment places extra emphasis on a manager's decision-making skills.

Natural disasters, such as the Great Flood of 1993, devastate vast acres of land and cause considerable loss of property. Unexpected events like natural disasters require numerous unanticipated decisions.

■ Conditions for Decision Making: Certainty, Risk, and Uncertainty

Three conditions are encountered when making business decisions.

Decision making is classified according to the amount of knowledge possessed about events and the likelihood that these events will occur. The three conditions encountered when making business decisions are certainty, risk, and uncertainty. If certainty exists, decision making is quite simple. The risk criterion involves the use of mathematical probabilities. If uncertainty exists, however, decision makers do not know which events will occur and cannot determine probabilities. The presence of uncertainty characterizes far more decisions than the conditions of certainty or risk do. Figure 4–2 differentiates among the three conditions of decision making and identifies the amount of vagueness that typically prevails in each case.

Certainty is an unusual characteristic of business decisions.

CERTAINTY This criterion does not usually characterize business decisions. **Certainty** implies that the decision maker knows which events will occur and

■ FIGURE 4–2   The Three Conditions of Decision Making

CERTAINTY	RISK	UNCERTAINTY
Decision makers **have** knowledge of events and results.	Decision makers do **not** know which events will occur.	Decision makers do **not** know which events will occur.
Select the largest payoff value.	Probabilities for various events **are** known.	Probabilities for various events are **not** known.

Increasing vagueness

can choose the one with the largest payoff value. For instance, managers at United Parcel Service know that the volume of packages handled by UPS increases during the Christmas season. To assure the most expedient service possible, they must make the decision to use more personnel and equipment to sort and deliver parcels during this seasonal period.

Probability is a key to the risk criterion.

RISK   When the condition of **risk** is present, the decision maker does not know which events will happen but can determine the probabilities that these events will occur. Accuracy of probability estimates is critical to successful usage of this criterion. Therefore, assessments should be determined carefully and as representatively as possible.

Let's consider an example. A farmer must decide whether to plant wheat, corn, or soybeans. The farmer knows that wheat grows best if wet weather prevails, corn does best under variable weather conditions, and soybeans have the greatest success when dry weather exists. A review of weather records indicates the probability of occurrence for each type of weather, and the farmer knows the payoff values for the various types of grain. Figure 4–3 presents all of this information and shows the calculated **expected values,** which are the sums of products of each probability multiplied by its respective value. The computations tell the farmer to plant wheat because it has the largest expected value ($26,000).

Uncertainty characterizes most business decisions.

UNCERTAINTY   Most business decisions can be categorized under this criterion. **Uncertainty** acknowledges that both events that influence decisions and accompanying probabilities are not known. Consequently, structured guidelines are not available, and vagueness predominates. This is the most complex decision-making condition. Think about the difficulty of deciding whether or not to make a large commitment of funds to do business in the People's Republic of China. Potential customers may not buy your product; the Chinese government could take over any facilities you may build. Or you may discover that things work out better than you anticipated and profits exceed expectations.

Uncertainty about human resources presents an especially challenging decision-making condition. Very talented persons may leave the firm, be promoted to other jobs within the firm, receive transfers to other localities, or retire, thereby necessitating decisions about their successors. "60 Minutes" has done quite well for CBS. During a recent season, the show earned more than $60 million;

■ **FIGURE 4–3**   Expected Values for the Farmer

CROP CHOICE	DRY WEATHER (PROBABILITY .20)		VARIABLE WEATHER (PROBABILITY .50)		WET WEATHER (PROBABILITY .30)		EXPECTED VALUE
Wheat	($5,000)(.20)	+	($20,000)(.50)	+	($50,000)(.30)	=	$26,000
Corn	($10,000)(.20)	+	($30,000)(.50)	+	($20,000)(.30)	=	$23,000
Soybeans	($20,000)(.20)	+	($8,000)(.50)	+	($10,000)(.30)	=	$11,000

one season, it represented the balance between profit and loss for the network.[19] Each of the leading correspondents (Mike Wallace, Andy Rooney, Morley Safer) is at least 60 years old, and Harry Reasoner, one of the original correspondents, passed away in 1991. Who will replace these aging newsmakers? According to Kevin Goldman of *The Wall Street Journal*: "It is an unprecedented predicament in network television. Shows usually die out long before their stars do."[20]

When faced with uncertainty, firms often strive to reduce costs. The Persian Gulf War and prevailing recession forced many companies to examine their expenses more carefully. In one year, Federal Express trimmed its travel costs by 55 percent, saving $3.3 million, and Unisys Corporation cut $20 million from its air-travel budget.[21] It is common practice to keep cost-cutting measures intact, even after problematic concerns are alleviated. As economic and political climates improve, companies become more willing to increase expenditures for money, equipment, and personnel. During the latter phases of a recession, managers start to assign overtime to current employees before they begin to add new employees to the payroll. If sales revenues continue to increase, more workers are hired because the perception of uncertainty is reduced.

Personal factors influence decisions.

When uncertainty is encountered, the personal characteristics of decision makers cannot be ignored. A cautious manager adheres to more conservative approaches than a risk taker does. Likewise, decision makers who have pessimistic attitudes view events and possible outcomes differently than those who have optimistic outlooks do. Some people rely on past ways of doing things. If a particular strategy has previously produced results, the decision maker is likely to apply the same strategy to situations perceived to be similar in nature.

THE ROLE OF GROUP DECISIONS

It is a common managerial practice to use groups to make decisions. The use of groups is frequently justified on the basis that "two heads are better than one." The complexities of doing business, technological advancements, and an emphasis on competitiveness all encourage firms to adopt group decision making policies.

Today's employees seek greater involvement in decisions that affect them. The number of **quality circles**—voluntary groups of workers who recommend solutions to job-related problems—has grown considerably. In less than a decade, the International Association of Quality Circles grew from 100 to over 7000 members.[22] Concern for developing teamwork and using workers in advisory roles has also increased. When faced with a need to change from a five- to seven-day production schedule, Baxter Healthcare Corporation established an employee advisory committee specifically designed to evaluate options and make recommendations on this matter.[23]

When are groups appropriate?

Several conditions favor using groups to make decisions.[24] A group functions best if a range of potential solutions is available for consideration. Cordiality among participants and a pleasant work environment are conducive to the group approach. Groups tend to function better when personal needs do not predominate. Also, distribution of rewards among the group as a whole, instead of to individuals, facilitates group decisions.

A PERSPECTIVE ON QUALITY

Group Decision Making at U.S. Steel

The Gary Works' plant of U.S. Steel won an RIT/*USA Today* Quality Cup for using teamwork to better communication, reduce product damage, and improve customer satisfaction. Group members visited customer facilities to learn about problems. Visits led to revised shipping and handling procedures: rubber pads to support steel coils during shipment, plastic rings to avoid crane damage, and signed tags to verify the condition of the coils during packaging and loading. As a result, the amount of steel rejected by automotive customers declined from 2.6 percent, worst in the industry, to 0.6 percent.

Each Monday, the group meets with management and personally discusses ways to resolve problems and improve product quality. A group member can call managers directly, and burdensome paperwork has been eliminated. Knowledgeable personnel can provide answers without bureaucratic hassles. Ford, a major customer, was concerned because zinc was flaking from steel purchased at the Gary Works. The remedy involved making an adjustment on trim rods. Also, Ford discovered that it incurred needless waste because a harmless residue was mistakenly believed to be rust.

ADAPTED FROM: James R. Healey, "U.S. Steel Learns from Experience," *USA Today* (April 10, 1992), pp. 1B–2B.

■ The Advantages and Disadvantages of Group Decisions

Figure 4–4 summarizes the advantages and disadvantages of using groups to make decisions. A key benefit of group decision making is the availability of people with different backgrounds and experiences. Problems can be considered from various perspectives, and complications in communication are minimized. Instead of getting bogged down with jargon, technical specialists and

■ **FIGURE 4–4** The Advantages and Disadvantages of Group Decisions

Advantages	Disadvantages
■ A variety of ideas and suggestions can be discussed.	■ The group approach consumes a considerable amount of time.
■ Alternatives can be considered from the viewpoint of group members who possess different backgrounds and experiences.	■ Some group members may not support or be committed to a recommended decision.
■ A considerable amount of information can be collected and reviewed.	■ Dominant personalities may unduly influence a decision.
■ Employee involvement encourages acceptance of the ultimate decision.	■ Some group members may sacrifice the best interests of the group for their own personal gains.
■ Participants gain greater insights into the complexities of the problem itself.	■ Some participants may not express their true beliefs or opinions in order to avoid possible disagreements.

Group decisions combine the skills and talents of several persons. Knowledge and experience are strengths in resolving complex problems.

other personnel can work together and seek the best results. At General Motors' Lake Orion plant, workers and engineers met to discuss full-sized models before production ever started. As a result of this decision, planning time was reduced by six months.[25]

When especially difficult decisions such as plant closings, personnel layoffs, and reorganizations must be made, the group technique enables members to gain a better grasp of the rationales used to reach conclusions. Involvement is an important factor in gaining support for decisions. Authors Linda J. Segall and Carol Meyers phrase it this way: "Not only is a group solution better than any one person's, but you don't have to 'sell' the solution to everyone; they already 'own' it."[26]

Because it places a greater emphasis on quality, the group concept is increasingly used as a decision-making process.[27] Cross-functional groups combine the knowledge of employees from separate units to resolve problems. At Precision Industries, for instance, workers from three departments met and decided how to streamline the computer invoicing system. Well-trained personnel can be given decision-making authority and assigned to self-directed groups, some of which even allow members to make hiring and firing decisions.

What hampers group decision making?

Group decision making does have its disadvantages. It can be quite time consuming. Despite efforts to develop cooperation and understanding, some members may not commit themselves to making the decision work. During deliberations, some people may monopolize discussions and pressure others to accept their views. Other group members may hesitate to communicate what they think or may say whatever they believe to be "acceptable" in order to avoid causing conflicts. In either case, relevant points may fail to be considered by the group.

GROUP DECISION TECHNIQUES

Groups differ in many ways. Some are quite small and are composed of close colleagues who interact on a regular basis. Others are large and consist of per-

GLOBAL VIEW

Decision Practices Around the World

Historically, U.S. managers have tended to lean toward individual accountability for decisions. Only recently, U.S. firms have given greater attention to the concept of teamwork and to the societal responsibilities of business. Decision practices in other countries have traditionally emphasized teamwork or have developed other unique approaches to decision making. Therefore, U.S. managers are challenged to accommodate dissimilar views toward the roles and obligations of business owners, labor, and government when companies from other countries are involved.

The popularity of employee participation in the decision-making process and consensus decision making is often attributed to the growth of interest in Japanese management techniques. As practiced by the Japanese, extensive consultation among decision participants consumes much time; once a consensus is reached, however, a decision is rapidly implemented. Some European countries, including Sweden and France, legislate employee involvement in company decisions. By contrast, employers in Italy and Spain give less emphasis to the solicitation of employee views. In general, European workers are usually more involved in implementing strategies than in developing them.

Boards like this Bavarian supervisory board, play major roles in decisions involving a company's future. The German concept of "codertermination" includes two sets of governing boards.

In most American companies, detailed job descriptions clearly outline job expectations. In Europe, operating managers have few written objectives. An organization's culture provides the guidance needed to attain its objectives. For these managers, "What truly matters is the set of broad and encompassing principles that keeps independent managers aligned with one another and with the company's overall goals." [Henzler, "The New Era of Eurocapitalism," p. 66]

In Germany, firms with stock traded on public exchanges are obligated to abide by the concept of "codetermination." According to this concept, companies have two governing boards: a management board to manage daily operations and a supervisory board to serve in an oversight role. At least one-half of the supervisory board's membership must represent workers. This board has the power to select persons for the management board and becomes involved with issues that have a major impact on employment. Unlike many American boards, the chair of the management board exercises less power and is considered to be more like a peer by other board members.

ADAPTED FROM: Herbert A. Henzler, "The New Era of Eurocapitalism," *Harvard Business Review* **70** (July/August 1992): 66; John Hill, Chris Lowery, and Tracy Kramer, "In Search of a European Management Style," *Proceedings: Southwest Division, Academy of Management* (1992): 156; and Jay W. Lorsch, "The Workings of Codetermination," *Harvard Business Review* **69** (July/August 1991): 108.

sons who have little (if any) personal contact and meet only sporadically. Despite differences in group composition, however, several techniques are available to assist groups in arriving at decisions. We will examine three of them in this section: the ordinary group technique, the Nominal Group Technique, and the Delphi Technique.

Three decision techniques help groups to make decisions.

■ *The Ordinary Group Technique*

The ordinary group technique is a common approach to group decision making.

Interpersonal dialogue among group members in an unstructured setting characterizes the **ordinary group technique.** The decision procedure is relatively straightforward. A group identifies the problem, develops and evaluates alternatives, and reaches a decision, which is generally based on majority vote. When this technique is applied, the leader's role is important: he or she explains the problem, answers questions, guides deliberations, and keeps the discussion on track so that it does not stray from the topic. The views of all participants should be considered, and sufficient control is necessary to assure that no group member is intimidated.

Brainstorming can be used to encourage communication of ideas, some of which may represent potential solutions to the problem. Assume a group is asked to recommend how productivity might be improved. Approximately 30 minutes to an hour can be set aside for people to express ideas. During this time, members are told to avoid criticizing the ideas presented by others, mention as many ideas as possible, and state all ideas that come to mind, regardless of their perceived merit. After this time period has concluded, members discard less useful ideas and further refine those they consider to be worthwhile.

What characterizes groupthink?

Some groups become quite cohesive, and members show great respect for the views of their colleagues. When this occurs, views of participants may not be sufficiently scrutinized. This phenomenon, referred to as **groupthink,** characterized the thinking of the Kennedy administration during the planning stage of the Bay of Pigs invasion and of President Richard Nixon's inner circle when confronted with the Watergate scandal. Both groups emphasized conformance and did not consider dissenting opinions.

How can groupthink be avoided? Several strategies are useful.[28]

■ Encourage participants to be skeptical and to question the appropriateness of suggestions.

■ Form two decision-making groups to provide a way to compare recommendations.

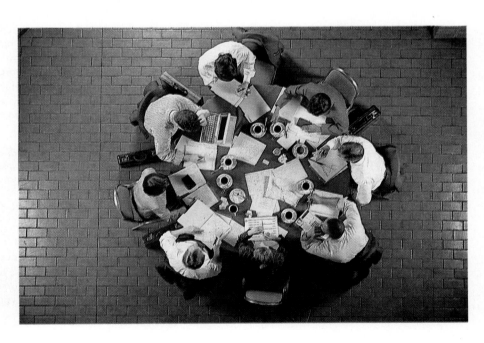

Brainstorming sessions provide opportunities for participants to share views and develop ideas and are sources of unique problem-solving suggestions.

- Hold "second-chance" meetings to give group members an opportunity to question a decision prior to its implementation.

■ *The Nominal Group Technique (NGT)*

When the **Nominal Group Technique (NGT)**—developed by Andrew H. Van de Ven and Andre L. Delbecq—is applied, a maximum of ten people meet together as a group to develop solutions to problems. Each problem must be presented in a well-structured format. For example, the group leader asks, "How can we do better work?" Such a question is too vague and will encourage many generalized responses. A more specific question might be, "How can we reduce errors in the assembly department and meet established quality standards?" When group members clearly understand the nature of problems or issues, they are more likely to make practical and worthwhile recommendations.

Participants in the NGT are asked to *write* down their personal solutions rather than to communicate them verbally. This procedure is designed to encourage freely expressed responses so that individuals will not be unduly influenced by others or intimidated by more dominant or vocal members of the group. The Nominal Group Technique generates a large number of alternatives from which a final solution can be selected. However, the NGT does have drawbacks. Personal interaction among group members is minimal. Furthermore, capable leadership is needed to conduct meetings and to guide participants through the process of reaching decisions.

The NGT generates many alternative choices.

The steps involved in the NGT process are relatively simple:

- Without consulting each other, group members write down their ideas concerning how to resolve a problem.

- These ideas are recorded on a flip chart or a chalkboard with no discussion of their merits.

- One at a time, ideas are discussed to clarify the group's understanding of them.

- A secret-ballot vote is taken, and the highest-ranked idea becomes the chosen solution.[29]

■ *The Delphi Technique*

The **Delphi Technique** was originated by Norman Dalkey and his colleagues at the RAND Corporation. When this technique is employed, questionnaires are mailed to collect responses and develop a consensus of opinions from experts who do not meet each other on a personal basis. The Delphi Technique consists of four steps:

Delphi panelists do not meet face to face.

- A problem is identified and disseminated to a panel of experts.

- Panelists independently write out solutions to the problem.

- These recommendations are tallied, and feedback from others is given to all panel members.

- The process is repeated until a consensus is attained.

Although the Delphi Technique can be time consuming and does not include the benefits of direct verbal communication, it does have advantages. By

REMEMBER TO COMMUNICATE

Accurate Information Is Essential

Information is a key ingredient of decision making. More often than you might imagine, people accept information as timely and accurate without reviewing pertinent details or seeking further clarification. Yet unexpected problems can arise. Let's consider the decision made by Doug Hess, who heads up an investment firm, to buy over 800 loans from the Federal Deposit Insurance Corporation.

After making this purchase decision, Doug discovered that 600 of the 800 loans contained errors. Although some loans had previously been paid, others were not completely owned by FDIC. He contacted the General Accounting Office, which examined 25 of Doug's newly purchased loans and found errors in 23 of them. The FDIC maintained that the difficulties were not widespread and eventually repurchased nearly 500 of the loans.

A failure to communicate created problems for Doug Hess and for FDIC. The key point here is not to assign blame but to emphasize the importance of avoiding miscommunication. Efforts to update records and recheck information for accuracy can save many headaches and worrisome frustrations.

SOURCE: Paul Wiseman, "Tangled Loan Records Trip FDIC," *USA Today* (August 22, 1991), p. 6B.

---

preserving anonymity, the problem of members' "saving face" is avoided. In addition, each panel member learns from the responses of others. Finally, the technique serves to overcome an obstacle encountered in interactive groups: Delphi allows experts to focus on making good decisions without diverting their attention to defend vested positions[30]

CREATIVITY AND THE WORKPLACE

What is creativity?

Creativity involves bringing together ideas, concepts, or information in new and different ways. Creative ideas have led to the development of many goods and services that we take for granted in our everyday lives.[31] For instance, in response to his daughter's inquiry about why pictures were not instantly available, Edwin Land originated the Polaroid camera. Frederick Smith of Federal Express came up with the idea of overnight delivery service while he was a student at Yale. Clarence Birdseye proposed freezing vegetables after a fur-trapping expedition, and Malcolm McLean conceived of containerized shipping to eliminate the loading and unloading of crates.

Numerous myths are associated with the concept of creativity. "Creativity is a sort of intangible psychic organ. . . . It is restricted to those who are 'geniuses.' . . . The creative individual is a kind of oracle."[32] In truth, all of us have some creative talents.

■ *Understanding Creativity*

Sources for creative ideas are unlimited. Creative suggestions can emerge from any of the problem-solving approaches, such as the Nominal Group Technique, discussed earlier. At times, experiences and circumstances can mix together to create an innovative solution. For example, Arthur Fry, a 3M employee, found it difficult to use pieces of paper to mark pages in his choir hymnal. One Sunday, he happened to think about a removable adhesive a friend had developed and the concept of Post-It Notes emerged. Even though 3M marketers and their distributors initially had reservations about the product, it became one of the top-selling office products in the world.[33] Fry had invented a new way to leave messages as well as a new way to mark pages.

■ *The Four Stages of the Creative Process*

The creative process consists of four stages.

The **creative process** is a way to mentally manipulate information in new and meaningful combinations; it consists of four stages.[34] Creative ideas do not necessarily flow smoothly in a neat, orderly fashion through each stage. Nevertheless, the process can provide you with an understanding of how ideas progress from inception to reality. Figure 4–5 shows the stages of the creative process.

The first stage, *preparation,* relates to defining the problem, gathering and reviewing information, and discovering a reason to do something differently. Preparation necessitates thought and detailed examination of accumulated data. Much effort and hard work takes place during this stage.

The second stage, *incubation,* consists of subconscious mental reflection about the problem and the data that must have been gathered.

During *insight,* which is the third stage, a spark of awareness occurs as a solution is recognized.

> Insight comes in many forms. It may appear as a flash of inspiration, as with Newton; or as a gradual awareness growing out of repeated hard work, as often occurs in poetry and art; or as the result of an apparent accident, as with the discovery of penicillin. It may be a word or words, symbols, figures, or feelings.[35]

■ **FIGURE 4–5** The Creative Process

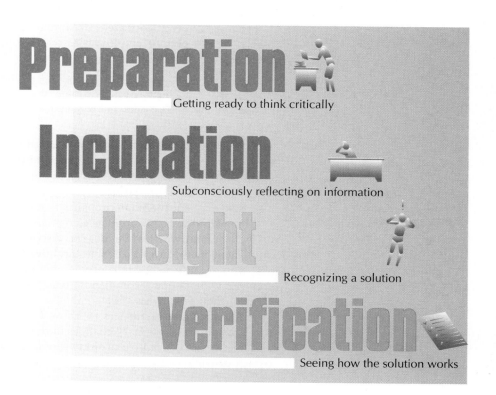

Preparation
Getting ready to think critically

Incubation
Subconsciously reflecting on information

Insight
Recognizing a solution

Verification
Seeing how the solution works

Verification is the final stage of the creative process. Here, the emphasis is on seeing how the solution works and on testing to learn if the insight is useful. At times, results may have to be modified to fit the circumstances. For instance, it is necessary to test a new computer chip to learn if it is reliable and commercially feasible. However, the chip may have to be redesigned to meet specific user needs.

What are creative people like?

What are the characteristics of creative people? These individuals challenge conventional practices, tolerate vaguenesses, and become very enthusiastic about things that interest them. They tend to be self-confident, flexible, and persistent. Based on some research studies, creative people appear to be driven by a belief that they can overcome obstacles and established authority.[36] Mary Kay Ash, founder of Mary Kay Cosmetics, was undeterred by the advice of financial advisers who did not support her aspirations.[37] Thomas J. Watson, Jr., former chairman of IBM, observed that major technological advances are often attributed to "wild ducks," which he describes as "those quirky, individualistic, highly intelligent employees who ignore bureaucratic procedures, shun set schedules, and resist attempts to make them more 'efficient.' "[38]

■ *Encouraging Creativity*

Creativity is important.

Creativity is a key to prosperity and competitiveness. Tomorrow's firms will be challenged to find creative solutions to increasingly complex problems. More organizational configurations will be altered to favor work teams and short-term alliances.

> The adaptive organization . . . will bust through bureaucracy to serve customers better and make the company more competitive. Instead of looking to the boss for direction and oversight, tomorrow's employee will be trained to look closely at the work process and to devise ways to improve upon it.[39]

Productivity is encouraged by a managerial philosophy that establishes objectives and permits employees to retain some discretion and exercise some creativity in order to attain them.

> The model manager of a creative work force is like an impresario who persuades and cajoles a highly motivated cast into working toward a common goal. Rather than set and enforce rules and regulations, he (or she) acts as teacher, coach, or even cheerleader.[40]

According to a Porter/Novelli survey, more than twice as many top executives consider being creative more important than being smart.[41] Creativity is a source of product innovativeness and improvements in product quality. Maytag's transmission for washers not only contains significantly fewer parts but also is so efficient that many repairpersons are unfamiliar with it.[42]

Managers can promote or hamper creativity.

Managerial decisions influence creativity.[43] It can be discouraging for workers who submit worthwhile ideas to discover that they are always expected to implement them. Employees who are given some time to evaluate a problem and who are not rushed into providing an immediate solution are more apt to come up with unique recommendations. Also, managers who take credit for the ideas of their employees stifle creativity.

It is difficult for managers to know which ideas will lead to major breakthroughs and revolutionary changes in the way things are done. Therefore, the possible merits of creative projects should not be taken lightly. One company turned down a worker proposal to develop a different type of personal computer. The idea was taken to Apple, and the Macintosh computer became a reality.[44]

CONSIDER THIS

1. Why is group decision making becoming more widespread?

2. What is the key to successful brainstorming sessions?

3. How can creative people encourage greater acceptance of their ideas?

USING INFORMATION TECHNOLOGY

Data consist of numbers and facts, which, by themselves, are meaningless. **Information** is a meaningful interpretation of data by decision makers. Assume Elmont Jewelry is considering the possibility of opening an upscale store in a shopping mall. These data about the community are available: the average age is 28, the average annual household income is approximately $27,000, and nearly one-half of the citizens commute to jobs in a nearby city. Each fact in itself does not reveal much about the community, but, when taken together, the information becomes relevant and provides insight into whether the new store should be opened. Management may decide that younger people with moderate incomes who live in close proximity to major big-city competitors do not provide a sufficient market for expensive jewelry.

Successful decision makers recognize the interdependent link among information, communication, and productivity. Information serves as a cornerstone for the analyses of possible choices. When information is unavailable, inaccurate, or misinterpreted, the likelihood of making a wrong decision increases. Inopportune decisions translate into lost customers, product defects, and even costly accidents; each negatively impacts productivity.

All levels of management, however, do not require the same information. Top management is especially concerned with economic forecasts, customer buying practices, and actions of major competitors to introduce new products or services. Mid-level managers use information to prepare summary reports, plan personnel requirements, and establish budgets or quotas. Supervisors use information to prepare daily reports, schedule employee work hours, and prioritize work-unit activities.

Future applications of computer technology are practically limitless. Automated systems enable managers to eliminate the human element in many routine decisions. As examples:

■ Desired levels of merchandise, such as books in a book store, can be maintained by programming a system to reorder whenever the quantities available for sale reach a certain level.

■ At Security Pacific, managers can select preferred formats for receiving information and establish models to determine possible outcomes for various proposed solutions to problems.

■ Resumix Incorporated produces software that "reads" the resumes of job applicants. In a matter of seconds, resume pages are scanned to determine the match between skills listed by applicants and those needed by employers.

■ Blockbuster Entertainment and IBM are cooperating to develop an information-storage system that allows customers to obtain copies of compact discs in a matter of seconds.[45] Implementation of this concept will eliminate the need for store managers to carry stocks of musical albums.

■ *Functions of Business Information Systems*

Managers may discover they have too much or too little information, none of which is available in a useful format. Although valuable, certain information might not be needed at the present time. Moreover, some information may be interesting and easily understood but of no value to the decision maker. As you can imagine, many complications can arise when communicating information to managers. Effective information systems help to alleviate these problems.

Business information systems serve several functions.[46]

1. Information has to meet user requirements; this means that it must be accurate, timely, and inclusive of a sufficient amount of detail.

2. It is advantageous for information to be shared among various units or departments of a firm.

3. Accessibility to a common source of information overcomes the difficulty of keeping separate data files and helps to develop and interpret different types of summary reports.

4. Flexibility of output enables information to be altered so that just the right amount of detail is available for users.

Why do we need information systems?

5. Interactive inquiry lets the computer and user communicate with each other. As a result, information can be obtained quickly, ideally without delays and inaccuracies.

Figure 4–6 summarizes the functions of information systems.

Managers' and employees' access to information are key factors in business success. The ongoing development of new technology will continue to influence business information systems.

■ Management Information Systems (MIS)

A **management information system (MIS)** gives managers the necessary information for them to do their jobs. Although it is not a requirement, practically all information systems are computerized. Management information systems are quite broadly oriented to serve entire units or departments rather than to provide specific information needed by any particular manager.[47]

Information generated by an MIS

Management information systems serve entire managerial units or departments.

- aids in the monitoring and controlling of managerial activities
- generates periodic reports
- provides special reports that draw attention to problems
- helps to formulate tactical plans[48]

For maximum success, managers and technical specialists should work together to develop management information systems. Greater understanding improves communication between those who develop systems and those who use them. Too often, systems are developed, implemented, and then used infrequently.

Several key questions should be answered during the MIS development phase:

■ **FIGURE 4–6** Functions of Business Information Systems

SOURCE: Paul L. Tom, *Computer Information Systems: A Managerial Approach with BASIC* (Glenview, IL: Scott, Foresman, 1989), p. 41. Copyright © 1989 by Scott, Foresman and Company. Reprinted by permission of Harper-Collins Publishers.

FUNCTION	INFORMATION SYSTEMS:
Satisfy the needs of users	■ Are accurate and timely
	■ Contain the appropriate level of detail
	■ Help in making projections
	■ Come from internal and external sources
Share common data	■ Are obtained in transaction systems
	■ Are integrated for management information reporting
	■ Are summarized and combined with external data for corporate planning
Integrate information flow	■ Go across organizational boundaries
	■ Address the decision made at each level of management
Provide flexible output presentation	■ Are tailored to the needs of the users
	■ Use various presentation media (graphs, charts, pictures, etc.)
Provide interactive inquiry and analysis	■ Converse with computer to obtain information
	■ Use information for immediate analysis and problem solving

- What types of reports are necessary?
- How often are they needed?
- Who is to receive these reports?

Obtaining proper equipment and scheduling training activities are also relevant concerns. Well-trained personnel are more likely to use the system most advantageously, express fewer complaints, and become active supporters of the MIS concept.

■ Decision Support Systems (DSS)

Decision support systems provide direct assistance to individual managers.

A management support system is generalized in nature to meet nonspecialized informational needs. A **decision support system** (DSS) assists managers who need more specialized types of information. The focus of decision support systems is to give individual support directly to decision makers who must deal with specific problem situations. Therefore, a DDS is narrower in scope and emphasizes the decision itself. Decision support systems are useful in resolving semistructured problems in which some, but not all, of the variables can be computerized.[49]

Let's consider how a DSS might work. The Fabriframe Corporation makes window panels and decorative interior doors for homes. Before investing a large sum of money to replace and upgrade equipment, the management of Fabriframe must decide whether to purchase precut lumber or buy new equipment that saws boards into desired shapes and lengths. A DSS can generate information on the current and previous costs of labor, shipping, and equipment. This is useful information for management because Fabriframe has not actually experienced potential complications, such as those caused by the lack of enough precut lumber on hand to fill unanticipated orders. However, although a DSS can generate valuable information from stored data, the manager is still responsible for making the ultimate decision.

■ Expert Systems

Expert systems provide if/then choices for managers.

Expert systems are computerized programs that use information to reason like very knowledgeable human experts. Unlike decision support systems, expert systems provide alternative solutions to unstructured or semistructured decision situations for which precise answers are not necessarily possible. In addition, expert systems are capable of providing reasons to support decision choices. The most common type of expert system is called a rule-band system. In it, "Rules specify actions that the system should take when conditions are present that satisfy the conditions of a rule."[50] For example, *if* (condition) sales revenue declines to a predetermined level, *then* (action) management should reduce overhead expenses by a specified amount.

Although business applications are in the infancy stage, expert systems have been successfully implemented in the workplace.[51] Digital Equipment Corporation (DEC) uses its XCON system to assure that orders for computer systems are configured so all component elements function together after installation. Remote Interactive Communication applies expert-system technology to spot potential breakdowns in copying machines and send repairpersons before problems occur.

Opportunities to use expert systems exist at all levels of management. The expert-system technique can be used to reduce decision time, develop complex scheduling arrangements, and facilitate implementation of strategies. Some areas of business have considerable potential for the application of expert systems.[52] Potential applications include circumstances involving the limited availability of people who possess needed expertise and situations in which job-related demands restrict the amount of time informed experts have to share their knowledge with others.

Recognize the characteristics of expert systems.

Successful expert systems serve managerial needs for information and have several general characteristics.[53] Such systems perform as well or better than human experts, are reliable, and render decisions in a timely manner that, in turn, gives managers sufficient response time. In practice, expert systems have advantages and disadvantages.[54] They provide consistent decisions within a specific area of application, improved understanding of the decision process, and cost reductions as a result of the reduced need for human resources. Nevertheless, expert systems are expensive to develop and maintain and, unlike humans, cannot incorporate common sense into the decision-making process. Also, it is often difficult to translate knowledge into "if/then" rules of logic.

THINK ABOUT IT

1. To those who are not responsible for implementing it, making a decision often appears to be an easy task.

2. It is worthwhile to ask relevant questions and gather information *before* making a decision. After-the-fact rationalization about a decision is often counterproductive.

3. In the real world, relatively few guarantees exist. Eventual realities can nullify an overwhelming number of reasons to pursue a particular course of action.

4. It is not necessarily beneficial to make the same decision just because another firm has done so.

5. If not hastily discarded, an "off-the-wall" idea may be more feasible than initially thought.

6. Decisions are always influenced by the experiences, attitudes, and opinions of those who make them.

7 Those who criticize a managerial decision frequently do not have access to all of the privileged information used by the decision makers.

8. Managers may be expected to implement decisions that do not coincide with their personal perspectives.

LOOKING BACK

You have studied about decision making and learned that creativity can benefit managers and organizations. Knowledge based on information-systems technology will become increasingly more valuable to managers. Now let's review the chapter objectives and briefly summarize several highlights for each of them.

Understand the behavioral aspects of decision making.

Decisions cannot be separated from the views and perspectives of those who make them. Behavioral aspects of decisions include experiences, attitudes and opinions, knowledge, emotions, circumstances, and personal intuitions. People have different outlooks, motives, and expectations—all of which impact decisions. Human capabilities are limited by the level of complexity and the number of variables involved in an issue.

Identify steps in the decision-making process.

The steps are to identify the problem, develop and evaluate alternatives, select the best alternative, implement the alternative, and follow up. Problem identification is critical because unidentified problems cannot be solved. It is worthwhile to generate as many alternatives as possible and to evaluate each of them carefully. After the preferred alternative is chosen, it is implemented. Communication is especially important in explaining rationales, in practicing fairness, and in demonstrating consideration for human feelings. Follow up, the final step, helps to assure that events are progressing as anticipated.

Describe the conditions of certainty, risk, and uncertainty.

Certainty, which is not a common condition of business decisions, implies that the decision maker knows which event will occur and simply chooses the largest payoff value. Under the condition of risk, nobody knows which events will happen, but the probabilities of occurrence are known. Most business decisions must be made in the face of uncertainty. Given this condition, the decision maker does not know which event will actually happen, and the concept of probability is meaningless.

Explain the approaches to group decision making.

The complexities of doing business, technological advances, and greater competitiveness encourage firms to make group decisions. The ordinary group technique, the Nominal Group Technique (NGT), and the Delphi Technique are among the approaches to group decision making. The ordinary group technique generally involves face-to-face interaction among group members. If the NGT is employed, members write down ideas, which are recorded and later discussed; the ultimate solution is determined by secret ballot. If the Delphi Technique is applied, questionnaires are mailed to collect responses, and a consensus of opinions is developed from a panel of experts who do not meet on a personal basis.

Discuss the role of creativity in the workplace.

Creativity involves the bringing together of ideas, concepts, or information in new and different ways. The creative process consists of four stages: preparation, incubation, insight, and verification. Creative people challenge conventional practices, tolerate vaguenesses, and become very enthusiastic about things that interest them.

Provide an overview of business information systems.

A management information system (MIS) provides managers with the information they need to do their jobs. An MIS is broadly oriented to serve the needs of entire departments or divisions. Decision support systems (DSS) focus on providing individual support directly to decision makers who must deal with specific problem situations. Information systems do have limitations, including the cost of computers, software, and training. Expert systems use information to reason like very knowledgeable human experts and provide alternative solutions to unstructured or semistructured decision situations.

KEY TERMS

brainstorming	groupthink
certainty	information
creative process	management information system (MIS)
creativity	
data	Nominal Group Technique (NGT)
decision making	nonprogrammed decision
decision support system (DSS)	ordinary group technique
delegation	programmed decision
Delphi Technique	quality circle
expected values	risk
expert system	uncertainty

REVIEW AND DISCUSSION QUESTIONS

1. Why is a manager's choice of doing nothing about a problem or issue considered to be a decision?
2. How do attitudes and opinions influence decisions?
3. Why do managers make faulty decisions?
4. What is the difference between a programmed decision and a nonprogrammed decision?
5. Why is follow up a necessary step in the decision-making process?
6. Why should a decision maker be knowledgeable about the conditions of certainty, risk, and uncertainty?
7. What are the advantages of group decision making?
8. What are the useful aspects of the ordinary group technique?
9. How can managers encourage creativity?
10. What stages are involved in the creative process?

CRITICAL THINKING INCIDENT 4.1

More Work: Is This a Joke?

Jill Corey, secretary to the director of training at Coleman International Corporation, is responsible for preparing correspondence, keeping records, developing schedules, and completing tasks on word-processing equipment. In addition to her specified duties, Sally Melanio, the director, has asked Jill to prepare very detailed reports and even conduct training sessions for other secretaries. Jill has built her reputation by consistently doing excellent work. According to her colleagues, Jill is a conscientious person who can handle a multitude of tasks and still meet deadlines.

Since joining the firm, Jill has taken evening courses. Three years ago, she completed requirements for a bachelor's degree in management. Last year, Jill applied for an entry-level management position at Coleman. However, the job was given to another applicant who did not have a college degree but did have several months of managerial experience. In Jill's opinion, the decision was not fair, but she has never reacted negatively. Her productivity has continued to excel; she even arrives early several days a week to assure that work is promptly completed.

Sally was appointed to her position because of a successful record as a practicing trainer. She gets along quite well with her bosses, largely because of a willingness to agree with their decisions. Also, Sally goes out of her way to praise them for their talent and managerial wisdom. A few months ago, Sally decided to request approval to hire an assistant training director. This person would handle many of her more routine problems and relieve her of some travel responsibilities. Just yesterday, the approval was granted.

At a coffee break, Polly VanHatten, an executive secretary, told Jill about the decision to staff the new position. Jill was surprised and responded, "More secretarial work; are you joking?" "No," Polly replied, "Sally assured management that you could handle any additional secretarial work without difficulty." Actually, Sally really has not considered how the new position might affect Jill.

Jill thinks about what has happened: "I wasn't selected for the management position, I probably could have handled the new assistant's job, and I am expected to do more and more work. My efforts don't seem to be appreciated. Maybe I should make an appointment with James Wentworth [the general manager] and tell him that it's unreasonable for me to be expected to do more work."

Discussion Questions

1. How effectively does Sally make decisions?
2. Since she did not get the entry-level management job, did Jill make a wise decision to continue her high level of productivity? Why or why not?
3. What can Sally do to improve her decision-making abilities?
4. Should Jill schedule an appointment with James to state her concerns?

CRITICAL THINKING INCIDENT 4.2

We've Got To Do Something

The Federal Credit Corporation was established to serve the credit needs of farmers and ranchers. Unfortunately, an economic downturn, adverse weather conditions, and large numbers of delinquent loans have had a negative impact on the agency. Although the number of foreclosures and farm sales has risen dramatically, some customers have attempted to restructure their loans and diversify operations in order to survive. Nevertheless, agency revenue is down significantly, and the board of directors must decide how to respond to the current situation.

Federal Credit encounters much competition from commercial banks, which are also a source of funds for borrowers who need short-term loans to buy cattle and other livestock. Commercial banks offer competitive rates, and the loan-approval process at a bank takes considerably less time than it does at the credit corporation. Nevertheless, Federal Credit is capable of granting much larger loans than banks and generally requires a borrower to put up less money as a down payment on a loan.

All of Federal Credit's board members recognize the importance of serving customer needs and are committed to the best interests of the organization. However, differences of opinion exist regarding the most appropriate course of action to follow. Manuel Solis believes that the board should accommodate customers, even though they are behind with their payments, and look ahead to the possibility of improved weather conditions next year. On the other hand, Jane Simpson argues that the organization itself cannot survive unless customers pay their debt obligations. Jane believes that increased care should be exercised to better assure customer credit worthiness and ability to repay loans.

Last month, the board asked Janet Musgrave, the president, to develop a possible reorganization. After much thought, Janet proposed to eliminate two vice-president and four loan-officer positions, while retaining all of the support staff. In regard to the criteria for granting credit, she took a neutral position to avoid confrontation with board members who had already taken a definite stance.

Yet Janet encounters unexpected disagreement from John Hargis, the most respected board member. He says, "When we eliminate loan officers, we are cutting our own throats because they are directly responsible for contacting potential customers and generating business." William Frakes, another board member, comments, "But John, our remaining loan officers can adequately serve the customers. We need to 'pull in our horns' and consolidate operations. To me

closing several offices in the smaller communities is a more logical approach."

As the discussion continues, Joan Collenge, chair of the board, contemplates what should be done. Because no consensus prevails, she considers whether a subcommittee should be appointed to further examine Janet's plan or recommend modifications. Another thought is to suggest that an outside consultant be employed to give an impartial opinion. Perhaps scheduling meetings with employees might help the board to arrive at a generally acceptable decision.

Discussion Questions

1. After hearing Janet's recommended plan, why should the board not vote immediately to make the final decision?

2. How should Janet react to the difference in the viewpoints of Manual and Jane?

3. What can the group do to avoid making an unfortunate decision?

4. What course of action should Joan ultimately favor to arrive at a decision?

 CRITICAL THINKING INCIDENT 4.3

Creativity and the Marketplace

McCollins Press, a specialty publisher of business texts, is a major firm in the college textbook industry. Stan Winters, a sponsoring editor, recently received a prospectus and several sample chapters for a new principles of management text from Bill Green and Gloria Petsarch, professors with considerable experience in managing employees and instructing students. The authors consider readableness and comprehensive coverage of relevant topics to be the strengths of their manuscript. They believe these are the most important factors considered by instructors who select textbooks.

Several teaching colleagues have read the chapters and commented favorably about the detailed explanations of concepts. One colleague was especially impressed with the presentation of emerging management concerns—topics not extensively discussed in competitive texts. To learn if the manuscript is easy for students to read, the authors sampled opinions of students currently enrolled in their courses. Anonymous responses indicated that students are quite enthusiastic about the readableness of the text.

To determine publication merits of the proposed text, Stan sent copies of the sample chapters to six reviewers who teach management courses and solicited their viewpoints. While three reviewers responded favorably, comments from

the others were rather neutral. Those who were positive toward the manuscript agreed with Bill and Gloria's assessment of its strong features. However, the other reviewers thought the chapters were too much like the content of texts already available in the marketplace. One reviewer remarked, "Why not try to be creative and really strive to distinguish the proposed text from the competition?"

Stan shared the reviewers' comments with the authors and asked for their reactions. Recently, Bill and Gloria met to discuss ways to revise and improve the manuscript. "We are capable people with a lot of desire to write a book. How can we be more creative?" asked Bill. After a moment's hesitation, Gloria replied, "I've got a few ideas, but there are a lot of well-written books with a variety of supplemental teaching aids. We've simply got to think of something different."

At this point, the conversation turned toward a discussion of ways to be more creative. Bill's suggestion was to market the entire text on a computer disk. Although many texts include cases and various types of student exercises on supplemental disks, it is highly unusual for an entire management text to be produced in this manner. Bill also mentioned the possibility of producing the text in a looseleaf notebook format and selling annual updates to students. Each year, the publisher might provide new review and discussion questions, application exercises, and other types of aids to learning. With this format, however, the authors would have to continually revise the content of the basic text and write new supplemental items.

Gloria was enthusiastic about developing a series of videotapes, each of which would cover one main idea presented in each chapter. She noted that videotapes could reinforce key points and encourage classroom discussion. Nevertheless, videotapes are expensive to produce and are not used by a number of instructors. According to survey data, only about one-third of potential adopters of the text have a strong interest in videotapes. However, these instructors teach at metropolitan colleges, have large classes, and represent considerable potential adoptions.

At McCollins Press, Stan has the final responsibility for the publication decision. He knows all too well that success depends on producing a text that meets adopter expectations but that can be differentiated from competing texts. A newly written text must produce sufficient sales to cover manufacturing and marketing expenses, which probably will exceed $100,000.

Stan considers possible approaches to creativity and is not especially receptive to the suggestions of Bill or Gloria. Yet he does not have any magic recommendations to offer them. Furthermore, Stan wonders if the authors are really flexible enough to implement any creative suggestions that might emerge after the manuscript is accepted for publication. Such suggestions often necessitate considerable rewriting, researching for background information, and revising of writing schedules—all of which cause frustration to persons who write textbooks.

Given the mixed reviews and his lack of personal excitement about the creative suggestions provided by the authors, Stan wonders whether to accept the project for publication. Yet McCollins needs a principles of management text to complement its current textbook offerings. Presently, Stan has no other manuscripts to consider; his invitation to submit chapters for a principles text was turned down by several established authors because they considered the marketplace to be too competitive. During the past year, Stan has not received any other unsolicited manuscripts from authors who want to write a management principles text.

Discussion Questions

1. Why is creativity an important publication consideration?

2. How can Bill and Gloria generate additional creative ideas?

3. Can a well-written text be successful in the marketplace without any special creative efforts? Explain your response.

4. Should Stan extend an offer to Bill and Gloria to publish the text? Why or why not?

NOTES

1. Amal Kumar Naj, "Some Manufacturers Drop Efforts to Adopt Japanese Techniques," *The Wall Street Journal* (May 7, 1993), p. A1.

2. "New Colleagues Dedicated to Teamwork, Quality," *Martin Marietta Today* 1 (1993), p. 11.

3. "Making Up Our Minds," *The Royal Bank Letter* 68 (September/October 1988): 3.

4. Stephen C. Harper, "Intuition: What Separates Executives from Managers," *Business Horizons* 31 (September/October 1988): 16.

5. "They Should Have Picked Mustang, 1957," *The Wall Street Journal* (August 15, 1989), p. B1.

6. Leonard R. Sayles, *Leadership: Managing in Real Organizations*, 2d ed. (New York: McGraw-Hill, 1989), pp. 16–17.

7. Diane Dodd-McCue, J. Kenneth Matejka, and D. Neil Ashworth, "Deep Waders in Muddy Waters: Rescuing Organizational Decision Makers," *Business Horizons* 30 (September/October 1987): 55–56.

8. Douglas R. Anderson, "Increased Productivity via Group Decision Making," *Supervision* 51 (September 1990):7.

9. Dana Milbank, "P&G Admits 'Error' in Effort to Trace Leaks," *The Wall Street Journal* (September 5, 1991), p. A3.

10. Kevin Maney and Julia Lawlor, "Companies Shifting to Thinner Ranks," *USA Today* (August 6, 1991), p. 1B.

11. Linda J. Segall and Carol Meyers, "Taking Aim at Problems," *Management Solutions* 33 (February 1988): 6.

12. Susan Antilla and Beth Belton, "Shearson Suspends 2 Executives," *USA Today* (September 6, 1991), p. 1B.

13. Lawrence R. Jauch and William F. Glueck, *Business Policy and Strategic Management*, 5th ed. (New York: McGraw-Hill, 1985), p. 25.

14. Susan Caminiti, "Sears' Need: More Speed," *Fortune* (July 15, 1991), pp. 89–90.

15. G. David Walker, et al., "America's Leanest and Meanest," *Business Week* (October 5, 1987), p. 79.

16. Laurie Hays, "A Taste of Capitalism at Russian Collective Brings Chaos and Strife," *The Wall Street Journal* (November 27, 1992), pp. A1, A4.

17. John Huey, "America's Most Successful Merchant," *Fortune* (September 23, 1991), p. 58.

18. Bruce Ingersoll, "Big U.S. Airlines Fly into Foreign Barriers over Expansion Plans," *The Wall Street Journal* (May 14, 1993), p. A1.

19. Kevin Goldman, "At '60 Minutes,' Men of the Hour Lack Successors," *The Wall Street Journal* (September 13, 1991), p. C1.

20. Ibid.

21. Desiree French, "Firms Keep the Brakes on to Curb Costs," *USA Today* (September 3, 1991), p. 1B.

22. Mitchell Lee Marks, "The Question of Quality Circles," *Psychology Today* 20 (March 1986): 44.

23. Lanny Blake, "Group Decision Making at Baxter," *Personnel Journal* 70 (January 1991): 76.

24. Gene E. Burton, "The Group Process: Key to More Productive Management," *Management World* 10 (May 1981): 15.

25. Jacob M. Schlesinger and Paul Ingrassia, "GM Woos Employees by Listening to Them, Talking of Its 'Team,' " *The Wall Street Journal* (January 12, 1989), p. A1.

26. Segall and Meyers, "Taking Aim at Problems," p. 7.

27. Bradford McKee, "Turn Your Workers into a Team," *Nation's Business* 80 (July 1992): 36–37.

28. Robert A. Baron and Jerald Greenberg, *Behavior in Organizations,* 3d ed. (Boston: Allyn & Bacon, 1990), pp. 501–502.

29. Stephen E. Catt and Donald S. Miller, *Supervision: Working with People,* 2d ed. (Homewood, IL: Richard D. Irwin, 1991), p. 294.

30. Fred Luthans, *Organizational Behavior,* 5th ed. (New York: McGraw-Hill, 1989), p. 544.

31. Rosabeth Moss Kanter, "Creating the Creative Environment," *Management Review* 75 (February 1986): 11.

32. Lesley Dormen and Peter Edidin, "Original Spin," *Psychology Today* 23 (July/August 1989): 49.

33. "Choir Member Sings the Write Notes, 1980," *The Wall Street Journal* (November 17, 1989), p. B1.

34. H. Joseph Reitz, *Behavior in Organizations,* 3d ed. (Homewood, IL: Richard D. Irwin, 1987), pp. 181–85.

35. Ibid., p. 184.

36. Fred V. Guterl, "The Art of Managing Creativity," *Business Month* 130 (October 1987): 36.

37. Mary Kay Ash, *Mary Kay* (New York: Barnes & Noble, 1981), pp. 4–5, 190.

38. Beverly Geber, "How to Manage Wild Ducks," *Training* 27 (May 1990): 29.

39. Brian Dumaine, "The Bureaucracy Busters," *Fortune* (June 17, 1991), p. 35.

40. Guterl, "The Art of Managing Creativity," p. 35.

41. Julie Stacey, "Get Smart, Be Creative," *USA Today* (September 2, 1992), p. 1B.

42. Robert L. Rose, "Maytag's Acquisitions Don't Wear as Well as Washers and Dryers," *The Wall Street Journal* (January 31, 1991), p. A6.

43. Richard Lombardo, "Breaking the Barriers to Corporate Creativity," *Training and Development Journal* 42 (August 1988): 64–65.

44. Guterl, "The Art of Managing Creativity," p. 37.

45. Kevin Maney, "Revolution in Store for Record Shops," *USA Today* (May 17, 1993), p. 1B.

46. Paul L. Tom, *Computer Information Systems: A Managerial Approach with BASIC* (Glenview, IL: Scott, Foresman, 1989), pp. 41–50.

47. Raymond McLeod, *Introduction to Information Systems: A Problem-Solving Approach* (Chicago: Science Research Associates, 1989), pp. 338–39.

48. Tom, *Computer Information Systems,* p. 40.

49. McLeod, *Introduction to Information Systems,* pp. 337–39.

50. James O. Hicks, Jr., *Management Information Systems,* 3d ed. (St. Paul: West, 1993), p. 171.

51. Ibid., p. 174.

52. McLeod, *Introduction to Information Systems,* p. 399.

53. Joseph Giarrantano and Gary Riley, *Expert Systems* (Boston: PWS-Kent, 1989), pp. 8–9.

54. Hicks, *Management Information Systems,* pp. 175–77.

 **SUGGESTED READINGS**

Alford, Peg. "Company Success Demands Creativity." *Business and Economic Review* 39 (January/March 1993): 19–21.

Bhide, Amar. "How Entrepreneurs Craft Strategies That Work." *Harvard Business Review* 72 (March/April 1994): 150–61.

Cosarello, Robert. "Seize the Opportunity in Latin America." *HR Magazine* 138 (September 1993): 56–57.

Davenport, Thomas H. "Saving Its Soul: Human-Centered Information Management." *Harvard Business Review* 72 (March/April 1994): 119–31.

Henderson, Rebecca. "Managing Innovation in the Information Age." *Harvard Business Review* 72 (January/February 1994): 100–105.

Hequet, Marc. "Creativity Training Gets Creative." *Training* **29** (February 1992): 41–46.

Lee, Chris. "Open-Book Management." *Training* **31** (July 1994): 21–27.

Metcalf, C. W., and Roma Felible. "Humor: An Antidote for Terminal Professionalism." *Industry Week* (July 20, 1992), pp. 14–19.

Shoemaker, Paul J. H., and J. Edward Russo. "A Pyramid of Decision Approaches." *California Management Review* **36** (Fall 1993): 9–31.

Stewart, Thomas A. "Welcome to the Revolution." *Fortune* (December 13, 1993), pp. 66–68, 70, 72, 76, 80.

PART TWO

FUNCTIONS OF MANAGEMENT

CHAPTER 5
Planning

Planning and strategic management are cornerstones of effective management. The concept of planning is described, and steps in the planning process are identified. The importance of corporate, business, and functional strategies is emphasized.

CHAPTER 6
Organizing

Organization is a key factor in the attainment of management objectives. This chapter examines traditional and new trends in organizational structures. Relevant aspects of job design are also discussed.

CHAPTER 7
Staffing and Training

Recruitment and selection of personnel are important to business success. Human resources are management's most valuable assets. This chapter focuses on understanding the staffing model as a key to the development of effective selection techniques and training activities.

CHAPTER 8
Leading

Leadership is a complex skill that requires careful study to be understood and practiced successfully. The trait, behavioral, and situational approaches to leadership are discussed. In addition, the appropriate usage of self-managed work teams is explained.

CHAPTER 9
Controlling

The basic principles and foundations of the control process are introduced in this chapter. The importance of effective control systems at various levels of management is described. Reasons why people resist control systems are also discussed.

CHAPTER 5

PLANNING

■ LEARNING OBJECTIVES

This chapter provides insights into planning—a crucial management function. You will study how plans evolve and learn how strategies are applied at various levels of a business. The specific learning objectives for this chapter are to:

- Differentiate among policies, procedures, and rules.
- Describe each step in the planning process.
- Explain the importance of strategic management.
- Identify the grand-strategy alternatives.
- Recognize strategies in the adaptation model.

■ CHAPTER OUTLINE

THE REAL WORLD — Corporate Giants Fail to Adapt Business Plans to a Changing Marketplace

Sears, IBM, and General Motors (GM) are among the most widely known corporate names in the world. In 1972 and again in 1982, IBM was the most valuable firm on earth in terms of stock-market valuations, and GM and Sears ranked among the top 13 companies. By 1992, however, all of these corporations disappeared from a market-value listing of the world's top 20 firms. IBM ranked 26, GM was 40, and Sears fell to 81. At IBM, the per-share value of stock declined from a high of $176 to a close of $50 at the end of 1992, representing a loss of billions of dollars in market value.

How did these giants of industry encounter difficulties? Although various elements contributed to their problems, the failure to adapt business plans to changing market conditions was a contributing factor.

Sears considered itself to be the premier retailer and did not pay sufficient attention to the rise of discount-store competitors, especially Kmart and Wal-Mart. Through its Allstate Insurance subsidiary and its acquisition of Dean Witter and Coldwell Banker, Sears implemented plans to diversify into the financial services industry. During 1993, the firm finalized plans to sell part or all of its interests in financial services. Also, Sears abandoned its 96-year-old catalog operation and planned to convert several hundred catalog outlets into retail stores. In addition, plans to market specialty products through direct mailing and return tabs on bill-payment envelopes were considered. As Sears abandoned catalog sales, competitors such as J. C. Penney, Montgomery Ward Direct, and Spiegel initiated plans to attract its former catalog customers.

As foreign competition increased the market share for smaller cars during the 1960s and 1970s, planning at General Motors continued to emphasize larger, more profitable vehicles. In the 1980s, reorganization led to design changes, replanned manufacturing, and additional bureaucracy. GM produced automobiles that did not mesh with customer tastes. Historically, automobile manufacturing has been characterized by high labor costs. GM's accounting method did not record future health expenses for retired employees as a current expense item. With revised accounting regulations, the corporation recorded a $33 billion charge for these benefits in 1992.

Over the years, IBM had emerged as a classic illustration of corporate growth and success. Between 1914 and 1992, IBM's stock experienced 39 stock splits or stock dividends. Two shares purchased in 1914 were worth almost a million dollars by the 1980s. At IBM, planning emphasized the production of mainframe computers. Failure to enhance development of reduced instruction-set computing (RISC), to recognize the extent of the demand for personal computers, and to abandon a commitment to full employment of personnel were detrimental to long-term corporate interests.

These companies will not disappear from the corporate landscape. However, some doubts prevail about their abilities to regain positions as front-runners in terms of growth, market share, and profits. Greater foresight cannot guarantee success but becomes increasingly relevant in a global marketplace. As you study Chapter 5, consider how effective communication helps planners to develop sound strategies and avoid pitfalls, such as using inaccurate information or failing to consider budget restrictions.

ADAPTED FROM: "After IBM," *Smart Money* 2 (April 1993): 75; Jean Sherman Chatzky, "Used People," *Smart Money* 2 (April 1993): 85; Carol J. Loomis, "Dinosaurs?" *Fortune* (May 3, 1993), pp. 36–42; Gregory A. Patterson, "Demise of Sears' Big Book Sparks Race by Catalog Retailers to Win Its Customers," *The Wall Street Journal* (May 26, 1993), p. B1; "Sears to Sell Coldwell Banker," *Wichita Eagle* (May 14, 1993), p. 7B.

Planning is essential to continued business success. Firms must continually review plans to remain competitive in an era of rapid change.

THE ROLE OF PLANNING

Planning is a key management function.

The key management function of **planning** involves looking ahead and preparing courses of action to attain business objectives. The importance of planning cannot be underestimated. A company is successful if its management can correctly anticipate future events. For example, Chrysler's plan to introduce the minivan was a resounding success and served a product need unmet by Japanese competitors. According to Hal Sperlich, who fathered the minivan, "If we hadn't done minivans, Chrysler would be gone—no question."[1] Planning directly relates to the management function of decision making.

> Planning identifies objectives. Decision making provides the will to achieve them. Unfortunately, these two skills are often exercised in isolation from each other. Planning without deciding is . . . sheer speculation. Deciding before planning is to act before you think—impulsiveness.[2]

How does planning benefit managers? It enables them to set expectations and priorities. Through planning, tasks can be completed without undue waste of time or money. Plans help companies to adjust to change. As an example, during the late 1970s, 11 national and nine local-route airlines served the United States. By 1991, eight carriers earned more than 90 percent of the sales revenues generated by airlines within the country.[3] Deregulation caused the number of airline carriers to decline and necessitated planning in a more competitive marketplace.

Plans help managers to be responsive to uncertain environmental conditions. Economic forecasts, past sales records, and local employment trends are useful to retail merchants who must plan ahead for holiday seasons. Planning is so vital that some say, "Failing to plan is planning to fail."

Planning includes three components: policies, procedures, and rules. **Policies** are quite general in nature. For example, it is generally a policy of banks to grant loans to creditworthy borrowers. A **procedure** refers to the step-by-step sequence of events needed to implement a policy. Banks require potential borrowers to complete an application, provide a statement of their financial condition, and meet certain borrowing requirements. **Rules** are more restrictive than policies or procedures. Rules are inflexible and usually must be followed without deviation. On monthly installment loans, banks could have a rule that payments must be received by the fifth business day to avoid a late fee.

Businesses encounter increasingly greater pressures to be competitive, emphasize quality, and boost productivity. According to the Bureau of Labor Statistics, the average annual rate of productivity growth between 1947 and 1973 was 2.6 percent; it has averaged only 0.8 percent per year since 1973.[4] Accelerated rates of technological change, shortened product life cycles, and a need to make realistic assumptions about future events do not make planning any easier.

Managers cannot overlook the realities of the marketplace.

Well-researched products are not necessarily market successes. Weyerhaeuser had high hopes for its UltraSoft brand of diapers, but poor planning and quality problems led to unanticipated complications. During the manufacturing process, machines spraying absorbent material malfunctioned and transformers overheated. In addition, the company experienced difficulties in obtaining contracts from vendors who supplied the materials from which the diapers were made.[5]

From both a domestic and an international perspective, the purpose of the planning function remains the same. However, the international domain includes economic, political, cultural, and technological factors that complicate the planning process. Managers need to remain focused on company objectives and to recognize the purpose of involvement in the international marketplace. A short-term emphasis on export-import arrangements often precedes direct investment or mergers.

Plans vary according to the types of products a firm seeks to market. For example, Coca-Cola and McDonald's have experienced much success in Asian markets offering essentially the same products available in America. Firms such as Unilever, Exxon, and General Electric are truly globalized and market an array of different products on a worldwide basis.

Intuition, rumors, and opinions are not substitutes for critical analysis. Consideration of available information serves to justify rationales for chosen courses of action. For instance, Lotus was the first American company to do business in South Africa after the U.S. government lifted its apartheid-related ban on new investments.[6]

Compared to the business environment of the United States, however, planners cannot overlook the economic, political, and bureaucratic realities encountered in South Africa. As a result of the political unrest there, shootings and beatings are not uncommon. Lengthy delays often occur in telephone installations and shipment arrivals. In addition, South African workers frequently demonstrate a lax attitude toward doing their jobs. Considering these complications, why did Lotus initiate plans to enter South Africa? The reason is that the country represents a vast market with much potential for sellers of computer technology and software.

■ Developing Effective Plans

Effective plans are important to organizational success. When future courses of action are not thoroughly discussed, a firm is not as likely to respond promptly or correctly as events unfold. Plans do not guarantee that goals will be reached, however, since the future generally includes the unexpected. For example, Edwin H. Land, inventor of the successful Polaroid camera, also introduced Polavision Instant Movies in 1977. The movie camera, was costly, did not have sound, and included less than three minutes of film. To make matters worse for Polaroid, the Japanese emphasized quality and marketed video recorders that could be played over and over on television sets.[7]

Formalized planning provides a structured approach that allows participants to express their views, react to the viewpoints of others, and understand the pros and cons of alternatives. Planners need sufficient flexibility to revise plans when necessary and to overcome obstacles when they arise.

Regardless of its relevance, planning is sometimes misunderstood. Several common myths prevail:

- Planning unduly wastes management time.
- Planning hinders a manager's flexibility.
- Planning does away with change.[8]

Although it consumes time, planning forces managers to think ahead and to focus their attention on unfinished tasks. Effective planning is a continual process that should not be perceived as a restraint to flexibility. Furthermore, the best of plans cannot eliminate change but instead help managers respond to it.

■ Key Concerns: Communication and Quality

Managers must communicate to obtain results.

COMMUNICATION   The development and implementation of plans are relevant concerns. However, successful planners cannot underestimate the importance of communication. Managers must possess practical knowledge as to what strategies imply about their particular areas of responsibility. If the intent of a strategy is clear to managers but unclear to employees, miscommunication is quite likely to occur. Time that is taken to answer questions and provide explanations is not wasted.

Support of other managers and subordinates is essential to gain approval of plans. Such support is especially relevant when plans involve multiple departments or operating units. Clarity of understanding is a foremost concern. When interpretations vary, unexpected difficulties usually arise. For instance, an assumption that another manager agrees with your view may turn out to be incorrect and necessitate time-consuming revisions of plans.

Understanding is a key to acceptance.

As plans are developed, managers may change their minds based on updated information, clarifications, and answers to their questions. The extent to which plans are perceived to be relevant, readily understood, or presented impressively influences whether they are approved or rejected. People tend to reject what they do not understand. Whenever plans are changed, the persons involved need to be informed.

QUALITY   Continuous quality improvement stresses the need to satisfy customers, provide value, and minimize product defects. It emphasizes that plans clearly specify standards and measurement criteria. Efforts to improve quality require sincere commitment by all persons from top managers to newly hired trainees. Deltapoint, a consulting organization, estimates that as many as 70 percent of all American firms do not attain expected results because their quality programs are poorly executed.[9] The following firms demonstrate a quality consciousness.[10]

■ At Motorola, top executives carry beepers to maintain around-the-clock contact with customers. (When providing microprocessors for a major customer, the company president resolved to return the customer's calls within ten minutes.)

■ Corning Incorporated activated a plan to eliminate product defects and discovered that chips in ceramic products occurred at the company's production facilities and were not caused during shipment.

■ The Limited, a specialty retailer, no longer simply records the numbers of items sold. The company also seeks to learn whether specific colors and types of merchandise meet customer expectations.

The need to survive makes planning a priority. Essential concerns include knowing the objective, avoiding complacency, understanding the nature of competitors, and emphasizing potential improvements.

Planning influences outcomes.

Planning influences outcomes. For example, as General Motors implemented its plant-closing agenda, either the Arlington (Texas) or Willow Run (Michigan) facility faced closure.[11] At Arlington, workers proposed a plan that included a three-shift schedule without overtime pay and changes in paint-shop work rules directly related to quality improvements. For example, previously, a senior employee could "bump" (replace) an employee who had less seniority. Therefore, a worker could be performing a job without being fully trained to do it.

- -

REMEMBER TO COMMUNICATE

Misunderstandings Impede Planning

Until it happens to them, many people do not realize the impact of financial and emotional strains caused by misunderstandings. Parties who are supposedly on the same side in a dispute can wind up as adversaries. Miscommunication impedes planning and complicates events to a greater extent than might ever be expected. Let's consider the case of a small chemical company, Senoret, its law firm, and the Environmental Protection Agency.

The EPA expressed concern about potential health dangers to children from the company's Terro brand of ant killer. The Roberts family, owners of Senoret, retained the services of a leading law firm, and a dual-track strategy was formed. While their lawyers initiated a request for a hearing to challenge the claim, Senoret sought to develop a child-proof dispenser for the product. Ultimately, negotiations were held between EPA and the lawyers for the company. According to the family, a settlement could have been reached if the terms had been known to them, since a product recall would not have been demanded. One of the lawyers refuted the assertion, and the miscommunication became a major issue in a dispute between the owners and their lawyers.

The Roberts family went to trial against the EPA to contest cancelling registration for the insecticide. Although viewpoints differed, the owners asserted that they were not fully informed about the legal costs. Their lawyers claim otherwise. Nevertheless, daily legal costs for the five-week hearing averaged over $3000. The total bill received for all costs related to the case was slightly over $375,000 in fees and approximately $81,000 in expenses. After paying $128,000, the family ceased to submit $15,000 monthly payments. The law firm sued the owners for breach of contract. The family filed a counter-suit alleging that their lawyers had neglected to inform them of financial risks and available alternatives. Incidentally, the Roberts family lost the original case against the EPA.

ADAPTED FROM: Milo Geyelin, "How a Small Company Fell Deeply into Debt to Its Own Law Firm," *The Wall Street Journal* (October 8, 1991), pp. A1, A8.

That rule would be changed. Arlington's plan also stressed a record of fewer product defects. Even though the Willow Run plant eventually decided to negotiate with management, Arlington's plan prevailed, and GM decided to close the Michigan plant.

THE PLANNING PROCESS

Planning is not a haphazard activity.

Without much thought or effort, some things work out as expected, possibly even better. On the other hand, it is unrealistic to think that issues will resolve themselves or that goals will be attained automatically. The planning process helps decision makers look ahead and consider how to respond to various circumstances that may arise. Managers develop plans to reach a variety of goals that can range from profit concerns to issues involving employee benefits. In a survey of over 2000 midsized companies, nearly 50 percent of the participants considered a major aspect of quality—improving productivity and efficiency—to be their top-ranked management objective. Managing growth (noted by 29 percent of the respondents) was the second most important objective.[12]

Planning consists of five steps.

The planning process consists of five steps.

1. Determine the goal.
2. Review the present situation.
3. Recognize limiting factors.
4. Develop the plan.
5. Implement the plan.

These steps are summarized in Figure 5-1. Although each of these steps may seem to be separate from the others, they are frequently interrelated in practice. A manager might consider the limitations of a plan at the time it is formulated. Likewise, during the early stages of the planning process, a manger could evaluate the particulars of how a plan is to be implemented. The following sections examine each step of the planning process in greater detail.

■ *Determine the Goal*

A **goal** is a result that the managers of a firm hope to achieve. Goals must be clearly specified; otherwise, time and effort will not necessarily be channeled in the right direction. Overall organizational goals include making a profit, providing quality products, and serving customer needs. On the plant floor, relevant goals include scheduling enough work for all shifts, reducing time lost due to breakdowns, and keeping the number of product defects and/or customer complaints to a minimum. Precise goals vary among businesses, but any goal provides a target against which progress and quality can be measured.

The nature of goals tends to differ. Some are rather broadly oriented and outline a general direction to be followed. Others are quite specific and narrowly focused. A convenience store owner decides to make fast-food items available to customers. Although this goal is not precise, it is a starting point from which more detailed plans can ultimately be formulated. Once the direction of the owner's plan has been determined, the planning process can emphasize such things as ordering necessary equipment and possibly hiring additional personnel.

Goals are an essential concern. If planners do not know what they are striving to accomplish, they cannot function. Nevertheless, some managers are not especially enthusiastic about setting goals. Others may believe they will be too harshly criticized if targeted goals are not reached. At times, managers may feel that their priorities are changing too rapidly to set goals. Accurate

What is to be done?

Goals specify targets to be reached.

■ **FIGURE 5-1** The Planning Process

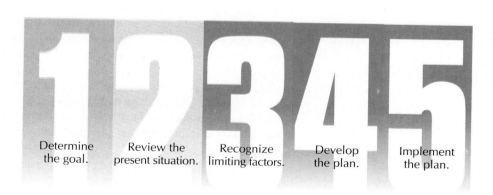

Determine the goal. Review the present situation. Recognize limiting factors. Develop the plan. Implement the plan.

communication helps managers to derive the maximum benefits from the planning process.

■ *Review the Present Situation*

What is the current status of affairs?

If there is a discrepancy between desired goals and the current status of affairs, planning activities to reduce this gap need to be considered. A continuous assessment of the status quo is relevant. Planners who fail to review current events can place an organization at a disadvantage. If sales are lagging and the management of a company delays plans to stimulate sales, its market share may be lost when other firms reduce prices to gain a competitive advantage. The comparison of past events with future expectations provides managers with insights about factors that can help as well as hinder planning efforts.

■ *Recognize Limiting Factors*

What barriers to the goal must be recognized?

When assumptions are correct, plans usually prove to be accurate, and actions can be carried out as anticipated. In practice, however, it is difficult to predict some events because of unknown factors, large numbers of interactive variables, or accelerating changes. Past records serve as a basis for making future forecasts. Yet economic factors, new or well-entrenched competitors, weather conditions, or any number of other elements in the business environment can cause forecasts to be inaccurate.

Human, equipment, and financial resources are potential limitations to planning because they can restrain preferred courses of action. Managers do not have unlimited numbers of employees or amounts of equipment at their disposal; they must function within budget allocations. At times, these restrictions may be accurately projected. The number of employees scheduled to retire each year or the amount of funds expended on mortgage payments are examples. Circumstances can, nevertheless, change; unforeseen events may necessitate the revision of plans. Prior experiences are valuable assets to planners. When making a budget presentation, for example, a manager who has previously prepared and defended budgets will be more likely to handle anticipated objections competently than a manager who has never participated in the budget process.

■ *Develop the Plan*

How is the goal to be achieved?

To formulate a plan, it is necessary to consider alternatives, specify tasks, set priorities, and assign responsibilities. This step involves "putting it all together" so that the plan becomes a useful tool. Often, it is worthwhile for a manager to consider "if/then" choices. For instance, if the firm adds a new product line, then space may not be available for some items currently carried in the inventory. Planners should be sure that their plans are workable. For example, an overall plan "to decrease customer complaints" is too general and should be restated more precisely as, say, "to reduce complaints by 10 percent."

As a plan evolves, a manager should not overlook possible pitfalls. Asking probing questions now may help to avoid time-consuming and costly difficulties later. It is important that planning be a continual process.

The real key to planning for uncertainty and change must be to accept the premise that the planning process is more important than the written plan, that the manager is continuously planning and does not stop planning when the written plan

A PERSPECTIVE ON QUALITY

A Plan Goes Awry

Coca-Cola invested $4 million of market research and 4½ years into the introduction of a soft drink called New Coke, which was designed to replace traditional Coke. Despite the time and effort spent to plan the new product, the older version was ultimately retained and reintroduced into the marketplace as Coke Classic.

As originally planned, Coke's new product was targeted to overcome Pepsi's victories in taste tests. New Coke was to represent the combination of the heritage of Coke with a new, improved taste. In May 1985, Coke's research showed that 53 percent of customers preferred New Coke. By July, the tide had turned; 60 percent favored the original formula.

The company was forced to do additional planning and consider the possibility of a two-cola (old and new) strategy. At the time, Coke feared discrediting the newer product by bringing back its traditional recipe. Through adept planning, the corporation hoped to increase its market share. The sweeter New Coke would be targeted to teen-agers; the taste of Coke Classic—the original Coke—would be aimed at the adult market.

This case shows that plans do not always work as expected and illustrates the importance of consumer satisfaction. Customer wrath far exceeded company expectations. Thousands of Coke drinkers wrote letters and called to express displeasure with the plan to abandon original Coke. One unhappy customer stated a blunt opinion: "You have fouled up by changing the only perfect thing in the world." [*U.S. News & World Report* (July 22, 1985), p. 12]

ADAPTED FROM: "Classic Comeback for an Old Champ," *U.S. News & World Report* (July 22, 1985), p. 12; Janet L. Fix, "Leaders Keep Growth in Focus," *USA Today* (August 13, 1992), p. 6B; John Koten and Scott Kilman, "How Coke's Decision to Offer 2 Colas Undid 4 ½ Years of Planning," *The Wall Street Journal* (July 15, 1985), p. 1.

is finished. . . . If the manager is not planning on a continuous basis—planning, measuring, and revising—the written plan can become obsolete the day it is finished.[13]

■ Implement the Plan

The final step is putting the plan into action.

The final step in the planning process is to put the plan into action. Communication is especially relevant at this stage. To implement a plan successfully, participants must know who is responsible for what. If prior steps have been carefully thought out, fewer complications will arise. It is necessary to monitor results. Changes may still have to be made because the plan is not working as originally envisioned or because new information is received.

TYPES OF PLANS

Plans can be categorized in three ways.

Plans can be categorized on the bases of time and level of management involvement. Strategic plans, the domain of top management, focus on a time horizon of one to five years or longer. Mid-level managers are concerned with intermediate plans, which range from several months to a couple of years. At the lowest managerial level, supervisors develop operational plans of much shorter durations. These plans may relate to activities of a day, a week, or a month but generally of less than one year. Figure 5–2 illustrates the relationships among short, intermediate, and long-term plans. Another type of plan, the contingency plan, emphasizes the importance of timely responses to unforeseen events.

It is convenient to classify planning responsibilities as shown in Figure 5–2. In practice, however, senior vice presidents consult with plant managers and division managers. Consequently, various managerial levels are not associated exclusively with only one type of plan. For instance, a manager might be asked to express the views of his or her employees toward a proposed revision of the performance-appraisal process. Sharing views facilitates understanding and avoids complications caused by miscommunication. A *Fortune* survey asked 212 CEOs of the largest U.S. firms what their companies had done to improve communication and productivity among employees. The top-ranked factor, according to 41 percent of the respondents, was to hold regular meetings with employees.[14]

■ *Strategic Plans*

Strategic plans provide the firm with a long-term sense of direction. These plans provide guidance and help a company to communicate its purpose to customers, owners, employees, and the general public. Strategic plans can involve major organizational changes. To illustrate, a firm may decide to diversify and enter new markets, merge with another company, or close plants at several locations. Such decisions change customary ways of doing things.

Strategic decisions also have the potential to alter the allocation of resources. Instead of using funds to purchase new equipment, management may decide to divert these funds to pay off debt. Personnel layoffs reduce the number of employees who work for the firm; permanent budget reductions require managers to find alternative ways to complete tasks.

Finally, strategic plans can have distant time horizons. For example, a firm may make the commitment today to build practical electric automobiles, but the cars will probably not become a reality for several years to come.

Managers give various explanations for not developing formal plans: plans do not need to be written down to be remembered; formal planning activities

■ **FIGURE 5–2** Relationships among Short, Intermediate, and Long-Term Plans

	SHORT-TERM PLANS	INTERMEDIATE-TERM PLANS	LONG-TERM PLANS
AMOUNT OF DETAIL INCLUDED	Very detailed	Somewhat detailed	Broadly stated
BUSINESS/ECONOMIC CONDITIONS	Comparably fewer uncertainties	Some uncertainty	Considerable uncertainty
TIME FACTOR	Under one year	Several months to two years	One to five years or longer
LEVEL OF MANAGEMENT	Lower	Middle	Top
NAME OF PLAN	Operational	Intermediate	Strategic

Executives of Parker Hannifin and Honda of America view a Honda Accord assembly line in Ohio. Strategic planning at top management levels is a key to the eventual successful production and marketing of goods and services.

Formal planning enhances productivity.

consume much valuable time. Is formal strategic planning the cause of increased productivity and achievement of desired results? "There is no such thing as a definitive study which proves that strategic management causes better performance. . . . But the majority of studies suggest that there is a relationship between better performance and formal planning."[15]

It is important for chief executive officers to communicate their support for strategic plans. This clarifies a firm's position and demonstrates commitment to chosen courses of action. Events do not always occur as expected; adverse circumstances can cause plans to be revised. When Citicorp encountered financial concerns in the early 1990s, the corporation absorbed losses and eliminated its dividend. While acknowledging the existence of problems, Citicorp's chairman, John Reed, stressed a need to plan for reorganization and to reconsider Citicorp's perspective of the credit function.[16]

Compared to American corporations, European firms tend to have longer-term planning horizons. The strategic plan for Hoechst, a German-based international chemical company, covers up to ten years. Specific steps include analysis of relevant data, delineation of alternatives, selection of preferred outcomes, and initiation of the plan. The company also uses mid-term and short-term operational plans and has a control system to monitor results on a quarterly basis. Hoechst places much emphasis on the attainment of a match between the company's product line and regional preferences among customers.[17]

Now let's define and briefly discuss the basics of intermediate, operational, and contingency plans. Then we'll cover the strategic management process—an application of strategic planning.

■ *Intermediate Plans*

Intermediate plans, which are largely a middle-management responsibility, cover a time frame between several months and two years. Compared to strategic plans, these plans are more limited in scope and of shorter duration. Mid-level managers must be knowledgeable about corporate goals so that specific

Intermediate and strategic plans should be correlated.

plans can be implemented to achieve them. Assume a department store chain adopts a major strategy to integrate additional apparel lines. Product managers must understand the rationale behind this strategy and accordingly assist department managers in making intermediate plans to ensure that the overall corporate strategy will be successful.

Intermediate plans include projects that middle managers consider important. According to a General Accounting Office survey, for example, Internal Revenue Service employees who were assigned to answer telephone questions posed by taxpayers gave correct answers to only 64 percent of selected questions posed to them.[18] Assuming that the survey is accurate, a manager might initiate an intermediate-range project to improve quality and better train IRS personnel. If the plan is successful, it will help to accomplish the long-term overall goal of improving communication with taxpayers.

■ *Operational Plans*

Operational plans focus on the short term.

Operational plans are developed at the lowest organizational level, focus on short-term time periods, and are narrowly defined. These plans involve such activities as making up daily or weekly work schedules, preparing a weekly or monthly budget, and developing a list of tasks for an employee to complete during the next week. The relevance of operational plans should not be overlooked; they provide managers with guidance for dealing with events in the immediate future. A failure to use operational plans directly and adversely affects a firm's ability to meet higher-level goals.

During the development of operational plans, the importance of communication should be considered. If schedules vary from week to week, employees need to know the days and times that they are expected to work. Managers must be aware if their expenses are not within budget allocations; therefore, budgets need to be accurate and kept up-to-date. Daily or weekly sales summaries serve as the basis for planning future orders. Whenever miscommunication is kept to a minimum, managers can avoid the additional planning needed to remedy misunderstandings and work that is incorrectly done.

■ *Contingency Plans*

Contingency plans facilitate immediate responses.

Contingency plans provide managers with alternative courses of action to follow. Such plans let managers react to situations without hesitancy. An emergency plan to vacate facilities is a practical example of contingency planning. Managers can develop contingency plans to guide them in making decisions about declining sales or to handle unexpectedly large numbers of customers. "The basic premise of contingency planning is that the organization plans ways to deal with unfavorable and favorable events *before* they occur."[19]

Changing events alter plans.

"We'll never need a contingency plan." "There's really a slim chance for that event to ever happen." "Contingency planning is too time-consuming." These statements demonstrate the views of some managers toward contingency plans. Yet the unexpected can happen and can have considerable impact on an organization. For example, the sudden retirement of basketball superstar Magic Johnson caused the Los Angeles Lakers to revise player-personnel plans and make adjustments needed to reach the team's objectives.

The development of contingency plans benefits managers.[20] They learn to think ahead and weigh potential outcomes; this somewhat alleviates the com-

A PERSPECTIVE ON QUALITY

Is 99.9% Good Enough?

Many research surveys specify that results are accurate within ±3 percent. Some persons may believe that companies can produce products with a defect rate of 1 percent and still be competitive. However, acceptance of 99.9 percent accuracy means

- 2 million documents will be lost by the IRS this year.
- 22,000 checks will be deducted from the wrong bank accounts in the next 60 minutes.
- 12 babies will be given to wrong parents each day.
- 268,000 defective tires will be shipped this year.
- Two plane landings daily at O'Hare International Airport in Chicago will be unsafe.
- 3,056 copies of tomorrow's *The Wall Street Journal* will be missing one of the three sections.
- 18,322 pieces of mail will be mishandled in the next hour.
- 20,000 incorrect drug prescriptions will be written in the next 12 months.

SOURCE: Reprinted with permission from the March Supplement 1991 issue of TRAINING Magazine. Lakewood Publications, Minneapolis, MN. All rights reserved.

plexities and pressures that arise from crisis management. Participation helps managers become aware of the pros and cons of problem-solving alternatives and encourages them to use different types of decision-making techniques.

UNDERSTANDING STRATEGIC MANAGEMENT

Strategic management involves planning for the long term.

Initially, **strategic management** involves the definition of an organization's mission and the identification of its long-term objectives. Next, strategies designed to achieve these objectives are developed and implemented. Finally, results are monitored to determine if desired outcomes occur.

The role of strategic management is receiving greater attention in today's increasingly complex business environment. It is critical for the management of a firm to look ahead and anticipate the impact of internal and external environmental factors on business operations. Figure 5–3 identifies the steps involved in strategic management.

■ Define the Mission and Identify Strategic Objectives

The **mission statement** "describes an organization's purpose, customers, products or services, markets, philosophy, and basic technology."[21] It is the basis for answering several major questions: What is our business? Who do we serve? What do we sell? For instance, the strategic concerns of Centerior Energy are to become more cost-effective and competitive, to improve its financial position, and to provide customers with lower-cost and high-quality service.[22] Figure 5–4 illustrates the missions of several corporations. Notice

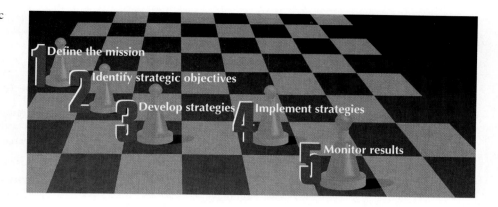

how these statements clearly communicate corporate purposes and obligations to various stakeholders—owners, customers, employees, and the general public.

Compared to goals, **strategic objectives** are more precise and emphasize the
outcomes to be attained if a particular strategy is followed. They identify target expectations in key result areas, such as market share, human resources,
and finance.

> Objectives are more specific than goals. Objectives steer the organization in the
> direction of these desires within the constraints of the SWOT (strengths, weak-

■ **FIGURE 5–4** Exemplary
Mission Statements

ESSO Imperial Oil (Canada)

The company's mission is to create shareholder value through the development
and sale of hydrocarbon energy and related products. (*Annual Report,* 1993)

Orange and Rockland Utilities

We choose to be a customer-driven company in which every employee is
empowered to provide our customers with unequaled energy value and services
and to provide our shareholders with a superior-quality investment. (*Annual
Report,* 1993)

Battle Mountain Gold Company

Using our core skills and technologies, we will seek to enhance shareholder
value through growth and industry leadership. We will succeed by exploring for
or acquiring reserves, constructing and operating profitable mines, and providing
challenging opportunities for our employees. We will apply our resources to the
fundamental obligations that we have to our shareholders, employees, communities, and the environment, while capitalizing upon opportunities in the Western
Hemisphere and the Western Pacific. (*Annual Report,* 1993)

Transamerica Corporation

To enhance shareholder value, through stock price appreciation and cash flow
from dividends, by being the premier provider of specialized financial and life
insurance products to individuals and organizations. (*Annual Report,* 1992)

Citizens Utilities

Our goal is to deliver ever-appreciating value to our shareholders, our customers,
and our employees. (*Annual Report,* 1993)

nesses, opportunities, and threats) of the firm within a strategic intent or strategic fit perspective.[23]

Later in the chapter, essentials of the SWOT analysis, which enables management to assess a firm's competitiveness, will be discussed.

At Centerior Energy, reaching long-term objectives involves three strategies.

■ *Financial Strategy* "To further strengthen our financial position by controlling operating costs, keeping down capital expenditures, and increasing income through off-system sales."

■ *Marketing Strategy* "To expand our partnerships with customers to help them improve energy efficiency and hold down their costs while we aggressively pursue new markets for electricity sales."

■ *Operating Strategy* "To continuously improve our operations to achieve the most profitable use of our facilities while acting as responsible stewards of the environment."[24]

■ *Develop and Implement Strategies*

There are levels of strategic management.

Strategies are developed at the corporate, business, and functional levels. **Corporate strategy** identifies the major thrust of an organization. **Business strategies** specify how each business unit or cluster of subunits should operate. **Functional strategies** involve courses of action for specific areas such as marketing, human resources, production, or finance.

A close relationship exists between the development and the implementation of a strategy. Successful strategies are generally well thought out and well executed. A poorly developed and implemented strategy is a recipe for failure. Managers who carefully consider the appropriateness of strategies are more likely to avoid potential complications. For example, some managers are prone to adopt new, trendy management fads that promise to increase competitiveness, productivity, and profits. For various reasons, including inadequate communication or implementation, lofty expectations may prove to be unrealistic.

According to a recent survey of responses from 4000 focus groups, both workers and customers considered trendy management theories—including such concepts as benchmarking, broadbanding (a consolidation of salary grades), and skill-based pay—to be minimally effective.[25] The importance of strategy execution is stressed by Samuel C. Certo and J. Paul Peter:

Unfortunately, when formulating strategies, managers are inclined simply to assume that effective implementation will occur. Yet it should be obvious that *what organizations actually do* is at least as important as *what they plan to do. . . .* The quality of a formulated strategy is difficult, if not impossible, to assess in the absence of effective implementation.[26]

Figure 5–5 highlights the principal tasks involved in implementing a strategy. Remember, managerial actions are the key to the successful application of the strategic management process. As an example, Farm Credit Services of Southeast Kansas, an agricultural lender, has adopted a flat organizational structure with minimal layers of management. Its president and senior vice president strive to maintain open communication with employees who are grouped together in self-directed work teams. A recently installed information system enables personnel to determine the exact status of a customer's account and to respond to commonly asked inquiries without referring to paperwork filed

■ **FIGURE 5–5** Principal Tasks Involved in Implementing a Strategy

SOURCE: Arthur A. Thompson, Jr., and A. J. Strickland, *Strategic Management: Concepts and Cases,* 7th ed. (Homewood, IL: Richard D. Irwin, 1993), p. 217. © 1993 by Irwin. Used with permission of the publisher.

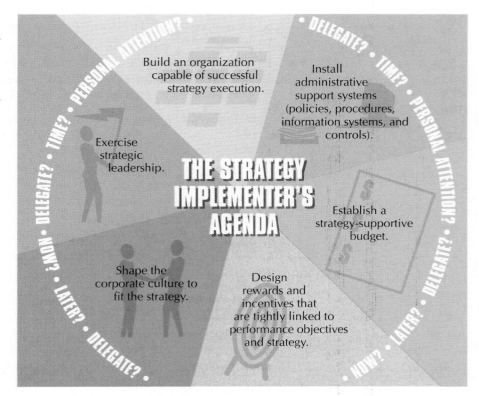

away in folders. Continuous training provides staff members with the up-to-date knowledge they need to do their jobs effectively. By focusing on getting results, the association anticipates increasing its share of a very competitive market.

■ *Monitor Results*

Feedback is essential.

Through monitoring, a manager learns to what degree a plan is achieving the desired results. When problems become apparent, plans need to be revised or rewritten. It is important to gain feedback and initiate needed changes as early as possible.

Sometimes, difficulties are not readily remedied. After Louis Gerstner, Jr., became Chairman of IBM, he quickly identified the company's sales strategy as a key problem area. Instead of reorganizing the marketing area, he decided to improve the existing system.[27] However, it may ultimately be necessary to alter the corporation's "one face" image and organize the sales staff according to industry lines (airlines, banking, and so on) or even divide IBM into a series of smaller companies.

Internal and external environmental factors do not remain static. Often, it is difficult to anticipate when key human resources will leave the organization and seek employment elsewhere. From an external perspective, the arrival of new competitors places a great deal of pressure on sales; unexpected government regulations can restrict profit margins, and new technology often renders products obsolete. Perceptive managers recognize the need to correct apparent deviations from plans in order to get results.

THE SWOT ANALYSIS

What is a SWOT analysis?

Consideration of a company's strengths, weaknesses, opportunities, and threats, called a **SWOT analysis,** allows management to assess the firm's competitive position. **Strengths** are capabilities in which strong advantages are perceived to exist; **weaknesses** negatively impact the likelihood of attaining desired results. **Opportunities** identify areas in which market shares can be gained, profits can be increased, or other objectives can be achieved. **Threats** represent potential obstacles, such as a poor economic climate or changing customer preferences, that adversely influence competitiveness.

Strategy selection depends on management's ability to maximize an organization's internal strengths and minimize its weaknesses. The external environment presents challenges that can curtail opportunities or minimize the negative consequences posed by possible threats. Figure 5–6 illustrates the factors to consider in the development of a SWOT analysis.

■ Identifying Strengths and Weaknesses

Efforts to identify strengths and weaknesses focus on five key functional areas: marketing, production/operations, finance and accounting, research and devel-

■ **FIGURE 5–6** Factors to Consider in a SWOT Analysis

SOURCE: From Peter Wright, Charles D. Pringle, and Mark J. Kroll, *Strategic Management: Text and Cases.* Copyright © 1992 by Allyn & Bacon (Boston). Reprinted by permission.

SOURCES OF POSSIBLE ENVIRONMENTAL OPPORTUNITIES AND THREATS

Economic forces	Social forces
Industry forces	Technological forces
Political/legal forces	

POSSIBLE ORGANIZATIONAL STRENGTHS AND WEAKNESSES

Advertising	Labor relations
Brand names	Leadership
Channel management	Location
Company reputation	Management
Computer information system	Manufacturing and operations
Control systems	Market share
Costs	Organizational structure
Customer loyalty	Physical facilities/equipment
Decision making	Product/service differentiation
Distribution	Product/service quality
Economies of scale	Promotion
Environmental scanning	Public relations
Financial resources	Purchasing
Forecasting	Quality control
Government lobbying	Research and development
Human resources	Selling
Inventory management	Technology

opment, and human resources. Better understanding enables managers to take advantage of the benefits to be gained from implementing successful strategies. A balanced perspective is essential because strengths do not always guarantee success and weaknesses do not necessarily imply certain failure. An example follows.

Known as a financially strong corporation, Coors was late in bringing low-calorie and top-of-the-line premium beers to the marketplace. While competitors expanded and built new facilities, Coors shipped beer from a single production plant in Colorado. At one point, the entire cost of a major plant expansion was paid for without any debt financing. In retrospect, Coors might have better utilized its strong financial position to overcome its disadvantage in the area of marketing (distribution).

Now let's examine several critical factors that are essential to successful strategic management.[28]

■ *Marketing* A firm's ability to utilize marketing-mix variables (price, product, promotion, and distribution) is critical. Marketing strength is demonstrated by companies that provide customers with desired products in a timely manner at competitive prices.

■ *Production/Operations* These factors involve technological effectiveness and the transformation of raw materials into finished products. To be successful, a firm must be able to compete in an increasingly global environment. The productive accomplishments of the Japanese have made American manufacturers pay greater attention to productivity. For example, the American automobile industry—a target of much criticism due to poor product quality—has improved. "In 1980, the average U.S. car had 250 percent more defects than a Japanese car. By 1990, that difference had shrunk to 50 percent."[29]

■ *Finance and Accounting* Relevant concerns in this area are the cost of funds, expenditures of monies, working capital requirements, and dividend-disbursement policies. Knowledge of a firm's financial strengths and weaknesses enables managers to best utilize its financial resources. Accurate accounting information gives managers a perspective on what is owned and what is owed.

To illustrate, organizations that are burdened with large amounts of debt are more restricted in their choice of alternatives than companies that have considerable cash reserves. Multinational companies operate in an environment of fluctuating international currency exchange rates. Also, the rules governing acceptable accounting practices vary from country to country.

■ *Research and Development (R&D)* A focus on new and improved products is a major R&D function. The R&D process evolves through various stages, from basic research to commercialization. Firms can approach the area of research and development from an offensive or a defensive perspective, or a combination of both.[30] Offensive approaches involve the application of innovative technology; defensive positions emphasize modifying products and adapting technology.

Some firms stress defense of the market for their present products and, at the same time, practice an offensive thrust to introduce their new products. While trying to preserve the current demand for its hamburger products, McDonald's also heavily promoted the introduction of Chicken McNuggets and McChicken sandwiches.

Sometimes, American firms do not maximize the use of available information. International competitors tend to focus more on the conclusions of government-sponsored research programs conducted by other countries and to have their research and technical personnel attend a greater number of international conferences.[31]

■ *Human Resources* Capable employees and managers are the lifeblood of an organization. Their contributions influence what a firm is able to accomplish. Recruitment, training, and management-development activities are important concerns. Personnel who understand the company's goals and who demonstrate a commitment to them are most valued assets. The General Electric Company uses its Management Development Institute to provide new college graduates, middle managers, and top executives with a better understanding of the company and to encourage cooperative efforts to meet corporate goals.

CONSIDER THIS

1. How can managers improve their effectiveness as planners?

2. Why should first-line managers be concerned with strategic planning?

3. What is the most important task for a manager to consider when implementing a strategy?

■ *Recognizing Opportunities and Threats*

The environment includes several sectors.

To successfully implement business strategies, the management of a firm must be responsive to the factors that affect its operations.[32] Let's briefly examine the seven primary sectors of the business environment.

■ *Socioeconomic Sector* Economic, social, and climatic factors are relevant. During favorable economic times, incomes rise and consumers are inclined to spend more or to assume greater debt burdens. Concerns about social issues, such as health care or education, can benefit some organizations and can have a negative impact on others. Weather conditions play a major role in the success or failure of agricultural businesses.

■ *Technological Sector* Technological advances shorten product life cycles and render products obsolete within short periods of time. Although they have become smaller in size, for example, today's semiconductor chips are much more powerful than those manufactured just a few years ago.

■ *Government Sector* Businesses are obligated to obey laws, and the expenditures necessary to comply with these laws may increase. In addition to its regulatory role, the government is a major purchaser of a variety of goods and services.

■ *Customer Sector* Firms serve user needs for products and services. Customer choices have a major influence on strategic plans. Peter F. Drucker has argued, "There is only one valid definition of business purpose: to create a customer."[33] Problems arise because customers stop making purchases, buy lesser quantities, or purchase other goods and services.

■ *Supplier Sector* The availability of materials, money, and human talent influences what a firm can and cannot accomplish. If the costs of these resources increase or if access to them becomes restricted, then the likelihood of a threat to the firm's productivity is increased.

■ *Competitor Sector* When a company's entry into the marketplace is costly, time-consuming, and resource-intensive, the possibility of threats to

Assembly of an Ocean Voyager takes a lot of advance planning, research, and development among different sectors. In addition, the planning process must ensure that the completed product will meet or exceed performance expectations.

its competitiveness declines. If competitors go out of business, then serving their former customers becomes a possible business opportunity for the firm.

■ *International Sector* The international arena represents a market for products as well as a potential source of labor and/or raw materials. To do business in some countries, however, a firm must accept political or social instabilities that create quite dissimilar business environments to those in the United States.

CORPORATE STRATEGY

Corporate strategies serve the entire organization.

After the corporate mission and strategic objectives are specified, top management must determine what the organization is to do. Corporate strategy, which commonly has a time horizon of three to six years, provides an overall sense of direction and specifies the primary plan of action to accomplish goals. Ameritech's corporate strategy is "to continually modernize and expand . . . basic network capabilities; to enter and grow businesses related to the information industry; and to invest . . . resources wisely in long-term diversification opportunities."[34] When choosing a corporate strategy, managers focus on the grand strategies of growth, stability, and retrenchment (or a combination of these) or on a portfolio strategy, such as the BCG matrix. A discussion of each of these approaches to implementing corporate strategy follows.

■ *The Grand Strategies*

Grand strategies identify the goals sought by a firm. Four grand strategies are commonly practiced: growth, stability, retrenchment, or a combination of these strategies. Grand strategies can also be used in the formulation of business-level strategies, which are discussed later in this chapter. Let's examine the characteristics of these grand strategies and consider the rationales for each.

GROWTH   To implement a **growth strategy,** the management of a firm focuses on acquiring additional market shares, opening more outlets, and introducing new products. Expansion, product innovativeness, and mergers are three means by which firms can become larger. Wal-Mart is an excellent example of an organization that has concentrated on growth and continues to open new stores each year. Given the risk and demand for investment needed to finance growth, why do companies formulate growth strategies? Various reasons are cited: the attainment of power, pressures from owners, and the need for organizational responsiveness to changing environmental conditions.[35]

Stability emphasizes the status quo.

STABILITY   An effort to preserve the status quo is the primary thrust of a **stability strategy.** Stability is frequently practiced by firms that cannot commit additional financial resources to expansion. The managements of these companies strive to improve existing products and defend their present market shares. American Express, a growth corporation of the 1980s, restructured its Travel Related Services division. The evolving stability strategy was to make Amex credit cards the industry's "gold standard" and to intensify efforts to get customers to charge more purchases on these cards.[36]

At times, retrenchment is necessary, and a firm must reduce its business activities.

RETRENCHMENT   Firms fail to reach goals for a number of reasons: insufficient resources, competitor reactions, lack of market demand, and ineffective management. A **retrenchment strategy** involves the reduction of a firm's activities and is evidenced by withdrawal from markets, personnel layoffs, curtailment of services, sales of assets, and cutbacks in expenditures. In 1990, General Motors reported its first yearly loss since 1980. Consequently, the auto giant cut the stockholder dividend, eliminated jobs, sought price concessions from suppliers, and announced plans to reduce its capital-spending budget.[37]

COMBINATION STRATEGIES   Grand strategies can be used in combination. **Combination strategies** are most commonly employed by large, diversified organizations. Kmart's actions illustrate the application of combination strategies.[38] At one time, Kmart owned an entire group of specialty retail businesses, including Payless Drug, OfficeMax, Sports Authority, Waldenbooks, and Pace Membership Warehouse. In the Dallas area, the Pace operation lost money, failed to compete with Sam's Club, and forced Kmart to retrench. During the same period of time, however, Kmart was growing and introduced its new Super K stores, which combine the features of a discount outlet and a supermarket.

■ *A Portfolio Strategy: The BCG Matrix*

The BCG matrix considers growth rate and market share.

When a **portfolio strategy** is employed, a corporation is viewed as consisting of multiple businesses with units that are dissimilar in nature. For example, RJR Nabisco's operations are quite diverse and range from tobacco to baking. The **BCG matrix,** developed by the Boston Consulting Group, compares high and low growth rate with high and low market share. The matrix, shown in Figure 5–7, classifies business units into one of four quadrants: stars, cash cows, question marks, or dogs.

■ *Stars*   Business units that demonstrate high growth and high market share are positioned in this category, which represents excellent long-term opportunities. Stars typically require short-term financing beyond the revenues they produce. Diet colas, light beers, and VCRs are examples of stars that may ultimately evolve into cash cows.

Stars	Question Marks
■ High growth	■ High growth
■ High market share	■ Low market share
Cash Cows	**Dogs**
■ Low growth	■ Low growth
■ High market share	■ Low market share

GROWTH RATE

MARKET SHARE

■ *Cash Cows* These low-growth business units garner large shares of the market. Cash cows do not require a commitment of additional finances. Revenues generated from them can be transferred to other operations, which is often referred to as "milking." Hershey chocolate bars, original Pepsi Cola, and Cheerios breakfast cereal are examples of cash cows.

■ *Question Marks* Question marks exhibit high growth and low market share. Managers of these business units have a choice: they can commit additional financial resources to these units due to their high growth or reduce spending due to their low market shares. The introduction of some prescription drugs illustrates this dilemma; they often possess much market potential but require considerable investment to commercialize.

■ *Dogs* Business units that operate in mature markets but show little profitability are called dogs. They have small growth opportunities and low market shares. Managers must either liquidate these businesses or sell them to other companies. The failure to remain competitive has been a major difficulty for American steel producers. Drive-in movies were once quite popular but could not compete with television and videotapes.

The BCG matrix gives managers insight into the twin concerns of growth rate and market share. However, the matrix is not without its limitations.[39] Some critics argue that the four-cell categorization is too restrictive and overly simplified. In practice, precise measures of growth rate and market share may not be readily available. Also, the relationship between market share and profitability varies among industries.

BUSINESS STRATEGY

A number of business strategies can evolve.

A business strategy is focused on attaining goals for each business unit or cluster of business units in the organization. Compared to a corporate strategy, a business strategy is less broadly oriented. Ameritech has a strategy for its various subunits, which together comprise the Ameritech family of companies. Ameritech Bell provides communication and long-distance telephone services; Ameritech Publishing produces telephone directories and other specialty publications. Business strategies can be quite diverse and range from an emphasis on growth to cutbacks at the other end of the spectrum.

What are SBUs?

Strategic business units (SBUs) are separate operating units designed to sell distinctive products or services to identifiable consumer groups.[40] As companies grow and diversify into various types of operations, it becomes unwieldly for a single manager to be responsible for many diverse units. It is more sensible to develop a managerial hierarchy for the various units.

Bristol-Meyer Squibb is so large that it is actually composed of four separate core businesses (pharmaceuticals, consumer products, medical devices, and nutritionals). It would be cumbersome for one manager to have the operating responsibilities for all of these separate areas. Italian-based GFT is a worldwide producer of designer apparel. Even though it consists of 45 companies and 18 plants, GFT strives to coordinate major organizational plans with those of its various business units. This approach provides flexibility and allows the firm to be sensitive to the planning needs of its individual subsidiaries.[41]

To be classified as a strategic business unit, a business unit must meet several criteria.[42] An SBU should:

- Sell products or services to external customers and experience the challenge of facing competition.

- "Stand on its own feet" and make its own decisions about financing, manufacturing, marketing, and so on.

- Perform in a way that lends itself to evaluation.

To summarize, SBUs operate on their own but are part of larger, more comprehensive organizations.

■ *The Adaptation Model*

A key feature of the **adaptation model** is that it matches business strategies with environmental conditions. Figure 5–8 shows three strategies—prospectors, analyzers, and defenders—and describes the environment associated with each of them. The reactor strategy is not suitable, since it cannot be maintained.

Defenders try to protect their markets.   **DEFENDERS** A **defender strategy,** which is feasible in stable environments, emphasizes competition in a relatively narrow market by selling a limited number of goods or services. A defender business strives to become very adept at com-

■ **FIGURE 5–8** Adaptation Strategies and Environmental Variables

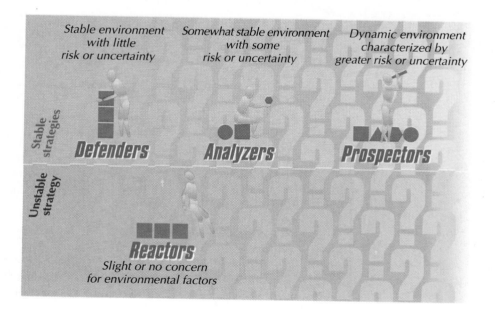

CHAPTER 5 *Planning*   **165**

municating a concern for quality and efficiency. For example, a garden center may concentrate on selling a limited variety of nursery items to upscale customers who value personalized suggestions and are willing to pay higher prices than those charged by discount stores. Fast-food franchises and convenience-store chains are other examples of firms that frequently practice defender strategies.

PROSPECTORS The **prospector strategy** advocates an active thrust to introduce new products and seek new customers. A prospector business gets optimal results in dynamic environments, which are characterized by risk and uncertainty. Under very competitive circumstances, for example, United Parcel Service has expanded its service area, arranged for convenient package-dropoff facilities at some retail stores, provided quick responses to resolve problems and complaints, and installed automatic package sorting to expedite deliveries.

Prospectors seek new business opportunities.

ANALYZERS Positioned between prospectors and defenders, the **analyzer strategy** "balances" stability with conditions that involve some risk and uncertainty. A key factor is the retention of customers for traditional products or services and the simultaneous expansion into new ventures. For example, Pepsico is often thought of as a soft-drink manufacturer. However, the company also has extensive operations in fast food (Kentucky Fried Chicken), Mexican food (Taco Bell), snack food (Frito-Lay), and pizza (Pizza Hut).

Analyzers represent a "middle position" between defenders and prospectors.

REACTORS The **reactor strategy** evidences failure. Ultimately, reactors must adopt one of the other three strategies or cease to function.[43] An inability to operate successfully can be attributed to poor economic conditions or to inappropriate managerial choices. In either case, an unsuccessful outcome is traumatic for a firm's management and its personnel. For example, deregulation contributed to problems in the savings and loan industry during the 1980s. The removal of government restraints enabled many S&Ls to make more speculative investments; a large percentage of these ventures did not work out and led to failures.

The reactor strategy cannot be maintained.

CONSIDER THIS

1. How can the BCG matrix be of the most value to managers?
2. What is the relationship between a firm's mission and its corporate strategy?
3. Referring to the adaptation model, why is the defender strategy feasible in stable environments?

■ *Porter's Framework*

Firms are challenged to excel at successfully responding to competitive pressures. Michael E. Porter, a Harvard professor and leading business strategist, emphasizes the important impact of competitive forces on industry profitability. Porter cites several competitive forces, which are illustrated in Figure 5–9. We will discuss each of them here.[44]

The actions of competitors cannot be disregarded.

■ *Threat of New Entrants* Various barriers impede entry into an industry, including such factors as economies of scale, "switching costs" (one-time costs of switching from one vendor or product to another), capital requirements, and government policies. If the barriers to entry are high or if new firms perceive strong retaliation from existing competitors, then the threat of

GLOBAL VIEW

Sandoz Buys Gerber: A Mutual Exchange?

What do baby food, pharmaceuticals, and chemicals have in common? More than you might think, if we are talking about the sale of Gerber Products to Sandoz AG of Switzerland. Gerber serves nearly three-fourths of the U.S. market for baby food but, despite several attempts, has not attained a desired level of penetration in international markets. On the other hand, Sandoz wants an opportunity to significantly increase nutritional sales in the United States.

As a growth strategy, the acquisition gives Gerber access to an existing international distribution system without battling strong competitors to establish a market presence. Gerber's entry into the international marketplace is especially important because the United States represents only 2 percent of the births in the entire world, and it has been a challenge for Gerber to increase its share of the domestic market. While the U.S. birth rate is declining, infants are also consuming less baby food. Sandoz benefits by gaining the respected Gerber brand name and an opportunity to complement its food business, which includes such well-known products as Ovaltine and Triaminic cough medicine.

Most companies develop plans for adopting up-to-date computer technology. Planning enables Sandoz International to be competitive in the international marketplace.

Gerber is not without experience in the international arena and has approximately 17 percent of the $1.5 billion market for baby food sold in jars. The company strives to accommodate cultural differences: sardines are mixed with baby food for the Japanese; artichokes are included to satisfy the preferences of French parents. Yet Gerber has encountered complications in the international marketplace. For example, the company previously used licensing agreements as its primary international marketing strategy. However, this approach led to lower profit margins and loss of product control to licensees responsible for marketing many types of products.

With this acquisition, Sandoz takes a different strategy than competitors such as Merck and SmithKline Beechem, which have acquired cost-containment companies. Instead, Sandoz seeks product diversification in an era of increasingly stiff competition. Future marketing decisions at Sandoz will probably focus on greater involvement with generic and nonprescription products, an objective that will require the acquisition of additional firms.

Was Sandoz wise to offer $3.7 billion—an amount nearly 50 percent higher than Gerber's prevailing market price and more than 30 times greater than its present earnings—to acquire the Gerber brand name? With the passage of time, the answer will become more obvious. Nevertheless, the offer communicated a message to dissuade other possible bidders and shortened the time needed to complete the transaction. Perhaps these factors were inherent considerations in the development of the premium-bid strategy.

ADAPTED FROM: Richard Gibson, "Gerber Missed the Boat in Quest to Go Global, so It Turned to Sandoz," *The Wall Street Journal* (May 24, 1994), pp. A1, A7; Richard Gibson and Margaret Studer, "Sandoz to Acquire Gerber in $3.7 Billion Agreement," *The Wall Street Journal* (May 24, 1994) p. A3; Micheline Maynard, "Swiss Firm to Buy Gerber for $4 Billion," *USA Today* (May 24, 1994) p. 1B; Margaret Studer and Ron Winslow, "Sandoz, Under Pressure, Looks to Gerber for Protection," *The Wall Street Journal* (May 25, 1994), p. B3.

new entrants to the industry is low. A considerable amount of capital is required to build a plant to generate electricity. Given this high entry barrier, the federal and state governments regulate electric utilities to assure that customer interests are considered. Dillions or Safeway (large grocery chains) can spread expenses over many stores—a luxury not available to the owner of a small, independent grocery store.

■ *Rivalry among Competitors* By offering better service, lower prices, and newer products, firms seek to attract customers from competitors. Originally, Ford's Model T was produced in one color, and few major changes were introduced in the automobile for a period of time. Perceiving an opportunity to gain market share, rival General Motors began production of the Chevrolet, a more stylish vehicle available in a variety of colors. Since deregulation, the airline industry has suffered fierce competition. In a recent three-year period, Delta spent approximately $700 million to compete with Eastern, which has since gone out of business.[45]

■ *Availability of Substitute Products* Although competition among producers exists (for example, Anheuser-Bush versus Coors), price increases are a reason for customers to buy other products (perhaps nonalcoholic beverages or wines). The tobacco industry offers a classic example of how pricing strategies influence consumer behavior. As the price of premium brands escalates, many smokers switch to lower-priced, generic brands.

■ **FIGURE 5–9** The Competitive Forces That Determine Industry Profitability

SOURCE: Reprinted with the permission of The Free Press, a Division of Macmillan, Inc., from *Competitive Advantage: Creating and Sustaining Superior Performance* by Michael E. Porter. Copyright © 1985 by Michael E. Porter.

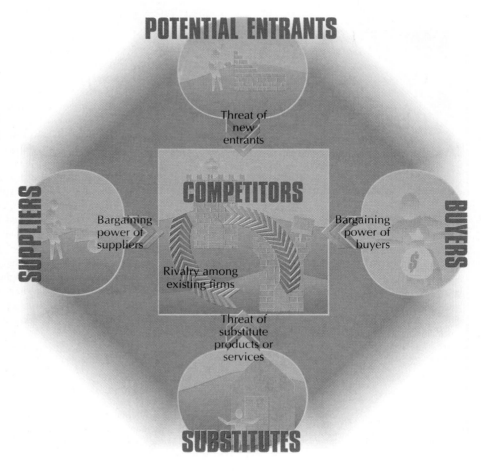

■ *Economic Strength of Buyers* Buyers seek to pay lower prices, obtain higher quality or additional services, and pit their competitors against one another. Factors that contribute to economic buying strength include an ability to purchase large-volume quantities and to acquire much information about market conditions. An economically strong buyer might also threaten to make a product rather than continue purchasing it from a supplier. When buying capability is concentrated, buyers can greatly influence prices and conditions of sale.

■ *Economic Strength of Suppliers* Through their ability to raise prices or lower product quality, suppliers exercise bargaining strength. If a needed product or component part is available from only one supplier and no substitute products exist, this supplier holds an enviable position. If a powerful supplier provides low-quality materials, then the company that purchases these materials will probably experience problems in its efforts to serve its customers and to maintain a competitive position.

In summary, five competitive forces influence a firm's success in gaining entry into an industry: high barriers to entry, lack of strong competition, unavailability of substitute products, and absence of strong buyers or sellers offer a maximum opportunity to generate profits. However, such ideal circumstances are not commonplace. Porter recommends three generic strategies to cope with a competitive marketplace and gain a comparative performance advantage.[46]

Three generic strategies influence competitiveness.

1. *Overall Cost Leadership* Low overall costs give a firm an advantage over its competitors. Porter emphasizes the importance of having a relatively high share of the market and of maintaining high cash margins for the purchase of new machinery or buildings. In the precious metals industry, for example, American Barrick has implemented a successful hedging program to afford protection against declines in the price of gold. The corporation generates sufficient funds to take advantage of business opportunities in Central and South America.

2. *Differentiation* A firm that applies the differentiation strategy attempts to provide products that have unique characteristics. Traditionally, Apple computer promoted user-friendliness as a differentiating feature to command premium prices.[47] However, Microsoft's introduction of its Windows software programs has reduced Apple's ability to capitalize on this strategy. Porter illustrates how firms successfully differentiate.

> Approaches to differentiating can take many forms: *design or brand image* (Fieldcrest in top-of-the-line towels and linens, Mercedes in automobiles); *technology* (Hyster in lift trucks, MacIntosh in stereo components, Coleman in camping equipment); *features* (Jenn-Air in electric ranges); *customer service* (Crown Cork and Seal in metal cans); *dealer network* (Caterpillar Tractor in construction equipment); or other dimensions. Ideally, the firm differentiates itself along several dimensions.[48]

3. *Focus* A firm using the focus strategy stresses low costs, product differentiation, or both approaches to a narrow target market. Many firms in the weight-loss business aggressively advertise special prices for diet plans and exercise programs. These efforts are specifically targeted to overweight persons. Montblanc pens and pencils are marketed as upscale products to appeal to executives and others who are willing to pay for exclusive writing instruments. Weinig, a German manufacturer of wood-molding equipment, makes a single product and markets it globally as a top-of-the-line item.

Prevailing business conditions provide opportunities but also limit a firm's ability to implement strategies. New products enable pharmaceutical companies to maintain high profit margins. Ultimately, such protection expires, and competitors may perceive demand to be large enough that they can introduce their own brands. At times, firms become "stuck in the middle" and are incapable of implementing any of the generic strategies. This position indicates an inability to be competitive and leads to declining profits. For example, most U.S. airlines have not been able to adopt successful generic strategies and have become unprofitable to owners.

Managers should think carefully before they choose a strategy to cope with a competitive marketplace.

 ## FUNCTIONAL STRATEGY

Functional strategies affect the activities of a firm's various functional units: marketing, production/operations, finance, research and development, and human resources. The successful implementation of these strategies will enable a company to compete effectively and exhibit sufficient flexibility to make adjustments in response to changing conditions in the business environment. "Whereas corporate- and business-level managers center their attention on 'doing the right thing,' managers at the functional level center their attention on 'doing things right.' "[49]

Functional strategies are results-oriented.

Let's consider an example. Marketing plans recognize ways in which businesses compete—through service, reputation, price, and the like. Production is concerned with encouraging product innovativeness and eliminating defects. Therefore, functional strategies for marketing and production at Ameritech Bell could emphasize gaining new customers, minimizing service interruptions, and pricing on a competitive basis. Ameritech Publishing might focus on assuring the accuracy of published telephone listings and stimulating the sales of additional specialty products.

THINK ABOUT IT

1. Those who plan for the future are likely to be prepared for it.

2. While they do contribute to successful outcomes, good plans do not guarantee them.

3. Past plans do not necessarily fit future circumstances.

4. Although planning does take time, avoidance generally consumes more time.

5. Plans may need to be revised—frequently—because expected events did not occur and the unexpected happened.

6. To be worthwhile, plans should be developed and used, not placed on a shelf to collect dust.

7. The failure to plan can be a blueprint for a plan to fail.

8. Assumptions can influence plans; however, all assumptions are not accurate.

 ## LOOKING BACK

Knowledge of the planning function is a key to becoming a successful manager. You have studied about the role and importance of planning. Now let's carefully review each of the learning objectives for this chapter.

Differentiate among policies, procedures, and rules.

Policies are broadly oriented, overall guidelines to action. Procedures are step-by-step orderings of events; procedures make policies operational. Rules are quite specific and inflexible; in practice, rules are usually followed without deviation. Managers need to recognize the purposes of these components and to understand how they contribute to effective planning.

Describe each step in the planning process.

The planning process includes five steps: determine the goal, review the present situation, recognize limiting factors, develop the plan, and implement the plan. Goals represent the outcomes that the organization wants to achieve. A review of the current situation provides an understanding of the gap, if any, between goals and the status quo. Limitations must be recognized because they represent potential barriers to market entry. Development involves weighing alternatives, specifying tasks, setting priorities, and assigning responsibilities. To be useful, plans must be put into action.

Explain the importance of strategic management.

The process of strategic management forces an organization to examine its purpose, specify its long-term objectives, develop and implement key strategies, and monitor results. Successful practice of strategic management enables managers to better understand how well their companies can compete in the marketplace. Also, strategic management helps managers to identify the changes that are required to improve competitiveness.

Identify the grand-strategy alternatives.

Firms practice four grand strategies: growth, stability, retrenchment, or a combination of these. Growth emphasizes acquiring market share, opening new outlets, and the introduction of new products. With a stability strategy, the firm strives to preserve the status quo. Retrenchment involves reduction in a firm's activities. Retrenchment occurs for numerous reasons, including insufficient resources and the actions of competitors.

Recognize strategies in the adaptation model.

Adaptation matches business strategies and environmental conditions. A defender protects narrow markets and commonly offers a limited variety of goods or services; this strategy is feasible for stable environments. A prospector strategy, which involves risk and uncertainty, is appropriate for dynamic environments. The analyzer strategy represents a middle ground between prospectors and defenders. It balances stability with conditions that involve some risk and uncertainty. Finally, a reactor strategy represents an unstable position and must ultimately become one of the other strategies for the company to continue to exist.

 # KEY TERMS

adaptation model	goal
analyzer strategy	grand strategies
BCG matrix	growth strategy
business strategy	intermediate plan
combination strategy	mission statement
contingency plan	operational plan
corporate strategy	planning
defender strategy	policy
functional strategy	portfolio strategy

procedure
prospector strategy
reactor strategy
retrenchment strategy
rule
stability strategy
strategic business unit (SBU)
strategic management

strategic objective
strategic plan
SWOT analysis
  strengths
  weaknesses
  opportunities
  threats

REVIEW AND DISCUSSION QUESTIONS

1. How does effective planning benefit managers?

2. What are the differences among policies, procedures, and rules?

3. What steps are involved in the planning process?

4. What is the relationship between the concepts of corporate strategy and functional strategy?

5. Why should planners understand the concept of grand strategies?

6. What is the purpose of a business strategy?

7. What are functional strategies?

8. How does the adaptation model assist managers?

9. Identify each quadrant of the BCG matrix and explain the differences among the quadrants.

10. What factors should be considered when developing a SWOT analysis?

CRITICAL THINKING INCIDENT 5.1

A Change of Plans

A year ago, Jean Carlyle was employed as office manager for Consolidated Express, a shipping company serving customers located in western parts of the United States. When she was hired, Sam Wilson, her boss, emphasized the importance of maintaining the company's reputation for prompt, dependable service to customers. As a result, Jean developed a plan to revamp the recordkeeping system. Implementation of the plan has caused a few complications, including the delayed billing of some customers, late posting of accounts receivable, and missed deadlines for paying invoices.

Sam is upset about these events, which he feels have gone on too long, and urges Jean to get them resolved quickly. She considers Sam's criticism to be unjust because many of the difficulties involve equipment failures that are beyond her control. In addition, Jean does not believe the troubles are as problematic as Sam thinks. In her view, Sam does not understand the complexities of the new technology or how much work is necessary to make the system function.

A couple of weeks ago, Sam informed Jean of the pressing need to reorganize the office staff and consolidate job responsibilities in order to eliminate two jobs. Such reorganization poses a challenge because the staff is already overworked due to previous cutbacks. Two days ago, Sam told

Jean to submit a plan that outlines how to best utilize some adjacent office space that became available when the sales staff recently moved to another location.

Jean became frustrated and asked Sam about priorities. He replied, "Jean, you're a capable person with the ability to get things done. Just stay on top of everything." In Jean's perspective, the discussion did not accomplish anything and was typical of Sam's responses. She considers him to be a disorganized person who gets behind with his own work but expects his employees to be organized and complete tasks on time.

The semiannual performance evaluation is coming up, and Jean is concerned. She strives to meet job expectations but experiences time pressures and changing expectations. Jean is hesitant to tell Sam how she really feels and risk getting a low evaluation. She thinks to herself, "I realize that circumstances necessitate change, but it would be nice to have some formally stated objectives and know the basis on which I'll be evaluated."

Discussion Questions

1. What is the relationship between the planning function and Sam's concern about dependable customer service?

2. How could Jean have minimized Sam's criticism of her implementation of her new plan for revamping the recordkeeping system?

3. During her performance evaluation, should Jean plan to tell Sam how she really feels? Explain your response.

4. How can Sam be encouraged to become a more capable planner?

 ## CRITICAL THINKING INCIDENT 5.2

Looking Ahead

The firm of Winters and Associates has been involved in commercial and residential property development for the past eight years. During this time, the company developed two medium-sized malls in Kansas communities and four residential projects on tracts of land in thriving Kansas City suburbs. These endeavors were successful and completed without any unexpected complications. A couple of weeks ago, Charles Winters, the president of the firm, learned about the possibility of buying the campus facility of a defunct college located in Havertown, an eastern Kansas community of 35,000 people.

Charles is intrigued with the potential of converting existing campus buildings into office space, senior-citizen housing, and a small shopping mall. He believes that vacant land on part of the campus can be sold as residential building lots for homes in the $125,000 to $150,000 price range. Enough land is also available to construct a small, picturesque lake. These uses of land and facilities conform to zoning regulations and the character of the surrounding neighborhood. No complaints or lawsuits related to utilization of the property are anticipated.

The property is appraised at $5 million, but it can be purchased for 70 percent of this amount with an all-cash offer. The seller is willing to negotiate the $5 million price and other terms of the sale. Construction and remodeling expenses are estimated at another $1 million and could be completed within nine months. The firm is not in a position to pay cash, but Charles believes an acceptable offer can be made, especially if contingent prepurchase arrangements can be reached with persons who are willing to buy the residential lots.

Havertown, a college community, is located at the intersection of two interstate highways and serves as a regional shopping center. In the past year, two major employers have closed plants there and the railroad has moved its shop operations to another locality. Despite these occurrences, property values have not substantially declined. Due to a recent property reappraisal, however, property taxes are anticipated to increase by approximately 20 percent.

Discussion Questions

1. How much thought has been given to the plan for developing the former campus facility?

2. What factors might necessitate revising a plan to purchase the facility?

3. What should Charles include in any contingency plan that might be developed?

4. Why is it important for Charles to review the content of the plan before it is finalized?

 ## CRITICAL THINKING INCIDENT 5.3

Where from Here?

Wilbur Johannes has worked as an electrician for several years and recently passed the examination to be certified as a master electrician—a necessary requirement to become owner of a firm that provides electrical services. Believing that the time is right, Wilbur has decided to go into business for himself. To get started, he must purchase the necessary equipment and stock supplies of frequently used items. His former employer has offered to sell Wilbur a service vehicle at a reasonable price and also is willing to sell him a "bucket" truck, which is used to reach high places such as street lights, towers, and multilevel buildings.

Wilbur thinks to himself, "How can I obtain enough equity funds to qualify for a small business loan?" Few alternatives exist; the only feasible one is to contact several relatives and offer them an attractive rate of interest to loan him the money. His wife's parents are the most promising lenders. They have observed Wilbur's ability to organize work tasks and consider his perseverance to be a valuable entrepreneurial trait. Without a loan, however, it will not be possible for Wilbur to start his new business.

Wilbur has always wanted to be his own boss but has no prior experience in developing a business plan or in completing the necessary forms to obtain a business loan. He contemplates whether to serve only residential customers or to bid on commercial jobs as well. Although commercial business is not as profitable, it provides stable employment because many projects take several weeks or longer to finish. Residential customers call more sporadically for services that can be completed within relatively short amounts of time.

Currently, no retail store within the locality specializes in the sale of lighting fixtures. Wilbur wonders if he should plan to open a retail outlet and combine the sale of fixtures with other products, such as mirrors and decorative glass items. By using a call-answering service and cellular telephones, the electrician business can be conducted without renting a building. An inventory of needed parts can be stored in the basement of his residence and carried in storage cabinets on trucks. Retailing, however, requires a ground-level storefront, preferably at a location that is easily accessible to customers. Also, employees must be available to wait on customers.

Although he dropped out for financial reasons, Wilbur learned a lot about computers during his two years at college. He has continued to be interested in computer technology and considers offering programming advice to commercial customers to attract and retain their electrical business. Although he could do much of the work himself, it will be necessary to hire another employee to implement this strategy. However, Wilbur thinks this approach is realistic because many computer majors at the local university seek part-time employment to supplement their college expenses.

Three other companies provide electrician services to the community. One firm is rather large and well-established; it serves residential as well as commercial customers. The other two companies are much smaller and concentrate on doing minor repair work for residential customers. Wilbur believes that both commercial and residential customers can be successfully targeted. From a competitive perspective, he considers his reputation for doing good work to be a major advantage.

To gain a market share, Wilbur anticipates pricing his services lower than his three competitors. In addition, he plans to place a display advertisement in the Yellow Pages of the telephone directory, to buy a television spot ad to be aired two times each evening over the local cablevision channel, and to have the truck and the service vehicle painted a distinctive color and display his company's name on them in large, easy-to-read letters.

Several individuals have expressed an interest in working for Wilbur. Martin Olivetti, a former colleague, is eager to become an employee. Martin is very knowledgeable and has considerable experience as an electrician, but he currently earns more money than Wilbur can pay him. Wilbur's brother, Gerald, has just moved to town and is not presently employed. Although he is a dependable worker, Gerald does not have much experience. Sally Ogden is interested in keeping books on a part-time basis and has previous experience in retailing.

Discussion Questions

1. In planning for his business, what factors should Wilbur consider?

2. Since he is already skilled and experienced at his profession, why is it still important for Wilbur to plan?

3. As it relates to planning his business, identify the most relevant long-term question for Wilbur to consider.

4. Why do short-term plans need to be developed for the new business to be successful?

5. Assuming Martin, Gerald, and Sally are hired, why should Wilbur involve them in the planning process?

NOTES

1. John Huey, "Nothing Is Impossible," *Fortune* (September 23, 1991), p. 136.
2. Frederick G. Harmon and Garry Jacobs, *The Vital Difference* (New York: AMACOM, 1985), p. 147.
3. "The Transportation Industry: A Deregulated Environment Creates Investment Opportunities," *Assessing the Investment Climate*, Merrill Lynch (October 18, 1991), p. 1.
4. David Craig, "Stock Plans Gain Favor as New Benefit," *USA Today* (September 24, 1991), p. 1B.
5. Alecia Swasy, "Diaper's Failure Shows How Poor Plans, Unexpected Woes Can Kill New Products," *The Wall Street Journal* (October 9, 1990), p. B1.
6. Brett Pulley, "As U.S. Firms Return to Land of Apartheid, Lotus Feels Its Way," *The Wall Street Journal* (May 26, 1993), pp. A1, A5.
7. Lawrence Ingrassia, "How Polaroid Went from Highest Flier to Takeover Target," *The Wall Street Journal* (August 12, 1988), p. 10.
8. Stephen E. Robbins, *Management*, 3d ed. (New York: Prentice-Hall, 1991), pp. 193–94.
9. Dick Schaaf, "Beating the Drum for Quality," *Training* Supplement **28** (March 1991): 8.
10. Amanda Bennett and Carol Hymowitz, "Firms Say They Put New Stress on Client Needs," *The Wall Street Journal* (October 6, 1989), p. B1.
11. Gregory A. Patterson, "How GM's Car Plant in Arlington, Texas, Hustled to Avoid Ax," *The Wall Street Journal* (May 6, 1992), pp. A1, A6.
12. "Top Management Goals," *Nation's Business* **79** (November 1991): 12.
13. Dale D. McConkey, "Planning in a Changing Environment," *Business Horizons* **31** (September/October 1988): 72.
14. Anne B. Fisher, "CEOs Think That Morale Is Dandy," *Fortune* (November 18, 1991), p. 84.
15. Lawrence R. Jauch and William F. Glueck, *Business Policy and Strategic Management*, 5th ed. (New York: McGraw-Hill, 1988), p. 19.

16. Carol J. Loomis, "How Does Reed Hang on at Citi?," *Fortune* (November 18, 1991), p. 120.

17. Jean-Pierre Jeannett and Hubert D. Hennessey, *Global Marketing Strategies* (Boston: Houghton Mifflin, 1992), pp. 590–92.

18. "Professional Income Tax Preparers Have Poor Performance," *Emporia Gazette* (February 18, 1991), p. 13.

19. McConkey, "Planning in a Changing Environment," p. 70.

20. Ramon J. Aldag and Timothy M. Sterns, *Management,* 2d ed. (Cincinnati: South-Western, 1991), p. 177.

21. Fred R. David, *Fundamentals of Strategic Management* (Columbus: Merrill, 1986), p. 84.

22. *Annual Report,* Centerior Energy Corporation (1990), p. 3.

23. James M. Higgins and Julian W. Vincze, *Strategic Management: Text and Cases,* 5th ed. (Fort Worth: Dryden, 1993), p. 71.

24. *Annual Report,* Centerior Energy Corporation (1992), p. 3.

25. Fred R. Bleakley, "Many Companies Try Management Fads, Only to See Them Flop," *The Wall Street Journal* (July 6, 1993), p. A1.

26. Samuel C. Certo and J. Paul Peter, *Strategic Management: Concepts and Applications,* 2d ed. (New York: McGraw-Hill, 1991), p. 131.

27. Laurie Hays, "IBM's Gerstner Holds Back from Sales Force Shake-Up," *The Wall Street Journal* (July 7, 1993), pp. 1B, 4B.

28. John A. Pearce and Richard B. Robinson, Jr., *Strategic Management: Formulation, Implementation, and Control,* 4th ed. (Homewood, IL: Richard D. Irwin, 1991), pp. 314–15.

29. John Hillkirk, "Workers Are the Key, Top Firms Find," *USA Today* (October 1, 1991), p. 2B.

30. Pearce and Robinson, *Strategic Management,* pp. 314–15.

31. Gregory G. Dess and Alex Miller, *Strategic Management* (New York: McGraw-Hill, 1993), p. 39.

32. Jauch and Glueck, *Business Policy and Strategic Management,* pp. 90–139.

33. Peter F. Drucker, *The Practice of Management* (New York: Harper & Row, 1954), p. 37.

34. *Annual Report,* Ameritech (1987), p. 1.

35. Jauch and Glueck, *Business Policy and Strategic Management,* pp. 207–208.

36. Bill Saporito, "The Bill Is Due at American Express," *Fortune* (November 18, 1991), pp. 99–100.

37. Micheline Maynard, "GM Gears Up for '91 with Dividend Cut," *USA Today* (February 5, 1991), pp. 1B–2B.

38. Bill Saporito, "The High Cost of Second Best," *Fortune* (July 26, 1993), pp. 99–100.

39. Pearce and Robinson, *Strategic Management,* p. 265.

40. Lloyd L. Byars, *Strategic Management,* 3d ed. (New York: Harper Collins, 1991), p. 16.

41. Robert Howard, "The Designer Organization: Italy's GFT Goes Global," *Harvard Business Review* **69** (September/October 1991): 29, 40.

42. Byars, *Strategic Management,* p. 16. Based on William H. Rothschild, "How to Ensure the Continued Growth of Strategic Planning," *Journal of Business Strategy,* (Summer 1980): 14.

43. Jauch and Glueck, *Business Policy and Strategic Management,* p. 241.

44. Michael E. Porter, *Competitive Strategy: Techniques for Analyzing Industries and Competitors* (New York: The Free Press/Macmillan, 1980), pp. 6–29.

45. Kenneth Labish, "What Will Save the U.S. Airlines?," *Fortune* (June 14, 1993), p. 98.

46. Porter, *Competitive Strategy,* pp. 35–41.

47. Charles McCoy and Key Yamada, "Apple's Woes Renew Worries about Price War's Bite," *The Wall Street Journal* (June 10, 1993), p. B8.

48. Porter, *Competitive Strategy,* p. 37.

49. Pearce and Robinson, *Strategic Management,* p. 5.

 # SUGGESTED READINGS

Filipowski, Dianne. "HR Guides Restructuring." *Personnel Journal* **72** (December 1993): 57.

Greengard, Samuel. "Don't Rush Downsizing: Plan, Plan, Plan." *Personnel Journal* **72** (November 1993): 64–77.

Henkoff, Ronald. "Getting Beyond Downsizing." *Fortune* (January 10, 1994), pp. 58–60, 62, 64.

Hof, Robert D. "Hewlett-Packard Digs Deep for a Digital Future." *Business Week* (October 18, 1993), pp. 72–75.

Jacob, Rahul. "Beyond Quality and Value." *Fortune* (Autumn/Winter 1993), pp. 8–11.

Kim, W. Chan. "Making Global Strategies Work." *Sloan Management Review* **34** (Spring 1993): 11–27.

Mintzberg, Henry. "The Pitfalls of Strategic Planning." *California Management Review* **36** (Fall 1993): 32–47.

———. "The Rise and Fall of Strategic Planning." *Harvard Business Review* **72** (January/February 1994): 107–14.

Power, Christopher, et al. "Flops." *Business Week* (August 16, 1993), pp. 76–80, 82.

Wallum, Peter. "A Broader View of Succession Planning." *Personnel Management* **25** (September 1993): 42–45.

CHAPTER **6**

ORGANIZING

■ LEARNING OBJECTIVES

Too often, managers fail to give much attention to how their company and departments are organized. Often, whatever organizational structure tradition has established is accepted without any review. However, the way firms are organized can influence their ability to succeed. Therefore, managers should possess an understanding of key elements of organization and a knowledge of how different approaches to organizing can help companies accomplish their goals. The learning objectives for this chapter are to:

- Explain the difference between line departments and staff departments in organizations.
- Identify common ways in which organizations practice departmentalization.
- Identify the key factors that should be considered when designing jobs, according to the job characteristics model.
- Distinguish process management from management by function.
- Explain how the modular approach to organizing works.
- Describe the virtual corporation approach to organizing.

■ CHAPTER OUTLINE

During much of the 1980s, many computer industry experts considered Hewlett-Packard (HP) to be a slow-moving, impassive company. Today, however, HP has become one of the most innovative and competitive computer makers around. In the past few years, the company has slashed its bureaucracy and accelerated product development. As a result, HP has been able to increase market share and tap new computer markets. According to Casey Powell, Chairman of minicomputer maker Sequent Computer Systems, Inc., "They're the toughest company we go after."

What has changed at HP? For one thing, the company has eliminated dozens of committees that previously evaluated all decisions. While these committees spent months discussing ideas, market opportunities were being lost. Now, the computer division is better organized, with more autonomy given to key departments. This change, in turn, has led to faster product development. For example, in 1991, the company replaced its entire line of computers with 21 new models, and they got to market in record time due to fast approval. "Before, it would have taken umpteen committees," says Vice President Willem P. Roelandts. In addition, the improvements in organizing at HP have helped increase profits for the company.

Due to rapid changes in technology and the need to achieve higher levels of quality, many companies must become better organized to be competitive. Organizational designs that empower employees produce high levels of productivity, product quality, and job satisfaction. To make the most of organizational designs, there should be direct communication channels between managers, employees, and customers.

ADAPTED FROM: Robert D. Hof, "Suddenly Hewlett-Packard Is Doing Everything Right," *Business Week* (March 23, 1992), pp. 88–89.

TRADITIONAL PRINCIPLES OF ORGANIZING

What is organizing? **Organizing** is the process of determining what tasks should be assigned to employees, how the tasks should be grouped into departments, and how resources can be appropriately allocated to accomplish organizational goals. Suppose, for example, you have an idea for a new product, service, or approach to doing something that you wish to pursue. Even if you are given all the employees and other resources you need to implement your idea, you still must be able to utilize and coordinate all of these resources. Part of that ability includes the important management function of organizing.

Being good at organizing is crucial to being a successful manager.

The pressures associated with strong global competition are forcing many firms to become more efficient and productive. To make these changes, it has been necessary for managers to employ innovative approaches to organizing. In addition to discussing the traditional approaches to organizing, innovations in this area will also be examined in this chapter.

■ *Formal and Informal Organizational Structures*

In reality, companies actually have two organizational structures. One is the formal structure; the other is the informal structure. The **formal organizational**

structure is based on the positions and functions in a company and is represented by the firm's organizational chart.[1] The formal structure of a company is served by the formal communication system, through which information can be made official. The chain of command of the formal structure influences the flow of downward, upward, and horizontal communication within the firm.

The **informal organizational structure** refers to the relationship patterns that develop as a result of the interests and informal activities of members of an organization.[2] The informal organization is served by the grapevine. The design of the informal structure is not dictated by management or found on an organizational chart. Instead, the informal organizational structure evolves naturally.

The informal structure can provide company employees with forms of recognition that the formal structure fails to offer. Coworkers, for instance, can make you feel important and valued even though you may not actually have an impressive job title or a lot of official power in a company. As another example, a new manager in one company found the department secretary to be a *very* valuable and powerful employee. The secretary had a thorough knowledge of the department's budget and what forms needed to be completed to get things done! However, the secretary was not even listed on the company's organizational chart.

Companies have an informal organizational structure that is served by the grapevine.

■ *Centralization and Decentralization*

In organizations, **centralization** exists when most important decisions are made by top managers. Conversely, **decentralization** occurs when lower-level employees engage in decision making. In highly centralized companies, top management maintains much control. As a result, it is common for these companies to have standardized operating procedures that apply to all departments. On the other hand, more empowerment exists in companies that are very decentralized. Lower-level employees in these companies can act quickly to solve problems on the job because they have been given the authority to make decisions.

Employees are empowered as part of decentralization.

Centralization and decentralization are not automatically good or bad. Managers need to consider which approaches can be most beneficial for different operational areas within a company. In this regard, forms of centralization and decentralization coexist in many companies. Consider, for example, some of the changes Jack Smith has made at General Motors since he became CEO of the company. Before, GM's chief car designer was not required to consult with many company officials. Now, the design process is more decentralized and the design boss works closely with other supervisors in engineering, manufacturing, and marketing. On the other hand, individual divisions in the company had created their own engineering procedures. Smith declared that a more centralized engineering approach would be implemented in an effort to create more common parts for use in different models of GM cars.[3]

■ *The Scalar Principle*

In organizations, the **scalar principle** suggests that a clear, step-by-step line of authority should connect every person from the top to the bottom of a company. Through this clear line of authority, everybody in an organization knows who reports to whom. The scalar principle, for example, dominates the organizational structure of the armed services in the U.S. military. The vertical line of authority that identifies the reporting functions of managers and employees throughout an organization is commonly referred to as the **chain of command.**

The organizational chart in Figure 6–1 shows the chain of command for The Global Manufacturing Company. The scalar principle dictates that upward and downward communication between managers and supervisors and their employees should strictly follow the chain of command. The Global Manufacturing Company plans to design and hand-build a prototype product—a one-of-a-kind item—to display at the next industry trade show. All company employees want to work on the prototype, but only a small group of workers will be chosen. The president of the company makes the final decision regarding who is selected to help design and assemble the prototype. Therefore, it could be argued that company employees who wish to work on the prototype should contact the company president directly.

However, this approach violates the chain of command shown in Figure 6–1 because the president is not the direct supervisor of the lower-level workers in the company. Furthermore, if every worker who wants to work on the prototype contacts the company president, the president will experience communication overload. Therefore, through the company's chain of command, the workers contact their immediate supervisor to request assignment to the prototype project. At this level in the organizational structure, some of the requests will be denied. The supervisors will then send their recommendations to the next level in the chain of command, their manager. Eventually, as this process continues, a short list of the best-qualified individuals will be presented to the company president for final approval.

For too many executives, an unanticipated result of the scalar principle is that they become isolated from and unaware of the thoughts and views of lower-level employees. In turn, this lack of relevant information can lead to poor decisions by top management. When confronted with this problem, some executives respond by saying, "I cannot talk to employees directly without dis-

Individuals in the chain of command can aid or hinder the flow of upward and downward communication.

To be well informed, top managers should encourage upward communication.

■ **FIGURE 6–1** The Chain of Command for The Global Manufacturing Company

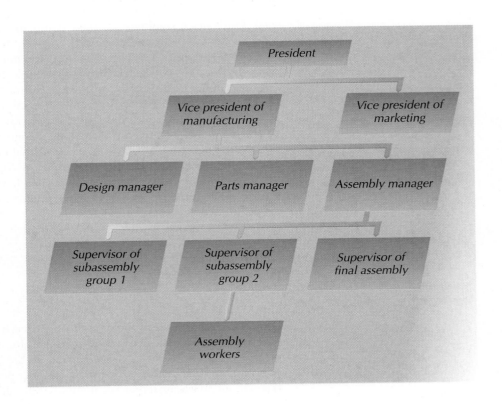

turbing the chain of command and insulting those individuals who are in charge of various departments and divisions." An appropriate way for you to deal with this dilemma as a senior manager is to discuss it with supervisors who are in charge at lower levels of the organization. Explain that you will continue to rely on them heavily to keep you informed. However, you will also need to periodically receive comments directly from employees on relevant issues that affect them. Also, you should explain to lower-level supervisors that you will quickly share with them what you learn from these direct contacts with their employees.

LINE AND STAFF STRUCTURES

Line departments contribute directly to the accomplishment of company goals.

Organizations have goals. The departments in an organization that contribute directly to the accomplishment of these goals are called **line departments.** In a manufacturing organization, for example, the primary objectives are to produce and sell a product. Therefore, the line departments in this firm would be those that are directly responsible for making and marketing the company's product. These departments are critical to the operation and success of the company. Organizations that contain only line departments are called **line organizations** and are structured as illustrated in Figure 6–2.

As an organization prospers and expands, it typically increases the number and complexity of the tasks it performs. To meet these new challenges, the line departments generally need special help, and staff departments are created to meet this demand. **Staff departments** provide specialized advice and assistance to members of line departments. Staff departments do not contribute directly to the accomplishment of organizational goals. Instead, they assist line departments.

■ **FIGURE 6–2** A Line Organizational Structure

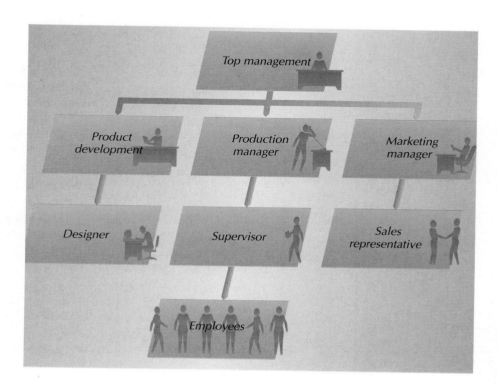

A PERSPECTIVE ON QUALITY

Office Design Can Enhance Communication

Research shows that the layout or design of offices influences the communication behavior of employees. An alternative to traditional offices with fixed walls and standard corridors can be found in the use of open offices. The phenomenon of open offices began in Germany and Sweden. It was then introduced in the United States as "office landscaping." (In some cases, low planters are used in open office designs as flexible barriers to separate work groups, which has given rise to this description.) In open offices, desks can be rearranged to facilitate communicative interaction among employees who work together on projects.

One advantage of an open-office design is that it can increase organizational effectiveness. When a high priority is assigned to collaboration and creativity on the part of employees, the possibility of using open offices should be considered by managers.

For example, when a group of product engineers was moved from traditional offices to open offices, it was found that both the quantity and quality of their ideas increased. In this case, the open plan allowed the engineers easier access to their colleagues by placing them in physical proximity to one another. The ease of collaboration resulting from the redesign of office space allowed for improved communication, which led directly to increased productivity. Similarly, a change to an open-office layout in a manufacturing firm resulted in an improved information flow—less time was spent on the telephone, doing paperwork, and in meetings, while more time was spent in face-to-face conversations.

In some situations, excessive noise may result from an open-office arrangement, making it inappropriate. In many cases, however, increased noise levels can be dealt with effectively by applying acoustical treatments to ceilings and walls and by carpeting floors.

SOURCES: Everett M. Rogers and Rekha Agarwala-Rogers, *Communication in Organizations* (New York: The Free Press, 1976), p. 102; Suzyn Ornstein, "The Hidden Influences of Office Design," *Academy of Management Executive* **3** (May 1989): 144.

Staff departments provide valuable assistance to line departments.

A human resources (personnel) department is a classic example of a staff department in a manufacturing company. The human resources department is not involved directly in the primary objectives of manufacturing and selling a product. However, the assistance of this department makes it possible for the primary objectives of the company to be met. To illustrate, the human resources department will recruit and hire employees to produce and sell the company's product.

According to Harold Stieglitz, staff employees frequently perform three general roles when assisting line personnel.[4]

1. *The Advisory or Counseling Role* In this role, the professional expertise of staff employees is utilized to help the organization analyze and solve problems. For example, a staff member in the legal department may provide the company with expert opinions on laws that govern commerce.

2. *The Service Role* When similar services are needed by several line departments, it makes more sense for one staff department to provide those services. For example, it may not be wise for each line department to hire people to train employees. One training department that serves all line departments may be more efficient and cost-effective.

3. *The Control Role* Line departments often rely on the professional expertise of staff employees to help assess the quality and effectiveness of organizational plans. For example, staff employees may assist in developing budgets, policies, rules, and operating procedures. In this role, the staff recommendations influence how various functions in the organization operate and cooperate.

In top management's relationships with line and staff departments, it is critical for good communication to exist. For example, not only does top management need to receive an uninterrupted flow of relevant information from line departments, but each line department needs to know how its work affects other line departments. In addition, as important decisions are being made, company executives must find out how these decisions will affect the operations of staff departments. It may, for example, be necessary to allocate additional resources to staff departments that are suddenly required to provide more assistance due to new company goals.

The traditional distinction between line and staff functions that characterizes organizational roles and departmental activities is becoming more and more blurred in a lot of companies. In the past, bloated bureaucracies in many companies isolated staff functions from market realities. However, downsizing in companies—a reduction in the number of individuals employed—has forced more staff departments to assume increased responsibilities for company performance. Furthermore, with increasing frequency, staff departments are expected to become self-supporting by selling their services competitively to line units.[5]

As a result of downsizing in companies, staff departments must accept more responsibilities.

DELEGATION

In organizations, **delegation** is the practice of empowering employees with the authority and responsibility to use organizational resources to accomplish assigned tasks. Within this definition, there is an important distinction between authority and responsibility. **Authority** is the right delegated to individuals in an organization to make job-related decisions, to perform duties, and to direct others to complete certain tasks. On the other hand, **responsibility** is an obligation by an employee to perform certain duties or to make sure they are completed. In other words, authority is a right, whereas responsibility is an obligation. Other issues related to delegation that are often overlooked include the need for accountability and the use of personal power.[6]

■ *Accountability*

Managers are accountable for the work that they delegate to others.

Although authority can be passed from manager to employee, managers are still accountable for the actions of their employees and for the completion of delegated tasks. A manager should not be able to escape, through delegation, the responsibility for how an employee performs an assigned task. Skilled managers, therefore, excel in assessing what tasks should be delegated to which employees. They are also good at determining what additional training employees need and at monitoring the progress of assigned tasks.

Managers must delegate tasks in order to accomplish important company goals. Specialized tasks, for example, should be delegated to employees who are especially knowledgeable about them. When delegating, managers need to clearly communicate exactly what is needed and expected.

■ *Personal Power*

Too often, unfortunately, managers are given the responsibility for accomplishing important tasks but only limited authority to do so. For example, office managers are hired to manage the business of an office. When these managers start their jobs, they typically find that they must supervise employees who have been hired by a previous manager and assume responsibility for equipment that they did not purchase. Likewise, managers often face situations in which they lack the authority to change key aspects of tasks that they are responsible for completing.

Effective managers use personal power to succeed in situations in which they must meet their responsibility with less than the desired level of authority. Specifically, they use their persuasive abilities and association through informal groups to accomplish organizational goals successfully.

■ *Obstacles to Delegation*

Although there are important advantages and benefits to be gained through appropriate delegation, efforts by some managers to delegate authority and responsibilities to employees are often lacking. Granted, some tasks are difficult to delegate. However, several common obstacles to delegation are controllable and can be overcome by managers.[7] For example, managers who fail to provide employees with adequate training make delegation difficult. Inadequate planning by managers eliminates many opportunities for orderly delegation. Managers who think, "Only I can do the job right" and are in the habit of performing routine tasks themselves preclude much appropriate delegation from occurring. Furthermore, expecting perfection and being unwilling to accept the reasonable risks associated with giving authority and responsibilities to others make delegation unlikely.

Excuses for not delegating are often weak.

A PERSPECTIVE ON QUALITY

Searching for a More Efficient Organizational Structure

Current examples abound of companies which have been placed in jeopardy due to the introduction of higher-quality products by competing firms. As a result, a large number of organizations are focusing on the management of quality in every aspect of their businesses. According to this broad view, known as the system-structural view of quality, a manager must be aware of the changing business environment and adapt appropriately by making necessary changes in the organizational structure.

Implementation of the system-structural view occurs in three stages. The manager must

1. Analyze external quality demands, past quality performance, resources available to improve quality, and quality levels offered by the competition.
2. Formulate a strategy for meeting quality challenges.
3. Implement the strategy to reach a desired level of quality performance.

As a result of the system-structural view, many U.S. companies are shunning vertical integration for more efficient organizational structures. Patricia McLagan, a management consultant, explains that too frequently companies utilize hierarchical structures that promote the philosophy that "People at the top think, and people at the bottom do." To correct this problem, she claims that these companies must move from autocracy to empowerment. Researchers Jay R. Galbraith and Edward E. Lawler III, agree. They explain that bureaucratic control is increasingly losing favor in companies. In its place, customer control, peer control, and automated formal controls are being substituted.

With this change, there is less need for control-oriented managerial units and the layers of management that go with them. The trend is for employees to work more directly with customers and to receive pay increases based on the results of customer-satisfaction surveys. However, Galbraith and Lawler note that most employees cannot really help organizations solve quality problems unless organizations themselves are changed. Important changes that are needed include giving employees sufficient power to make decisions concerning quality and providing them with the necessary information to make wise decisions. Employees also need proper training to understand important quality issues.

Progressive companies are finding it desirable to change their organizational structures or designs in ways that decentralize many activities that were originally centralized at corporate headquarters. For example, paint is purchased by the department in charge of painting the product because its employees understand what is needed to produce high-quality painting. This type of decentralization enhances efforts toward continuous quality improvement.

ADAPTED FROM: P. George Benson, Jayant V. Saraph, and Roger G. Schroeder, "The Effects of Organizational Context on Quality Management: An Empirical Investigation," *Management Science* **37** (September 1991): 1107–24; Bob Smith, "The Dark Side of Corporate America," *HR Focus* **69** (October 1992): 1, 8; Jay R. Galbraith, and Edward E. Lawler, III, *Organizing for the Future* (San Francisco, CA: Jossey-Bass, 1993).

■ Determining What to Delegate

Skilled managers realize that delegating allows them to maximize their potential and perform their jobs in an effective manner. They also understand that many of the obstacles to delegation can be overcome. Therefore, instead of wondering, "Should I delegate," managers need to ask themselves, "What should I delegate?" The following suggestions may help to provide an appropriate answer to the latter question.[8] Determine which tasks should not be delegated and which tasks can be delegated; for example, some duties cannot be delegated because they involve the discussion of confidential information. Problems that require the personal expertise of the manager should not be delegated. In addition, if a problem must be addressed immediately, there may be no time for delegation.

However, many tasks often performed by managers can be delegated effectively to employees. For example, when completing paperwork and routine duties, managers should ask themselves, "Could these tasks be performed just as quickly and effectively by others?" In many cases, such duties can and should be delegated. Furthermore, issues brought to a manager's attention that deal with technical matters frequently can be delegated to an employee who is more knowledgeable on the subject. Even if a manager is quite capable of completing a challenging task, there is still strong justification for delegating that duty to a competent employee. Through the delegation of such tasks, managers provide employees with important opportunities to gain valuable experience and to develop professionally.

As a manager, when you do decide to delegate, make sure that your employees clearly understand what is being delegated to them and what is expected from them. How much clarification you need to provide will depend on the situation. However, when there are problems with the completion of delegated tasks, the problems can often be traced to poor communication.

The most productive managers are good at delegating.

CONSIDER THIS

1. Some managers are detail-oriented and focus on specifics. Other managers look at the broad picture and focus on abstract ideas. Which type of manager is likely to be better at organizing and why?

2. Staff departments, such as the training (personnel) department, are often the first to experience budget cuts when companies are looking for ways to reduce costs. How wise is this strategy?

3. What traits, if any, do you have that make you reluctant to delegate responsibilities to others?

SPAN OF MANAGEMENT

A wide span of management can often create communication overload for a manager.

In organizations, **span of management** refers to the number of employees a manager is responsible for supervising. Also known as **span of control,** span of management can influence whether organizations have relatively flat or tall organizational structures. As shown in Figure 6–3, a **flat organizational structure** occurs when there are few levels of hierarchy and many employees report to one manager. A common communication problem plaguing flat organizational structures is *communication overload:* so many employees report to one person that the manager can be overwhelmed with requests for information. Although the manager has a lot of control in this situation, it is difficult for a flat organization to expand because too many demands are placed on the manager. Therefore, as businesses make the decision to expand, they usually add additional hierarchical levels of authority with more workable spans of management. The result is a taller organizational structure.

■ FIGURE 6–3 Examples of Flat and Tall Organizational Structures

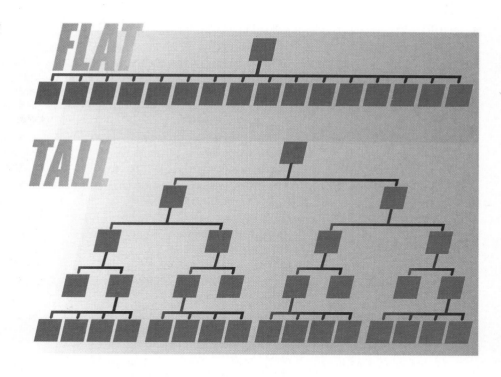

As the levels of hierarchy in a company increase, span of management often decreases.

A **tall organizational structure** has several hierarchical levels and many managers to oversee the completion of a variety of tasks. The expectation is that the large number of managers will be able to provide the careful attention to detail required to complete goals with high-quality results. Unfortunately, as the levels of the hierarchy increase, tall organizational structures typically face the inherent communication problem of *communication distortion*. Specifically, as messages travel vertically through the different levels of the organizational structure, they can and often do become altered or distorted in ways that lead to miscommunication.

What is the optimal span of management, or the largest number of employees a manager can effectively manage? There is no precise number. In reality, it depends on many factors. Certainly, one factor is the skill and experience of the manager. Some other key factors that can influence span of management are identified in Figure 6–4.

DEPARTMENTALIZATION

The manner in which employees are assembled in organizations can influence how effectively they perform their duties. Specifically, the technique of grouping jobs and resources into departments to complete assigned goals is called **departmentalization.** Five common ways in which organizations practice departmentalization are by function, product, customer, geographic location, and matrix design.

■ *Departmentalization by Function*

In organizations, **departmentalization by function** is the grouping of employees with similar jobs into the same department; that is, employees who perform the

■ FIGURE 6–4 Factors Influencing Span of Management

FACTOR	FACTOR TENDS TO INCREASE SPAN OF MANAGEMENT WHEN:	FACTOR TENDS TO DECREASE SPAN OF MANAGEMENT WHEN:
1. Similarities of functions	1. Employees perform similar job functions.	1. Employees perform dissimilar job functions.
2. Geographic concentration	2. Employees work in close proximity to each other.	2. Employees work in geographically distant locations from each other.
3. Complexity of functions	3. Employees perform tasks that are simple and routine.	3. Employees perform tasks that are complex and varied.
4. Capability of employees	4. Employees have high levels of task-relevant competencies.	4. Employees are deficient in necessary task-relevant competencies.
5. Coordination	5. Employees' work activities require little supervision by manager.	5. Employees' work activities require much supervision by manager.
6. Planning	6. Manager's planning responsibilities are routine and easy to complete.	6. Manager's planning responsibilities are complex and difficult to complete.
7. Organizational assistance	7. Manager receives ample administrative assistance.	7. Manager receives little or no administrative assistance.

ADAPTED FROM: Harold Koontz, "Making Theory Operational: The Span of Management," *Journal of Management Studies* 3 (October 1966): 237–38.

same function work together. These functions usually represent specializations. For example, basic functions in profit-making organizations typically include production, finance, marketing, and human resources, as shown in Figure 6–5. When employees who perform common tasks are grouped together, they are able to learn from each other and to share ideas about improving their performance. Furthermore, when priority is given to technical efficiency and quality, departmentalization by function can be especially appropriate.[9]

Departmentalization by function is common in many companies because it has two key advantages. First, it permits employees to specialize and become experts in a certain area. Second, it simplifies the supervisors' tasks because each one is only responsible for understanding and coordinating the duties of one functional task or skill.

However, there are some disadvantages associated with departmentalizing by function. First, employees who specialize in a particular function may show great interest in the goals of their department but ignore the broader goals of the organization.

Second, overall decision-making time is slow. To illustrate, suppose the production department in a company has a backlog of orders. After analyzing how best to deal with the situation, management decides that more employees need to be hired. Although a solution to the problem has been determined, action cannot be taken immediately. The human resources department must be contacted. Time is then required to decide how the jobs will be advertised and filled.

> There is a natural tendency for companies to departmentalize by function.

Third, specialized departments lead to stereotyping of employees in those departments. This tendency can limit communication among departments and produce conflict when they do interact. Limited interaction fosters bottlenecks in the flow of work from one department to another.[10]

■ *Departmentalization by Product*

Various products offered by a company may be unique enough to require different management strategies for success.

Organizing or grouping jobs according to the product being produced is referred to as **departmentalization by product.** Large corporations, for example, often produce several lines of products aimed at different customers. To illustrate, three product units controlled by PepsiCo are Kentucky Fried Chicken (KFC), Taco Bell, and Pepsi. Each of these products has special production and marketing demands. A large manufacturer of avionics, for example, will often offer three product lines for use in commercial, general, and military aviation. Typically, a separate department is established in the company for each of these distinct product lines. As a matter of fact, companies that manufacture and sell technologically sophisticated products frequently are organized into product divisions.[11]

Several advantages are associated with departmentalization by product.[12] When the product is the center of attention, all tasks performed in the department can be coordinated around this common focus. Likewise, since decisions made in a department relate to a single product line, decision making can usually occur quickly. The common focus on the product also permits employee responsibilities to be clearly defined. Furthermore, the experience of being associated with the production of a product from beginning to end helps to develop broadly trained managers.

There are also disadvantages to organizing by product.[13] When departments concentrate on their product, it is easy for them to lose sight of and interest in the broader goals of the organization. In addition, this tendency toward isolation hinders coordination between divisions. It also can be costly to organize by product because each self-contained division needs its own management structure and other specialists.

■ *Departmentalization by Customer*

An organization engages in **departmentalization by customer** when management groups jobs according to the customers who purchase the company's goods and services. A bank, for example, can be expected to have different groups of customers. Some customers want auto loans, and other customers seek commercial loans; home builders approach the bank for construction loans. The bank may establish different departments to meet the special needs of these distinct groups of customers. A major advantage of departmentalization by customer is that it allows companies to meet the specific needs of different types of customers.

The needs of distinct groups of customers can influence how a company is organized.

■ *Departmentalization by Geographic Location*

Some companies find that geographic regions have different needs for their products and must be managed differently.

Specifically, **departmentalization by geographic location** occurs whenever a firm organizes activities based on geographic location. Companies that are physically dispersed are frequently organized according to geographic territory. A building-products manufacturer may, for example, divide the U.S. market into three regions. This manufacturer would treat the western, midwestern, and eastern regions of the country as separate markets, each with its own regional manager. In turn, it is necessary for regional managers to understand the special needs of the customers in their geographic regions. For example, the manager of the western region must let the manufacturer know what types of building products will sell best in the western part of the United States.

Departmentalization by geographic location has specific advantages.[14] It allows a company to develop area markets aggressively. The unique needs of regional markets and customers can also be better understood and met on a regional basis. In addition, geographic territories provide excellent training grounds for managers.

However, there are also disadvantages associated with departmentalization by geographic location.[15] When several geographic regions are operating, it can be difficult to maintain uniform and consistent company practices. Many general managers and a large staff are often needed to operate several autonomous territories for a company. As a result, duplication of staff services often occurs. Last, it can be difficult for company headquarters to exercise control over the ways in which local operations function. From a communication standpoint, managers of geographic regions must not assume that headquarters understands the individual needs of each region. Instead, these managers need to carefully describe how their geographic regions differ from one another. Likewise, the company headquarters needs to maintain close and frequent contact with regional managers to stay well informed about the different markets.

■ *Departmentalization by Matrix Design*

In a matrix design, employees may report to two or more bosses.

A **matrix design** establishes work groups based on a dual focus within a company.[16] For example, instead of grouping jobs according to either function *or* product, a company may decide to organize jobs according to both function *and* product. As a result, in a matrix design, employees may report to two or more bosses.

Under a straight-line chain of command, each employee typically has one supervisor. Managers in this type of traditional organizational structure focus on achieving greater levels of efficiency in their departments, where the same tasks are performed on a generally continuous basis. When the organization begins work on a special or unique project, a capable person is put in charge of the project and given the title of "project manager." This person forms a project team from specialized employees assigned to the project. The managers of established departments continue to perform their normal duties while providing some limited assistance to the project team.

When an organization takes on increasing numbers of special projects, the managers of established departments cannot cope with increased demands from the project managers. At this point, top management may begin to implement a matrix design. With this change, the traditional departments take on a new role. Specifically, they now exist mainly to support the special project teams.

For example, consider a company that manufactures only wooden office furniture. A special order for bedroom furniture is accepted. Special orders for dining-room and living-room furniture follow. As its success in different markets increases, the company is inundated with special projects. As a result, the company adopts the matrix design shown in Figure 6–6.

The first few special projects were just a sideline for the various departments that existed in the company. However, as the number and importance of the special projects increase, roles change to the point where the departments are viewed as supporting the different projects. Thus, the projects draw from the pool of resources available in the departments. The object, however, is to schedule the various projects in such a manner that they do not all request identical resources from the same departments at the same time.

Special forms of coordination are necessary to make a matrix design operate effectively.

The department and project managers in a matrix design both report to the general manager. They must work together on a cooperative basis for the matrix configuration to succeed. The department manager has authority over employees with technical specialties. As a result, it is essential for department managers to have strong communication skills.

■ **FIGURE 6–6** Matrix Design for Furniture Manufacturing Company

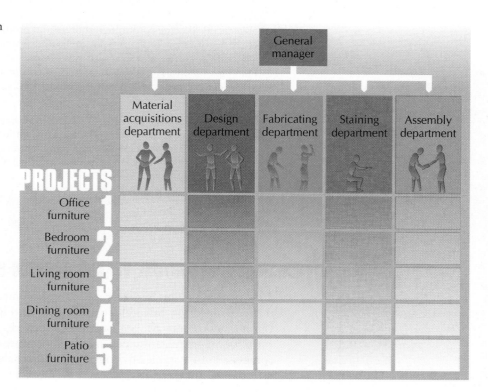

A Multinational Is Also Multidomestic—by Matrix Design

A business cliche that is guiding the management of an increasing number of international companies is, "Think global, act local." Asea Brown Boveri (ABB), a Swiss-Swedish corporation, practices this approach. ABB is a leading supplier of equipment to the electric-power industry and the largest manufacturer of railway vehicles in the world. ABB employs 223,000 people in 140 countries and coordinates a $1.9 billion annual R&D budget. The business dealings of ABB span so many international borders that the company appears stateless, yet its presence in local countries is so strong that ABB also seems multidomestic. As Percy Barnevik, the CEO of ABB, explains, "We strive to be a local company everywhere."

Barnevik has worked to flatten management layers in the company and weave them into a matrix system. The fact that ABB has a relatively flat organizational structure with few layers of management separating the CEO from workers on the shop floor has two advantages. First, it results in improved communication. Second, it enhances the ability of the corporation to have a close involvement with its customers. ABB vice presidents oversee eight core business segments for the company. There are 50 major business areas within each segment. Each business area has a leader who is responsible for maximizing business globally. In addition to this network structure of business areas, the corporation has a geographic country structure composed of ABB member companies. In a specific country, therefore, various local companies are actually subsidiaries of a member company. Specifically, the presidents of ABB's 1300 local companies have two managers: the leader of a business area and the national member company president.

This matrix structure has three advantages for ABB. First, it allows local companies to place foremost importance on meeting the needs of their local customers. Second, interconnections with other ABB companies in a business area enable managers at ABB to strategically allocate corporate resources and production capacity. Third, managers in different factories get to learn from each other, even while they are in competition. In essence, the organizational structure of ABB fosters competition and cooperation.

The research efforts of ABB must also be coordinated across the corporation's various business segments. As Craig Tedmon, ABB executive vice president for R&D explains:

> I have learned there is tremendous strength in cultural and national diversity, strength that exceeds normal homogenous cultures and national situations. To take advantage of this, you have to communicate, communicate, communicate. It's complicated because there are not only language differences but also cultural differences. But it can lead to greater strength, if you harness it.

SOURCE: Ted Agres, "Asea Brown Boveri—A Model for Global Management," *R&D Magazine* **33** (December 1991): 30–34.

MECHANISTIC STRUCTURE VERSUS ORGANIC STRUCTURE

How structured or bureaucratic must a company be to operate most effectively? Pioneering research to help answer this question, conducted by Tom Burns and George M. Stalker, determined that the appropriate bureaucratic form for an organization depends on the nature of the company's external environment.[17] In a stable environment, a "mechanistic" or bureaucratic structure is better. Conversely, in an uncertain environment that is rapidly changing, a much less bureaucratic or "organic" structure is more appropriate.

McDonald's restaurants have been very successful in using a mechanistic structure. There are set procedures for most aspects of running a McDonald's restaurant. As a result, the company can predict with a high degree of certainty that most customers will have positive experiences while dining, such as at this McDonald's on Wall Street in New York City.

In stable business environments, companies can rely on the continuous use of set operating procedures.

In a **mechanistic structure,** employees specialize, job descriptions are precise, authority and power are centralized at the top, many formal rules and policies exist, and downward communication dominates. When appropriate, a mechanistic design can contribute greatly to a company's success. Consider, for example, the phenomenal success of McDonald's restaurants.

The basic process of preparing and serving hamburgers is not one that changes quickly or frequently. As a result, a mechanistic design works well in this stable business environment. McDonald's maintains strong central control over its restaurants. There are set procedures for almost every aspect of running a McDonald's, and these procedures are uniformly applicable to almost all of the company's restaurants. A McDonald's meal can be counted on to taste about the same almost anywhere you find it. McDonald's has become a symbol of stability by capitalizing on the appropriateness of its mechanistic form.[18]

In an **organic structure,** employees assume responsibility for a wide array of tasks, job descriptions are informal and general, authority is decentralized, minimal formal rules exist, and communication is encouraged both vertically and horizontally. When changing conditions exist in an organization's external environment, an organic structure may be appropriate for the company. For example, consider the changing external environment experienced by Pella, the manufacturer of high-quality designer windows and doors.

In a changing external business environment, a company must be prepared to change the way it does business.

For 68 years, Pella has been the choice of custom builders of luxury homes. Prosperity in the construction business enabled Pella's revenues to grow at an annual rate of 9 percent for 37 years. In 1988, however, revenues and profits at Pella collapsed. The U.S. economy entered into a prolonged slowdown that squeezed much of the growth out of the construction industry. In its factories, Pella instituted continuous quality-improvement procedures. Productivity jumped 25 percent, and Pella was able to cut in half the time it takes to fill orders. The company also launched a moderately priced line of windows that it sells through discount home-supply stores. With revenues and earnings back up, Pella's strategy to be more organic both in its design and in the way it functions is proving to be a wise one.[19]

JOB DESIGN

There are many different types of jobs in organizations, and how these jobs are structured or designed can influence how well they are performed. **Job design** determines what tasks are to be performed, how they are to be completed, and the expectations, responsibilities, and authority associated with the job. In mechanistic organizations that are bureaucratic, jobs are often specialized. A classic example of a specialized job is an assembly-line job in a manufacturing company. Although such jobs have high levels of standardization, as will be discussed, they can be designed to be intrinsically interesting and they can encourage innovation and creativity.

■ *Job Specialization and Standardization*

Can a bureaucratic, hierarchical organization use great discipline to implement detailed standards as part of specialized jobs and, at the same time, encourage employee innovation and commitment? Researcher Paul S. Adler believes that it can, and he cites the New United Motor Manufacturing Inc. (NUMMI) plant in Fremont, California, as proof.[20] NUMMI is a reborn General Motors assembly plant. At the old GM plant, more than 80 industrial engineers developed assembly-line norms for management to impose on the work force. Over time, the GM-Fremont plant developed a reputation for being the worst plant in the world! Specifically, productivity at the plant was exceedingly low, quality was awful, and the absenteeism rate was greater than 20 percent. It was not uncommon for the list of unresolved grievances to exceed 5000. Operations finally ceased in 1982 when GM closed the plant.

Now, the plant produces Toyota Corollas and some GM automobiles under a joint venture between Toyota and GM. Toyota is responsible for daily operations at the plant. Employees must work harder at NUMMI than they had at the old GM plant. They must also meet much higher standards for quality and efficiency. However, absenteeism is down to 3 percent, grievances have declined greatly, and more than 90 percent of the plant's employees indicate that they are "satisfied" or "very satisfied" with their work.

These surprising results are due in large part to the production system and the way jobs are designed at NUMMI. Managers at the plant, for example, encourage an active suggestion program by employees. Teams of employees study individual suggestions and implement specific improvements. Workers are trained to do different jobs and are allowed to shift from one task to another. The plant has roughly 350 production teams, each composed of about seven people and a leader. Managers at the plant provide and assist the production teams with their expertise in problem solving.

Workers at NUMMI have learned techniques of work analysis that can lead to improvement on the job. The job-design process at the plant works as follows. Team members time each other with stopwatches, searching for the safest, most efficient way to perform each task. They use the analytical tools they have been taught, their own experiences, and suggestions from plant engineers to create job standards. A similar analysis is performed on the same tasks by more than one team. The resulting analyses are then compared, and detailed specifications for each task are prepared.

This method of standardizing work gives control over jobs to the individuals who perform them and empowers the plant's work force. As a result, work-

Employees need to be taught how to analyze work processes for the purpose of improving quality.

Job design can influence how well jobs are performed. In mechanistic organizations, jobs are often specialized. Workers performing assembly-line jobs can be empowered to stop the assembly line if quality problems develop and can contribute problem solving skills as part of their routine responsibilities.

ers at the plant become experts at job analysis and work stations become centers of innovation. In 1991, plant workers offered more than 10,000 suggestions. Management implemented over 80 percent of them. Frequent analysis, standardization, reanalysis, refinement, and new standardization produces a very structured system of continuous improvement.

Results at NUMMI show that disciplined standardization does not inevitably lead to coercion, resentment, and resistance. Unionized auto workers at NUMMI have demonstrated a strong desire for excellence. As a matter of fact, quality is much higher at NUMMI than at any other GM plant. NUMMI is a very bureaucratic organization, but much vertical and horizontal communication is encouraged at the plant to develop consensus on many decisions. As a matter of fact, the open communication that exists in the plant enhances the ability of NUMMI to quickly identify production problems and to harness the power of teamwork.

High levels of standardization can be established in a way that still promotes creativity in a company.

■ *Beyond Specialization*

Managers face the challenges of making tasks meaningful to employees so they will be motivated to perform their jobs well. Four traditional alternatives are available to meet this challenge: *job rotation, job enlargement, job enrichment,* and use of the *job characteristics model.*

Job rotation helps employees to develop and improve their understanding of different jobs.

JOB ROTATION   **Job rotation** is the systematic movement of employees among various jobs in an organization in order to broaden their experiences. Through job rotation, employees are exposed to different jobs and learn the interrelationships among them. Employees often become acquainted with new people in the company and are exposed to various processes and technologies. Job rotation also helps to increase the problem-solving and decision-making skills of employees. The needs and capabilities of each employee should determine which assignments he or she is given in job rotation. Also, the length of time spent at different jobs should be flexible enough to take into consideration how fast each employee is learning each job.[21]

Goodyear Tire and Rubber Company uses job rotation to train college graduates. The graduates can accept up to six assignments to different departments. A new chemical engineer, for example, might elect to work in fabric development, chemical materials development, research, central process engineering, process development, or chemical production.[22]

JOB ENLARGEMENT Job enlargement increases the number of tasks to be performed in a job. The additional tasks are usually taken from other jobs that have been eliminated. Part of the logic behind job enlargement is that the additional tasks keep workers busy, and busy workers do not have time to be bored. Boredom, however, is more a function of how workers feel about the work they perform than of how much work they have to perform. Adding a lot of simple tasks to an already simple job does not change the nature of the job much.

The best type of job enrichment involves increased employee responsibility, authority, control, and accountability.

JOB ENRICHMENT Job enrichment involves increasing the responsibility, scope, and challenge of the work performed in a way that gives workers more control over how they do their jobs.[23] If a job is highly structured and the employees who do the work are generally told what to do, they will probably become dependent, unmotivated, poor performers. However, if their jobs are redesigned and enriched by giving them more responsibility, authority, and control and holding them accountable for their decisions, employee performance will often improve. The jobs of workers at NUMMI were enriched in these ways, and their motivation and performance increased dramatically.

THE JOB CHARACTERISTICS MODEL The job characteristics model, developed by J. Richard Hackman and Greg R. Oldham, suggests that the design of jobs should take into consideration the workers' competency, their need for personal growth, and their level of satisfaction with the work context.[24] Hackman and Oldham explain that when employees are well matched to their jobs, they will naturally try to do well because they find their work satisfying. Poor performance by these employees produces unhappy feelings, and the employees will try harder to experience success to feel good about themselves again. In essence, there is internal motivation for these employees.

Managers need to create an environment that provides workers with a strong internal motivation to perform well.

According to Hackman and Oldham, **internal motivation** is influenced by three conditions.

1. How meaningful the work is to the employee

2. The degree to which the employee is accountable for the outcome or success of the work performed

3. The amount of feedback or knowledge of results that the employee receives about personal performance

If all three of these conditions or factors exist, strong internal motivation will probably result. Conversely, poor performance by employees is likely when their jobs are not meaningful, lack accountability, and offer little feedback.

There are five core job characteristics that affect the three conditions of internal motivation: skill variety, task identity, task significance, autonomy, and feedback. A job, for example, that is characterized by skill variety, task identity, and task significance will typically be perceived as meaningful. This job incorporates several different activities that involve unique skills (*skill variety*), the employee completes the job from beginning to end with an identifiable outcome (*task identity*), and the work performed has a significant impact on the lives of others (*task significance*). If a job offers *autonomy*, the employee will probably experience responsibility for the quality of the work performed. In other words, to feel accountable, the employee needs to be given freedom, independence, and discretion in scheduling tasks and in determining the procedures to be used to complete the work. Last, the employee needs *feedback* on the effectiveness of work performed.

The essence of internal motivation, according to Hackman and Oldham, is that positive feelings result from good performance and negative feelings result from poor performance. Unfortunately, if the motivating potential of a job is low, internal motivation can also be expected to be low and the employee's feelings will probably be unaffected by personal performance. Therefore, the design of such a job offers little incentive to employees to perform well to feel good. Interestingly, however, for individuals to respond positively to complex and challenging jobs, their "growth needs" must be strong. **Growth needs** refer to an individual's needs for personal accomplishment, for learning, and for improvement.[25] Employees who have the necessary knowledge and skills to perform a job, who have strong growth needs, and who experience context satisfaction (like their work environment) will respond positively to enriched and challenging jobs. Figure 6–7 illustrates the job characteristics model and indicates the key factors to consider in designing jobs.

Employees who have a need for personal accomplishment tend to respond positively to challenging jobs.

■ **FIGURE 6–7** The Job Characteristics Model

SOURCE: J. Richard Hackman and Greg R. Oldham, *Work Redesign* (Reading, MA: Addison-Wesley, 1980), p. 90. © 1980 by Addison-Wesley Publishing Company, Inc. Reprinted by permission of the publisher.

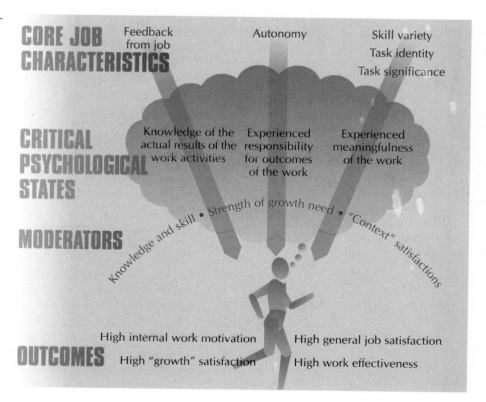

THE NEW FLEXIBLE ORGANIZATION

Changes in the way many companies are organized will be necessary as global competition intensifies.

Fundamental changes are occurring in the organizational designs of many companies.[26] The impetus for such changes is the need to accommodate the rapid pace of technological developments, global competition, and the dawning of a knowledge-based economy. As a result of these developments, increasing numbers of companies are abandoning the traditional monolithic and rigid organizational designs. The emerging organizational designs are ones that can accommodate innovation and change in an effective manner.

The delayering and downsizing that occurred in companies during the late 1980s and into the 1990s initially was triggered by the need to cut costs. However, the proliferation of information and communication technologies has increasingly reduced the need for middle managers. One benefit of this delayering is an enhanced ability on the part of companies to respond faster to competitive and market changes.

Today, top managers find it especially important for their companies to be versatile and flexible. In this regard, companies must be able to

- Change course quickly to maximize opportunities and to side-step threats
- Utilize various capabilities to do different things as unique situations develop
- Endure while exposed to unforeseen difficulties caused by change

Companies that are flexible have the best chance of seizing market opportunities quickly.

Today, companies must seize market opportunities quickly, introduce new products frequently, and respond immediately to competitive pressures. To do so, a trend in organizational design, especially in high-technology companies, is the creation of generally interdependent business units within a company. The organizational designs that provide the best forms of direct communication channels between managers, employees, and customers are being given the greatest attention.

■ *Breakthrough in Organizing*

Three areas of influence are merging to produce a new design for the twenty-first-century organization.[27] First, mounting evidence indicates that self-managing teams (to be discussed in Chapter 8) and other methods of empowering employees generally produce significant gains in productivity, quality, and job satisfaction. Second, it has been shown that productivity can be improved by focusing on business processes rather than on functional departments. Third, increased ability exists to rapidly disseminate information in organizations. Based on these insights, management experts foresee the traditional vertical organization of many companies changing to a process-oriented, horizontal organization.

Two key aspects of the horizontal organization are an *empowered labor force* that can design its own jobs and *process management*. According to Marvin Weisbord, a noted expert on organizational development, "The people who do the work should have in their hands the means to change to suit the customer."[28] Furthermore, Weisbord indicates that self-management in an empowered labor force routinely produces 40 percent increases in output per employee-hour.

Three unique characteristics distinguish **process management** from management by function.

1. Instead of focusing on intradepartmental objectives, process management looks at how well the various integrated functions in a company are working together.

2. Employees who possess different skills work together as a team to accomplish tasks, instead of performing functions in a series.

3. In process management, information is provided directly to where it is needed, without going through a hierarchy that can distort messages and cause miscommunication.

A process-oriented design is very economical.

The process-oriented horizontal organization does not have traditional department heads, such as "manager of sales." Instead, there is a manager of "getting-things-to-customers," who integrates sales, shipping, and billing. Here, the intent is to work for customers, not for bosses in the organization. As a result, the self-directed work teams do most of their own hiring, scheduling, and other managerial tasks. Douglas Smith, of the consulting company McKinsey & Co., estimates that organizations can cut their cost base by one-third or more if they adopt a process-oriented organizational design. For the twenty-first-century organization, training and empowering employees replace control as the key task of management.

A new horizontal organizational design has been utilized in the black-and-white film-manufacturing program at Kodak for over two years. The program's 1500 employees do not work in traditional departments. Instead, the program has what is called "the flow." At Kodak, the flow contains streams that serve customers and are judged according to standards of customer satisfaction. One such standard is on-time delivery. Employees in this program work in self-directed teams. Before the change to process management, the black-and-white film operation had operating expenses of 15 percent above budgeted cost, required more than 40 days to complete an order in some cases, and was late in filling one-third of its orders. In 1991, under process management, the operation was so frugal that its expenses were 15 percent below budgeted cost, and it succeeded in cutting response time in half.

CONSIDER THIS

1. Would you feel most comfortable as a manager with a large span of management in a flat organization or with a narrow span of management in a tall organization? Explain.

2. Why is it difficult for managers who like to provide a lot of direction and control to succeed when they have a wide span of management?

3. What do you think is the biggest obstacle to getting companies to make an appropriate switch from a vertical structure to a process-oriented, horizontal design?

■ *The Modular Approach*

Companies need to focus their efforts on what they do best.

Many companies are finding that to succeed, they need to move away from vertical integration and adopt a modular approach that allows them to focus on what they do best.[29] Specifically, the modern **modular approach** to organizing concentrates a company's efforts and resources on core activities in which it has special expertise and contracts required services to others. Use of the modular approach is enabling more companies to avoid the burdens of operating unprofitable plants and maintaining inefficient bureaucracies.

The success of the modular approach can readily be observed, for example, in the U.S. apparel industry. Profitable companies in this industry typically focus on their abilities to design and market apparel items. They often contract or outsource the production of these items to suppliers in foreign countries. Reebok, for instance, owns none of the plants that manufacture its shoes.

Outsourcing noncore activities offers two advantages to modular companies. First, it minimizes the financial investment needed to produce new products quickly. Second, it enables companies to funnel their scarce capital into areas where they have a competitive advantage, such as hiring the best people to design new products or enhancing customer service. Donald Beal, Chief Executive Officer of Rockwell International, affirms that, "Without a doubt, focusing on a core competency—and outsourcing the rest—is a major trend of the 1990s."[30]

Trying to do everything as a company exposes weaknesses.

In addition to apparel companies, outsourcing is flourishing in the electronics industry. Dell Computer, for example, benefits greatly from being modular. The company owns no manufacturing plants. Instead, it leases two small factories for the purpose of assembling computers from outsourced parts. With no need to purchase plants, Dell can spend much of its money on marketing and service and sell directly to customers through the use of a toll-free number.

Even in vertically integrated manufacturing companies, there is much interest in outsourcing. The Chrysler Corporation, for example, is refining how it uses modular methods. In addition to buying many parts from outside suppliers, Chrysler is requesting that its suppliers deliver preassembled sections ranging from complete antilock brake systems to door panels. Now, Chrysler designs its cars to be built in modules. "Assembling in sections is a lot cheaper than making parts ourselves and buying the rest from hundreds of companies," explains Thomas Stallkamp, Chrysler's Vice President in charge of procurement. As more modular companies are observed to outperform vertically integrated titans, it is becoming clear that the modular approach is not just a fad.

THE VIRTUAL CORPORATION

The pressures to come up with needed resources and to complete important tasks faster has caused most managers in companies with traditional hierarchies to think, "There must be a better way to get things done."[31] Several leading business experts believe the virtual corporation is the best way for many companies to organize. A **virtual corporation** is a temporary combination of independent companies that are linked by information technology to allow them to share skills, reduce costs, and enter new markets. The term "virtual" originates from the computer industry; "virtual memory" refers to computer storage capacity that appears to be greater than the memory capacity that actually exists.

Different companies are brought together as part of the virtual corporation.

To illustrate how the concept of a virtual corporation works, suppose you design a new type of lock that unlocks at the touch of a person who has an authorized fingerprint. You form a corporation called Lockprint and hire five employees. Lockprint does not have the machinery to manufacture the new lock. Even if you had the money to buy a manufacturing plant, you would not know what machines to purchase. Therefore, you form an alliance with a company that does have appropriate spare manufacturing capacity and has a reputation for high quality. You form another alliance with a premier marketing company to market your new lock. Even the paychecks for your five employees are issued through a capable outside company.

Through these different collaborations, you have leveraged your tiny work force into a powerful company with the flexibility to quickly exploit the niche market for touch-activated locks. The alliances formed by Lockprint Corporation will last only as long as they are needed. To an outsider, Lockprint looks like a single company with a large manufacturing capacity but it actually does not own a single machine. Although this example is greatly simplified, it illustrates the basic application of the virtual corporation.

Many large corporations are finding that the virtual concept works well for them. MCI, for example, uses partnerships with approximately 100 companies to help it compete successfully for major contracts with corporate customers. Through these partnerships, MCI's goal is to provide customers with one-stop shopping for products to satisfy their communications needs. Corning Inc. has also been successful in putting together alliances. The company's 19 partnerships have enabled it to develop and sell new products more quickly than it could without the alliances. As Corning's chairman, James Houghton, explains, "Technologies are changing so fast that nobody can do it all alone anymore."

Agreement with this assessment has led Applied Materials Inc., maker of semiconductor manufacturing equipment, to develop a collaborative web of suppliers. Since each supplier does something especially well, Applied Materials is not required to excel at everything itself. James Morgan, Chief Executive Officer of the company, points out that, "It's easier to manage a bigger business if others are managing pieces for you."[32]

If the collaborative efforts of virtual corporations are to work, the companies considering such alliances must develop a significant level of trust in each other. Likewise, managers in virtual corporations must be good at building relationships and putting together deals that benefit all parties involved. Demand for managers who can work well in the unique environment of virtual corporations is expected to improve as these organizations increase in numbers.

> The alliances formed by a virtual corporation exist only as long as they are needed.

> If a virtual corporation is to succeed, the companies forming alliances must trust each other.

REENGINEERING

In some cases, it is best to start over from scratch when reorganizing a company. Organizational reengineering relies on this approach.[33] Specifically, **reengineering** is the design and implementation of wide-ranging changes in business processes to produce breakthrough results. The top managers in an organization, who are responsible for reengineering, ask themselves, "If we could start all over again, how would we run this company?" Then, with intense dedication, they make the company fit their vision. Reengineering plans should be designed from an outward perspective, looking inward and considering how customers want to interact with the company.

The need for and implementation of reengineering efforts occurred at General Telephone Electric (GTE), for example, when the company found its

REMEMBER TO COMMUNICATE

Don't Be Fooled by Smoke Screen Communication

Guard against smoke screen communication. Specifically, **smoke screen communication (SSC)** is any message designed to obscure rather than to inform. In organizations, especially large ones, SSC may be used to confuse and trick someone through miscommunication.

To demonstrate how smoke screen communication works, the word chart shown in Figure 6–8 is used by Harold, a supervisor who wants to persuade his manager to increase his department's budget. To use the chart, Harold selects one word from each of the three columns. The three selected words are "compatible digital capability." In writing his letter, Harold states, "Without an increase in funding for my department, we will lose our compatible digital capability." Surely, no responsible person would want the company to lose its "compatible digital capability!" Furthermore, this phrase sounds so impressive and sophisticated that a person may be reluctant to question it.

Of course, communication in organizations is not enhanced by the use of SSC, and its use for the purpose of deceiving others is not encouraged. However, when you are exposed to SSC in the future, you will better understand the scheme. Do not be intimidated by SSC; instead, simply ask for clarification and that will usually clear away the smoke.

ADAPTED FROM: William V. Haney, *Communication and Interpersonal Relations: Text and Cases,* 6th ed. (Homewood, IL: Richard D. Irwin, 1992), pp. 288–89.

annual revenues from telephone operations were threatened by new competition. To compete effectively, management concluded that the company needed to dramatically improve its customer-service operations. In the past, when a customer called the company to report a problem with telephone service, a repair clerk took the information from the customer, filled out a repair order, and sent it on to others to fix the problem. Customers, however, wanted all of this done while they were on the telephone.

A company must understand the needs of its customers before engaging in reengineering.

■ **FIGURE 6–8** Word Chart for Smoke Screen Communication (SSC)

SOURCE: William V. Haney, *Communication and Interpersonal Relations: Text and Cases,* 6th ed. (Homewood, IL: Richard D. Irwin, 1992), p. 288. Reprinted by permission.

COLUMN ONE	COLUMN TWO	COLUMN THREE
0. integrated	0. management	0. options
1. total	1. organizational	1. flexibility
2. systematized	2. monitored	2. capability
3. parallel	3. reciprocal	3. mobility
4. functional	4. digital	4. programming
5. responsive	5. logistical	5. concept
6. optimal	6. transitional	6. time-phase
7. synchronized	7. incremental	7. projection
8. compatible	8. third-generation	8. hardware
9. balanced	9. policy	9. contingency

To make this change, the company had to reorganize its customer-service process. First, repair clerks at GTE were trained to use the testing and switching equipment. The clerks were then told that they would be evaluated on the basis of how often they took care of problems without referring them to others, rather than on the basis of how many calls they handled. The next step was to combine sales and billing services with repair, so that most customer needs could be handled with one call. This reengineering effort produced nearly a 30-percent increase in productivity for GTE in the early 1990s.

A reengineering strategy should be devised at the top of a company but implemented from the bottom. It is difficult to start reengineering from the bottom of an organization because vested interests may block change. Reengineering must be led by top management. The authority to usher change through from beginning to end is necessary. However, lower-level employees need to be involved in designing the reengineering changes because they have to make the new design work. For reengineering to succeed, top managers must be visionaries who are good at communicating the need for change to those who will design the new procedures and processes.

THINK ABOUT IT

1. When determining how a company should be organized, it is wise to ask, "What structure will best minimize confusion in the organization?"

2. The willingness of a manager to delegate responsibilities to employees is a prerequisite for employee development.

3. Managers who are reluctant to delegate authority may appear to be very busy, but they often are far less productive than managers who are effective at delegating.

4. It is not uncommon for employees in small companies to be more satisfied with their jobs than employees in large corporations are. The difference in job satisfaction is often due to the fact that the structure of small companies makes it easier for employees to recognize the importance of their work.

5. Not only are the structures of organizations changing, but their boundaries are becoming more fluid as well. The trend is toward a system in which a retail sale at a store automatically triggers an order from the manufacturer to replace the sold merchandise.

6. Organizations without an empowered work force fail to make the most effective use of their human resources.

7. Customer control is becoming the dominant form of control in organizations, and the trend is for employees to work in direct contact with customers.

8. More continuous improvement occurs in companies when the focus is on employees working in teams instead of alone.

LOOKING BACK

Common ways in which organizations are organized and structured have been discussed. In addition, new trends in organizing were examined. At this point, it is appropriate to review the chapter objectives.

Explain the difference between line departments and staff departments in organizations.

The departments in an organization that contribute directly to the accomplishment of the company's goals are called line departments. Staff departments provide specialized advice and assistance to members of line departments.

Identify common ways in which organizations practice departmentalization.

The common ways in which organizations practice departmentalization are by function, product, customer, geographic location, and matrix design.

Identify the key factors that should be considered when designing jobs, according to the job characteristics model.

According to the job characteristics model, the design of jobs should take into consideration the workers' competency, their need for personal growth, and their level of satisfaction with the work context. Employees who are well matched to their jobs will experience an internal motivation that is influenced by how meaningful their work is to them, by their level of accountability, and by how much feedback they receive. Five core job characteristics that affect the three conditions of internal motivation are skill variety, task identity, task significance, autonomy, and feedback. Furthermore, for employees to respond positively to complex and challenging jobs, their growth needs must be strong.

Distinguish process management from management by function.

Three characteristics distinguish process management from management by function. First, instead of focusing on intradepartmental objectives, process management looks at how well the various integrated functions in a company are working together. Second, employees who possess different skills work together as a team to accomplish tasks, instead of performing functions in a series. Third, in process management, information is provided directly to where it is needed, without going through a hierarchy that can distort messages and cause miscommunication.

Explain how the modular approach to organizing works.

The modular approach to organizing concentrates a company's efforts and resources on core activities in which it has special expertise and contracts required services to others.

Describe the virtual corporation approach to organizing.

The virtual corporation is a temporary combination of independent companies that are linked by information technology to allow them to share skills, reduce costs, and enter new markets.

KEY TERMS

authority
centralization
chain of command
decentralization
delegation
departmentalization
   by customer
   by function
   by geographic design

by matrix design
by product
flat organizational structure
formal organizational
   structure
growth needs
informal organizational structure
internal motivation
job characteristics model

job design
job enlargement
job enrichment
job rotation
line department
line organization
mechanistic structure
modular approach
organic structure
organizing

process management
reengineering
responsibility
scalar principle
smoke screen communication (SSC)
span of management (span of control)
staff department
tall organizational structure
virtual corporation

REVIEW AND DISCUSSION QUESTIONS

1. What is the difference between a centralized and a decentralized organizational structure?
2. Why is the distinction between line and staff functions becoming blurred in many companies today?
3. What communication problems seem to be inherent to flat versus tall organizational structures?
4. Why is departmentalization by function common in many companies?
5. What is the logic behind job enlargement, and why does this logic often fail?
6. Why don't all employees respond positively to jobs that are complex and challenging?
7. Why are many companies abandoning their traditional vertical organization in favor of a process-oriented, horizontal organization?
8. How does the modular approach enable companies to become more efficient and competitive?
9. How does the concept of a virtual corporation enable companies to act quickly to take advantage of new market opportunities?

CRITICAL THINKING INCIDENT 6.1

The New Manager

For the last five years, Warren Morris has been a research scientist for the Southwest Petrochemical Company. About a year ago, Warren was promoted to a managerial position within the company. He is responsible for managing a medium-sized department that conducts research on the environmental impact of various drilling technologies in different worldwide geographic locations.

As a research scientist, Warren worked an eight-hour day and received praise for the quality of his work. Initially, he was excited about the opportunity to become a manager. Warren had high hopes that employees would perform well

under his guidance and that he would soon be recognized as a manager with the potential for future advancement. Unfortunately, after less than a year in his new position, Warren is experiencing several problems and great frustration with his managerial performance.

In his job as manager, Warren is expected to act as a liaison between the company and state environmental agencies. It is critical for him to be aware of the environmental policies that the state is likely to adopt so the company will be prepared to deal with them. Warren must also make personnel decisions concerning who will be hired and what work duties will be assigned to which employees. Unlike his previous job as a research scientist, Warren now finds that he works much longer than eight hours a day. As a matter of fact, after working for ten hours, Warren often realizes that he has failed to accomplish many of the duties he had expected to complete on that particular day. Actually, many other managers with larger departments in the company perform better than Warren.

The employees in Warren's department are also struggling. In too many cases, they are not aware of new approaches that would help them perform their tasks more productively. Warren is aware of the most effective ways in which many tasks should be performed by his employees. However, Warren will often perform the task himself rather than take the time to train the employee. Even when employees possess needed skills, Warren's failure to plan ahead frequently creates a situation in which they are given too many tasks at once. In these cases, Warren must take over some of the tasks himself so they will be completed on time. These situations do not bother Warren much, however, because in many cases, he believes that only he can do the job right.

Warren has a habit of performing routine tasks that can easily be accomplished by others in his department. He has become so accustomed to performing many of these duties himself that he seldom considers assigning them to his employees. When he does relinquish a task, Warren's expectation of perfection practically guarantees that he will be dissatisfied with the way in which an employee performs the job. Then, instead of showing his employees how to complete routine departmental duties to his satisfaction, Warren takes back the responsibility for performing these tasks. The initial excitement of being a manager has faded for Warren, and he now wonders if he will succeed in his new job.

Discussion Questions

1. What mistake is Warren making as a new manager?
2. Why is Warren failing to delegate departmental responsibilities properly?
3. What changes do you recommend that Warren make to increase the likelihood that he will succeed as a manager?

CRITICAL THINKING INCIDENT 6.2

Fine Tuning a Merger

The recent merger of two firms has created a need for the combined companies to be reorganized. Susan Roberts, a management consultant, has been hired to make suggestions on how the reorganization should occur. Susan learns that the merged organization has two manufacturing plants: the East Plant and the West Plant. The demand for products produced at each plant is increasing rapidly. As a result, each plant is expanding in size and hiring new employees.

The duties performed by employees at the East Plant are very similar. As a matter of fact, the workers there voluntarily switch jobs periodically to change their work routines and seldom find it difficult to perform the different duties. Employees at the West Plant cannot switch tasks with one another easily because their jobs are generally very dissimilar.

The jobs that must be performed at the East Plant are considered to be simple and routine. Training for new employees at this plant is short and easy to complete. At the West Plant, however, the tasks are complex and varied. Finding skilled employees to fill the new jobs created at the West Plant is not easy. When inexperienced individuals are hired to fill these jobs, they must receive extensive training before they can perform their assigned tasks satisfactorily.

The planning required to keep the East Plant operating at peak performance is not that great. The technology required to produce the products manufactured at this plant is not sophisticated, and the required materials are generally easy to get on short notice. Changes seldom need to be made in the products produced there.

However, the opposite is the case at the West Plant. Product redesign occurs frequently as the technology associated with the products produced at this plant advances. Furthermore, the materials for these products can be expensive; much planning is required to determine when less-expensive substitute materials may be available and in what quantities. In addition, the work performed by employees at the West Plant must be highly coordinated, compared to the minimal coordination needed at the East Plant.

The managers in the merged organization routinely experience information overload. This problem results from an expanded work force and the fact that many of the managers in the merged organization prefer to maintain close control over their employees. Any reorganization that occurs must address the problem of information overload and consider the appropriate level of control to be maintained by managers.

Discussion Questions

1. Should Susan recommend a wide or a narrow span of management for the East Plant? Why?

2. Should Susan recommend a wide or a narrow span of management for the West Plant? Why?

3. What strategies should Susan recommend to reduce the problem of information overload that managers in the two plants are experiencing?

CRITICAL THINKING INCIDENT 6.3

A Growing Company

The Omega Craft Company manufactures small, high-quality, fiberglass fishing boats. The company is very successful in this market. Over the past couple of years, however, many of the departments in the company have been expending more of their human and material resources on special, unique products that the company has agreed to produce. For example, due to its expertise in building fiberglass molds, the company began to accept a few special orders to produce custom fiberglass hot tubs and spas. The quality of these products pleased buyers, and the company soon received more orders for similar items. Now the hot tubs and spas produced by the company appear to have a promising future.

The company also received a request to build a custom fiberglass hull for a specially designed competition speedboat. Keith Selby, President of Omega Craft, thought it would be good advertising to have the name of the company displayed prominently on the hull of a speedboat entered in competition races, so the company agreed to produce the hull. After the custom speedboat won several important races, Keith received requests from other designers to have the company build their hulls out of fiberglass. The meticulous work involved in manufacturing these hulls permitted Omega Craft to charge high prices for these projects, which yielded substantial profits for the company. The high quality of these custom hulls began to be noticed by others in the racing industry, and it was not long before new orders for fiberglass hulls were received.

Omega Craft began to take on other special projects. One project that Keith is committing a lot of company resources to is the building of fiberglass parts for kit cars. The kit cars allow regular automobile chassis to be customized to look like expensive sports cars. Keith has created a separate division for the kit cars because he believes this product has the potential for huge growth. The new division has several departments, each of which is devoted to the kit-car products.

Unfortunately, the kit-car division is experiencing many problems. The company is learning that building fiberglass body panels and other parts for kit cars differs from building racing hulls. The company is very good at building fiberglass molds. However, it is not so good at maintaining color consistency in large production runs or at filling orders for parts on time. Also, its costs are high in the kit-car division. Keith is becoming frustrated because he thinks his company is losing its "golden touch" with fiberglass.

Discussion Questions

1. Why is Omega Craft successful with its boats but not with its kit-car parts?

2. Would the concept of a virtual corporation be appropriate for the kit-car division? Why or why not?

3. Although Omega Craft is successful at building fishing boats, what problems will this company probably experience as it expands?

NOTES

1. Keith Davis and John W. Newstrom, *Human Behavior at Work: Organizational Behavior,* 8th ed. (New York: McGraw-Hill, 1989), p. 362.

2. Ibid.

3. Alex Taylor III, "GM's $11 Billion Turnaround," *Fortune* (October 17, 1994), pp. 54–74.

4. Harold Stieglitz, "On Concepts of Corporate Structure," *Conference Board Record* 11 (February 1974): 7–13.

5. Homa Bahrami, "The Emerging Flexible Organization: Perspectives from Silicon Valley," *California Management Review* 34 (Summer 1992): 41.

6. Stephen C. Bushardt, David L. Duhon, and Aubrey

R. Fowler, Jr., "Management Delegation Myths and the Paradox of Task Assignment," *Business Horizons* **34** (March/April 1991): 37–43.

7. Ibid., pp. 32–33.

8. Don Caruth and Trezzie A. Pressley, "Key Factors in Positive Delegation," *Supervisory Management* **29** (July 1984): 6–11.

9. R. L. Daft, *Organization Theory and Design* (St. Paul, MN: West Publishing Company, 1983), p. 227.

10. Arthur A. Thompson, Jr., and A. J. Strickland III, *Strategy Formulation and Implementation,* rev. ed. (Homewood, IL: Richard D. Irwin, 1983), p. 324.

11. Theodore T. Herbert, "Strategy and Multinational Organization Structure: An International Relationships Perspective," *Academy of Management Review* 9 (April 1984): 263.

12. John A. Pearce II and Richard B. Robinson, Jr., *Management* (New York: Random House, 1989), p. 312.

13. Ibid.

14. Arthur A. Thompson, Jr., and A. J. Strickland III, *Strategy Formulation and Implementation* (Dallas, TX: Business Publications, 1980), p. 227.

15. Ibid.

16. The material on matrix design is drawn from David I. Cleland, *Matrix Management Systems Handbook* (New York: Van Nostrand Reinhold, 1984), pp. 13–29.

17. Tom Burns and George M. Stalker, *The Management of Innovation* (London: Tavistock, 1961).

18. Penny Moser, "The McDonald's Mystique," *Fortune* (July 4, 1988), pp. 112–16.

19. Ronald Henkoff, "Moving Up by Downscaling," *Fortune* (August 9, 1993), p. 72.

20. Material in the section entitled "Job Specialization and Standardization" is drawn from Paul S. Adler, "Time-and-Motion Regained," *Harvard Business Review* **71** (January/February 1993): 97–108.

21. Kenneth N. Wexley and Gary P. Latham, *Developing and Training Human Resources in Organizations,* 2d ed. (New York: Harper Collins, 1991), pp. 163–64.

22. Ibid., p. 164.

23. Paul Hersey and Kenneth H. Blanchard, *Management of Organizational Behavior,* 6th ed. (Englewood Cliffs, NJ: Prentice-Hall, 1993), p. 74.

24. J. Richard Hackman and Greg R. Oldham, *Work Redesign* (Reading, MA: Addison-Wesley, 1980), pp. 71–98.

25. Ibid., p. 85.

26. Material in the section entitled "The New Flexible Organization" is drawn from Bahrami, "The Emerging Flexible Organization," pp. 33–52.

27. Material in the section entitled "Breakthrough in Organizing" is drawn from Thomas A. Stewart, "The Search for the Organization of Tomorrow," *Fortune* (May 18, 1992), pp. 92–98.

28. Thomas A. Stewart, "The Search for the Organization of Tomorrow," *Fortune* (May 18, 1992), p. 3.

29. Material in the section entitled "The Modular Approach" is drawn from Shawn Tully, "The Modular Corporation," *Fortune* (February 8, 1993), pp. 106–15.

30. Shawn Tully, "The Modular Corporation," *Fortune* (February 8, 1993), p. 106.

31. Material in the section entitled "The Virtual Corporation" is drawn from John A. Byrne, Richard Brandt, and Otis Port, "The Virtual Corporation," *Business Week* (February 8, 1993), pp. 99–103.

32. Byrne, et al., pp. 100–01.

33. Material in the section entitled "Reengineering" is drawn from Thomas A. Stewart, "Reengineering: The Hot New Management Tool," *Fortune* (August 23, 1993), pp. 41–48.

SUGGESTED READINGS

Burdett, John O. "The Magic of Alignment." *Management Decision* 32 (1994): 59–63.

Clark, Tim. "Chiat 'Virtual Office' Swells." *Advertising Age* (August 1, 1994), p. 44.

Cravens, David W., Shannon H. Skipp, and Karen S. Cravens. "Reforming the Traditional Organization: The Mandate for Developing Networks." *Business Horizons* 37 (July/August 1994): 19–28.

Fagiano, David. "Don't Throw the Baby Out with the Bath Water." *Management Review* 83 (August 1994): 4.

Lamont, Bruce T., Robert J. Williams, and James J. Hoffman. "Performance During 'M-Form' Reorganization and Recovery Time: The Effects of Prior Strategy and Implementation Speed." *Academy of Management Journal* 37 (February 1994): 153–66.

Lawler, Edward E., III. "From Job-Based to Competency-Based Organizations." *Journal of Organizational Behavior* 15 (January 1994): 3–15.

Martinsons, Aelita G. B., and Maris G. Martinsons. "In Search of Structural Excellence." *Leadership & Organizational Development Journal* 15 (1994): 24–28.

Mitroff, Ian I., Richard O. Mason, and Christine M. Pearson. "Radical Surgery: What Will Tomorrow's Organizations Look Like?" *Academy of Management Executive* 8 (May 1994): 11–21.

Rieley, James B. "The Circular Organization: How

Leadership Can Optimize Organizational Effectiveness." *National Productivity Review* 13 (Winter 1993/1994): 11–19.

Welge, Martin K. "A Comparison of Managerial Structures in German Subsidiaries in France, India, and the United States." *Management International Review* 34 (First Quarter 1994): 33–49.

CHAPTER 7

STAFFING AND TRAINING

■ LEARNING OBJECTIVES

Human resources are critical to the success or failure of organizations. Without capable personnel, firms cannot provide the high-quality goods and services demanded by today's customers. Effective training increases productivity, reduces miscommunication, and enhances a firm's ability to be competitive. The learning objectives for this chapter are to:

- Understand the staffing process.
- Explain the purpose of equal employment opportunity (EEO) legislation.
- Differentiate between internal and external recruitment practices.
- Identify the techniques used in the selection process.
- Discuss various types of job-training methods.
- Specify methods to evaluate training activities.

■ CHAPTER OUTLINE

THE REAL WORLD *Training—A Business Response to the Educational Shortfall*

Organizations strive to obtain the best possible candidates to fill available positions. Each year, corporate America spends vast sums, as much as $40 billion or more, on training and development activities. Nevertheless, concerns are expressed about the inabilities of some workers entering the labor force to apply basic reading, writing, and arithmetic skills.

- In a single year, only 800 of 3700 entry-level job applicants passed Southwestern Bell's employment test.

- Only 16 percent of 21,000 candidates for beginning positions passed New York Telephone's basic reading and reasoning skills exam.

- Slightly more than 13 percent of prospective employees passed Michigan Bell's reading and mathematics test for clerical positions.

- When Ingersoll-Rand upgraded technology to further automate manufacturing equipment, more than one-half of its 300 hourly employees lacked the basic skills to learn the new jobs.

- To place one teller who was required to complete a training program successfully as a prerequisite of employment, New York's Chemical Bank interviewed 40 high-school graduates.

The business world has responded to the shortfall in educational expectations in various ways, including monetary support to schools and colleges, company-school partnerships, donations of equipment, and internships. For example, the Boston Compact—a well-known business-school system alliance—offers an incentive-based program to improve the quality of high-school education that provides employment opportunities to its graduates. Honeywell has a long tradition of providing equipment and technical support to education; in a single year, its contributions amounted to $2.9 million.

Johnsonville Foods, an innovative Wisconsin-based sausage maker, exemplifies a "learning organization." Instead of relying on training techniques that stress the mastery of functions in specific sequences, a learning organization encourages employees to think for themselves and to use ideas to develop solutions. Instead of simply observing what workers do, managers in these organizations assume the roles of coaches and facilitators. Workers make the decisions about how tasks can best be completed. Greater commitment to job performance, more loyalty toward the firm, and improved service and product quality are key outcomes that result from learner involvement. The "bottom line" has been impressive, leading to a higher return on assets and a significant growth in sales for these companies.

According to a survey of 645 firms conducted by the Hudson Institute and Towers Perrin, the major reason job candidates are not hired is that they have poor writing or verbal skills. Yet two-thirds of these firms spent under $2000 per year on training initial-entry personnel, and only 8 percent of them had remedial training programs.

Differences of opinion prevail regarding how people can be more adequately prepared to function in the workplace. Regardless of the approach recommended, there is merit to the observation that employees are undervalued assets.

The importance of training cannot be overemphasized. To provide quality products and serve customer needs, businesses must have well-trained personnel.

ADAPTED FROM: Elizabeth Ehrlich, "Business Is Becoming a Substitute Teacher," *Business Week* (September 19, 1988), pp. 134–35; Philip J. Harkins, "The Changing Role of Corporate Training and Development," *Corporate Development in the '90s, Training* supplement (1991): 26–29; Linda Honold, "The Power of Learning at Johnsonville Foods," *Training* 28 (April 1991): 55–58; Pamela Kruger, "A Game Plan for the Future," *Working Woman* 15 (January 1990): 74–78; Karen Pennar, "It's Time to Put Our Money Where Our Future Is," *Business Week* (September 19, 1988), pp. 140–41; Bill Richards, "Wanting Workers," *The Wall Street Journal* (February 9, 1990), p. R10; Janice C. Simpson, "A Shallow Labor Pool Spurs Business to Act to Bolster Education," *The Wall Street Journal* (September 28, 1987), p. 1; "Work Force 2000: Talk, Talk, Talk," *Training* 28 (May 1991): 84.

STAFFING: PEOPLE AND JOBS

Staffing is a key to productivity.

Staffing is the process through which an organization attracts, hires, and retains a sufficient number of people to meet its stated goals. A key objective is to match the skills needed to do jobs with human-resource capabilities. The importance of this objective cannot be overemphasized because it is through the efforts of managers and employees that quality is attained and productive work is accomplished. Ideally, staffing enables a firm to hire persons who will be committed to their jobs and loyal to their employers.

Because new hires, transfers, promotions, and terminations are routine business procedures, managers must carefully consider the need for effective staffing practices. Persons who possess certain job skills might be in short supply; an unexpected downturn in sales could require layoffs. A promotion (or termination) usually means that the successful (or unsuccessful) person's former position must be filled. Firms are obligated to abide by employment-related legislation, which serves to assure equal employment opportunities in the workplace. Effective staffing strategies also can reduce or minimize absenteeism, turnover, and costly mistakes on the part of employees.

The personnel department performs a staff function.

Larger firms have personnel or human-resource departments to assist with staffing responsibilities. In recent years, these departments have assumed increasingly important roles in forecasting personnel requirements, documenting relevant employment records, and assuring compliance with equal employment opportunity legislation. At times, conflicts do arise between the personnel department, which performs a staff function, and line managers. These problems often result from communication difficulties and inaccurate assumptions about employee responsibilities.

Success depends on people.

Staffing is a mutual concern to both employees and employers due to their dependent relationship. Employees need jobs and, when possible, seek to work for organizations that provide stable employment, equitable wages, and desirable working conditions. Employers want to hire qualified people who will make quality contributions toward the attainment of corporate objectives. In the mid-1990s, job-applicant qualifications are an emerging problem. Many potential employees do not possess desirable levels of reading, writing, and arithmetic skills.

> Though only a relatively small percentage of Americans have trouble reading or writing a simple passage and counting out bus fare, a distressing number can't do much more than that. The Federal Education Department estimates that the United States has 17 million to 21 million functional illiterates— people whose meager skills aren't up to [the] demands that life and work place upon them.[1]

■ *The Staffing Model*

This chapter presents an overview of human-resource needs, recruitment, selection, and training. Figure 7–1 illustrates the components of the typical staffing model. Staffing is performed by all companies. A key purpose is to hire knowledgeable personnel who are dedicated to the concept of making continuous efforts to improve service or product quality.

Firms have different goals and therefore different human-resource needs.

A firm's human-resource needs are influenced by strategic plans, which specify the major goals that the company seeks to accomplish. A growth-oriented real estate business will probably need additional salespeople, closing agents,

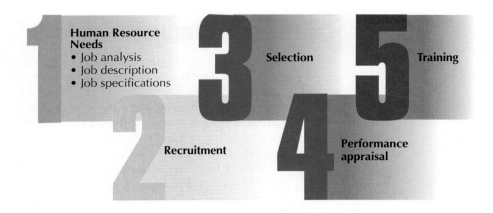

FIGURE 7–1 The Staffing Model

Human Resource Needs
- Job analysis
- Job description
- Job specifications

1

2 Recruitment

3 Selection

4 Performance appraisal

5 Training

and a secretarial staff. Conversely, a firm that must consolidate operations because of a merger will generally require fewer personnel and often reduce the number of existing employees through layoffs. Three tools are available to help managers meet human-resource needs. The *job analysis* is a process that assimilates information about a particular job; based on these data, more detailed *job descriptions* and *job specifications* are developed. These human-resource tools will be discussed in more detail in the next section.

After human-resource needs and job duties are determined, applicants must be recruited to fill positions. These persons may already be employed at other jobs within a company or may be sought from sources outside the firm. A primary objective of recruitment is to assure that the firm attracts a sufficiently large number of applicants from which appropriately qualified persons can be chosen. Sometimes the selection process involves formalized testing; it almost always includes preemployment interviews. In practice, both individuals and committees make selection recommendations.

New personnel must be trained. Employees who have little or no prior experience require extensive training; others may not need as much formal training. All employees must understand the policies, procedures, and rules related to their jobs. More and more employers are inclined to seek persons who speak at least one foreign language and who have some familiarity with cultures other than their own. At Coca-Cola, for example, emphasis is placed on "the ability to develop and supply globally people who have the experience, skills, and values to help the company achieve its objectives."[2]

Performance appraisal is the review of how well employees are doing their jobs. A key aspect of the appraisal process is the improvement of on-the-job performance through feedback to subordinates. As firms increase in size, they are more likely to have formal appraisal systems. However, effective managers continuously appraise employees on an informal basis.

The recruitment and selection processes match applicants and jobs.

New employees must be trained to perform on the job.

■ *Equal Employment Opportunity (EEO) Legislation*

The purpose of **equal employment opportunity (EEO) legislation** is to prevent discrimination in job selection or in the assignment of job duties after employees are hired. Many EEO laws originated during the 1960s in an era that focused on creating equal workplace opportunities for minorities, women, older employees, and the handicapped. The Civil Rights Act of 1964 represents a major effort by the federal government to assure that race, color, sex, religion, or national origin do not bias employment decisions in the workplace.

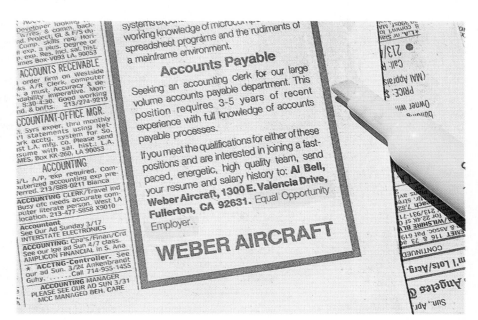

Businesses advertise the fact that they offer equal employment opportunities (EEO) in order to attract women and minorities to their operations.

A prejudicial attitude differs from a discriminatory action.

All persons do not have similar backgrounds, experiences, beliefs, or values. Consequently, they also do not share similar views about others. Friends, associates, bosses, family members, and subordinates influence personal beliefs and opinions. Inaccurate stereotypes can negatively alter behavior. Consequently, it is important to differentiate between prejudice and discrimination.

Prejudice is an *attitude* toward a person or group that is based on incomplete information. For example, someone might form a positive or negative attitude about the work ethic of a particular racial group without having personal interactions with any member of the group. **Discrimination** refers to either favorable or unfavorable *actions*. Discrimination is a necessary part of staffing because selecting a job candidate discriminates against all other applicants. However, if the selection of an employee is based on one or more of the factors designated as inappropriate by EEO legislation, it is unlawful. The following laws serve to promote fair employment practices and assure equal opportunity for members of protected groups.

- *Equal Pay Act of 1963.* Gender cannot be used as a basis for compensation discrimination. The law mandates equal pay between the sexes for performance of equal work duties.

- *Title VII of the Civil Rights Act of 1964.* When making employment decisions, it is illegal to discriminate on the basis of race, color, sex, religion, or national origin.

- *Age Discrimination in Employment Act of 1967* (as amended). Persons who are 40 or older are protected from employment discrimination solely on the basis of their age.

- *Rehabilitation Act of 1973* (as amended). Persons cannot be discriminated against on the basis of physical and/or mental handicaps.

- *Pregnancy Discrimination Act of 1978.* "Pregnancy, childbirth, or related medical conditions" cannot be used as a basis for discriminating against women.

■ *Americans with Disabilities Act of 1992.* When making employment decisions, employers cannot discriminate against disabled employees or against qualified persons with disabilities who apply for jobs.

Illegal discrimination involves unequal treatment, perpetuating outcomes of previous discrimination, or causing adverse impacts on protected classes.[3] Unequal treatment is a deliberate action based on bias. A decision to employ Caucasians and not to hire Hispanics is an example of unequal treatment. As a result of past discriminatory practices, women and minorities may continue to be disadvantaged in terms of pay, promotion opportunities, and seniority privileges.

ADVERSE IMPACT   **Adverse impact** is the application of an employment practice that unjustly affects the members of one or more protected groups. If a high-school diploma is not a condition of employment, for example, then requiring one will have a disproportional impact on certain minorities to a greater extent than on whites. In general, adverse impact involves **disparate impact,** which implies discrimination against a group, or **disparate treatment,** which is discrimination against an individual. Several criteria have been developed to demonstrate adverse impact in the workplace.[4]

■ *Comparative Statistics.* This approach compares employment ratios for members of protected and nonprotected groups. According to the "80-percent rule," adverse impact exists if members of any race, sex, or ethnic group represent less than four-fifths of the group having the highest selection rate.

■ *Labor Market Statistics.* To avoid allegations of illegal hiring practices, a company's labor force should approximate the race or gender percentages that prevail in the relevant labor market. These percentages can be based on the locations where current or prospective employees live or on the area from which employment applications are solicited.

■ *Concentration Statistics.* Illegal discrimination is evidenced if members of protected classes all perform the same type of job or have similar job titles.

Employers do have defenses against charges of adverse impact. They may be able to show that job-selection predictors are valid. Another defense is to establish **bona fide occupational qualifications (BFOQ),** which demonstrate that only a member of a certain group can perform the job task. For example, hiring a woman to model women's fashions or to supervise dressing facilities for women at an athletic club is justifiable.

Women, minorities, older workers, and the handicapped have been targets of discrimination. Age discrimination is the most rapidly growing sector of bias claims in the workplace. In one six-year period, the number of age-discrimination complaints doubled.[5] The extent of allegations involving unfair workplace discrimination is evidenced by the growing number of cases filed with the Equal Employment Opportunity Commission, a government enforcement agency that processes 52,000 complaints per year.[6]

According to a Korn/Ferry-UCLA survey, fewer than 5 percent of senior management positions were held by women and minorities, two percentage points higher than reported a decade earlier.[7] The term **glass ceiling** frequently refers to invisible, artificial barriers that limit career advancement for women and members of minority groups. Many reasons, ranging from outright discrimination to perceptions of inadequate managerial capabilities, are given for the existence of the glass-ceiling phenomenon. A U.S. Department

Illegal discrimination must be avoided in the workplace.

of Labor report cited informal (such as word-of-mouth) recruitment, insufficient management-development activities, and lack of responsiveness toward equal employment practices by senior managers as major factors.[8] From a realistic perspective, however, the choice of managerial style does not appear to be gender-related.[9]

AFFIRMATIVE ACTION PROGRAMS (AAPS)   **Affirmative action programs (AAPs)** attempt to correct prior workplace discrimination against women and minorities. The intent is to establish goals so that firms will employ members of these groups in percentages that reflect those that currently exist in the labor pool from which all workers are selected. Affirmative action legislation does not set quotas for hiring unqualified personnel but serves to "communicate clearly the message that a company is an equal opportunity employer."[10]

AAPs provide job opportunities.

Components of affirmative action programs include utilization and availability analyses, specified goals, and time guidelines.[11] A utilization analysis indicates the actual numbers of women and minorities that are employed by a firm. An availability analysis reveals the number of these people who are available to work in a particular labor market. Data from each analysis are compared to show whether or not women or minorities are under-utilized in a firm. Goals involve efforts to remedy employment imbalances, and time guidelines specify target dates for implementing AAPs. A formal, written AAP is needed if a firm has a government contract in excess of $50,000 and employs 50 or more people. The program may be established voluntarily or can be required by a court consent decree. Management plays a key role in the development of effective AAPs.

> It appears that in order for AAPs to have a chance to succeed, they must be written down and they must be vigorously supported and communicated by top management. Without top-management support, it is difficult to show that there is a good faith effort being exerted to deal with discrimination.[12]

HUMAN-RESOURCE NEEDS

Organizations are constantly challenged to use human resources wisely. Through human-resource planning, the management of a firm determines if current employees are utilized to their fullest potentials and prepares for changes in personnel requirements that may arise in the future. The process involves reviewing present employee assignments, assessing future needs, and developing plans to meet them.[13] A focus on human-resource needs is advantageous because it forces a firm to plan and enables it to be in a better position to attract people who possess desired job skills.

■ Job Analysis

What is job analysis?

Job analysis is the process of identifying and recording job tasks and the human qualifications required to do them. Through job analysis, information is provided to firms to enable them to comply with laws in hiring, promoting, and appraising personnel.[14] To minimize biases, information should be collected from the employees who actually do the work as well as from their supervisors. Job analysis justifies the rationale for a position and identifies various reporting relationships between managers and employees. A review of job-analysis data guides decisions involving work-design changes and is a basis for planning and implementing employee-development programs. Job analysis is the key resource for the development of job descriptions and job specifications.

Various kinds of information are relevant to job analysis, including knowledge of the tasks and activities involved in completing jobs. The types of equipment or tools necessary to perform jobs should be specified. If an ultimate appraisal of work efforts is to be effective, sufficient information should be available so that job performance standards can be established. In summary, job analysis involves compiling information about jobs and the skills needed to do them.

How is job information collected?

There are a number of ways to collect the information needed to prepare job analyses. Commonly used methods include observing work behaviors, asking questions, and identifying major job duties. It is important to obtain accurate information about the jobs that are to be examined. These methods of information collection can be used in combination; however, such an approach frequently consumes a considerable amount of time. Consequently, time-benefit considerations are important and should also be evaluated.

■ Job Descriptions

A job description should specify what the jobholder is to do.

Job descriptions are written statements that outline the duties and responsibilities involved in performing jobs. They include general descriptions of job duties and illustrate the types of activities completed by jobholders. Each job description should clearly communicate job expectations. Whenever tasks are altered or responsibilities are changed, a job description should be revised and updated to reflect these modifications. If employees know what their jobs entail and what is expected of them, mistakes and miscommunications are less likely to occur. Consequently, the management of a firm is apt to experience fewer problems related to job dissatisfaction and low morale, both of which contribute to poor quality and low productivity.

The perception of formal job descriptions varies throughout the world. In the United States, compared to many other countries, business practices are more legalistic and place a greater emphasis on carefully defined employment relations between employers and employees. To the Japanese, for example, the American version of describing management jobs is too restrictive; in Japan, managers are expected to do whatever needs to be done to accomplish an objective or resolve a problem.[15] This management approach, which demonstrates considerable commitment to an employer, is not easily understood by American managers, who may change jobs frequently and have less loyalty to a particular company.

■ Job Specifications

Job specifications state the human skills that are needed to do a certain job.

Job specifications state in detail the qualifications a person must have to perform certain job duties. These qualifications involve knowledge, skills, experience, and education requirements. For instance, real estate salespeople and nurses must be licensed to practice their professions. An accounting firm may only be interested in hiring candidates who are CPAs (Certified Public Accountants) for full-time career employment. Specifications must be job-related and should be listed in terms of minimally acceptable requirements. Unless it is necessary to do a job, it is inappropriate to specify that jobholders must possess a certain credential, such as a college degree. Figure 7–2 displays brief illustrations of the job description and job specifications for a systems analyst position.

■ **FIGURE 7–2** Job Description and Specifications for a Systems Analyst Position

SOURCE: Stephen E. Catt and Donald S. Miller, *Supervision: Working with People*, 2d ed. (Homewood, IL: Richard D. Irwin, 1991), pp. 343–44. Used with permission of the publisher.

Job Description

Job Title
Systems Analyst

Department
Programming and Systems Analysis

General Description
Responsible for systems analysis and design, programming specifications and development, and systems implementation and documentation

Duties and Responsibilities
1. Prepare complete studies of assigned systems, including
   a. review of work assignments
   b. analysis of work flow
   c. study of work-load pattern
   d. study of backlogs and overload points
2. Prepare feasibility studies
3. Prepare programming specifications for the necessary programs for the system(s)
4. Prepare complete systems documentation for assigned systems
5. Work with the programming staff to make certain that programming specifications are completed in an efficient manner
6. Maintain appropriate files in a professional fashion

Job Specifications

Job Title
Systems Analyst

Qualifications
Education: Minimum of baccalaureate degree in a field such as business, accounting, or management information systems
Experience: At least two years as a systems analyst
Programming experience in widely used computer languages
Skills: Technical writing ability required
Identify alternative courses of action and make timely decisions based on factual information and logical assumptions
Retain perspective while working on detail
Demonstrate creativity and initiative in completing work assignments
Develop and maintain good working relations with systems users

RECRUITMENT

Recruitment is the process of building a "pool" of applicants from which to choose persons for employment. The purpose of the recruitment process is to attract people who possess the job qualifications desired by a firm and who may accept invitations for employment. Practically all employers are seeking newly hired personnel who will stay on the payroll for an extended period of time.[16] Although formal recruitment programs are considered to be a function of personnel or human-resource departments, all managers and employees can informally serve as recruiters, especially by making positive comments about their employers.

Recruitment is expensive but essential.

Formal recruitment activities are expensive and time-consuming for job applicants as well as for the personnel who are responsible for staffing vacant positions. One study indicates that direct recruitment costs average $3212 per employee.[17] According to one estimate, a corporate recruitment manager takes ten hours to complete a typical recruiting assignment.[18]

Firms that serve international markets often hire people who can interact with customers who have diverse cultural and language backgrounds. Nevertheless, business knowledge and communication skills are still emphasized. For example, Unilever, a major transnational consumer products firm, makes a special effort to recruit job applicants who can work cooperatively as team members and accept a consensus-oriented corporate philosophy.[19] Companies with reputations for recognizing and rewarding service abroad have a recruitment advantage when staffing positions that require time to be spent at international locations.

Hiring managers should give accurate job previews and should not "over-sell" a job.

Potential new employees should be given a realistic preview of what a job entails. In their enthusiasm about a candidate or haste to get a position filled, hiring managers can "oversell" the duties that are actually performed on a job. They might ascribe more importance to the position than really exists or over-generalize about future promotional opportunities. Such actions are not recommended because they create unrealistic jobholder expectations and ultimately lead to low morale, absenteeism, and turnover among employees.

SOURCES OF EMPLOYEES

Job candidates can be located within the ranks of current employees (internal) or outside an organization (external). Each source has assets and limitations that are worthy of consideration. Much information about currently employed applicants is available to the firm. However, considerable infighting can occur among potential candidates for a position. External applicants often bring new ideas and ways of doing things to a company, but they also usually require a longer adjustment period to become accustomed to a new job environment. Figure 7–3 summarizes these and other advantages and disadvantages of internal and external sources of job applicants.

■ Internal Recruitment

Are qualified people already "on board"?

Promotions, transfers, job rotation, and rehires are internal sources of job applicants.[20] Compared to job rotation and rehires, promotions and transfers tend to be for more permanent types of positions. Internal recruitment motivates good job performance because it creates opportunities for career advancement. It is less expensive to recruit employees internally than it is to initiate recruitment programs to attract persons from outside the company.

Promotions are especially noteworthy because they formally recognize past performance and evidence a commitment on behalf of an employer. In some organizations, training is used to prepare employees for possible promotions. A record of consistent accomplishments and a demonstrated ability to handle increasingly greater responsibilities is often evidenced by persons who get promotions to better, higher-paying positions.

■ External Recruitment

Employers should target recruitment activities.

Employers have a wide range of external sources to use to recruit personnel, including referrals, employment agencies, schools, and trade associations.[21] An

■ **FIGURE 7–3** Advantages and Disadvantages of Internal and External Sources of Employment

SOURCE: Reprinted by permission from page 191 of *Personnel/Human Resource Management*, Sixth Edition, by Robert L. Mathis and John H. Jackson. Copyright © 1991 by West Publishing Company. All rights reserved.

ADVANTAGES	DISADVANTAGES
Internal	
■ Morale of promotee	■ Inbreeding
■ Better assessment of abilities	■ Possible morale problems for those not promoted
■ Lower cost for some jobs	■ "Political" infighting for promotions
■ Motivator for good performance	■ Need strong management-development program
■ Causes a succession	
■ Have to hire only at entry level	
External	
■ "New blood," new perspectives	■ May not select someone who will "fit"
■ Cheaper than training a professional	■ May cause morale problems for internal candidates
■ No group of political supporters in organization already	■ Longer "adjustment" or orientation time
■ May bring industry insights	

employer can encourage present employees and others to refer friends and acquaintances to be interviewed for employment opportunities. Referral programs, which may be formal or informal, have been successful for many companies. State and private employment agencies are sources of job applicants. State agencies offer job-counseling sessions, administer job-related tests, and provide placement services to persons who request them. Private agencies charge a fee that is paid by the job seeker, the employer, or both. They serve persons with widely varied experiential backgrounds, ranging from individuals who have considerable professional experience to those who possess few

Recruitment fairs provide mutual learning opportunities: Potential job applicants become knowledgeable about companies, and recruiters become acquainted with prospective employees.

GLOBAL VIEW

Staffing and the International Environment

To remain competitive, many businesses strive to find new markets in other countries. These firms need personnel who are knowledgeable about international cultures and ways of conducting business. Over time, greater numbers of managers will have at least some international experience, and more employers will provide such experience as part of the grooming process for future top executives.

Through its International Graduate Trainee Program, Gillette International staffs and trains for positions located throughout the world. The company's international subsidiaries recruit business students at local colleges and provide six months of training before sending them to the United States for additional professional development. Those who complete the program are offered trainee positions and return to their home countries. Nearly one-half of the program's graduates have earned promotions to important managerial positions with the company.

The growing globalization of business operations often involves training employees to work in other countries. Firms increasingly need personnel who are familiar with international business practices.

Gillette's strategy enables the company to train its own employees rather than recruit executive-level persons at considerably higher salaries. According to Gillette's international personnel director, the ideal job candidate "is someone who says, 'Today, it's Manila. Tomorrow, it's the United States. Four years from now, it's Peru or Pakistan.' " [Laabs, "The Global Talent Search," p. 40]

Managers should not underestimate the importance of making successful transitions to live in other cultures. According to a Conference Board survey, business knowledge, a high level of tolerance as well as flexibility, and an ability to work with others are among the most important factors. A variety of approaches are used to prepare persons for international assignments. Some firms actually hold training sessions at overseas locations. Others make special efforts to include training exercises that emphasize awareness of cross-cultural considerations.

What qualities influence the selection of persons for overseas positions? Research conducted by International Orientation Resources indicates that 90 percent of all employers consider technical knowledge to be the most relevant quality. Managerial capability ranked second; language skills ranked a distant fifth.

To experience success abroad, is it necessary for managers to speak a foreign language? Companies seem to have different philosophies. At Colgate, fluency in another language is regarded as a vital factor. Before leaving for another country, personnel at the 3M Corporation are encouraged—but not required—to know another language.

ADAPTED FROM: Beverly Geber, "The Care and Breeding of Global Managers," *Training* **29** (July 1992): 32–37; Jennifer J. Laabs, "The Global Talent Search," *Personnel Journal* **70** (August 1991): 38–42, 44.

job skills. Executive recruitment firms are widely used to search for managerial talent.

High schools, vocational/technical schools (vo-techs), and colleges are sources of job prospects. Vo-techs are excellent places to recruit people who have technical skills in specific fields, such as automobile repair or printing.

Colleges prepare students for initial-entry careers in a variety of academic disciplines. However, college-recruitment programs need to be reviewed to assure their effectiveness.

> Recruiting at colleges and universities is often an expensive process. The significant figures to review are the costs associated with hires versus the costs associated with nonhires. If an organization is spending more than two-thirds of its recruiting budget on individuals who never join the company, the recruiting program needs serious revamping.[22]

Trade associations represent another source of employees. In addition to the publication of periodicals and newsletters, associations hold conferences that provide employers with the opportunity to form acquaintanceships. Also, service on various committees sponsored by associations enables contacts with others to be developed. Like applicants, recruiters can build "networks" of persons who might be interested in employment. According to one survey, as many as 60 percent of all job candidates use networking to find new jobs.[23]

Firms with reputations for providing quality products and services have an advantage in recruiting talented personnel. Many job applicants equate the marketplace success of employers with career employment possibilities for themselves. Merck, a pharmaceutical firm, has consistently ranked at the top of *Fortune*'s most admired corporations. Among its products are high-demand blood-pressure and cholesterol drugs. Merck's commitment to research and development enables the firm to attract bright, capable people. Its former CEO, P. Roy Vagelos, once observed, "The competition in our field is enormous, and the more original thinkers we have, the better I like it."[24]

Recruiters can build "networks" of potential employees.

SELECTION

The selection process determines who gets the job.

Selection refers to choosing a successful job candidate from the potential employees being considered by a firm. A good match between applicants and jobs serves the interests of employees and employers. Employees are likely to do better work and to derive greater personal satisfaction from their jobs. Employers benefit because qualified employees are most likely to meet company objectives.

■ *Selection Techniques*

Let's examine several techniques used in the selection process. The selection decision is critical and generally involves communication skills. Tom Peters, author of *Thriving on Chaos* observes

> Grocer Stew Leonard considers retailing experience or skills at the cash register to be secondary. . . . "We can teach cash register. We can't teach nice," says Stew. . . . At retailer Nordstrom, regional vice president Betsy Sanders reports that the chief criterion is not prior retailing experience but "friendliness." . . . Tom Melohn, co-owner of North American Tool & Die, recalling interviews with candidates for one clerical job, explains: Most applicants began by asking about hours, money, and other mechanics. The one he picked, however, "asked all kinds of questions about our approaches and procedures."[25]

Firms do not necessarily follow the same sequence of activities when selecting new personnel. However, the selection process generally includes application forms, recommendations and references, employment testing, and interviews. For managerial positions, results based on performance at an assessment center may be considered.

APPLICATION FORMS Application forms, which represent an initial expression of interest in employment, serve two purposes.[26] They provide information that can be used to screen candidates (and kept in personnel files for referral purposes), and they include various types of information about an applicant: name, address, Social Security/telephone number, educational record, and work history. At times, application forms even contain introductory information to help applicants understand job expectations. For example, the application blank for a fast-food restaurant chain lists job tasks that include taking out trash, mopping floors, and keeping restrooms clean.

Computers are playing an increasingly greater role in the employment process. Advanced technology enables applications to be scanned for information that is then entered into a computer system. The resulting database is used to match desired job skills and applicant characteristics. Automated processing is especially useful to large employers like Coors Brewing, a company that receives more than 40,000 job applications each year.[27] Proponents of computerized scanning point to several advantages.[28] Candidates are likely to be evaluated more fairly, and computers make fewer mistakes than humans do. Job seekers receive faster notice concerning the status of applications, and information can be stored in a computer system for an extended period of time.

JOB REFERENCES When seeking employment, applicants are often asked to list the names, addresses, and telephone numbers of several references. This practice is quite common; however, caution should be exercised.[29] The candidates themselves choose the references; it is unlikely that a name given will be listed unless a positive reference is expected. Some people are hesitant to make negative comments, especially when their remarks could cause a person not to get a job. In addition, a person listed as a reference may comment about the candidate but not actually be in a position to know the answers to the questions posed by the employer.

Many employers hesitate to make statements about the job performance of current or former employees due to possible lawsuits. Inquiries about references are often referred to personnel or human-resource departments, which generally confirm only job titles and dates of employment. Without written permission, some firms will not give out any information about current or former employees. In practice, the value of references is sometimes questionable.

EMPLOYMENT TESTING A variety of employment tests is used to evaluate the suitability of applicants for job openings. The foremost concerns of testing programs include the accurate prediction of job-related performance abilities and compliance with equal employment opportunity (EEO) legislation. Proficiency, aptitude, psychomotor, and simulation (work-sample) tests illustrate the extensive nature of possible testing options.

Candidates must demonstrate a specified level of proficiency for some jobs. To be considered for a secretarial position, a person might have to type at least 60 words per minute. To become a mail carrier, an individual must take an examination, part of which measures his or her ability to sort mail for delivery.

Candidates must apply to be considered for a job.

Because candidates choose their own references, employers should be cautious about positive feedback.

Testing predicts the on-the-job performance of a candidate.

When a job requires eye-hand coordination to assemble small objects, a job candidate may be required to pass a psychomotor test.

Tests should be valid and reliable.

Employment tests are not without complications. The administration of a testing program can be expensive. In addition, tests must exhibit **validity** (actually measure what they say they measure) and **reliability** (evidence consistency over a span of time). For instance, tests can be developed to simulate work tasks that are actually performed on a job. Generally, employment tests are designed for specific jobs and consequently are considered to be valid job-performance predictors.

INTERVIEWS   The interview is a very common component of the selection process. Almost all employers want to meet applicants on a personal basis to discuss job openings. This technique is characterized by many subtleties, including the personal likes and dislikes of interviewers. Sometimes recruiters reach a hiring decision during the first few minutes of an interview, even before sufficient information has been exchanged. The following guidelines will help you, as a manager, to conduct interviews.

■ Review each applicant's file. Focus on the skills, relevant experiences, and special talents needed to perform the job.

■ Develop a list of interview questions based on job-related factors. Unless you need to clarify a specific point, do not ask needless questions about information that is already available to you.

■ Make each candidate feel welcome. Create a cordial work atmosphere and minimize potential interruptions.

■ Provide opportunities for applicants to ask questions. Interviews are a "two-way street" for both obtaining and giving information.

■ Do not make promises that cannot be kept. Be careful not to make comments that might be unnecessarily encouraging about employment possibilities.

■ Be courteous and thank each candidate for coming to the interview. Even if the person is not hired, you want him or her to have a favorable impression of the company.

As a job applicant, an essential first step is to learn about the prospective employer. Corporate annual reports include much valuable information about company objectives, types of products produced, and financial results. Smaller companies frequently provide informational brochures and pamphlets about their operations. To increase the likelihood of successful employment interviews, these guidelines are useful.

■ Dress for the occasion. Clean clothing, shined shoes, and a well-groomed appearance are the hallmarks of appropriate dress.

■ Arrive promptly. Plan ahead and anticipate possible traffic congestion or the need to locate parking facilities.

■ Practice good body posture. Do not slouch in the chair or nervously rub your hands together.

■ Act enthusiastic about the job opportunity. Remember, interviewers look for applicants who are excited about the possibility of working at their firms.

■ Sell yourself. Do not be afraid to mention strong points or to stress your qualifications for the job.

REMEMBER TO COMMUNICATE

CEOs as Role Models

Chief Executive Officers (CEOs) are role models for the behaviors and practices of managers and employees throughout organizations. If CEOs demonstrate effective communication skills and emphasize the importance of communication, potential problems are identified more readily, and employee concerns are resolved more expediently. The role of internal communication is a key factor in determining corporate success in the 1990s. "Internal communication—talk back and forth within the organization, up and down the hierarchy—may well be more important to a company's success than external communications." [Rice, "Champions of Communication," p. 111]

Some corporate executives are not especially adept at the practice of effective communication. However, several CEOs exemplify how communication skills can be used to train, solicit feedback, and improve bottom-line results.

- Bob Crawford, CEO of Brook Furniture Rental, stresses the development of an open-communication environment. He personally leads many training sessions and elicits employee ideas to improve operations.

- J. Stark Thompson, CEO of Life Technologies, strives to convey a "graphic picture or image" of tailoring communication to specific employee groups.

- Mike Walsh, CEO of Union Pacific Railroad, emphasizes increased training for lower-level managers and ties part of their compensation to improved communication with subordinates.

- Sam Walton, founder of Wal-Mart stores (now deceased), wanted his personnel trained to be merchants who know profit and expense data so their departments can be run as if they were personal businesses.

- James Orr, CEO of UNUM Corporation, implements week-long training programs, which include the topic of communication. He personally spends a minimum of one day a week at each program.

In an era of big banking and bank mergers, small banks can thrive and compete, partly because they recognize the necessity to communicate with customers. Likable bank personnel and personalized service are two reasons for the success of fly-in (by airplane) banking at the First State Bank in Rio Vista, Texas, a community of 546 people. By using newspaper ads to attack the impersonality of larger competitors, Bank of A. Levy in California attracted some 400 customers, who represented more than $10 million in deposits, away from the big banks.

ADAPTED FROM: Michael Allen and Peter Pae, "Despite the Mergers of Many Big Banks, Tiny Ones May Thrive," *The Wall Street Journal* (October 9, 1991), pp. A1, A6; John Huey, "America's Most Successful Merchant," *Fortune* (September 23, 1991), p. 54; Faye Rice, "Champions of Communication," *Fortune* (June 3, 1991), pp. 111–12, 116, 120.

- Thank the interviewer. Always express appreciation for the interviewer's time. Also, it is appropriate to mail a brief note of thanks.

Interviewers must avoid illegal questions.

In preemployment interviews, questions that illegally discriminate among job candidates cannot be asked. It is necessary for employers to comply with EEO legislation and to assure equal opportunity to all applicants, regardless of race, color, religion, sex, age, or national origin. Figure 7–4 presents some examples of inappropriate preemployment inquiries.

SOURCE: Excerpted from "A Guide for Preemployment Interviewing," prepared by the Kansas Division of Personnel Services. The chart was compiled by Clifford Coen, University of Tennessee, and was originally published in the December 1976 Newsletter of the American Association for Affirmative Action (revised).

1.	Ancestry or national origin	Inquiries into applicant's lineage, national origin, descent, birthplace, or native language. National origin of applicant's parents or spouse.
2.	Religion	Applicant's religious denomination or affiliation, church, parish, pastor, or religious holidays observed.
3.	Citizenship	"Of what country are you a citizen?" Whether applicant or parents or spouse are naturalized or native-born U.S. citizens. Date when applicant or parents or spouse acquired U.S. citizenship.
4.	Education	Any inquiry specifically about the nationality, racial, or religious affiliation of a school. Inquiry as to how foreign-language ability was acquired.
5.	Conviction, arrest, and court record	Any inquiry related to arrests. Asking or checking into a person's arrest, court, or conviction record if not substantially related to functions and responsibilities of the particular job in question.
6.	Military record	Type of discharge.
7.	Race and color	Applicant's race. Color of applicant's skin, eyes, hair, etc., or questions directly or indirectly indicating race or color.

CONSIDER THIS

1. What is the most common mistake that job applicants make during preemployment interviews?

2. How can managers prepare themselves to interview prospective employees?

3. Why should managers be knowledgeable about recruitment practices?

ASSESSMENT CENTERS   The comprehensive evaluation of prospective employees and of current employees being considered for promotion or career-development programs characterizes an **assessment center.** The techniques available at an assessment center can include "personal interviews, management games, leaderless group discussions, individual presentations, mock interviews, . . . and personality and interest inventories."[30] Trained assessors and managerial personnel observe performances and prepare evaluations. Even though these techniques can be time-consuming and costly, assessment centers are a valuable screening tool. Compared to other employee-selection methods, research studies indicate that the techniques employed at these centers can quite accurately predict job performance.[31]

THE ROLE OF TRAINING

Training is a key to competitiveness in the marketplace.

Training involves acquiring the knowledge, skills, and abilities needed to do job tasks. In a competitive marketplace that emphasizes increasing quality and reducing costs, training has grown in importance. As a field, it attained prominence soon after World War II. By the 1970s, training directors became more common and began to report to upper-level management. During the late

Many corporations are involved with "adopt-a-school" programs. Corporate participation demonstrates an active concern for and support of students who will become employees of the future.

1980s, the public costs of programs to provide worker training comprised at least one percent of the Gross Domestic Product in West Germany and in Sweden but only 0.3 percent of the GDP in the United States.[32] By the 1990s, U.S. organizations with at least 100 employees were spending $45.5 billion per year to provide formal training for 39.5 million persons.[33] Business schools have experienced an increase in the demand for custom-tailored management-training courses.

The business community has expressed concern about the educational capabilities of workers. In a survey of 4200 employers in the state of Washington, almost one-third were dissatisfied with basic and technical skills. Nearly 40 percent considered communication skills and general knowledge of workers to be less than desirable.[34] From preschool to graduate school, the corporate support of education appears to be increasing. According to a *Fortune* survey of 500 industrial and 500 service firms, almost one-quarter has donated $1 million or more to education; 83 percent of all top managers actively participate in educational reform.[35]

Businesses spend vast sums on training.

For businesses to be productive and competitive, capable personnel and the ability to adapt to changing circumstances are essential. Firms will increasingly be challenged to be quality conscious and to adopt innovative work practices. Let's consider employee responsibilities at Corning's Blacksburg, Virginia, plant.

The educational capabilities of workers may not meet business expectations.

> Employees put in a demanding 12 ½-hour shift, alternating three-day and four-day weeks. They make managerial decisions, impose discipline on fellow workers, and must learn three skill "modules"—or families of job skills— within two years or lose their jobs. This is far different from the traditional U.S. manufacturing plant, where workers are placed in narrow jobs, must follow orders blindly, and are protected by union work rules.[36]

Who gets trained? According to a survey of firms with 50 or more employees, executives, professionals, and middle managers average over 40 hours of training each year. Conversely, administrative personnel and office/clerical workers average 22 or fewer hours of annual training.[37] The Commission on the Skills of the American Workforce has estimated that funds spent on blue-collar training may be as little as 10 percent of the training expenses provided by businesses.[38] In the future, personnel at all levels of the organization will receive more training. Given the inevitable technological advancements and greater pressures to achieve objectives, employees will be retrained more frequently.

As business becomes more globalized, greater interactions will occur among personnel trained in various parts of the world. Even though they possess similar technical skills, many workers will have considerably different cultural backgrounds. For example, Japan's Omron Corporation, a manufacturer of parts used in automation systems, employs Chinese software engineers in Shanghai who are not familiar with Western economic principles. Although they have adequate job skills, these engineers do not necessarily understand the need to consider market-related factors—an essential concern for selling products in Western countries.[39] Workers who design products and those who market them can be trained to recognize the importance of producing and distributing products that include features demanded by customers.

Awareness of diverse backgrounds and experiences is essential to successful training outcomes.[40] Employers who overlook cultural beliefs, customs, and expectations are likely to experience misunderstandings that may lead to difficulties in the international business arena. Compared to the United States, cultural ambiguity is the norm in the Middle East, Asia, and Latin America. It is important to avoid negative criticism of other cultures and not to prejudge unfamiliar instructional practices. For example, there is a great contrast between classroom instruction in Japan and in America. Japanese learners are accustomed to the lecture approach and, unlike Americans, may initially be somewhat hesitant to actively participate in training activities that emphasize lively discussion and exchange of dialogue between instructors and trainers.

A successful trainer recognizes that people learn at different rates of speed and in different ways. Patience, planning, and common sense are keys to training international employees. Consistency and self-discipline are needed to learn a foreign language. Efforts to become familiar with the history, geography, and politics of a nation or region are worthwhile and also indicate sincerity to new acquaintances in host countries. Few, if any, people who receive their first international assignment are completely prepared for the experience. However, several strategies increase the likelihood of meeting the challenge and can also be useful when training personnel who originate from other countries.

- As a minimum prerequisite, try to learn a few simple phrases in the host country's language: hello, goodbye, thank you, and good luck.

- Maintain a sense of humor. Language confusion is likely to occur, but do not let it devastate personal or business relationships.

- Recognize the prevailing ways of doing business. Americans strive to complete transactions as soon as possible, but extended negotiations, often accompanied by delays, are commonplace in many cultures.

- Caution against using confusing jargon, such as "What's up?" "Has she taken off?" Although they would probably be understood in the United States, such questions are not easily comprehended by persons who are unfamiliar with the English language.

Technological advancements will make retraining mandatory.

Successful trainers recognize differences among learners.

■ Speak slowly and distinctly. Many Americans talk too rapidly and run their words together, thereby causing miscommunication even in conversations among persons who are fluent in English.

Figure 7–5 lists several benefits of training. Training can reduce time and costs to make a company more productive; training can also increase job satisfaction and encourage positive attitudes toward jobs. Trainees have dissimilar personalities, are motivated differently, and learn at varying rates. For example, some trainees may quickly grasp technical skills but be slower to learn more abstract concepts.

Trainers have varied backgrounds and experiences. They may be human-resource professionals, managers, nonmanagerial employees, or outside consultants. Figure 7–6 summarizes the advantages and disadvantages of using various types of trainers. In general, differences involve costs, extent of familiarity with a firm, and amount of up-to-date knowledge possessed. Trainers are the key factor in the success of training efforts. Therefore, they must know subject-matter content and instructional methodologies.

RECOGNIZING TRAINING NEEDS

Competition for resources can have a negative impact on the amount of funds that an organization allocates to training. Consequently, identifying training needs and meeting them in a timely fashion are essential concerns. Let's examine several ways in which training needs can be recognized.[41]

■ *Worker Suggestions* A common technique is to ask workers for suggestions. Although their opinions are too frequently overlooked, the people who actually do the jobs are a valuable source of information about how job performances can be improved. Questionnaires or personal interviews can be used to collect desired information.

Why train?

Who does the training?

■ **FIGURE 7–5** Benefits of Training

Training . . .
- Promotes awareness of the important relationship between continuous quality improvement and organizational success.
- Demonstrates how productivity gains translate into better customer service, lower costs, and higher profits.
- Empowers employees to become involved in product or service quality and promotes job satisfaction.
- Clarifies company goals and employee job expectations, thereby encouraging positive attitudes and higher morale among employees.
- Alleviates the likelihood of problematic rework caused by miscommunication and human error.
- Enhances the skills and competencies of employees so that they can develop professionally and earn promotions to positions of greater responsibility.
- Minimizes injuries due to job-related accidents.
- Reduces the amount of time needed to complete job duties.

TYPE OF TRAINER	ADVANTAGES	DISADVANTAGES
Human-resource professional	Knows organization and its unique problems	May be too close to the organization and its members
	Knows participants and can use existing relationships with them	May have more pressing responsibilities
	Often has state-of-the-art knowledge	May not be objective about problems
	Committed to solving the organization's problems	
	Requires low out-of-pocket costs	
Manager	Committed to solving the organization's problems	May be ineffective as a trainer
	Requires low out-of-pocket costs	May lack state-of-the-art knowledge
	Has good knowledge of the organization and its employees	May have more pressing responsibilities
		May not be objective about problems
Nonmanagerial employee	Has good knowledge of the organization	May lack detailed knowledge of problems
	May have good relationships with trainees	May lack experience as a trainer
		May have more pressing responsibilities
Outside consultant	Has specialized knowledge	Lacks knowledge of organization
	Knows state-of-the-art techniques and information	May rely on packaged programs rather than tailoring programs to organizational needs
	May be more objective about organizational situation	Calls for higher out-of-pocket costs

SOURCE: Judith R. Gordon, *Human Resource Management* (Boston, Allyn & Bacon, 1986), p. 272. Copyright © 1986 by Allyn & Bacon. Used with permission of the publisher.

■ *Quality of Output* Production records include information regarding product defects, shipment delays, and personal-injury accidents. By examining finished products and listening to customer comments, many valuable insights about product quality can be learned.

■ *Job-Related Examinations* In some professions, such as real estate sales or nursing, an examination must be successfully passed to hold a position. Additional continuing education is commonly required to assure that professionals update their job skills. In some industries (nuclear power, airline, or railroad), government agencies and company policies mandate periodic competency examinations for certain jobs. Regardless of the profession, summary statistics frequently reveal areas where additional training is necessary.

■ *Performance Appraisals* Evaluation of employee job performance identifies strengths and weaknesses. During appraisal interviews, managers have

A PERSPECTIVE ON QUALITY

Successful Diversity Training

More and more firms are becoming aware of the importance of diversity training. Prudential, Avon, and Hewlett-Packard are examples of major employers that have implemented successful programs. At Prudential, all middle- and upper-level managers complete two days of diversity training. Avon sponsors a Managing Diversity Program for all employees, regardless of their position in the company. Hewlett-Packard uses training modules and prepares executive overviews, which are a part of the orientation program for new employees.

Several considerations enhance the likelihood of providing successful diversity training. Taking advantage of a diverse work force prepares a company to use human resources to their fullest potential and supports the concept of providing quality goods and services to customers. Several suggestions are useful.

- Solicit top-management support for diversity awareness. Such commitment is critical to success because it establishes the importance of diversity and provides a sense of direction.
- Strive to recognize the needs of workers. For example, job sharing, flex-time scheduling, or day-care facilities might be especially valued by female employees. What is perceived as a minority issue might really be a gender or lifestyle issue.
- Seek continuous improvement of communication to assure that all employees know how success will be appraised.
- Institute a mentoring program to help acquaint personnel with the company culture and organizational expectations.
- Encourage managers to value workplace diversity. A key strategy is to reward, through recognition, those who attain diversity objectives.
- Educate personnel to be aware of the benefits to be gained from a diverse workplace.

ADAPTED FROM: Shari Caudron, "Training Can Damage Diversity Efforts," *Personnel Journal* **72** (April 1993): 54–61; Benson Rosen and Kay Lovelace, "Fitting Square Pegs into Round Holes," *HR Magazine* **39** (January 1994): 86–93.

opportunities to ask subordinates how training might increase their effectiveness.

Training includes many topics.

What types of training do businesses emphasize? According to a *Fortune* survey, new employee orientation is the most common type of training.[42] Other major training programs cover such topics as performance appraisal, leadership, interpersonal skills, and the operation of new equipment. Less than one-third of the survey respondents provide training related to creativity, purchasing, reading skills, or foreign language. Numerous employers do recognize a need for training to improve the health and welfare of their human resources. Over 39 percent of those surveyed offer training sessions in smoking cessation, substance abuse, and stress management.

More and more businesses are recognizing the value of diversity in the workplace. Diversity implies that all employees have opportunities to develop professionally and to maximize their contributions to employers. Although sometimes viewed as race or gender issues, diversity is broader in scope and

Greater diversity characterizes the workplace.

encompasses many types of personal differences, including age, sexual orientation, physical or mental disabilities, social status, and religious preference. Diversity training serves to alleviate many fears, stereotypes, and prejudices and to increase the ability of all personnel to become more effective and valued human resources. The goal of diversity training is to create an environment in which differences are recognized, so that knowledge and capabilities can be used to advance a firm's interests. Successful diversity training requires organizational commitment and the use of skilled trainers who can address employee concerns without creating a divisive workplace environment.

 # TRAINING METHODS

Selection of a training method or combination of methods merits careful consideration.

> To train successfully, it is essential to plan and organize, assure trainer competency, and provide availability of appropriate instructional materials, aids, and facilities. . . . Since interests and motivations are not alike, trainees differ in their responsiveness to various methods."[43]

Lecture methods and videotapes are widely used in training sessions.

A variety of training methods are available. Over the years, the lecture method has been employed quite extensively; however, videotapes are increasingly used in training sessions. Based on a survey of firms with 100 or more employees sponsored by *Training* magazine, the most highly used methods of training were videotapes, lectures, one-on-one instruction slides, and role plays.[44] Over 80 percent of the companies surveyed use videotapes and lectures. Few respondents use video conferencing, teleconferencing, or computer conferencing. Let's examine several popular training methods.

■ *On-the-Job Training*

On-the-job training includes job instruction training (JIT), job rotation, and special assignments. It actively involves learners, accommodates differences in learning abilities, applies directly to job duties, and rates quite low in terms of costs.[45] On-the-job training does necessitate interrupting normal work duties and does consume instructional time.

JIT includes four steps.

JOB INSTRUCTION TRAINING (JIT)   As shown in Figure 7–7, **job instruction training** features a characteristic four-step approach. This method is designed to train learners who have little, if any, familiarity with the duties performed on a specific job. Job instruction training is especially useful when trainees must be taught how to perform repetitive job tasks.

The JIT process is composed of four steps.

1. Anxieties are alleviated, and learners are encouraged to have positive attitudes toward training.

2. Step-by-step instruction is presented, with an emphasis on telling, showing, illustrating, and questioning.

3. Learners are given the opportunity to perform the job tasks under a trainer's supervision.

FIGURE 7–7 Job Instruction Training (JIT)

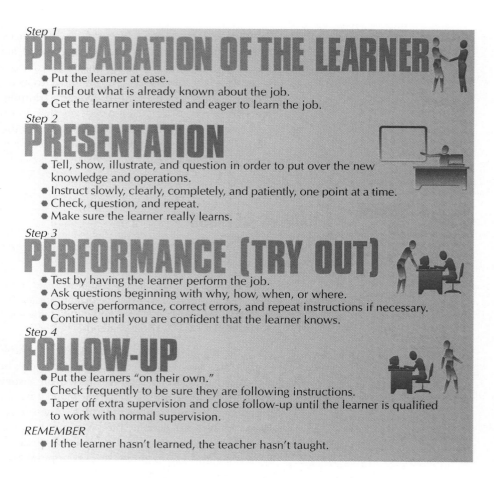

Step 1
PREPARATION OF THE LEARNER
- Put the learner at ease.
- Find out what is already known about the job.
- Get the learner interested and eager to learn the job.

Step 2
PRESENTATION
- Tell, show, illustrate, and question in order to put over the new knowledge and operations.
- Instruct slowly, clearly, completely, and patiently, one point at a time.
- Check, question, and repeat.
- Make sure the learner really learns.

Step 3
PERFORMANCE (TRY OUT)
- Test by having the learner perform the job.
- Ask questions beginning with why, how, when, or where.
- Observe performance, correct errors, and repeat instructions if necessary.
- Continue until you are confident that the learner knows.

Step 4
FOLLOW-UP
- Put the learners "on their own."
- Check frequently to be sure they are following instructions.
- Taper off extra supervision and close follow-up until the learner is qualified to work with normal supervision.

REMEMBER
- If the learner hasn't learned, the teacher hasn't taught.

4. During the follow-up step, learners are "put on their own," and direct supervision is gradually reduced.

JOB ROTATION Moving learners among a series of jobs is called **job rotation.** This method provides trainees with firsthand experiences at operating various types of equipment or understanding how different units of a firm operate. Over time, a new management trainee might be assigned to the manufacturing, marketing, or finance departments to learn how each unit functions and to better understand the relationships among them. Knowledge gained—not just the amount of time spent at a position—is the key consideration in job rotation. It is an excellent method for crosstraining learners to do several kinds of jobs. When employees can perform various jobs, managers have more flexibility in making job assignments, and trained personnel are available for possible job replacements.

Knowledge gained is the key factor in job rotation.

Job rotation is a major method of management development used by Japanese companies. A wide variety of experiences provides valuable managerial insights and prepares personnel to assume future managerial responsibilities. American managers and blue-collar employees who work in Japanese firms are viewed differently. Compared to U.S. employers, Japanese employers are more willing to provide blue-collar employees with job-rotation training because they are considered by the Japanese to be more loyal and less likely to quit their jobs.[46]

SPECIAL ASSIGNMENTS When the **special assignment method** of on-the-job training is employed, learners are assigned nonroutine work responsibilities to gain experience and develop job/career skills. For example, a subordinate who demonstrates managerial potential might be asked to prepare a report on how productivity and quality can be improved. When trainees do not control their own work flow, such as on assembly lines, special assignments are not feasible.

The interests and abilities of trainees should not be overlooked when making assignments.[47] Employees who have difficulty completing their regular job duties are not likely candidates for special assignments. Also, managers should not use this method to assign tasks they dislike to others. If managers are accessible, provide guidance, and readily respond to questions, special assignments can be enriching learning experiences for trainees.

■ Off-the-Job Training

Many times, training occurs away from the job site or work station. **Off-the job training** includes lectures, case studies, role playing, an audiovisual techniques. These methods may be combined to increase the effectiveness of a training program. For example, a question-answer or discussion format can be easily integrated into a lecture. Role playing actively involves learners who might be videotaped for future review and critique.

Lectures tend not to actively involve learners.

THE LECTURE METHOD Knowledgeable trainers who are able to clarify and explain content material are the keys to the successful implementation of the **lecture method,** which emphasizes spoken presentations. In practice, lectures are often supplemented with videotapes, overhead transparencies, or handout materials. The lecture method is relatively inexpensive and can be used to train a large number of persons at the same time. However, this method does not accommodate individual learning abilities and relies extensively on the comprehension of verbal messages.

Preparation is the key to successful training via the lecture method.

Excellent lecturers prepare thoroughly. They read relevant materials, outline the content of lectures, prepare supplemental handouts when appropriate, and review carefully before making presentations. There is no substitute for preparation if the lecture method is to be employed successfully. The effectiveness of lectures is increased if trainers speak clearly, summarize periodically, and provide opportunities for learner participation. If trainees ask questions, exchange perspectives, and discuss the implications of material presented in lectures, the training is likely to be more beneficial to them.

CASE STUDY METHOD Many college students are familiar with the **case-study method,** whereby trainees are given information that describes certain decision-making circumstances and asked to recommend solutions. This method encourages learners to develop problem-solving skills and is often used as a group exercise to encourage teamwork. In practice, trainees are asked to present written and/or oral reports summarizing their analyses of case data. Consequently, presenting case studies also helps trainees to improve their written and verbal communication skills. When confronted with real-world events, however, critics claim that learners will not necessarily take the same courses of action that they practiced in their case-study exercises.

ROLE PLAYING Acting out roles for various types of decision-making circumstances illustrates **role playing.** Trainees who role-play gain experience handling events similar to those encountered by managers. For instance, a trainee might be assigned the role of a manager who must terminate a subordinate or discipline an employee for a major violation of company rules. If the exercise is videotaped, participants and trainers can view how the managerial role was performed and possibly recommend suggestions for improvement or behaviors to avoid.

If role playing is to be successful, the trainer must give clear instructions, strive to achieve a realistic setting, and provide worthwhile feedback to learners. Role playing is a flexible technique that is adaptable to practically any workplace event, including interviewing job candidates, handling difficult employees, or appraising job performances. Sufficient time should be set aside for instructors, participants, and observers to critique the exercises. Much learning can occur through such evaluative discussions. Trainees can exchange views and gain insights from both positive and negative comments about their role playing.

Role playing actively involves learners.

AUDIOVISUAL (AV) TRAINING Audiovisual (AV) **training,** which involves the use of videotapes, slides, and audio cassettes is being employed more and more

AV methods add variety to training.

A PERSPECTIVE ON QUALITY

Training as a Quality-Improvement Strategy

The need to train personnel and update job skills will continue to accelerate during the 1990s. The late W. Edwards Deming, a renowned quality expert, stressed the importance of training as a quality-improvement strategy. However, the American Society for Training and Development estimates that fewer than 10 percent of all employees are given formal training by employers. Progressive firms use training to increase competitiveness, improve quality, and provide job satisfaction.

- At L-S Electro-Galvanizing, winner of a RIT/*USA Today* Quality Cup for small businesses, quality is an essential aspect of integrated process control. All workers take two weeks of training in fundamental statistics and have an opportunities to earn higher salaries by completing more advanced courses. A company goal is to assure versatility by crosstraining all workers.

- With 100 percent quality as a goal, Federal Express has introduced an interactive videodisc system to train 90,000 workers. This approach has saved the company over 80 percent of the cost necessary to provide customary classroom instruction.

- As evidence of poor quality became apparent, the Will-burt Company required employees to acquire geometry skills and improve reading abilities. At first, employee resistance was encountered, but the requirement ultimately led to the creation of an in-house program for awarding an associate degree. The training reduced absenteeism and workers' compensation claims, but the major benefit has been increased employee loyalty to the firm.

ADAPTED FROM: Susan Dentzer, "How to Train Workers for the 21st Century," *U.S. News & World Report* (September 21, 1992), pp. 72–74, 76, 78; Beverly Gerber, "Improving the Quality of White-Collar Work," *Training* 27 (September 1990): 29–34; James Kim, "Employees Call Shots," *USA Today* (April 10, 1992), p. 4B.

extensively by companies to meet their training needs. Some firms prepare their own audiovisual training aids, but most companies use professionally prepared materials. Audiovisual methods add variety to training programs. They can be tailored to meet specific training needs and can be used repetitively. Videotape technology allows trainees to view themselves and receive immediate feedback.

Audiovisual training is often combined with lectures and discussions. For example, a brief lecture might be used to introduce a topic and emphasize important points to remember. After a videotape presentation, discussion serves to clarify misunderstandings, provide additional information, and answer trainee questions.

Audio cassettes have emerged as a training method and are especially useful to convey generalized concepts: how to be a better leader; how to motivate yourself and others; how to develop and maintain a positive attitude. Convenience is a major advantage of audiotapes. Trainees can listen to them while driving to and from work or relaxing at home.

CONSIDER THIS

1. In the next decade, what changes in training methodology are likely to occur?

2. How can managers improve their capabilities as trainers?

3. Who is responsible for company efforts to train personnel?

EVALUATION OF TRAINING

Evaluation is not a precise science.

Evaluation is a relevant component of the training process. Yet much training is not evaluated, largely because evaluation is an after-the-fact occurrence and requires a commitment of time and effort.[48] Many variables affect how well trainees learn, including personal interests and ambitions, preferences for certain instructional methodologies, and individual learning abilities. As a result, evaluation is not a precise science and subtle considerations are not always recognized.

> For example, the "work versus perk" (putting forth energy and effort versus the view that training is perceived as a reward) aspect of training may never be stated by an organization but is part of the decision process for at least some program sponsors and participants.[49]

Why evaluate training?

The purpose of training is to enhance productivity and quality. Managers need to know whether current training methods achieve organizational objectives or if additional programs or modifications to existing ones are necessary. Both formal and informal methods are used to evaluate training programs.[50] Let's examine each of these methods in turn.

■ *Formal Evaluation*

There are pros and cons to using questionnaires.

One formal-evaluation technique—the questionnaire—includes a series of questions that solicit participant reactions to training activities. Generally, participants are asked to complete questionnaires at the close of training sessions. Questionnaires are a very common evaluative tool and do provide immediate feedback. However, they do not really measure the amount of learning that has occurred or indicate if the training will change future job behaviors.[51]

Examinations are another formal-evaluation technique. Some firms may require candidates to attain a certain score to demonstrate their proficiency to perform certain job responsibilities. In some fields, such as insurance or financial planning, examinations must be passed to use professionally recognized designations (for example, Chartered Property and Casualty Underwriter or Certified Financial Planner). As an instrument of evaluation, the examination documents attained levels of proficiency.

Examinations do measure learning.

If relevant job-performance records are kept, the pre- and post-training productivity of individuals or groups can be compared. These comparisons use relevant criteria, including absenteeism, injuries, personnel turnover, product defects, and counts of items produced. Rather than rely on the opinions of trainers and trainees, evaluation is based on actual measurements and serves to document whether training is effective. If training achieves its purposes, this documentation can be cited among the reasons to justify budgetary requests for future training funds.

■ *Observation and Informal Evaluation*

Managers should notice how well employees do their jobs.

Managers have many opportunities to observe the job performances of employees. These observations help to evaluate previous training and provide insights into the need for additional training. Even though the employees in a department may have attended several seminars, an office manager might observe continued inefficiencies in processing invoices or handling billing complaints and determine that further training is needed to remedy these problems.

Persons who participate in training are almost always willing to comment informally about their experiences. Although individuals have different likes and dislikes about training methodologies, a pattern of consistency often emerges in their views toward a specific course, workshop, or seminar. Numerous positive remarks indicate a favorable view toward a training experience. A large number of negative comments may be a signal for managers to ascertain why these views prevail. Informal comments are only one aspect of evaluation. Trainees may find a particular trainer personable and enjoy his or her training session but not benefit from it in terms of actual job-related learning.

THINK ABOUT IT

1. The views that job applicants express at preemployment interviews do not always correspond to their on-the-job behaviors.

2. Job candidates do not have a second opportunity to make a first impression.

3. To prospective employees, completing job-application forms is a first step toward getting a job. From an employer's perspective, this is the first step in screening out candidates.

4. Employees do not learn just because training sessions are enjoyable. Some trainers tell funny jokes, relate interesting "stories," and have pleasing personalities. However, this does not necessarily mean that the trainees are learning job-related skills or behaviors.

5. During difficult economic times, training activities are tempting targets for budget reductions. However, short-term savings may contribute to greater long-term costs.

6. Nothing can be a substitute for demonstrated job-performance excellence. A record of job accomplishments is a valuable personal asset.

7. Position titles do not always accurately describe job duties and responsibilities.

8. There are no perfect jobs or job candidates. All jobs have advantages and disadvantages; all applicants have strengths and weaknesses.

Staffing decisions are critical because employee performance is a major factor in determining whether an organization's objectives are attained. Through training, employees update job skills and acquire new knowledge. Once again, let's review the chapter objectives.

Understand the staffing process.

In addition to determining human-resource needs, the staffing process involves activities related to recruitment, selection, training, and performance appraisal. Based on information provided through job analysis, job descriptions and job specifications are prepared. Job descriptions list the duties and responsibilities of a position; job specifications indicate the human skills needed to do a job. Recruitment practices develop a "pool" of candidates from which to select persons for job vacancies.

Explain the purpose of equal employment opportunity (EEO) legislation.

EEO legislation is designed to prevent unfair discrimination in the staffing process and in the assignment of job duties. Much emphasis was placed on EEO legislation following the Civil Rights Act of 1964, which makes it illegal to base employment decisions on race, color, sex, religion, or national origin. Other EEO laws serve to prevent sex-based compensatory differences for performing equal work duties and unfair discrimination on the basis of age or physical or mental factors.

Differentiate between internal and external recruitment practices.

Through internal recruitment, job vacancies are filled from within the firm. Although information about current employees is readily available, much infighting can occur among potential job candidates. Transfers, promotions, rehires, and job rotation are examples of internal sources of job applicants.

External recruitment seeks to attract applicants from sources outside the firm. Employee referrals, schools and colleges, employment agencies, newspapers, and trade associations illustrate the variety of available sources. Review Figure 7–3, which compares the advantages and disadvantages of internal and external sources of employment.

Identify the techniques used in the selection process.

Application forms, job references, employment testing, and interviews are common components of the selection process. Application forms solicit personal information about applicants and can be kept on file for future reference. Job references are persons who are familiar with applicants and can comment on their qualifications for employment. Employment tests are used to measure applicant suitability for job openings. Interviews are generally face-to-face exchanges of information and provide both applicants and interviewers with opportunities to ask and answer questions about a position.

Discuss the various types of training methods.

On-the-job training includes job instruction training (JIT), job rotation, and special assignments. Job instruction training, which is predominantly used to train people to perform repetitive tasks, involves a four-step approach: preparation, presentation, performance, and follow-up. When job rotation is employed, trainees are moved among jobs to gain a variety of experiences and to better understand company operations. The special-assignment method, which is appropriate only when trainees have some control over the flow of work, uses the performance of nonroutine job responsibilities to train employees and to give them career-enriching experiences.

Lectures, case studies, role playing, and audiovisual (AV) techniques are examples of off-the-job training methods. The success of trainers who employ the lecture method depends on their skillful use of verbal communication and their knowledge of the subject being taught. Case studies present trainees with the opportunity to analyze data and recommend solutions. Role playing gives participants experience in acting out roles comparable to real-world situations. Videotapes, slides, and audio cassettes are examples of audiovisual methods, which are increasingly used to train personnel.

Specify methods to evaluate training activities.

Questionnaires, examinations, and comparisons of job-performance records are formal methods of evaluating the effectiveness of training. By observing employees as they do their jobs, managers can appraise prior training activities and gain insights into possible needs for future training. Also, employees are usually willing to comment informally about their views toward training programs they have attended.

KEY TERMS

adverse impact
affirmative action program (AAP)
assessment center
audiovisual (AV) training
bona fide occupational qualifications (BFOQ)
case-study method
discrimination
disparate impact
disparate treatment

equal employment opportunity (EEO) legislation
glass ceiling
job analysis
job description
job instruction training (JIT)
job rotation
job specification
lecture method
off-the-job training

on-the-job training
prejudice
recruitment
reliability
role playing

selection
special-assignment method
staffing
training
validity

REVIEW AND DISCUSSION QUESTIONS

1. Why is staffing considered to be a key to corporate success?
2. How are a firm's human-resource needs influenced by its strategic plans?
3. Why should job descriptions and job specifications be developed?
4. How do recruitment practices affect selection decisions?
5. What are the advantages and disadvantages of recruiting from internal sources?
6. During preemployment interviews, what types of questions should interviewers avoid asking?
7. For the purpose of employment testing, what is the difference between validity and reliability? Why are these concepts important?
8. Why are assessment centers a recommended method for training managers?
9. What major benefits are derived from training?
10. Why is job instruction training (JIT) a recommended method for training employees to perform jobs that involve repetitive tasks?

CRITICAL THINKING INCIDENT 7.1

Who's Next?

For the past three years, Wilma Roush has managed the St. Louis district for Haywards, the largest family-style restaurant chain in the Midwest. Previously, she was a hotel manager for Seabrook Inns, a group of hotels located on the East Coast. Wilma liked the hotel industry but accepted the job at Haywards because it permitted her to live closer to her family.

At Haywards, Wilma has been quite successful. Her proposal to offer a low-budget menu for cost-conscious customers was adopted and has successfully increased sales revenue. In addition to receiving several large bonuses, Wilma was honored as "District Manager of the Year" two years ago.

One day, Stan Willis, the regional manager and Wilma's boss, returned from lunch and received a phone call. The caller was Omar Lopez, the executive vice president of a major competitor. He indicated that Wilma was a finalist for a regional manager's position in the Kansas-Missouri area and wanted to ask questions about her work record. Surprised, Stan paused and said, "Well, Wilma has done a fine job for us, and I really hope you do not hire her." Shortly thereafter, the conversation ended, but Stan still could not concentrate on doing his own work.

Stan thinks to himself, "Wilma's done a super job—resolved problems, motivated people, and increased sales—but we've rewarded her for these efforts. In fact, Wilma may be our highest-paid district manager, and she has only been with us for three years." Furthermore, Stan is concerned because Wilma has never discussed being dissatisfied with her job at Haywards or even mentioned the possibility of applying for other positions.

"Should I call Wilma to find out why she applied for that job?" Stan asks himself, but he concludes that she might consider such an action inappropriate. Yet if something has upset Wilma, Stan wants to know about it. Also, he contemplates whether she should be given another raise to encourage her to remain with Haywards.

Wilma is not displeased with Stan. They share similar managerial philosophies, and she appreciates the encouragement he has given her. After learning of the job opening, Wilma made a spur-of-the-moment decision to apply because it offered a faster track to top management than was available at Haywards. She did not expect to be considered seriously as a candidate and did not believe the prospective employer would be making inquiries about her.

If Wilma leaves, Stan will be faced with finding a replacement for her. He does not know whether he would promote one of his own restaurant managers or look for a promising candidate outside the organization. Nevertheless, Stan knows it will be difficult to find a person who possesses Wilma's enthusiasm and ability to work with people. He thinks to himself, "If she leaves, who's next?"

Discussion Questions

1. How should Stan have responded to Omar's inquiry?
2. What, if anything, should Stan say to Wilma about receiving the call from Omar?
3. In addition to the career-advancement opportunity, what factors should Wilma consider if Omar makes her a job offer?
4. Assuming that Wilma does leave Haywards, how should Stan go about recruiting her replacement?

 # CRITICAL THINKING INCIDENT 7.2

Greater Expectations

Judy Grimes has worked as a secretary to Don Burris, the personnel manager at IBC Communications, for the past seven years. Her duties include typing letters, memos, and reports. In addition, she performs a variety of tasks, such as filing correspondence, processing employment applications, and initially screening most job applicants. A year ago, the department's receptionist and a part-time secretary were victims of a personnel reduction caused by adverse economic conditions. Since then, Judy has assumed the responsibility for the work formerly done by these two persons as well.

Recently, IBC installed a new company-wide computer system. Management then announced that all work, including internal communication among offices, was now to be processed by computer. Although she is an excellent typist, Judy is not accustomed to working with computers. However, she is a willing learner who realizes it is necessary to become well-versed in understanding this technology.

Don, Judy's boss, is impressed with her ability to organize tasks, handle a heavy workload, meet deadlines, and cooperate with others. He believes she is capable of filling an office-manager position, which is expected to become available within the next year because of a merger between IBC and a smaller competitor. Even though he wants Judy to remain in her current position, Don believes she has the talent for career advancement.

Don wants Judy to have additional training, especially experiences that will assist her professional growth. Because of Judy's increased job responsibilities, the new computer system, and changes caused by the merger, it is unlikely that excess time will be available for formal training activities. Don understands the organizational pressures to keep expenses down and be competitive; however, he is thinking about asking his boss for permission to hire a part-time employee to assist Judy.

Judy likes her job, believes she has an excellent boss, and feels fortunate to be employed. Yet she is concerned about her future and the possibilities of being promoted. She thinks to herself, "Over the years, I've done good work. Maybe I should expect greater rewards in terms of pay and advancement."

Discussion Questions

1. What type of training is recommended for Judy?
2. How could the special-assignment method be used to train Judy?
3. Should Judy be considered as a potential candidate for the office-manager position? Explain your response.
4. If approval is granted to hire a part-time employee, what duties should be stated in the job description for the position?

CRITICAL THINKING INCIDENT 7.3

We've Got a Problem

Four years ago, Helen Seymour invested her life savings and founded Beauty Cosmetics. Subsequently, the firm has prospered and evolved into a regionally recognized producer and distributor of cosmetics. Products are sold on the "party plan" through a network of beauty consultants, each of whom is trained by the person who brought him or her aboard. Originally, this approach worked because the organization was small and managers could follow-up to see that newcomers were trained properly. However, prosperity has created difficulties.

During the past two years, the number of customer complaints has increased significantly. Dissatisfaction relates to misinformation about products, use of "hard-sell" sales techniques, and failure to explain how products are to be used. Helen believes that most of these problems can be attributed to inadequate training, and she realizes a need to take action before the reputation of Beauty Cosmetics is damaged. Consequently, she plans to revise and simplify the consultant's training manual, which is given to each person who affiliates with the company. To assure familiarity with products and understanding of sales techniques, she is also considering development of a product/sales "training skills checklist" that must be signed by each recruiter and newly hired consultant before the newcomer can represent Beauty Cosmetics. Helen wonders if there are training options that she might be overlooking and thinks to herself, "We've got a problem."

Discussion Questions

1. How effective is the existing approach to training at Beauty Cosmetics?

2. What training options could Helen be overlooking?

3. Will a simplified consultant's training manual and the proposed "training skills checklist" remedy difficulties with customers? Explain your answer.

4. How can recruiters of new consultants become better trainers?

5. What is the most important training priority at Beauty Cosmetics?

SOURCE: Donald S. Miller and Stephen E. Catt, *Human Relations: A Contemporary Approach* (Homewood, IL: Richard D. Irwin, 1989), pp. 334–35.

NOTES

1. Janice C. Simpson, "A Shallow Labor Pool Spurs Businesses to Act to Bolster Education," *The Wall Street Journal* (September 28, 1987), p. 1.

2. Jennifer J. Laabs, "The Global Talent Search," *Personnel Journal* **70** (August 1991): 40.

3. Terry L. Leap and Michael D. Crino, *Personnel/Human Resource Management* (New York: Macmillan, 1989), pp. 70–71.

4. Randall S. Schuler and Vandra L. Huber, *Personnel and Human Resource Management*, 4th ed. (St. Paul, MN: West Publishing Company, 1990), pp. 146–48.

5. Sydney P. Freedberg, "Forced Exits? Companies Confront Wave of Age-Discrimination Suits," *The Wall Street Journal* (October 13, 1987), p. 33.

6. "Why Drive on Job Bias Is Still Going Strong," *U.S. News & World Report* (June 17, 1985), p. 68.

7. "The Glass Ceiling," *HR Magazine* **36** (October 1991): 91.

8. Ibid., p. 92.

9. Tom Lester, "A Woman's Place," *Management Today* (April 1993): 48.

10. David J. Cherrington, *The Management of Human Resources*, 3d ed. (Boston: Allyn & Bacon, 1991), p. 204.

11. Schuler and Huber, *Personnel and Human Resource Management*, pp. 111–14.

12. John M. Ivancevich and William F. Glueck, *Foundations of Personnel Human Resource Management*, 4th ed. (Homewood, IL: BPI/Irwin, 1989), p. 101.

13. Stephen P. Robbins, *Management,* 3d ed. (Englewood Cliffs, NJ: Prentice-Hall, 1991), pp. 355–57.

14. Schuler and Huber, *Personnel and Human Resource Management,* pp. 74–75.

15. Bob Filipczak, "Working for the Japanese," *Training* **29** (December 1992): 25.

16. Michael A. Hitt, R. Dennis Middlemist, and Robert L. Mathis, *Management: Concepts and Effective Practice,* 3d ed. (St. Paul, MN: West, 1989), p. 280.

17. Andrew Bargerstock, "Low-cost Recruiting for Quality," *HR Magazine* **35** (August 1990): 68.

18. "Perspectives," *Personnel Journal* **69** (August 1990): 12.

19. Floris A. Maljers, "Inside Unilever: The Evolving Transnational Company," *Harvard Business Review* **70** (September/October 1992): 49.

20. Randall S. Schuler, *Managing Human Resources,* 4th ed. (St. Paul, MN: West Publishing Company, 1989), pp. 148–51.

21. Ibid., pp. 153–56.

22. Schuler and Huber, *Personnel and Human Resource Management,* p. 122.

23. Julie Stacey, "Behind the Job Search," *USA Today* (November 1, 1990), p. 1B.

24. Alison L. Sprout, "America's Most Admired Corporations," *Fortune* (February 11, 1991), p. 57.

25. Tom Peters, *Thriving on Chaos* (New York: Perennial Library/Harper & Row, 1987), pp. 380–81.

26. Donald P. Crane, *Personnel,* 4th ed. (Boston: Kent, 1986), p. 205.

27. Larry Stevens, "Automating the Selection Process," *Personnel Journal* **70** (November 1991): 59.

28. Julia Lawlor, "Scanning Resumes: The Impersonal Touch," *USA Today* (October 3, 1991), p. 7B.

29. Stephen E. Catt and Donald S. Miller, *Supervision: Working with People,* 2d ed. (Homewood, IL: Richard D. Irwin, 1991), p. 345.

30. Crane, *Personnel,* p. 213.

31. Ramon J. Aldag and Timothy M. Stearns, *Management,* 2d ed. (Cincinnati: South-Western, 1991), p. 313.

32. Nancy J. Perry, "The Workers of the Future," *Fortune* (1991/The New American Century), p. 72.

33. Chris Lee, "Industry Report, 1990," *Training* **27** (October 1990): 30.

34. "More Signs of Skills Shortage," *Training* **28** (July 1991): 14, 16.

35. Joel Keehn, "How Business Helps the Schools," *Fortune* (October 21, 1991), p. 161.

36. "Sharpening Minds for a Competitive Edge," *Business Week* (December 17, 1990), p. 74.

37. "Who Gets Training?" *The Wall Street Journal* (July 17, 1987), p. 19.

38. John Hoerr, "With Job Training, a Little Dab Won't Do Ya," *Business Week* (September 24, 1990), p. 95.

39. Ford S. Worthy, "Tapping Asia's Brainpower," *Fortune* (October 7, 1991), p. 165.

40. Michael J. Marquart and Dean W. Engel, "HRD Competencies for a Shrinking World," *Training & Development* **47** (May 1993): 59–60, 62.

41. Donald S. Miller and Stephen E. Catt, *Human Relations: A Contemporary Approach* (Homewood, IL: Richard D. Irwin, 1989), p. 348.

42. Jack Gordon, "Where the Training Goes," *Training* **27** (October 1990): 61.

43. Miller and Catt, *Human Relations,* p. 319.

44. Gordon, "Where the Training Goes," p. 54.

45. Judith R. Gordon, *Human Resource Management* (Boston: Allyn & Bacon, 1986), p. 274.

46. Filipczak, "Working for the Japanese," p. 28.

47. Miller and Catt, *Human Relations,* p. 323.

48. David J. Cherrington, *The Management of Human Resources,* p. 372.

49. Glenn M. McEvoy and Paul F. Buller, "Five Uneasy Pieces in the Training Evaluation Puzzle," *Training and Development Journal* **44** (August 1990): 42.

50. Miller and Catt, *Human Relations,* pp. 329–31.

51. Judith R. Gordon, *Human Resource Management,* p. 284.

SUGGESTED READINGS

Armstrong, Larry, and others. "The Learning Revolution." *Business Week* (February 28, 1994), pp. 80–86, 88.

Broadwell, Martin M. "Seven Steps to Building Better Training." *Training* **30** (October 1993): 75–81.

Caudron, Shari. "Teamwork Takes Work." *Personnel Journal* **73** (February 1994): 41–46, 48.

Fierman, Jaclyn. "The Contingency Work Force." *Fortune* (January 24, 1994), pp. 30–34, 36.

Fitzgerald, William K., and Scott Allen. "Personal Empowerment: Key to Manager's Development." *HR Magazine* **38** (November 1993): 84–86, 89.

Lierman, Bruce. "How to Develop a Training Simulation." *Training and Development* **48** (February 1994): 50–52.

Nowack, Kenneth M. "360-Degree Feedback: The Whole Story." *Training and Development* **47** (January 1993): 69–72.

Overman, Stephanie. "Hiring Bakers by the Dozens." *HR Magazine* 39 (February 1994): 55–56, 58.

Soloman, Charlene Marmer. "Staff Selection Impacts a Global Success." *Personnel Journal* 73 (January 1994): 88, 91, 94, 97, 99, 100–101.

Ulrich, Dave. "A New HR Mission: Guiding the Quality Mindset." *HR Magazine* 38 (December 1993): 51–54.

CHAPTER **8**

LEADING

■ LEARNING OBJECTIVES

Organizations require effective leadership to survive and prosper. Under the guidance of capable leaders, the potential of human resources is developed. As a matter of fact, history contains many instances in which new leadership in an organization has inspired an existing work force to excel. However, leadership is a complex skill that requires careful study to be understood and practiced effectively. The learning objectives for this chapter are to:

- Define leadership.
- Explain the trait approach to leadership.
- Identify and describe key theories of the behavioral approach to leadership.
- Identify and describe important theories associated with the situational approach to leadership.
- Describe a self-managing work team.

■ CHAPTER OUTLINE

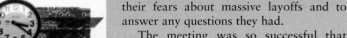

Any executive who likes to mix business with pleasure has to envy Roger Penske. An auto-racing enthusiast, Penske is able to direct a premier auto-racing team and also manage a multibillion-dollar-a-year business conglomerate. What makes his dual focus even more unique and amazing is that he is highly successful in both endeavors. His effective leadership has been especially apparent at Detroit Diesel, which builds heavy-duty truck engines.

Roger Penske bought the Detroit Diesel Corporation from General Motors in 1988. At that time, Detroit Diesel had accumulated millions of dollars in losses and its share of the heavy-truck market had plummeted. On purchasing the company, Penske took immediate steps to improve the morale and confidence of its work force. Specifically, he convened a meeting of employees to calm their fears about massive layoffs and to answer any questions they had.

The meeting was so successful that Penske continues to meet often with union leaders. In addition, he schedules time each year for a series of small-group meetings with all Detroit Diesel employees. According to Penske, these meetings help the work force to better understand how the company operates and what needs to be done for it to succeed. The same workers and senior management that had foundered before at the company relate well to Penske's efforts to keep them informed.

With Roger Penske in charge, the decision-making process at Detroit Diesel is fast—just like in the racing pits. For example, plant manager James Morrow thought the dingy workers' cafeteria should be renovated and requested $500,000 for the project. In the past, the company took weeks to review such a proposal. However, when Penske received the request, he immediately toured the cafeteria. At the end of his inspection, he told Morrow to increase his funding request and to hire the people who build restaurants for the McDonald's Corporation to do the remodeling.

Today, the Penske Corporation has 12 officers who help to manage the operations of Detroit Diesel, Hertz-Penske Leasing, several automobile dealerships, and Team Penske auto racing. Some would say that running such a diverse conglomerate with only 12 individuals to oversee things is nearly impossible. However, according to Dan Luginbuhl, a Penske vice president, Roger Penske's strategy of letting his people run their own units has proved the skeptics wrong.

Roger Penske, CEO of Detroit Diesel, gives managers flexibility while maintaining a detailed understanding of each unit's operations. In each year from 1969 to 1994, Penske entered a car in the Indianapolis 500 mile race.

ADAPTED FROM: Joseph B. White, "Revved Up: How Detroit Diesel, Out from Under GM, Turned Around Fast," *The Wall Street Journal* (August 16, 1991), pp. 1, A5; Matt DeLorenzo, "Roger Penske: Multi-Talented Entrepreneur Just Keeps on Growing," *Automotive News* (January 18, 1988), pp. 1, 54; David Versical, "Racing Helps, But Penske Builds on Firmer Base," *Automotive News* (July 25, 1988), p. 59; Robert T. Grieves, "Penske Prepares," *Forbes* (October 3, 1988), p. 192; Laura Landro, "Hard Driver: Roger Penske's Passion, Auto Racing, Becomes Penske Corp. Symbol," *The Wall Street Journal* (August 9, 1983), pp. 1, 20.

 # LEADERSHIP DEFINED

Organizations are in search of good leaders. Fortunately, through proper education and training, students of management can learn how to provide the capable leadership that is in great demand. Leadership is much more than giving orders or being in charge. Specifically, **leadership** is the process of directing and influencing the activities and behaviors of others through communication to attain goals. Effective leadership and success on the job are closely linked for most managers.

In all likelihood, a managerial position will require you to establish goals and to motivate employees to accomplish these goals. Furthermore, it is through communication with employees that the process of influencing others occurs. "We hear a lot these days about vision as the key to leadership and the driving force behind organizational transformation. But a leader makes the vision a reality only if he or she can communicate it to others by directing their attention to it."[1]

Effective leadership can be and often is the key factor that determines whether an organization and its programs are effective. Consider, for example, efforts to implement continuous quality-improvement programs in companies. What separates programs on quality improvement that work from those that do not work in most firms? The answer, in many cases, is the leader of the company. Dan Ciampa, CEO of Rath and Strong, a consulting firm, indicates that his company's research shows that a quality program that does not have strong support from the chief executive will probably fail.[2]

Leaders must accomplish goals by working through others.

MANAGEMENT VERSUS LEADERSHIP

The terms *management* and *leadership* are used interchangeably by many individuals. However, by definition, there are important distinctions between the two concepts. As indicated earlier in the book, **management** involves using human, equipment, and information resources to achieve various objectives. On the other hand, leadership focuses on getting things done through others. Thus, you manage things (budgets, procedures, and so on), but you lead people.

Management can be viewed as a broader concept than leadership. Managers, for example, must assess complex organizational problems, set goals, and develop strategies for accomplishing these goals based on available resources. Employees represent one of several resources with which managers may be concerned. To illustrate, when managing the operations of a large corporation, the CEO of the company must devote time to many issues that may range from securing adequate financing to evaluating legal issues facing the company. On the other hand, as Figure 8–1 indicates, leaders focus more narrowly on interacting with people and influencing them to accomplish certain goals.

Providing effective leadership is one of the many responsibilities of most managers.

■ **FIGURE 8–1** Leadership versus Management

What does it take to be a good leader? As we will see, this question has intrigued leadership researchers for years.

THE TRAIT APPROACH TO LEADERSHIP

In the 1800s and early 1900s, it was commonly believed that great leaders were born, not made. This view evolved to refocus on the traits of successful leaders, without regard to whether such traits were inherited or acquired. Specifically, the **trait approach** to leadership seeks to identify key characteristics found in all successful leaders. During the early part of this century and into the 1950s, the personal characteristics of effective leaders were studied closely by researchers.[3] Often, the unstated goal was to develop a precise formula of characteristics that could be used to identify individuals who would be good leaders. In essence, the trait approach grouped all successful leaders together without examining the specific situation each faced.

Four problems, however, plague the trait approach.

1. Just being in a leadership position requires a manager to behave differently than his or her employees. However, changes in behavior brought about by the requirements of a job do not indicate that the manager has leadership skills.

2. The possession of any group of leadership traits by a manager does not automatically assure success. Unfortunately, examples abound of managers who failed on the job even though they looked good on paper.

3. The trait approach does not consider the nature of the leadership situation itself. As a result, all leadership situations are viewed as being the same, which is not the case in reality. Few, for example, would claim that a successful religious leader must have exactly the same traits as a successful military officer.

4. Not all successful leaders are exactly alike. Some managers are tall, well educated, extroverted, patient, and people-oriented. However, a manager who is short, poorly educated, introverted, impatient, and task-oriented may also be successful in accomplishing goals. Presently, no single personality trait or set of traits consistently differentiates leaders from nonleaders.

These problems aside, however, researchers with revised expectations are showing renewed interest in the trait approach to leadership. No group of traits is expected to guarantee that a leader will be successful. However, evidence indicates that the possession of certain core traits significantly contributes to a leader's success.[4] These core traits include drive, the desire to lead, honesty and integrity, self-confidence, cognitive ability, and knowledge of the business.[5]

■ *Drive* Successful leaders generally exert a high level of effort on the job. They are ambitious and derive satisfaction from the successful completion of challenging tasks. These leaders have the energy to work overtime and the tenacity to persevere. Furthermore, they take initiative and do not just wait for things to happen.

Consider, for example, Linda Wachner, Chief Executive Officer of Warnaco, a Fortune 500 industrial company that manufactures apparel. Wachner has been described as America's most successful businesswoman.[6] When Wachner took over Warnaco, she injected the company with energy and focus. She is generally described as a good listener and a hard worker. As

If only certain traits were needed to be a successful leader, it would be easy to identify those who would make good leaders.

Leadership researchers are beginning to restudy the trait approach.

Wachner explains, "I know I push very hard, but I don't push anyone harder than I push myself."[7]

■ *Desire to Lead* Successful managers typically like being leaders. They want the additional responsibility that goes with being a leader. The power that leaders wield is also of interest to many managers.

■ *Honesty and Integrity* To cement a trusting relationship between themselves and their followers, successful leaders know that it is important to be truthful and reliable. They are open with employees, and they do what they say they will do.

Not all leaders are alike, but there are certain core traits that contribute to a leader's success.

■ *Self-confidence* A manager must analyze much information and consider many aspects of a problem in order to make an important decision. Low self-confidence would incapacitate a person in this regard. Therefore, self-confidence is usually necessary to succeed as a leader.

■ *Cognitive Ability* The ability to make wise decisions is obviously a valuable leadership trait. In a study at AT&T, for example, cognitive ability was found to predict managerial success 20 years later.[8] Also, part of a leader's credibility depends on the employees' perception of that person's intelligence or cognitive ability.

■ *Knowledge of the Business* Effective leaders usually are familiar with the products or services that their companies offer. Without this knowledge, it would be difficult for leaders to react to the technological and market changes that affect their companies. For this reason, new managers should work diligently to become well educated about their company and industry.

It is important to note that even these core traits alone will not guarantee successful leadership. "Traits only endow people with the potential for leadership."[9] However, these core traits help leaders to develop a vision for the organization and turn that vision into reality.[10]

THE BEHAVIORAL APPROACH TO LEADERSHIP

Another perspective, based on the view that leaders are made, not born, led to the development of the **behavioral approach** to leadership, which focuses on behaviors that differentiate effective leaders from ineffective leaders. The logic of this approach is that if key behaviors of effective leaders can be isolated, a blueprint for success as a leader may be created. Thus, managers who fail to demonstrate the correct behaviors for effective leadership can be trained to behave appropriately. Early leadership research at Ohio State University and the University of Michigan influenced the development of the behavioral approach to leadership. This research, along with an interest in determining the best leadership style for managers to use, also led to the development of the Leadership Grid, which will be discussed later in this section.

The way leaders behave influences how successful they are in leading others.

■ *The Ohio State Leadership Studies*

In 1945, the Ohio State leadership studies were initiated. Researchers associated with these studies identified two significant dimensions of leader behavior: initiating structure and consideration. **Initiating structure** refers to actions taken by a leader to set goals, to structure how a job is to be performed, and to closely monitor the performance of employees. **Consideration** refers to leader behavior that demonstrates friendship, warmth, respect, and mutual trust in the relationship with employees.[11]

As illustrated in Figure 8–2, the two dimensions of leader behavior are viewed as distinct and separate. Furthermore, high and low levels of initiating structure and consideration are possible. As a result, the different combinations of these two dimensions produce four leadership styles.

Early research identified two important dimensions of leader behavior.

■ The University of Michigan Leadership Studies

At about the same time the leadership investigations at Ohio State were occurring, leadership studies at the University of Michigan were being conducted. The Michigan researchers independently identified two broad classifications of behavior associated with successful leaders: production orientation and employee orientation. Managers with a **production orientation** focus their attention on the tasks to be completed, develop detailed steps for performing the tasks, closely supervise their employees, and view employees primarily as tools of production. Managers with an **employee orientation** believe that the quality of the relationships with their employees is of paramount importance and that their employees should be treated with respect and encouraged to be involved in decision-making activities. Interestingly, these two major behavioral orientations are very similar to the two important dimensions of leader behavior identified through the Ohio State leadership studies.

■ **FIGURE 8–2** The Ohio State Leadership Model

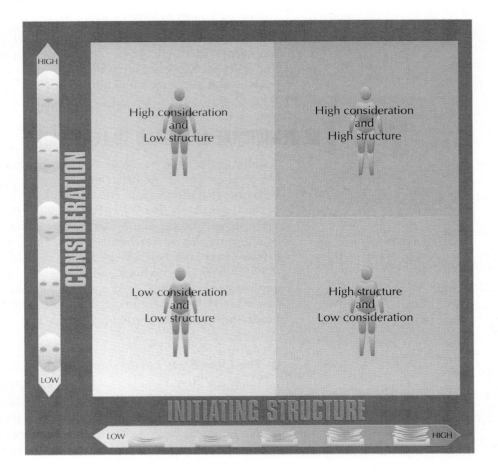

GLOBAL VIEW

Empowerment as a Growth Strategy

Deciding how to expand internationally is a challenging issue faced by companies with opportunities to enter foreign markets. For many of these companies, empowerment can be a powerful growth strategy. However, the use of empowerment may require a change in the executive's traditional role.

Consider the BSD company, which develops and installs software for the inventory control of materials that are considered hazardous and toxic. The company started with two employees: a computer programmer and a former fire chief. Initially, these two individuals sold and installed their inventory control systems to large fire districts. As sales grew, the ex-fire chief hired former employees. The computer programmer taught new recruits the necessary programming skills. The former fire-department employees liked doing business with customers who were their former colleagues. To grow, the company needed to move into new geographic areas. However, the former fire-department personnel did not want to turn their current customers over to somebody else in order to develop new territories. They felt a personal interest in their former colleagues and wanted to make sure they got the support they needed.

Instead of deciding what should be done, the president of BSD turned the problem over to the employees who would have to make the decision work. The employees decided to hire a new team that would sell to smaller fire districts in their own geographic area. The experienced employees carried out their decision by accepting the responsibility for training and monitoring the new employees. Before long, the company had 42 employees, organized into 12 work teams. In two years, BSD grew to almost $20 million in sales and excellent profitability.

In 1988, the president of BSD was contacted by the manager of a large European port that had experienced several toxic spills. The manager indicated that the port needed the service of BSD. The port job would generate $25 million in sales and would allow the company to enter a new growth market. However, the job was 7000 miles from BSD headquarters. The president of BSD wondered how the company could do an effective job that far away.

While analyzing the problem, the president remembered how BSD had dealt with the difficulty of expanding into new geographic areas previously by hiring and training a new team. The company used the same strategy again. In essence, BSD once again hired a new team by entering into a joint-venture partnership that enhanced its ability to accept and effectively complete the European port job. Since then, several other port authorities have requested the help of BSD. As a result, BSD has entered into additional joint-venture partnerships. The company has since grown to 54 offices around the world, with 50 joint ventures ranging from Moscow to Singapore.

According to management researcher James Belasco, what can be learned from the BSD example is that empowerment results from situational decisions; that is, leaders must search for situations that allow their employees to make decisions and solve problems. The president of BSD challenged the company's employees to assume increased responsibilities and learn from them, thereby creating empowerment opportunities. When employees want to make decisions, are willing to accept the consequences of their decisions, and have the necessary information and training to make decisions, a strong case exists for allowing them to do so.

ADAPTED FROM: James A. Belasco, "Empowerment as a Growth Strategy," *Management International Review* **32** (Second Quarter, 1992): 181–88.

Employees like to feel valued and important. When jobs are stressful or frustrating, employees especially appreciate their managers' show of support for them. Employees also respond positively when managers demonstrate confidence in them.

Team management is the best leadership style, according to the Leadership Grid.

■ *The Leadership Grid®*

In creating the original Managerial Grid, which was renamed the Leadership Grid® in 1991, Robert R. Blake and Jane Srygley Mouton built on the leadership studies at Ohio State University and at the University of Michigan. Like the Managerial Grid, the new **Leadership Grid** states that the most effective managers have a high concern for both people and production.[12] This approach to managing others, shown in Figure 8–3, is identified by the Lead-

■ **FIGURE 8–3** The Leadership Grid

SOURCE: The Leadership Grid® figure from *Leadership Dilemmas— Grid Solutions* by Robert R. Blake and Anne Adams McCanse (formerly the Managerial Grid figure by Robert R. Blake and Jane Srygley Mouton). Houston, TX: Gulf Publishing Company, p. 29. Copyright © 1991 by Scientific Methods, Inc. Reproduced by permission of the owners.

1,9 Country Club Management
Thoughtful attention to the needs of people for satisfying relationships leads to a comfortable, friendly organization atmosphere and work tempo.

9,9 Team Management
Work accomplishment is from committed people; interdependence through a "common stake" in organization purpose leads to relationships of trust and respect.

Middle of the Road Management 5,5
Adequate organization performance is possible through balancing the necessity to get out work with maintaining morale of people at a satisfactory level.

1,1 Impoverished Management
Exertion of minimum effort to get required work done is appropriate to sustain organization membership.

9,1 Authority—Compliance
Efficiency in operations results from arranging conditions of work in such a way that human elements interfere to a minimum degree.

Concern for People — High 9, 8, 7, 6, 5, 4, 3, 2, 1, Low

Concern for Production — Low 1 2 3 4 5 6 7 8 9 High

ership Grid as a 9,9 or team management leadership style. Concern for production, the horizontal axis of the Grid, ranges from 1 (a low level of concern) to 9 (a high degree of concern). In the level 9 case, "production" refers to any outcome or result that employees are hired to accomplish. Concern for people is the second dimension, or vertical axis of the Grid, and ranges from 1 (little concern for people) to 9 (much concern for people). Here, concern for people refers to how leaders feel about and treat their employees.

When the two axes of the Leadership Grid intersect, a third dimension relating to motivations is created.[13] This dimension is bipolar and ranges from a plus (+) end, which indicates the things we are motivated to achieve, to a negative (−) end, which indicates the things we wish to avoid. Through the addition of the third motivational dimension, two additional leadership styles, *paternalism* and *opportunism,* are created which are not present in the two-dimensional grid seen in Figure 8–3.[14] Paternalistic, or 9+9, management occurs through the simultaneous use of the 1,9 and 9,1 grid styles. The paternalist tries to motivate employees to be productive through reward and punishment by selecting the stern, demanding approach of the 9,1 style and, at the same time, by being kind and benevolent in a 1,9 way for compliance. Opportunistic management combines any or all grid styles, depending on what the leader determines to be the best approach in terms of self interest. A summary of the seven leadership styles within the Leadership Grid is contained in Figure 8–4.

■ **FIGURE 8–4** Summary of Leadership Grid Styles

SOURCE: Robert R. Blake and Jane Srygley Mouton, *The Managerial Grid III.* Houston, TX: Gulf Publishing Company, Chapters 1–7 (as modified here). Copyright © 1985 by Scientific Methods, Inc. Reproduced by permission of the owners.

1,1	**Impoverished Management,** often referred to as **laissez-faire leadership.** Leaders in this position have little concern for people or productivity, avoid taking sides, and stay out of conflicts. They do just enough to get by.
1,9	**Country Club Management.** Managers in this position have great concern for people and little concern for production. They try to avoid conflicts and concentrate on being well-liked. To them, the task is less important than good interpersonal relations. Their goal is to keep people happy. (This is a soft Theory X approach and not a sound human relations approach.)
9,1	**Authority-Obedience.** Managers in this position have great concern for production and little concern for people. They desire tight control in order to get tasks done efficiently. They consider creativity and human relations to be unnecessary.
5,5	**Organization Man Management,** often termed **middle-of-the-road leadership.** Leaders in this position have medium concern for people and production. They attempt to balance their concern for both people and production, but are not committed to either.
9+9	**Paternalistic "Father Knows Best" Management,** a style in which reward is promised for compliance and punishment is threatened for noncompliance.
Opp	**Opportunistic "What's in It for Me" Management,** in which the style utilized depends on which style the leader feels will return him or her the greatest self-benefit.
9,9	**Team Management.** This style of leadership is considered to be ideal. Such managers have great concern for both people and production. They work to motivate employees to reach their highest levels of accomplishment. They are flexible and responsive to change, and they understand the need to change.

Blake and Mouton have long claimed that the 9,9 managerial orientation is the one best style or approach for managers to take when leading employees. They state that through the use of a 9,9 approach, communication between the manager and employees is enhanced. In addition, they believe conflict is more easily resolved, employees are more committed, and creativity blossoms when a team-management style is employed.[15] Blake and Mouton also claim that managers generally identify the 9,9 approach as the best overall leadership style for achieving excellence, regardless of the situation. However, several leadership researchers believe that the leadership situation itself determines the best leadership style for a manager to use.

A team management leadership style enhances communication between managers and employees.

THE SITUATIONAL (CONTINGENCY) APPROACH

According to the **situational (contingency) approach** to leadership, a leader should analyze a particular situation to determine the appropriate leadership style to employ. Situational leadership theorists do not believe there is one best leadership style; they think the style is dictated by the situation. Established situational or contingency leadership theories include Tannenbaum and Schmidt's leadership continuum, House's path-goal theory, Fiedler's contingency model of leadership, and Hersey and Blanchard's situational leadership model.

■ *Tannenbaum and Schmidt's Leadership Continuum*

Over 30 years ago, Robert Tannenbaum and Warren H. Schmidt introduced a continuum of leadership that has had a significant influence on the development of the situational leadership concept.[16] This **leadership continuum,** shown in Figure 8–5, indicates several different leadership behaviors that are available to managers. These behaviors range from the manager making the decisions to the manager delegating important responsibilities to subordinates.

The amount of freedom that managers designate to their employees varies along the continuum. Managers who adopt leadership behaviors on the left of the continuum are considered authoritarians and are called boss-centered leaders. Leadership behaviors on the right of the continuum are characterized as democratic and are applied by subordinate-centered leaders. An example of a subordinate-centered leader is Wayne Calloway, CEO of PepsiCo. To enhance quality, Calloway tells his employees to look for ways to improve things, even if current methods are "not broke."[17]

Leaders are often classified as authoritarian or democratic.

Knowing the range of available leadership behaviors is important. However, managers also need to understand what they should consider when determining how to lead. As a result, Tannenbaum and Schmidt have identified three factors, or forces, for managers to consider when deciding which leadership behavior to use: forces in the manager, forces in the subordinate, and forces in the situation.

The leadership style that works best for a manager depends in part on the manager's personality.

FORCES IN THE MANAGER Generally, there are four forces operating within a manager's personality that influence how the manager makes decisions. The manager's value system represents the first force. Managers who genuinely believe employees should have input in decision-making activities will embrace the right side of the leadership continuum. Managers who believe that they alone should make the decisions will lean toward the left side of the continuum when selecting leadership behaviors.

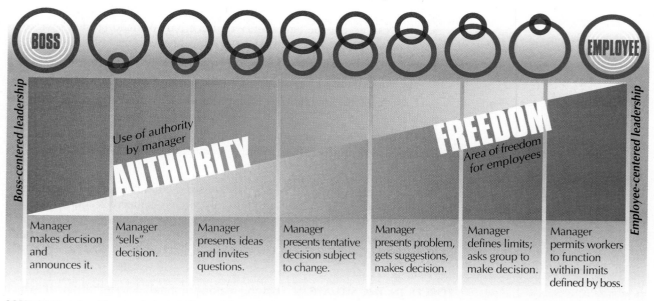

■ **FIGURE 8–5** Tannenbaum and Schmidt's Continuum of Leadership Behavior

BOSS   EMPLOYEE

Boss-centered leadership   Employee-centered leadership

Use of authority by manager

AUTHORITY

FREEDOM

Area of freedom for employees

| Manager makes decision and announces it. | Manager "sells" decision. | Manager presents ideas and invites questions. | Manager presents tentative decision subject to change. | Manager presents problem, gets suggestions, makes decision. | Manager defines limits; asks group to make decision. | Manager permits workers to function within limits defined by boss. |

SOURCE: Reprinted by permission of *Harvard Business Review*. An exhibit from "How to Choose a Leadership Pattern" by Robert Tannenbaum and Warren H. Schmidt (May/June 1973). Copyright © 1973 by the President and Fellows of Harvard College; all rights reserved.

The second force is the level of confidence managers have in their employees. Managers who trust their employees and believe they have the expertise to solve problems on the job are likely to select a subordinate-centered form of leadership behavior. However, some managers believe that if you want something done right, you have to do it yourself. This view results in boss-centered leadership behavior.

The extent to which the leader is domineering is the third force that influences how a manager makes decisions. Some managers like to give a lot of orders and make every attempt to exercise authority over employees. Other managers are team players; their natural inclination is to share decision-making responsibilities with employees.

The fourth force is tolerance for ambiguity. Managers who like to know how work is progressing during all stages that lead to completion of a project will retain close control over decision-making responsibilities. On the other hand, managers who do not mind that uncertainty is a characteristic of delegating responsibility will be more willing to give employees increased control over decision-making activities.

The personality of employees should also be considered when a manager selects a leadership style.

FORCES IN THE SUBORDINATE Subordinates are influenced by forces associated with their personalities. The better a manager understands these forces, the more skilled he or she will be at selecting the appropriate leadership behavior from the leadership continuum. Specifically, Tannenbaum and Schmidt believe that greater decision-making freedom can be given to employees if

1. They have a strong need or desire for independence and to be accountable for the quality of their performance.

2. They indicate a willingness to assume responsibility for decision making

on the job, especially if they demonstrate the ability to take on this responsibility.

3. They can accept the uncertainty that is a part of making their own decisions, rather than rely on directions from a supervisor.

4. The problem they are working on is important and of interest to them.

5. They understand and identify with the goals of the organization.

6. They have the appropriate training and skills needed to deal with the problem.

7. They are ready to accept decision-making responsibilities. However, giving employees much responsibility quickly can cause them to fail and lose confidence in themselves.[18]

In leadership situations in which most of these conditions do *not* exist, managers probably should lean toward adopting a boss-centered leadership behavior. After all, when employees show little interest in making decisions and expect the manager to be the decision maker, it may be necessary to be a boss-centered leader.

The values and traditions of an organization influence the leadership options that are considered appropriate for managers.

FORCES IN THE SITUATION Before making a final determination of which leadership behavior to adopt, the manager should examine the general leadership situation. Tannenbaum and Schmidt have identified four forces that affect the manager that stem from the leadership situation.

First, a manager should consider the values and traditions of the organization. The second force relevant to the situation is group effectiveness. The manager should consider how effectively employees work together as a group and should also determine how much experience they have had working together. Established work groups that are made up of employees with similar backgrounds will be better equipped to take on challenging tasks than new groups of employees with dissimilar backgrounds. Also, the manager should evaluate the group's level of confidence in its ability to handle increased decision-making freedom.

The third force to be considered is the problem itself. Specifically, the manager needs to determine whether the problem is too difficult for the group to handle on its own. It is inappropriate to ask a work group to attempt to solve a problem that its members do not have the training or knowledge to understand. In this case, the manager should select a boss-centered leadership approach and dictate a solution.

Much can be accomplished in companies when employees are empowered.

However, if employees are capable of dealing with a problem, they should be empowered to do so. For example, as part of a continuous quality-improvement program at Pepsi-Cola East, company president Mike Lorelli sought input from employees at all levels on how things could be improved. In response, drivers of the company's trucks reported that grocery stores wanted faster delivery of their soda orders. To meet this request, the drivers and inventory managers worked together on the problem. As a result, delivery time has been cut from three days to one, and customers are happier. The change also saves Pepsi money.[19]

Successful total quality management (TQM) programs require effective leadership.

The need for leaders who can adopt behaviors that will enable their company's total quality management (TQM) programs to succeed has never been greater. As a matter of fact, it has been said that "Leadership is the real wellspring of quality."[20] Specifically, it is critical that managers engage in the following eight behaviors if quality-improvement programs are to be successful in their organizations:

REMEMBER TO COMMUNICATE

Adapting to Communication Styles

While analyzing a leadership situation to identify an appropriate leadership style, managers should also understand and adapt to the communication styles of employees. In examining communication styles, it is important to realize that no single style will probably describe any person perfectly. However, many employees can be broadly categorized as using open or closed communication styles.

Open Communicators

In organizations, employees who are open communicators show a willingness to express their views and indicate an interest in receiving feedback from others. These employees are equally interested in both the needs of others and in the needs of the organization. It is safe to say that employees who are open communicators are interested in their supervisor's views on work-related issues. As a manager, for example, your views on industry trends will be of interest to employees who are open communicators, and they will be receptive to constructive criticism from you. Furthermore, open communicators typically want to be assigned challenging tasks and to receive recognition from their manager for work done well.

Closed Communicators

Employees who are closed communicators often feel more comfortable working alone on a task rather than with other people. They seldom request feedback from others or volunteer information. The failure of closed communicators to express their expectations to others frequently causes them to be disappointed by the actions of associates. Employees who are closed communicators are often anxious and prefer situations that provide them with psychological safety. They are reluctant to offer an opinion and cautious when they do state their views.

Generally, closed employees feel safe when their manager eliminates the need for them to make decisions. They like to get information directly from their boss rather than from the grapevine. Furthermore, closed communicators are sensitive to criticism and like specific directions.

ADAPTED FROM: Cherly Hamilton, *Communication for Results,* 4th ed. (Belmont, CA: Wadsworth, 1993), pp. 71–97.

1. Work with employees to decide what the company should be.
2. Focus quality effort on customer service, not on cost cutting.
3. Show willingness to change everything.
4. Set up pilot programs where employees learn how to solve problems.
5. Let workers make changes they suggest.
6. Reward employees for improving the way the company serves its customers.
7. Keep workers informed of the success or failure of the quality program.
8. Stay actively involved throughout the quality effort.[21]

Time pressure is the fourth force relevant to many leadership situations. When managers believe they must make decisions quickly, there may not be time to involve employees and respond to their input.

Tannenbaum and Schmidt realized that several factors interact to influence the leadership behaviors that are appropriate for managers. Many situational leadership researchers have concluded that successful leadership is a function of the leader, the follower, and the situation.

CONSIDER THIS

1. Think of a person you consider to be a good leader. What leadership traits do you observe in this person?

2. Why, in your opinion, are many people who could be leaders reluctant to accept leadership roles?

3. What should a leader do to earn the trust and loyalty of subordinates ?

■ *House's Path-Goal Theory of Leadership*

The path-goal theory of leadership, developed by Robert J. House, is an outgrowth of expectancy theory.[22] According to expectancy theory, two factors have great influence over how employees behave. First, employees estimate the rewards they will receive from behaving a certain way. Second, they decide how valuable the rewards are to them.[23] As a result, it is reasonable to expect that employees will work hard if they believe their efforts will help them to acquire things that they value.

Employees can be expected to work hard to achieve goals that are important to them.

Building on this expectation, **path-goal theory** proposes that a manager's leadership style will be motivating to the extent that employees believe it will help them to achieve things that they value.[24] Furthermore, the theory explains how the following four types of leadership styles affect the motivation of employees.[25]

1. *Directive Leadership* The manager who uses a directive leadership style explains to employees what is expected of them, how they are to do their jobs, and how they will be evaluated. The employees are expected to follow the rules and regulations established by the manager. When job demands are ambiguous, directive leadership behavior by the manager is satisfying to employees. However, it is considered to be a hindrance to them if they have a clear task.

2. *Supportive Leadership* The manager who uses a supportive leadership style shows concern for the well-being of employees and is perceived to be friendly and approachable. Employees notice that the manager attempts to make their jobs as enjoyable as possible. These efforts are especially satisfying to employees whose jobs are naturally stressful and frustrating.

3. *Participative Leadership* The manager who employs a participative leadership style involves employees in the decision-making process. Instead of waiting for input to be offered by employees, the manager consults directly with them to get their suggestions. The employees also observe that their suggestions are given serious consideration by the manager.

Employees tend to be more committed to goals they have set than to goals set for them.

According to path-goal theory, participation by employees clarifies the paths to various goals or rewards that are valued. Having input concerning what will be done and how it will be done gives employees increased control over how things proceed on the job. Furthermore, employees tend to be committed to decisions that they have been involved in making. These factors are theorized to promote hard work and strong performance by employees.

Employees who lack training or have an ambiguous job need directive leadership from their manager.

4. *Achievement-Oriented Leadership* The manager who employs an achievement-oriented leadership style sets high goals for employees and expects them to contribute their best efforts to the job. Although managers who use this approach are very demanding, they also show a great deal of confidence in their employees. In short, the theory holds that employees become more confident when they observe their manager showing confidence in them. In one study, for example, employees who perform ambiguous, nonrepetitive tasks were studied. A positive relationship was found to exist between the manager's level of achievement orientation and the employees' expectations of effective performance. When the achievement orientation of the manager was greater, the employees were more confident that their efforts would result in effective performances.[26]

CONTINGENCY VARIABLES According to House, two contingency variables should be considered by a manager when selecting an appropriate leadership style: the personal characteristics of subordinates and the environmental pressures of the job.[27] In relation to the first contingency, path-goal theory asserts that employees will accept a manager's leadership style to the extent that it is satisfying for them to do so. Interestingly, employees who believe that their behavior determines what happens to them are most satisfied with a participative leadership style. Employees who believe that what happens to them is due generally to luck or chance are most satisfied when their manager uses a directive style of leadership.

Employees who possess the skills needed to do a job well prefer that their manager use a participative leadership style.

Another important personal characteristic to consider is how competent employees perceive themselves to be on the job. Employees who perceive that they are able to do a job well are less likely to view leader directiveness as acceptable. Individuals who believe that they lack the needed skills to do a job, however, will probably prefer a manager who engages in much directive behavior. These employees believe that the manager's directive behavior will help them to succeed and obtain valued rewards.

The second contingency variable refers to uncontrollable aspects of the employees' environment that affect their satisfaction and performance. For example, employees typically do not have much control over the extent to which their jobs are routine and structured. Therefore, if a job is routine and well understood by an employee, attempts by a manager to offer guidance as to how to perform the job will be perceived negatively.

The importance of path-goal theory for managers is that it emphasizes the need to clarify the paths that employees should take to obtain the goals and rewards that they value. For example, employees can be expected to be interested in such things as receiving formal recognition for accomplishments, increased pay, and promotion. The manager should clearly explain how these things can be accomplished. Furthermore, the manager needs to be flexible in selecting a leadership style based on the personal characteristics of employees and on environmental characteristics. For instance, employees who lack training and have an ambiguous job are going to need directive leadership from their manager. Also, managers should understand that their leadership style will be viewed as satisfying to employees to the extent that it helps them accomplish the goals they value.

Employees prefer that their manager select a leadership style that helps them to achieve their goals.

■ *Fiedler's Contingency Model of Leadership Effectiveness*

Fred E. Fiedler, a pioneer researcher in the area of situational leadership theory, realized that the ease with which a leader can exert influence varies depending on the leadership situation. As a result, Fiedler's **contingency model of leadership effectiveness** theorizes that the appropriate leadership style depends on the leader's personality and on how favorable the leadership situation is to the leader. Specifically, this model states that a manager's success in leading a work group is contingent on the task or relationship motivation (personality) of the leader and on the extent to which the leader has situational control and influence.[28]

According to Fiedler, managers should consider their personality and the extent to which they have situational control and influence when selecting a leadership style.

LEADER PERSONALITY Fiedler broadly characterizes leaders as being primarily either relationship-motivated or task-motivated in their style of leadership. To measure the extent to which a manager is either relationship- or task-motivated, the manager is asked to think of all the coworkers he or she has ever known and to select the one with whom the manager has had the most difficulty. This person is identified by Fiedler as the least-preferred coworker (LPC). Next, the manager describes the LPC by completing an 18-item questionnaire based on his or her perception of this person.

A manager whose combined ratings of the LPC are low is classified as task-motivated. Such a manager focuses primarily on production or on getting the job done and views any coworker negatively who gets in the way. On the other hand, a manager whose ratings of the LPC are high is viewed as relationship-motivated. Specifically, such a manager is primarily people-oriented and wants to have good relationships with subordinates.[29] Even if a people-oriented manager cannot work well with a particular employee, the manager will still want to have a friendly relationship with that person. In addition to determining the nature of the leader's personality, Fiedler indicates that the amount of situational control the leader has should also be examined when identifying appropriate leader behavior.

Some leadership situations provide the manager with more control and influence than others.

SITUATIONAL CONTROL AND INFLUENCE   The extent to which the leadership situation provides the manager with control and influence is referred to as **situational control**. The type of leadership situation a manager faces plays an important role in determining the extent to which a particular leadership style will be successful. The three factors or elements that comprise situational control, in order of importance, are leader-member relations, task structure, and leader position power.

1. *Leader-Member Relations*   Specifically, **leader-member relations** refer to how much support and loyalty a manager receives from members of a work group. This dimension can be measured by asking group members to provide evaluation ratings of their leader or by using a so-called group atmosphere scale completed by the leader. The scale, which is used more frequently, asks the manager to estimate leader-member relations with his or her work group. A manager who has good leader-member relations with a work group is trusted and liked by the group. Moreover, the group is willing to follow the manager's directions. However, a manager who is experiencing poor leader-member relations will find it difficult to influence employees.

2. *Task Structure*   The nature of the task to be performed can also be an important determinant of how much control and influence a leader has. **Task structure** represents the extent to which a job is clearly defined and contains step-by-step procedures for success. A manager can exercise much more authority over how employees perform structured tasks than over how they perform unstructured tasks.

A leader's influence is determined in part by the degree to which employees' jobs are structured or unstructured.

3. *Leader Position Power*   In organizations, **leader position power** refers to the amount of formal authority a manager has to make decisions and give orders to employees. In part, leader position power is determined by the degree to which a manager can hire or fire, promote or demote, recommend sanctions, or force subordinates to comply with orders.[30]

Managers who are given a lot of responsibility and who are allowed to make important decisions are usually viewed as having high position power. The job of a manager with high position power is easier than the job of a manager who must struggle with low position power. However, a manager may compensate for low position power with high personal power. For example, a person who manages an office staffed by volunteer workers has little position power but may be well-liked and respected by the staff. As a result, compliance by the volunteers occurs simply because they believe in the manager and want to contribute to what he or she is trying to achieve.

Each of the three dimensions of situational control, according to the contingency model of leadership effectiveness, are divided into two levels. Leader-member relations can be viewed as good or poor, tasks are structured or unstructured, and position power is judged as high or low. Situational control is highest when a manager has good relations with his or her employees, a structured task, and high position power. Conversely, situational control is lowest when a manager has poor relations with his or her employees, an unstructured task, and low position power.

CONDITIONS FOR EFFECTIVE LEADERSHIP   As we have already discussed, leaders vary not only in personality but also in the amount of situational control they experience. Given such potentially different orientations, it is natural to ask, "Which leadership approach should a manager use?" According to Fiedler's contingency model, the correct answer is, "It depends." As a matter of fact, Fiedler's research indicates that both task- and relationship-motivated leaders perform well in some instances and poorly in others.

As shown in Figure 8–6, task-motivated managers (low LPC) need either high or relatively low situational control to perform best, but relationship-motivated managers (high LPC) perform best when situational control is moderate. The logic behind these findings is as follows. Task-oriented managers are determined to get the job done, one way or another. Their self-esteem is derived more from measurable performance than from how their employees perceive them. If the work group supports the task-oriented manager's strategy, he or she will step back and let the group implement the strategy. These managers can be very pleasant when things are going their way. However, they are going to make sure the work is completed, even if their employees don't like the job or how it is being done. Therefore, under conditions of low support, high task orientation may be the only way to get the task completed.

When situational control is moderate the manager may face a somewhat skeptical work group, a partially unclear task, and a situation in which employees who are fired may not be easy to replace. Relationship-motivated managers perform best under such conditions. They are able to deal with interpersonal relationships effectively and to cope with difficult employees. Furthermore, their creative ability allows them to demonstrate innovation when they are faced with challenging tasks.[31]

Task-motivated and relationship-motivated leaders both perform well in certain situations.

■ **FIGURE 8–6**   How the Effectiveness of Two Leadership Styles Varies with the Situation

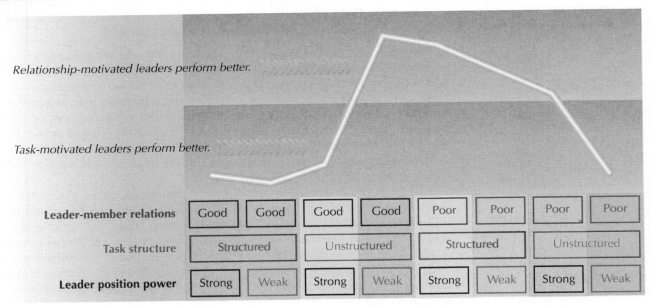

Leader-member relations	Good	Good	Good	Good	Poor	Poor	Poor	Poor
Task structure	Structured		Unstructured		Structured		Unstructured	
Leader position power	Strong	Weak	Strong	Weak	Strong	Weak	Strong	Weak

Relationship-motivated leaders perform better.

Task-motivated leaders perform better.

SOURCE: Fred E. Fiedler and Martin M. Chemers, *Leadership and Effective Management* (Glenview, IL: Scott, Foresman, 1974), p. 80. Adaptation of an exhibit from "Engineer the Job to Fit the Manager" by Fred E. Fiedler, *Harvard Business Review* (September/October 1965). Copyright © 1965 by the President and Fellows of Harvard College; all rights reserved. Reprinted by permission of *Harvard Business Review.*

A PERSPECTIVE ON QUALITY

A Managerial Perspective on TQM

Senior managers who make a commitment to total quality management (TQM) for their organizations must realize that this decision will require them to live in a fishbowl. One reason for this scrutiny is that employees will be looking for proof that top managers really support TQM and are willing to practice what they preach. A second reason is that if the emphasis on quality does not produce positive results, the senior managers who backed the new focus will become a lightning rod for blame.

John W. Johnstone, CEO of Olin Corporation, has learned firsthand what it is like to lead a company through the TQM process. According to Johnstone, the quality process at Olin has the following key goals.

- Make sure everyone in the company, including the CEO, places customer satisfaction as their highest priority.
- Create a corporate culture that is customer-driven.
- Capitalize on the unique qualities of the company's different lines of business.
- Involve 100 percent of employees, including the CEO, in the commitment for continuous improvement.

Olin launched its TQM effort with a large training program. Johnstone thought that the quality training provided to employees would necessarily lead to new behaviors on the job. However, he found that the desired behavioral changes did not last long unless the culture of the organization supported them.

Furthermore, the prevalent culture of an organization often reflects top management's commitment—or lack of it—on various issues. As a matter of fact, according to quality expert W. Edwards Deming, 80 percent of the opportunity for improvement in an organization rests with its management. Therefore, to make TQM work, top managers must be committed to it, must communicate a vision for their organization, and must provide employees with necessary training.

ADAPTED FROM: John W. Johnstone, "A Point of View: Life in a Fishbowl— A Senior Manager's Perspective on TQM," *National Productivity Review* **11** (Spring 1992): 143–46.

According to Fiedler, there are eight types of situational control. These types of situational control and their favorableness to the leader are shown in Figure 8–7. The implication of Fiedler's contingency model of leadership effectiveness is that if you can modify your job as manager to best fit your natural leadership style, you will be most effective. According to Fiedler, there is no one best leadership style. Instead, leadership effectiveness depends on an appropriate match between leader personality and situational control.

■ Hersey and Blanchard's Situational Leadership Model

Influenced in part by the Ohio State leadership studies, Paul Hersey and Kenneth H. Blanchard developed their **situational leadership model.** This model considers the readiness level of an employee to be the critical factor in determining an appropriate leadership style for most leadership situations.[32] Here, "readiness" refers to an employee's level of ability and willingness to accom-

Hersey and Blanchard believe that the readiness level of employees determines which leadership style a leader should select.

SITUATION	DEGREE OF FAVORABLENESS OF SITUATION TO LEADER	LEADER-MEMBER RELATIONS	TASK STRUCTURE	LEADER POSITION POWER
1	Favorable	Good	Structured	High
2	Favorable	Good	Structured	Low
3	Favorable	Good	Unstructured	High
4	Moderately favorable	Good	Unstructured	Low
5	Moderately favorable	Poor	Structured	High
6	Moderately favorable	Poor	Structured	Low
7	Moderately favorable	Poor	Unstructured	High
8	Unfavorable	Poor	Unstructured	Low

SOURCE: Reprinted by permission from Edwin B. Flippo and Gary M. Munsinger, *Management,* 5th ed. (Boston: Allyn & Bacon, 1982), p. 342.

plish a specific job or task.[33] When leading a group of employees, a manager must determine an overall level of readiness for the group in general. Available leadership styles in the situational leadership model contain different degrees of task behavior and relationship behavior for a leader to use.

Task behavior is defined as a leader's efforts to specifically indicate the duties and responsibilities of employees.[34] Thus, the leader tells employees what job to do and when, where, and how to do the job.[35] On the other hand, **relationship behavior** refers to the leader's efforts to maintain open communication with employees through listening, facilitating, and being supportive.[36]

FOUR POSSIBLE LEADERSHIP STYLES The situational leadership model contains four different leadership styles for managers to use.[37]

1. *High Task and Low Relationship Behavior* When this style of leadership is used, the manager tells employees exactly what to do and roles are specifically defined. This blend of leader behavior is called the "telling" style. In using it, the manager relies heavily on one-way, downward communication. Although some relationship behavior occurs, there is no doubt that the manager calls all the shots.

2. *High Task and High Relationship Behavior* With this leadership style, there is more two-way communication between the manager and employees. Through this two-way interaction, the manager tries to persuade employees that their jobs should be performed in a certain way. As a result, this approach is called the "selling" style of leadership. The manager still makes most of the decisions and provides much direction, but a strong effort is made to make sure the employees understand the reasoning behind decisions. By selling employees on why things have to be done a certain way, it is easier to gain their cooperation.

3. *Low Task and High Relationship Behavior* In using this approach, the manager gives employees much input into the decision-making process.

Therefore, this is called the "participating" style of leadership. Here, the manager still makes the final decisions, but employees are encouraged to play an important role in setting goals and developing strategies to get the job done.

Low relationship behavior does not mean no relationship behavior.

4. *Low Task and Low Relationship Behavior* By engaging in little task and relationship behavior, the manager is generally taking a hands-off approach. In return, the employees are given much responsibility and authority to make decisions. The manager usually sets major goals, but much leeway is given to employees to decide how they will accomplish the goals. As a result, this approach is called the "delegating" style of leadership.

The situational leadership model, which incorporates these four leadership styles, is shown in Figure 8–8. To use the model, determine the point on the readiness continuum that you believe represents the level of readiness of your employees to perform a certain job. From that point, construct a perpendicular

■ **FIGURE 8–8** Situational Leadership Model

SOURCE: Paul Hersey and Kenneth H. Blanchard, *Management of Organizational Behavior: Utilizing Human Resources,* 6th ed., © 1993, p. 257. Adapted by permission of Prentice-Hall, Englewood Cliffs, NJ.

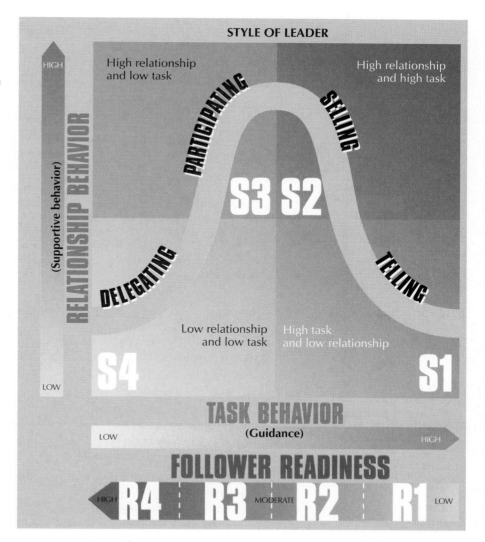

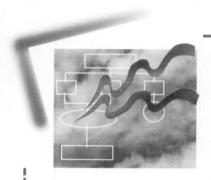

REMEMBER TO COMMUNICATE
Ensure That Predictions Will Come True

As the manager of a growing wholesale food-supply company, Jim Casey was responsible for locating an additional warehouse to store the company's expanding inventory. Jim found a warehouse that was of suitable size; it just needed repainting. A local painter, Sam Walker, quoted Jim a very low price to repaint the interior of the building. Jim asked, "How soon can you start?" Sam responded, "Monday of next week." Jim then asked, "How long will it take you to do the painting?" Sam answered, "It will take me two days." They shook hands on the deal. Jim then made arrangements to have a shipment of inventory delivered to the new warehouse the next Wednesday.

On Monday, during his lunch hour, Jim drove by the warehouse. Through a window, he could see Sam painting. Wednesday morning, Jim got a call from an employee who said that the arriving inventory could not be delivered to the new warehouse because Sam was not finished painting. Jim drove to the warehouse where he had the following conversation with Sam.

Jim: You said you would start painting on Monday and that it would take you two days.

Sam: That's right.

Jim: Here it is Wednesday, and you are still painting!

Sam: I'll finish today.

Jim: You were supposed to be finished yesterday, and I scheduled deliveries today.

Sam: You should have checked with me before you made that decision. I wasn't able to work here yesterday. I said the painting would take two days. I didn't say it would be two consecutive days. I painted Monday, and I'll finish painting today, Wednesday. That's two days.

Even if Jim's decision to schedule deliveries to the new warehouse on Wednesday was reasonable, the problem could have been avoided through better communication. When you make important decisions based on the *predicted* actions of others, it is wise to confirm your plans with key individuals. This recommendation is especially appropriate when others have not specifically stated they will do certain things; instead, their actions are only implied.

line to a point of intersection with the curved line. The area in which this intersection occurs indicates the appropriate leadership style for you to use with your employees.

CONSIDER THIS

1. Think about the leadership style that you prefer to use when you are in a leadership position. How would you characterize what appears to be your natural style of leadership?

2. What leadership approach do you think has the best chance of working well in the majority of situations that leaders face?

3. Is it easier to lead a large number of independent or dependent employees? Why?

TRANSFORMATIONAL LEADERSHIP

Some leaders have a special ability to inspire and motivate employees.

Some leaders possess such dynamic personal qualities that they can literally transform a company. It is more than a selected leadership style that makes them so successful. Employees are inspired by them. These unique leaders have the special distinction of being transformational leaders in their companies. **Transformational leadership** occurs when leaders inspire and motivate followers to put aside their individual self-interests and work diligently to accomplish organizational goals.[38]

For example, Lee Iacocca is widely recognized as an individual who has demonstrated transformational leadership. When Iacocca became Chairman of the Chrysler Corporation, the company was on the brink of bankruptcy. However, Iacocca was able to motivate employees and mobilize individuals to help him transform Chrysler into a profitable company.

Another undisputed transformational leader is Bill Gates, CEO of Microsoft Corporation. A multibillionaire, Gates admits that he is the greatest single influence in his company's corporate culture. He doesn't worry about haircuts or fashion, and he seldom takes vacations. Instead, Gates works 15-hour days pursuing excellence in an industry in which his company dominates. Gates is described as "high horsepower and high energy."[39]

Management consultant Richard Byrd cautions that a new frame of reference is needed to understand what it takes to be a successful leader in a complex organization. Specifically, Byrd believes that five categories of skills are important for leaders.

1. *Anticipatory Skills* Learning what to expect from the business environment and preparing for those events.

2. *Visioning Skills* Having a meaningful purpose that followers can be persuaded to embrace with enthusiasm.

Bill Gates (left), CEO of Microsoft Corp., has been described as "ultra-competitive." As co-founder of Microsoft, Gates developed the company into one of the most profitable enterprises in the world. Gates uses his transformational leadership abilities to redirect the company's vision as necessary.

3. *Value-Congruence Skills* Bringing the values of employees into line with the mission of the company.

4. *Empowerment Skills* Providing employees with opportunities to accept increasing amounts of responsibility in ways that maximize their ability and potential.

5. *Self-Understanding Skills* Knowing your own strengths and weaknesses and striving for continuous development and improvement.[40]

Transformational leaders are prepared to change the culture of an organization in ways that enable them to begin to achieve their vision. As a manager, the degree to which you can clearly communicate your vision to your employees will significantly influence your ability to succeed as a transformational leader.[41]

GENDER AND LEADERSHIP STYLE

Women hold many managerial jobs in companies.

Throughout U.S. industries, the percentage of managerial jobs held by women has more than doubled since 1970.[42] In addition, large numbers of women are continuing to acquire the experience and professional training needed for positions as managers. As women move into more managerial jobs, is there reason to expect them to lead differently than men do?

The issue itself is controversial, and conflicting answers to this question abound. However, research on gender and leadership style has yielded interesting information. For example, a review of research comparing the leadership styles of male and female school principals found identifiable differences. Specifically, the female principals made greater use of a democratic or participative leadership style and less use of an autocratic or directive style than male principals did.[43]

Leadership researcher Judy Rosener indicates that women managers are now drawing on the skills they have acquired from their own experiences instead of

The number of women who hold managerial positions continues to increase. The need for skilled leadership from both men and women in companies is strong. Managers can benefit from doing a self analysis and then capitalize on their strengths.

automatically adopting the traditional leadership styles used in male-dominated jobs.[44] In a survey of male and female leaders, Rosener found that the female respondents described themselves in ways that are characteristic of "transformational" leaders. These women generally attributed their power to the personal characteristics they possessed. However, the men surveyed tended to describe themselves as leaders who "command and control." The men relied a lot on the power associated with their positions as leaders.[45]

Cynthia Epstein, a professor at City University of New York, cautions that female managers may not actually lead much differently than male managers, although they might perceive that they do.[46] One study of approximately 19,000 employees in almost 100 organizations examined the gender-leadership issue. In the study, female employees rated female managers higher than male managers on 19 out of 25 questions on a leadership survey. Male employees rated female managers higher on 23 of 25 questions on the same survey.[47] One thing is certain, however, successful leaders in organizations include both men and women.

Successful leaders include both men and women.

 # RECOMMENDATIONS FOR EFFECTIVE LEADERSHIP

Successful managers have found that certain leadership practices are appropriate for a variety of leadership situations. The following leadership recommendations will aid you in leading others as a manager.

1. *Carry through with Decisions* When you announce that you are going to do something, do it! Employees want to be able to depend on you as a manager. Managers who fail to do what they say they will do, lose the respect of employees. It is better not to promise something than to dash the expectations of others.

Failure to adequately train employees can be costly in the long run.

2. *Train Employees* It is amazing how many companies spend large sums of money on buildings, inventory, and marketing but fail to adequately train employees. Poorly trained employees are not able to perform effectively. Provide employees with proper training and give them appropriate responsibilities based on their abilities.[48]

3. *Show Respect for Employees* A management consultant recently interviewed clerical employees in a large corporation. Some of the employees did not like their jobs. The consultant asked an especially dissatisfied employee, "Why do you stay here?" The employee answered, "I stay because my boss makes me feel important. She respects me, and I don't want to let her down." Employees value the respect a manager shows for them, and they will work hard to retain it.

4. *Provide the Necessary Resources for Employees* When employees need resources to perform their jobs well, they will evaluate you as a manager on the basis of how effectively you obtain these resources from top management. Employees want to feel that their manager is a strong advocate of their needs when he or she deals with top-level executives.[49]

5. *Demonstrate Confidence in Employees* If a manager demonstrates that he or she believes in employees' abilities, they will be encouraged to perform well. Assess the skills of your employees and provide them with tasks that allow them to demonstrate those skills in a successful manner. If possible, move those who cannot perform well to jobs where they can achieve success.[50]

6. *Set a Good Example* When you assume the job of a manager, you become a role model to employees, and your behavior will be watched carefully by them. You will set the work tone by your behavior or actions. For instance, if you work hard and are productive, others associated with you will feel obligated to do the same.

Carefully evaluate the goals set for employees.

7. *Set Realistic But Challenging Goals* Managers should examine the appropriateness of employees' goals. For example, consider whether the goals are realistic. Unrealistic goals only set employees up for failure; they will lose motivation for a goal they consider to be futile. Furthermore, goals that are too easy fail to challenge employees to achieve their potential.

8. *Be Fair and Consistent* Employees expect managers to treat them fairly when making job assignments, distributing overtime work, rotating unpopular duties, and so on. When employees sense that a manager is fair, they tend to develop loyalty and a willingness to exert extra effort for him or her. Managers should also be consistent in the ways in which they enforce rules and policies on the job. Showing favoritism in this respect can destroy morale.

It is a manager's job to periodically check the progress of employees who are completing important assignments.

9. *Monitor the Progress of Important Tasks* In addition to assigning tasks and establishing completion dates, managers are also responsible for following up on important assignments. Some employees are more motivated and capable than others. Therefore, the amount of time required to monitor the work of employees will vary. However, managers are responsible for checking on the progress of important work assignments to make sure they are being completed correctly.

SELF-MANAGING WORK TEAMS

In general, leadership involves working with and through others to accomplish important organizational goals. This view of leadership recognizes the power of teamwork. Leaders in large corporations such as Xerox, Procter & Gamble, GM, and TRW are finding that they can accomplish much by delegating responsibilities to self-managing work teams.[51]

A **self-managing work team** is a group of well-trained and cross-trained employees who have the specified responsibility and authority to complete a well-defined task. Since the employees are cross-trained, each one has the ability to perform several activities. It is important to note that a self-managing team is different from a project-management team. The distinction is that project-management teams exist only temporarily, whereas self-managing teams are a permanent structure in an organization. Once a project is completed, project-management teams disband, but self-managing teams have a continuous function to perform.

Self-managing teams have ongoing tasks to perform but require little supervision from top management.

Self-managing teams need very little supervision from top management. In essence, top management decides *what* task the team should be working on, but the team determines *how* it will complete the task. As long as a self-managing team meets its goal, top-management generally leaves the team alone. The result is that middle managers in most organizations can oversee several self-managing teams.

■ The Benefits of Self-Managing Work Teams

Even within a large organization, self-managing work teams can re-create the entrepreneurial spirit that exists in the start-up stage for most small compa-

A PERSPECTIVE ON QUALITY

The Self-Managing Team—A Success Story

For more than 20 years, the Executive Offices Company has produced fine office furniture. Over the last decade, however, orders for custom-designed furniture made from unique materials and having special finishes to match a room's decor have been increasing at the company. In the past, the company did its best to fill the custom orders, but it was a hit-and-miss proposition. For example, at best, the prices quoted by some of the company's salespeople were wild guesses. Too often, the prices accepted by customers were ones that ultimately provided little profit. Furthermore, not all of the salespeople were adept at conveying customer needs to the company designers. Employees working in the design and manufacturing segments of the company also had mixed views on the custom orders. Some designers and assemblers were excited about working on one-of-a-kind products. Others, however, preferred the standard company line.

As orders for custom-designed furniture became substantial, the company made a fateful decision—it established a self-managing work team to handle custom-designed orders exclusively. Only the most appropriate employees were appointed to the team. Assigned, for example, was the salesperson most adept at pricing the custom work, the designer who was especially creative at conceptualizing new furniture styles, a craftsperson with a special talent for producing one-of-a-kind parts, and three assemblers who were especially skilled at working with new designs and materials.

Another wise decision made by top management was to give the self-managing team the authority it needed to price jobs, design the furniture, purchase necessary materials, and schedule its work. The team members each had special skills, and they cross-trained each other. As a result, all the members became knowledgeable about most aspects of the jobs performed by the team. In essence, the team became a self-contained group that basically ran itself.

Interestingly, the custom-order business has become a highly profitable venture for the Executive Offices Company. Furthermore, the company has achieved a nationwide reputation for providing quality custom furniture, due to the excellent performance of its self-managing team.

ADAPTED FROM: Thomas Owens, "The Self-Managing Work Team," *Small Business Reports* **16** (February 1991): 55–56.

Self-managing work teams enhance efficiency and productivity within any organization. Middle managers in small or medium-sized companies frequently oversee several self-managing teams. In large companies, self-managing teams create an entrepreneurial spirit among team members.

nies.[52] As a result, team members typically generate a high level of energy, commitment, and performance. Furthermore, these teams allow company operations to be streamlined in a way that often provides added flexibility, quality, and cost savings. These and other benefits can allow an organization to achieve excellence and be very competitive.

■ *Creating Self-Managing Teams*

The success of self-managing teams is not magical or automatic. However, if you, as a manager, adhere to the following implementation process, the chances that a self-managing team will flourish in your organization will be increased.[53]

Self-managing teams are ideal in situations that require group creativity and teamwork.

■ *Define the Function* Self-managing work teams are ideally suited to handle challenges that require creativity, a variety of skills, and teamwork. However, when establishing a self-managing work team, you, as the manager, should make sure that the duty to be performed by the team is clear. There also needs to be early agreement as to where the scope of authority for the team begins and ends.

■ *Determine the Required Skills and Resources* The makeup of the team is critical. Determine what skills are necessary for the team to complete its assigned function successfully. At this point, focus on the required skills, not on what skills employees in the organization currently possess. Also, consider what resources the team will need. The list of resources will eventually be important when a budget is developed for the team.

■ *Select Team Members* The group should have enough employees to perform its duties well, but no more employees than necessary. Recruit team members from employees who possess the needed skills contained on the skills list you have prepared. No employee should be forced or coerced to join the team; you only want willing participants. In some cases, you will find that the employees you are able to recruit do not possess all the needed skills from the skills list. As a result, you may need to provide the existing group members with new skills training or hire people who already possess these skills.

■ *Select a Team Leader* Like other groups, a self-managing work team needs a team leader to conduct meetings and coordinate efforts with outside groups. When the team is first formed, top management may initially appoint a leader just to get things going. However, once the team builds some momentum, team members may elect a leader. The role of team leader can also be rotated among various team members. Periodically, the team leader may decide that outside consultants need to be added as temporary members of the team. These temporary members provide needed technical support to help the team accomplish a difficult task or assignment.

THINK ABOUT IT

1. Think about the leadership style you would feel most comfortable using—that is, your natural leadership style. Consider the types of managerial jobs in which this leadership style would be appropriate.

2. Any time you attempt to influence the behaviors of others, you are engaging in some form of leadership. You do not have to be assigned a specific job title in an organization to demonstrate leadership.

3. Some people subscribe to the view that if you want something done right, you have to do it yourself. If you adhere to this view, it will be difficult to maximize your leadership potential.

4. Be cautious when you select measures for effective leadership. For example, a coach who has a winning season but fails to develop younger players on the team will not be successful in the long run.

5. As a leader, you may not be able to please everyone with your decisions or actions. However, never engage in behavior that will cause you to lose the respect of others.

6. If, as a manager, you use your leader position power to force employees to perform duties in certain ways, you will be practicing coercion more than leadership.

7. As a leader, you should "practice what you preach." Employees will regard your level of commitment to accomplishing goals as an indication of how hard they should work to assist in goal achievement.

8. A leader is also a persuader. Do your homework as a leader so you can make a strong case for the actions you try to persuade others to take.

Different approaches to leadership have been identified and discussed in this chapter. Each approach raises important concepts for managers to consider as they engage in leadership activities. At this point, it is appropriate to review the chapter objectives.

Define leadership.

Leadership is the process of directing and influencing the activities and behaviors of others through communication to attain goals.

Explain the trait approach to leadership.

The trait approach to leadership seeks to identify key characteristics found in all successful leaders. No single personality trait or set of traits consistently differentiates leaders from nonleaders. However, certain core traits significantly contribute to a leader's success. These core traits include drive, the desire to lead, honesty and integrity, self-confidence, cognitive ability, and knowledge of the business.

Identify and describe key theories of the behavioral approach to leadership.

The behavioral approach to leadership focuses on behaviors that differentiate effective leaders from ineffective leaders. The Ohio State leadership studies and leadership research at the University of Michigan have identified two broad classifications of behavior associated with successful leaders: an emphasis on production and quality relationships with subordinates. In turn, the Leadership Grid states that the most effective managers have a high concern for both production and people.

Identify and describe important theories associated with the situational approach to leadership.

According to the situational approach to leadership, there is no single best leadership style. Instead, the situation determines the appropriate leadership style.

Established situational or contingency leadership theories include

■ Tannenbaum and Schmidt's leadership continuum, which illustrates leadership behaviors that reflect the varying levels of authority exercised by managers. Forces in the manager, subordinates, and situation determine which leadership behaviors are selected.

■ House's path-goal theory of leadership proposes that a manager's leadership style will be motivating to the extent that employees believe it will help them to achieve things that they value.

■ Fiedler's contingency model of leadership effectiveness theorizes that the appropriate leadership style depends on the leader's personality and on how favorable the leadership situation is to the leader.

■ Hersey and Blanchard's situational leadership model considers the readiness level of an employee to be the critical factor in determining an appropriate leadership style.

Describe a self-managing work team.

A self-managing work team is a group of well-trained and cross-trained employees who have the specified responsibility and authority to complete a well-defined task.

KEY TERMS

behavioral approach
consideration
contingency model of leadership
  effectiveness
employee orientation
initiating structure
leader-member relations
leader position power
leadership
leadership continuum
Leadership Grid
management

path-goal theory of leadership
production orientation
relationship behavior
self-managing work team
situational (contingency) approach
situational control
situational leadership model
task behavior
task structure
trait approach
transformational leadership

REVIEW AND DISCUSSION QUESTIONS

1. How is management distinguished from leadership?
2. What are some of the problems that plague the trait approach to leadership?
3. What contribution has the trait approach made to the understanding of leadership?
4. According to Blake and Mouton, what is the best leadership style for managers to use?
5. How were the results of the Ohio State University and the University of Michigan leadership studies similar?

6. According to Tannenbaum and Schmidt, what forces in a leadership situation should a manager consider when determining the appropriate way to lead?

7. According to the contingency model of leadership effectiveness, a manager's success in leading a work group is contingent on what factors?

8. According to Fiedler's research, why do task-motivated leaders generally perform best when their situational control is either high or relatively low?

9. According to the path-goal theory of leadership, what determines whether a manager's leadership style will be motivating to his or her employees?

CRITICAL THINKING INCIDENT 8.1

Designing a Leadership Approach

Tony Russell started the Manhattan Fashions clothing manufacturing company in New York seven years ago. The company designs and manufactures its own lines of men's and women's clothing. When he began his business, Tony did much of the design work himself. However, as the company prospered and grew, Tony realized he did not have time to design clothes and run the business so he hired several designers to create new fashions. When the company was small, Tony felt comfortable in his role as owner and manager. Now, however, the company has many employees and Tony is not sure how to best manage the business. He must lead two distinctly different groups of employees.

One group is the designers. These individuals are highly trained and experienced in designing men's and women's fashions. They are proud of their designs, they take their work very seriously, and they are well paid. Their designs are originals. As a result, the designers see themselves as artists working on custom projects. They know the emphasis in the design department is on quality, and Tony provides them with the time and artistic freedom to produce outstanding designs. The designers like their jobs and the status that goes with creating original fashions.

Tony determines which designs actually go into production. The selected designs are sent to the manufacturing plant, where patterns are created. From the patterns, cloth is cut to exact specifications; it is then transferred to the employees who operate the commercial sewing machines.

Constructing each style of clothing is a fairly routine and uninteresting job. The second group of employees—the workers who operate the sewing machines—construct clothing from the same pattern over and over until a specific order is filled. Operating the sewing machines requires little skill and does not pay well. The job is very structured, and

the operators that Tony has hired do not express an interest in assuming a lot of responsibility. Due to the monotony of the job, it is easy for workers to lose their concentration. As a result, the quality of their work needs to be monitored closely to maintain high standards.

One day, as Tony discusses his business concerns with a close friend, Dale, the following conversation occurs.

Tony: I know how to design, but I'm not sure I know how to lead.

Dale: What do you mean?

Tony: I like to think that I can assign tasks to people and then go on to other things, knowing that they will get the job done. However, that doesn't always work.

Dale: Maybe some of your employees don't understand their jobs as well as they should.

Tony: That's not the problem. Designing stylish clothing is more difficult than manufacturing clothing, but most of my problems are in the manufacturing plant.

Discussion Questions

1. According to Hersey and Blanchard's situational leadership model, how do the job-relevant levels of readiness differ for the designers and the sewing-machine operators?

2. Why is Tony having problems in the manufacturing plant? State the most likely reason.

3. How should Tony attempt to lead the employees in his company?

CRITICAL THINKING INCIDENT 8.2

Three's a Charm

The Safford Landscaping Company is owned by Mike, Joanne, and Dan Safford. As commercial landscapers, the Saffords install and maintain landscaping for new residential homes, resorts, and commercial businesses. Mike is the sales manager, Joanne is the office manager, and Dan is the construction manager.

As sales manager, Mike has formed a sales staff that is good at identifying customers' needs and showing them how the company can meet those needs. A big part of Joanne's job is devoted to designing landscaping plans for Dan to follow. Joanne has hired a very capable office staff, and her employees are able to do their jobs well without a lot of close supervision.

The employees Dan has hired, however, differ in many respects from the ones employed by Mike and Joanne. To save money, Dan recruits workers who have little or no landscaping experience. The fact that the workers are inexperienced is fine with Dan because he likes to be in control. Dan's philosophy is, "If you want something done right, you have to do it yourself." Therefore, all important decisions concerning the installation of landscaping by his employees are made by Dan. In addition to deciding what will be done and how it will be done, Dan closely oversees the work of his employees. He is very much a "get the job done" type of person. Although Dan spends a lot of time checking on what the landscaping workers are doing, he does not try to develop rapport with them. According to Dan, "It should always be clear who is in charge, and that distinction is lost if the boss starts to get close to the employees."

Dan thinks most of his employees are lazy because, in his opinion, they do not work as hard as they should, and he is not always pleased with their work. For example, at one job site, Dan noticed that a worker added one more sprinkler to the water line than was shown on the landscaping plans. The worker believed that the water pressure in the area was sufficient to accommodate the modification, and he thought the additional sprinkler would provide better water coverage. Although the worker's assessment of the situation was correct, Dan was furious that the employee did not request permission before installing the additional sprinkler. In front of the other workers, Dan chastised the employee for not following the landscaping plans. Dan exclaimed, "Extra sprinklers cost money that we didn't budget for in this job!"

In general, the Saffords are pleased with the performance of their company. Joanne and Mike like their jobs and their employees. As Joanne explains, "I feel like my office staff works with me, not for me. We accomplish a lot as a team." Dan, on the other hand, is not so content. He does not believe his employees show much initiative. "They could do a lot more than they do," Dan laments. "I shouldn't have to tell them how to do everything, but I don't think they are ever going to be ready to accept greater responsibility. I guess that's just the way it will always be in this job," Dan concludes.

Discussion Questions

1. How appropriate is Dan's leadership style for the employees he must lead?

2. What is your reaction to Dan's statement that he doesn't think his employees are ever going to be ready to accept greater responsibility?

3. What recommendations can you make that will enable Dan to become a more effective leader?

CRITICAL THINKING INCIDENT 8.3

Changing Weather Patterns

The Weathertronics forecasting company is a private firm that provides long- and short-term weather forecasts for any area of the globe. There is a large demand for the company's services. Wall Street commodities traders, for instance, are very interested in how favorable the weather will be for growing everything from coffee beans to wheat. Manufacturers of products that vary in demand based on the weather are also interested in the forecasting provided by Weathertronics.

The weather analysts employed by Weathertronics have an ambiguous job. Weather forecasting, especially in the long term, is not a precise science. This fact is known by anyone who has ever planned an outdoor activity based on a favorable weather report only to have things canceled due to rain! The weather forecasts issued by Weathertronics are more accurate than most available weather predictions. However, to achieve this distinction, the company's analysts must evaluate reams of technical data collected by various means. There is no single formula that will always convert these data into a completely accurate weather forecast. Instead, the analysts employed by Weathertronics must continuously refine their forecasting techniques and build on their collective wisdom to create superior weather predictions.

Corporate clients pay high fees to the company for its weather forecasts. In return, they expect the analysts' forecasts to be far more accurate than the reports that the National Weather Service gives out for free. Once the analysts provide a weather forecast to a client, their job is not done. They must continue to monitor new data relevant to that forecast and provide the client with updates on anything that could affect their forecast. These high expectations and requirements make the weather analysts' jobs very stressful.

The weather analysts employed by Weathertronics see themselves as competent, but many are young and realize they can benefit from all the help they can get. Specifically, they understand the importance of getting reactions from other company analysts to their forecasts before releasing them to clients. The weather analysts are aware that they are judged in general terms by their track records. However, they personally do not receive direct feedback from the corporate clients who purchase their forecasts. That feedback is provided directly by the clients to the top managers at Weathertronics. Furthermore, the analysts are not very clear about how their salary increases or promotions are determined by the company.

Weathertronics is now faced with the task of hiring a new manager to direct the activities of the weather analysts. Neither top management nor the analysts are pleased with the performance of the current manager, Jeff Atkins, who is resigning. Apparently, Jeff was not very good at goal setting or providing assistance to the analysts so that they could do their jobs well. The company needs to hire a new manager who will be an effective leader.

Discussion Questions

1. According to path-goal theory of leadership, what key aspects of the weather analysts' job at Weathertronics should be considered in determining an appropriate leadership style for the new manager?

2. What is known about the analysts that will be important in determining an appropriate leadership style?

3. What leadership approach does path-goal theory suggest for the new manager?

NOTES

1. "Can Academic Types Provide a Leadership Paradigm?," *Behavioral Sciences Newsletter* (March 24, 1986), p. 1.

2. Rick Tetzeli, "Making Quality More Than a Fad," *Fortune* (May 18, 1992), p. 12.

3. For an excellent review of trait research in leadership, see Ralph M. Stogdill, *Handbook of Leadership: A Survey of Theory and Research* (New York: The Free Press, 1974), pp. 35–91.

4. Shelley A. Kirkpatrick and Edwin A. Locke, "Leadership: Do Traits Matter?," *Academy of Management Executive* 5 (May 1991): 49.

5. The identification and description of these six traits are drawn from Kirkpatrick and Locke, "Leadership: Do Traits Matter?," pp. 49–56.

6. Susan Caminiti, "America's Most Successful Businesswoman," *Fortune* (June 15, 1992), pp. 102–108.

7. Ibid., p. 104.

8. Kirkpatrick and Locke, "Leadership: Do Traits Matter?," p. 55.

9. Ibid., p. 56.

10. Ibid., p. 48.

11. Ralph M. Stogdill and Alvin E. Coons, eds., *Leader Behavior: Its Description and Measurement*, Research Monograph No. 88 (Columbus, OH: Bureau of Business Research, Ohio State University, 1957), p. 75.

12. Robert R. Blake and Anne Adams McCanse, *Leadership Dilemmas—Grid Solutions* (Houston, TX: Gulf Publishing Company, 1991), p. 234.

13. Ibid., p. 26.

14. Ibid., p. 30.

15. Robert R. Blake and Jane Srygley Mouton, *Corporate Excellence through Grid Organization Development* (Houston, TX: Gulf Publishing Company, 1968), p. 29.

16. Robert Tannenbaum and Warren H. Schmidt, "How to Choose a Leadership Pattern," *Harvard Business Review* 51 (May/June 1973): 162–80.

17. Tetzeli, "Making Quality More Than a Fad," p. 12.

18. Tannenbaum and Schmidt, "How to Choose a Leadership Pattern," pp. 175–78.

19. Tetzeli, "Making Quality More Than a Fad," pp. 12–13.

20. Charles R. Day, Jr., "Total Quality Leadership," *Industry Week* (October 7, 1991), p. 7.

21. Tetzeli, "Making Quality More Than a Fad," p. 13.

22. Robert J. House and Terence R. Mitchell, "Path-Goal Theory of Leadership," *Journal of Contemporary Business* 3 (Autumn 1974): 81.

23. Robert J. House, "A Path-Goal Theory of Leader Effectiveness," *Administrative Science Quarterly* 16 (September 1971): 322.

24. House and Mitchell, "Path-Goal Theory of Leadership," p. 84.

25. Discussion of the four leadership styles is based on House and Mitchell, "Path-Goal Theory of Leadership," pp. 83–91.

26. House and Mitchell, "Path-Goal Theory of Leadership," p. 91.

27. Discussion of contingency variables is based on House and Mitchell, "Path-Goal Theory of Leadership," pp. 85–88.

28. Fred E. Fiedler, "The Contingency Model and the Dynamics of the Leadership Process," in *Advances in Experimental Social Psychology,* Leonard Berkowitz, ed. (New York: Academic Press, 1978), pp. 59–66.

29. Ibid., p. 9.

30. Fred E. Fiedler, "Engineer the Job to Fit the Manager," *Harvard Business Review* 43 (September/October 1965): 117; Fiedler, "The Contingency Model and the Dynamics of the Leadership Process," p. 65.

31. Gary Johns, *Organizational Behavior: Understanding Life at Work,* 3d ed. (Glenview, IL: Scott, Foresman, 1988), p. 319; Fred E. Fiedler, Martin M. Chemers, and Linda Mahar, *Improving Leadership Effectiveness: The Leader Match Concept* (New York: John Wiley, 1976), pp. 9–29.

32. Paul Hersey and Kenneth H. Blanchard, *Management of Organizational Behavior: Utilizing Human Resources,* 6th ed. (Englewood Cliffs, NJ: Prentice-Hall, 1993), pp. 183–219.

33. Ibid., p. 189.

34. Ibid., p. 185.

35. Ibid., p. 186.

36. Ibid., p. 187.

37. Ibid., pp. 188–94; Paul Hersey and Kenneth H. Blanchard, *Management of Organizational Behavior: Utilizing Human Resources,* 4th ed. (Englewood Cliffs, NJ: Prentice-Hall, 1982), p. 153.

38. Bernard M. Bass, "From Transactional to Transformational Leadership: Learning to Share the Vision," *Organizational Dynamics* 18 (Winter 1990): 21.

39. Kathy Rebello and Evan I. Schwartz, "Microsoft," *Business Week* (February 24, 1992): 62–63.

40. Richard E. Byrd, "Corporate Leadership Skills: A New Synthesis," *Organizational Dynamics* 16 (Summer 1987): 34–43.

41. Bernard M. Bass and Bruce J. Avolio, "Transformational Leadership and Organizational Culture," *Public Administration Quarterly* 17 (Spring 1993): 112–21.

42. Terry C. Blum, Dail L. Fields, and Jodi S. Goodman, "Organization-Level Determinants of Women in Management," *Academy of Management Journal* 37 (April 1994): 241.

43. Alice H. Eagly, Steven J. Karau, and Blair T. Johnson, "Gender and Leadership Style among School Principals: A Meta-Analysis," *Educational Administration Quarterly* 28 (February 1992): 76–102.

44. Judy B. Rosener, "Ways Women Lead," *Harvard Business Review* 68 (November/December 1990): 119–25.

45. Ibid.

46. "Debate: Ways Men and Women Lead," *Harvard Business Review* 69 (January/February 1991): 150–51.

47. "Women Managers Rate Higher Than Male Counterparts," *Personnel Journal* 73 (July 1994): 17.

48. Charles Brewton, "The Best Bosses Don't Just Manage—They Lead," *Hotel and Motel Management* (April 8, 1991), p. 36.

49. Ben Pitman, "How Do I Motivate and Lead My People?," *Journal of Systems Management* 42 (March 1991): 34.

50. Jay A. Conger, "Leadership: The Art of Empowering Others," *Executive* 3 (February 1989): 18.

51. The information on self-managing work teams in this section is derived from Thomas Owens, "The Self-Managing Work Team," *Small Business Reports* 16 (February 1991): 53–65.

52. Ibid.

53. Ibid.

SUGGESTED READINGS

Antonioni, David. "Managerial Roles for Effective Team Building." *Supervisory Management* 39 (May 1994): 3.

Bass, Bernard M., and Bruce J. Avolio. "Transformational Leadership and Organizational Culture." *Public Administration Quarterly* 17 (Spring 1993): 112–21.

Blum, Terry C., Dail L. Fields, and Jodi S. Goodman. "Organization-Level Determinants of Women in Management." *Academy of Management Journal* 37 (April 1994): 241–68.

Capowski, Genevieve. "Anatomy of a Leader: Where Are the Leaders of Tomorrow?" *Management Review* 83 (March 1994): 10–17.

Carr, Clay. "Empowered Organizations, Empowering Leaders." *Training & Development* 48 (March 1994): 39–44.

Dannemiller, John C. "Getting Leaders to Lead." *Industry Week* (April 18, 1994), p. 27.

Deming, W. Edwards. "Leadership for Quality." *Executive Excellence* 11 (June 1994): 3–5.

Isgar, Tom, Joyce Ranney, and Sherm Grinnell. "Team Leaders: The Key to Quality." *Training & Development* 48 (April 1994): 45–47.

Kinni, Theodore B. "Leadership Up Close." *Industry Week* (June 20, 1994), pp. 21–25.

White, Joseph B. "Developing Leaders for the High-Performance Workplace." *Human Resource Management* 33 (Spring 1994): 161–68.

CHAPTER 9

CONTROLLING

■ LEARNING OBJECTIVES

This chapter discusses the basic principles and underlying foundations of the management control process. The learning objectives for this chapter are to:

- Understand the main role of the control function in management.
- Explain the control process.
- Identify various types of control systems.
- Discuss how controls vary, depending on the managerial level.
- List the characteristics of an effective control system.
- Examine why people tend to resist control systems.

■ CHAPTER OUTLINE

During the Great Depression in the 1930s, only 4.7 percent of the then 11,777 savings and loan (S & L) institutions failed. Yet in July 1989, almost 30 percent of the S & Ls were insolvent or had been taken over by the federal regulatory system. Why did they survive the Great Depression and not the inflation and high interest rates of the 1980s? What went wrong?

Although savings and loan institutions made up the largest number of bank failures in the 1980s, many commercial banks also failed. Here, depositors line up for FSLIC repayment in New York City, September 1987.

To understand this question, it is necessary to take a look at the history behind the S & Ls. During the 1700s, there were no S & Ls. Back then, commercial banks focused primarily on financial commerce and did business only with the elite. As the working class increased in number, however, the demand for housing finance rose proportionately. In the 1830s, the S & Ls were created to supply that demand.

In early 1920, Regulation Q ensured that commercial banks paid depositors lower interest rates than S & Ls did. The S & Ls needed only to use the bulk of their funds to finance housing, which allowed them to compete against commercial banks. In 1934, the Federal Savings and Loan Insurance Corporation (FSLIC) was established. It insured depositors up to $5000 per account in the 1930s; this insurance rose in increments each decade until it reached $100,000 per account in the 1980s. At this time, monitoring by the depositors was no longer a great necessity and was virtually eliminated. The institutions became their own monitors, backed up by periodic inspections by an agency of the federal government.

The S & Ls prospered until the 1980s, when interest rates became very volatile. This caused problems for institutions like S & Ls that were carrying fixed, long-term, low-interest mortgages. The ways in which individual S & Ls managed their internal controls to make up the difference between their long-term, low-interest mort-

—Continued

THE IMPORTANCE OF CONTROL

All anyone has to do to realize the importance of the control function in management is to look at the huge number of businesses that have failed primarily because they lost financial control. The savings and loan failures are classic examples of businesses that failed to establish management control systems that would have prevented many of the abuses that occurred.

One excellent example of such abuse is Centrust Savings of Miami and David Paul, who took charge of Centrust in 1983. According to the Resolution Trust Corporation (RTC)

> Mr. Paul used the Thrift's money to buy a $7 million yacht and financed his purchase of a home in an exclusive area in Miami. Paul also squandered nearly $30 million on an art collection and spent lavishly on silver lobster crackers, Baccarat Crystal, and gifts from Tiffany.[1]

The problem of lack of management control even goes beyond the S & L crisis. Every day, both in the newspapers and on the television, the media informs

gages and the new high interest rates was what literally went wrong with the S & Ls.

The S & Ls that concentrated most of their monies in traditional investments, such as house mortgages, mortgage-backed securities, and consumer deposits, to try to make up the difference in low-interest mortgages and high interest rates continued to be solvent in the 1990s. Those S & Ls that became insolvent had

1. Invested highly and recklessly in nontraditional investments, primarily in the forms of commercial loans and real estate investments that they knew very little about.

2. Poor loan-documentation procedures and inadequate credit analyses.

3. Violated federal regulations and did not have accurate appraisals for loans secured by real estate.

Only 3–4 percent of all insolvent S & Ls failed as a result of outright fraud or abuse.

The cost of the S & L mismanagement has been high. The FSLIC estimates the cumulative cost of deals completed in 1988 alone at $37.1 billion. According to Treasury Department estimates, which include financing costs, this cost in 1990 was $90 billion and the cost over 30 years will be $157.6 billion. It appeared that this trend was changing in 1992, which marked the third consecu-

tive year of declines in S & L failures. It is too soon to tell, however, but San Francisco economist and writer R. Dan Brumbaugh and other analysts point out that much of the record profits of $4.05 billion for 1992 was driven by the unusually wide gap between short-term and long-term interest rates.

What went wrong, who is to blame, and how could so many S & Ls lose control of their financial situations? This chapter attempts to answer these questions by analyzing the subject of control in management.

ADAPTED FROM: *The Bradenton Herald,* Associated Press (January 2, 1993), p. B1; William C. Ferguson and Reid Nagle, "The FSLIC Crisis: What Can We Learn from It?" *Savings Institutions* **110** (June 1989): 62–67; William A. Hamilton and Penny R. Hamilton, "A Bank Is Only as Good as Its Bankers," *Bankers Monthly* **107** (January 1990): 81–83; George J. Benston and George G. Kaufman, "Understanding the Savings-and-loan Debacle," *The Public Interest* (Spring 1990): 79–95; Serge Bellanger, "Looking Behind the Thrift Crisis," *The Banker's Magazine* **172** (July/August 1989): 60–64; Banning K. Lary, "Insolvent Thrifts: A National Crisis," *Banker's Monthly* **78** (March 1989): 29–32; Terese Kruezer, "Born-Again Banks: Four Fabulous Turnarounds," *Banker's Monthly* **107** (April 1989): 14–18; J. Noel Fahey, "Grade A Institutions Far Outnumber the Bad," *Savings Institutions* **110** (January 1989): 38–44; William A. Stone, "Lessons from the Thrift and Commercial Bank Industries," *Internal Auditor* **47** (June 1990): 32–40; Gary Hector, "S & Ls: Where Did All Those Billions Go?," *Fortune* (September 10, 1990), pp. 84–86.

---

us of new business failures in such industries as the airline industry. There are also the all-too-familiar disasters in the public sector, ranging from the explosion of the Challenger to the meltdown at Chernobyl, and what appears to be a chain of never-ending financial abuses by government contractors.

Control "monitors" the effectiveness of the other management functions.

Control is the fifth basic management function. The **control function** "monitors" the other four management functions—planning, organizing, staffing, and leading—to ensure their effectiveness. In the control phase, management begins to formulate plans and strategies as a result of either negative or positive control findings. Without an effective control system, the desired results and goals of any organization would virtually be doomed to failure.

Through the control phase, management is made aware of changes in the firm's external or internal environment. Declining sales, increasing product-rejection rates, rising costs, lower profits, excessive employee turnover, and absenteeism are just a few of the problems that management can identify by constantly monitoring controls. The control system also identifies positive results that are above the goals or objectives anticipated by management. These results should also be analyzed by management so that the trend can continue.

THE ROLE AND DEFINITION OF THE CONTROL PROCESS

The definition of "control" indicates that it is a "process" that tells management how the firm is doing.

Control may be defined as the process that helps to ensure that the firm's plans and objectives are being achieved or to determine that adjustments must be made in order to reach them. Through the control process, information is gathered that tells managers at all levels whether the activities they have designed to accomplish specific organizational goals and objectives are working. Thus, the control and planning functions are very closely related to one another. By gathering this information and comparing it to the desired results, management can make changes in present plans if the results are not being obtained. A good control system should also help managers determine *why* goals are not being met. By knowing the cause of the failure, effective corrective action can be taken and the same problem hopefully will not occur again. Control activities should relate directly to tactical and operational plans; these plans, in turn, directly relate to long-term strategic plans.

THE CONTROL PROCESS

An effective communication system is at the heart of every truly effective control system. Only if everyone understands the control process and if sound, accurate information is gathered, analyzed, and communicated to all parties concerned will management have a good control system in place.

Although the control process naturally varies among different firms and different industries, the actual steps in the process are basically the same.

1. Top management generates long-term strategic goals and plans.

2. Middle and supervisory managers generate short-term tactical and operational plans and objectives.

3. Identify standards from strategic, tactical, and operational plans and objectives.

4. Measure performance.

5. Compare performance to the standard.

6. Take corrective action if necessary or continue current course of action.

Steps 1 and 2 are preliminary but essential to the control process Steps 3 through 6 as shown in Figure 9–1.

All business organizations follow these steps in the control process, but they handle each stage in considerably varied ways. The organization's external competitive environment, for instance, may force firms who are in a very dynamic and rapidly changing industry to design a control system that has very broad and flexible objectives and standards. The rapidly changing computer industry, where technological breakthroughs occur frequently, would require such a system. On the other hand, firms that operate in a very stable and slow-moving environment, such as a public utility company, would be able to quantify objectives and standards very specifically.

■ *Setting Performance Standards*

Step 1 is setting performance standards.

If the firm is using a planning system, such as the management-by-objectives (MBO) planning process, then the objectives normally will be quite specific.

Performance standards are sometimes more easily quantified for certain professions than for others. An important question is how often to gather samples for comparison. This laboratory researcher at British Petroleum America is checking samples and gathering data on an ongoing basis.

■ **FIGURE 9–1** Steps in the Control Process

Top management generates long-term strategic goals and plans.

Middle and supervisory managers generate short-term tactical and operational plans and objectives.

The control standards are identified from the planning objectives.

Performance is measured periodically.

A comparison of performance to standards is made.

Either corrective action is taken, the standard is changed, or action is continued.

Regardless of the type of planning used, **control standards** for every position and objective must be set.

These standards should be communicated in clear, specific, numerical terms and should be measurable. For example, a quantity standard could be sales per month and the number of products rejected during each day's production run. A profitability standard could be a stated percentage of rate of return on investment in a given year. A cost standard could be a stated percentage of cost reduction by a given date.

Some control standards are stated in terms of a range of acceptable tolerances, as is true in a manufacturing setting. Quality controls of this type are discussed in detail in Chapter 13. Finally, some performance standards are derived from such industry benchmarks as computer sales, which is $500,000 per sales person in Europe.

Although some positions and objectives are relatively easy to quantify or state in numerical terms, it is much more difficult to set control standards for positions that are not directly involved with the production or marketing of a product or service. For example, what is the minimal acceptable standard of job performance for a secretary or a laboratory research scientist or a school teacher? Some aspects of each of these positions can be stated in numerical terms, but it is very difficult to come up with specific and clearly definable standards for every aspect of these jobs.

When this occurs, a manager must determine what contribution this person or position makes to the firm and then find some way to convert this contribution into a standard, even if it is subjective in nature. Regardless of the difficulty, standards must be set that are as specific as possible, that are clearly communicated and understood by the people involved, that are acceptable to the people in these positions, and that are measurable.

■ *Measuring Performance*

Once the standards are known, then management must decide exactly what information is to be gathered, how it is to be gathered, and how frequently it is

REMEMBER TO COMMUNICATE

Point Out Problems Right Away

A few years ago, a commercial airliner crash-landed a few miles short of a Portland, Oregon, airport runway, killing ten people on board. The plane had run out of fuel. The report to the Air Transportation Safety Board contained some interesting items.

- The plane had been circling the airport for quite some time, while the crew tried to fix a landing-gear problem.
- Both the copilot and the flight engineer were aware of the plane's extremely low fuel level.
- Transcripts from the cockpit flight recorder indicated that the warnings given to the captain by the crew were very subtle, gentle, and extremely differential. They were either never heard, or they were never respected.

This disaster obviously illustrates the need to strongly encourage subordinates to speak up openly when they see problems occurring.

ADAPTED FROM: Michael Mayo Charles, "The Wrong Approach," *Flying* (July 1990): 113.

Step 2 is determining what information to gather.

Determine a method that can be used to gather performance data accurately.

How often should information be gathered?

to be gathered. Some of the information needs of an organization are very obvious. As examples, sales, costs, profits, and production rates are all easy to quantify and relatively easy to collect. In the more subjective areas, gathering information becomes more difficult. For example, what information should be gathered to determine the efficiency of a firm's clerical staff? Clearly, a lot of thought and imagination are required to come up with accurate, useful information in this area.

Normally, information is gathered from personal observations, oral or written reports, or computer-generated reports, which summarize data gathered either mechanically or manually. Personal observations are somewhat subjective in nature. If they are done very methodically and definite identifiable points are observed, however, personal observations can attain at least an acceptable degree of accuracy. Similarly, to be useful, an oral or written report must be in a format that relates well to the standard being measured; reports should not contain too much or too little information. The upward communication of information should always be strongly encouraged in order to avert a disaster like the one in the "Remember to Communicate."

Finally, how often to gather the data must be determined. The activities and/or standards to be measured will answer this question. For example, if IBM introduces a new laptop computer and has established a goal to achieve 20 percent of the laptop market by 1997, then gathering market-share data every six months will probably be acceptable. If, however, quality-control data related to production on an assembly line is to be gathered, then every product may have to be checked at each stage of assembly if it is highly technical in nature and relatively expensive to produce.

■ Comparing Performance to the Standard

Step 3 is comparing performance to the standard.

Management must be sure that all of the information gathered is accurate and definitely relates to the standard against which it is being compared. Of course, some **deviations from the standard** are going to occur. Once the data are compared to the standard, management must establish an acceptable range of variation from that standard. Any deviations in excess of the acceptable range of variation must be further analyzed in order to determine why they are exceeding the acceptable range of the performance standard.

For example, let's assume you are the sales manager of a group of salespeople who sell marine electronics to boat manufacturers nationally. You receive the sales report for the month of May, as shown in Figure 9–2. If your management policy is to analyze the reasons for any variations that exceed ±10 percent, then you would have to ask why Bradick's sales are so high and Sullivan's sales are so low.

What are some reasons for variations from the standard?

Some possible reasons for these variations could be differences in the sales of boat manufacturers; economic variations in different parts of the country; inaccurate information gathered; new competitors; aggressive promotion in certain areas of the country by a current competitor; or a poor sales effort by Sullivan and a superior sales effort by Bradick. You must determine what the reason is so that you can complete the final stage in the control process correctly and communicate the results to all personnel. You could also compare the data gathered to your own history, to close competitors, to industrial averages, and even to similar operations that are not direct competitors.

■ Taking Corrective Action

Step 4 is taking corrective action.

When taking corrective action, management should first determine that the *cause* for the variation has been accurately determined. Many times, managers simply see the *symptom,* or what is happening. They must learn to ask, "What is causing this situation to occur?"; the proper choice of corrective action is then usually fairly obvious. For example, if sales are off and management has determined that increased competitive promotions have caused the downturn, then the firm may need to increase promotions.

Sometimes the cause will be beyond the manager's control. The standard itself must then be revised. For example, it is quite common for a number of firms to set sales quotas for salespeople in anticipation of an increased level of economic activity. If the economy declines rather than improves, it would be ridiculous to think that lost sales could be made up by simply increasing promotion. Here, the sales quota, or standard itself, needs to be adjusted. Whatever form of correction is taken, management must carefully communicate the reasons for the change to the people affected by it.

Preventive action can eliminate recurrent negative deviations from the standard.

Every organization also needs to try to take **preventive corrective action.** This action can take two forms: (1) instituting routine maintenance programs,

■ **FIGURE 9–2** May Sales Report for the Marine Electronics Company

SALESPERSON	MAY SALES GOAL	ACTUAL SALES	VARIATION BETWEEN SALES GOALS AND ACTUAL SALES (%)
Bradick	150,000	182,000	+17.6
Palmer	200,000	182,000	− 9.1
Johnson	170,000	168,000	− 1.2
Clark	250,000	268,000	+ 6.8
Sullivan	210,000	171,000	−22.8

or (2) determining the cause of negative deviations and then developing a plan or program to try to eliminate reoccurrences.

Getting employees involved in this process can be very beneficial. If employees are encouraged to communicate possible causes of and solutions to negative deviations, not only can future problems be avoided but the preventive-action program is also more likely to be positively accepted by the employees. For instance, if it is determined that a production milling machine starts to have problems with its electric motor within 10,000–12,000 hours of usage, then it is wiser to replace the motors after 10,000 hours instead of waiting for the motor to fail, which could certainly cause a production hardship.

A manager should communicate to his or her employees why a preventive action is necessary and how it will help them in the future, so that their support for the program is won. By utilizing this type of program, managers can concentrate on solving new problems rather than rehashing the same old ones over and over again.

The control system must also address positive findings. If the variation is above the stated standard, the manager should determine whether or not this is a temporary or a one-time variation. It would also be good to know if this variation is caused by a single occurrence or by a series of fortunate circumstances. Or is the positive variation due to a more permanent reason, such as the permanent withdrawal of a competitor from the marketplace? If this is the case, the new opportunity must be seized and an aggressive marketing plan should be devised to immediately broaden the firm's market share.

CONSIDER THIS

1. Where do performance standards come from, and why is it so important that they must be clearly understood by everyone?

2. How do you determine what information to gather, how often to gather it, and where to get it?

3. Why is preventive corrective action so important?

THE IMPORTANCE OF COMMUNICATION IN THE CONTROL PROCESS

It is important that communication be clear, specific, and understood by everyone involved in the control process. All of the participants must understand exactly how the control process works, why it is necessary, how significant deviations from the control standard occur, and what to do about them when they do occur. If managers and employees do not understand all stages of the control process very clearly, then problems like the ones experienced by Kaypro Computers can occur.

Kaypro Computers entered the computer field in the 1980s and became an overnight success story. To manage the firm's rapid growth, Andrew Kay turned to his family; his two sons, wife, brother, and even his 94-year-old father helped to run the organization.

Problems started to occur, however, when communications and control broke down. David Kay, the youngest son and the marketing director, states that he found it nearly impossible to get his father, Andrew, to stop buying inventory that the company did not need. (The family literally had to erect a circus tent to warehouse the millions of dollars of excess inventory. Since it was extremely difficult to adequately secure the tent, thefts and shrinkages occurred throughout the next year.) In turn, Andrew Kay felt that he could no longer ask David any questions without feeling threatened by his son's answers. Both men felt that they had no control over the situation.

At the end of 1988, David Kay quit the family business and became a consultant. Kaypro eventually closed due to its financial problems. These results were disastrous and illustrate how vital communication is to the effective control of business operations.[2]

TYPES OF CONTROL SYSTEMS

Control systems take many forms. Some of the more common types of control systems involve:

1. Controls of the *functional areas* within the firm: human resources; production; marketing; information; financial activities.

2. Controls based on the timing of the control procedure during the production process: feed-forward controls; concurrent controls; post-action controls.

3. Controls based on the level of management: strategic controls; tactical controls; operational controls.

■ Control of the Functional Areas

The functional areas of human resources, production, marketing, information, and financial activities must all be controlled very carefully.

All levels of management are engaged in human-resource control.

HUMAN-RESOURCE CONTROLS   Human-resource control consists of a large variety of control techniques and is done at all levels of management throughout the company. Since the quality of the personnel to a large degree determines an organization's effectiveness, management must start by making sure that good controls are in place during the hiring procedure. Once qualified employees are hired, they must be trained and developed to their fullest potentials. Some of the control procedures that help managers in the area of staffing and employee evaluation are performance appraisals, day-to-day observations, guidance to help correct weaknesses and perfect competency, and well-planned job-qualification measures. (These procedures were covered in detail in Chapter 7.)

Managers must explain very carefully why changes need to be made.

The only way that a manager can encourage employees to develop to the point that they achieve their highest performance levels is to monitor their performances, progress, and weaknesses and to effectively communicate these observations to them. A good example of this is a professional football team. First, the team owners carefully draft the best player available. Then they set up a very structured training program. Finally, they evaluate the performance of every player on every down played in the game. This evaluation is communicated to each player, and corrective action in the form of a new training program is developed.

Efficiency and quality are critical today.

PRODUCTION CONTROLS   No matter what the product or service is, the firm needs to produce it efficiently and at the highest level of quality possible.

Production controls can be done before, during, or after a production process. This manager at CSX Corporation carefully monitors production controls.

Production-control techniques attempt to maximize efficiency and quality in every area of the production process. Purchasing, inventory control, quality control, scheduling, and waste management are just some of the more common areas of production control.

As worldwide competition increases for virtually every product and service produced today, only the most efficient and quality-conscious firms will be able to effectively compete in the very near future. The Perspective on Quality illustrates some of the quality-control techniques currently being utilized. Each of these areas is discussed in more detail in Chapter 13.

MARKETING CONTROLS Marketing controls are concerned with all aspects of the marketing area. There are controls on the cost, revenue, market share, and profit of each product or service offered in the marketplace. Market controls help managers to determine when a product should be discontinued and which products should be given additional emphases.

Customer service is vital to all organizations.

Marketing controls also are used to maintain adequate levels of customer service, and this area is receiving increased attention as competition continues to increase. One key to an effective marketing-control system is to have a continuous customer feedback system in place. Only by constantly communicating with customers can management quickly determine changes in customer satisfaction with a firm's products and services.

Finally, firms that fail to properly control how their sales agents and representatives do business may be in for quite a shock. MetLife recently agreed to pay a $20 million fine and $76 million in restitution to 60,000 customers nationwide. MetLife agents in some parts of the country were selling whole-life polices as retirement savings plans. According to an appointed insurance investigator in Florida, these problems happened because of "MetLife's lack of sales supervision and a tacit approval of aggressive sales tactics."[3]

Access to information must be controlled.

INFORMATION CONTROLS Every manager or employee needs certain information in order to do his or her job effectively. A decision has to be made, how-

A PERSPECTIVE ON QUALITY

A New Vision of Quality Control

Quality control in a manufacturing setting is constantly being analyzed, and new ways to improve it are constantly sought after. One new element here is the new way many manufacturers are utilizing "vision systems" in their process-control area. Vision systems utilize laser beams to accurately measure parts or products passing by them.

Since the early 1980s, companies like General Motors have been using vision systems to scan and reject parts that failed to meet their quality-control standards. Likewise, Texas Instruments has been using vision systems to inspect component parts provided by outside suppliers.

Now, however, in addition to utilizing vision systems to inspect component parts, many manufacturers are using them to monitor the entire manufacturing process. To accomplish this, they are tying their vision systems in with industrial programmable controllers (computers), which then gives them a connection between the inspection process and the manufacturing process.

For example, this new type of vision system is used by Intel, a manufacturer of computer chips. Since even a minute flaw in a chip can have grave consequences, Intel has to have virtually instantaneous knowledge of any deviations in their manufacturing process. To achieve control standards of this magnitude, Intel uses some artificial-intelligence programs that draw on information fed them by the vision system. The system tells them not only when they have a problem, but where the problem is coming from in the manufacturing process.

This new type of control system is closer to the type of systems utilized by Asian manufacturers. Rather than have one large vision system at the end of an assembly line to inspect completed products, this company has several smaller vision systems located throughout the manufacturing process to inspect products periodically. If deviations to quality standards are seen, the entire line is stopped and the part of the manufacturing process that is causing the problem is fixed before any more defective parts or products are produced.

The future of linking vision systems to some form of computerized processing device is indeed great. Only time will tell how sophisticated these control devices will become.

ADAPTED FROM: Bob Francis, "A New Vision of Quality Control," *Datamation* (April 1, 1990), pp. 70–72.

ever, as to what specific information different employees and managers can access. Needless to say, there is a lot of sensitive information to which only top management or a given area of the firm should have access. With the ever-increasing use of computers to store and retrieve information, management must be sure that limited access codes are developed. Also, in order to maintain accuracy and confidentiality, management must control what forms of information are entered into the computer. Finally, the level of sophistication of a firm's management information system needs to be thoroughly analyzed, so that the information given to managers and employees truly helps them to make the best possible decisions in the fastest and most cost-effective manner.

FINANCIAL CONTROLS   The importance of understanding the financial area of a firm cannot be overstated. All managers, in both small and large companies, must be familiar with financial statements and financial controls; if they are not, their careers in management will be very short. The financial controls in any organization are obviously very crucial, since they, more than any other

Managers need access to timely and accurate information in order to do their jobs effectively. Managers also share the results with employees so that everyone clearly understands.

control system, indicate the success or failure of a firm. Small businesses, in particular, sometimes neglect the financial area.

Normally, financial controls consist of two parts: budgets and ratio analysis. We will discuss each of these aspects of financial control, in turn, in the following sections.

BUDGETS

Budgets are developed in order to effectively plan, communicate, and control the future activities of an organization for a given period of time. Budgets are stated in numerical terms and are normally done on an annual basis, although both longer and shorter time frames are also budgeted. There are several types of budgets, including operating budgets, cash-flow budgets, capital expenditure budgets, and miscellaneous or nonmonetary item budgets.

There are many types of budgets.

The operating budget is usually the master budget for a firm.

1. The **operating budget,** the most common type of budget, is basically an estimate of all the revenues and expenses that will be incurred by an organization during the up-coming year. In order to develop an operating budget, an expense budget and a sales or revenue budget are done for each department, division, or product area. The operating budget attempts to estimate potential profits and is normally used as the master budget for the entire firm.

2. **Cash-flow budgets** illustrate whether the firm is generating enough revenues on a monthly basis to cover its monthly expenditures. The revenues of most successful businesses fluctuate from month to month, so money from retained earnings must be budgeted well in advance to cover expenses in months when revenues are lean. Many times, businesses are short of cash because too many of their accounts receivables are outstanding at the same time that their fixed and operating expenses continue to grow. Finally, cash-flow budgets indicate if any excess cash is available for either short-term or long-term investment purposes. Management needs to communicate the firm's cash-flow situation to employees so they can understand why business

Cash-flow budgets indicate months in which business revenues either exceed or fall short of expenses.

purchases and other financial outlays can only be made during certain months.

3. Capital expenditure budgets are utilized to purchase major capital items, such as plant expansions, major pieces of machinery or equipment, or vast amounts of inventory. Since these are large expenditures, they are normally budgeted over several years to allow top management to keep control of them. In most major corporations, some capital expenditures are made every year; in smaller firms, they may rarely be made.

Capital expenditure budgets involve major purchases.

4. Nonmonetary or miscellaneous budgets are also utilized to allocate resources other than cash. As examples, floor space, hours of labor, and materials and supplies are all budgeted out on a physical basis first; later, these units are converted to cost figures and included in each department or product expense budget. Since cash is not the only scarce resource in most organizations, it only makes sense to budget these other items out also, thereby ensuring that each department or area is receiving its fair shares of them. If management clearly communicates this process to its employees, there will probably be less resentment among departments.

There are also budgets for nonmonetary items, such as floor space.

■ *The Advantages and Disadvantages of Budgets*

The primary advantages of good constructive budgeting are that it

- Helps any organization control its expenditures
- Indicates and communicates to everyone what areas, products and/or services, and objectives the firm is valuing at the current time
- Allocates the firm's resources in a fair and equitable manner
- Is a good way to measure the firm's performance monetarily

What are the advantages of budgets?

What are the disadvantages of budgets?

The disadvantages of budgeting also have to be considered. Primarily they take a lot of time to prepare and are, therefore, costly. Many times, managers inflate budgets, "knowing" that they will be cut later. Also, budgets can even be wasteful; department managers may quickly spend the remainder of their budgets at the end of the year out of fear that next year's budget will be reduced if they do not spend all of this year's budget. Managers are also sometimes "evaluated" unfairly when they exceed their budgets due to circumstances beyond their control.

And finally, budgets tend to be restrictive in nature in that they only consider the monetary aspects. Sometimes even though the costs outweigh the revenues, if the expense increases customer satisfaction and loyalty or gives the firm a competitive advantage, the expenditure still may be the right move to make. Managers must encourage and be receptive to upward communication from their employees, who may have very justifiable reasons why they need more resources or why exceeding the departmental or product budget makes sense—and may save money—in the long run.

■ *Zero-Based Budgeting*

Zero-based budgeting requires every item to be justified.

One of the most recent attempts to overcome some of the problems with budgets is zero-based budgeting. Many departmental budgets are prepared each year by simply adding to last year's line-item figures. Therefore, many budgets constantly grow without being reevaluated in terms of the necessity for these increases. **Zero-based budgeting** tries to eliminate this problem by forcing every manager to justify the necessity for and the cost of every line item.

Many major corporations, such as Ford, Texas Instruments, and Xerox, have adopted zero-based budgeting and claim large savings as the result of it. However, this method is very time-consuming and can anger a lot of managers who have to justify things that they feel are obviously important to their operation. To solve this problem, a clear and relatively simple communication procedure needs to be established to outline how items can be easily justified.

RATIO ANALYSIS

Ratio analysis tells management how the firm is doing compared to similar firms in the industry.

A very important communication tool for any type of business is **ratio analysis.** Ratios communicate to management how the firm compares in terms of its financial condition to similar firms in the same industry. Ratios indicate what relationship two different numbers, taken from either the firm's balance sheet or income statement, have to each other.

As illustrated in Figure 9–3, a firm's **balance sheet** indicates the overall financial condition of the firm at a given date in time. It lists the firm's assets,

■ **FIGURE 9–3**   Marine Tech Balance Sheet December 31, 19XX

ASSETS			
Current Assets:			
Cash		$118,400	
Accounts Receivable		197,200	
Notes Receivable		47,000	
Supplies		3,800	
Prepaid Insurance		2,700	
Inventory		217,000	
Total Current Assets			$586,100
Fixed Assets:			
Property (Plant and Equipment)			
Land		$95,500	
Plant and Equipment	$400,000	360,200	
Less: Accumulated Depreciation	39,800		
Total Fixed Assets			455,700
Total Assets			$1,041,800
LIABILITIES AND OWNER'S EQUITY			
Current Liabilities:			
Accounts Payable		$24,300	
Salaries Payable		12,000	
Income Tax Payable		13,400	
Notes Payable		198,000	
Total Current Liabilities			$247,700
Long-term Liabilities			
Mortgage Payable		$298,700	
Notes Payable		120,000	
Total Long-term Liabilities			418,700
Total Liabilities			$666,400
Owner's Equity			375,400
Total Liabilities and Owner's Equity			$1,041,800

its liabilities or debts, and the amount of equity the owner(s) have in the firm. As illustrated in Figure 9–4, the **income statement** indicates the amount of profit or loss that a firm has achieved over a stated period of time. It lists the firm's sales and other revenues, if any, and all of the firm's expenses. Both of these statements are extremely important to the analysis of a firm's financial condition.

In addition to comparing a firm's own past ratios to its current ratios (past performance to current performance), a firm's current ratios can also be compared to industry ratios. Comparisons of a company's balance-sheet and/or income-statement ratios to industry ratios provide fairly reliable indicators of how a business stacks up against other similar firms in the industry. Ratio analysis is also studied carefully by lending institutions before they make loans to customers and by potential buyers if the owners of a business decide to put it up for sale.

Ratio analysis is typically done in four common areas.

- Liquidity ratios (the firm's ability to meet short-term debts)
- Leverage ratios (the amount of debt utilized to purchase the firm's assets)
- Operating or activity ratios (how efficiently a firm's assets are being used)
- Profitability ratios (how efficient a firm is at earning a profit)

We will discuss each of these types of ratios in turn.

■ *Liquidity Ratios*

The firm's current creditors look at liquidity, or the firm's ability to pay its debts right now.

Liquidity ratios are very important to the firm's current creditors, especially the short-term creditors. A **liquidity ratio** indicates the firm's ability to pay its

■ **FIGURE 9–4** Marine Tech Income Statement for the Year Ending December 31, 19XX

REVENUES		
Sales Revenues	$1,790,400	
Less: Sales Returns and Allowances	80,100	
Net Sales		$1,710,300
COST OF GOODS SOLD		
Beginning Inventory	$189,000	
Purchases	990,000	
Total Goods Available for Sale	$1,179,000	
Less: Ending Inventory	217,000	
Total Cost of Goods Sold		962,000
Gross Profit		$748,300
EXPENSES		
Sales Promotion Expenses	$47,900	
Capital Consumption Allowance	16,400	
Administrative Expenses	59,000	
Salaries	124,000	
Total Expenses		$247,300
Net Income before Taxes		501,000
Federal Taxes		285,350
Net Income		$215,650

current debts. If a firm is attempting to obtain a line of credit from a supplier, this is the ratio in which the supplier would be most interested. The most common liquidity ratio is the **current ratio** (current assets divided by current liabilities). This figure indicates how many times larger the value of a firm's assets are than the amount of liabilities the firm has at the time.

For example, in the balance sheet in Figure 9–3, the total current assets are $586,100 and the total current liabilities are $247,700. We divide current assets by current liabilities ($586,100/$247,700), which yields a current ratio of 2.37. This means that the firm has more than two times as many assets as it does liabilities. Although averages vary from industry to industry, 2.0 is the commonly accepted current ratio for the manufacturing industry. A ratio 2.0 or higher for a manufacturer would be considered good by most creditors.

The acid test ratio shows how well a firm can pay its bills without making any more sales.

An even stricter liquidity ratio is the **acid test ratio,** which removes the value of a firm's inventories from its current assets. This ratio reflects how well the company can pay for its operating expenses without selling any of its products. For example, in the balance sheet in Figure 9–3, the current assets less the inventory are $369,100 and the current liabilities are $247,700. The acid test ratio is $369,100/247,700, which gives a ratio of 1.49. Since current assets still outweigh current liabilities, this ratio communicates to creditors that this firm is probably able to pay its current liabilities without too much difficulty.

■ *Leverage Ratios*

The leverage ratio indicates a firm's level of total indebtedness.

The **leverage ratio,** also sometimes referred to as a **debt ratio,** indicates the percentage of debt financing that a firm used to purchase its assets. A firm's total liabilities (total debt) are divided by its total assets to derive this percentage. Again, industry averages vary considerably. Industries that operate in a very stable and predictable business environment may have very high ratios of debt to assets; the reverse is true for firms that operate in a very dynamic and unpredictable business environment.

For example, the total liabilities from the balance sheet in Figure 9–3 are $666,400 and the total assets are $1,041,800, so $666,400/$1,041,800 yields a leverage percentage of 0.64, or 64 percent. In general, if this percentage is lower, a firm is better able to withstand business slowdowns and still pay its creditors. Again, to determine its real meaning, this ratio needs to be compared to the leverage ratios of other similar firms in the industry.

■ *Operating or Activity Ratios*

Operating ratios indicate business activity.

An **operating** or **activity ratio** indicates how well the firm is utilizing its assets. These ratios deal primarily with inventories and sales to assets. One of the most common operating ratios is the **inventory turnover ratio,** which indicates how many times during a given year a firm turned over or sold its average inventory. The inventory turnover ratio is determined by dividing the average inventory (Beginning Inventory + Ending Inventory/2) into net sales.

For example, the beginning inventory in the income statement in Figure 9–4 is $189,000 and the ending inventory is $217,000, so the average inventory would be $406,000/2, or $203,000. If net sales are $1,710,300, then $1,710,300/$203,000 yields an inventory turnover ratio of 8.43. This means that the firm sold the equivalent of its entire average inventory almost 8 ½ times during the year. Normally, this ratio is lower for high-priced durable goods and higher for low-priced nondurable goods. A high turnover ratio normally indicates efficient use of the company's inventory and high sales figures.

The total asset turnover ratio indicates how efficiently a firm uses its assets.

A second type of operating ratio, the **total asset turnover ratio,** indicates how efficiently a firm is using its assets to generate a given level of sales. It is found by dividing the firm's net sales by its total assets.

For example, net sales in the income statement in Figure 9–4 are $1,710,300 and total assets in the balance sheet in Figure 9–3 are $1,041,800. Thus $1,710,300/$1,041,800 yields a total asset turnover ratio of 1.64. This means that each dollar of the firm's assets generated $1.64 in sales. The higher this figure is, the better. The lower the total amount of assets needed to generate a given sales level is, the more efficiently the firm is utilizing its assets.

Profitability Ratios

ROI is the percentage of the return the firm is receiving on its investment.

Profitability ratios indicate how efficiently the firm utilizes its assets to generate a profit. The most popular profitability ratio is **return-on-investment (ROI),** which is derived by dividing a firm's net income or net profit (after taxes) by its total assets. The ROI ratio shows the rate of return (a percentage) that a firm is getting for every dollar it is investing in assets.

For example, the net income in the income statement in Figure 9–4 is $215,650 and the total assets in the balance sheet in Figure 9–3 are $1,041,800. The profitability ratio, or rate of return, for the firm is then $215,650/$1,041,800, or 20.7 percent. The higher this percentage is the better, since it communicates to the firm's owners what their return was for their investment.

Breakeven Analysis

Breakeven analysis is a crucial step in investment or new product/service analysis.

One final financial control utilized by virtually every firm is the **breakeven analysis,** which determines what level of sales or revenues a business must generate to cover all of its total costs. Breakeven analysis is normally one of the first things to consider when investors are developing startup plans for a new business or when a firm is planning to introduce any new product or service.

The breakeven analysis involves both fixed costs and variable costs, which, when added together, equal total costs. A firm's fixed costs do not vary with production or sales; they consist of such items as the monthly rent or mortgage payment, utilities, and insurance premiums. Variable costs do vary with production or sales; they include such items as labor, materials, and costs of component parts.

The management of any organization knows that before it can make a profit on any product or service, it must cover all of the firm's fixed and variable costs. The question then becomes, How many more units of this product or service does the firm realistically think it can sell at a given price in a given market area? To find the **breakeven point (BEP)** at which a firm's total costs are covered, we use the formula

$$\text{Breakeven point (in units)} = \frac{\text{Total fixed costs}}{\underset{\text{(per unit)}}{\text{Selling price}} - \underset{\text{(per unit)}}{\text{Variable costs}}}$$

Let's assume that a person plans to open a retail store to sell tropical plants. If the total fixed costs to open the store are $40,000, the variable cost per plant is $12.00, and the selling price per plant is $20.00, then the breakeven point would be

$$\text{BEP (in units)} = \frac{\$40{,}000}{\$20.00 - \$12.00} = \frac{40{,}000}{8.00} = 5000 \text{ plants}$$

The breakeven point in sales would be $5000 \times \$20.00 = \$100,000$, as shown in Figure 9–5. At the breakeven point on the graph, total revenues equal total costs. This point occurs when 5000 units (plants) have been sold (at $20.00 per plant), generating $100,000 in revenues. If the firm sells less than 5000 units (plants), it will experience a loss. Once the firm sells more than 5000 units, it will start to earn a profit. These figures will help our investor to estimate whether going into this business will be profitable or not, considering the market and the competitive situation.

You should be aware of the following assumptions about and limitations of breakeven analysis.

1. Although it is helpful to know the breakeven point, no one goes into business to "break even." Even nonprofit organizations need to acquire income in excess of costs in order to grow and expand. Most managers want to know, How many units must the business make or sell to earn, for example, $20,000 in profit? This point of profit can be determined by simply adding the firm's profit goal to its fixed costs. For example

■ **FIGURE 9–5** Breakeven Analysis

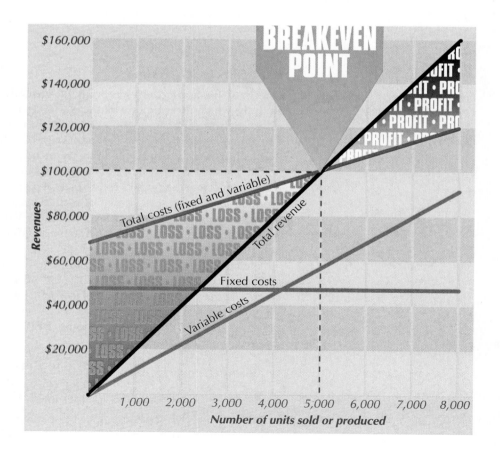

$$\text{Profit goal} = \frac{(FC)\ \$40,000 + (PG)\ \$20,000}{(SP)\ \$20.00 - (VC)\ \$12.00} = \frac{60,000}{8.00} = 7500 \text{ plants}$$

where FC = Fixed costs
       PG = Profit goals
       SP = Selling price
       VC = Variable costs

What are some limitations of BEA?

2. The straight fixed-costs line and the 45° total revenue and variable-costs lines in Figure 9–5 indicate a constant fixed pattern. In reality, fixed and variable costs change as volume increases; normally some adjustment in unit price must be made to generate larger sales volumes. Since the graph assumes constant costs and a constant sales price at all levels of volume, there is some margin for error.

3. Breakeven points for every product or service are constantly changing as competitive pressures force firms to adjust their prices and suppliers change the costs of both fixed and variable items. This means that any breakeven point is probably going to have a fairly short life.

Does all this mean that figuring breakeven points is worthless? No, it simply means that this analysis—like most management rules of thumb—is useful but imperfect.

CONSIDER THIS

1. Why do some firms not believe in doing extensive budgeting?

2. How does a manager determine whether a firm's ratios are good or bad?

3. How can the results of a firm's breakeven analysis be deceiving?

CONTROL SYSTEMS BASED ON TIMING

The second type of control system classifies the controls in terms of when they are used in the production or creation of a product or service. Three types of controls are based on timing: feed-forward, concurrent, and post-action controls.

■ Feed-Forward Controls

Feed-forward controls are preventive in nature.

Feed-forward controls, also known as **preliminary controls,** are designed to be preventive in nature: their purposes are to make sure that the necessary resources are supplied and that potential problems with the production process are anticipated. Many feed-forward controls ensure that suppliers of raw materials and component parts deliver them at the right quality level, in the proper quantities, and on time. The desired quality levels must be carefully and accurately communicated to suppliers so that there are not any misunderstandings.

For example, before a construction company starts to build a home, the general contractor must develop a complete construction schedule and an estimate of the materials and equipment needed. Both the estimate and the schedule indicate what types of personnel are needed; what specific construction materials must be ordered; what quality and quantity levels are specified for the materials;

GLOBAL VIEW

Financial Controls

Keeping tight controls on the costs of producing both existing and new products is hardly news in today's manufacturing setting. Yet, the Japanese seem to approach this area much differently than most American and European companies do, and the results indicate a superior cost-control tactic.

In terms of existing products, companies like Isuzu Motors utilize what they call a "tear-down" approach. Competitive products are literally taken apart piece-by-piece and analyzed for types of material, production method, and assembly method. Actual probable costs can then be determined for each competitor's components. Isuzu may then make the costs of Toyota's steering mechanism and Nissan's brake assembly their own target costs for these same components.

Although some American manufacturers occasionally employ this tear-down procedure, Japanese firms routinely use it as an integral part of cost-control policy. This enables them to keep up with any new competitive ideas and also to stay competitive costwise—not only in today's marketplace, but in tomorrow's as well.

ADAPTED FROM: Ford S. Worthy, "Japan's Smart Secret Weapon," *Fortune* (August 12, 1991), pp. 72–75.

and what equipment is needed. The schedule indicates when each of these activities should take place. Then, prior to each activity, the contractor can make sure that the materials meet the specified quality levels and arrive in the proper quantities and that the right people with the right equipment are at the job site at the right times.

Although feed-forward controls of this nature do help to prevent production problems, they are subject to multiple unpredictable circumstances and/or changes in the situation that cannot be controlled. For example, construction may be delayed by bad weather, equipment breakdowns, or materials supplied in incorrect quality or quantity levels.

■ Concurrent Controls

Concurrent controls help to offset unforeseen circumstances. These controls assess progress as the product or service is developing. In the construction of a home, for example, actual construction must stop at given, predetermined intervals and be checked by a local building inspector before further construction can continue. This is an example of a "yes-no" concurrent control which is used in many manufacturing and construction settings.

What is a yes-no control?

Concurrent controls are vital to the success of any product and are also used in the delivery of services. Probably the most common form of concurrent control in the service industry is management's direct observation of the procedures that take place during the delivery of service by a technician or therapist. Needless to say, concurrent controls are extremely vital if mistakes, errors, and problems are to be kept to a minimum. A manager must communicate why these controls are necessary if he or she honestly expects employees to accept and comply with such regulations.

■ *Post-Action Controls*

Future plans are modified from post-action controls.

The last type of control based on timing, the **post-action control,** assesses the results after the product or service has been completed. Based on this evaluation, plans and procedures are often modified to try to elicit a better level of performance. Post-action controls in the construction of a home would take the form of the final inspection before a certificate of occupancy is issued.

Many times, post-action controls will point out glaring problems or even indicate potential financial losses that the organization was not aware of at the time. Post-action controls also provide a source of feedback to the firm's employees in terms of how well they have performed their jobs. This information must be communicated to employees in a timely and accurate manner. Employee appraisals are an example of this type of control.

CONTROLS BASED ON THE LEVEL OF MANAGEMENT

The type of control system changes as the level of management changes:

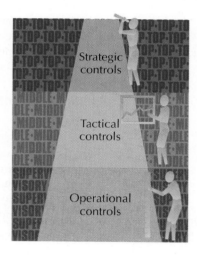

Top managers, who engage in long-range strategic planning, use different types of controls than supervisory-level managers do, since they are concerned with daily operations.

■ *Strategic Controls*

Strategic controls focus on changes in the business environment.

Strategic controls assess the long-range plans and strategies that top management has developed and implemented. Since these are long-term plans, the controls themselves consist primarily of monitoring changes in the firm's financial statements, financial ratios, and the business environment and determining how these changes will impact on the business in the future. Flexible strategic control systems should be set up to gather information that allows top management to see "emerging patterns" that they can react to intuitively. Top management should avoid restrictive, explicit control systems that are too formal and "cut and dried."[4] Control at this level is also concerned with the overall performance of strategic business units (SBUs), product lines, and subsidiaries.

Top managers must be sure that they are interpreting the data correctly. For example, EuroDisney, outside Paris, lost $930 million for fiscal year 1993. EuroDisney officials blamed the loss on a recession and on high interest rates. An analysis of the situation, however, indicated managerial errors by top officials who tried to employ the same marketing practices at EuroDisney that they had used in Florida at Disney World. The analysis also indicated that EuroDisney officials were slow to realize that this system would not work well in Europe. Errors were made in pricing and merchandising; also, European consumers did not react favorably to the exclusion of beer and wine with meals at EuroDisney restaurants. Virtually all of these errors have now been corrected.[5]

■ Tactical Controls

Tactical controls look at the performance of a given product or store or division.

Tactical controls are concerned with monitoring the performance of individual stores, divisions, or products to be sure that their objectives and strategies are progressing as planned. Control points here would consist of store, product, or division sales, costs, profits, growth rates, and budget analyses, which are presented in the form of reports to top management. These reports are very useful to top managers in their strategic planning. Middle managers must be sure to communicate the true results of the performance of their product, division, or store to top management.

■ Operational Controls

Operational controls are established by supervisors and are more explicit than controls at the strategic level are. Many times the information gathered through operational control systems indicates the need to make changes in a store, product, or divisional strategy.

For example, business shrinkage through employee theft—how important is it, and to what degree does management need to establish a control system to prevent it? Here is one reaction to the problem.

> Internal business shrinkage occurs when employees, not outsiders, shrink a firm's cash and inventory. Up to $200 billion is stolen each year from the business place. The Chamber of Commerce estimates that one-third of small-business failures are due to expenses evolving from employee theft. Without effective internal controls, employees can be tempted into committing dishonest acts, as they simply take advantage of opportunities to "get away with something" unchecked.
>
> What should be done? Management must analyze the organization and its current control environment and
>
> 1. Know how the organization operates.
>
> 2. Pinpoint weak links susceptible to internal theft.
>
> 3. Develop an overall internal control system that integrates defenses against the corporate weaknesses of fraud or theft.[6]

Operational controls focus on individual or work-group performance levels.

Operational controls are established to assess the performances of individuals or work groups against predetermined standards. The management by objectives (MBO) process is commonly used as an employee performance-appraisal method. Since employees and managers jointly determine goals for the employee, the results will clearly indicate whether or not they have met the goal. Management must be sure to communicate the results of such evaluations to their employees very carefully, so changes can be made, if necessary.

Keeping employees' records and measuring results of their labor through data storage and computer analysis is a common operational control technique used by many companies.

Operational controls measure very specific results, such as sales, quantity produced, quality, costs, and profits for a specific time frame. This information indicates whether the actual plans and strategies devised by top management are working or not. This level of management is receiving more and more emphasis, as indicated by the advent of more participative management styles.

Operational controls are receiving increasing emphasis.

An example of an operational control system is one that deals with the common problem of unauthorized long-distance telephone calls, which cost businesses millions of dollars per year.[7] The majority of unauthorized phone calls are charged to specific departments, which makes this a supervisory-level management control problem. To curb the costs of unauthorized telephone use, a manager only needs to

1. Tighten switchboard access.

2. Block calls to areas where the company does not conduct business.

3. Educate switchboard operators about fraud schemes, and review personnel practices.

4. Watch phone bills closely for excessive volume.[8]

 # CHARACTERISTICS OF A GOOD CONTROL SYSTEM

In establishing an effective control system, management should be sure not only that it gives the right information on a timely basis but also that it does not create negative feelings and reactions among the employees who are directly affected by it. Although different business situations require different control strategies, some common characteristics seem to be present in virtually all effective control systems. They include the following.

What are some common characteristics of good control systems?

1. *The control must fit the organization and task characteristics.* Research indicates that the most effective type of control strategy depends, to a large degree, on the dynamics of the business environment and on the preciseness

with which specific objectives can be measured. The more available specific performance documentation is, the greater the tendency is to rely on explicit controls.[9] Conversely, businesses that operate in an environment where it is very difficult to measure specific objective performance find that a more informal style of control works best. For example, a research laboratory would have an informal control system in place. Whatever the business environment, the controls must fit the situation.

2. *The control system must provide timely and accurate information.* Many times, the question is asked, "How frequently must controls be applied, and to what degree of accuracy does our control system have to be?" The main considerations here are costs, potential losses, and potential dangerous outcomes. For example, a milk-processing plant may only have to spot check five quarts of milk every 15 minutes for quality and proper fill level; furthermore, the level of accuracy of the fill information may be $\pm \frac{1}{2}$ ounce. Contrast this to the timeliness and accuracy of a control system used during a surgical open-heart procedure. Although highly accurate and constant monitoring is absolutely essential in this case, the cost of developing a control system to this degree of accuracy for the milk producer may be impractical in view of the results to be gained.

The degree of accuracy in a control system will vary.

3. *The control system must be acceptable and clearly communicated to and understood by the people directly involved with it.* If the control system is not clearly communicated to the employees who operate it, or who are being measured by it, they will resent the system and even try to subvert it. People need to fully understand what a control system is measuring and why the firm needs this information. In addition, the system should not measure factors that the employees cannot control or change, or resentment is sure to build up against the system. Employee involvement in developing the control system is essential.

Employees will only accept controls that they understand fully.

4. *The control system should be cost-effective.* It does not make much sense to invest $10,000 in an electronic scanning device if the highest probable amount of annual loss is $5000. Also, additional controls almost always increase personnel costs and slow down productivity to some degree. Thus, the control systems need to be viewed not only in terms of initial costs but also in terms of additional operating costs. The total cost of the control system should then be measured against potential losses.

5. *The control system needs to monitor strategic elements of the business.* So often, businesses do a wonderful job of controlling the nickels and dimes but have very poor control over areas in which substantial sums of money are invested. For example, the managers of a manufacturing firm recently analyzed the control systems throughout the company. They found that they were employing three people in the accounting department to examine and verify the expense accounts of their sales force and management team. Their annual potential losses in this area was estimated at less than $10,000. At the same time, the losses that they were experiencing from poor inventory control had reached $100,000 annually. The work force for inventory control consisted of one person.[10]

Management must be sure to control areas where significant financial losses could occur.

No business can control everything down to the last cent. Even if it could, the number of controls needed to accomplish this would virtually handcuff an organization. Control systems should be placed in the most strategic areas, where potential losses could be significant and where the increased costs, in terms of time and personnel, are well worth it.

6. *Control systems should be difficult to manipulate.* In a lot of organizations, there are always going to be people who will do almost anything to "look good" or to avoid "looking bad." It is also possible that a person in the organization may resort to outright stealing if the opportunity arises. Management must be sure that the firm's control systems have built-in checks and balances to account for these types of employees. For example, more than one person should be required to verify cash, inventories, or sales.

The E. F. Hutton money-laundering case in 1987 is a good example of how unethical employees can subvert a control system in order to acquire financial gain. Federal law requires brokerage houses and banks to file a "Currency Transaction Report" for cash transactions of $10,000 or over. The "CTR," as it is commonly called, it is a control device that helps ensure that the money is recorded for tax purposes. Thus, it can be used as a tool against organized crime, which frequently generates large amounts of cash.

At E. F. Hutton, certain customers were coming in with cash far in excess of $10,000. Some E. F. Hutton brokers would then break the bundles of cash up into amounts under $10,000. They would, in turn, give them to secretaries who would take them to a local bank and get a cashiers check for the amount of cash given them. These cashiers checks were used to purchase unregistered bearer bonds for the customer.

This practice was discovered only when one of the secretaries was mistakenly given a bundle of cash which was larger than $10,000. The Securities Exchange Commission then investigated and found that this practice had occurred at least 17 times in the past. The result of this investigation led to E. F. Hutton being fined $1.2 million. The moral of this story: You too will pay a price for subverting federal controls.[11]

Good managers know that if a control system indicates that an employee's performance is not what it should be, they need to work on the performance and not on the person. As a manager, do not discourage employees from bringing their problems or errors to you by criticizing them every time they do, or you will find that your controls are being subverted and your losses are a lot higher than necessary. Upward communication should always be encouraged, as this is a prime source of information for management.

RESISTANCE TO CONTROL SYSTEMS

Obviously, every organization needs good control systems and benefits from them, but there are some inherent problems when very tight controls are in place. In addition, people as a whole naturally resist being controlled, and they do it in a number of different ways.[12] Every good manager needs to be aware of this and should avoid overcontrolling employees whenever possible. Some of the problem areas related to control systems include the following.

1. *Strict output control systems definitely increase job tension and stress levels.*[13] The negative outcomes that result when employees suffer from excessive stress are well documented. Managers must try to minimize stress reactions by communicating the rationale for the controls to employees. Management should also only control strategic areas that really demand regulation.

2. *Employees may engage in "gaming" tactics or behaviors that appear beneficial to management but really are not.* For example, if a salesperson's only

A PERSPECTIVE ON QUALITY

Overcontrol Can Be Expensive

The cost to regulate and control the hospital industry is growing at such a rapid rate that it is no wonder that health-care costs have gotten out of control. Take, for example, Sequoia Hospital, a 430-bed, not-for-profit general hospital in the San Francisco area.

Between 1966 and 1990, the average patient load has remained the same. The staff, however, has increased 175 percent in size, due primarily to all the new regulations and requirements that the government has mandated. Sequoia Hospital has hired 140 full-time employees just to comply with all of these regulations.

On top of this, all health care paid for by the government must be reviewed by an outside, independent agency. Providing duplicate records, x-ray data, billing information, and so on, is very expensive. Medicare funds undergo a third audit just for them. Each of the auditing agencies issue directives and demand that information be provided on multiple-copy forms by everyone from the pharmacist to the doctors and nurses.

The "bottom line" is that annual costs at Sequoia Hospital run $7.8 million just to meet these regulations.

ADAPTED FROM: Sidney Marchasin, "One Hospital Tells the Cost of Regulation," *The Wall Street Journal* (June 26, 1990).

---

control point is sales volume, he or she may try a variety of tricks or schemes, or even lie to customers, to get new sales. In the long run, of course, this behavior will have very negative consequences for the company.

3. *Information manipulation can take several different forms.* "Smoothing" occurs when employees try to "even out" sales figures or costs over a period of time so they look more consistent. For example, if a construction superintendent is running over budget on one project and under budget on another, he or she may just try to "smooth" the costs out by charging one project for costs incurred on the other project. "Focusing" occurs when employees enhance and expound on some information that is beneficial but hardly mention or omit negative outcomes. Employees also may intentionally submit inaccurate reports with inflated figures, "knowing" that their budget or funds request will be cut.

Some of the possible reasons for resistance to control appear to be overcontrolling managers, an overemphasis on a single control point rather than on several key points, and the establishment of unrealistic performance objectives by management.

1. **Overcontrol** occurs when the management of an organization attempts to rigidly control business areas of relatively minor importance or when the control procedures are ridiculously detailed. Some control over procedures may be necessary to maintain efficiency and to standardize results. However, if a manager attempts to dictate and control every movement, word spoken, and even mannerism of his or her employees, a lot of resistance will result.

A controversial example of such managerial intrusion is electronic monitoring, which basically hooks an employee's telephone and computer into a single system that monitors keystroke speed, errors, length of time on the phone, what is said on the phone, and length of time when nothing is happening. Most employees feel this type of control system has gone beyond

Information can be manipulated in several different ways.

How does an organization overcontrol?

monitoring and is really an invasion of privacy. As one employee stated, "I felt like I was in prison." Employers, on the other hand, believe that monitoring provides feedback and permits hands-on coaching and skills development.

However, there appears to be a point at which monitoring can turn into overcontrolling.[14] People want some personal control over how they do their jobs. If the management of a firm wants to increase creativity, innovation, and problem-solving abilities among employees, then managers must give them as much freedom as possible to do their jobs in their own ways.

2. If a firm only uses a single control point, or stresses one control point excessively over the others, then that point will be the only aspect of the employee's performance that he or she really cares about. The organization must stress multiple control points and give them values equal to their importance. Also, the control points shouldn't conflict with each other excessively, or resistance and game playing among employees will result.

3. Sometimes objectives are set that, at the time, seem fair and realistic. Then, for some reason, the situation changes, but the objectives do not. If employees view objectives as totally unrealistic, then they are either going to ignore them or resort to some type of game playing. Managers need to listen to employees and even solicit their feedback on how they feel about the objectives. Management must be willing to change objectives as situations change, or resistance is sure to follow.

If only one control point is used, it will be the only aspect of performance that employees care about.

Management must adjust objectives as factors change.

THINK ABOUT IT

1. Many medium- and large-sized organizations set up elaborate control systems but still suffer significant losses due to corrupt and dishonest employees or managers.

2. Control is a management function that needs to be constantly monitored and occasionally fine-tuned if a control system is to be truly effective.

3. Management control is not just financial control. Managers also need to carefully control equipment, product quantity and quality, supplies, information, inventories, and the time and effort of their employees.

4. As worldwide competition increases in virtually every product and service area, the need to be flexible, creative, and innovative in the marketplace becomes increasingly important. To develop these skills, managers must move toward self controls and away from bureaucratic controls.

5. When attempting to control any function within the firm, the use of multiple control points is always superior to the use of single control points.

6. A key to the effectiveness of any control system is to make sure you, as a manager, have communicated very clearly to the employees involved how the system works and why it is necessary. Ask for input from employees, since they are the ones who are most knowledgeable about their given job tasks.

7. Remember, it is possible to overcontrol, which can create employee resentment and, in most cases, is not cost-effective.

8. It is only natural for employees and first-level managers to resist a firm's control systems somewhat. We all like to have the freedom to do things our way.

9. In the most effective cash control systems, more than one person is responsible for handling and recording cash.

10. Sometimes the controls that are really the most beneficial to the firm are the ones that are preventive in nature and eliminate problems before they start.

LOOKING BACK

You have studied the basic principles and underlying foundations of the management control process and examined several types of control systems. Now let's review the chapter objectives and briefly summarize several highlights for each of them.

Understand the main role of the control function in management.

The control function is very closely related to the planning function. When managers develop their plans in order to accomplish their predetermined objectives, they are also establishing the control standards against which data will be compared. The control process tells managers at all levels whether the activities they have designed to accomplish specific organizational goals and objectives are working.

Explain the control process.

The control process itself is certainly going to vary from business to business. However, all organizations utilize some form of control in four specific areas: identifying standards from strategic, tactical, and operational plans and objectives; measuring performance; comparing performance to the standard; and taking corrective action.

Identify various types of control systems.

There are many types of control systems. They vary depending on the level of management, the functional area being controlled within the firm; the timing of the control process within the production process; and the management control strategy desired.

Discuss how controls vary, depending on the managerial level.

Top management is, of course, primarily concerned with long-term strategic goals and plans; here, the control points have to be very broad and flexible. At the middle-management level, much more specific tactical plans are formulated, and time frames are normally specified in terms of one year or one-quarter of a year. Finally, operational plans, which are implemented by first-level managers or supervisors, are very specific and have very short time frames; daily, weekly, and even hourly numbers are recorded.

List the characteristics of an effective control system.

Although good control systems do vary, depending on the specific situation, virtually all of the truly effective ones exhibit the following characteristics. The control system

- "Fits" the organization and the task characteristics
- Provides timely and accurate information
- Is acceptable to and clearly understood by all personnel
- Is cost-effective
- Monitors strategic elements in the business
- Is difficult to manipulate

Examine why people tend to resist control systems.

Since people tend to naturally resist being tightly controlled, they may attempt to subvert a control system. Managers need to communicate to their employees why they must follow control procedures and what the consequences will be if they fail to do so. Management must realize that resistance to the control system can take several different forms, including "gaming" and information manipulation. Possible reasons for these tactics include overcontrol of employees, overemphasis on a single control point, and the establishment of unrealistic performance objectives by management.

KEY TERMS

acid test ratio
balance sheet
breakeven analysis
breakeven point (BEP)
budget
capital expenditure budget
cash-flow budget
concurrent controls
control function
control standard
current ratio
deviation from the standard
feed-forward (preliminary) controls
financial controls
human-resource controls
income statement
information controls
leverage (debt) ratio

liquidity ratio
marketing controls
nonmonetary (miscellaneous) budget
operating (activity) ratio
  inventory turnover ratio
  total asset turnover ratio
operating budget
operational controls
overcontrol
post-action controls
preventive corrective action
production controls
profitability ratio
ratio analysis
return-on-investment (ROI)
strategic controls
tactical controls
zero-based budgeting

REVIEW AND DISCUSSION QUESTIONS

1. What is the main function of the control process?
2. How are the planning and control functions connected to each other?
3. How are the four basic steps in the control process related to each other?
4. Why does communication play such a critical role in the control process?
5. What is the breakeven point both in units and in dollars if a firm's fixed costs are $10,000, its variable costs are $15.00 per unit, and the selling price is $25.00 per unit?
6. How can top management keep middle- and first-level managers from continually increasing every new budget?
7. What information does a liquidity ratio provide to management? In addition to the managers of a firm, who else might be interested in this ratio?
8. If a firm has a leverage ratio of 0.85 and the industry average is 0.70, is this good or bad for the firm? Why?
9. List at least four characteristics of all good control systems.
10. Why might some employees attempt to subvert a control system?

CRITICAL THINKING INCIDENT 9.1

The Bread Box Restaurant

Jackie Ode is a divorced, single parent of two small boys, ages two and four. Jackie has worked at the Bread Box Restaurant in Waylands, West Virginia, for the past six years as a waitress. Her job performance has always been very good, and she is well-liked by both her coworkers and the customers.

Ralph Leonard is the owner and manager of the restaurant. One day, Judy Osborne, another waitress, came into Ralph's office to tell him that he might want to check Jackie's waitress checks against her cash receipts a little more closely.

Ralph began to check Jackie's receipts and waitress checks personally; over the next seven days, he found slight discrepancies each day. To confirm his thoughts, he put an extra $20.00 in the till during her break on the evening she was running the cash register. When Jackie totaled out that night, she reported no overage. Ralph then confronted Jackie: he told her what he had done and what he had found during the past week.

Jackie finally broke down in tears and admitted taking the $20.00. After further questioning, Jackie admitted taking money over the past six to eight months. She said that there had been times when business was slow and she just couldn't make ends meet on her salary and tips. She thought that she

probably had taken between $2000 and $3000 over this period of time. Jackie went on to say that she always intended to pay the money back and that, in her mind, she was not stealing but just borrowing from the restaurant. In fact, on one occasion, she actually did return $50.00 that she had "borrowed" earlier in the year.

Ralph knows how difficult it is to raise a family on just a waitress's tips and salary. He also knows that because Waylands is a small town, it will be very difficult for Jackie to get another job once word gets out about what she has done. Ralph turns to you, a trusted friend, for advice.

Discussion Questions

1. What do you think Ralph should do about this matter? What are the main issues that he must deal with?

2. What are the pros and cons of keeping Jackie on as an employee? Of firing her? Which action do you recommend and why?

3. Do you feel it was ethical for Ralph to put $20.00 in the cash register to try to catch Jackie?

CRITICAL THINKING INCIDENT 9.2

Sail Right, Inc.

Sail Right, Inc., is a medium-sized manufacturer of sailboats and sailboat accessories. Sail Right currently manufactures small sailboats that range from 18 feet to 30 feet in length. The managers of the company are considering adding a new line of sailboat sails, which would be much larger and more expensive to manufacture than the firm's present line. Before they commit to producing this new sail, however, they want you to determine the breakeven point (BEP). You are given the following data.

Monthly Fixed Costs

1. Mortgage allocation: 1000 sq. ft. @ $8.00 per sq. ft.
2. Utilities: $1000 per month

3. Insurance: $100 per month
4. Salary allocation for top management: $2000
5. Depreciation of equipment and machinery: $3000

Monthly Variable Costs (per unit)

1. Raw materials: $150
2. Labor (direct): $100
3. Sales and marketing: $50
4. Shipping costs: $40
5. Office expense: $10

Selling Price: $750 per unit (sail)

The management of Sail Right is also wondering how the firm compares financially to other manufacturers in the industry. To find out, you must complete the first column of the following table, using the figures shown here on the company's balance sheet and income statement. Then compare these ratios with the industry averages given in the second column of the table and tell the managers if Sail Right's ratios are good, fair, or poor in relation to them.

RATIO	SAIL RIGHT	INDUSTRY AVERAGE	COMPARATIVE RATING
Liquidity ratio		2.0	
Leverage ratio		0.55	
Inventory turnover ratio		4.5	
Total assets turnover ratio		2.25	
Return on investment (ROI)		17.8%	

Sail Right, Inc.
Balance Sheet
December 31, 19XX

ASSETS

Current assets:		
Cash	$138,000	
Accounts Receivable	342,000	
Inventory	419,000	
Total Current Assets		$899,000
Fixed Assets:		
Land, Plant, and Equipment	$708,000	
Less: Accumulated Depreciation	54,000	
Total Fixed Assets		654,000
Total Assets		$1,553,000

LIABILITIES AND OWNER'S EQUITY

Current Liabilities:		
Accounts Payable	$152,100	
Salaries Payable	124,000	
Total Current Liabilities		$276,100
Long-term Liabilities:		
Mortgage Payable	$289,000	
Notes Payable	287,000	
Total Long-term Liabilities		576,000
Total Liabilities		$852,100
Owner's Equity		700,900
Total Liabilities and Owner's Equity		$1,553,000

Sail Right, Inc.
Income Statement
For the Year Ending December 31, 19XX

REVENUES

Sales Revenues	$1,718,000	
Less: Sales Returns and Allowances	106,000	
Net Sales		$1,824,000

COST OF GOODS SOLD

Beginning Inventory	$328,000	
Purchases	902,000	
Total Goods Available for Sale	$1,230,000	
Less: Ending Inventory	249,000	
Total Cost of Goods Sold		981,000
Gross Profit		$843,000

EXPENSES

Salaries	$157,000	
Administrative Expenses	32,000	
Depreciation	36,000	
Marketing and Sales Expenses	42,000	
Total Expenses		– $267,000
Net Income before Taxes		576,000
Federal Taxes		– 201,600
Net Income		$374,400

Discussion Questions

1. Find the BEP, both in terms of the number of sales that must be sold (units) and in terms of total sales dollars.

2. Find the breakeven points in Question 1 if the company wants to make a per-month profit of $5000.

 # CRITICAL THINKING INCIDENT 9.3

Home Federal Savings & Loan

Home Federal Savings & Loan, a medium-sized savings and loan (S & L), started doing business in 1950 in downtown Toledo, Ohio. Like all of the savings and loan institutions at that time, Home Federal was heavily involved in making home loans to the people living in the Toledo area. Over the years, Home Federal made a consistent but modest profit and served the community well.

When banking deregulation came about in the early 1980s, the president, Harry L. Taylor, believed very strongly, as many other bankers did, that only the large banks and savings and loans would survive in the future. To survive, Taylor was convinced that Home Federal must immediately launch an extensive expansion program to keep the larger commercial banks and savings and loans from coming into the Toledo area and "stealing" the market. In order to accomplish this expansion program, Taylor devised the following plan.

1. Sell 30–40 percent of the institution's home mortgages in the secondary mortgage market at the best possible

price. This would give the Home Federal the cash liquidity it needed for the expansion program.

2. Locate existing savings and loans in the Toledo area that are having financial problems. These institutions are exactly what the large competitors would like to purchase to get into the Toledo market. Home Federal must "beat them to the punch" and purchase as many of these S & Ls as possible right away.

Taylor presented his plan to the Home Federal's board of directors, who were somewhat dubious at first. However, Taylor finally convinced the board that this was truly the only way to survive the onslaught of major competitors expected in the Toledo area. The directors reluctantly approved the plan.

Taylor put his plan into action immediately. He sold 38 percent of the Home Federal's mortgages at the best price available, although they were discounted more than he had hoped. Next, he and his staff located six savings and loans in the Toledo area that were in financial difficulty. Taylor started negotiations with all six; within three months, he had decided that he wanted to purchase four of them. All four were located in older areas of Toledo, and all were currently losing money.

Taylor knew that the $20 million dollars needed to purchase these new branches represented virtually all of the funds available for Home Federal to lend. He also knew that none of these savings and loans had made profits for the past three years. Taylor really believed, however, that they could be turned around by instituting an aggressive marketing program that would contain new incentives for both consumers and companies to do business with these new branches.

Taylor privately wanted to purchase these savings and loans very badly. When he presented them to the board for approval, which he had to do because of the size of the transactions, he falsely told the directors that they had to act very quickly since other banks were interested in purchasing these S & Ls. Although Taylor did not know this to be a fact, deep down he felt that if Home Federal dragged its feet on these purchases, it would lose them to the competition. The board questioned Taylor on their poor profit records, but he convinced them that they were strictly due to poor management. The board then approved the purchases for fear of losing them to the competition.

Taylor's plan was now intact. Home Federal had grown from a medium-sized, $200-million savings and loan to one of the largest S & Ls in the Toledo area. The company now had assets of over $600 million and four new branches. Almost all—98 percent—of the institution's funds that could be loaned were committed. For the first time ever, Home Federal could seriously consider making commercial loans. Taylor's dream of joining the "big boys" had finally materialized.

Nine months later, however, things started to change. First, the new branches were becoming more and more of a financial drain. They all continued to lose money, even after an extensive and relatively expensive marketing program over the past six months. It was becoming increasingly apparent that the new branches were losing money because the neighborhoods in which they were located were in rapid states of decline and there simply were not any new customers to be had. All of the businesses that Home Federal spoke with said that they did not want to return to these areas of the city until they were substantially renovated and crime there was reduced.

The real crunch came, however, when the economy started into a recession due to high inflationary pressures. All lending institutions were forced to raise interest rates, thereby slowing the volume of all loans to a virtual trickle while operating costs rose dramatically. The actual operating losses for the third quarter were $2 million dollars, and the projected losses for the fourth quarter were large enough to spell the collapse of Home Federal.

Home Federal's board of directors has now turned to you, a management consultant, for an analysis of what happened and how they can get out of this mess.

Discussion Questions

1. What is the heart of the real problem here?
2. Who is responsible for causing this problem to occur?
3. How can Home Federal stop this problem from getting any worse right now?
4. What is your long-term solution to this problem?
5. What is your contingency plan in case your first solution fails?

NOTES

1. Gary Hector, "S & Ls: Where Did All Those Billions Go?," *Fortune* (September 10, 1990), p. 88.
2. J. Pitta, "We Had a Communication Problem," *Forbes* (May 28, 1990), p. 346.
3. "$20-Million Fine Urged for MetLife," *The Sarasota Herald-Tribune* (March 7, 1994), p. B7; Rob Wells, "MetLife to Pay $20,000,000 Fine," *The Sarasota Herald-Tribune* (March 9, 1994), p. D2.
4. Michael Goold and John J. Quinn, "The Paradox of Strategic Controls," *Strategic Management Journal* 11 (January 1990): 4–55.
5. Gary Delsohn, "Mickey Le Pew? At EuroDisney,

Kingdom's Spell Is Less Than Magic," *Sacramento Bee* (July 25, 1993), p. A1.

6. Lucian G. Conway and Joe A. Cox, "Internal Business Shrinkage," *Baylor Business Review* 5 (Summer 1987): 9–10.

7. Stephen Davis, "Phone Bilks: How to Prevent Unauthorized Charges," *Working Women* (September 1990): 96.

8. Ibid., p. 96.

9. Bernard J. Jaworski and Deborah MacInnis, "Marketing Jobs and Management Controls: Toward a Framework," *Journal of Marketing Research* 26 (November 1989): 408.

10. Richard Binsacca, "Cutting Direct Costs," *Builder* (March 1991): 142.

11. Peter Phipps, "E. F. Hutton Penalized for Money-Laundering," *The Wall Street Journal* (July 17, 1987), p. E14.

12. Jaworski and MacInnis, "Marketing Jobs and Management Controls: Toward a Framework," pp. 409–10.

13. Ibid., p. 409.

14. Mark D. Frefer, "Is Your Computer Spying on You?," *Glamour* (November 1991), pp. 132–33.

 ## SUGGESTED READINGS

Ayres-Williams, Roz. "Mastering the Fine Art of Delegation." *Black Enterprise* (April 1992): 91–93.

Dalton, Dan R. "Corporate Governance: Who Is in Control Here?," *Business Horizons* 32 (July/August 1989): 2–10.

Garofalo, Michael J. "How Strategies Can Get Lost in the Translation." *Business Month* 134 (October 1989): 82–83.

Hall, Robert. "Driven to Perform." *Success* (January/February 1994): 10.

"I Spy." *INC.* (April 1994): 110.

Kellinghusen, Georg, and Klaus Wubbenhorst. "Strategic Control for Improved Performance." *Long-Range Planning* 23 (June 1990): 30–40.

Kerr, Jeffrey L. "Strategic Control through Performance Appraisal and Rewards." *Human Resource Planning* 11 (September 1988): 215–23.

Koretz, Gene. "How the Car-Leasing Explosion Burns Uncle Sam." *Business Week* (September 2, 1991), p. 16.

Makosz, Paul G., and Bruce W. McCuaig. "Is Everything Under Control? A New Approach to Corporate Governance." *Financial Executive* 6 (January/February 1990): 25.

Mezias, Stephen J., and Mary Ann Glynn. "The Three Faces of Corporate Renewal: Institution, Revolution, and Evolution." *Strategic Management Journal* 14 (February 1993): 77–101.

Morck, Randall, Andrei Shleifer, and Robert W. Vishny. "Alternative Mechanisms for Corporate Control." *The American Economic Review* 79 (September 1989): 842–52.

"Phar-Mor Files Plan." *Bradenton Herald* (July 30, 1994), p. 1A.

Pontell, Henry N., and Kitty Calavita. "White-Collar Crime in the Savings and Loan Scandal." *The Annals of the American Academy of Political and Social Science* 525 (January 1993): 31–45.

Rechner, Paula L. "Corporate Governance: Fact or Fiction?" *Business Horizons* 32 (July/August 1989): 11–15.

Sheridan, John H. "MRP II Still a Sound Control Strategy?" *Industry Week* (July 3, 1989), pp. 39–45.

Sherrill, Robert. "S & Ls, Big Banks, and Other Triumphs of Capitalism." *The Nation* (November 19, 1990), pp. 589–623.

"Six Steps to Saving a Troubled Business." *Income Opportunities* (April 1994): 123.

Thayer, Lee. "Organization—Communication: Emerging Perspectives." *Administrative Science Quarterly* 35 (June 1990): 397–98.

Toth, Elizabeth L., and Nick Trujillo. "Reinventing Corporate Communications." *Public Relations Review* 13 (Winter 1987): 42–51.

PART THREE

THE MANAGERIAL ENVIRONMENT

CHAPTER 10
Motivating Job Performance

The concept of motivation is explained, and various motivational theories are discussed. This chapter describes how managers apply strategies to motivate themselves and others. Empowering employees, developing morale, and giving recognition are among the techniques presented.

CHAPTER 11
Social Responsibilities and Ethics

The role of social responsibilities and ethics in today's business environment is examined. An understanding of the benefits and costs of social responsibility is emphasized, and the importance of ethical behavior for managers is stressed. Alternative ways to improve social responsibilities and ethics are discussed.

CHAPTER 12
International Management

This chapter examines the increasing globalization of business. Relationships between trade barriers and international competition are explained. Ways to manage successfully in an era of greater emphasis on international management are also presented.

CHAPTER 13
Production/Operations Management

The critical importance of establishing effective operations management in production or service businesses is discussed. A need to recognize the merits of producing high-quality, low-cost goods and services is stressed. This consideration is essential to survival and growth in an increasingly complex business environment.

CHAPTER 10

MOTIVATING JOB PERFORMANCE

■ LEARNING OBJECTIVES

Motivation is a key to the accomplishment of goals. The truly motivated person *wants* to do something. Understanding motivation is vital to the development of positive interpersonal relationships, both personally and professionally. Even though each individual's needs are internal, managers create workplace environments that can highly motivate job performance. Some insights into how this can be accomplished are provided in this chapter. The learning objectives for this chapter are to:

- Define motivation and understand the motivation process.
- Discuss several commonly recognized motivation theories.
- Examine how communication influences motivation.
- Explain the concepts of self-motivation, empowerment, and goal setting.
- Understand how morale affects job performance.

■ CHAPTER OUTLINE

Successful motivation programs focus on involving employees, being responsive to suggestions, and recognizing accomplishments. Workers have valuable insights to contribute and often relish the opportunity to express their views. At Black & Decker, employees are invited to submit suggestions and, in addition, to research the potential savings and benefits of these suggestions. In a single year, this program saved Black & Decker $580,000 and is expected to save the company another $3 million in the future. Other positive results include better communication, more effective teamwork, and improved rapport among personnel.

Cotton States Insurance, which primarily serves customers living in several southern states, recognized a need to improve customer service, increase teamwork, and reward attainments. Instead of relying on external consultants, the employees themselves developed a motiva-

tion program. A committee of ten workers focused on promoting the theme of "Together We're Better." Various levels of incentives (Employees of the Quarter, Employees of the Year, and daily recognition awards) were offered to stimulate interest and encourage performance. This program not only generated positive attitudes among employees but also reduced turnover by 45 percent in two years.

At Pacific Gas & Electric (PG&E), workers volunteer suggestions, recommend changes, and make job-related decisions. These actions have increased motivation, improved quality, and saved money. Changes were implemented to increase employee involvement and to encourage greater productivity. The company eliminated a layer of management and focused on providing customer satisfaction. The Coast Division was the first unit to implement the program, and customer satisfaction there increased by 12 percent over a three-year period. Moreover, fewer accidents occurred, and the number of union grievances declined at this division.

Both Black & Decker and PG&E involve employees in researching their own suggestions to determine if they can feasibly be implemented. This strategy provides workers with a greater understanding of the problem-solving process and enables them to learn from personal experience why management cannot respond positively to all suggestions from employees. To provide research guidance, a committee of managers at Black & Decker advises employees and recommends useful sources of published information.

SOURCES: Regina Eisman, "Workers Iron Out Suggestions," *Incentive* **164** (June 1990): 86–87; Steven B. Kaufman, "Empowerment at Pacific Gas & Electric," *Training* **28** (August 1991): 47–48; John Millsaps, "Creating Motivation Programs from Within," *Personnel Administrator* **33** (June 1988): 113–14.

Motivated employees signal "thumbs up." They are key links to improved quality, greater productivity, and higher levels of customer satisfaction.

UNDERSTANDING MOTIVATION

What is motivation?

Motivation is an internal process through which human wants, needs, and desires are satisfied. Each person is unique and possesses different experiences, attitudes, and opinions. For most people, the need to work is a fact of life; they must earn money to support themselves and their families. Some workers devote their best efforts to the accomplishment of job tasks and perform beyond reasonable expectations. Others contribute minimal effort to their jobs, and a few workers perform so poorly that they must be terminated. The priorities placed on job security, wages, potential for advancement, and preferred hours of employment vary widely among people. Understanding how to motivate yourself and others is a challenge to your managerial skills.

■ The Importance of Motivation

People are a firm's most valued asset.

Human resources are essential to an organization's success in the forms of increased productivity, greater competitiveness, and improved quality of goods and services. Therefore, managers should learn to recognize what factors are important to employees. Today's workers value meaningful work, give more attention to leisure activities, seek personal feedback, and exhibit impatience about gaining career success.[1] According to a survey of top corporate officers, personal challenge, the importance of a job, and career advancement were the most-cited reasons for changing jobs.[2] Employees who are treated with respect, encouraged to excel, and rewarded for their efforts are more likely to demonstrate motivated job performance.

> Workers who are content with their jobs, who feel challenged, who have the opportunity to fulfill their goals will exhibit less destructive behavior on the job. They will be absent less frequently, they will be less inclined to change jobs, and, most importantly, they will produce at a higher level.[3]

To be competitive, firms must motivate employee performance.

As organizations prepare to compete in the 1990s, many employees will have less job security, fewer opportunities for promotions, and more job-related stress. Nevertheless, the needs to motivate employee performance and emphasize product and service quality will continue to be top-priority concerns. For example, Coleman, the well-known maker of camp stoves and lanterns, focused on improving efficiency and reducing materials stocked in inventory. Previously, Coleman required two months to fill a major order; today, the company can ship such an order in a week. Assembly workers at Coleman can stop operations and correct problems without reducing their wages for lost time.[4]

The objective of the motivation process is to satisfy needs.

■ The Motivation Process

■ FIGURE 10–1 The Motivation Process

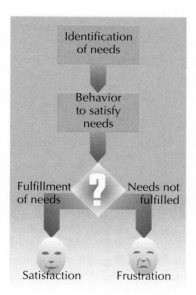

People initiate behaviors to fulfill **needs,** which are perceived to represent unsatisfied psychological, physiological, or social deficiencies.[5] The nature and importance of needs varies widely. You might value an automobile as a status symbol and do a lot of overtime work to purchase a new one every other year. In contrast, a colleague may avoid all overtime work and place no importance on a vehicle as a status symbol. Motivation is complicated, and some behaviors are not easily explained or readily understood.

Figure 10–1 illustrates the motivation process, which begins with the identification of needs. Once needs are identified, behaviors seek to satisfy them. Assume you are a salesperson but want to become a sales manager. Your behavior is directed toward demonstrating your expertise, developing a rapport with customers and colleagues, and impressing the managers who will be participating in the selection decision. All of these considerations are relevant because they directly or indirectly influence whether or not you get the job. If you are chosen, a need is fulfilled, and you experience satisfaction. If another person is selected instead of you, then your need will remain unsatisfied and frustration will occur.

PERSPECTIVES ON MOTIVATION

All behavior is motivated.[6] Managers are challenged to motivate employees to achieve organizational and personal goals. By the nature of their positions, managers play key roles in influencing employee behaviors. As management guru Peter F. Drucker observes

> Management is about human beings. Its task is to make people capable of joint performance (working together), to make their strengths effective and their weaknesses irrelevant. This is what organization is all about, and it is the reason that management is the critical, determining factor.[7]

Managers are role models.

Most highly motivated managers are enthusiastic about their work and have a positive attitude toward others. Developing and maintaining cordial human relationships is an important factor in the creation of a motivated work environment. Employees observe the behaviors of their manager, so he or she should not make thoughtless remarks or overlook opportunities to praise performance. Assume your boss has just returned from a two-week vacation. During this time, you have been working hard (including extra uncompensated hours) to get tasks finished and avoid missing deadlines, but some paperwork still remains on your desk. The boss remarks, "It's good to be back. I see all of the work did not get done. What have you been doing?" How would your supervisor's remarks make you feel? You would probably conclude that your efforts were not appreciated.

Consider the four Cs of motivation.

An understanding of the four **Cs of motivation** provides insight into behaviors.[8]

1. Confidence is a sense of sureness about personal ability to do something. During the 1990 season, Bill Parcells, coach of the New York Giants, permitted his team to try for first downs on fourth-down plays more than any other National Football League coach. His game plan reflected confidence in the abilities of his players and may have contributed to the team's success as an eventual Super Bowl champion.[9]

2. Competence refers to having the know-how needed to complete tasks. A skilled technician who knows how to repair broken dry copiers will experience more success and less anxiety on the job than a person who attempts trial-and-error solutions.

3. Commitment involves being persistent and sticking with tasks until they are finished. Entrepreneurs who start their own companies often work an inordinate number of hours and make many personal sacrifices to assure business success.

4. Challenge is a desire to work toward the completion of assignments or goals. The challenge to acquire new skills and become more knowledgeable is a reason for learners to put forth effort.

From a global viewpoint, are people motivated by similar work goals? Although research results are somewhat inconclusive, an extensive survey of respondents from seven countries (Belgium, Great Britain, Israel, Japan, the Netherlands, the United States, and West Germany) has revealed much consistency among opinions.[10] Data were analyzed according to gender, age, and organizational level (employee, supervisor, or manager). Regardless of gender or age differences, "interesting work" and "good pay" were the top-ranked work goals. In terms of organizational level, "interesting work" was the single-most valued factor. Employees and supervisors ranked "good pay" second, but managers ranked it fifth. The researchers concluded that pay was a more important motivator at lower levels of the organization.

■ *Management Perspectives*

What motivates employees?

Managers and their employees do not necessarily have similar perspectives on job-reward factors. Figure 10–2 shows disagreement between the factors valued by employees and those considered to be important by supervisors. Specifically, note the difference between the supervisor and employee rankings of "good wages" and "interesting work." Compared to workers, managers place greater importance on salary as a motivational tool. Yet research shows that many factors valued by workers are nonmonetary in nature.

> When asked to name the characteristics that make a job rewarding to them, time and again workers rank above salary qualities such as interesting and challenging work, recognition and appreciation from superiors for work well done, a feeling of being in on key decision making, and job security.[11]

Don't overlook nonfinancial incentives.

During difficult economic times, managers encounter pressures to reduce financial incentives. To compensate, they may stress intellectual challenges, give employees greater flexibility to do their jobs, and encourage worker participation. In the late 1970s, employee involvement at Public Service of New Mexico was almost nonexistent. By the early 1990s, however, the primary focus of the company's human-resource strategy was directed toward employee participation and giving greater decision-making authority to first-line managers.[12]

What a manager expects is often what a manager gets.

Management expectations can influence motivation. In a classic study, the job performances of insurance agents directly corresponded to the expectations of their managers. The sales of agents who reported to managers with high

■ FIGURE 10–2   Motivation: Employees versus Supervisors

A sample of industrial workers was asked to rank ten "job-reward" factors. In addition, supervisors ranked the same factors, based on their perception of how workers would rank-order them.

Actual Worker Rankings	Supervisor Perceptions of Worker Rankings
1. Interesting work	1. Good wages
2. Full appreciation of work done	2. Job security
3. Feeling of being in on things	3. Promotion and growth in the organization
4. Job security	4. Good working conditions
5. Good wages	5. Interesting work
6. Promotion and growth in the organization	6. Personal loyalty to employees
7. Good working conditions	7. Tactful discipline
8. Personal loyalty to employees	8. Full appreciation of work done
9. Tactful discipline	9. Sympathetic help with personal problems
10. Sympathetic help with personal problems	10. Feeling of being in on things

SOURCE: Kenneth A. Kovach, "What Motivates Employees? Workers and Supervisors Give Different Answers," *Business Horizons* 30 (September/October 1987): 59–60.

Managers and employees are challenged to meet and exceed expectations. At CSX Corporation, achievement of "100 Days of Safety" is recognized.

expectations increased significantly. The productivity of agents supervised by managers with low expectations actually declined. The study concluded that

> If managers believe subordinates will perform poorly, it is virtually impossible for them to mask their expectations. . . . Clearly, the way managers *treat* subordinates, not the way they organize them, is the key to high expectations and high productivity.[13]

Given the trend toward globalization, managers are increasingly challenged to motivate employees in multicultural and multinational environments. Business practices vary among countries and influence a manager's choice of motivational alternatives. For instance, U.S. workers are susceptible to termination as the result of poor job performance or layoffs or mergers. In Britain and France, a high degree of unionization prevails; employees there are more permanently tied to employers, thereby limiting management's option to terminate personnel for other than criminal charges.[14] Differences among management styles further complicate efforts to motivate employees. "Swedes may be frustrated by French executives who don't believe in consensus management. Hierarchical Germans may not blend well with more emotional Italian executives."[15]

■ Communication Considerations

"I work extra hard, but my efforts aren't rewarded." "Unclear directions cause too many frustrations." "The boss doesn't tell me what she wants; I can't read her mind." Such comments evidence ineffective communication and are frequently repeated by many employees. Communication influences motivation to a greater extent than is often realized. Employee productivity is affected by the comments and actions of managers. "Indeed, managers often communicate most when they believe they are communicating least."[16]

When communicating, show that you care.

Lack of communication creates anxiety, unclear messages create confusion, and miscommunication needlessly consumes time. In addition, the tone of a

A PERSPECTIVE ON QUALITY

Motivation Improves Productivity

Motivation is a key factor in attaining quality performance to benefit employees and employers. A continual emphasis on quality is becoming an expectation in today's business environment. Companies cannot afford to lose their market shares to competitors and must be alert for opportunities to attract new customers. At Eaton Corporation's Lincoln, Illinois, plant, worker suggestions resulted in savings of $1.4 million, and these employees earned $44,000 in credits to exchange for various types of merchandise. By improving productivity and reducing defects, personnel at Whirlpool's Benton Harbor facility received an extra $2700 per person.

Promotions, increased job responsibilities, and other personal desires are incentives to quality job performance. However, prevailing economic conditions cannot be ignored. In the mid-1980s, Whirlpool announced plans to close the entire Benton Harbor unit except for the tooling and plating shop, which was given an opportunity to continue on one condition: output must improve. This mandate provided the necessary motivation to get results. Over a four-year period in the shops, productivity increased more than 19 percent, and rejected parts declined to an amazingly low 10 per million produced.

At Eaton, a team of maintenance people became frustrated with the continued equipment breakdowns and the company's practice of hiring out the repairs to be done. The team constructed two machines on their own at a cost the to company of $173,000, less than one-third the cost charged by outside repairpersons. The machinery can perform routine tasks, thereby freeing employees for more challenging work activities.

Competition provides an impetus to change. The success of Japanese automakers motivated Chrysler to learn from them. Although Chrysler conducted several crash tests of prototype vehicles (each costing $350,000), only one such test was completed at Mitsubishi Corporation of Japan.

SOURCES: Thomas F. O'Boyle, "A Manufacturer Grows Efficient by Soliciting Ideas from Employees," *The Wall Street Journal* (June 5, 1992), p. A1; Bradley A. Stertz, "Detroit's New Strategy to Beat Back Japanese Is to Copy Their Ideas," *The Wall Street Journal* (October 1, 1992), p. A10; Rick Wartzman, "A Whirlpool Factory Raises Productivity—and Pay of Workers," *The Wall Street Journal* (May 4, 1992), pp. A1, A4.

message is important. In a gruff voice, your boss says, "Show some initiative and get started on the project; it won't get done by itself." Does this make you look forward to getting to work? Probably not, because the message combines a "put down" with a request. Now suppose your boss says, in a more conciliatory manner, "How about getting started on the project? We need it completed as soon as possible, and you're the person for the job." This message is certainly more likely to motivate you.

Communication serves as a medium for giving directions, getting suggestions, and providing feedback. If managers are accessible, employees are more likely to rely on them for information and pay less attention to rumors and to the grapevine. Effective communication helps managers to understand the needs and wants of their employees. *Fortune* magazine polled 212 CEOs of major corporations and asked what they had done to improve communication and stimulate productivity. Initiation of regular meetings with workers (41 percent) and implementation of quality-improvement programs (20 percent) were the most-mentioned activities.[17]

1. Why is employee motivation so frequently regarded as a major concern in the work-place?

2. What is the most important factor to recognize about motivating employees?

3. How can managers better understand the motivational needs of their employees?

THEORIES OF MOTIVATION

Motivation can be examined from different perspectives.

Various theories have been developed to explain motivation. McGregor's Theory X and Theory Y emphasize the role of assumptions about behaviors. Abraham H. Maslow proposes a hierarchical order for the fulfillment of needs; this research serves as the basis for Clayton Alderfer's ERG theory. Frederick Herzberg focuses on the work environment and on the motivational implications of work itself. Expectancy theory examines the relationship between the valuation placed on rewards and the likelihood of attaining them. Equity theory is based on perceptions of fairness in the allocation of rewards. Finally, reinforcement theory considers how the use of reinforcers can encourage or discourage behaviors.

The works of Maslow and Herzberg exemplify **content theories of motivation,** which are concerned with identifying the specific internal needs that motivate individuals. On the other hand, equity, expectancy, and reinforcement theories illustrate **process theories of motivation,** which are designed to "describe and analyze how personal factors (internal to the person) interact and influence each other to produce certain kinds of behavior."[18] Scholars and researchers continue to search for explanations of how people are motivated. Let's discuss the widely known and accepted theories of motivation.

■ *McGregor's Theory X and Theory Y*

According to Douglas McGregor's Theory X and Theory Y, assumptions of managers influence their behaviors toward employees. **Theory X** is a traditional management approach that emphasizes control to assure compliance. According to Theory X, managers make these assumptions.

Theory X emphasizes management by control.

- Subordinates dislike work and consequently will avoid it.

- Workers do not or will not accept responsibility.

- Employees are not ambitious and desire to be led.

- To assure organizational goals are attained, employees must be closely supervised and controlled.

Theory X managers practice an autocratic management style and may use the threat of punishment to induce employee productivity. Communication is one-way (downward), and the work environment is characterized by minimal manager-employee interactions.[19]

In contrast, **Theory Y** emphasizes management through employee input and delegation of authority. According to Theory Y, managers make these assumptions.

- People want to work, and work is a natural activity.

Exceptional performance leads to accomplishments. Receiving an award in the presence of colleagues is a powerful motivator.

Theory Y recognizes human capabilities.

■ Workers are willing to accept responsibilities.

■ Employees are ambitious and demonstrate initiative to achieve objectives.

■ With positive motivation, subordinates can be encouraged to attain goals.

Managers who adhere to Theory Y solicit ideas from their employees and delegate responsibilities to them. Communication is multidirectional, and managers interact frequently with employees.[20] Compared to Theory X, Theory Y has the greater potential to develop positive job relationships and motivate employee performance. At AT&T's Universal Card Services, named among the 1992 Baldridge National Quality Award winners, employees have the authority to solve most problems on their own without management intervention. A positive motivational approach is practiced, and rewards are given for doing tasks correctly. The quality program recognizes the need for employees to believe that their work contributions are important. At Universal, turnover among service representatives is only one-fifth of the industry average, which ranges from 40 to 50 percent.[21]

■ *Maslow's Hierarchy of Human Needs*

Maslow's hierarchy includes five levels of human needs.

Abraham H. Maslow's theory of motivation, shown in Figure 10–3, includes five levels of human needs.[22] This theory is commonly referred to as **Maslow's hierarchy of human needs.** These needs are arranged in a hierarchical order: lower-order needs are fulfilled before motivation is directed toward the satisfaction of higher-order needs.

Once satisfied, a need is no longer motivational; at a later time, however, it can emerge to be fulfilled once again. For example, assume you change employers and move across the country to accept a new position. At the time you are moving, your needs for affiliation and acceptance by others, which previously had been satisfied, are probably unfulfilled, at least for a short duration of time. Let's examine each of Maslow's need levels.

If you are hungry and thirsty, what else matters?

SURVIVAL NEEDS **Survival needs** include food, shelter, air, water, and clothing, all of which are considered to be essential to life. Until physiological needs are

FIGURE 10–3 Maslow's Hierarchy of Human Needs

Reaching the maximum potential for growth and fulfillment
SELF-ACTUALIZATION NEEDS

Gaining self-esteem and receiving esteem from others
ESTEEM NEEDS

Feeling accepted by others; having a sense of belonging
SOCIAL NEEDS

Wanting security and protection from dangers
SAFETY & SECURITY NEEDS

Seeking food, shelter and clothing
SURVIVAL NEEDS

met, individuals are not motivated to attain higher-order needs. If a family breadwinner earns minimum wages, it may be difficult to ensure that basic needs are met. Corporate downsizing and reorganization have interrupted the careers of many workers and frequently have necessitated the termination of their employment. The potential for accidents and injuries, which may lead to an inability to perform job duties, is an inherent risk in such occupations as construction and mining.

SAFETY AND SECURITY NEEDS   The **safety and security needs** of all employees must be met. Employees have the right to be free of physical and economic dangers. Legislation, such as the Occupational Safety and Health Act, promotes a safer and healthier workplace. Economic downturns, corporate mergers and restructurings, and technological advancements impact job stability. However, many workers have considerable assurance of steady employment with little likelihood of experiencing physical harm. For these persons, Maslow's second-level needs are fulfilled.

Affiliations make life worthwhile.

SOCIAL NEEDS   People fulfill their **social needs** by seeking affiliations with others; they value a sense of belonging. On their jobs, workers have many opportunities to form social relationships. These arise formally (assignments to work teams) or informally (friendships and company-sponsored recreational activities). Working with others and being accepted as a member of the group is an example of how this type of need can be satisfied.

ESTEEM NEEDS   Esteem needs—improving self esteem and gaining recognition from others—are important elements of personal growth and development. If you are named an "outstanding employee" as a result of your excellent job performance, you will probably feel good about yourself. Furthermore, congratulations expressed by colleagues, friends, and the boss should cause you to experience feelings of pride and self-confidence.

Few people are self-actualized.

SELF-ACTUALIZATION NEEDS   Self-actualization needs represent the pinnacle of Maslow's hierarchy and involve reaching the maximum potential for growth and fulfillment. Few, if any, people are truly self-actualized. However, self-actualization serves as an ideal toward which motivated behavior can be directed. William Gates, III, founder of Microsoft Corporation and a self-made billionaire, exemplifies a self-actualized person. A Harvard dropout, Gates and a friend started Microsoft, a company that has grown into a world-renowned manufacturer of software for personal computers. As astute conversationalist, Gates is known for his ability to ask probing questions.[23] Other seemingly self-fulfilled persons include the late Ewing Kaufman, founder of Marion Laboratories and former owner of the Kansas City Royals baseball team, and Billy Graham, a noted evangelist.

Maslow's theory is widely accepted and easily understood. It illustrates a logical progression for the fulfillment of individual needs. However, the theory is difficult to test.

> Maslow did not take it upon himself to develop measures of "operational definitions" of the need categories, and some of them—particularly the self-actualization need—have presented major difficulties to researchers trying to give the theory an honest and fair test.[24]

Some critics consider Maslow's five-category hierarchy to be overly detailed and recommend a more simplified categorization.[25]

■ ERG Theory

Clayton Alderfer modified Maslow's approach and developed the **ERG theory** of motivation. Alderfer condensed Maslow's five categories of needs to three: existence (E) needs, relatedness (R) needs, and growth (G) needs.

■ *Existence needs* include basic necessities, such as food, air, and water, and are similar to Maslow's survival and safety/security needs.

■ *Relatedness needs* focus on interpersonal relationships—a feeling of being accepted by others, having their respect, and gaining positive recognition from them. Relatedness needs are similar to Maslow's social needs.

■ *Growth needs,* which include Maslow's self-actualization and esteem needs, are illustrated by efforts to make creative work contributions and to develop professionally to the fullest extent possible.

Compared to Maslow's hierarchy, Alderfer's model is probably more representative of actual human behavior. Maslow's hierarchical arrangement emphasizes the fulfillment of needs in an orderly progression from lower- to higher-order needs. According to ERG theory, however, multiple unmet needs can simultaneously motivate behavior. For example, an employee who holds a low-

GLOBAL VIEW

Motivation and Cultural Differences

The United States is known as the land where successful entrepreneurs can rise from rags to fame and riches through their personal efforts. Americans value individualism. In the workplace, rewards and recognition are often based on individual job-performance accomplishments. In contrast, many Asian cultures emphasize the importance of group affiliations. In China, the needs of the State receive the highest priority. Even when they deserve recognition, Japanese workers do not like to be singled out for praise in front of their peers.

In the United States, loss of employment is not an unusual event. Personnel can be terminated for any number of reasons. Some managers may use the possibility of termination as a motivational strategy to improve job performance. Other countries, however, have a different philosophy of employer-employee relations. The Japanese are

Group recognition acknowledges achievements and encourages additional job-performance excellence by the group. In some foreign cultures, group rewards represent a primary way of motivating personnel.

known for the practice of lifetime employment, whereby the employee spends an entire career with a single company. Many European workers are closely bound to employers through labor agreements and government regulations. Consequently, motivational appeals need to be meshed with prevailing cultural norms.

U.S. managers are noted for communicating in a direct, to-the-point manner; their employees do not expect a lot of time to be spent on "small talk." However, this is not the case in all cultures. Often, too much abruptness may signify a lack of interest or insincerity and inhibit a manager's efforts to motivate. In some Hispanic cultures, for instance, conversation about family, topics of mutual interest, or local events is expected to precede discussion of business matters.

In the United States, direct feedback from supervisors is part of formal job-performance appraisals. Most American employees are not pleased to receive negative criticism—quite in contrast to the Japanese approach in which job-related feedback is commonly shared on an informal basis during after-hour social gatherings. Japanese managers respond to critical comments, and their employees interpret this as a signal that their supervisors are still concerned about them. However, the really important feedback comes from the human-resource department, which makes the major personnel decisions in Japanese firms.

SOURCES: Paul Epner, "Managing Chinese Employees," *China Business Review* **18** (July/August 1991): 25; Bob Filipczak, "Working for the Japanese," *Training* **29** (December 1992): 24–25; William G. Ouchi, *Theory Z* (New York: Avon, 1982): 15–18.

wage job and has a concern about job security (existence needs) may also seek to be accepted by colleagues and earn their approval (relationship needs).

Also, failure to meet a higher-order need may cause an individual to become frustrated, regress, and direct effort toward previously satisfied lower-order needs. For instance, an employee who has trouble developing satisfactory interpersonal relationships might strive to earn more income, even though the person already enjoys a comparatively high standard of living. Furthermore, it is possible that a higher-order need may be dominant over a lower-order need.

■ Herzberg's Two-Factor Theory

Frederick Herzberg's research centered on the workplace itself.[26] Herzberg analyzed data obtained from engineers and accountants and used critical incidents to identify motivators and hygiene factors that corresponded to the good and bad feelings that they had about their jobs.[27] In Herzberg's view, **motivator factors** contribute to job satisfaction and accordingly serve to motivate. Conversely, **hygiene factors,** often called **dissatisfiers,** represent potential sources of job dissatisfaction. Although employees want to have good salaries, positive relations with the boss, and up-to-date equipment, the presence of these factors does not necessarily mean that they will work harder and be more productive at their jobs.

Opportunities for advancement, achievement, and recognition are examples of motivator factors. Unlike hygiene factors, motivator factors do not solely help workers to avoid job dissatisfaction. Motivator factors also encourage employees to be productive. For example, the potential for promotion (a motivator factor) encourages a worker to excel, but if no such opportunity exists, employee motivation is not directly affected. On the other hand, the quality of supervision (a hygiene factor) does not encourage motivation but is a source of job dissatisfaction if an employee perceives it to deteriorate. Figure 10–4 illustrates various motivator and hygiene factors.

Herzberg's research has influenced management's practice of motivation theory. The theory provides a basis for enriching jobs to make work more meaningful and fulfilling. Nevertheless, Herzberg's work has been criticized because his sample was limited to respondents from only two types of employment categories. In addition, various subsequent research studies have concluded that money can indeed serve to motivate job performance. "His model describes only the content of work motivation; it does not adequately describe the complex motivational process of organizational participants."[28]

Motivator factors encourage employee productivity.

■ Expectancy Theory

According to **expectancy theory,** motivation is influenced by the relationship between the desire for preferred outcomes (value) and the likelihood of attaining them (expectancy). Primary considerations involve effort, performance, and outcomes.[29] Possible expectancies range from zero to 1.0. A high probability indicates considerable likelihood that an expectancy will occur; with a probability of zero, there is no chance of occurrence.

Value and expectancy influence motivation.

■ **FIGURE 10–4** Herzberg's Two-Factor Theory

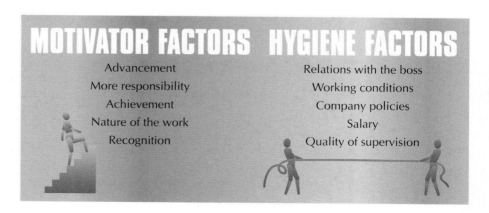

MOTIVATOR FACTORS

Advancement
More responsibility
Achievement
Nature of the work
Recognition

HYGIENE FACTORS

Relations with the boss
Working conditions
Company policies
Salary
Quality of supervision

REMEMBER TO COMMUNICATE

Heaven Communicates a Customer-Oriented Message

Located in Commack, New York, Rudy Massa's Gasoline Heaven service station sells over 7 million gallons of gasoline per year. Each day, the station purchases two loads of gasoline from its supplier, an amount equivalent to what many stations buy in a week. With a concern for quality and service, the station was enlarged to 34 pumps. Attendants are available to fill customer's gas tanks; mechanics are on duty; and practically any credit card is accepted.

Attractiveness of the facility has not been forgotten, as numerous plots of flowers decorate the premises. During the Christmas season, calendars are given to customers. Rudy is particular about the appearance of attendants, who cannot look messy. Restrooms are examined for cleanliness several times each day, and even the boss has been known to clean them. These amenities communicate a positive customer-oriented message and are part of the process for motivating drivers to stop at Gasoline Heaven.

Rudy Massa likes the challenge of keeping lines of rush-hour commuters moving through the station. In fact, he uses a window beside his desk to give instructions to attendants. The window has no screen because Rudy thinks it would be a needless obstacle to effective communication. He's motivated to keep things running smoothly and generally works as long as ten hours per day, up to seven days per week. In fact, he even decided not to take a free vacation to Puerto Rico awarded by Gulf Oil for being the company's top sales performer.

ADAPTED FROM: Allanna Sullivan, "Cheap Gasoline and Full Service? It Must Be Heaven," *The Wall Street Journal* (May 24, 1991), p. A1.

Probability assessments are based on perceptions of anticipated results. If you study hard and understand the subject matter, it is reasonable to set a high probability to your chance of getting a good grade on an exam. On the other hand, if the course content is difficult and you do not do any of the homework assignments, it is more reasonable to assign a very low probability to your chance of earning an A on the exam. The key is to recognize that probability assessments are totally dependent on the perceptions of persons who make them.

Assume you are selling health insurance and have learned that a major local employer wants to change insurance companies to obtain lower rates. You offer competitive rates and schedule an appointment to make a sales presentation. It is very likely that your efforts will lead to a sale; the effort-to-performance expectancy is high. You think success will occur about eight times out of ten.

Performance leads to valued outcomes.

You must make the sale (performance), but the major reward (outcome) is the commission you will earn. Based on past experience, you know a check will arrive about a month after the sale is completed; therefore, the performance-to-outcome expectancy is 1.0, which indicates certainty. In this example, the reward has a high valence (value) to you, and you possess the selling skills to complete the task.

Let's summarize why motivated performance occurs.

■ High effort-to-performance expectancy (Your efforts lead to completion of the sale.)

- High performance-to-outcome expectancy (The sale assures you a commission.)

- High valuation of the reward (You place considerable value on the money earned from making the sale.)

When employing expectancy theory, several factors are noteworthy.[30] The theory recognizes the importance of individual differences in skills and abilities. It considers how role perceptions influence performance. For instance, managers and subordinates may have quite different perspectives about job expectations. Consequently, actual job performance may vary because of miscommunication, not lack of motivation. Managers can encourage motivation by closely relating rewards to performance. This implies a need to communicate clearly so that employees understand how rewards are earned.

■ *Equity Theory*

Motivation depends on a sense of fairness.

Based on the work of Stacy Adams, **equity theory** is concerned with an individual's perception of fairness. According to the theory, employees strive for equality and make subjective comparisons of their inputs and outcomes to others in similar circumstances. *Inputs* represent what individuals contribute to their jobs, such as knowledge, skills, abilities, and training. *Outcomes* refer to what individuals receive from their jobs, such as salary, benefits, promotion opportunities, and recognition.

Let's consider an example of the application of equity theory. Jerry Jones and Peter Hawkins are computer technicians who work for the same employer. They have identical positions, similar job experiences, and equivalent training. However, Peter earns $200 per month more than Jerry, who does not consider the situation to be equitable. A sense of equity prevails only when the input/outcome ratio is perceived to be the *same* as that of a comparison reference person. If Peter were more experienced or considered to be better qualified for the job, then Jerry might easily justify the salary difference as being equitable.

Several alternatives are available to reduce perceptions of inequity. If rewards are less than equitable, employees (like Jerry) might ask for a raise or not put forth as much effort. People who know they are overcompensated (like Peter) might work harder to justify the differential. Sometimes, workers alter their views and accept their situations, or they compare themselves with another reference person. The actions of any individual depend on various factors: personality, attitude, future expectations, and so on. Figure 10–5 illustrates responses to perceptions of equity and inequity.

People compare their situations to those of others.

Equity theory has several implications for managers.[31] Workers must consider the reward system to be fair. Managers cannot control the comparisons that employees make to determine equity. For instance, if an employee receives the highest raise given by her manager, she still may not consider it equitable if a friend holding a similar job at another company receives a much larger raise. The comparison aspect of equity theory is quite relevant.

> It is not only important how much an individual is being paid but how much the person is being paid compared to other people he or she identifies with. . . . It does mean that high performance (high inputs), especially, must be consistently rewarded at a high level. It also means that poor or shoddy performance should not be rewarded if high performers are to be satisfied.[32]

■ **FIGURE 10–5** Responses to Equity and Inequity

SOURCE: David D. Van Fleet, *Behavior in Organizations* (Boston: Houghton Mifflin, 1991), p. 66. Copyright © 1991 by Houghton Mifflin Company. Used with permission.

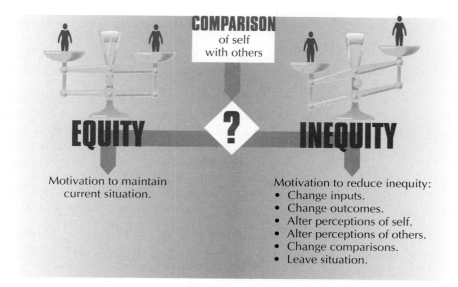

■ *Reinforcement Theory*

Reinforcement theory examines the consequences of past experiences on subsequent behaviors. If behaviors are rewarded, they will be repeated. Employees learn not to repeat unrewarded behaviors. In administering rewards, managers play key roles in the reinforcement of responses. Assume you start taking evening courses to learn more about business. Subsequently, the boss increases your pay and lets you develop your own work schedule. Since your initiative led to favorable results, you will continue to enroll in evening courses.

The theory includes four types of reinforcement: positive, negative, punishment, and extinction.[33]

Differentiate among four types of reinforcement.

■ *Positive Reinforcement* **Positive reinforcement** in the form of rewards recognizes desired behaviors. Examples include granting a bonus for achieving a specified level of productivity and praising a person who works late to assure that an important deadline is met.

■ *Negative Reinforcement* **Negative reinforcement** focuses on behavior to avoid undesirable consequences. To illustrate, an employee expends much effort to finish an assignment in order not to upset the boss. If this undesirable outcome is successfully avoided, then the employee will repeat the behavior in the future.

■ *Punishment* **Punishment** in the form of penalties minimizes undesirable behaviors. If your paycheck is reduced as a result of excessive absenteeism, you will get the message that this behavior is not appropriate. Criticism and ostracism by managers are two other examples of punishment. A major difficulty with this type of reinforcement is a tendency for those who are punished to become angry or resentful.[34]

■ *Extinction* When formerly rewarded behaviors cease to be recognized, **extinction** occurs and unwanted behaviors diminish. If a manager stops paying attention to an employee's overly negative comments about the company, the person will ultimately stop making them.

Managers need to recognize the relationship between reinforcement and motivation.[35] As a motivational tool, rewards are more effective than punishment. A close link between accomplishments and rewards increases the likelihood that highly motivated behaviors will continue. Assume you earn a bonus for sales in January but do not receive it until August. At this point, too much time has elapsed for the reward to have the maximum positive impact on your productivity. Clearly communicated expectations are easier to reinforce because they are more likely to be understood.

Reinforcement can be applied on a continuous or an intermittent basis. With **continuous reinforcement,** every correct response is reinforced. In business settings, this is too impractical and **intermittent** (or **partial**) **reinforcement** is applied. Four intermittent reinforcement schedules are commonly used.[36]

■ *Fixed-Ratio Schedule* The **fixed-ratio schedule** administers a reward after a preselected number of correct responses. For example, a bank teller gets a reward after every 1000 error-free transactions. Since the teller knows the frequency of reinforcement, productivity may decline after a reward is received. However, productivity increases as the next opportunity for a reward approaches.[37]

■ *Variable-Ratio Schedule* The **variable-ratio schedule** randomly reinforces behavior according to an average number of responses. For example, a lathe operator is rewarded after producing an average of 25 units. However, the next reward might be given after 10, 15, or 30 additional units are produced. Since workers do not know exactly when the reinforcement will be administered, they are constantly motivated. "Variable-ratio schedules tend to produce a very high rate of response that is vigorous, steady, and resistant to extinction."[38]

■ *Fixed-Interval Schedule* The **fixed-interval schedule** approach reinforces behavior after a specified amount of time has expired. Paychecks issued every Saturday or once each month illustrate this schedule. Since employees know exactly how often to expect rewards, more highly motivated performance occurs just before a reward and tends to decline immediately afterward. The interval of time should not be unduly lengthy because expiration of too much time nullifies a close response-reward relationship.

■ *Variable-Interval Schedule* The **variable-interval schedule** varies the time between reinforcement of behaviors. For example, manager John Jacobsen randomly visits work areas to inspect employee performance. Yesterday, John made only one trip; today, he visited on two occasions; tomorrow, he plans three visits. Subordinates do not know when to expect John, since his visits are unannounced. This schedule tends to encourage relatively high levels of employee performance.

Figure 10–6 summarizes the characteristics of the various reinforcement schedules. Note how each schedule influences productivity and behavior. For example, the fixed-interval schedule is less likely than the other techniques to produce high and stable employee performance. In general, we can conclude that ratio schedules are more likely to motivate behavior.

Although the data are inconclusive, it appears that the ratio reward schedules—fixed or variable—lead to better performance than either of the two interval schedules. Ratio schedules are more closely related to the occurrence of desired behaviors than interval schedules, which are based on the passage of time.[39]

SCHEDULE	FORM OF REWARD AND EXAMPLE	INFLUENCE ON PERFORMANCE	EFFECTS ON BEHAVIOR
Fixed interval	Reward on fixed time basis; weekly or monthly paycheck	Leads to average and irregular performance	Fast extinction of behavior
Fixed ratio	Reward tied to specific number of responses; piece-rate pay system	Leads quickly to very high and stable performance	Moderately fast extinction of behavior
Variable interval	Reward given at varying periods of time; unannounced inspections or appraisals and rewards given at random times each month	Leads to moderately high and stable performance	Slow extinction of behavior
Variable ratio	Reward given for some behaviors; sales bonus ties to selling X accounts, but X constantly changing around some mean	Leads to very high performance	Very slow extinction of behavior

Reprinted by permission from *Organizational Behavior*, 7th ed., p. 157 by Don Hellriegel, John W. Slocum, Jr., and Richard W. Woodman. Copyright © 1995 by West Publishing Company. All rights reserved.

■ *Motivation Theories: Implications for Managers*

Without a doubt, motivated job performance is essential, and managers play important roles in the motivation process. Even though content varies, the theories are complementary in an attempt to explain motivation. The needs approach of Maslow and Alderfer and Herzberg's two-factor theory stress *what* motivates behavior. The expectancy, equity, and reinforcement theories focus on *how* motivated behavior occurs.

Based on Maslow's hierarchy and on ERG theory, satisfaction of needs is a key factor for managers to consider when determining how to motivate personnel. Herzberg encourages managers to look beyond the factors that contribute to job dissatisfaction and to focus on such things as achievement, advancement, and responsibility—all of which influence job satisfaction. For example, managers can often exercise some discretion in giving workers more control over their work duties; the workers, in turn, become more productive and experience greater personal fulfillment.

Equity theory emphasizes managerial awareness of employee viewpoints concerning fairness and inequities. Employees consider how well management treats them compared to others, especially peers, in the organization. Expectancy theory gives managers insights into the relationships among effort, performance outcomes, rewards, and goal attainment. Therefore, managers need to communicate job-related expectations to their employees and help them to perceive how excellent work leads to desired rewards. A key aspect of reinforcement theory is that managers recognize the importance of reinforcing desired behaviors and select appropriate reinforcement schedules.

A PERSPECTIVE ON QUALITY

Teach Employees to Be Peak Performers

Einstein once said, "If you can't say something simply, you don't really understand it." Charles Garfield has studied 1500 peak performers for 20 years and has determined that they all have a set of basic characteristics in common.

"As a business, we needed to have a vision of what we could become," says Kathy Stratton of Scott Paper in Philadelphia. . . . "Vision is one of the main qualities that peak performers exhibit as individuals. There are also personality types you find in companies: hippos, who just sit around; tigers, who are go-getters; and elephants, who are trainable." Garfield tied Scott's goals for its employees to its business goals. Now the company focuses on what its sales mission is, how to apply it at the job level, and how it fits with the business.

The key to applying the principles of peak performance to a large organization is to establish a clear direction and focus that people can relate to every day. For Scott, it meant communicating that focus to employees across the country. The direction has been clear and consistent from the top and has been reinforced visibly. From small district meetings to the top levels of the company, people are focused on why things are done the way they are and what the company's goals are. "Peak performance isn't just some latest hot button, but an ongoing process," says Stratton.

"Our sales force needed a proper utilization of selling tools—reprints and abstracts of medical literature, for example," says Eugene Jones, who retired last year from Upjohn, where he had served as director of sales training.

The idea of self-worth is a big part of this approach. Peak performers have high self-images—yet our salespeople face rejection day in and day out. . . . Garfield showed us that if they got behind the idea of peak performance, routine rejections wouldn't bother them so much. . . . Unless a person has a positive attitude and is goal-oriented, he or she is not going to be a peak performer.

Henry Givray, Vice President of Smith, Bucklin and Associates in Chicago, explains his company's use of Garfield's research.

As we move forward into a period of growth, we need to get more people participating in the company's direction who are more capable of solving problems. You achieve that result by having management share information with more people in the organization, while staying focused on a clear, compelling vision of what you want the organization to be. Now we're moving toward a more formal, guided process for that—and the challenge is to make it happen so that it's not bureaucratic and stifling.

SOURCE: "Teach Your Employees to Be Peak Performers," *Personnel Journal* **70** (June 1991): 78. Copyright © 1991. Reprinted with permission of *Personnel Journal*, Costa Mesa, CA. All rights reserved.

From an operational viewpoint, motivational implications should be considered during the selection of personnel, design of jobs, and development of reward systems. When selecting and orienting personnel, performance expectations and evaluation criteria should be clearly explained. Meaningful job duties, positive work environments, and employee participation all help to motivate personnel. Similarly, well-designed reward systems provide opportunities to earn personal recognition, build greater job security, and enhance career development.

1. Which theory best explains the motivation of today's workers?

2. What can managers do to maintain perceptions of equity or fairness among employees?

3. Why do so few people attain Maslow's level of self-actualization?

MOTIVATION TECHNIQUES

Highly motivated people typically work hard and devote considerable energy to the attainment of their goals. More and more organizations are encouraging employees to become involved in problem solving, seeking their recommendations and loyalty, and granting them greater authority to make decisions. From a communication perspective, recognition of accomplishments is a powerful motivator. High morale is a characteristic of most people who are known for their ability to complete tasks. Let's examine how techniques are applied to motivate human resources.

■ Self-Motivation

Managers who cannot motivate themselves are likely to have difficulty trying to motivate their employees. Attitude is a major factor in self-motivation.[40] Rather than dwelling on negative possibilities, a focus on positive outcomes helps to overcome obstacles and inevitable disappointments. A willingness to learn from experiences and to be persistent contributes to achievement and satisfaction.

What motivates you?

Self-motivation involves an examination of oneself in terms of needs, wants, and interests. Many people who excel appear to possess insight into their own behaviors. Frequently, they have a real liking for their jobs. For example, one year Jessie Thatcher, a retail salesperson, sold 480 Buicks and had $5.3 million in total sales. When interviewed, she commented about always having a love for cars and indicated she spent 60–70 hours weekly at her place of employment.[41] When a goal is meaningful and valued, self-motivated efforts are more likely to occur.

An agreement with yourself should be kept.

The concept of a **self contract** is a factor to consider in motivating yourself. In essence, this is a written agreement you make with yourself to do certain tasks. For example, you might make a contract with yourself to take at least one college course each semester until you complete a degree. The written aspect gives the contract more importance, makes it more permanent, and forces you to confront reality (courses must be completed before the degree can be granted). Also, progress is easily monitored; you record the completion of each course and know where you stand.

■ Empowering Employees

Many firms are empowering employees.

Empowerment refers to "giving workers at all levels the knowledge, confidence, and authority to use their own judgment to make important decisions."[42] When employees are empowered, the managerial role changes from order giver and decision maker to coach and adviser. Managers must be willing to concede

Motivated employees are vital business assets. Knowledgeable and trained workers are empowered and exercise much discretion regarding how to do their jobs.

some of their traditional prerogatives, especially power and authority; employees need to understand how to examine information and formulate recommendations. Successful empowerment depends on management's ability to explain expectations so that employees know what objectives are to be attained.

It is difficult to do a job without knowing what to do.

Training is a key aspect of empowerment. Trained personnel are knowledgeable about the management processes used to make choices and implement decisions. For example, the Committing to Leadership program sponsored by American Airlines helps workers realize the importance of quality. It "underscores the airline's commitment to customer satisfaction and teaches employees that everyone at the company has the responsibility to ensure that passengers are happy. Workers learn about taking initiatives in solving problems."[43]

Many middle-management positions have been eliminated as firms seek ways to reduce expenses and become more competitive. Today, middle managers who remain often encounter greater pressures for results, and many show a lesser degree of loyalty to their employers. To retain capable managerial talent, some companies make a priority effort to note management concerns and recognize the value of empowerment. This involves learning what middle managers think, granting them the flexibility to develop solutions, and permitting these solutions to be implemented.[44]

Managers should not overlook the views of their employees.

Employees are a valuable source of recommendations for reducing costs and increasing job satisfaction. For instance, the hospital industry is challenged to resolve problems involving cost and quality issues. The Kaiser Permanente Medical Care Program in Oakland, California, achieved a 20-to-one return on money allocated to an employee suggestion program. Some hospitals encourage the development of cross-departmental teams to formulate suggestions.[45]

Toyota's experience illustrates the impact of receptiveness to worker views.

In 1965, Toyota received 9000 employee suggestions, about one per worker, and used 39 percent of them. In 1980, Toyota received 850,000 suggestions, about 19 per worker, and used 94 percent of them. That's the power of employee involvement. The dramatic increase can be attributed to managers learning to "listen to the ideas of their employees."[46]

Attaining goals is essential to business success. Worthwhile and challenging goals are most likely to motivate managers and employees.

■ *Goal Setting*

Goal setting focuses on making a conscious effort to achieve specified goals. This technique involves employees and provides opportunities for them to ask questions, express opinions, give criticisms, and receive feedback. When goal setting is in place, workers know what they are trying to accomplish and have a basis for allocating their time and effort.

> Knowing what you're supposed to do will put you at a powerful advantage over most people. It used to be that jobs were clearly defined and very straightforward. Today's white-collar worker . . . must be clever enough to unravel the mystery of how his or her success will be measured.[47]

Several characteristics are important to effective goal setting.[48] Specific and challenging goals that employees accept are most motivational. Feedback is also relevant because it enables workers to assess their progress in reaching goals. When workers are given a sense of direction, fewer misunderstandings occur and less time is lost by concentrating efforts on inappropriate tasks.

Consider how to measure goal achievement.

Let's assume that a company goal is "to increase productivity and improve quality." This goal is quite general and probably not of much practical value. Let's revise it and restate the goal as "to increase the number of units produced by 10 percent with five percent fewer defects." Since this new goal is specific and also measurable, it serves as a reference guideline for subsequent decisions.

Challenging goals are necessary to motivate employee performance.

If goals are too easily reached, they will not motivate workers. Consider the experience of winning whenever you play cards; soon, the thrill no longer exists, and the game becomes boring. In goal setting, a similar response pattern prevails. Goals must be at least moderately challenging. If goals are perceived as too difficult or as completely unattainable, workers will give up and not try to reach them. Remember, the employees themselves set various levels of challenge. A goal of five sales per day may be viewed as too difficult by one worker but as easily attainable by another.

To sustain their motivation, employees must perceive goals as worthwhile or valued. Otherwise, a "so what" attitude can evolve, and performance declines. Employee participation in goal setting increases the likelihood of goal acceptance.[49] This view is based on the premise that workers are more likely to support goals that they have helped to develop.

■ Building Organizational Morale

The generalized attitude of an employee group toward the company, management, or job-related factors is referred to as **organizational morale.** It is influenced by many things, including salary, job tasks, colleagues, and managers.[50] High organizational morale involves a feeling that job contributions are worthwhile. Similarly, group morale is greater when members work cooperatively together and take pride in their accomplishments. The actions of managers play a major role in organizational morale. "Employees expect a just reward for their contributions and fair treatment for their efforts. If that doesn't happen, they'll lower their evaluation of managerial fairness and commitment."[51]

Many factors affect morale in the workplace.

Concerns and factors in the business environment influence organizational morale. Worries about health or personal problems affect employee attitudes. Likewise, the lack of up-to-date equipment or a failure to provide adequate work facilities contributes to low worker morale. Morale is affected by relevant comparisons. As an example, assume the members of the fabricating department ask management to replace their word processor with a computer. The request is denied, and they give little thought to the matter until a colleague informs them that all of the other departments already have computers. As a result, the morale of the members of the fabricating department is likely to deteriorate.

Managers cannot be "everything to everybody."

Most managers are limited in their abilities to initiate major organizational changes. They must abide by company directives and operate within budget allocations. However, an important relationship exists between managerial actions and the morale of subordinates. To determine what employees believe matters most on their jobs, 3500 workers were surveyed. The factor cited most frequently was "having a boss you can respect," which was ranked above satisfying work, pay, and opportunities for advancement.[52] Respect between employees and managers is a two-way street. Managers who respect their employees are more likely to be successful morale builders. Let's examine several strategies to improve organizational morale.

GIVING RECOGNITION Employees appreciate receiving positive recognition for their accomplishments. Handwritten notes of praise, personal compliments, and public acknowledgment are relevant nonmonetary morale builders. Think how you would react if your boss (or even his or her boss) gave you a compliment for doing excellent work. You would probably experience feelings of pride and satisfaction. Recognition helps to build self-confidence and generally encourages additional efforts to excel. Recognition also helps to generate positive sentiments toward managers and the company. Cultural differences should not be overlooked in terms of giving recognition. For example, most American workers like to receive personal praise for their performances on the job. Employees from some Asian cultures, however, believe that recognition should go to their peer group and not to its individual members.

GAINING PERSPECTIVES   Employees want to be treated fairly and to be given opportunities to express their views. High organizational morale is associated with managers who are accessible and responsive to worker concerns. Some managers have an **open-door policy:** their employees are invited to come in and discuss topics of interest. This is how the practice works at Delta Airlines.

> The open-door policy sets the tone. Former president Tom Beebe explains: "My rug has to be cleaned once a month. Mechanics, pilots, flight attendants—they all come in to see me. If they really want to tell us something, we'll give them the time. They don't have to go through somebody."[53]

Managers employ the concept of **managing by walking around (MBWA)** to become better acquainted with employee job responsibilities and problems. Such a setting is more informal and conversational in nature; managers who visit employees at their work stations are likely to learn quite a lot about job interests and quality concerns.

Managers can practice MBWA at all levels of a firm. An incident involving Sam Walton, founder of Wal-Mart, indicates how a manager can learn from an informal discussion with workers.

> One night, Walton couldn't sleep. So he went out and bought four dozen dough-nuts at an all-night bakery. At 2:30 A.M., he took them to a distribution center and chatted with Wal-Mart shipping dock workers. From this talk, he discovered that two more shower stalls were needed at that location.[54]

In many Japanese firms, tables and chairs are arranged with no dividers to physically separate workers from their bosses. Such an approach enables managers to know if job assignments are being completed and to become better acquainted with the strengths and weaknesses of their employees. Young Japanese managers learn the importance of maintaining positive interactions with peers. Participation in work groups motivates them to develop positive attitudes toward coworkers and employers, which promotes high morale. William G. Ouchi, an expert on Japanese management, observes that the "intimate, subtle, and complex evaluation by one's peers" is a major factor in the success of Japanese organizations.[55]

EMPHASIZING THE POSITIVE   Managers routinely encounter challenges: equipment will unexpectedly malfunction; projects do not get finished as planned; deliveries do not always arrive as scheduled. Despite the many obstacles that can occur, a positive attitude will encourage those you manage to have higher morale. "In practice, many managers do not realize how much their attitudes influence subordinates. Negativism, inconsiderateness, and apathy are not conducive to development of a progressive work environment."[56]

THINK ABOUT IT

1. Job satisfaction does not necessarily imply high levels of worker motivation.

2. Managers and employees often have dissimilar opinions about factors that motivate job performance.

3. A strong determination to succeed helps workers overcome frustrations and attain goals.

4. Attitude is a key word. Positive attitudes focus on opportunities; negative attitudes emphasize disappointments.

5. Empowering employees alters management's role. Instead of giving orders, managers advise, coach, and act as facilitators.

6. Perceptions of fairness vary among workers. What one employee considers equitable may differ considerably from the perspective of another employee.

7. It is easier to discuss effective motivation techniques than to practice them.

8. Managers who practice "management by walking around" gain firsthand knowledge of employee concerns. It is better to learn about problems from your subordinates than from your boss.

LOOKING BACK

You have studied various concepts and theories of motivation—a topic of considerable importance in an era of concern about productivity and competitiveness. Let's examine the learning objectives listed at the beginning of this chapter to give you an opportunity to review your understanding of the chapter content.

Define motivation and understand the motivation process.

Motivation is an internal process through which human wants, needs, and desires are satisfied. Figure 10–1 illustrates the motivation process. Individuals strive to satisfy identified needs. When these needs are fulfilled, satisfaction occurs. If needs remain unfulfilled, individuals become frustrated.

Discuss several commonly recognized motivation theories.

McGregor's Theory X and Theory Y are based on assumptions about behaviors. Theory X, a traditional approach, emphasizes the importance of control. According to Theory Y, employees have ambitions, want to work, and willingly accept responsibility.

In Maslow's view, needs are arranged in a hierarchical order from survival, safety and security, and social needs to esteem and self-actualization needs. Fulfillment of basic needs precedes satisfaction of higher-level needs. Another researcher, Frederick Herzberg, developed a two-factor theory. Hygiene factors, such as salary, working conditions, and quality of supervision, represent sources of dissatisfaction. Motivator factors, including advancement, achievement, and recognition, are the real stimuli to motivate job performance.

The expectancy and equity theories are other widely recognized theories of motivation. Expectancy theory is based on the relationship between the value placed on outcomes and the likelihood of attaining them. If a reward is valued, a high effort-to-performance expectancy and a high performance-to-outcome expectancy lead to motivated performance. Equity theory is concerned with perceptions of fairness. A sense of equity exists only when the ratio of inputs to outcomes is perceived to be the same as that of a comparison reference person.

Reinforcement theory examines the consequences of past experiences on subsequent behaviors. Positive reinforcement, negative reinforcement, punishment, and extinction are methods of reinforcing behaviors. Intermittent schedules of reinforcement include the fixed-ratio, variable-ratio, fixed-interval, and variable-interval schedules. Review Figure 10–6, which summarizes the characteristics of reinforcement schedules.

Examine how communication influences motivation.

Lack of communication creates anxieties. If messages are unclear, confusion occurs, and miscommunication consumes a considerable amount of time. The tone of a message can convey negativism and, in turn, cause less-motivated efforts on the part of the receiver. Effective communicators experience fewer problems related to rumors and grapevine. In addition, they are more likely to recognize the wants and needs of their employees.

Explain the concepts of self-motivation, empowerment, and goal setting.

Self-motivation involves looking at an individual's own needs, wants, and interests. Managers who cannot motivate themselves will have difficulty motivating others. Empowering employees gives them greater authority to make decisions about job tasks. Workers who become more involved in doing their jobs should also become more motivated. Goal setting focuses on making a conscious effort to achieve specified goals. When workers have goals, they can direct their time and energy toward reaching them.

Understand how morale affects job performance.

When morale is high, people take pride in their work and feel that job contributions are valued. Poor attitudes, lack of necessary equipment, and inadequate work facilities can negatively impact productivity. Giving recognition, gaining perspectives of employee views, and emphasizing positive factors are strategies to boost organizational morale and, in turn, improve job performance.

KEY TERMS

content theories of motivation	fixed-interval schedule
continuous reinforcement	fixed-ratio schedule
Cs of motivation	goal setting
challenge	growth needs
commitment	hygiene factors
competence	intermittent reinforcement
confidence	management by walking around
dissatisfier	(MBWA)
empowerment	Maslow's hierarchy of human needs
equity theory	motivation
ERG theory	motivator factors
esteem needs	needs
existence needs	negative reinforcement
expectancy theory	open-door policy
extinction	organizational morale

positive reinforcement
probability assessment
process theories of motivation
punishment
reinforcement theory
relatedness needs
safety and security needs
self-actualization needs

self contract
social needs
survival needs
Theory X
Theory Y
variable-interval schedule
variable-ratio schedule

REVIEW AND DISCUSSION QUESTIONS

1. Why is motivation a complex topic?
2. How do the assumptions of Theory X differ from those of Theory Y?
3. Why do so few people attain Maslow's level of self-actualization?
4. How can managers motivate themselves?
5. What is the difference between Herzberg's motivator factors and hygiene factors?
6. In equity theory, what is the importance of a comparison reference person?
7. What are the important differences among the four types of reinforcement?
8. Discuss the fundamental premise of expectancy theory.
9. How does the concept of employee empowerment change the role of a manager?
10. What can managers do to improve the organizational morale of their employees?

CRITICAL THINKING INCIDENT 10.1

Things Change

Two years ago, Carol Watson completed her college degree and accepted employment as an account executive at New-World Travel Agency, a well-known company serving the Kansas City and St. Louis metropolitan areas. Recently, New-World was absorbed by Travel and Cruises International, a larger company with customers located throughout the Midwest. Since the takeover, Carol's sales quota has been increased and her commission schedule has been reduced. Also, Travel and Cruises provides less attractive employee benefits for its personnel.

Bryan Hodges is the new manager. He is an aggressive individual who emphasizes sales as the most important criterion of success. Bryan arbitrarily sets sales expectations and seldom solicits suggestions from employees. While cor-

dial, he tends to be somewhat aloof and spends the majority of his time in his office doing paperwork.

Carol is disappointed with the new quota system and revised compensation plan. She thinks to herself, "Why am I expected to do more but be paid at a lower rate?" In addition, she is uncomfortable with Bryan's style of management. The former manager was accessible, volunteered assistance, and took a personal interest in her career progress. Because of the changes in her business environment, Carol's sales have declined and she has become increasingly withdrawn.

June Glasgow is a colleague who also worked for New-World. June is knowledgeable, experienced, and successful. Others describe her as a goal-oriented, energetic person; she works hard and requires little supervision. A couple of days ago, June and Carol had lunch together. During the conversation, Carol asked June what she thought about the changes that have occurred. June replied, "I don't like the new pay plan or really care much for Bryan. I just do my best and ignore what I can't control."

Bryan has observed that Carol's sales have slipped. He is somewhat perplexed because the economy has gained momentum and greater numbers of potential customers have recently located in the area. Since the new compensation plan was a directive from upper management, Bryan has not given it much attention. Also, he has not considered the negative reaction to the benefits package, since he never worked for New-World. Bryan wonders, "How can Carol be motivated?"

Discussion Questions

1. In terms of motivation, why do Carol and June react differently to the takeover by Travel and Cruises International?
2. How can Bryan become knowledgeable about the basis of Carol's motivation?
3. Why is Bryan perplexed about Carol's job performance?
4. Specifically, how can Bryan motivate Carol?

CRITICAL THINKING INCIDENT 10.2

I'm Stuck Here

Harriett Elliott supervises the checkout counters at the local outlet of Westside Stores, a major discount retailer. Another part of her assignment is to assist customers by answering questions and helping them to locate merchandise. Harriett has held this position for the past seven years; two years ago, she received a storewide award for giving courteous service to customers. On many occasions, customers have complemented her for doing a good job and also told management about her helpfulness.

Within the past week, numerous complaints have been received about Harriett, including remarks about her slow service, time-consuming mistakes, and rudeness. Wilma Santiago, the assistant manager, was surprised to learn of the complaints and discussed them with Harriett. Basically, Harriett asserted that the customers were too fussy and expected too much of her. Then she said, "Considering the length of time I've worked here, I've probably had fewer complaints than anybody." Wilma indicated the need for Harriett to avoid future complaints and extended an invitation to her to come in and discuss any problems or concerns.

Actually, Harriett is frustrated because she does not feel her efforts have been rewarded. Her salary raises have been meager and distributed according to length of service, not productivity. Furthermore, the opportunity for a promotion is rather slim; the next available higher-level job is held by Ron Rinneman, who is expected to remain in the position for the next few years.

Harriett shared her feelings with Alice Baumgardner, a friend and coworker. Alice responded, "You always have to do your best and demonstrate a positive attitude toward everyone." Harriett agrees but admits her frustrations have recently gotten out of control. "Alice, I am proud of my record, but despite all of my efforts, things have not really worked out like I had anticipated. I can't let the negativism continue."

In the meantime, Wilma is wondering what can be done to help Harriett. She discussed the situation with Tom Rice, the store manager. He recommended telling Harriett that further complaints cannot be tolerated and will result in the termination of her employment. "But Tom," Wilma said, "Isn't your recommendation too harsh for an employee who has such a good overall record with us? Shouldn't I try to get more information from Harriett before giving her such an ultimatum?"

Discussion Questions

1. How can Harriett gain control over her frustrations and avoid being so negative?
2. What can Wilma do to motivate Harriett?
3. Do you agree with Tom's recommendation? Explain your response.
4. Is Harriett likely to regain her enthusiasm and be motivated if she changes jobs and works for another employer? Explain your response.

CRITICAL THINKING INCIDENT 10.3

The Star Performer

Sally Thomas has one of the most outstanding sales records ever achieved at Nationwide Cosmetics, a direct distributor of cosmetic products. A year ago, she was promoted to district manager, largely because of her outstanding record.

Rhonda McIntyre, the regional sales manager and Sally's boss, is concerned about performance in Sally's district. There has been a significant decline in sales volume and a considerable turnover of sales representatives. On inquiry, she learns that many employees consider Sally's attitude to be somewhat arrogant and antagonistic. Although they consider Sally helpful and willing to be of assistance, her employees feel that she is impatient and expects too much from them.

Rhonda has discussed these opinions with Sally. But Sally still believes that she has each employee's interest at heart and is trying to get every person to understand the need to work long hours and push hard for results. After all, these are the key factors that have contributed to her success. Rhonda tries to convince Sally that all of her employees will not be superstar producers, but Sally feels that her workers need to set high goals and strive to attain them.

Rhonda thinks that Sally has the potential to be a successful manager, especially since she appears to like her job and enjoys sharing her knowledge with others. But, Rhonda contemplates, "Everyone cannot be the star performer."

Discussion Questions

1. What factors motivated Sally to achieve her outstanding sales record?

2. How can Sally be a star performer but be seemingly ineffective at motivating her employees?

3. Does Sally have the potential to be a successful manager? Explain your response.

4. Sally's employees are using her as an excuse for their own ineffective job performances. What is your response to this statement?

5. Would you like to have Sally as your manager? Why or why not?

SOURCE: Donald S. Miller and Stephen E. Catt, *Human Relations: A Contemporary Approach* (Homewood, IL: Richard D. Irwin, 1989), p. 159.

NOTES

1. Robert W. Goddard, "Motivating the Modern Employee," *Management World* 13 (February 1984): 9.

2. J. A. Livingston, "Survey Shows Who Reaches Top Jobs," *Wichita Eagle-Beacon* (November 10, 1986), p. 6D.

3. Kenneth A. Kovach, "What Motivates Employees? Workers and Supervisors Give Different Answers," *Business Horizons* 30 (September/October 1987): 65.

4. Brian Dumaine, "Earning More by Moving Faster," *Fortune* (October 7, 1991), pp. 89–91, 94.

5. Don Hellriegel, John W. Slocum, Jr., and Richard W. Woodman, *Organizational Behavior,* 6th ed. (St. Paul, MN: West Publishing, 1992), p. 205.

6. David W. Richardson, "Search to Find Proper Motivating Techniques for Differing Types of Individual Employees," *Merchandising* 10 (January 1985): 102.

7. Peter F. Drucker, "Management and the World's Work," *Harvard Business Review* 66 (September/October 1988): 75.

8. Donald S. Miller and Stephen E. Catt, *Human Relations: A Contemporary Approach* (Homewood, IL: Richard D. Irwin, 1989), pp. 135–36.

9. Frank K. Sonnenberg, "If a Tree Falls in the Woods," *Industry Week* (June 17, 1991): 85.

10. Izhak Harpaz, "The Importance of Work Goals: An International Perspective," *Journal of International Business Studies* 21 (First Quarter 1990): 76–86.

11. Connie Wallace, "The Fine Art of Using Money as a Motivator," *Working Woman* 15 (January 1990): 126.

12. Amanda Bennett, "When Money Is Tight, Bosses Scramble for Other Ways to Motivate the Troops," *The Wall Street Journal* (October 31, 1990), p. B1.

13. J. Sterling Livingston, "Pygmalion in Management," *Harvard Business Review* 66 (September/October 1988): 124.

14. Donald R. Utroska, "Management in Europe: More Than Just Etiquette," *Management Review* 81 (November 1992): 24.

15. Ibid., p. 22.

16. Ibid.

17. Anne B. Fisher, "CEOs Think That Morale Is Dandy," *Fortune* (November 18, 1991): 83.

18. Hellriegel, Slocum, and Woodman, *Organizational Behavior*, p. 220.

19. Gerald M. Goldhaber, *Organizational Communication*, 3rd ed. (Dubuque, IA: Wm. C. Brown, 1983), pp. 84–86.

20. Ibid.

21. John Waggoner, "AT&T Card Aimed High from Start," *USA Today* (October 15, 1992), p. 28.

22. Abraham H. Maslow, *Motivation and Personality* (New York: Harper & Row, 1954).

23. Andrea Gabor and others, "The U.S. News 100: Market Bonanzas," *U.S. News & World Report* (July 6, 1987): 48–49.

24. Dennis W. Organ and Thomas S. Bateman, *Organizational Behavior*, 4th ed. (Homewood, IL: Richard D. Irwin, 1991), p. 65.

25. Ibid.

26. Frederick Herzberg, *Work and the Nature of Man* (New York: Thomas Y. Crowell, 1966).

27. Fred Luthans, *Organizational Behavior*, 5th ed. (New York: McGraw-Hill, 1989), p. 243.

28. Ibid., p. 244.

29. David D. Van Fleet, *Behavior in Organizations* (Boston: Houghton Mifflin, 1991), p. 67.

30. Robert A. Baron and Jerald Greenberg, *Behavior in Organizations*, 3d ed. (Boston: Allyn & Bacon, 1990), pp. 89–91.

31. Hellriegel, Slocum, and Woodman, *Organizational Behavior*, pp. 230–31.

32. Carl R. Anderson, *Management*, 2d ed. (Boston: Allyn & Bacon, 1988), p. 248.

33. Baron and Greenberg, *Behavior in Organizations*, pp. 40–41.

34. O. Jeff Harris and Sandra J. Hartman, *Human Behavior at Work* (St. Paul, MN: West Publishing, 1992), p. 200.

35. J. Clifton Williams and George P. Huber, *Human Behavior in Organizations*, 3d ed. (Cincinnati: South-Western, 1986), pp. 132–33.

36. M. Joseph Reitz, *Behavior in Organizations*, 3d ed. (Homewood, IL: Richard D. Irwin, 1987), pp. 55–56.

37. Baron and Greenberg, *Behavior in Organizations*, p. 46.

38. David J. Cherrington, *Organizational Behavior: The Management of Individual and Organizational Performance* (Boston: Allyn & Bacon, 1989), p. 140.

39. Hellriegel, Slocum, and Woodman, *Organizational Behavior*, p. 188.

40. Miller and Catt, *Human Relations: A Contemporary Approach*, p. 148.

41. "Best Sellers," *Ambassador* 18 (June 1985): 40.

42. Erika Penzer, "The Power of Empowerment," *Incentive* 165 (May 1991): 97.

43. Ibid., p. 99.

44. Anne B. Fisher, "Morale Crisis," *Fortune* (November 18, 1991), p. 76.

45. Paula Eubanks, "Employee Suggestion Programs Boost Morale and Bottom Line," *Hospitals* (May 20, 1991): 46.

46. Howard E. Hyden, "Winning Organizations," *Executive Excellence* 8 (July 1991): 20.

47. Leonard Sandler, "The Successful and Supportive Subordinate," *Personnel Journal* 63 (December 1984): 44.

48. Gary Johns, *Organizational Behavior*, 3d ed. (New York: HarperCollins, 1992), pp. 226–27.

49. Baron and Greenberg, *Behavior in Organizations*, p. 93.

50. Miller and Catt, *Human Relations: A Contemporary Approach*, p. 152.

51. Joseph A. Petrick and George E. Manning, "How to Manage Morale," *Personnel Journal* 69 (October 1990): 86.

52. Suzy Parker, "What Matters Most on the Job," *USA Today* (January 24, 1990), p. 1B.

53. Thomas J. Peters and Robert H. Waterman, Jr., *In Search of Excellence* (New York: Warner Books, 1982), p. 253.

54. Petrick and Manning, "How to Manage Morale," p. 87.

55. William G. Ouchi, *Theory Z* (New York: Avon, 1982), pp. 23–25.

56. Miller and Catt, *Human Relations: A Contemporary Approach*, p. 153.

SUGGESTED READINGS

Galagan, Patricia A. "Think Performance." *Training and Development* 48 (March 1994): 47–51.

Hakim, Cliff. "Boost Morale to Gain Productivity." *HR Magazine* 38 (February 1993): 46–49.

Hudy, John J. "The Motivation Trap." *HR Magazine* 37 (December 1992): 63–67.

Kimmel, Michael S. "What Do Men Want?" *Harvard Business Review* 71 (November/December 1993): 50–63.

Koonce, Richard. "One on One." *Training and Development* 48 (February 1994): 34–40.

Moskal, Brian S. "Company Loyalty Dies, A Victim of Neglect." *Industry Week* (March 1, 1993): 11–12.

Sherman, Stratford. "Are You as Good as the Best in the World?" *Fortune* (December 13, 1993): 95–96.

Smith, Lee. "The Executive's New Coach." *Fortune* (December 27, 1993): 126–128, 130, 132, 134.

Verespej, Michael A. "The 'Psychology of Entitlement': It Must be Broken." *Industry Week* (April 5, 1993): 35–36.

Vogl, A. J. "Carrots, Sticks, and Self-Deception." *Across the Board* 31 (January 1994): 39–44.

CHAPTER 11

SOCIAL RESPONSIBILITIES AND ETHICS

■ LEARNING OBJECTIVES

In this chapter, we will study the social responsibilities and ethics of businesses in today's world. The learning objectives for this chapter are to:

- Define and understand what social responsibility means.
- Discuss and appreciate the costs and benefits that a socially responsible business incurs in today's competitive environment.
- Understand the different ways to measure social responsibility in the business world.
- List and discuss some common ways to improve social responsibility.
- Define and discuss the role of ethics in business today.
- Appreciate and explain some of the factors that affect ethics in business.
- Identify some ways to improve managerial ethics.

■ CHAPTER OUTLINE

On March 24, 1989, when the oil tanker Exxon Valdez ran aground in Alaskan waters, spilling 10 million gallons of crude oil, it made the *news*. Later, when the Coast Guard released the story to the press, it made the *headlines*. It was interesting gossip. It appeared that the third mate was at the helm, where he had no license to be, and the captain was below, where he should not have been.

Perhaps the public could have overlooked the irresponsibility that led to the accident. How Exxon bungled

Oil tankers off the coast of Alaska are still a common sight, even after the horrific Exxon Valdez oil spill in 1989.

the cleanup, however, made the *history books*. It appeared that Exxon was not equipped to handle such a large spill. "There was no cleanup equipment on the scene for the first 18 hours," according to Alaska's governor, Steve Cowyer. Experts say the spill could have been cleaned up in ten hours if the right equipment had been available.

What did the cleanup cost? It took 20 months and cost Exxon some $2.2 billion, but it did not end there. On May 2, 1994, the first civil trial involving 14,000 plaintiffs (Alaskan fishermen and women and property owners) began in Anchorage Federal Court. On June 13, the federal jury in that civil trial found Exxon guilty of "recklessness" in the 1989 oil spill. In September, the federal jury ordered Exxon to pay $5 billion in punitive damages.

This is not the only mistake Exxon made that year. In late December 1989, Exxon suffered an explosion and fire at a major Louisiana oil refinery. Something was said about malfunctioning equipment. However, Exxon managed to keep this mistake out of the public eye.

Then on New Year's Day in 1990, a 12-inch pipeline running under the Arthur Kill Waterway, which separates Staten Island and New Jersey, ruptured and spewed out 567,000 gallons of No. 2 heating oil. Apparently, the safety system was known to be defective, so when the alarm rang and the plant system automatically shut down, the workers did not believe there was a leak. They shut off the alarm and manually reopened the values. Some of the oil was recovered, and some of it evapo-

—Continued

SOCIAL RESPONSIBILITY DEFINED

If any society is truly going to advance its people, then every major sector of that society must become more socially responsible, regardless of the individual costs. Social responsibility in the business sector will only occur if the people who run the businesses accept this fact. Businesses today must clearly and continuously communicate to employees that their firms will adhere to socially responsible principles, or it will never happen.

Social responsibility is very difficult to define. Actions that you, as a manager, see as socially responsible may be viewed by others as socially irresponsible. As examples, firms that can be considered either socially responsible or socially irresponsible manufacture war weapons and products that pollute the atmosphere, or sell unsafe cars, or produce unhealthy foods that contain high percentages of fat, sodium, or cholesterol.

Social responsibility in the business world may be defined as "actions and decisions which consider the legal, economic, and societal factors in both the

Business decisions and actions that consider both organizational and societal factors are collectively defined as socially responsible.

rated. Much of it permeated the shoreline and coastal wetlands, killing many of the birds and fish in the area. "It's a Mini-Alaska," noted New York Attorney General, Robert Abrams. In many ways it was. The incident again attracted public attention. People began to boycott Exxon products. Environmentalists demanded reform.

The Exxon Valdez catastrophe made us vividly aware of the dangers and costs of oil spills, and it brought with it some progress toward change. Environmentalists are now stressing the need for vessel traffic systems (VTS), which are radar systems like those used for air-traffic control, to minimize accidents at sea. Also, legislation has been implemented that requires all ships carrying oil to have double hulls—an inner hull and a second outer hull—by the year 2015.

The problem, however, is that not very many companies are socially responsible enough to implement either of these solutions, so the saga continues.

- In December 1992 a Greek tanker, The Aegean Sea, ran aground at La Coruna, Spain, and spewed 21 million gallons of oil on the Spanish shorelands.

- In January 1993, the American tanker, the Braer, ran aground on the Shetland Islands (the northernmost territory of Britain) and spilled 25 million gallons of oil on the shores of one of the most renowned bird sanctuaries in the world.

- In August 1993, the freighter, The Balso 37, collided with two incoming barges in Tampa Bay about 2 ½ miles west of the Sunshine Skyway Bridge, which is located in Saint Petersburg, Florida. The Barge Ocean 255 caught fire and lost 9.4 million gallons of jet fuel, gasoline, and diesel fuel. The second barge, Barge 155, spilled about 210,000 gallons of its 5 million gallon cargo of heavy No. 6 fuel oil.

Unfortunately, not one of these tankers or barges had a double hull. If the companies transporting these sea vessels had demanded that double hulls be manufactured, the oil spills would have been small and the damage to the environment would have been minimal. So the costs of social irresponsibility continue. The question is, Will we learn from these mistakes?

ADAPTED FROM: "Five Years Later, Alaskan Losses Focus of Exxon Valdez Civil Suit," *The Bradenton Herald* (May 1, 1994), p. A3; Robert Engler, "Portrait of an Oil Spill," *The Nation* (March 5, 1990), pp. 300–302; Keith Hammonds, "A Verdict That Could Sully Exxon's Credit," *Business Week* (June 27, 1994), p. 38; J. Lieblich, "Exxon Befouled," *Fortune* (April 24, 1989), p. 16; Eugene Robinson, "Tanker Spews Oil on Shetland Coast," *Washington Post* (January 6, 1993), p. B1; Barbara Rudolph, "Exxon's Attitude Problem," *Time* (January 22, 1990), p. 29; Caleb Solomon, "Exxon Is Told to Pay $5 Billion for Valdez Spill," *The Wall Street Journal* (September 19, 1994), pp. A1–A8; Calab Solomon, "Jury Finds Exxon Reckless in Oil Spill," *The Wall Street Journal* (June 14, 1994), p. A1; Sam Starnes, "Future Oil Spills Foreseen," *The Bradenton Herald* (August 15, 1993), pp. B1–B2.

short and long run as well as organizational interests."[1] This does not mean that businesses today are not concerned with profits; it simply means that profits are the reward for serving society well but not a sole end in and of themselves. This definition of social responsibility means that the managers of a firm must consider more than just the question, "Is what we are doing legal and profitable?" They must also ask, "Are we meeting society's expectations in terms of what we are producing and how we are producing it?"

Many businesses have been socially responsible in the past, but many have not. Some business leaders today even try to rationalize their behavior by pointing out how much more socially responsible they are than their predecessors were. Today, the public's opinion of companies that are not socially responsible is extremely negative and can definitely translate into lost business and profits for a firm:

The timing is so right for people to become more interested in social responsibility. Why is it so right? We are tired of drugs and crime, politicians and TV evangelists whom we cannot trust, an American car that is nothing but junk, health care and insurance costs we cannot afford, and an environment that is killing us slowly, but surely. Yes, we are finally getting mad enough to force change in business ethics and social responsibility. Here are a few examples.

■ A millionaire named Phil Sokolof wrote about his own heart attack and pleaded with cookie and cereal makers to dump the oil. He also put out a newspaper ad at a cost of $200,000 with Cracklin' Oat Bran Cereal pictured under the headline "The Poisoning of America." Within one month, Kellogg Company, the maker of Cracklin' Oat Bran, decided to take the coconut oil out.

■ The consumer group Voter Revolt won the narrow passage of Proposition 13. This law literally cut automobile and home insurance rates by 20 percent in California. "A new brand of citizen activism is underway," says Ralph Nader. Nader is currently working on legislation similar to California's Proposition 13 for several other states.

■ For months after the Exxon Valdez oil spill in Alaska, the public saw blackened beaches and oil-soaked birds on TV. Disk jockeys around the country urged Exxon gasoline cardholders to relinquish their cards, and more than 10,000 Americans did.

■ The American Nurses Association wrote to express dismay over the fact that student nurses were shown in their underwear on the TV show "Nightingales." Chrysler Corporation and Sears, Roebuck and Company quickly backed out as sponsors because they did not want to be associated with a television program that women viewed as sexist.

■ According to Gene Pokorny, a pollster for Cambridge Reports/Research International, "surveys indicate that Americans increasingly are willing to pay higher prices for environmentally friendly products and avoid doing business with companies they believe are hurting the environment."[2]

Were early business leaders ethical?

Today, when we look back at some of the early business leaders, such as J. P. Morgan, Jay Gould, and Cornelius Vanderbilt, we have a tendency to condemn them as men who exploited resources and people to gain large profits. However, many historians, including University of Rhode Island professor Maury Klein and Hofstra University business historian Robert Sobel, point out that these early entrepreneurs were simply operating under the laws and rules of the business world that were in place at the time. In short, standards change over time; Morgan, Gould, and Vanderbilt simply conducted business within the law and employed the acceptable practices of the day.[3] What constitutes socially responsible behavior, therefore, must always be viewed in conjunction with the social and cultural aspects of the time period in question.

There is still a great need for additional legislation to make firms more socially responsible.

The business world is constantly trying to adjust as society attempts to outlaw socially irresponsible actions through legislation. Many socially irresponsible activities by both individuals and business firms technically are not illegal but do permit people or companies to profit at the expense of others. For example, hiring practices that discriminated against minorities, women, and the physically challenged were common until laws were passed that made them illegal. Although some businesses may still discriminate against these groups, most firms no longer do. The list of violations is simply endless and includes everything from various types of pollution to deceptive marketing schemes to defraud the public:

Even though there has been a very definite movement toward being more socially responsible by the majority of the business world, a survey conducted for

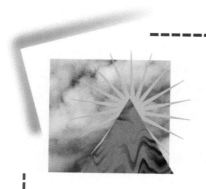

A PERSPECTIVE ON QUALITY

Social Responsibility Earns Customer Confidence at Stride Rite

Stride Rite Corporation is best known as a manufacturer of baby and children's shoes. But Stride Rite is living proof that a company can be socially responsible, produce a very high-quality product, charge a relatively high price for its product, and still be very profitable.

Stride Rite's most well-known social investment was started in 1971, when it opened the first corporate child-care center in the United States. This center now serves the entire local community of Roxbury, Massachusetts, as well as the employees, in a large, old factory in this very rough Boston neighborhood. In addition to this day-care center, Stride Rite also has a very extensive family-leave policy for its employees and an intergenerational center for infants and elderly parents of both employees and community members. The company also provides public-service scholarships. Stride Rite even convinced one of its joint-venture firms in Thailand to open a day-care center there.

Stride Rite also tries very hard to be socially responsible in the ways in which it produces its shoes and serves its customers. Stride Rite's former chairman, Arnold L. Hiatt, stated, "We're unashamedly out to make a profit, and we're very concerned with children's health. We run our business on both concerns." Stride Rite shoes are designed with a "long-standing, quasi-medical dedication to foot care." Even when selecting new suppliers overseas, the company is very careful to make sure that the factories are upgraded and that the work force is operating at a craftsman level. The managers of Stride Rite realize that these improvements will increase the cost of their shoes, but they feel that the higher quality of their product is worth the additional cost.

When servicing customers, the same type of quality issues arise. Former chairman Arnold Hiatt stated that what really impressed him about the firm when he first came on board was the amount of consumer confidence in a pair of Stride Rite shoes. The typical customer strongly believed that a store specializing in Stride Rite shoes would look after their child's feet in the most professional manner possible. Even today, Stride Rite managers indeed view this as their responsibility.

To maintain this level of consumer confidence, Stride Rite offers training sessions for both new and existing dealers. The training for new dealers is extensive, covering every aspect of running a Stride Rite shoe store, but a major emphasis is placed on how to properly measure children's feet so the correct shoes are sold to them. The company also insists that its dealers do not sell their customers new shoes if the old ones still fit and are in reasonably good condition. The management at Stride Rite firmly believes that only by serving customers well can a company hope to be successful and contribute to a healthy, caring society.

ADAPTED FROM: Andrew Stark, "What's the Matter with Business Ethics?," *Harvard Business Review* **71** (May/June 1993): 48; Nan Stone, "Building Corporate Character," *Harvard Business Review* **70** (March/April 1992): 95–104.

Ford Motor company by HRN, a management consulting firm in Philadelphia, gave some surprising findings. Ford wanted to find out what the environmental priorities were of key leaders in business, education, government, environmental advocacy groups, and the media. HRN sent out 6868 surveys and received 2172 completed surveys back. The results indicate the following.

■ 70 percent "strongly disagreed" that business will "voluntarily" take steps to protect the environment.

- 80 percent felt industry should be held *liable* for environmental damages and cleanup costs.

- 85 percent felt the federal government, rather than the state government, should take the lead in setting environmental standards.

- 90 percent called on the U.S. government to create *economic incentives* to encourage conservation and to develop new energy sources.

- 90 percent felt that the *environment* would be the public's top priority in the 1990s.

Top environmental issues specifically were 79 percent taking care of the ozone layer, 78.6 percent improving air quality, 74.5 percent dealing with hazardous waste disposal, 74.2 percent reducing acid rain, and 73.9 percent reducing auto emissions.[4]

Society continues to pass tougher and tougher laws to try to ensure that the business sector not only complies with the standards of society but begins to take the lead in shaping our environment. To offset negative perceptions engendered by business abuses, firms need to strongly communicate to the public sector what they are presently doing to become more socially responsible.

OPPOSING VIEWS ON SOCIAL RESPONSIBILITY

Social performance has evolved over the past 30 years. As Figure 11–1 illustrates, social responsibility can progress through four separate and distinct phases as a business organization grows in its acceptance of social responsibility.

■ *Economic Responsibility*

The first phase or viewpoint of social responsibility is the doctrine of **economic responsibility**, which has Milton Friedman as its strongest proponent, who is a Nobel laureate in economics. Friedman states that the sole social responsibility of a business manager is to maximize the firm's profits within the "rules of the game." Friedman apparently sees business managers as people who are strictly responsible to their stockholders. Since stockholders are only concerned with maximizing profits, it is therefore management's responsibility to be sure that this occurs.

Friedman notes that any use of a firm's resources for social activities simply makes the firm less competitive and undermines its primary objective. Friedman seems to view social responsibility as a subversive doctrine, not as a complementary doctrine. In other words, firms are being socially responsible if they maximize profits to stockholders, thereby ensuring steady employment for workers and a steady supply of goods and services to society. Anything else in terms of funding social issues is simply stealing from the stockholders.[5]

Many firms have gone beyond being just economic organizations.

Although on the surface Friedman and his followers appear narrow-minded about social responsibility, their basic point of keeping the firm profitable is valid. However, many large corporations have evolved beyond pure and simple economic organizations. In fact, they have established very definite political dimensions through their sponsorship of lobbying groups and political action committees. Certainly, political groups led by corporations have helped to shape many of our current laws and acceptable societal standards in such areas as employee safety, environmental protection, and antidiscriminatory hiring

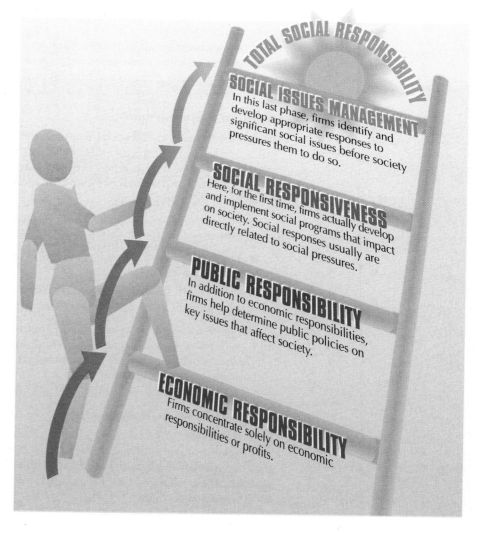

practices. Since corporations are involved in shaping these and other social issues, it is only right that they take on some responsibility for them.⁶

■ *Public Responsibility*

In the public responsibility phase, firms strive for profits and feel the need to assist in public-policy development.

The second phase of social responsibility is what can be called the **public responsibility** phase. In this phase, the managers of a business do recognize the need for the firm to be economically profitable, but they also feel a responsibility to help to shape public policies on major social issues. Such managers believe that since their firms' profits are derived from the marketplace and since their firms' actions to achieve these profits impact the marketplace, they should be willing to help to develop public policies that have broad implications for society as a whole. Such a policy might relate to workers who have acquired immune deficiency syndrome (AIDS).

Defining public policy is very difficult.

The problem that business managers encounter in this phase is that it is too difficult to determine on what issues they should help to define public policy. If social responsibility is defined in the narrow sense of helping with only those issues for which new laws must be legislated, then this course of action may be too restrictive to permit businesses to interact meaningfully with society. If, however, businesses try to help society in the broadest sense of social responsibility, which includes all of the mechanisms that cause social changes, then the management of a firm must become involved with all of society's problems. Different management groups currently support both positions.

■ Social Responsiveness

In the social responsiveness phase, firms take action and implement social programs.

In the third phase, called **social responsiveness,** businesses actually respond to public pressure by implementing social programs that can make a tangible impact on society. At this point, business managers go beyond mere philosophical discussions and actually respond to social problems in meaningful ways. Some good examples include

- Heinz Corporation spent $8 million over three years to replace its nonrecyclable ketchup bottle with one that is recyclable.
- Star-Kist Seafood stated it would not buy tuna from fishing firms that use nets that also kill dolphins.
- Conoco Oil stated it will convert to the use of only double-hulled tankers for shipping all of its oil.[7]

Business managers must continually monitor how their corporate objectives and society's objectives interrelate. They must also make sure that they are keeping in touch with society's current social issues and are identifying socially responsible ways to respond to them.

■ Social Issues in Management

In the social issues in management phase, firms identify major current social issues and establish appropriate social responses to them.

In the last phase of social responsibility, the **social issues in management** phase, managers must constantly scan the firm's internal and external environments so they can identify changes in social issues as early as possible. Once they are recognized, these changes can be analyzed to determine the most appropriate social response to them:

As budget cuts continue to slash America's educational programs, more and more American corporations and businesses are picking up this social responsibility. Some excellent examples across the nation follow.

- *Miami, Florida:* Dade County Schools, with the assistance of many businesses, have set up satellite learning centers for 300 kindergarten, first-, and second-grade students. The corporations fund the space; the school system funds the certified teacher, classroom supplies, and equipment. In 1990 alone, this saved the Dade County Schools $1 million.
- *San Francisco, California:* McKesson Corporation, a distributor of pharmaceuticals, entered into a partnership with the Alamo Park High School to establish an academic and on-site work-experience program. McKesson provides individual tutors to help students in areas of academic weakness. Students spend eight hours per week in an entry-level work experience on-site at McKesson.
- *Denver, Colorado:* The Community College of Denver has implemented a computer-training course especially for the physically challenged. It is sponsored by the State of Colorado and a business advisory council. The state pays for the tuition; the college provides the space, instructors, and support staff; IBM and other companies donate the computers; and Martin Marietta and other businesses supply volunteers and leadership.[8]

By examining current social issues, a business will be able to make sure that it is on the leading edge of being a truly socially responsible firm. Firms also need to communicate to the public sector what social issues they are addressing and how they are responding to them, so society at large will view the business sector in a more positive manner.

THE BENEFITS AND COSTS OF BEING A SOCIALLY RESPONSIBLE FIRM

Almost everyone agrees that businesses need to be socially responsible, at least to some degree. However, the socially responsible firm can encounter some possible costs as well as some definite benefits.

The following list summarizes the *benefits* to a firm of being socially responsible.

A socially responsible firm accrues many benefits.

1. *It can be very profitable.* More and more consumers are strongly supporting socially responsible firms and actively boycotting socially irresponsible firms. A good example is Ben & Jerry's Ice Cream, which is priced higher than almost all competing brands. This company receives thousands of letters a week from fans who say they are willing not only to pay a premium price for the quality of the ice cream but also to buy Ben & Jerry's products because of the tremendous commitment the firm has made to the community and the environment.[9]

2. *The firm's image can be improved.* Since consumers highly value positive social programs, firms that implement or contribute to such programs gain respect and admiration from the public, which lead to greater consumer awareness and customer loyalty.

3. *It minimizes the probability that more restrictive legislation will be passed.* Government legislation is aimed directly at socially irresponsible firms. If more firms become socially responsible, less legislation will be proposed to restrict and regulate how businesses operate.

An employee of Houston Industries tests artificial oyster reefs built in Galveston.

4. *Stockholders benefit, since the price of the firm's stock usually rises.* Socially responsible firms are far less open to public criticism, thereby making them more solid investments. This creates greater demand for their stock and raises its value. The Council on Economic Priorities, a New York-based research and advocacy group, ranks major manufacturers on the basis of how they handle many social issues. The Council then publishes the results in a guide entitled "Shopping for a Better World." The main purpose of this nonprofit group is to influence investors.[10]

5. *Helping to solve some of society's problems creates a better environment.* Both the firm's working environment and the community's environment are enhanced by socially responsive businesses. Employees are proud to work for socially responsible firms, and communities respect and support them.

6. *Helping to prevent problems from growing is a logical approach.* Social problems start slowly and then grow over time until they impact on everyone in a community. By intervening early, firms can help to solve problems quickly and cheaply.

7. *Joint cooperation between business, government, and society helps everyone.* Society needs help in solving social problems. Although the government is a large contributor to social programs, it encounters limitations. Getting businesses involved in social issues provides the best opportunity to solve social problems. Then all three sectors win.

8. *In most cases, the benefits of being socially responsible far outweigh the costs.* Virtually all of the costs of being socially responsible can be overcome if the firm conducts social programs properly and communicates regularly with the public about them. The costs must always be weighed in light of the benefits, especially long-term gains.

The following list summarizes the possible *costs* to a firm of being socially responsible.

1. *The financial costs of social programs may be passed on to consumers in the form of higher prices.* Raising prices makes the firm less competitive, reduces its profits, and opens the door for domestic and foreign competitors who are not socially responsible. However, higher prices do not necessarily mean reduced profits. In fact, social programs can even be profitable for the firm if the consuming public views them favorably. But the public must also respond by purchasing more of the firm's products and by showing the firm greater customer loyalty, thereby increasing its market share. To get this type of reaction from consumers, the business firm needs to communicate to the public what it is doing and why.

2. *Social programs may not be cost-effective.* In some cases, the costs of the programs may exceed the positive returns to the company in the short run, but this is almost never true in the long run. Businesses today must take the long-term view. A good example is provided by Johnson & Johnson. The company removed Tylenol from the market after several people died when someone tampered with the product. The cost of this removal and the development of a tamper-proof package was $100 million. The long-run outcome, however, was very positive, and the action literally saved the product from extinction.

3. *Social programs may cause the firm to stray from its main purpose of efficiency and profitability.* However, social programs do not necessarily hinder profitability and efficiency and can indeed be profitable. In such instances, they do not contradict the firm's main purpose.

Some costs are attached to being a socially responsible firm.

4. *Business social programs may be harmful or even illegal.* Very well-meaning firms, when instituting social programs designed to help to alleviate a social problem, may actually break the law. For example, a firm could institute an affirmative action program to employ more minorities and women; however, this program could actually discriminate against white men. This problem can be overcome if the firm carefully checks appropriate guidelines with the regulatory agencies before implementing such a program.

5. *There is a general lack of public support for being socially active.* The public as a whole is not deeply involved in social issues. However, a significant percentage of consumers does support businesses that are socially responsible. The important point here is that consumer support for social awareness in business is growing. The public outcry against firms that commit socially irresponsible acts is proof. Also, if the business community communicates with the public regularly about what firms are doing to help solve pressing social issues, then public support will certainly grow.

In summary, *INC.* magazine polled the business community and asked two very pertinent questions. The following results appear to indicate that at least three-fourths of the firms surveyed really believe in being socially responsible.[11]

Question 1: What is your reaction to the idea that beyond being successful as businesses, "good" companies have an obligation to "give back to society"?

Results:

I agree. Business can't be separated from other forms of social interaction. Social responsibility is good business.	76%
It's a good idea for companies that have the resources, but it's not an obligation.	22%
It's hype and posturing, just a passing fad.	2%

Question 2: Would you continue socially responsible practices even if you found out they were cutting into your profits?

Results:

Yes	68%
I would probably discontinue some of them.	22%
No	10%

CONSIDER THIS

1. Since more and more businesses are becoming socially responsible, why do we need more federal legislation in this area?

2. Why is it wrong for businesses to only concentrate on making a profit when that is their main reason for going into business in the first place?

3. Can socially responsible firms really compete with firms that are not spending any money on social programs?

MEASURING SOCIAL RESPONSIBILITY

A stakeholder is any person or group of people affected by the firm's decisions and actions.

First, management must determine the main individuals or groups, commonly termed **stakeholders,** to be considered when the firm engages in various business activities. A stakeholder can be anyone who is affected by the decisions and activities of the organization. Examples of people who make up these stakeholder groups follow, in the order in which most businesses consider them to be important: stockholders, employees, managers, customers, suppliers, financial sources, local business communities, competitors, government agencies, and people in the surrounding community (see Figure 11–2). Managers need to monitor how socially responsible their firms have been to each of these stakeholder groups by communicating with them on a regular basis.

Once it has been determined how socially responsible an organization is to its stakeholders, management must then try to determine how the firm is responding to society as a whole on a number of key current social issues. Some important areas of focus are listed here.

Businesses today can respond to a number of important social issues.

■ *Environmental Issues* **Environmental issues** deal primarily with pollution of the air, water, or land. Not only do socially responsible firms not pollute any of these natural resources; they also are involved in cleaning up the pollution caused by others. For example, the Minnesota Mining and Manufacturing Company is a true leader in environmental conservation with its pollution-prevention and waste-recovery programs.[12]

■ *Energy Concerns* **Energy concerns** consist of everything from developing conservation programs to actively engaging in research to find alternative forms of energy.

■ *Quality of the Work Environment* The **quality of the work environment** refers to how managers and employees are treated in a number of different areas. The most important areas are the manager-worker relationship, wages and benefits, job security, promotion opportunities, amount of recognition and financial incentives, participation in work-related matters, degree of communication throughout the firm, amount of autonomy on the job, and amount of concern for producing a true quality product or service.

These areas of social responsibility can even be expanded to companies that operate worldwide. In the United States, IBM exemplifies this area of social responsibility through programs that assist employees in caring for

■ **FIGURE 11–2** Stakeholders in a Typical Corporation

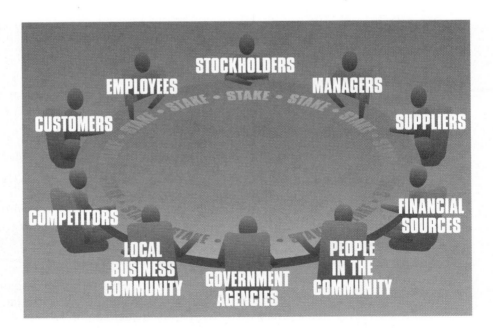

elderly relatives or mentally or physically challenged children. IBM is also recognized for the way in which it relates to employees with AIDS.[13]

■ *Equal Employment Opportunities* By law, businesses must provide **equal employment opportunities.** All of their hiring, promotional, and dismissal practices must be nondiscriminatory. The American workforce is becoming more and more multicultured. Affirmative action programs encourage firms to employ and promote minorities, women, and physically challenged people. Exemplary equal opportunity employers include General Mills, American Express, AT&T, and IBM.[14]

■ *Community Support* **Community support** includes everything from volunteering the time and talents of managers and employees to directing financial contributions for local community projects. Best Western International's prison work program is a good example of community support.[15]

■ *Social Investments* **Social investments** include everything from charitable donations to the actual sponsorship of social programs to help alleviate social problems. The Gannett Company gave $2 million to programs across the nation designed to teach adults to read.[16]

The real problem in evaluating any particular firm's social responsibility on the basis of these factors is that it varies tremendously, depending on the area in question. For example, a firm may treat its stockholders, managers, and employees properly but engage in questionable competitive practices; at the same time, the same firm may be extremely active in energy-conservation and pollution-control programs. Even the Stride Rite Shoe Corporation has been criticized for closing its plants in the New England area and moving its production overseas.[17] One possible answer to this problem is to give each of the six areas of social responsibility a point value from −10 to +10. Negative points could be given for socially irresponsible actions; zero points, for no positive or negative actions; and positive points, for socially responsible actions. A firm's total points would place it on a continuum of social responsibility, where

A worker restores low income housing through a grant from British Petroleum America, Inc.

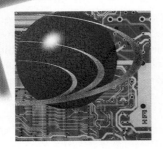

GLOBAL VIEW

The Social Responsibility of Doing Business

Today, many American managers are not just taking social responsibility seriously within their own businesses. They are also forcing suppliers in the international marketplace to conform to their firms' standards or they will not do business with them.

For example, Home Depot recently sent a questionnaire to all of its suppliers worldwide asking them if they employed children or prison convicts. The company gave them an ultimatum to respond within 72 hours.

Some other companies that are forcing their suppliers to be more socially responsible include the following.

- Sears is refusing to import any products from China that are produced by forced laborers.

- Phillips-Van Heusen is terminating all orders from apparel suppliers who do not meet their ethical, environmental, and human rights codes.

- Dow Chemical now demands that its suppliers conform to U.S. pollution and safety laws, not just to their local laws.

- Levi Strauss and Company has instituted tough standards of conduct for all 600 of their suppliers worldwide. To be sure that their suppliers conformed to these standards, the company conducted personal inspections of all 600 of them. Levi Strauss dropped 30 suppliers, exacted reforms from another 120 firms, and completely pulled out of Myanmar, a country in Southeast Asia, because of the government's human-rights violations.

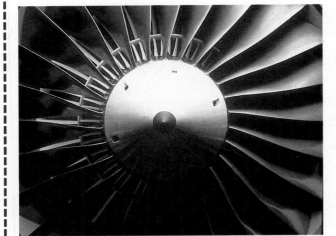

BMW's turbine engine was designed to improve air flow and thus save fuel use by jet airplanes.

ADAPTED FROM: John McCormick and Marc Levinson, "The Supply Police," *Newsweek* (February 15, 1993), pp. 48–49.

the point range extends from −60 to +60, as indicated in Figure 11–3. By comparing the total point values of different firms, some assessment of their social responsiveness could be made.

WAYS TO IMPROVE A FIRM'S SOCIAL RESPONSIVENESS

A firm's social responsibility starts at the top.

Improving a firm's social responsiveness has to start at the top of any organization. Earlier in this chapter, we discussed some of the costs and benefits of being socially responsible and learned that social responsiveness can be profitable and is not necessarily just a cost item.

First and foremost, if a company is going to become socially responsible, top management must accept this point and then strongly communicate it to everyone in the entire firm. A number of studies verify this point. One survey on ethics conducted by author David Freudberg analyzed the relationship between public service and long-range corporate profitability. All of the companies in the study had been in business at least 30 years and had a written set of principles relating to their public service policies. The 15 publicly-traded companies

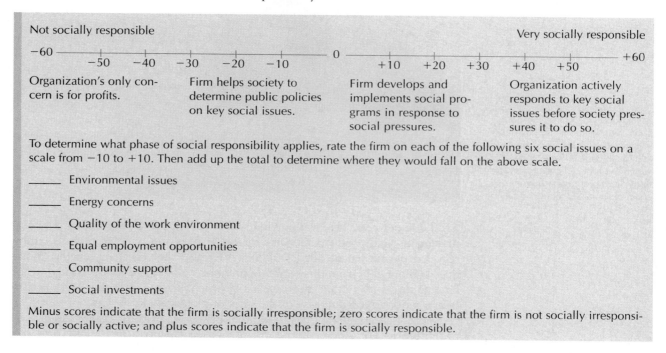

To determine what phase of social responsibility applies, rate the firm on each of the following six social issues on a scale from −10 to +10. Then add up the total to determine where they would fall on the above scale.

_____ Environmental issues

_____ Energy concerns

_____ Quality of the work environment

_____ Equal employment opportunities

_____ Community support

_____ Social investments

Minus scores indicate that the firm is socially irresponsible; zero scores indicate that the firm is not socially irresponsible or socially active; and plus scores indicate that the firm is socially responsible.

registered average growth and profits of 11 percent over the 30-year period ending in 1982. In contrast, the Fortune 500 companies showed average growth and profits of 6.1 percent during the same time period. These results definitely suggest a long-term financial payoff.[18]

James O'Toole, a professor at the University of Southern California's Business School, notes in his book, *Vanguard Management,* that over the long term, socially conscious business firms will do better than firms that are not socially responsible. O'Toole cites John Deere & Company, McDonald's Restaurants, and Levi Strauss and Company as examples of socially conscious firms who have continued to lead in their respective fields while engaging in socially responsive programs.[19] Possibly the best example, however, is the ice-cream company Ben & Jerry's Homemade Ice Cream, Inc. This firm started in 1978 with a $12,000 investment and had revenues of over $100 million in 1991. Since 1985, Ben & Jerry's has given 7.5 percent of their pretax profits to worthy causes its employees help to select.[20]

Although studies have tried to refute the claim that social responsibility is profitable, most of them have revealed no significant differences between the profitability of firms that are socially responsible and firms that are socially irresponsible. If this is true, then the *worst* that can happen to a socially responsible firm is that it will be just as profitable if it is socially responsible as it will be if it is socially irresponsible.[21]

In 1990, DuPont Canada, Inc., hooked onto the social-responsibility bandwagon by implementing an environmental plan complete with specific commitments for the next decade. DuPont has learned through the years that it can indeed do more in the environmental area and that there are benefits to being socially responsible. For example, at its Kingston site, DuPont sent 6 million pounds of waste nylon to a landfill every year, at a cost of $0.02 a pound—or

Research indicates that being socially responsible is basically a "can't lose" proposition for a firm.

Anita Roddick, CEO of The Body Shop, founded an entire line of personal care products based on natural and organic ingredients, none of which use artificial chemicals. The Body Shop products and profitable chain of shops are found worldwide.

$120,000 per year. This waste nylon is now recycled into engineering polymers that make such products as parts for office furniture, kitchen utensils, and a recycled plastic fence called DuPont's VEXAR® polyethylene fencing. What does DuPont gain from this recycling program? Not only does the company not have to throw away that unused plastic, which is very costly; but DuPont also boasts a 50-percent increase in the sales of its fence line.[22]

Another company that has found that being socially responsible can also be profitable is The Body Shop, a British-based cosmetic firm. This firm has avoided excessive beauty claims in its advertising and has actively demonstrated that it does no animal testing. As a result, The Body Shop has seen its sales grow by 50 percent per year on average during the past decade. Then there is Loblaws, a Canadian grocery chain; its managers saw sales rise from 10 percent to 60 percent after the products received the company's environmental seal.[23]

■ *Cause-Related Marketing*

In cause-related marketing, a firm increases sales by tying a company's products to a social cause or charity.

Is cause-related marketing basically good or bad for society?

In general, firms that announce that they give a certain amount or percentage of profits or sales to designated causes receive a very good public response. One approach to being a socially responsible business, which has been both praised and criticized, is termed **cause-related marketing,** in which firms tie in with charitable organizations or take on social problems that are in dire need of financial support. Many times, the organization's products naturally "fit" the charity or social cause. The idea, of course, is to elicit sales by appealing to the consumers to help a particular cause when they buy a particular product.

This type of social response has evolved primarily because corporations are finally realizing that they have been trying to communicate things to the public that are important to the corporation but that may not be important to consumers. As a result, corporate advertisers are beginning to tie the sales of their products to corporation donations to specific charities or public concerns. For example, Johnson & Johnson has allied a number of their products with the Children's Miracle Network.

Johnson & Johnson has also created its own cause-related program, Shelter Aid, specifically to benefit women, children, and families—the company's primary customers—who are in need of shelter. Four Johnson & Johnson units were involved in this project: J & J Baby Products, J & J Personal Products, J & J Products, and McNeil Consumer Laboratories, all of which represent

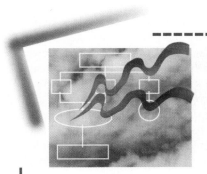

REMEMBER TO COMMUNICATE

How to Implement Social Responsibility

Once a business decides to become socially responsible in the community, it needs to take several steps to assure success.

- ■ The top managers of the business need to agree on a direction. What social causes do they want to support, and what course of action will the firm take?

- ■ Business leaders must check to see if a precedent or common practice has been set.

- ■ The coordinators of the social program must involve management and other employees in decision making. Coordinators should assign responsibilities to line employees in the organization to ensure that they become committed to the cause. Built-in rewards should be available when goals are accomplished.

- ■ The goals of the organization must match the firm's philosophy about the specific social responsibility, cause, or issue.

- ■ The coordinators of the social program must involve and constantly communicate with all individuals or groups inside and outside the company whose interests are at stake, such as customers, key suppliers, and employees.

- ■ The coordinators must communicate constantly with the community. The community must *perceive* that the business is acting in a socially responsible manner.

- ■ The coordinators must audit and evaluate the progress of the social program and must be sure that all the people involved are informed of this progress and of any changes in the firm's goals.

ADAPTED FROM: Thomas F. Garbett, "Look What We're Doing for Humanity," *Across the Board* (May 19, 1989), pp. 45–52; J. E. Newall, "Managing Environmental Responsibility," *Business Quarterly* **55** (Autumn 1990): 90–94; Karen Springen and Annetta Miller, "Doing the Right Thing," *Newsweek* (January 7, 1991), pp. 42–43.

nine different brands. All of the participating brands experienced "significant market share increases" said Maug Heffler, J & J's Director of Promotion. In fact, Stayfree experienced a "dramatic sales increase" across its entire line of feminine-care products. The promotion itself resulted in a $1.5 million donation—possibly the largest donation ever made by a package-goods manufacturer to a single event.[24]

Although the benefits to both charities and businesses from this type of social involvement are obvious, there are also some genuine concerns. First, a lot of people are afraid that companies will become increasingly reluctant to donate to any charity or cause that does not have some obvious marketability for them. Second, if these types of promotions do not produce substantial results for the company, the charity or cause could be quickly dropped, leaving it in a financial bind. These problems do not appear to be happening right now, but there is no guarantee that they will not occur in the future.

Some potential problems can arise from cause-related marketing.

One other type of cause-related marketing is of social significance. In **advocacy promotions,** the business firm tries to build customer goodwill and develop a better public image by promoting causes that are not naturally tied in to its products. Some examples include firms like DuPont, which advocates the theme "Look what we're doing for humanity" in its advertisements. DuPont has also aired commercials that show Bill Demby, a double amputee, playing basketball on his high-tech, artificial legs. Other business firms have

Advocacy promotions aid social causes that do not have a direct marketing tie-in to the firm's products.

jumped on patriotic themes; one promotional campaign describes U.S. dependence on foreign oil as the "Kiss of Death." In each case of advocacy promotion, the business firm is communicating its social responsiveness. But the real question is, "Are these firms truly being socially responsible?" Certainly cases could be made for each side, but we will only know for sure in the long run.[25]

Once the managers of an organization recognize that having a social conscience can be profitable, they should develop a written set of objectives and policies indicating how the firm intends to be socially responsible. These objectives and policies need to be fully communicated to all managers and employees in the firm and implemented in a way that company actions speak truthfully to the issues.

As Figure 11–4 indicates, there are many different ways to respond to social issues. It is very difficult to determine the most effective or most socially responsible response to the issues at hand.

> It is very important to communicate a firm's social objectives to all members of the organization.

CONSIDER THIS

1. Why is it so difficult to accurately measure the social responsibility of a firm?

2. What are some of the most important current social issues that should concern businesses?

3. Is cause-related marketing an acceptable way to be socially responsible? What about advocacy marketing?

■ **FIGURE 11–4** Some Ways to Be Socially Responsive

ADAPTED FROM: Trevor Armbrister, "When Companies Care," *Reader's Digest* (April 1989), pp. 25–30; Alessandra Bianchi, Michael P. Cronin, and Anne Murphy, "Socially Responsible Entrepreneur—Pam Del Duca," *INC.* **14** (December 1992): 103; Ellyn E. Spragerus, "Making Good," *INC.* **15** (May 1993): 114–22.

FIRM	SOCIAL RESPONSE
Xerox Corporation	Raised $580,000 to help Nexus, a drug and alcohol abuse center in Dallas, Texas.
The Delstar Group	The sole proprietor of a small gift shop, Pam Del Duca formed a partnership with three nonprofit organizations and opened six new stores. Each organization gets a percentage of the store's gross income for ten years.
Just Desserts	A San Francisco bakery got 35 other small businesses to "adopt an elementary school." Over 700 volunteers, primarily from these firms, painted and refurbished rooms in schools located in low-income areas of the city.
Piper Jaffray	Maintained a large vegetable garden to feed the hungry in Spokane, Washington.
Rhino Records	This small company in California encourages employees to volunteer to undertake charitable activities. The company gives Christmas week off with pay to everyone who does at least 16 hours per year of volunteer work. More than 100 employees participate in this program each year.
Barnett Bank	Raised close to $800,000 for a new Ronald McDonald House in Jacksonville, Florida.
Shell Oil	Had volunteers help the poor and elderly with home repairs and yard work in Houston, Texas.

MANAGERIAL ETHICS: PROBLEMS IN DEFINING ETHICAL BEHAVIOR

We have just discussed social responsibility, or how businesses should respond to current social problems. We will now talk about **ethics,** or how individuals, businesses, or entire industries behave in their daily interactions with the marketplace.

Defining ethics is a very difficult job. Ethics involve rules, values, laws, and even personal rights. One thing is clear, however: Business ethics is not just a technique; it is a total philosophy of management that has very practical and daily applications. In this text, ethics will be defined as "the rules of conduct and moral principles and values that define how individuals and businesses conduct business."[26] Basically, there are three levels of ethics.

■ The First Level of Ethics: The Law

The **law** is established to try to prevent the worst known types of unethical behavior. Such activities as falsifying financial records, bribing public officials, or deliberately deceiving the public through false advertising are all illegal business practices. The law helps to define acceptable business behavior, but laws are subject to different interpretations. Also, laws are often passed only after repeated violations of accepted business practices have occurred, thereby creating a legislative backlog.[27]

■ The Second Level of Ethics: Policies, Procedures, Rules, or Guidelines

Virtually every type of institution in this country abides by **policies, procedures, rules, or guidelines** that are described in written or verbal form. Schools, churches, the military, the government, and businesses of all types have internal policies, procedures, and rules that indicate proper behaviors in a large variety of circumstances. Although such guidelines, in conjunction with the law, help to further define the ethical behavior of a business, they are still not sufficient to solve all of the problems that can occur.

The business culture that has been established over time definitely influences how managers and employees conduct a firm's activities beyond the written guidelines. The specific actions that are recognized and rewarded and those that are ignored or punished definitely impact on how employees will respond. Also, rewarding good achievements without considering *how* employees accomplished them encourages unethical behavior. Being ethical in business activities, although not always well received, must be actively encouraged if potentially hazardous unethical behavior is to be eliminated from the workplace.

■ The Third Level of Ethics: Moral Stance

The third and most difficult level of ethics to interpret consists of the **moral stance** a person takes when dealing with situations that are not covered by the law or by policies, procedures, or rules. How individuals respond to matters in this area depends, to a large degree, on the personal values and beliefs they have developed through their families, religion, and life experiences.

The real problems associated with making good ethical decisions usually occur when individuals must address issues on this third level. Most people can handle problems when clearcut solutions to them are provided by laws or written guidelines. But individuals encounter additional pressures and usually do

The most difficult ethical problems are encountered on the third level of ethics: moral stance.

A PERSPECTIVE ON QUALITY

"Blowing the Whistle"

Have you ever "blown the whistle" on your boss? Have you ever wanted to? Whistle blowers are becoming more and more prominent in businesses today. Why? Because people are tired of unethical business practices. Let's look at two examples.

- Syntex Corporation, a large pharmaceutical company, recently lost a $17.5 million lawsuit brought by a scientist who was fired after he voiced concerns about the harmful side effects of the company's new ulcer drug, called Enprostil. The court found that Syntex did withhold evidence from regulatory agencies while waiting for approval to sell the drug in the United States. The court agreed that Syntex fired the scientist to silence his concerns about the drug's safety.

- Textron Lycoming has agreed to pay the U.S. government $17.9 million for supplying the U.S. Coast Guard with problem-plagued helicopter engines. Robert Ballew, an employee of the firm, notified government investigators of problems with the engines. The engines were operating at temperatures higher than they were designed to withstand, and overhauls on the engine were needed four times as often as they should have been.

These examples should help us to take a closer look at people who "blow the whistle" on their bosses. Who are they? Research suggests that they are not very different from you or me. When people blow the whistle, it is generally for a very serious reason. A product, service, or behavior may be a danger to someone, or may involve a large sum of money, or may be a frequently repeated offense.

So what does this tell us as managers? It says that we cannot afford to ignore these people. We must listen to whistle blowers *before* a disaster happens. We must encourage communication by anonymous reporting systems or by using impartial omsbudspersons. We must keep the communication channels open. We must not make our employees feel threatened if they report wrongdoings. After all, auditors and quality-control supervisors are expected to report wrongdoings. So why not make it an expectation of all your employees, and sit back and reap the benefits?

ADAPTED FROM: Alex Barnum, "Syntex Hid Results of Ulcer Drug Tests," *San Jose Mercury News* (August 15, 1990); Janet P. Near, "Whistle-Blowing: Encourage It!" *Business Horizons* (January/February 1989): 21–25; Robert Weisman, "Whistle-Blower to Get $2.7 Million," *Hartford Courant* **32** (July 11, 1990), pp. C14, D1.

not function as effectively when they must rely on their own personal experiences to make business decisions and solve ethical problems.

As we think about how to act ethically based solely on our own personal experiences, a good procedure to follow is the Four-Way Test, which was originated in the 1930s by Herbert J. Taylor and is currently the ethics guide of the Rotary Clubs International. The Four-Way Test consists of four questions.

1. Is it the truth?
2. Is it fair to all concerned?
3. Will it build goodwill and better friendships?
4. Will it be beneficial to all concerned?[28]

Think of some of the major ethical problems that have occurred in the business sector and made headlines in the past. Many of them could probably have been avoided or minimized by asking one or more of these four questions. Some examples follow.

- Fraudulent or misleading advertisement—"Is it the truth?"
- Insider trading and illegal profit-making—"Is it fair to all concerned?"
- An unsafe product produced without proper testing—"Will it build good-will and better friendships?"
- A hostile corporate takeover and subsequent dismantling—"Will it be beneficial to all concerned?"

 # FACTORS THAT AFFECT MANAGERIAL ETHICS

Good business ethics, like social responsibility, starts at the top.

In a study done by Marshall Clinard, 64 retired executives from 51 Fortune 500 companies were asked why some corporations became corrupt while others stayed honest. The two main reasons given were the poor ethical practices of top management and competition or greed, both of which are operative in the Bank of Credit and Commerce International (BCCI), which boasts, among its clientele, some of the biggest names in drug trafficking and terrorism.[29]

The need for top management to set the tone in regard to corporate ethics and to clearly communicate it to everyone involved has been cited in several research studies. A study done by The Business Roundtable, which surveyed more than 100 of its member companies, reported that "no point emerges more clearly than the crucial role of top management."[30]

Good ethics can be profitable.

The question that begs to be asked then is, "Does good ethical behavior translate into increased profits?" There appears to be considerable evidence that the answer is yes! A *Dallas Times Herald* survey found that 97 percent of the business respondents answered this question in the affirmative.[31]

An example of good ethical behavior creating more profits is provided by Jack McDonald, Chief Operating Officer for Centex Corporation, which is involved in construction, gas, oil, and cement. McDonald recently stated enthusiastically that hard work and creativeness, along with being honest and ethical, are the keys to success and high profits. Under McDonald's leadership, Centex's sales almost doubled from $645 million to $1.18 billion during a seven-year period.[32]

When we look closely at unethical business practices, two results are notable.

1. The company only derives short-term advantages or gains from unethical actions.

2. Over the long run, skimping on quality and service does not pay.[33]

3. George Harvey, Chairman of Pitney Bowes in Stanford, Connecticut, states that unethical decisions can drive customers away, demoralize employees, and irritate local communities, ultimately hurting company performance and profits. "When you do something good for customers, they'll tell their neighbors; however, when you've done something wrong . . . hey, they tell a lot of people."[34]

Finally, the penalties for unethical behavior can be extremely severe for both the organization and the top executives personally, if they are caught and convicted.

Visitors enjoy Florida Power Corp.'s Crystal River Mariculture Center.

The Beechnut Nutrition Corporation recently pled guilty to 215 felony counts for selling phony apple juice. Beechnut received a $2.2 million fine, and two of the implicated executives received stiff fines and relatively severe prison terms for their role in this consumer scam. The ironical part of this story is that they could have possibly avoided this situation had they just listened to their own Director of Research and Development, Jerome LiCari, who showed top-management executives strong evidence that Beechnut's main supplier was adulterating its apple-juice concentrate. LiCari urged top management to switch suppliers in order not to jeopardize this product and an entire new product line of nutritional baby foods. When top management ignored his advice, LiCari quit the firm and notified the authorities. He was absolved of any personal responsibility. Beechnut is now suffering even further from millions of dollars in lost sales on its entire line of baby foods due to the negative publicity the company received regarding a single product—its apple juice.[35]

CONSIDER THIS

1. What are the three levels of ethics?

2. Aren't individuals or firms being ethical as long as they are obeying all applicable laws?

3. What are the main reasons why businesses become unethical?

WAYS TO IMPROVE MANAGERIAL ETHICS

When we look at how large and small companies alike are utilizing managerial ethics to engage in more straightforward business practices, we see that quite a variety of methods are being employed, including

- Writing a code of ethics
- Setting up a permanent ethics committee

- Employing ombudspeople
- Establishing "hot lines" to process reports of unethical behavior
- Conducting in-house ethics seminars
- Making training programs available to all employees and managers

Here is a step-by-step approach to setting up a good ethics program.

Although the number and different combinations of ethical programs are vast, the following step-by-step program was developed by the Business Round-table and others who surveyed over 100 companies in order to give you, as a manager, a logical approach to establishing an effective, on-going business ethics program.

■ Step 1: The Role of Top Management

Top management must be openly committed to ethical conduct and must provide constant leadership in tending and renewing the values of the organization. Managers can communicate their commitment to ethical business behavior in a variety of ways, including policies, directives, speeches, company publications, and especially actions. Every sector of the company and all of the firm's stakeholder groups must be made aware of the core values of the firm's ethics program. To ensure that this is an on-going process, top managers must carefully groom potential candidates for top management in ethical conduct.

■ Step 2: The Establishment of a Code of Ethics

Basically, a code of business ethics does two things:

1. It tells employees how to act in various situations.
2. It makes it clear to employees that they will be expected to recognize the ethical dimensions of the corporate policies and actions.[36]

In a survey appearing in *Business Week 1000,* 84 firms sent in copies of their codes of ethics. Although the range of items included was extensive, three basic clusters, or groups of related items, were identified. A final group of unclustered, or unrelated, items was then developed from this survey.

Cluster 1:	"Be a dependable organization/citizen." Items here included, "Demonstrate honesty, respect, courtesy, and fairness to customers, suppliers, and other employees."
Cluster 2:	"Don't do anything unlawful or improper that will harm the organization." Items here included, "Conduct all business in compliance with relevant laws, regulations, and policies."
Cluster 3:	"Be good to your customers." Items here included, "Strive to provide products and services of the highest quality" and "Perform assigned duties to the best of your ability and in the best interest of the company and its stakeholders."
Unclustered items:	"Exhibit standards of personal integrity and professional conduct." "Conserve resources and protect the environment in areas where the company operates."[37]

The following example of Martin Marietta's code of ethics exemplifies many of these items.

■ To our employees, we are committed to just management and equality for all, providing a safe and healthy workplace, and respecting the dignity and privacy due all human beings.

- To our customers, we are committed to produce reliable products and services at fair prices that are delivered on time and within budget.

- To the communities in which we live, we are committed to be responsible neighbors, reflecting all aspects of good citizenship.

- To our shareholders, we are committed to pursuing sound growth and earnings objectives and exercising prudence in the use of our assets and resources.

- To our suppliers, we are committed to fair competition and the sense of responsibility required of a good customer.[38]

Good codes of ethics emphasize the free and open communication of all information. Steve Jobs, formerly of Apple Computer, who now operates a company called Next Inc., states that he strongly believes in open communication within the firm. At Next Inc., all employees have complete access to almost all information in the company, including other employees' salaries. Jobs states that only when employees understand the entire master plan for the firm will they be able to make effective decisions that are in line with the company's values.[39]

■ *Step 3: The Process of Implementation—Making Ethics Work*

This step has two main purposes: (1) to ensure compliance with company standards of conduct, and (2) to instill a strong conviction among managers and employees that good ethics is a key to an organization's survival and profits. Some of the various approaches here include

- Management involvement and oversight

- Attention to value and ethics in recruiting and hiring practices

- Communication programs to inform and motivate employees, customers, and the general public

- An emphasis on corporate ethics in education and training programs

- Recognition and rewards for exemplary employee or managerial performance

- An ombudsperson or someone in the company who can go directly to top management with problems or complaints; hotlines for comments and complaints to encourage communication of unethical acts

- Special focus on vulnerable sectors and jobs

- Periodic certification of adherence to organizational standards

- "Ethical audits" to ensure compliance by personnel on at least an annual basis

- Enforcement procedures, including discipline and dismissal for violations

Open communication is the key element in implementing any ethics program.

Openness in communication is deemed fundamental, as is building a relationship of trust. Employees should feel it is their *duty* to report violations, and channels for doing so should be available to them.

■ *Step 4: Involvement and Commitment of Personnel at All Organizational Levels*

Participative involvement at all levels in the company helps to assure commitment and understanding among employees. Also, as employees interact with each other about what they feel is valuable about the firm, they develop higher levels of trust and pride in the business. Finally, as levels of trust increase, employees feel more involved in business activities and they focus more on job-related ways to increase quality and productivity.

■ Step 5: Measuring Results

In a social audit, a firm looks at how many of its social goals were accomplished during the past year.

There is no exact way to measure the end results of a business ethics program. The two most commonly accepted methods are surveys and **social audits.** The Packard Commission has recommended the use of independent assessments on an annual basis in the defense industry to assess corporate ethics. Company executives can also assess the effectiveness of their corporate ethics programs through observations, through the company's reputation in the community, and through its performance in the marketplace. The ultimate measurements will emerge only over a long period of time.[40]

■ Ethics Violations—The Penalty Phase

U.S. corporations and businesses are starting to readily engage in formal ethics programs. The Center for Business Ethics at Bentley College in Waltham, Massachusetts, recently found that 45 percent of the 1000 largest U.S. companies now have ethics programs or ethics workshops, up from 35 percent just five years ago.[41]

One reason for the increased interest in business ethics programs is stiffer penalties for unethical actions.

This increasing focus on ethics in the workplace is not necessarily occurring because all of these businesses have suddenly discovered their collective social consciousness. As of November 1, 1991, new sentencing guidelines have gone into effect that double the average fine for firms found guilty of such crimes as fraud. However, if the guilty firm cooperates with prosecutors and if its policies meet the guideline standards, then the company's fines will be much lower. In fact, if a firm is fined, say, $1 million but has a comprehensive business ethics program in place (including a code of conduct, an ombudsperson, a hot line, and mandatory training seminars for executives), then the fine could be reduced to as little as $50,000.[42]

Unfortunately, all of the ethics policies and programs in the world will not totally stop unethical business behaviors. People who are intent on violating the policies of a firm for their own personal gain may get away with it for awhile. However, if they continue their unethical business practices long enough, they will be caught, and the penalties for both the company and the individual wrongdoer are rising rapidly.

How a company reacts to an ethical crisis is also very important:

An ethical crisis can come from a number of different sources, including dishonest, disgruntled, or incompetent employees; managerial incompetence; product tampering; or even terrorism. How a business reacts to a crisis is critical if the firm is going to reduce any resulting negative publicity or financial losses.

Harland Warner, an executive with a Washington public relations firm that specializes in crisis management, gives the following guidelines for handling a crisis.

1. First and foremost, tell the truth. The truth eventually comes out, and if you have lied, your integrity is shot.

2. If you are in doubt about doing something, do not do it. A business cannot afford any more errors in a time of crisis.

3. Show concern and understanding. This is the least a company can do at this time, and usually the public demands it.

4. Act as fast as possible. A contingency plan for crisis management should be in place. Warner states that about one-half of the Fortune 500 companies now have such plans.[43]

Some examples of firms that have handled ethical crises poorly include Exxon (see chapter-opening feature The Real World); Sears, which was cited for charging customers for auto services that were not needed; and Denny's Restaurant, which was cited for discriminating against minorities. In each case, the firms moved slowly and failed to address the problems at the top-management level until substantial negative publicity had occurred.

Firms that have handled ethical crisis properly include Johnson & Johnson in the Tylenol tampering incident; Northwest Airlines, which went public on a specific bomb threat on a flight from Paris to Detroit; and PepsiCo, which quickly defused reports that cans of Pepsi contained syringes by proving the reports to be a hoax. In each of these cases, the firms acted quickly, told the truth, and took appropriate action.[44]

■ *Dealing with Ethical Dilemmas on an Individual Basis*

Finally, we must answer the question, "What is the right way to deal with ethical dilemmas on an individual basis, especially when an employee is working for a firm that is not particularly ethical? This question can be answered in several ways:

Here is a personal way to deal with ethical problems on the job.

1. Make sure there is a conflict. Make sure both you and your boss have all the facts. Check the contract to see if the activity is permitted.

2. Decide how much you are willing to risk. Do a cost-benefit analysis. Look at everyone involved, and ask yourself what the harm and benefit is to each group.

3. Make your move. If the unethical action is important enough for you to take a risk, tell your boss you cannot do it. Do not make accusations to your boss. Let him/her save face.

4. If there is trouble, get help. If your boss says you *have* to do it anyway and you feel that you cannot, then you should go to some influential person in the company. Try not to go directly above your boss's head.

5. Consider a job change. If the people you turn to for help do not have a problem with the situation, then perhaps you need to quit. Evaluate your boss's values. If they conflict with yours, then leaving may be the best answer.[45]

Ethical problems and dilemmas will always be with us, and every individual, manager, and business must find an effective way to deal with them. As new world markets open up, new ethical problems will present themselves. The time to prepare to handle these problems is right now, so they can be dealt with swiftly and properly when they do arise.

THINK ABOUT IT

1. Even though more businesses are becoming more socially responsible, surveys still indicate a very strong need for federal legislation to reward or penalize firms for being either socially responsible or socially irresponsible in the marketplace.

2. The benefits of being socially responsible far outweigh the costs. Once companies realize this, there will be a lot more socially responsible firms.

3. A firm must first take care of its stakeholders and then decide how to appropriately respond to important social issues.

4. Evaluating a firm's social responsiveness can be very difficult. Most firms are strong in some social areas and weak in others.

5. While charities and some social causes do benefit from cause-related marketing programs, this may be a questionable way for firms to respond if they really want to be socially responsible.

6. Once a firm commits itself to becoming socially responsible, it needs to develop written objectives and policies and fully communicate them to all stakeholder groups.

7. The real problems associated with making good ethical decisions occur when a person is confronted with situations that are not covered by any laws, rules, regulations, or policies.

8. Ethical behavior always starts at the top of the organization and is communicated to the lower levels through the words *and* actions of management.

9. Unethical companies may gain some benefits in the short run, but unethical business practices always catch up with them in the long run.

10. A person who decides to deal with an ethical problem on an individual basis should think the problem through carefully and plan for all possible contingencies.

You have learned about the social and ethical responsibilities of businesses in today's world. Now let's review the learning objectives for this chapter and briefly summarize several highlights for each of them.

Define and understand what social responsibility means.

First of all, being socially responsible means looking beyond the concerns of the firm to the needs of society. It also means actually making sacrifices in order to help society solve some of the difficult problems that it faces today. Finally, it means monitoring the main social issues of the day and developing and implementing programs to address them.

Discuss and appreciate the costs and benefits that a socially responsible business incurs in today's competitive environment.

Although some costs are incurred, at least in the short run, the evidence clearly indicates that being socially responsible can be quite profitable. As society becomes more and more socially conscious, a firm really will not have any other choice but to become socially responsible. We have already seen numerous examples of severe consumer backlash at socially irresponsible firms.

Understand the different ways to measure social responsibility in the business world.

Measuring socially responsible firms is difficult, since a firm may often be very socially responsible on some issues and somewhat socially irresponsible on others. The main areas in which to evaluate a firm's social responsiveness are environmental issues, energy concerns, quality of the work environment, equal employment opportunities, community support, and social investments.

List and discuss some common ways to improve social responsibility.

First, top managers must commit themselves to molding a socially responsible firm. Once this is done, objectives and policies must be established and clearly and fully communicated, through both words and actions, to all stakeholder groups. Finally, the firm's top managers must determine which social areas they feel most strongly about and develop and implement programs to do what they can to solve selected social problems.

Define and discuss the role of ethics in business today.

Ethical standards determine how an individual or a business will behave in the marketplace. Ethics is really an entire philosophy of behavior that has daily practical applications. The ethics of a business can be clearly seen in its policies, procedures, and rules, which dictate how the firm transacts business on a daily basis.

Appreciate and explain some of the factors that affect ethics in business.

Research indicates that the main factors that affect the ethical behavior of businesses are the ethics of top management, the competitive business environment, and greed on the part of the owners of the firm. Other factors that are starting to have a much larger influence in this area are (1) new legislation, which contains very severe penalties for ethics violations, and (2) an ever-growing awareness of the unethical behavior of businesses and public boycotts of these firms and/or their products.

Identify some ways to improve managerial ethics.

There are a number of different ways to improve the ethical behavior of a business firm. Some of the more common methods include writing a code of ethics, setting up ethics committees, establishing "hot lines" to process reports of unethical behavior within the company, conducting in-house ethics seminars, developing training programs for all employees and managers, and utilizing ombudspeople.

 **K**EY TERMS

advocacy promotion
cause-related marketing
code of business ethics
community support
economic responsibility
energy concerns
environmental issues
equal employment opportunity
ethics
law
moral stance

policies (procedures, rules, guidelines)
public responsibility
quality of the work environment
social audit
social investment
social issues in management
social responsibility
social responsiveness
stakeholder

REVIEW AND DISCUSSION QUESTIONS

1. What are the four phases of social responsibility?
2. What are the main benefits of being socially responsible?
3. What are the real costs of being socially responsible?
4. Why is it so important that social responsibility start with top management?
5. What are some of the ways in which management communicates its social responsiveness stance?
6. How does a firm benefit from advocacy promotions?
7. What are some of the main factors that affect managerial ethics?
8. How can a firm improve its managerial ethics?
9. What are some of the factors that an individual should consider when challenging an ethical problem?

CRITICAL THINKING INCIDENT 11.1

What Is John Waterman's Dilemma?

John Waterman has been in the real estate business for the past four years, selling residential homes and building lots. He has managed to make a modest living during this time, but he knows that if he is ever going to make really big money, he is going to have to ally himself with a real estate developer, which will not be easy. Most developers have their choice of real estate agents, since the developments usually sell out in six months to a year. Agents can make four or five times their normal commission during this length of time by overselling general real estate.

One day, John was having lunch with a friend who was also a real estate agent. His friend mentioned that he had heard that there was an opening for a real estate agent at the Whispering Pines Condominium Development. John was naturally very interested and asked his friend why the position was not filled already. John's friend said that he had heard that the condos there were not selling all that well because they were a little overpriced and adjacent to a questionable area of low-rent housing.

John thanked his friend for the lead and drove right down to the development. The owner interviewed John and showed him around the grounds. John was impressed with the layout of the condos and all of the development's amenities. Just before the interview ended, the owner explained to John the new marketing plan that was expected to really get sales moving. The plan consists of three main points.

1. The condos are to be advertised as if they are on sale; each one will be "marked down" from $119,000 to $89,900. John Waterman knows that the condos were originally priced at $85,900 apiece. The developer intends to mark all the condos up to $119,000 for one week prior to announcing his new sale price.

2. The condos are to be financed at a 5-percent interest rate, which is one-half the normal rate. The developer explains that he is going to tell customers that he borrowed money from some wealthy people and that is why he can finance the condos so cheaply. In reality, there will be a balloon payment in the mortgage after five years, at which time the customer will have to refinance the entire mortgage. The developer's borrowing costs for the five-year period will be covered by $3000 of the $4000 price increase (from $85,900 to $89,900) per condo.

3. The developer is going to offer $1000 rebates to all purchasers. He feels that this tactic works great for car dealers—so why not for condos? The cost of each rebate will be covered by the remaining $1000 of the price increase.

Although John knows that these tactics are used in real estate sales occasionally, he really wonders if he wants to do business in this manner. He turns to you, a trusted friend, for advice.

Discussion Questions

1. Assuming that the developer's marketing plan is now in place, what ethical questions does it raise?
2. What possible problems could arise in this situation?
3. Would you recommend that John take the position?

Was American Pesticide, Inc. Negligent?

On June 7, 1992, American Pesticide, Inc., experienced a chemical disaster that was truly a nightmare come true. American Pesticide, an American manufacturer of the pesticide Roach Proof and other chemicals, has a plant located just outside Mexico City, Mexico. One morning, the city awakened to find more than 1000 people dead and over 10,000 people injured from a poisonous gas leak at the plant.

The cause of the pesticide leak is still not completely known. The Mexican government was quick to blame the management of American Pesticide for gross negligence and incompetence. The plant was run by an all-Mexican crew; due to declining profits, the employment training program standards had been lowered considerably. American Pesticide officials blamed the leak on a faulty valve in the underground tanks that were used to mix the gas. One report stated that two workers, seen at the location of the suspected leak, fled instead of fixing it.

Whatever the cause, the damage claims from the accident seriously threaten American Pesticide's existence. The Mexican government, which quickly declared itself the representative of all of the victims, is seeking financial settlements for the Mexican people at the average per-capita income rate of U.S. workers, instead of at the per-capita income rate of Mexican workers.

American Pesticide is facing another problem as well. Although the company carries insurance, the insurer is threatening to cancel coverage if it can prove that American Pesticide caused the accident due to "gross negligence."

American Pesticide officials insist that this plant was built to the same safety standards as their plants in the United States and other countries. However, a similar plant in Texas has a computerized safety system, which the Mexico City plant does not have. The company was also supposed to install sirens that would warn local residents of any dangerous leaks like the one that occurred. The company stated that they had not had time to install a siren system at this plant.

American Pesticide's rebuttal was that, by law, local Mexican government officials were supposed to monitor the safety of the plant constantly so that accidents like this would not happen. This, in fact, was the reason the U.S. courts refused to hear any of the lawsuits filed in this case. However, after four years in the Mexican courts, a $189 million settlement is being considered. This is a big price to pay for American Pesticide, but it is not nearly as great a price as the Mexican people paid who lost their lives as a result of this disaster.

Discussion Questions

1. Do you feel that American Pesticide was acting in a socially responsible manner in this case?

2. In what ways, if any, was American Pesticide negligent? Was anyone else to blame for the accident?

3. What options can American Pesticide exercise to solve this problem? Which option do you recommend and why?

So Who Really Was to Blame?

The cause of the 1986 Challenger tragedy is now clear. An O-ring seal failed to perform as designed due to subfreezing temperatures prior to liftoff. The design failure that caused the explosion, killing the six Challenger crew members and the teacher, had been spotted in October 1977. NASA's review of the design concluded that it was unacceptable and some other type of seal should be considered.

Problems with the seals were recorded on at least nine shuttle flights prior to the Challenger mission. Morton Thiokol, manufacturer of the solid rocket boosters, ignored these reports. Even in 1985, when Thiokol's own engineers noted damage to the seals and found that low temperatures aggravated the problem, the situation was only identified as critical and never dealt with at that time. The rationale was that the O-ring seal design was noted for its cost-effective use of materials. It was the cheapest possible material that would withstand the stress, and the booster only had to fly for two minutes. So the warnings were ignored, and the Challenger was launched on January 28, 1986. The teacher and the crew were killed when the O-ring failed.

An investigative team comprised of veteran engineers scrutinized contractor operations. They noted that Thiokol's use of construction waivers and deviations was commonplace. Management would not let anything interfere with production. They did not want to inform NASA of problems of any kind, so they suppressed reports. If a hazard could not be resolved, they did not want it submitted. Thiokol's management was aware of the coverups.

Although it is easy to point the finger of blame at Thiokol, the case can also be made that the real reason for this disaster was that the space-shuttle program was underfunded. When you are dealing with "lowest bidders"—and Thiokol was the lowest bidder—cutting costs is paramount. In fact, this is the reason solid-rocket boosters were used rather than safer liquid-rocket boosters, even though the liquid-rocket boosters were in NASA's original plan.

Other people point out that Thiokol should have redesigned the boosters once they knew that the O-ring was partially failing on previous flights. But as Michael Josephson, of the Josephson Institute for the Advancement of Ethics, states, "Very often engineers will tend to overstate risks, and managers tend to use safety margins to be less cautious." The booster only had to last for 120 seconds. Redesigning the booster has cost NASA over $500 million. Is it reasonable to expect Thiokol to absorb cost overruns of this size?

In exchange for a $10-million reduction in award fees, Thiokol was exonerated from any legal blame by NASA. After the investigation, not one of Thiokol's managers was dismissed because of the accident.

Discussion Questions

1. In what areas did Thiokol display poor—or at least questionable—ethics?

2. Is it reasonable to state that the real cause of the Challenger disaster is the way in which contracts are awarded through the lowest-bid process? Explain your answer.

3. Is it reasonable to expect a company to absorb $500 million in cost overruns to correct a design problem that has seen a lot of success? Explain your answer.

4. How can NASA improve the way in which it awards contracts so disasters like this one can be avoided in the future?

5. What is your reaction to the fact that none of the managers at Thiokol were dismissed? Do you agree or disagree with this decision? Justify your answer.

ADAPTED FROM: Tom Bancraft, "Two Minutes," *Financial World* (June 27, 1989), pp. 28–32.

NOTES

1. Steven L. Wartick and Philip L. Cochran, "The Evolution of the Corporate Social Performance Model," *Academy of Management Review* 10 (1985): 758–60.

2. Josh Baran, "Every Day Is Earth Day," *Public Relations Journal* (April 1991): 22; Ronald Grover, "Fighting Back," *Business Week* (May 22, 1989), pp. 34–35; Joseph LaCovey, "Business Changes Its Ways," *Public Relations Journal* (April 1991): 23.

3. Robert Teitelman, "Through the Glass Darkly," *Financial World* (June 27, 1989), pp. 46–47.

4. Copyright © June 1990. Reprinted by permission of *Public Relations Journal*, published by the Public Relations Society of America, New York, NY, p. 16.

5. Wartick and Cochran, "The Evolution of the Corporate Social Performance Model," 758–69.

6. Ibid., pp. 763–66.

7. Steven Thomma, "Products," *St. Paul Pioneer Press-Dispatch* (April 22, 1990), p. 13A.

8. Trevor Armbrister, "When Companies Care," *Reader's Digest* (April 1989), pp. 25–30; Anne Moncreiff,

"The Corporate Classroom," *U.S. News & World Report* (July 30, 1990), pp. 8–9.

9. Yvonne Daley, "Social Goals Help VT Firms Profit," *Boston Globe* (December 15, 1991), p. 3C.

10. Henry Gilgoff, "USX, Others Panned in Group's Rankings," *Pittsburgh Press* (January 9, 1991), p. 1B.

11. Christopher Caggiano, "The INC. FaxPoll—Is Social Responsibility a Crock?," *INC.* 15 (May 1993): 15.

12. Rick Brown, "Companies That Care," *Parents* 63 (December 1988): 23.

13. Ibid.

14. Ibid.

15. Ibid.

16. Ibid.

17. Joseph Perena, "Stride Rite Shoe Corporation," *The Wall Street Journal* (May 28, 1993), p. A1.

18. Larry L. Axline, "The Bottom Line on Ethics," *Journal of Accountancy* 170 (December 1990): 87–91.

19. "Nice Guys Finish Last," *The Economist* (July 2, 1988), p. 58.

20. Jennifer J. Laabs, "Ben & Jerry's Caring Capitalism," *Personnel Journal* (November 1992): 50–57.

21. Kenneth E. Aupperle, Archie B. Carroll, and John Hatfield, "An Empirical Examination of the Relationship between Corporate Social Responsibility and Profitability," *Academy of Management Journal* **28** (1985): 446–63.

22. J. E. Newall, "Managing Environmental Responsibility," *Business Quarterly* (Autumn 1990): 90–94.

23. Karen Springen and Annetta Miller, "Doing the Right Thing," *Newsweek* (January 7, 1991), pp. 42–43.

24. Laurie Freeman and Wayne Walley, "Marketing with a Cause Takes Hold," *Advertising Age* (May 16, 1988), p. 34.

25. "America's Corporate Flag-Waving: Rednecks Redux," *The Economist* (July 21, 1990), pp. 68–69.

26. Thomas G. Labrecque, "Good Ethics Is Good Business," *USA Today* (May 1990), pp. 20–21.

27. Ibid.

28. Penney Schwab, *Daily Guideposts* (Carmel, NY: Guideposts Associates, 1991), p. 22.

29. Paul Magnusson, "Ex-Bosses Criticize Firms' Ethics," *Detroit Free Press* (May 16, 1983).

30. Roger D. Oswald, "The Challenge Is Being Addressed; The Effort Must Continue," *The Business Roundtable* (February 1988): 4–10.

31. Axline, "The Bottom Line on Ethics."

32. Katie Ripley, "Is It Possible to Get Rich in Business and Still Be Ethical?," *Juneau Empire* (April 4, 1990), p. 1B.

33. Labrecque, "Good Ethics Is Good Business," pp. 20–21.

34. Richard Green, "The Right Thing to Do," *Advocate* (June 30, 1985), p. 6G.

35. Joseph A. Raelin, "Professional and Business Ethics: Bridging the Gap," *Management Review* **78** (November 1989): 39–42.

36. The Business Roundtable, *Corporate Ethics: A Prime Business Asset* (The Business Roundtable, 1988), pp. 4–5.

37. Ronald Robin and others, "A Different Look at Codes of Ethics," *Business Horizons* 32 (January/February 1989), p. 68.

38. "Corporation Schedules Workshops in Ethics Program," *Martin Marietta Today*, no. 1 (1986), p. 1.

39. John Craddock, "Are Ethics Now in Style for Corporate America?" *St. Petersburg Times* (February 10, 1991): 1A–2A.

40. The Business Roundtable, *Corporate Ethics: A Prime Business Asset*, pp. 6–10.

41. Bruce Hager, "What's Behind Business' Sudden Fervor for Ethics," *Business Week* (September 23, 1991), p. 65.

42. Ibid.

43. John J. Oslund, "More Firms Doing Well by Doing Good," *Minneapolis Star and Tribune* (June 1, 1992), p. 1B.

44. James Russell, "The First Rule in Dealing with Corporate Crises—Always Tell the Truth," *The Bradenton Herald* (August 16, 1993), p. 3.

45. Pat Amend, "The Right Way to Deal with Ethical Dilemmas," *Working Woman* 13 (December 1988): 19.

SUGGESTED READINGS

Anderson, Duncan Maxwell. "From China, Principles of Strategy and Deception for Entrepreneurs." *Success* (March 1994): 46–51.

Davidson, Jacqueline. "Responsibility Reaps Rewards." *Small Business Reports* (February 1993): 56–64.

Elmer-Dewitt, Philip. "Anita the Agitator." *Time* (January 25, 1993), pp. 52–54.

Hamilton, Joan O'C. "Managing by Values." *Business Week* (August 1, 1994), pp. 46–53.

Himelstein, Linda. "A Warning Shot to Scare Polluters Straight." *Business Week* (November 22, 1993), p. 60.

Laabs, Jennifer J. "Ben & Jerry's Caring Capitalism." *Personnel Journal* (November 1992): 50–57.

McGarvey, Robert. "Do the Right Thing." *Entrepreneur* (April 1994): 64–67.

Michaels, James W., and Phyllis Berman. "My Story—Michael Milken," *Forbes* (March 16, 1992), pp. 78–95.

Pizzolatto, Allayne Barrilleaux, and Cecil A. Zeringue, II. "Facing Society's Demands for Environmental Protection: Management in Practice." *Journal of Business Ethics* 12 (1993): 441–47.

Reynolds, Larry. "A New Social Agenda for the New Age." *Management Review* (January 1993): 39–41.

Rice, Berkeley. "One Doctor's RX for the Recession." *Medical Economics* (August 17, 1992), pp. 49–51.

Spragins, Ellyn E. "Making Good." *INC.* (May 1993), pp. 114–22.

Stodghill, Ron, and others. "Why AIDS Policy Must Be a Special Policy." *Business Week* (February 1, 1993), pp. 53–54.

Vyakarnam, Shailendra. "Social Responsibility: What Leading Companies Do." *Long Range Planning* 25 (October 1992): 59–67.

Welles, Chris, and Michele Galen. "Both Sides Took Their Lumps in the Milken Hearings." *Business Week* (November 19, 1990), pp. 114–15.

CHAPTER 12

INTERNATIONAL MANAGEMENT

■ LEARNING OBJECTIVES

The world of business is truly becoming a global affair. Currently, there is tremendous global competition in virtually all goods and services. The intensity level of this competition is definitely going to increase as trade barriers of all types continue to disappear worldwide. The learning objectives for this chapter are to:

- Understand how the field of business has evolved into a truly global scene.
- Identify some of the major changes in international markets.
- Examine how multinational firms have evolved.
- Discuss global competition in the service industry.
- Differentiate between cultural and environmental trends, and realize how they can impact the management of a foreign business.
- Find out how to apply American management principles to an international business world.
- Identify some definite problem areas that must be considered before a domestic firm becomes a multinational corporation.

■ CHAPTER OUTLINE

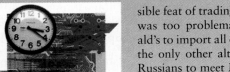

Despite being mired in a gloomy, dying economy, January 31, 1990 was an exciting day for many Russians. Why? Because a McDonald's Restaurant opened in the middle of Pushkin Square in the heart of downtown Moscow. Extremely long lines of curious people funneled through McDonald's doors, not knowing what to expect. What they saw was a huge, clean, brightly colored restaurant with a seating capacity of at least 700 people. Teenagers in black slacks and maroon T-shirts and "How can I help you?" buttons were everywhere. Everyone was smiling, the food was good, and the customers could pay in rubles. Much of what confronted the Muscovites seemed rather quaint and had not been seen in other Russian restaurants.

Since McDonald's was so different than any other Russian restaurant, how did it become such a success in the troubled city of Moscow in early 1990? It did not happen overnight. McDonald's started talking to the Russians about opening its restaurants there in the late 1970s. The timing was not right, and nothing materialized. But George Cohon, Chairman of McDonald's Canadian subsidiary, was the negotiator, and he was a man who did not give up easily. Cohon brought in the Moscow City Council as a partner, and a joint venture agreement was ultimately signed in April 1988.

But this was only the beginning. The $50 million project was probably the most difficult and challenging restaurant opening in history. The lack of quality control on raw materials in Russia initially forced McDonald's to lower its level of acceptable standards. The almost impossible feat of trading rubles for hard currency was too problematical to permit McDonald's to import all of its raw materials. Thus, the only other alternative was to train the Russians to meet McDonald's standards.

So McDonald's acted. First, McDonald's staff members actually had to teach the Russian farmers how to farm. They imported potato and cucumber seeds from the Netherlands and taught the Russians how to harvest and pack the produce without bruising it. McDonald's experts taught Russian cattle farmers how to raise leaner, higher-quality beef. The Russian distribution system was extremely poor. To maintain food standards and keep the supply of food stuffs flowing, McDonald's built a $40-million food-distribution plant just outside Moscow. This plant had its own bakery, dairy, meat-processing plant, and microbiology lab. McDonald's own trucks transported supplies to keep them readily available. By early 1990, McDonald's could buy all of its raw materials within Russia and had a stable, dependable distribution system. McDonald's standards could now be maintained.

Finally, to assure success, 30 Russian restaurant managers, who were now new McDonald's employees, were trained to familiarize all new employees with the company's standards of quality, politeness, and service. Trainees were given videos and manuals (written in Russian) on everything from how to mop floors to the proper way to assemble a Big Mac. So when the doors opened in January of 1990, McDonald's new staff was ready to show Moscow a new kind of restaurant and a new way to do business.

Now that Russia is in the process of converting to a capitalistic economy, some of the problems discussed here will be alleviated. However, it will be many years before doing business in Russia is as simple as doing business in the United States.

ADAPTED FROM: Ann B. Blackman, "Moscow's Big Mac Attack," *Time* (February 5, 1990), p. 51; Michael Dobbs, "Moscow Plays 'Ketch-up,'" *The Washington Post* (February 1, 1990), p. G5; Jeffrey M. Hertzfeld, "Joint Ventures: Saving the Soviets from Perestroika," *Harvard Business Review* 69 (January/February 1991): 80–91; Thomas Moore, "For the Leninists, It's Mac in the U.S.S.R.," *U.S. News & World Report* (February 12, 1990).

When McDonald's restaurant opened in Moscow in 1990, they introduced fast food and a whole new way of operating a business to the Russian people.

THE CHANGING GLOBAL BUSINESS SCENE

After World War II, the United States was in the tremendously enviable position of having its entire economy in excellent condition. Economies throughout Europe and a lot of Asia were significantly damaged during those war years. Consequently, for the next two and one-half decades, U.S. businesses had virtually no foreign competition.

Since the 1970s, however, this picture has changed dramatically. European and Asian countries have rebuilt their economies utilizing state-of-the-art technology. They have invaded the U.S. market in virtually every product area and in many service areas—and, in many cases, they are winning. Consider the following data.

Many U.S. industries are losing market share to foreign competitors.

In 1980, U.S. automakers had captured 71.3 percent of the domestic automobile market. By 1990, this market share had dropped to 62.5 percent, and it is still declining daily. In the service field, the United States has also lost ground. In 1980, the two largest banks in the world were U.S. banks. Today, eight of the top ten banks are Japanese; the largest American bank, Citicorp, ranks eleventh. In the area of high technology, there has also been tremendous slippage. In 1980, the United States produced 94 percent of the computers that were sold in this country. Today, this market share has dropped to 66 percent.[1]

And the list goes on and on—in product after product and in service after service. Although there are some bright spots—the United States does have some technological strengths—the U.S. market share is slipping in too many areas that are going to be critical in the future. And in some important areas of endeavor, such as consumer electronics, this country has virtually been pushed out of the field.

Although the present picture is somewhat gloomy, there are some encouraging signs.

There are some encouraging signs of an American resurgence in the international marketplace.

1. Productivity in U.S. manufacturing rose 3.9 percent per year during the 1980s. In 1992 and 1993, U.S. factory workers surpassed both German and Japanese workers[2]—the best performance by American workers since World War II.

2. U.S. exports rose 77 percent in the 1980s, including a record $398 billion in 1990. Growth in exports appears to be continuing as the dollar weakens and American manufacturers fight back with quality products of their own.

3. Many U.S. business firms are now ready to "do battle" on foreign soil, including Japan. In a survey by Deloitte and Touche, 42 percent of the responding manufacturers said they are ready to take on the Japanese in Japan right now.[3]

4. In 1992, Latin America and Asia (minus Japan and China) became a larger market for U.S. exports than Western Europe and Japan combined. This trend is expected to continue.[4]

■ *How Can U.S. Firms Become More Competitive Internationally?*

There really is not any question about what U.S. business firms need to do to become more competitive internationally. Management must concentrate on four key factors: strong customer focus, improvement of quality and productivity, development of human resources, and continuous improvement stressed

Management must focus on four factors if the firm is to become more competitive internationally.

in every area of the firm. If a company is going to survive in today's business world, doing these things is no longer an option.

CUSTOMER FOCUS   **Customer focus** means that managers look at the firm's products or services from the customer's point of view and strive to give customers innovative features and offer them added value. In order to determine what features are most desirable to customers, a strong avenue of communication must be established with them. We see some good examples of applications of customer focus in the business world.

- In 1985, Detroit sold only 1300 cars in Japan, while BMW sold 6000. One of the main reasons for these low sales is that U.S. automakers refused to put the steering wheel on the right side of the vehicle, where the Japanese are accustomed to having it.
- Coca-Cola tried for 12 years to gain a substantial foothold in Japan. When they finally changed all of their products except Coca-Cola Classic to fit the Japanese preference for a sweeter taste, they became successful.[5]

IMPROVED QUALITY AND PRODUCTIVITY   Improved quality and productivity can only occur if the business is synchronized. The entire process from design to production to suppliers and even to customer service must be quality-oriented. Once businesses learn how to make it right the "first time," both quality and productivity improve. The competition is constantly improving and each firm must also improve on a continuous basis.

THE DEVELOPMENT OF HUMAN RESOURCES   The knowledge and productivity of a firm's human resources—its employees—must be improved through con-

Pichit Larpboonlert of Kanchoke Ltd. Partnership is a distributor for the U.S. company SKF in Samutprakarn, Thailand.

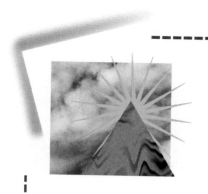

A PERSPECTIVE ON QUALITY

Japan's Leading Business Is Committed to Quality Worldwide

In 1989, Yamazaki Mazak Corporation, a Japanese manufacturer of machine tools, lasers, and robots, won the award as Japan's leading business based on a never-ending commitment to quality and efficiency in all of its plants worldwide. The manufacturer currently has plants in Japan, Europe, and North America.

Yamazaki's Computer Integrated Manufacturing (CIM) system is truly state of the art. The firm has spent an average of 10 percent of sales for the past ten years on the development of technology and computer systems. The firm pioneered the use of a mainframe computer with Computer Aided Design (CAD) and Computer Aided Manufacturing (CAM).

Yamazaki Mazak's $110 million plant in Kentucky has been a model for other U.S. plants since 1974. The manufacturer originated the idea of the demand-oriented production system. When an order is received with this system in place, all items necessary to make the product are automatically ordered from suppliers. Labor is assigned, and machine time is automatically scheduled. All the necessary paperwork is set up, and production is started.

The computerized system tracks the product through the system, so that everyone knows exactly where everything is at all times. Some of the computer-controlled machines continue to work even after most employees have gone home, keeping production on schedule at all times. Mazak's president, Brian J. Papke, also estimates that 70–90 percent of the parts in the finished products are U.S.-made.

Yamazaki has an extensive customer-communication system, which continuously collects and analyzes customer requests, comments, and suggestions to ensure even higher product quality and customer satisfaction in the future. Truly, Yamazaki Mazak is one international firm that is setting new standards worldwide and will be a fierce competitor in any market that it decides to enter.

ADAPTED FROM: Chris Gall, "Yamazaki Mazak," *Financial World Partners* (September 17, 1991), p. 4; Zachary Schiller and Roger Schreffler, "Look Who's Taking Japan to Task," *Business Week* (June 4, 1990), p. 64.

---

stant education and training. Managers must realize that their employees are their only true competitive advantage. A firm's products, technology, and everything else can be copied, but the people in the organization cannot be duplicated.

Management should be aware of three important points here.

1. The person who does a job is normally the person who is most knowledgeable about the job.

2. Employees must be encouraged to participate in the decision-making process and to use all of their talents on the job. Communication must flow easily and continuously between all levels of management and the employees.

3. Management must realize that its main role is to support workers by giving them the proper training, materials, equipment, and leadership.

CONTINUOUS IMPROVEMENT   Continuous improvement in every area of the business must be constant. A firm needs to adopt this belief as a part of its organizational culture. If management does not constantly strive to improve, the business will quickly be left behind by its competitors.

CURRENT TRENDS IN THE INTERNATIONAL MARKETPLACE

Three important trends will definitely have a tremendous impact on the business environment.

1. *Elimination of Trade Barriers* There is a definite trend to bring down trade barriers of all types among all nations. On April 2, 1993, for example, Chile and Venezuela signed a trade pact that will eliminate many customs duties between the two countries over the next four years.[6] It certainly appears that we will have truly barrier-free competition worldwide in the not-so-distant future.

2. *Regional Trading Areas* The second trend is the creation of **regional trading areas**—geographic areas without trade barriers—through free-trade agreements. These agreements include the European Economic Community Agreement (EC), which eliminated all physical, technical, and fiscal trade barriers between the common market European countries on December 31, 1992; the U.S./Canadian Free Trade Agreement (FTA); and the North American Free Trade Agreement (NAFTA) between the United States, Canada, and Mexico.

3. *New Markets* The third trend is the emergence of new markets in eastern Europe and Russia. Both the size and the potential of these markets is enormous, and they will become even more desirable as their economies become better adjusted to a market-based economy.

> Regional trading areas are geographic areas without trade barriers.

■ GATT and Other Agreements to Reduce Trade Barriers

The lowering of trade barriers began with the General Agreement on Tariffs and Trade (GATT)—a set of trading rules consigned by 117 nations that collectively account for over 90 percent of the world's trade. The GATT rules are continuously being revised to further facilitate trade with all countries throughout the world.[7] In December 1993, after seven years, the largest round of GATT negotiations came to an end. During these negotiations, tariffs and subsidies were slashed even further and GATT's name was changed to the World Trade Organization,[8] effective July 1, 1995.

Along with GATT, two other recent agreements are of concern to European nations. First, the 1986 single European Act paved the way for free trade within the European Community (EC) after 1992. This agreement promises to make Europe much more powerful economically.

Also, in December 1991, the European Community drew up the Maastricht Treaty, which is designed to establish a single European currency and a central bank by the end of 1999. However, this treaty still needs to be ratified by the 12 member nations of the EC. On June 2, 1992, Denmark had a referendum vote against the Maastricht Treaty. However, in May 1993, a second referendum vote passed easily. To win approval, the EC had to give Denmark the same option it gave Great Britain: to opt out of using the single currency.[9]

■ The European Community (EC)

> EC stands for the European Community. The EC is a large, unified European market.

The **European Community (EC)** is an alliance of the 12 common-market European nations as one large international market. This unified market began to operate on December 31, 1992,[10] with the establishment of the **European Economic Community Agreement (EEC)**. At that time, all trade barriers, customs delays, and even differences in national standards for products were eliminated.

Current members of the EC include Belgium, Denmark, France, Germany, Greece, Italy, Ireland, Luxembourg, the Netherlands, Portugal, Spain, and the United Kingdom, as illustrated in Figure 12–1. In addition, Austria, Finland, Switzerland, and Sweden have already applied for full EC membership, and Norway is expected to apply very soon.[11]

The significance of this new unified market is truly impressive. The removal of trade barriers among these European nations has created the largest single regional market in the world. In 1995 alone, just the 12-member European Community is expected to have over 347,000,000 consumers, compared to 256,000,000 for the United States and 126,000,000 for Japan.[12]

The EC will make Europe more competitive worldwide.

Although both the size and the wealth of the European Community are significant, possibly the important aspect to this new regional market is its competitive element. Companies in the EC will now be able to generate large economies of scale production runs like never before, which will also make them much more competitive in the United States, Japan, and the rest of the world. Competition within the EC will increase substantially, making the surviving business firms "lean and mean." Competition in the EC has already been increased by the development of ISO 9000, which is a series of comprehensive, international, quality management standards set up by the European Community. As discussed in Chapter 13, ISO 9000 will definitely affect the United States and other foreign corporations that try to do business in Europe.

■ **FIGURE 12–1**   Current Member Countries of the European Economic Community Agreement (EEC)

Companies, like Parker Hannifin's Digiplan Division in Colchester, England, can benefit from the European Economic Community Agreement (EEC).

■ *The U.S./Canadian Free Trade Agreement (FTA)*

The U.S./Canadian Free Trade Agreement (FTA) is already proving to be both successful and meaningful. Created in 1988, this agreement covers all goods and services that were not being freely traded at that time. This amounts to approximately 25 percent of all commerce between the two countries. The Free Trade Agreement (FTA) is a ten-year plan; different aspects of it are to be phased in each year.

Since the United States and Canada are each other's best customers, this agreement is very significant for both countries. Currently, the United States buys 73 percent of Canada's exports and Canada purchases 22 percent of all U.S. exports.[13]

Although the Free Trade Agreement is good for both countries in many areas, some new problems have arisen due to increased competition since the inception of the FTA. First, the strongest manufacturing and service firms tend to be dominant in both countries now that all trade barriers have been removed. This, of course, means that some "foreign" competitors may cause some domestic businesses to close, which in turn will result in a loss of domestic jobs in one country or the other. Second, it may not be necessary for some firms to continue to operate plants in both countries now that U.S./Canadian tariffs have been eliminated. For example, Gerber Products Company, Whirlpool (appliances), Gillette (razor blades), and Burlington Industrial closed plants in Canada and moved them to the United States, consolidating them with current U.S. plants. On the other hand, firms such as General Motors and Pet Inc. have moved north to Canada creating new jobs for Canadians.[14]

■ *The North American Free Trade Agreement (NAFTA)*

On November 17, 1993, Congress passed the North American Free Trade Agreement (NAFTA), which took effect on January 1, 1994, forming the largest single trading partnership in the world. Even the European Economic

GLOBAL VIEW

NAFTA and Free Trade

The 2000-page North American Free Trade Agreement (NAFTA) has created the largest free-trade region in the world to date. The three participating North American countries, however, may be only the tip of the proverbial iceberg. When then U.S. President George Bush signed the initial free-trade agreement among the United States, Canada, and Mexico, he clearly had his eyes on a much larger free-trade zone.

> Because of what we've begun here today, I believe the time will soon come when free trade is possible from Alaska to Argentina. If we are equal to the challenges before us, we can build in the Americas the world's first completely democratic hemisphere. Just think about that; think of the example for the rest of the world.

President Bush called NAFTA, "The first step toward fulfillment of a dream—a free-trade zone encompassing the entire Western Hemisphere, including Central and South America and the nations of the Caribbean."

ADAPTED FROM: "Bush Signs Mexican Trade Accord," *The Bradenton Herald* (December 18, 1992), p. A3.

Community Agreement is smaller. The North American block contains 355 million people and has a gross national product (GNP) of $6.4 trillion, compared to the 12-member Economic Community with 324 million people and a GNP of $4 trillion.[15] And this free-trade area may prove to be even larger.

All trade barriers among the three countries participating in NAFTA (the United States, Canada, and Mexico) will be eliminated over a 15-year period. Tariffs on more than 9000 products were eliminated immediately, and 65 percent of all products will be tariff-free by January 1, 1999. Some specific products, such as agricultural products, will be given the maximum of 15 years to "adjust" to a duty-free status.[16]

Although the size of an agreement like NAFTA is impressive, it raises some issues that worry a lot of people in both the United States and Canada. Of particular concern is the **Maquiladora program** started by the United States and Mexico in 1965 to create jobs for Mexico. The Maquiladora program encourages U.S. firms that use American-made parts to establish plants just across the border in Mexico. Firms in the United States ship American parts to their plants in Mexico for final assembly. When the finished goods are completed, they are shipped north to the United States. Under this special program, each product is taxed only on the "value added" by the assembly process, not on the value of the product as a whole. Although this program benefits both countries to some degree, it poses some obvious problems as well.

In Mexico, U.S. firms can assemble their products very cheaply, which makes them much more competitive in foreign markets. However, the bottom line is that the United States is losing jobs to Mexico. It is difficult to state the specific number of unskilled, assembly-line jobs that the United States has lost to Mexico to date. However in 1990, Maquiladora industries consisted of approximately 2000 plants that employed more than 500,000 Mexican workers.[17]

The only true and permanent solution to the problem of losing U.S. jobs to Mexico is to educate and train American assembly-line workers to perform more productive and higher-skilled tasks. There are always going to be countries that

Adding Mexico could make North America the largest free-trade area.

Maquiladora workers, who earn substantially lower wages than U.S. workers for equivalent tasks, work at a Whirlpool appliance assembly plant in Mexico.

can supply cheaper labor forces. In addition, many economists consider the rapid advancement in automation to be a far greater threat to low-skilled American workers.[18]

Like the Free Trade Agreement (FTA) between Canada and the United States, NAFTA appears to help both countries by removing barriers to trade. But just as the FTA posed some problems for and required some adjustments between U.S. and Canadian firms, NAFTA certainly presents some problems and raises some issues for Mexican and U.S. firms. In 1994, the Mexican economy faltered, raising concerns about how much the U.S. will gain from NAFTA. However, in January 1995, the U.S. coordinated an economic assistance program that has been put in place to bolster the peso: a $53 billion bailout of the Mexican economy in the form of a loan guarantee, in part from the International Monetary Fund (World Bank), including $20 billion from the U.S. Treasury. In the long run, however, both countries could be stronger economically and competitively, as U.S. capital and equipment move south and Mexican labor provides the means to make American products more cheaply so that they become more competitive worldwide.

■ New Markets in Eastern Europe and Russia

The last major trend in the international marketplace is the transformation of Russia and the eastern European countries to capitalism. As the eastern European countries privatize their industries, the opportunities for western countries to buy into these markets will never be easier.

Eastern Europe may offer some good opportunities for low-wage manufacturing.

Many investors can see that these countries offer low-wage manufacturing areas where products could be made for export. Gerber Products Company, for example, recently purchased 60 percent of Alima of Poland, eastern Europe's leading fruit-juice and baby-food producer, just for this cost advantage. Many other western firms are considering joint ventures for the same reason.[19]

There are negative aspects to the purchase of eastern European companies. Some firms carry very large amounts of bad debt; many businesses are unable to provide even basic social services to the communities in which they are located. PepsiCo was "surprised" to learn that after it purchased Wedel, a large Polish chocolate firm, it also was responsible for operating a health clinic, a rehabilitation center, two nursery schools, a recreational center, several hotels, and housing for retirees. Although the new capitalistic government will eventually allow PepsiCo to dispose of these services, the company must keep them for now because no current alternatives exist.[20]

The potential of the Russian market may be too good to be true.

The breakup of the Soviet Union and the beginning of the new Russian Commonwealth have created a work force of virtually millions of well-educated, hard-working people who, in essence, need everything. Although many of their manufacturing systems are somewhat primitive by western standards, they are not all that way. In Russia, in fact, there are many world-class research laboratories.[21] Russia, the Ukraine, and the Baltic states also jointly contain the world's largest reserves of gold, timber, oil, and some critical minerals.[22]

The business opportunities are obvious, but the problems currently facing new investors may be equally large. For the most part, the Russian Commonwealth's industrial technology is well behind western standards, so new investors will be required to heavily invest in renovating and modernizing these plants. The Russian Commonwealth's distribution and communication systems are very inadequate by western standards. Several new laws also both help and hinder foreign investment; for example, the high tax structure is obviously a detriment. Finally, although current Russian managers are quite dedicated and perform their present jobs competently, they have almost no knowledge of marketing, business strategy, or commercial accounting.[23]

CONSIDER THIS

1. What is NAFTA, and what impact will it have on U.S. businesses?

2. How will the European Economic Community affect foreign competitors?

3. What does the transformation of Russia and the eastern European countries to capitalism mean to U.S. businesses?

THE GROWTH AND DEVELOPMENT OF INTERNATIONAL MANAGEMENT

Some U.S. business firms still adhere to the belief that an American firm really does not need to get involved in international markets. After all, dealing with international markets can pose a lot of problems, and the managers of these firms may feel that they are doing just fine in their present domestic markets. In short, why does a business even need to seriously consider international marketing?

The answer to this question is both simple and complex. The simple part of the answer is that a firm may not have any choice; the opportunity may be so profitable that it literally would be foolish to pass it up. The complex part of the answer is that doing business internationally may be very difficult due to differences in the business environment.

Let's look at some of the things that are currently happening that may change the way you think about international markets.

There are some good reasons for a firm to "go international."

1. *Markets are regionalizing in terms of free trade.* This creates more competition from new companies that were not of major concern previously due

to such regulations as protective tariffs. If these firms are going to attack the market share why not attack them first?

2. *Manufacturing firms and other suppliers must grow with U.S. companies that market abroad or lose overseas business to local foreign suppliers.* Losing this new business may come back to haunt a domestic manufacturer if the new foreign supplier later decides to expand its operations to the United States.

3. *The cost of developing new products in some fields has risen dramatically.* It is not a sound business practice for one supplier to spend a great deal of money establishing new product technology so that competitors can simply pick it up and benefit from it. An example of a new-product joint venture of this type is the alliance between Boeing, Fuji, Mitsubishi, and Kawasaki to build the new 777 jet passenger airplane. As Larry Clarkson, Senior Vice President of Boeing, stated, "The day of Boeing being a sole producer of a Boeing product has passed. It simply takes too many dollars, has too high of a risk, and has a very limited customer base."[24]

International markets can extend the life of some products.

4. *Selling products internationally is a way to extend product life cycles.* Many products that are in a mature stage in the United States may be in the introductory stage or growth stage overseas. For example, phone service in Venezuela, Argentina, and Mexico is very poor and unreliable. Since revenues from all of the Baby Bells in the U.S. is expected to increase by only 2.7 percent, these international markets have to look very enticing.[25]

5. *New markets are opening up that will not last forever in terms of their ease of entry.* So often, small- and medium-sized firms think they are not large enough to enter the international marketplace. What the management of these firms fails to see is that a business can begin overseas operations on a very limited, almost risk-free basis. As the international market develops, a firm can switch to alternative forms of business ownership/control to take advantage of the opportunities at hand. Since domestic markets are becoming more and more saturated, the need to find new foreign markets is truly growing.

DIFFERENT FORMS OF INTERNATIONAL MANAGEMENT

A firm can enter the international marketplace in a variety of ways. Each method of entry has different levels of owner control and owner risk. The three main types of firms operating in the international marketplace are

What is the difference between an international firm, a multinational firm, and a global firm?

■ **International business firms,** which establish any type of business relationship with entities in a foreign country. This relationship may be as simple as exporting goods or services to a foreign agent or broker or as extensive as actually establishing wholly-owned foreign subsidiaries.

■ **Multinational firms,** which have made significant commitments in the form of international investments, either in fixed assets or in contractual agreements, that produce a significant amount of their revenues and profits. Multinational firms normally tailor their products or services to the individual markets in specific countries. The Ford Motor Company is an example of a multinational firm.

■ **Global firms,** which see the entire world as their market. Firms at this level produce relatively uniform products for the entire world and usually have significant investment commitments worldwide. Coca-Cola is an example of a global firm.

Normally, most firms first enter the international marketplace by utilizing a domestic-market approach. As Figure 12–2 illustrates, a firm usually establishes itself in a foreign market by progressing through the domestic-market methods of operation until it grows large enough internationally to try a multinational approach. Finally, the firm's management may consider a global approach.

■ *The Domestic-Market Approach to International Management*

Most firms start going international by simply exporting their goods or services.

When a firm of any size decides to enter the international marketplace, it is most common for management to begin by employing the first **domestic-market management approach.** This approach usually consists of exporting the firm's current products to a **foreign agent** or **broker.** Unfortunately, this

■ **FIGURE 12–2** Three Principle Methods of International Management (Methods of Operations)

DOMESTIC-MARKET ORIENTATION IN INTERNATIONAL MARKETS	MULTINATIONAL ORIENTATION IN INTERNATIONAL MARKETS	GLOBAL ORIENTATION IN INTERNATIONAL MARKETS
1. Sell to an *agent* or *broker,* who resells to the marketplace.	1. Form *joint ventures* or *partnerships* with foreign nationals to produce and market products or services specifically designed for a given market.	1. Form *global strategic partnerships* between two giant corporations that meet the following criteria.
2. Establish a *licensure agreement,* which grants a foreign firm the right to manufacture or market the firm's products, utilize its brand name, etc. A fee plus continuing royalties are received for this agreement.	2. Establish *wholly owned subsidiaries* for manufacturing, marketing, or both. Different products are produced to meet local demands.	a. They have a common, long-term strategy and produce products aimed at worldwide dominance.
3. Sign a *manufacturing contract,* which allows a foreign supplier to manufacture the domestic firm's product according to the domestic firm's specifications. Profits are shared under this arrangement.		b. The relationship is reciprocal. Both corporations share their strengths.
		c. Their joint efforts cover all markets throughout the world.
		d. The relationship is horizontal, not vertical. Technology and other resources are freely exchanged.
		e. The companies maintain their basic national identities.
		2. Establish *wholly owned subsidiaries* that are very vertically integrated (from manufacturer to retailer) and that produce one uniform product for worldwide distribution.

ADAPTED FROM: William R. Fannin and Arvin F. Rodrigues, "National or Global?—Control vs. Flexibility," *Long Range Planning* **19** (October 1986): 84–88.

method allows the manufacturer very little control over how its products are marketed once they are sold to the agent or broker. On the plus side, risk to the firm is minimal because products are normally sold on a cash basis.

The next most common domestic-market method of operation is to establish a **licensure agreement**. Here, a firm grants certain rights to another firm to use its brand name, symbols, product specifications, or other identifying characteristics in either the manufacturing or the marketing of its products. Disney World, for example, has many licensure agreements which, for a fee and usually continuous royalties, allows other firms to utilize Mickey Mouse® on all types of clothing articles. Under this form of management, more control is secured. However, the risk increases because the firm holding the licensure agreement is not the manufacturer in this market.

The third way to employ a domestic-market approach is to sign a **manufacturing contract** with a foreign manufacturer. Here, the domestic, parent firm shares its profits with a foreign manufacturer; in return, the domestic firm establishes a local presence in the foreign market without making a major investment of capital. With this contract, the foreign manufacturer produces the product under the domestic firm's supervision. Again, control increases but so does risk, since these contracts are usually for extensive periods of time and disagreements may occur.

■ The Multinational Approach to International Management

Once the management of a firm decides to enter a foreign international market on an even more established basis, the next logical step is to take a **multinational management approach**, in which the business firm moves away from producing its original domestic products and starts to modify them to meet the cultural demands of the foreign markets that the firm is entering. Here, the firm is making a strong commitment to the international marketplace in terms of sales and profits and, in many cases, fixed investments. The two most common ways to become a multinational firm are to form joint ventures or partnerships and to establish wholly-owned subsidiaries.

Joint ventures or **partnerships,** the most common form of international management, are formed when one firm actually purchases a minority, a majority, or an equal portion of a foreign firm. The two firms technically become partners. Normally, the foreign firm provides local market expertise and may receive favorable tax benefits and generate greater consumer acceptance. The investor firm provides new technology, access to a new market for the foreign firm, and new strategies for attacking different markets. Some examples of joint ventures include the formation of the NUMMI plant by General Motors and Toyota and U.S. Steel's joint venture with Kobe Steel in Japan. As in any partnership, each firm's role and responsibilities in a joint venture must be clearly communicated to all parties to the agreement.

The **wholly-owned subsidiary** in the multinational firm is normally given quite a bit of operational freedom from the U.S. parent firm. Many times, multinational corporations employ several local nationals as members of the management team and an almost totally local sales force. The idea is to try to get the government and people of the local country to accept the multinational by providing jobs and products for the local economy. Honda's plant in Maryville, Ohio, Chrysler's plant in Mexico, and Ford's plant in England are all examples of multinational operations. Here, of course, the risk to the invest-

Licensure agreements are quite common today in foreign markets.

A multinational approach means changing the product to fit the local market.

Wholly-owned subsidiaries are major investments in a foreign country.

ing firm is substantial, since large financial commitments are made. However, the parent firm is in control because it owns and operates the plant.

■ *The Global Approach to International Management*

The final approach to international management is the **global management approach.** Here, the two basic methods of operation are the wholly-owned subsidiary and the global strategic partnership. Utilizing wholly-owned subsidiaries on a global basis involves a lot of **vertical integration.** The firm then has complete control; it owns or controls the manufacturer, distributors, retailers, and/or marketing firms. The emphasis is not on modifying products to fit different markets but on developing a single-product marketing strategy worldwide.

The global approach tries to dominate world markets with a single-product marketing approach.

Finally, the most recent way for a firm to approach global markets is through the use of **global strategic partnerships.** These partnerships are far more than just joint ventures, which concentrate on single national markets. A global strategic partnership stresses worldwide leadership by developing a single-product marketing strategy that is designed to dominate its product or service area. An example of a global strategic partnership is General Electric and France's state-owned SNEEMA, which have joined together to produce a low-pollution engine for high-performance aircraft. The two firms are sharing the $800 million in development costs and hope to dominate all markets worldwide in this product area.[26]

GLOBAL COMPETITION IN THE SERVICE INDUSTRY

The United States is the world leader in selling services.

The United States has lost considerable ground in the manufacturing sector but is still the leader in selling services worldwide. In 1990, for example, American service firms generated a $31.9 billion trade surplus, which could grow to $100 billion by the end of the decade.[27]

The United States has some excellent strengths to export in the form of retailing and computer services, and the nation is making substantial gains in several other service areas. For example, Exxon has become the largest U.S. based multinational company, with $63 billion in foreign sales.[28] In terms of employment, the service industry again leads the way. Since 1970, 29 million new jobs have been created and more than 80 percent of them were in the service sector.[29] The service sector is the area that U.S. businesses can point to with pride, and the potential exists for even greater growth in the service industry.

Many kinds of services can be exported.

Due to technological advancements, the variety of services that can be exported is incredible. For example, one New York law firm has points of law researched overnight in Seoul by English-speaking Korean lawyers, who transmit their findings by satellite to the American law firm's database facility in Chicago by the next morning. The information is even used by the firm's partners in their London office before the New York lawyers get to work the next day. In addition, doctors in Houston diagnose patients in Brazil, using a CAT scan transmitted by satellite,[30] and New York Life sends some of its insurance forms to Ireland to be processed.[31]

Although the United States is strong in many service-related fields, foreign competition can be just as devastating in the service sector as it is in

GLOBAL VIEW

Service Companies Dominate the World Economy

Service companies continue to dominate the world economy in all areas from transportation to banking, from retail to construction. Services in the early 1990s accounted for over 60 percent of the gross domestic product (GDP) and most of the new jobs created in the industrial countries of the globe.

The United States, with 12.7 percent of the world market, is the top exporter of services. These U.S. services rose to nearly $8 billion toward the end of the 1980s. It is expected to grow to $100 billion by the end of the 1990s.

The services that U.S. companies are concentrating on are

Bharat Pandya of Poona, West India has been a distributor of SKF bearings since 1949. A company's longevity can be determined by its provision of a needed service.

- *Computer Services.* The United States has the edge in the $95-billion market for data processing, custom software, and other computer-related services. Exports recently exceeded imports by a 31-to-1 margin.

- *Retailing.* The United States clearly dominates in retailing. Of the world's 50 largest retail enterprises, 19 are American, among them are the top three companies.

- *Insurance.* Insurance remains mostly a domestic business. However, the American International Group (AIG) collects 40 percent of its premiums abroad.

- *Airlines.* American Airlines is gaining competitively on British Airways, the leading international carrier worldwide. American has lower costs and a huge computerized system.

- *Air-Courier Services.* Brussels-based DHL controls most of the international air-courier business. However, UPS is quickly stealing its customers by driving down costs.

- *Banking.* In 1989, Japan had 24 percent of the banking market, compared to 22 percent for the United States. However, in early 1990, Japan began reversing expansion.

- *Industrial Construction.* The United States is still one of the world's top international contractors, but its market dropped from 45 percent in 1980 to 25 percent in 1987.

ADAPTED FROM: Sarah Smith, "Cover Stories," *Fortune* (June 5, 1989), pp. 67–68; Nora E. Field and Ricardo Sookdeo, "The Global Service 500—Introducing a New List," *Fortune* (August 26, 1991), pp. 166–85; John Rutledge, "Economic Outlook," *U.S. News & World Report* (October 21, 1991), p. 72.

Although the United States currently dominates in the service industry, it may not always be that way.

the manufacturing sector. As economist and Nobel laureate Robert M. Solow at the Massachusetts Institute of Technology states, "Americans have no more natural advantages in producing financial services than in producing color TVs. We are in danger of losing our edge."[32] Europe, Japan, and even Singapore have made tremendous strides to try to gain a substantial foothold in the U.S.

service areas of retailing, banking, construction, and hotel management. Since 1980, these countries have quadrupled their investments in service enterprises in the United States, and this trend is expected to continue.

There appear to be five megatrends that virtually guarantee that international competition in the service industries will continue to grow in the future.

1. **Technological Advancements** Tremendous advancements in technology make the transmission of all types of data as close as the telephone.

2. **Globalization of Manufacturing** As both U.S. and foreign manufacturers build plants outside their home countries, their service firms in the home country will follow them.

3. **Increased Income** European and Asian consumers are experiencing strong economic growth and, therefore, increases in their incomes. As incomes rise, consumers worldwide spend more on services.

Five major trends will influence the service sector internationally.

4. **Deregulation of Government Barriers** Both the United States and many foreign countries have removed barriers and restrictions against foreign firms that compete in selected industries.

5. **Removal of Trade Barriers** The removal of all trade barriers among nations has already begun, and more countries in Europe have already applied for membership in the European Community.[33]

International competition is expanding both in the United States and on foreign soil. American service companies must continue to strive to grow in terms of efficiency and productivity.

ASSESSING ENVIRONMENTAL DIFFERENCES

Environmental differences can be categorized into three basic areas.

Obviously, managing a business in a foreign country is going to be quite a bit different than managing one at home. Differences can be found in three basic areas: the political and legal environment, the cultural environment, and the economic environment.

■ *The Political and Legal Environment*

When an American company decides to establish an international firm, one very critical area that must be considered is how the firm will be viewed by the political and legal systems in that country. In terms of tax laws and various government regulations, many foreign firms are not treated the same as domestic firms. An American Management Association survey respondent named David W. Johnson, head of Gerber Products Company, stated:

Unstable, sometimes even hostile governments may await foreign investors.

> When you are classified as a foreign company, it means you are regarded with degrees of suspicion and with doubt about your motivations. The playing field is not always level. The local government infrastructure, which must support and approve many business actions, is sometimes circumspect and slow. It can result in a competitive disadvantage.[34]

Another factor to consider is the stability of the government and its degree of hostility toward foreign investors. Government reaction to international business operations can range from outright expulsion of the firm and confiscation of its property (as happened in Iran after the deposition of the Shah in 1979) to a simple requirement that foreign firms employ a certain percentage of nationals. This type of risk has greatly diminished over the last decade, however. Fewer than 20 foreign investments were confiscated in the 1980s, compared to 423 in the 1970s.[35]

PROTECTIONISM Many governments, including the U.S. government, utilize *some form* of **protectionism** to grant domestic firms a more favorable competitive position. Protectionism can take any one of the following forms.

■ *Tariffs* **Tariffs** are stated fees or taxes that must be paid on all imported products brought into the country. Tariffs are designed to give domestic products a price advantage. The United States currently has tariffs on textiles, onions, and shoes, among other items.[36]

■ *Quotas* **Quotas** limit the number of foreign products that a firm may import. In many cases, the quota relates to a percentage of the total market sales for that product market.

Tariffs, quotas, and subsidies are all forms of protectionism.

■ *Subsidies* **Subsidies** consist of government payments to domestic firms that are under intense foreign pressure. Several major Japanese industries are subsidized. The United States currently has both import quotas and export subsidies on many agricultural products.[37]

Nationalism is very difficult for a foreign investor to overcome.

■ *Nationalism* **Nationalism** occurs when consumers strongly support their own country's products over competitive foreign products, even when the foreign product is better or less expensive. Unfortunately, as companies merge with other foreign companies and move their plants all over the world, it may be difficult to determine which product is imported and which product is domestic.

Picture yourself on the town council in Greece, New York. Your job as a council member is to decide which dirt remover to purchase for the town of Greece. You have only two stipulations: (1) Try to purchase from the lowest bidder, and (2) do not buy from a foreign company. That sounds easy enough, or so you think. So you do your homework and end up with only two bidders. The first bid is from Komatsu Dresser Company, an American-Japanese joint venture. The second bid is from John Deere & Company. You immediately think that a John Deere excavator would be very American. However, you discover that they make their John Deere excavators in a joint venture with Hitachi. The engines are made in Iowa, but the machines themselves are made in Japan. After further research, you uncover the fact that Komatsu Dresser Company's headquarters is in Lincolnshire, Illinois, and that 95 percent of its excavators are made in the United States. Which one do you buy? Which one is the American company?[38]

All forms of protectionism fail to address the real problem at hand.

Initially, a protectionist government policy may seem like a good way to save domestic firms and jobs from foreign competitors that may market superior products. Protectionism does not address the real problem, however. During the 1980s, protectionist policies did help American automakers to gain back their share of that market because the Japanese were excluded from it to some degree. To counter this, Japanese automakers built plants in the United States, thereby negating the quotas and tariffs altogether. The result, of course, was that the Japanese gained back the market share they lost earlier. Instead of relying on artificial trade barriers, U.S. automakers must realize that the only way to be successful is to challenge the competition through responsiveness to the marketplace in terms of service and product quality.

BRIBES AND PAYOFFS　One legal problem that is commonly encountered is the practice of bribes and payoffs. Although they are legal in many foreign countries, these are illegal practices in U.S. companies under the Foreign Corrupt Practices Act, enacted in 1977. However, the U.S. law has been amended to ease some company obligations and to clarify many points. For instance, it is not illegal to make payments to officials to "facilitate" routine government actions, such as providing utilities, or to quickly inspect shipments. However, it is illegal to pay officials to not inspect shipments at all.[39] The management of an international firm must know what is legal and what is not legal in order to operate within the legal systems of both the United States and a foreign country.

■ *The Cultural Environment*

Comprehending the cultural environment can be very difficult for a foreign investor.

The cultural differences between two countries may pose the most difficult problems to foreign investors. A business can usually acquire relatively reliable information regarding the laws and procedures in a foreign country. Cultural differences, however, are difficult to explain to foreigners and, in many cases, are very subtle. If a business is to succeed, its management must know and respect the cultural differences of the country in which the firm is to do business.

A good example of cultural differences between countries recently occurred when two separate but identical seminars were conducted—one for Japanese managers and one for American managers—all of whom were working for Japanese companies in the United States. The Japanese seminar consisted of 25 male Japanese managers, who arrived wearing almost identical dark suits. Even though the room temperature was very warm, none of them removed their suit coats. Their ten-minute coffee break lasted exactly ten minutes. They did not ask any questions until they got to know each other better during lunch. They were very courteous and were always polite.

The same seminar was given to 25 American managers. This group included eight women and 17 men. On entering the very warm meeting room, several of the men removed their suit coats. The ten-minute coffee break lasted for more than 20 minutes. Participants asked questions early and often, and several aggressively contradicted what the speaker had to say. As the late cofounder of Honda, Fakeo Fujisama, stated, "Japanese and American management practices are 95 percent the same and differ in all the important aspects."[40] Although this statement was obviously intended to be somewhat humorous, it does infer how different these two cultures really are in the business world.

Communication problems are common when doing business in foreign markets.

One of the most obvious cultural differences deals with communication, especially language differences. When doing business with someone from another culture, *how* something is said is as important as *what* is said. Consider the following examples.

■ Americans and Japanese (our number-two trading partner) view some common, nonverbal gestures quite differently. To Americans, people who pause before replying are probably being very critical of what was just said. Americans expect people who are trustworthy to respond directly and immediately. The Japanese, on the other hand, distrust such fluency. They are more impressed by someone who gives careful thought to a question before making a reply. Most Japanese are very comfortable with a period of silence before they answer a question. Most Americans have great difficulty with such pauses and often try to fill in these gaps with additional conversation.

Doing business with people from other cultures requires familiarity with their customs and attitudes toward business, and some knowledge of their language.

The American characteristics of frankness and openness are often misunderstood. The Japanese think it is not only polite, but very sensible, to be discreet about sensitive information. They confide in people only after they know the person and trust their willingness to keep certain information confidential. Americans who boast proudly that they are "their own person" and who exhibit other individualistic characteristics will be viewed as antisocial and not to be trusted by the Japanese, who value team-oriented people.[41]

■ Canadians, our number-one trading partner, are more low-key than Americans. Canadians take considerable time when speaking and select their words very deliberately. They often consider Americans to be pushy and reckless.

A foreign firm must not just be aware of cultural differences; it must relate to them.

■ Mexicans, our number-four trading partner, buy from their first cousins and sell to their sisters' husbands first. Family ties are strong in Mexican communities, making it difficult for U.S. competitors, especially sellers.[42]

■ South Koreans, our seventh largest trading partner, often speak out more frankly and bluntly than Americans and are very emotional, laughing one minute and screaming the next. South Koreans may have an easier time dealing with Americans than with the Japanese, who have difficulty dealing with emotional people in a business setting.

■ The Brazilians, our number-one trading partner in South America, are by far the most dynamic. They do not know the meaning of silence. They talk constantly and make frequent physical contact: touching, poking, and patting. It would be interesting to watch Americans and Japanese, who never touch one another, doing business with Brazilians.

To avoid communication problems, especially in a foreign country, management must be extremely careful to choose words that clearly and concisely convey the objectives and concerns of the firm. Selecting the wrong words can be embarrassing and, if an incorrect message is received, not very profitable.

Being capable of conversing in the native language of the country in which the firm is doing business has some obvious advantages. Not all English words

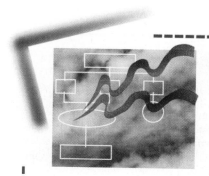

REMEMBER TO COMMUNICATE
Business Blunders Can Be Expensive

- Would you buy a car if you thought its name meant "does not go?" That is what Latin Americans thought of the Nova. "Nova" in Spanish means "does not go." Needless to say, the Nova did not sell well in Latin America.

- Would you take a flight to Brazil that advertises "rendezvous lounges" when in your language "rendezvous" means "a place to have sex"?

- Would you buy a can of vegetables with a green or white label if green is a symbol of disease in your country, as it is in Africa, and white is a symbol of death, as it is in Japan?

- Would you buy cans that you thought contained ground-up babies, as members of an illiterate African nation believed when they first saw baby-food cans with pictures of cuddly infants on the label?

These business blunders that proved expensive are contained in a novel collection of 200 or more documented blunders researched by David Ricks, who was chairman of the Ohio State University International Business Program in the 1980s.

Ricks also discusses blunders that result from problems with translation. Some examples are

- "Body by Fisher" changed to "Corpse by Fisher."

- "Come alive with Pepsi" changed to "Come alive out of the grave."

- A "car wash" changed to "car enema."

These blunders may be amusing, but they can also be very costly according to Ricks, who verifies the validity of every one that he uncovers. Ricks notes that in many cases, the people who blundered are no longer employed by their respective companies. Thus, cultural blunders can be costly to the individual as well as to the company.

ADAPTED FROM: John Pfeiffer, "How Not to Lose the Trade Wars by Cultural Gaffes," *Smithsonian* **18** (January 1988): 145–53.

Serious firms learn the languages of the countries in which they do business.

translate as we would like them to, and sometimes a lot of the true meaning of what someone intends to communicate is lost in translation. Expecting foreign counterparts to speak English is unrealistic and may even be interpreted by the people in a particular country as having no respect for them or their language.

■ The Economic Environment

There are four basic areas of economic difference for the foreign investor.

There are four basic areas of economic differences for the foreign investor to consider.

1. *Income Levels* In assessing economic differences, management can first look at the average income levels for the foreign population as a whole if a firm plans to market their goods or services in that country. The range of average incomes among countries varies widely. Since the level of income in a country primarily determines the quality and quantity of goods or services that can be marketed there, this point is very critical. Some countries have huge populations and obvious need for a given product or service. If the people as a whole cannot afford to buy a particular product or service, however, then there is no market for it.

GLOBAL VIEW

Cultural Differences between Japanese and American Managers

American individualism and Japanese conformity are causing problems in the workplace. In fact, the dichotomy created by these contradictory personality traits is beginning to be viewed as a cultural tug-of-war. Each side needs to understand the other side's differences and use them to its advantage. What are those differences, and why do they seem to be so difficult to overlook in the workplace?

■ Probably the ultimate difference between the Japanese and the American manager is priority toward work and family. In a Japanese firm, company loyalty is a top priority. To stay two or three hours after work and discuss ideas is commonplace. Many ideas that come up in meetings are devised between 6 and 8 o'clock in the evening and are expected to be approved in meetings the following day. In contrast, American managers are more inclined to work an eight-hour day so they can have time to spend with their families. Thus, the American manager tends to be isolated from his or her Japanese counterpart.

In 1992, business leaders overcame cultural differences in order to reach an alliance between IBM of the United States (left), Toshiba of Japan (middle), and Siemens of Germany (right).

■ A second important cultural difference is personal and work-related attitudes. In the Japanese company, group involvement is necessary and confrontations are not allowed. Overachievers and underachievers often blend into the group; thus, the weakest are protected and the strongest are held back. Promotions come automatically, as long as the job gets done and the workers conform to their roles. On the other hand, the American is used to striving for independence and may even become aggressive to get a point across. Americans view their experience and talent as their greatest work assets and believe that they should be rewarded for these assets. Experience and talent are important to the Japanese, but conformity and working together peacefully are more important.

■ A third cultural difference that causes problems in the workplace is the decision-making process. In many Japanese companies, the decision-making process is slow and much research and discussion takes place before a decision is made. Orders are not carried out unless everyone involved has signed off in advance. And to a Japanese manager, "yes" may have several different meanings, including "maybe," "I understand," "I'm listening," and "yes, I agree." So "yes" may not really mean "Yes, let's do it"; it may just mean that more research needs to be done before a decision can be reached. In the American company, however, the decision-making process is swift and is often communicated from the top down. To Americans, "yes" means "yes." In other words, a "yes" on a decision means "Let's do it."

ADAPTED FROM: Kerry Pechter, "Can We Make a Deal?," *International Business* (March 1992): 46–50; Jon Pepper, "Japanese Bosses Wary of Executive Gogetters," *Detroit News* (March 26, 1990).

2. Tax Structure   The tax structure within the foreign country is another major economic point to consider. In many countries, firms have much different tax rates applied to foreign firms than are applied to domestic competitors. Since tax structures and tax rates vary so widely from country to country, it is imperative for any business that is planning to invest in a foreign country to check them out very closely.

Tax structures vary widely in different countries.

3. Inflation Rate   The inflation rate is another large economic factor that must be carefully studied. Inflation in the United States has remained relatively stable, but we do not have to venture very far to find examples of countries where inflation has run rampant. Russia, eastern Europe, Mexico, and Brazil all have experienced very high inflation rates.

4. Fluctuating Exchange Rates   The exchange rates of some currencies can fluctuate so widely that a foreign investor can literally be wiped out financially on that basis alone. The **foreign exchange rate,** or the value of the home country's currency in terms of another country's currency, can change daily, depending on the supply and demand for each country's currency. If the government of a country starts to print too much currency, as Mexico did, the inflation rate soars and the value of that currency consequently declines.

The foreign exchange rate determines the value of the country's currency in terms of another country's home currency and can vary daily.

CONSIDER THIS

1. What communication problems does a firm commonly encounter when doing business in a foreign market?

2. What is meant by nationalism? How does it affect foreign competitors?

3. Why is the foreign exchange rate so important to the operation of a foreign business?

MANAGING IN THE INTERNATIONAL BUSINESS WORLD

Global competition is literally changing how U.S. organizations are managed, both at home and abroad. Some of the factors that contribute to changes in management techniques are ever-advancing technology, shorter product life cycles, and high-speed communications. Time factors in all areas of business are getting shorter and shorter.

Changes in so many areas are causing U.S. firms to change how they manage.

All of these changes add up to a new business environment that is forcing managers to replace old management styles with new ones. This new approach stresses constant, on-going communication, which, in turn, produces

■ Extremely high levels of employee involvement

■ Flexible organizational structures that adapt to market changes

■ Inspiring leadership at all levels

■ On-going staff-development programs

■ Design-control procedures that are understandable and acceptable to everyone in the firm

What we are talking about here is a shift in management values. Although the old values of honesty, trust, and hard work are certainly still valid, to be truly effective, the new international manager must be a visionary who is able to convince everyone in the firm of the need to realize specific organizational objectives. Commitment is becoming a very important watchword in the business world.[43]

■ *Planning*

The management of an international firm must utilize many of the planning methods outlined in Chapter 5. In addition to these basic techniques, the managers of an international organization must be sure that their plans fit in with the distinct cultures of the member countries in which they are doing business. Company strategies must be planned and developed not only to fit the competition but also to account for the competitive playing field.[44]

U.S. firms must think on more of a long-term basis when developing strategic plans.

Long-term strategic planning is generally done worldwide; however, the length, amount of detail, and degree of flexibility of these strategic plans do vary. International companies as a whole need to think and plan on more of a long-term basis. Typically, U.S. firms plan three to five years ahead for short-term results, and their current losses to competitors are proof of the lack of effectiveness of this approach.

Thomas Mandel, a consultant at Business Future Program at SRI International in California, estimates that the demand for advice on how to plan and develop business strategies beyond the year 2000 is growing at a rate of 20 percent per year. The main reason for this growth, Mandel says, is that, "In such an unstable environment, people get anxious." The antidote to anxiety is long-term planning, which requires the cultivation of what one futurist calls "the art of conjecture."[45]

The local government can also influence an international firm's long-term planning.

The role of the government in a firm's planning process can also be a major factor to contend with in the business world. In countries such as India, the array of government regulations and bureaucracies is very large and must be considered in a foreign investor's planning process.

■ *Organizing*

Adaptability and flexibility are essential elements of today's organizational structures.

The way in which managers organize U.S. companies so that they can compete successfully on a global basis is also going to require a major overhaul. The rate of change is accelerating so quickly that a U.S. organization must be designed to adjust and adapt to an alteration in the business environment very quickly and easily, regardless of its location. Organizing for this kind of change sometimes resembles total chaos rather than a nice, tightly controlled business operation.

Years ago, when a firm decided to compete on a global basis, management usually set up "clones" of itself in foreign countries. This style of international management is becoming quite obsolete because it fails to utilize all of the firm's capabilities worldwide.[46]

The new international management model organizes all of the divisions of a company into one company worldwide. For instance, when Whirlpool Corporation purchased the $1 billion European appliance manufacturer N. V. Phillips in 1989, corporate management transformed the two companies into one large global firm. As a result, the new Whirlpool set the pace and the price structure for the global appliance industry.

However, new products may still need some variations to accommodate special local market needs worldwide. If product-development specialists from every country in the company are consulted, common basic models can be designed that utilize the best product technologies and manufacturing processes. For example, Whirlpool recently won a contest sponsored by a group of U.S. utility companies for developing a new, super-efficient, chlorofluorocarbon-free refrigerator. The developing of this new product was worldwide. The insulation technology came from Whirlpool's European affiliates; the compressor technology from its Brazilian affiliates; and the manufacturing and design expertise from its U.S. affiliates.[47]

The management of an international firm must also create a whole new organizational style that is extremely responsive to foreign customers, employees, and suppliers. This organizational style is becoming popular in the United States as well. For example, at the Campbell Soup plant in Maxton, North Carolina, virtually every employee has been trained in Deming's statistical process-control methods (to be discussed in Chapter 13). The business then utilizes self-managed teams that meet with vendors and set their own schedules. These teams even propose capital expenditures, complete with internal rates of return. For example, one team was allowed to purchase a new $112,000 machine to process celery, which has a 30-percent rate of return; a 16-percent increase in productivity resulted in one year.[48]

Obviously, international organizational structures must redesign their communication systems to reflect the decision-making process, with increased amounts of participation at all levels, increased flexibility to respond to rapid changes in the business environment, and instituted control procedures that vary from very loose to strict control. Perhaps the toughest job facing international managers is to realize that they will have to manage differently in a foreign country if they are going to be as successful abroad as they are at home.

> Whatever direction the organizational structure takes, it must be acceptable to the employees.

Every person in every country feels that his or her way of doing business is right. The only way to make the entire company more efficient is to show management why and how the company—and everyone in it—benefits from this new organizational style. To do this, top management must communicate with employees continuously and get them involved so they can see the results first-hand. There must also be financial incentives and other "rewards" to help encourage all employees and managers to reach for new goals.

■ *Staffing*

Staffing is a critical function of any organization. Management must realize that no matter where in the world their firm is doing business, competitors can replicate its technology, copy its products, generate large sources of capital, and even duplicate its marketing programs. The one true difference between competing firms is the quality of their human resources.

> Labor laws may be quite different in a foreign country.

Top management is going to have to do a better job of selecting highly skilled managers and employees and developing them to their utmost potential. Only then will a firm be able to gain a true long-term competitive edge. When staffing overseas, the management of a firm must be aware of the national labor laws. For example, managers at Findley Adhesives, Inc., in Wauwatosa, Wisconsin, found the company was required to pay a Swedish employee three months severance pay after he was fired from its plant in Sweden.[49]

> The question of whether to send American managers abroad or to hire foreign managers is not easy to answer.

The question of whether to send an American manager abroad or to hire a foreign national for the position can also be a difficult one. It is always helpful to have a manager in charge of a foreign business who is well-known to the parent company, but there usually is a price to be paid for this arrangement. Most firms must offer salary incentives and cost-of-living adjustments, which can be very expensive. The Allen Bradey Company estimates these costs at $200,000 per year.[50] Also, about one-quarter of all managers who are sent abroad experience personal problems that cause them to cut short their overseas assignments.[51] In a recent survey of 50 Fortune 500 firms, it was found that companies selected employees for assignments abroad on the basis of their technical expertise 90 percent of the time. However, the personal characteristics that show the highest success rate overseas are cultural sensitivity, interpersonal skills, adaptability, flexibility, previous overseas experience, and interest.[52]

Hiring a native or a foreign national to run a company abroad is a good way to acquire knowledge about the local market in question. The main problem here is how to attract a competent national, especially if the firm is not very large or particularly well known.[53] Despite this problem, many human-resource experts in international staffing agree that it is better for most firms to send only a few expatriates to develop local talent. This reduces costs and leads to fewer cross-cultural problems.

> A firm's domestic hiring procedures may not be effective in a foreign country.

Finally, hiring foreign nationals may be quite difficult for American employers. Some countries require that a certain percentage of foreign nationals make up the labor force of an international firm. Some countries, like Russia, have labor shortages due to declining birth rates. Also, it is difficult to find trained or educated employees in some countries.

■ Leading

> The managers of a new international organization must consider the culture of a country when selecting a leader.

Good leadership is an extremely important attribute if a business firm is going to be competitive, much less dominate foreign markets. First and foremost, the managers of the new international organization must realize that the particular leadership style that motivates employees to honestly commit themselves to the firm varies tremendously, depending on the culture of the foreign country. To generate this type of commitment, management must

■ Know what style of leadership the employees expect and what style they are willing to accept. In France, for example, managers tend to be quite Napoleonic and discourage informal relations among employees. In contrast, Italian managers tend to be quite flexible and view informal employee networks as very important. German managers tend to "go by the book" and are usually quite regimented.[54] Whatever management style is employed, it must be acceptable to the employees.

■ Recognize that the type of employee-incentive system used in the United States is typically not as effective in Europe or Japan. Most employees in these countries feel that additional economic incentives, such as bonuses, are not as important as the provision of a good, stable place of employment that offers competitive salary and benefits packages.

■ Encourage employees to accept participative management in the "right spirit." Employee participation in managerial decisions is essential only in some countries, including Japan, Sweden, and the United States. Managers should carefully suggest or request that employees help to implement a particular management approach and take an honest interest in their attitudes and views. Participative management can help to develop team spirit and make the solution to a problem everybody's idea.[55]

Employee participation must be very carefully implemented if it is to be effective.

The effectiveness of leadership is clearly shown in the case of Jaguar, the British automobile manufacturer. In the early 1980s, Jaguar was in trouble in the marketplace. The relationship between management and the employees was so poor that managers did not even dare to go onto the production floor without formally going through union channels first. Then Jaguar brought in new leadership in the form of a chief executive officer named John Egan.

In a desperate bid for survival, Egan went to the employees and explained the current problems at Jaguar and what management was planning to do to try and solve them. But most important, he asked for their help and their input. Egan established weekly briefings to keep communication channels open and used films to demonstrate to employees what problems customers and dealers were complaining about. He also cut back on the number of inspectors to try to show the employees that he had faith in their ability to solve these problems on their own. Finally, new bonus schemes linked to productivity were instituted as well as a new attitude on the part of managers toward the employees.

The results have been truly remarkable. Manager-employee relations are now very cordial. Today, Jaguar is the number-two selling European import, second only to Mercedes in the U.S. automobile market.[56]

■ Controlling

Internal self-control is the new way to control an operation.

A new type of control system is required as a company becomes more and more involved in global competition. When faced with shorter product life cycles worldwide and other environmental changes, control in any country is eventually going to have to come from within the individual employees. Since true control always comes down to this, managers must have an organizational control system in place that is understandable and acceptable to their employees. Although the items that are most tightly controlled will vary, the basic control system described in Chapter 9 is workable in most countries.

For example, at Nixdorf AG, a German computer manufacturer, lower-level managers are allowed to "wheel and deal" as they like as long as they stay within general corporate guidelines. As the head of their human-resource department puts it, "We are a strongly market-oriented company . . . operating in a competitive environment that has extremely short time spans for decision making."

Managers at Nixdorf need and are given some freedom to decide how much to pay a new employee, based on their need and the value of the person to the company. Also, managers are encouraged to take initiatives without fear of recrimination. One example of this occurred during the 1970s, when a group of managers and employees tried to design a new electronic learning system for the state-run school system. The project lost $2.5 million before it was shut down, but no jobs were lost because of the failure.[57]

■ PROBLEM AREAS FACED BY A FIRM ENTERING THE INTERNATIONAL MARKETPLACE

Even though international and global markets appear very inviting and in some cases almost mandatory, all firms must be aware of the dangers and potential problems. Basically, there are four potential problem areas.[58]

There are some dangers involved with entering a foreign market.

1. The first area of concern is selecting the right market. Once a firm decides to enter a particular market, there is always the danger that one or several external environmental concerns will change. Political changes, economic changes, shifts in demand away from the firm's product, new competitors entering the market, and even a lack of acceptance by the local market are only a few of the problems that can make market selection a complete disaster.

New competitors are coming from unexpected places.

2. New competitors can emerge from a number of places. For example, Malaysia is now the world's third largest producer of semiconductors. Even in the United States, we find unexpected competitors like the Hungarian buses that service the people and streets of Portland, Oregon.

3. Economic reforms may take a lot longer than expected and may never be as successful as hoped. Dealing with structural barriers of all types can be tremendously difficult. Many eastern European countries, including Russia, have very poor infrastructures by U.S. standards. Things that Americans take for granted—adequate water and sewage installations, highways and transportation systems, and even telephone systems—may be totally inadequate for some firms to establish a business in a particular country.

Infrastructures in a country include all utility, transportation, and communication systems.

4. The last, and possibly the greatest, risk area is getting into the marketplace too late. Japan is already the biggest foreign investor in Southeast Asia, and Germany is the leader in eastern Europe. You can be sure that neither of these countries are going to voluntarily relinquish their leadership roles or make it easy for new investors to come into their "new" countries.

THINK ABOUT IT

1. One reason the United States is currently playing catch-up to foreign competitors is the fact that the nation had little or no foreign competition from the end of World War II until approximately 1970.

2. The international marketplace is changing rapidly. A trade-free world may be right around the corner. If this does occur, the United States will face competition like the country has never seen before.

3. Not every firm should be directly involved in the international marketplace, but international markets do affect all firms to some degree.

4. Although the United States is still the current leader in most service areas, the nation could easily lose its leadership position here just as it has in many product areas.

5. Going into a foreign country and establishing any kind of business always represents a certain degree of risk.

6. Cultural differences may be very subtle and even difficult to identify, but their meanings are often profound.

7. Because of the emerging international management scene, businesses are going to have to change the ways in which they currently manage in all five of the basic management-function areas.

LOOKING BACK

We have examined international management and the increase in global competition as barriers to trade are removed worldwide. Now let's review the learning objectives for this chapter and briefly summarize several highlights for each of them.

Understand how the field of business has evolved into a truly global scene.

As trade barriers continue to disappear worldwide, intense competition can only be expected to continue. Companies and firms in the United States are experiencing a lot of new competition in the service industry as technology makes these services just a phone call away from anywhere in the modern world.

Identify some of the major changes in international markets.

The first major change involves a shift in many product areas away from U.S. dominance and toward foreign dominance. The second major change involves the formation of regional trading areas which have no trade barriers. Finally, the world is witnessing massive changes in eastern Europe and Russia as they move their economies toward a free-enterprise system.

Examine how multinational firms have evolved.

Most firms enter the international marketplace by simply exporting goods or services to an agent or broker. The next step normally involves a licensure agreement in which certain rights are granted. Third, a manufacturing contract with a foreign manufacturer is set up. Joint ventures or partnership agreements are usually the next step, but wholly-owned subsidiaries are another alternative. Finally, a firm may take a global approach in the form of wholly-owned subsidiaries or global strategic partnerships.

Discuss global competition in the service industry.

Global competition in the service industry is growing rapidly. Japan and Europe have both made substantial investments in service-related areas, and all indications are that they will continue to invest even more.

Differentiate between cultural and environmental trends, and realize how they can impact the management of a foreign business.

Environmental differences can affect the way that a firm does business in a foreign country. In the political and legal environment, foreign countries have numerous laws that apply to foreign investors, and not many of them are favorable. In the cultural environment, language and gestures are two important areas of cultural difference that a firm must learn about and deal with on an on-going basis. In the economic environment, differences include average incomes, tax structures, inflation rates, and even currency exchange rates.

Find out how to apply American management principles to an international business world.

All five management functions must be adapted to a foreign environment.

    1. In terms of planning, firms must do more long-term planning and must consider environmental differences.

2. In terms of organizing, the new business structure must be acceptable to the work force. The degree of employee participation must be appropriate for the workers in a specific country.

3. In terms of staffing, the top managers of U.S. firms are going to have to do a better job of initially selecting both managers and employees. Local laws and regulations must be closely adhered to and known in advance.

4. In terms of leading, good leadership means honest, open communication with all workers and the use of incentive systems that are appropriate for the particular country. Most of all, the leadership style must be acceptable to the employees.

5. In terms of controlling, a firm's control system must be acceptable to workers and, in many cases, should even encourage some risk taking and innovative challenges.

Identify some definite problem areas that must be considered before a domestic firm becomes a multinational corporation.

First, the management of a firm must select the right market for its product and situation. Second, management must be aware that new competition can come from anywhere, not just from the major industrialized countries. Third, the economic reforms going on in less-developed countries may take an extremely long time to show results. Finally, being too late to enter a market can have disastrous consequences; a firm may be completely locked out of the competitive arena.

KEY TERMS

customer focus
domestic-market management
  approach
European Community (EC)
European Economic Community
  Agreement (EEC)
foreign agent (broker)
foreign exchange rate
global firm
global management approach
global strategic partnership
international business firm
joint venture (partnership)
licensure agreement
manufacturing contract
Maquiladora program
multinational firm

multinational management approach
nationalism
North American Free Trade
  Agreement (NAFTA)
protectionism
quota
regional trading area
subsidy
tariff
U.S./Canadian Free Trade Agreement
  (FTA)
vertical integration
wholly-owned subsidiaries
  (multinational and global)
World Trade Organization (formerly
  known as General Agreement on
  Tariffs and Trade or GATT)

1. What factors led to the U.S. decline in so many different product areas during the 1970s and 1980s?

2. What are the four key elements that U.S. companies must address if they are going to become more competitive internationally?

3. Why will most firms probably be involved in international markets, at least to some degree?

4. What are the different forms of international management?

5. How important is the service industry to international markets?

6. What are the three main areas of environmental differences that a firm must consider before doing business in a foreign country?

7. What impact has the international scene had on the way in which U.S. businesses manage their foreign firms?

8. Briefly, what kind of changes are managers going to have to make, in each of the five functional areas, when they start operating in a foreign country?

9. What are some of the general guidelines which most businesses will follow upon entering the international scene?

10. What are some of the real dangers that a business must be aware of before becoming an international firm?

CRITICAL THINKING INCIDENT 12.1

The Southern Fruit Drink Company

The Southern Fruit Drink Company is a well-established, family-owned southern firm that has been manufacturing fruit juices in Atlanta, Georgia, for over 70 years. During this time period, Southern has gradually increased the size of its distribution area until it currently includes virtually all of the major markets east of the Mississippi River. Top management has considered trying to enter markets west of the Mississippi but has never really had the excess capacity to produce enough of the company's products to service those markets. In approximately six months, however, that is all going to change when Southern's new plant in Orlando, Florida, comes on line.

The new plant will more than double Southern's capacity. The plant will also mass produce a brand new product called Southern Sparkle, which is a carbonated drink made up of several different fruit juices mixed together. Test market results in Atlanta indicate that this product will reach a whole new market segment. Southern Sparkle seems to appeal very strongly to younger, somewhat affluent people who think conventional orange or grapefruit juice is too boring. Consumers will pay a premium price for Southern

Sparkle, compared to competitive carbonated fruit drinks, all of which contain only one fruit juice.

Erin Monahan, the oldest daughter of Terry Monahan, the current CEO of Southern, has recently graduated from college with a degree in marketing. Erin is very interested in international markets—in particular, those in eastern European countries that have only recently opened up to foreign investors. She is convinced that Southern should forget about the West Coast of the United States for now and jump into the eastern European markets before someone else beats the company to them. Erin has accumulated all kinds of data related to these markets—everything from population growth to per-capita income. She believes that this market is wide open at this time. But if Southern doesn't move fast, some competitor will get in there and tie up the biggest retailers and distributors. If that happens Southern will, in effect, be locked out.

Erin is particularly excited about Southern's newest product, Southern Sparkle, and its potential impact on the eastern European markets. She feels that since eastern Europeans have never been exposed to a carbonated fruit drink, the novelty effect in and of itself will virtually guarantee the product's success.

Erin's father Terry is not so sure that entering an international market is the right move to take at this time. He thinks Southern should try to open up the western part of the United States first.

Discussion Questions

1. What are some specific factors that Terry should know before he agrees to Erin's proposal to enter international markets?

2. What are some reasons for and against marketing Southern in eastern Europe versus the western part of the United States?

3. Which market do you think Southern should attempt to enter? Why?

CRITICAL THINKING INCIDENT 12.2

Trail Rite Manufacturing Moves South

A little over three years ago, the top management of Trail Rite Manufacturing decided to move their complete manufacturing and assembly process to Mexico. Today, the firm faces possible bankruptcy.

For years, top managers at Trail Rite saw the firm's costs rise repeatedly as the labor union demanded higher and higher wages. At the same time, foreign competitors continued to lower their costs through automation and productivity increases that were truly remarkable. Trail Rite, based in Los Angeles, California, was the largest manufacturer of travel trailers in the western part of the United States. For many years, the company enjoyed a reputation as a manufacturer of high-quality travel trailers. Although Trail Rites' products were always priced above the market average, their quality allowed the company to maintain this price level.

Recently, however, two new competitors entered the market. Both of them provide high-quality products that are similar to Trail Rite's at substantially lower prices. One of the new competitors is from Canada; its plants are nonunion and the equipment in them is state-of-the-art. The second competitor, an American manufacturer located in Arizona, also has a nonunion labor force, and its labor rates are significantly lower than Trail Rite's. The Arizona competitor also has several subassemblies manufactured in Mexico; these inexpensive component parts are then shipped to the United States to be installed in the competitor's trailers. If Trail Rite did not figure out a way to lower its costs to compete with these new companies, it would soon be out of business.

With these thoughts in mind, Trail Rite's management made the decision to move its entire organization to a small town just north of Mexico City. At first, it looked like an excellent move. An abundant labor supply was willing to work for Trail Rite at one-tenth the wage rate in Los Angeles. Land on which to build the plant was readily available and reasonably priced. Both the local government and the Mexican federal government welcomed Trail Rite with open

arms. It was not until the plant was built and production had begun that the problems started to occur.

First, finding suppliers in Mexico that could reliably provide raw materials and finished component parts was almost impossible. In addition, the labor force was extremely unskilled and required massive amounts of training. Many workers could not read or write, so training manuals were useless. The workers also demanded a two-hour lunch break so that they could take a siesta and had very poor time-management habits. Absenteeism was double the American rate, and turnover was three times as high. The workers would either quit right on the spot or take two or three days off if a supervisor criticized them in any way. Needless to say, both production and quality at Trail Rite were taking a real beating.

The final blow came from the government. First, a new minimum-wage law was passed that tripled the wages of all employees who worked for a foreign firm. New tax laws were then passed that raised taxes on profits on a progressive scale that reached 90 percent at a ridiculously low figure. Finally, in an attempt to curb some of Mexico's monetary problems, the federal government devalued the peso by 75 percent; Trail Rite lost 75 percent of the value of its physical plant overnight. Trail Rite cannot just sell and get out of Mexico, yet staying simply appears to be a slower death sentence for the company.

Discussion Questions

1. What basic cultural, political, and economic factors did Trail Rite fail to foresee?

2. What options does Trail Rite have at this point in time?

3. What is your recommendation to the management of Trail Rite?

CRITICAL THINKING INCIDENT 12.3

First Quality Tools Goes Global

First Quality Tools is an old, established midwestern company that is a good example of a small-business success story. The name First Quality built a very high quality image, and every tool the manufacturer sold was made right here in the U.S.A.

All of this began to change just a few years ago when First Quality started exporting to European distributors and quickly found its foreign sales growing faster than its sales in the United States. In fact, foreign sales amounted to over 30 percent of total sales in 1993, and foreign sales are now growing at almost twice the rate of domestic sales.

Although it may seem easy for First Quality to simply continue to export tools to international markets, the company's new chairman, Emilio L. Carlsson, does not feel that this is a good approach. Emilio states, "Factories should be close to the customers they serve. This eliminates tariffs and, more important, gives the impression that the manufacturers are local companies. It also reduces delivery time and allows us to capture new manufacturing techniques that we can use in our factories back home."

As an example of how beneficial this management approach can be, Emilio points to the new "cold-forming" process that First Quality acquired when it purchased this technology from National Hand Tool in Taiwan. The process significantly reduces time and waste during the production of forged metal products, such as sockets. The cold-forming process is now used in all of First Quality's plants in the United States.

While there are some advantages to purchasing existing factories abroad, there are also some obvious disadvantages. One factory that the management of First Quality considered purchasing in England looked very promising at first, but it did not look so promising when the real costs were analyzed.

Another problem that First Quality faces in the international marketplace is that not all foreign countries agree on a particular tool design. For example, in England, customers want saws that have wooden handles and very "hard" teeth; in France, they want saws with plastic handles and rather "soft" teeth that can be sharpened with a file when desired. First Quality is currently trying to satisfy both markets with a compromise saw that has a plastic handle and "hard" teeth.

Finally, many members of First Quality's management team have literally been "born and raised" in the company. They know that if the firm's foreign investments were diverted to U.S. plants, they would be creating jobs for Americans. In fact, a new, increasing trend is that many tools that used to be produced in the United States and exported to foreign markets are now being imported to the United States from foreign factories. Some First Quality managers are wondering how long it will be before their jobs are exported, too.

Discussion Questions

1. What are the pros and cons of establishing factories in foreign countries?

2. At what point do you think a firm should definitely consider putting a factory in a foreign country?

3. What is your opinion of First Quality's compromise between the two types of saws preferred by French and English customers?

NOTES

1. Thomas A. Stewart, "The New American Century—Where We Stand," *Fortune* (Spring/Summer 1991), p. 13.

2. Joseph Spiers, "Exports Will Rise Again," *Fortune* (October 18, 1993), pp. 19–20.

3. Stewart, "The New American Century," p. 14.

4. Howard Banks, "America's New Trading Partners," *Forbes* (November 8, 1993), p. 35.

5. Tom Peters, "Closed Minds Can't Open Markets," *U.S. News & World Report* (March 3, 1986), p. 59.

6. Nicole Sneed, "Trade Pact Signed," *The Bradenton Herald* (April 3, 1993), p. A8.

7. "Succeeding in International Markets," *Nations Business* 80 (March 1992).

8. Bob Davis, "Trade Pact Is Set by 117 Nations, Slashing Tariffs, Subsidies Globally," *The Wall Street Journal* (December 16, 1993), p. A4.

9. John Templeman et al., "One Big Currency—and One Big Job Ahead," *Business Week* (December 23, 1991), pp. 40–42.

10. Peter Gumbel, "Denmark Approves European Unity

Pact," *The Wall Street Journal* (May 19, 1993), p. A10.

11. Robert Shapiro, "Building 'Fortress Europe'?" *U.S. News & World Report* (February 29, 1988), p. 42.

12. Gregory F. Treverton, "The Year of European (Dis)Unification," *Current History* **91** (November 1992): 353–57.

13. Monroe W. Karmin, "Unhappy Birthday for a Free-Trade Pact," *U.S. News & World Report* (February 5, 1990), pp. 54–59.

14. Ibid.

15. Peter C. Newman, "The Challenge from Mexico," *MacLeans* (June 25, 1990), p. 68.

16. Robert Rankin, Jennifer Lin, and Christopher Marquis, "House Approves NAFTA," *The Bradenton Herald* (November 18, 1993), pp. A1–A4.

17. John Rutledge, "Economic Outlook," *U.S. News & World Report* (May 13, 1991), p. 58.

18. Tim Carrington, "Trade Policy Stumbles on Rich vs. Poor States," *The Wall Street Journal* (June 21, 1993), p. A1.

19. Andrew Popper, "Eastern Europe Tries to Stoke Up Its Fire Sale," *Business Week* (October 21, 1991), pp. 52–53.

20. Ibid.

21. Jeffrey M. Hertzfeld, "Joint Ventures: Saving the Soviets from Perestroika," *Harvard Business Review* **69** (January/February 1991): 80–90.

22. Ibid.

23. Ibid.

24. Jeremy Main, "Making Global Alliances Work," *Fortune* (December 17, 1990), pp. 121–26.

25. Peter Coy, "Dialing for Dollars, Far from Home," *Business Week* (January 13, 1992), p. 99.

26. Howard V. Perlmutter and David A. Heenan, "Cooperate to Compete Globally," *Harvard Business Review* **64** (March/April 1986): 136–52.

27. John Rutledge, "Economic Outlook," *U.S. News & World Report* (October 21, 1991), p. 72.

28. Ronald K. Shelp, "Redirecting North American Trade and Industrial Policy," *Vital Speeches of the Day*, delivered before the Retail Council of Canada, Toronto, Canada (April 7, 1986).

29. "U.S. Firms with the Biggest Foreign Revenues," *Forbes* (July 23, 1990), p. 362.

30. Shelp, "Redirecting North American Trade and Industrial Policy."

31. Stewart, "The New American Century," p. 20.

32. Sylvia Nasar, "America Still Reigns in Services," *Fortune* (June 5, 1989), pp. 64–65.

33. Ibid.

34. Stewart, "The New American Century," p. 22.

35. Thomas A. Stewart, "How to Manage in the New Era," *Fortune* (January 15, 1990), pp. 58–68.

36. Spencer Hayden, "A Word from the Managers: Execs Discuss Problems of International Business," *Management Review* (September 1989): 35–38.

37. Ibid.

38. *The Bradenton Herald* (January 25, 1992), p. A1.

39. Hayden, "A Word from the Managers," pp. 35–38.

40. Ford S. Worthy, "When Somebody Wants a Pay Off," *Fortune* (Pacific Rim 1989), pp. 117–18.

41. "Management in America—Do It My Way," *The Economist* (November 24, 1990), pp. 75–76.

42. John Pfeiffer, "How Not to Lose the Trade Wars by Cultural Gaffes," *Smithsonian* **18** (January 1988): 145–53.

43. Rosemary Armao, "A Novel Collection of Business Blunders," *The (Ft. Pierce) News Tribune* (October 28, 1980), p. A8.

44. Mark L. Goldstein, "Just Managing Won't Be Enough," *International Management* (January 1986).

45. Lawrence G. Tapp and Lawson Mardon, "Europe 1992: Canadians Get Ready!" *Business Quarterly* (Summer 1990): 10–12.

46. Anne B. Fisher, "Is Long-Range Planning Worth It?," *Fortune* (April 23, 1990), pp. 281–84.

47. Keith Alexander, "Borderless Management," *Business Week* (May 23, 1994), pp. 24–26.

48. Regina Fazio Maruco, "The Right Way to Go Global," *Harvard Business Review* (March/April 1994): 135–45.

49. Stewart, "The New American Century," p. 22.

50. Michael Selz, "Hiring the Right Manager Overseas," *The Wall Street Journal* (February 27, 1990).

51. Charlene Marmer Solomon, "Staff Selection Impacts Global Success," *Personnel Journal* (January 1994): 88–97.

52. Selz, "Hiring the Right Manager Overseas."

53. Solomon, "Staff Selection Impacts Global Success," pp. 88–97.

54. "The Business of Europe," *The Economist* (December 7, 1991), p. 64.

55. "Is Traditional Management Dead?" *International Management* (January 1986): 22–25.

56. Ibid.

57. Ibid.

58. Stewart, "How to Manage in the New Era," pp. 58–72.

▮ S UGGESTED READINGS

Browning, E. S. "Computer Chip Project Brings Rivals Together, but the Cultures Clash." *The Wall Street Journal* (May 3, 1994), p. A1.

Cohen, Warren. "Exporting Know-How." *U.S. News & World Report* (August 30/September 6, 1993), pp. 53–58.

Farrell, Christopher. "America Needs Protection from the Protectionists." *Business Week* (February 10, 1992), p. 31.

Gibson, Richard. "Gerber Missed the Boat in Quest to Go Global, So It Turned to Sandoz." *The Wall Street Journal* (May 24, 1994), pp. A1–A8.

Harbrecht, Douglas, and Susan B. Garland. "Will NAFTA's Big Brass Band Ever Get in Step?" *Business Week* (October 4, 1993), p. 34.

Hofheinz, Paul. "Europe's Tough New Managers." *Fortune* (September 6, 1993), pp. 111–15.

Mamis, Robert A. "You Had to Be There." *INC.* (January 1994): 69–70.

Neff, Robert. "Turning the Screw on Japan." *Business Week* (April 11, 1994), p. 28.

Peak, Martha H. "Developing an International Style of Management." *Management Review* (February 1991): 32–35.

Rossant, John. "The Perils of Privatization." *Business Week* (May 16, 1994), pp. 48–49.

CHAPTER 13

PRODUCTION/OPERATIONS MANAGEMENT

■ LEARNING OBJECTIVES

This chapter focuses on the crucial importance of establishing effective operations management in a production or service setting. Foreign competitors are present in virtually all goods and service industries. It is absolutely necessary for the United States to produce high-quality, low-cost goods and services in the most efficient way possible in order to survive in today's marketplace. The learning objectives for this chapter are to:

- Define the role and importance of operations management.
- Examine the pros and cons of applying production/operations management principles to the service industry.
- Describe how strategic decisions in operations management have changed due to increased competition.
- Outline the basic steps involved in establishing a new product or service facility.
- Describe how to control production/productivity, quality, and inventories.
- Explain how scheduling, purchasing, and cost management are accomplished.

■ CHAPTER OUTLINE

THE REAL WORLD *Saturn—A Production-Management Model*

The Saturn, manufactured by General Motors (GM), may be the biggest revolution in the auto industry since Henry Ford introduced the assembly line. After eight years of planning and $3.5 billion of steady investment, the first Saturn automobile came off the final assembly line at the Saturn complex in Spring Hill, Tennessee, in the early 1990s. What makes the Saturn so different from other cars? The automobile's appearance or performance is not what is so sensational. It is how Saturn was initially planned and designed and how it is now produced on the assembly line that make it different and revolutionary in the U.S. automobile industry.

Eight years earlier, when the Saturn Corporation was in the initial planning stages for the Saturn, GM desperately needed to find an automobile that could compete with the Japanese compact and subcompact cars. General Motors was steadily losing its U.S. market share to this foreign competition and began to realize that drastic

changes in management and production were necessary.

First, GM acquired Electronic Data Systems (EDS), a computer service located in Texas, to help plan and set up a computerized system. Next, GM set up a joint venture with Fanuc LTD, a Japanese robot company, to perfect a robot system. Most importantly, the management of GM set up a joint venture with the United Auto Workers (UAW) to assist in getting the job done.

The joint venture with the UAW was perhaps the most revolutionary managerial change at Saturn. In all other U.S. automobile manufacturing plants, management seemed to have an adversarial relationship with their assembly-line workers. The Saturn Corporation set out to change that focus. In 1985, GM and the UAW signed a labor-management agreement unlike any other in the United States. The terms follow.

- Each UAW member was promised a salary that was at least equal to the average annual earnings of hourly paid workers at other automobile plants.

- 20 percent of this wage would be contingent on meeting productivity and quality targets set jointly by the company and the union.

- Workers who exceeded these targets would receive bonuses.

- Initial training of 300 to 700 hours and 12 days of additional training per year would be available to workers.

- UAW members and GM members would be "full partners," and all decisions—from designing parts to choosing dealers—would be made by consensus.

By the time the Saturn automobile came off the assembly line, UAW workers and management were working
—Continued

General Motors unveiled its Saturn division in 1991—and new ways to produce cars and structure company management.

DEFINING PRODUCTION/OPERATIONS MANAGEMENT

Every organization produces some type of product or service by taking organizational inputs, transforming them in some way, and coming up with outputs in the form of goods and services. This operations management process is outlined in Figure 13–1.

Production management is the management of the production of tangible products.

Production management describes the management techniques utilized by firms that make only tangible products. Since, in reality, the service industry makes intangible products, the term **operations management** has evolved to describe how both product and service industries are managed during the basic operations management process.

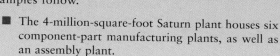

together. At that time, only a few grievances were reported to be on file.

In addition to these revolutionary changes in labor-management relations, changes in the production of the Saturn were also somewhat innovative. Some examples follow.

- The 4-million-square-foot Saturn plant houses six component-part manufacturing plants, as well as an assembly plant.

- A computerized production system extends from the dealer to the production floor.

- Flexible manufacturing methods have permitted many changes to be made on the assembly lines and are expected to cut assembly-line time from 55 hours to 21 hours per car.

- Robots are being used to weld and install windshields, rear windows, wheels, and doors.

- Parts to be assembled are purchased "just in time" for new production runs, thereby eliminating stockpiling costs.

Saturn's advertising slogan is "A New Car—A New Way of Doing Business." So what has this "new way of doing business" done for Saturn? Like many new cars, Saturn had a rocky start. In its first year, 1991, Saturn built just 50,000 cars—one-third of GM's original projection. So far, the overall statistics for Saturn look good, and it appears that General Motors is beginning to reap the benefits of its investment in the model. Saturn's sales have fluctuated, but the general trend is favorable. Customer satisfaction continues to increase. The J. D. Power and Associates 1995 Customer Satisfaction Index rated Saturn in first place, ahead of all other American and foreign cars. This is the fourth year in a row that Saturn owners have ranked within the top four in this survey.

Much of the customer satisfaction with Saturn can be attributed to the special treatment General Motors offers to Saturn buyers. Many dealers give new Saturn buyers a big send-off cheer and invite them back for weekend barbecues and car clinics. To top this off, in June 1994, Saturn went so far as to have a homecoming for all Saturn owners at its manufacturing plant in Spring Hill. Some 44,000 Saturn owners showed up. To General Motors, this was a round of applause.

It appears that Saturn is beginning to look toward a promising future, and GM is indeed watching. The manufacture of General Motor's new Olds Aurora, which is slotted to become the step-up model for Saturn owners, incorporates many of the production techniques learned at Saturn. If all goes well, Saturn could truly be the model for automobile production management in the future.

ADAPTED FROM: Alan L. Adler, "Saturn Winning Back Import Buyers, Aims for Profit in '94," *The Bradenton Herald* (November 1, 1993), A9; Brian S. Akre, "Saturn Owners Love Their Cars," *The Bradenton Herald* (June 16, 1995): A7; William J. Cook, "Ringing in Saturn," *U.S. News & World Report* (October 22, 1990), pp. 51–54; Beverly Geber, "Saturn's Grand Experiment," *Training* (June 1992): 27–35; Kathleen Kerwin, "Forget Woodstock—These Folks Are Headin' to Spring Hill," *Business Week* (June 27, 1994), p. 36; Kathleen Kerwin, "GM's Aurora," *Business Week* (March 21, 1994), pp. 89–90; Ross Laver, "Joining Hands," *McClean's* (April 15, 1991), pp. 46–47; Dan McCosh, "Inside Saturn," *Popular Science* 237 (August 1990): 62–65; "Saturn SC," *Consumer Reports* 55 (July 1992): 427; Tony Swan, "Saturn Story," *Popular Mechanics* (October 9, 1991), pp. 38–39; David Woodruff, "At Saturn, What Workers Want Is . . . Fewer Defects," *Business Week* (December 2, 1991), pp. 117–18; David Woodruff and others, "Saturn," *Business Week* (August 17, 1992), pp. 85–91.

Operations management includes all three levels of management.

Operations management includes all five of the basic management functions. These functions exist at all three levels of management, as described in Chapter 1. How effectively these functions are carried out in the production or service operation is the main emphasis of this chapter.

THE ROLE AND IMPORTANCE OF OPERATIONS MANAGEMENT

Like never before, the survival of American industries is under attack from foreign competition. Many U.S. factories and service organizations that were once successful businesses have closed their doors. Managers of today's production

■ **FIGURE 13–1** Simplified Operations Management Processes

INPUTS
Raw materials, labor, equipment, etc.

TRANSFORMATION PROCESS
Assembling, analyzing, testing, etc.

OUTPUTS
Products or services produced

PRODUCT EXAMPLE

DRESS MANUFACTURER

Patterns, cloth, thread, zippers, buttons, machines that cut and sew and install buttons, labor to run the machines, management to organize and oversee everything, and a facility to do it all in.

Materials are purchased, designs are drawn, fabric is cut and sewn, zippers and buttons are installed, product is checked for quality, boxed, and shipped to stores.

A woman's dress

SERVICE EXAMPLE

BANKING SERVICES

Tellers, managers, bookkeepers, loan officers, desks, teller windows, funds, computers, telephones, and a facility in which to operate.

Funds are taken into various types of accounts, loans are carefully analyzed and extended or rejected, investments are made, and various services are provided.

Banking services in the form of loans, checking and savings accounts, etc.

and service firms face competition for the consumer's dollar that is truly worldwide in virtually every area.

Competition is worldwide.

As all types of trade barriers begin to disappear, U.S. firms are entering a competitive arena that will force managers to devise innovative products and services. To survive, American companies must utilize state-of-the-art technology to produce products and services at the lowest possible costs and must maintain unheard of levels of product quality and customer service.

How badly have foreign producers hurt American industries? During the 1980s, the United States lost market shares in many basic industries, including the following:[1]

	PERCENT OF U.S. MARKET SHARE	
	1979	**1989**
■ Computers	94%	66%
■ Semiconductors	90	67
■ Machine tools	77	54
■ Color TV sets	92	74
■ Apparel	86	74

On top of this, even in the product areas, where American companies are holding their own, we are seeing an increasing influx of foreign parts.

Japan outspent the United States for the first time in new plant and equipment in 1989 and may emerge as the world's top industrial power by the year 2000 or soon thereafter.[2] For a long time, American businesses believed that the advanced growth of industry in Japan was due to the country's culture, strong central-government support, and increased use of technology, which has lowered the costs and increased the quality of Japanese products. However, the real source of industrial growth in Japan can now be seen to be a well-designed strategy that is based on the use of excellent manufacturing and management processes.[3] This fact has been verified over and over again, as we see Japanese companies like Sony utilize American workers in their plants in the United States. The answer to the problems facing U.S. industries seems clear: either learn to manage your firms more efficiently or you will be eliminated.

Good management is the answer to foreign competition.

The question could be asked, "Can *anyone* match the Japanese in terms of efficiency and product quality?" The answer is a resounding *yes*, as the following example illustrates.

At the Ford Taurus plant in Atlanta, Georgia, workers are producing cars at the rate of one new Taurus every 17.6 worker-hours. This far and away exceeds any European plant, which averages 35 worker-hours per car, or the average General Motors (GM) plant, which averages 21 worker-hours per car. Instead, the workers at the Ford Taurus plant come extremely close to matching the typical Japanese plant, which averages 17-worker hours per car. How did Ford achieve this tremendous rate of productivity at its Taurus plant without sacrificing quality? Here are some of the contributing factors.

- Morale is extremely high at the plant, and a very close working relationship exists between management and the workers.

- Joint committees work on problems together and receive monetary incentives if they contribute cost-saving ideas.

- All employees participate in the plant's plan, and job security increases as the cars sell to satisfied customers who make repeat purchases.

- Upward communication is very evident. Through a number of employee suggestions, costs have been decreasing at the rate of 5–6 percent per year, which not only saves the plant money but, in many cases, also improves product quality.

- Workers have positive attitudes both toward the product and toward management, which is obviously the main reason for Ford's success at this plant.[4]

As this example illustrates, foreign competition can be met and even beaten, but *only* if operations management is carried out very carefully and, most important, with the assistance and cooperation of the work force.

In operations management, the planning process consists of making a number of critical decisions. These decisions ultimately lead to the development of a master plan from which the firm will operate. Decisions are made at the strategic level first, then at the tactical level, and finally at the operational level. This process is basically the same for a product-oriented or a service-oriented firm. The total planning process is illustrated in Figure 13–2.

FIGURE 13–2 The Planning Process in Operations Management

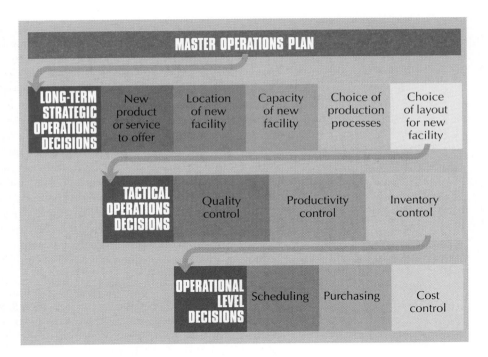

OPERATIONS MANAGEMENT IN THE SERVICE INDUSTRY

One main way for a company to succeed in the service field is for management to identify and constantly monitor the degree to which customers are satisfied with the benefits they receive when they purchase the firm's services. Unlike products, services are not tangible. The *benefit* of the service is really what a service company offers to its customers.

The service industry, although it is very large and continues to grow, is in trouble in terms of the consistency of the quality of the services—and therefore the benefits—that it offers. Since services cannot be inventoried and must be produced on request, some inconsistencies in quality are to be expected. However, a service firm must determine what *range* of quality is acceptable to it and to its customers. To do this, a firm must communicate with its customers on a regular basis.

The basic mass-production, service-industry model places the least emphasis on the people who deliver the services. This traditional model stresses technology and cost-cutting programs in every area of operation. The end result has been the creation of an entire industry full of jobs that are usually so simple and boring that they could be done by almost anyone, regardless of intelligence, experience, or training. These jobs often pay poorly, offer few benefits, and, for the most part, are dead-end jobs. The results of creating jobs of this nature are clear: large employee turnover and excessive absenteeism, which lead to high customer dissatisfaction and flat or falling sales and profits.

A new model for service organizations that has produced some excellent results places a new emphasis on the ways in which employees are treated and on the value of good customer service. This new model

■ Makes large investments in training employees

Why is the service industry in trouble?

A new service model emphasizes employee treatment and customer service.

Entrepreneur Rachel Borish turned a service industry job (making brownies) into her own successful business.

■ Employs extensive recruiting and hiring practices to attract able, trustworthy employees

■ Uses technology to support front-line employees, not to replace them

■ Links compensation to performance

■ Hires supervisors who communicate, coach, and develop employees and do not just monitor them

The payoff for the service firm is that well-trained, well-compensated employees perform better on the job. They need less supervision, increase customer loyalty and satisfaction, and reduce turnover and absenteeism costs significantly.

Taco Bell is a good example of a service organization that has adopted this new philosophy of service management. Between 1988 and 1990, Taco Bell's sales grew 60 percent and its profits grew 25 percent—in sharp contrast to McDonald's, which has earned profits of less than 6 percent during the same time period. Here are some of the reasons why.

■ Taco Bell emphasizes servicing customers, not manufacturing meals. Its food-preparation process has been automated; employees now only assemble the product, thereby eliminating long hours of chopping and cooking.

■ Taco Bell's managers have been freed from doing 15 hours of paperwork per week. They are told to communicate with and support employees, not just to direct and control them.

■ Managers spend more than 50 percent of their time training and developing Taco Bell employees.

■ Managers are eligible to earn bonuses of up to 225 percent of the industry average salary, and the paychecks of front-line workers at Taco Bell are typically above the industry average.

■ The recruitment and selection procedures at Taco Bell are designed to attract employees who value teamwork and responsibility.

- Individual managers are given much more authority and freedom to run their Taco Bell restaurants.

- Store managers are expected to spend significant amounts of time communicating with Taco Bell customers in order to model good service to employees and to get in touch with how customers feel about the service and products they are receiving.[5]

No single strategy works effectively in every service organization. However, there are numerous examples of firms that put their faith in the belief that able, satisfied, front-line employees are the keys to sales and profits in the service industry.

STRATEGIC DECISIONS IN OPERATIONS MANAGEMENT

At this time, refer back to the long-term strategic operations shown in Figure 13–2. As you can see, if both product and service organizations are going to survive, let alone grow, their managers must know the answers to the following strategic operations management questions.

- What products and services will be in demand in the future?

- What kind of resource inputs will be needed to produce these products or services?

- How should the resources be organized and managed in order to produce these products or services as efficiently as possible?

- What will the competitive products or services look like in the future?

Employees can be a manager's best source of the information he or she needs to make a strategic decision.

In what ways can firms get some assistance in answering these questions? First, in any firm, managers must realize that the best resources for these answers are their own employees. To succeed, top management must establish a solid communication system with its managers and their employees. The top managers of a firm should never limit themselves to consulting *only* with their managers and employees on strategic operations decisions. They must realize that employees and managers at all levels may be their best source of new ideas. Why? Simply because they are so close to the operation of the firm and naturally have a vested interest in its success.

One firm that has had success at managing in this manner is Tenneco, Inc., a large, diversified, energy-based company. Tenneco, which started in 1943, has doubled its income and assets nearly every five years and is currently one of the youngest firms among *Fortune*'s list of the 20 top U.S. companies.[6]

One of the things the top management of Tenneco does that is somewhat unique is to conduct brain-skill assessments to try to identify two different groups of "thinkers" among the firm's managers: "intuitive" managers and "thinking" managers. Intuitive managers are very good at generating new ideas. Thinking managers are very effective at evaluating the intuitive managers' ideas and pointing out solutions to problems or opportunities to pursue. At Tenneco, the two groups initially work separately. First, the intuitive group generates a list of possible ideas. Then the thinking group analyzes them. Finally, the two groups are brought back together to further refine and assess project ideas and problem solutions.

The Tenneco example certainly has merit. If a firm is really going to be successful, ideas need to be generated by all employees—not just by managers.

■ New Product and Service Development

How does management determine which new products to develop?

In strategic operations management, the first crucial question to answer is, What new products and/or services will be in demand in the marketplace in the short- or long-term future? For example, it is estimated that the world's current automobile manufacturers are going to have to trim product-development times by 25–33 percent and product-development costs by 50 percent to keep pace with the top automobile manufacturers five years from now.[7]

New small-market segments are forming faster and faster, and manufacturers as well as service providers must continually determine what products and services these new markets demand. To do this, a carefully planned, on-going communication system must be in place with a firm's customers. Without such a system, the firm will lose its market share to the competitors who identify these new needs and provide for them.

Product-development times are getting shorter and shorter.

How have competitors been able to achieve more rapid product-development times and low product-development costs? The answer appears to be that, for quite a while now, the design and development of new products in Japan has involved all departments of the firm in the process. Thus, as new products are designed, the marketing department participates heavily and the production department is there to ensure that the design of the new product is simplified in terms of the manufacturing process. Communication between the departments must be clear in order to minimize design and production problems. This procedure results in savings during the manufacturing process. It is estimated that the close coordination of departments in Japanese firms has reduced the hours that engineers require to develop new products between one-half to two-thirds that of their U.S. competitors.[8]

However, U.S. manufacturers are starting to close this gap. All three of the big U.S. automakers, along with companies like Honeywell and the Allen-Bradley Company, have scrapped the traditional method of new-product development. These U.S. companies and many more have developed parallel engineering programs, in which all of the departments work together to design

Product design is a crucial step in development and determines how products and services will be produced and maintained.

products that fit the consumers' needs and the company's manufacturing process. General Motors, for example, estimates that this new system has reduced engineering costs on the average project by 35 percent.[9]

Clearly, a totally integrated approach is needed that involves everyone in new product or service development. This approach should not only include all departments within the firm but also key suppliers. If they want to minimize problems, the managers of a firm need to communicate their ideas and concepts very clearly to everyone involved with the project, including their outside suppliers.

Finally, **computer-aided designs (CAD)** or other sophisticated computer programs are being used extensively in new-product development. The use of computers virtually eliminates the need to build numerous prototype models and allows the designer to actually view the new product three dimensionally on the computer screen.

Everyone must be involved in new-product development.

CONSIDER THIS

1. How is production management similar to operations management? Different from operations management?

2. What special problem does the service industry have that product industries do not have?

3. Describe the best way to conduct new-product planning. Who should be involved in this process?

■ *Determining Where to Locate a New Facility*

Once management has decided which new products or services the firm is going to produce, the next phase of the strategic operations management process is to plan for one or more new facilities, if they are indeed needed. A firm's existing facilities may be adequate to manufacture another product or provide an additional service. Management may only need to add another shift of employees, authorize current employees to work overtime, or subcontract significant portions of the manufacture of the new product or the provision of the new service out to vendors.

First, management must determine if the firm needs to expand existing facilities or build new ones to produce a new product or service.

If an entire new facility is needed, however, the following questions must be answered.

■ Where will the facility be located?

■ What size or capacity will the facility be?

■ What type of production process will be utilized?

■ What will the physical layout of the facility be?

Where to locate a new facility is a very important managerial decision. Many times, the type and/or nature of the product or service a firm produces will indicate some obvious choices. Several factors to consider are

Management must consider several points when planning a new facility.

1. The need to be close to a particular market or supplier

2. The need for inexpensive labor or energy

3. The availability of a large number of highly skilled employees

4. The importance of climate and general living conditions

5. Cost considerations in terms of land, construction, taxes, and so on.

Service organizations have found that the need to be extremely close to their markets is crucial. Also, many manufacturers of component parts find that their primary customers want parts to be delivered on a "just-in-time" (JIT) basis. (This concept will be covered in detail in the next section.) Their delivery schedules force these manufacturing firms to build new facilities extremely close to their main customers.

The cost of utilities has caused many manufacturers of large, durable products to select locations where the cost of energy is relatively inexpensive. For example, the Tennessee Valley Authority—a facility run by the federal government that provides inexpensive electricity to customers—was a major factor in GM's decision to locate its new Saturn plant in Tennessee.

If the cost or availability of certain types of labor is a main consideration, then a firm that produces products like clothing, which is a labor-intensive good, may decide to locate its manufacturing facilities in a foreign country where the cost of labor is cheaper. On the other hand, if highly skilled labor in a specific field is a critical component of the production process, then a location such as the Silicon Valley in California, which contains a large number of technically qualified employees in the computer industry, may be the best choice.

If none of these factors are of paramount importance, then the decision of where to locate a new facility may be made primarily on the basis of building and operating cost considerations or even climate and general living conditions. Normally, of course, some list of crucial criteria will be developed in which each factor is assigned appropriate weight, depending on its importance, and then various sites will be evaluated on the bases of these criteria. A good example of making a site selection follows.

Saturn's 4-million square foot facility site is the largest manufacturing complex that has ever been constructed at one time anywhere in the world. Why was Spring Hill, Tennessee—a small town of 1400 people—the site chosen for this huge complex?

The Saturn Corporation was looking for a place near a railroad that had water transportation and access to at least two interstate highways. Spring Hill met all of these requirements. Also, every day the factory would need 4 million gallons of fresh water, half a million pounds of steam, and 80 megawatts of power. Spring Hill is in a state where power and water are provided by the Tennessee Valley Authority at very inexpensive rates.

Tennessee also boasts a pro-business government, no state income tax on wages and salaries, and a hard-working labor force. Certainly, Saturn was influenced by these benefits.

Another selling point for Spring Hill was the fact that a large Nissan plant is located 30 miles away in Smyrna and the successful Bridgestone Tire Company is in La Vergne, which is 30 miles in another direction. These two Japanese companies have achieved unusually high productivity and quality rates in Tennessee, which surely would have impressed Saturn's management team.

Lastly, the Saturn facility required a considerable amount of real estate. Land in Spring Hill, Tennessee, is reasonably priced, which probably sealed the deal.[10]

■ *Determining the Size or Capacity of the New Facility*

How does management determine what size a new facility should be?

Once the location for a new facility has been selected, the size or capacity of the facility must be determined. This decision is based on the anticipated demand for the new product or service. It must be made as accurately as

Parker Hannifin carefully planned the location, size, and layout of its Tube Fittings Division in Brookville, OH.

possible to minimize costs. The need to expand or contract the facility in the future must also be assessed.

Demand estimates may be forecasted by employing a number of different methods. **Quantitative methods,** such as analyzing previous sales patterns for a trend, looking at economic indicators, or utilizing mathematical models, are based on known numeric data and are valuable if these data are available. **Qualitative methods** are often used when solid numeric data are not available. These methods are based on the judgment of people who have considerable knowledge in the area in question. The sales force, key executives, and suppliers can all provide valuable insights. It is important for managers to communicate as much information as possible to all of these people. Whenever possible, quantitative and qualitative methods are employed in conjunction to try to obtain the most accurate demand estimate possible.

Once top managers arrive at a good demand estimate, they can figure out how large a factory or restaurant or retail store needs to be to accommodate the demand. Although this sounds easy, demand for virtually all products and services fluctuates on an hourly, daily, or monthly basis, which makes the capacity decision much more difficult. Management must try to determine what size will generate the largest amount of sales or revenues and still minimize costs.

Quantitative data utilize known numeric facts.

Qualitative data utilize people's judgment.

■ *Determining How to Produce a Product or Service*

Process planning, or determining exactly how a product or service is going to be produced, is the third decision that management must make when planning a new facility. Such questions as what and how much equipment will be needed, how many of various types of workers will be needed, how the product or service will flow throughout the facility, and how production will be controlled must be answered.

The production of almost any type of product or service can usually be handled in one of several alternative ways. For example, should a factory use a mass-production assembly line or work groups to assemble a product? Should

Management must determine the best way to produce a new product or service.

a retail store utilize self-service or professional salespeople to provide merchandise to customers? In many cases, the very nature of the product or service will help to answer these questions, but the choice is not always clear.

CIM usually utilizes CAD and CAM in the production process.

COMPUTER DESIGN AND MANUFACTURING SYSTEMS How much of the production process to automate—and at what level of sophistication—must also be determined at this time. *Computer-integrated manufacturing (CIM)* is a very broad term that entails utilizing computers at various stages of product development and the manufacturing process. Computer Aided Design (CAD) programs and **computer-aided manufacturing (CAM)** programs are used to actually manufacture the product. In CAM programs, computer-controlled machines and robots perform virtually all of the manufacturing operations previously done by workers. Real state-of-the-art CIM integrates CAD and CAM programs in all manufacturing operations—from new-product design to ordering and handling materials, to assembling products, and even to preparing them for shipment. This type of computer-integrated manufacturing system can also be used to set up **flexible manufacturing systems (FMS)**. These small groups of computer-controlled machines have the flexibility to produce a variety of products in small, medium, or large production runs.

Finally, Texas Instruments (TI) has discovered a new way to use computers in manufacturing. They are building what they call "the virtual factory." In this system, all the engineering specs and invoices will be sent electronically, so that any product can be built at any time at any TI factory worldwide. Already, TI's product designers can transmit designs and equipment setup instructions to automated manufacturing sites globally. For example, TI keeps its big million-dollar chip testers in the Philippines, but they are controlled by test engineers in Houston.[11]

Are robots the answer to production problems?

ROBOTICS IN THE MANUFACTURING AND SERVICE SECTORS **Robotics,** the use of computer-controlled robots, is becoming an integral part of the production process. What makes robots unique is their "programmability." Machines have to be retooled (dismantled and reinstalled) to make more than one design item on an assembly line—a very costly and time-consuming process. Robots can now do the same jobs with a flexibility that allows them to work on many different items on one assembly line with little or no down time.

Robots can help to increase product quality. At GM, for example, robots measure car-body welds against specifications, taking 1000 readings in less than a second. When errors occur, humans are notified![12]

Robots and other computers are not strictly limited to the production sector. The use of robots in the service sector has also increased tremendously. Robots are now being used to do everything from diagnosing medical problems to helping prepare meals in a Japanese restaurant. Japan has a shortage of blue-color workers, and robots are used in many Japanese businesses. For example, take the fish section of a Seibu Department store in the western suburb of Tokyo. Fusada Kohji, a worker in the store, helped to set up "Sushi Robot." This robot can methodically mold rice into balls and add a sprig of radish. After a human helper garnishes each rice ball with a strip of raw fish, the robot wraps them in cellophane and places them on a conveyor belt for another helper to pick them up. According to Fusada, it would take as many as three cooks to keep up with this robot. He states that without "Sushi Robot," the business would not be operational.[13]

One of the biggest problems associated with the use of robots in the service sector is the fact that this sector has what experts refer to as a "highly unstructured environment." A robot in a factory can be programmed to perform certain repetitive tasks over and over; a robot in a service organization faces a constantly changing environment. Thus, service-sector robots require improved vision and, in some cases, even artificial intelligence to make the proper decisions based on what they see or sense. As computers grow more and more sophisticated, robots will have these abilities.

Current uses of robots in the service sector include cleaning nuclear waste dumps; inspecting, repairing, and even dismantling nuclear reactors; cleaning up chemical accidents; and inspecting oil rigs. Future robots will be able to cut timber, clean bathrooms, cook meals, cut grass, shovel snow, produce pharmaceuticals in space, and even mine the moon. The technology needed to perform all of these tasks, and even more, is just around the corner.[14]

AUTOMATION—AN ASSESSMENT Although the use of automation has increased considerably in recent times throughout the world, decisions on its cost-effectiveness, reliability, and suitability must be carefully weighed. Automation, in many cases, seems to have been beneficial. However, General Motors (GM) discovered that automation alone was not the whole answer. A Detroit, Michigan, Cadillac plant called Hamtramck was virtually fully automated. It opened in 1985 with 260 robots for welding and painting cars, and 50 automated guided vehicles were installed to carry parts to different areas of the plant. There were television cameras, computers, and laser-based measuring systems to check quality. It was a manufacturer's dream.

However, the result was a disaster. The production lines ground to a halt for hours while technicians tried to debug the software. When they did work, the robots often began dismembering each other, smashing cars, spraying paint everywhere, or fitting the wrong equipment together. The automated guided vehicles, installed to replace forklifts, sometimes refused to move. After one year, the technology was still so unreliable that the plant was producing about 30 cars per hour instead of the predicted 60. GM was forced to change its ways at Hamtramck. The company removed some of the high-tech equipment, perfected what was left, and gave more control to the workers.[15]

■ Determining the Layout for the New Facility

The production layout is the actual physical positioning of equipment, personnel, materials, finished goods, offices, and other organizational elements. The main objective here, of course, is to develop the most efficient and productive layout possible that minimizes costs and maximizes production. The production layout should be carefully examined in both product and service organizations. There are four basic layout designs and an infinite number of variations on each of them.

There are four basic product layout designs.

THE PRODUCT LAYOUT The first basic layout design, the **product layout,** is best exemplified by the common assembly line. The product layout works well when very standardized products are to be mass produced. The manufacturing design is very efficient: every component part is sequentially laid out in a step-by-step procedure. Thus, the product layout allows for specialization of labor, which increases efficiency and reduces costs through economies of scale.

The disadvantages of this layout design include extreme employee boredom and the inability to customize products or services. Automobiles, appliances, and even some routine services, such as taking a physical exam in a large medical clinic or registering for college, are normally laid out in this manner.

THE PROCESS LAYOUT   The **process layout** allows a product or service to be customized. In this layout design, equipment and people are grouped together, depending on the function. Firms that utilize various departments of specialization exemplify the process layout. This type of layout is very good for manufacturing products or offering services that require a lot of flexibility and variations. A machine shop that produces products according to a customer's given specifications is a good example of the process layout. An automotive service center that diagnoses an automobile's problem and then refers it to the proper department or area for service is another example.

Most service operations use the process layout.

THE FIXED-POSITION LAYOUT   In the **fixed-position layout,** people, equipment, and materials are brought to the product being manufactured or serviced because it is too large or cumbersome to move. A custom-built home on a lot is a good example of this type of layout. Airplanes and large boats or ships are also normally produced this way. In the service sector, appliance repair and lawn maintenance are done this way. The fixed-position layout is more expensive and less efficient than the mass-production or product layout, but the nature of the product or service requires that it be produced in this manner.

THE CELLULAR OR GROUP-TECHNOLOGY LAYOUT   The last and newest layout design is the **cellular** or **group-technology layout.** This type of layout groups clusters of machines and workers into small cells, which feed each other products after completing various processes. These cells are really work teams, and workers trade positions whenever they need to do so, encouraging close teamwork and worker flexibility. This type of layout will probably be used considerably more in the future.

TACTICAL DECISIONS IN OPERATIONS MANAGEMENT

At this point, refer back to the tactical operations decisions portion of Figure 13–2. After all of the strategic decisions have been made, management can move on to the tactical decisions involved in developing the firm's master operations plan. Controlling quality, productivity, and inventories are important items in producing either a product or a service.

■ *Quality Control*

TOTAL QUALITY MANAGEMENT (TQM)   Today, **total quality management (TQM)** is employed in a number of firms that want to be more competitive and efficient while maintaining quality in their products. There are many variations, but virtually all TQM systems

All TQM systems have eight main features.

1. Are customer-driven
2. Focus on quality, with an emphasis on continuous improvement
3. Concentrate on improving work processes

4. Try to eliminate rework by making it right the first time

5. Involve extending the mindset of everyone involved and sharing all vital information

6. Emphasize teamwork and the empowering of people to work on their own

7. Invest in the training and recognition of everyone in the firm

8. Require inspired leaders who have a vision to communicate it in actions, not just in words.[16]

Total quality management reverses the old management cliché from "If it ain't broke, don't fix it" to "If it ain't broke, do fix it." Today's managers must constantly communicate to their employees that no matter how well something is currently being done, it can always be improved. This is the basis of the Japanese principle of *Kaizen*, or continuous improvement, discussed in Chapter 2.

DEMING'S STATISTICAL PROCESS CONTROL   It appears that W. E. Deming, who died in December 1993, will be remembered most as the originator of the **statistical process control** approach to quality control. It is one of the earliest formal variations of total quality management (TQM). Deming's principles were first accepted by the Japanese in the early 1950s as they rebuilt their country after World War II. Although American firms failed to listen to Deming's ideas, Japan quickly accepted them. Even today in Japan, the most prestigious award for quality is named the Deming award.

Deming's quality concept is more than just statistics.

Although Deming's quality procedure is based on a statistical process, it is much more than just a statistical control procedure. It is a management philosophy that embraces total company commitment. Statistical process control starts with good communication at top management and moves down to everyone in the firm. Every worker and manager must be totally committed to providing the highest quality product or service possible, and they must include suppliers and customers in the chain if it is going to work. Customers must be contacted continually to monitor their satisfaction and to see if their needs and expectations are being fully met.

Similarly, suppliers must be brought in and told exactly what quality requirements are needed. If they cannot meet them on a dependable basis, they should be replaced. Long-term contracts with good suppliers are becoming increasingly common, giving suppliers even more incentives to come up to the firm's standards. For example, to do just that, Ford Motor Company has recently pared its supplier base from 10,000 to under 2000.[17]

Once everyone in the chain from suppliers to customers is committed and involved and the firm has an effective communication system in place, then management has a chance to see some impressive gains in improved quality, higher productivity, and lower costs. Companies like Ford, General Motors, and Xerox have all seen increases in productivity and decreases in costs when total quality programs are instituted. Doing it right the first time reduces the amount of rework and leads to higher productivity, which results in lower product-development/manufacturing costs and more satisfied customers. This allows a firm to capture a larger share of the market and provide more job security for everyone involved. **Deming's chain reaction** is illustrated in Figure 13–3.

Deming's approach works equally well in a manufacturing firm or in a service organization. Frank V. Murphy III, Executive Vice President and Chief Operating Officer at Morton Plant Hospital in Clearwater, Florida, has insti-

FIGURE 13–3
W. E. Deming's Chain Reaction

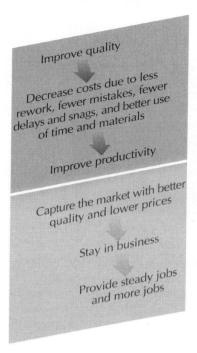

tuted a quality-control concept in three separate hospitals that includes full commitment of all levels of management, improved communications, managerial tools, reward and recognition, education and training, definition of outcomes, and measurement of customer satisfaction. Murphy also notes that the hospital staff members must continually improve their response times and give better service to their customers.[18] Deming's 14 points for management are listed in Figure 13–4. While Deming's name is associated closely with TQM, his ideas are even larger than this one approach to management, also focusing on productivity and management/labor relations.

IMPLEMENTING TQM   On the surface, it does not appear that total quality management is difficult to implement the first time. Unfortunately, TQM does not always produce positive results. In fact, according to a survey of 500 companies conducted by Arthur D. Little, only 36 percent of the firms that recently instituted TQM said that it significantly boosted their competitiveness.[19] Some companies that have developed excellent total-quality programs discovered that the cost of these programs even outweighed the return on profits. The Wallace Company, for instance, was a co-winner of the 1990 Malcolm Baldrige National Quality Award, but the company filed for Chapter 11 bankruptcy two years later when its costs soared.[20]

Apparently, many firms fail to get positive results from TQM due to the way in which the program is planned and implemented. Firms that are new to TQM often think all they have to do is copy firms that have developed state-of-the-art TQM programs. This copying technique, commonly called **benchmarking,** has produced positive results but can also produce negative results if not done

FIGURE 13–4   Deming's 14 Points for Management

SOURCE: Stanley J. Modic, "What Makes Deming Run?" *Industry Week* (June 6, 1988), p. 84. Reprinted with permission of the publisher, Penton Publishing, Cleveland, OH.

1. Create constancy of purpose for the improvement of product or service.
2. Adopt a new philosophy of total quality.
3. Cease dependence on mass inspection.
4. End the practice of awarding business on the basis of the price tag alone; instead, minimize total cost by working with a single supplier.
5. Improve constantly and forever every process for planning, production, and service.
6. Institute training on the job.
7. Adopt and institute leadership.
8. Drive out fear.
9. Break down barriers between staff areas.
10. Eliminate slogans, exhortations, and targets for the work force.
11. Eliminate numeric quotas for the work force and numeric goals for management.
12. Remove barriers that rob people of pride of workmanship, including the annual rating or merit system.
13. Institute a vigorous program of education and self-improvement for everyone.
14. Put everybody in the company to work on accomplishing the desired transformation.

Railway cars are real-life images of W. E. Deming's chain reaction at work: a continuous chain that links suppliers to customers.

correctly. First introduced by Xerox Corporation, benchmarking, or "the continuous process of measuring products, services, and practices against the companies recognized as the industry leaders," must be very carefully implemented or firms that are new to TQM may try to do too much too fast.[21] If all of a firm's employees are not well trained in quality principles, such as empowered work teams, then trying to implement TQM principles immediately will just produce chaos.

Then what is the proper way to implement TQM? First, there is not a single formula that works for everyone. Companies advance in stages, much like a learning curve. As a firm reaches a new level of performance, it must utilize new techniques to improve further.

One TQM technique that is currently very popular is to measure the **Return on Quality (ROQ)**. American Telephone and Telegraph (AT&T), for example, must demonstrate that a new quality program will create at least a 30-percent drop in defects and a 10-percent return on investment, or top management will not approve it. AT&T has found that when customers "perceive" that the quality of its service has improved, financial returns usually improve as well.[22]

Reengineering is rethinking the entire production or service process.

Another technique utilized by the management of a firm like PHH Fleet-America is to analyze the business in terms of every process and define the key ones that are essential to its operation. These key operations are benchmarked against competitors and customer expectations. Each area is then considered for **reengineering**—rethinking the total work flow, including the procedures implemented, the people involved, and the systems used to accomplish tasks. Benchmarking, when used with reengineering, restrains management from making the mistake of projecting business operations too far into the future—say, trying to leap ahead ten years in one year.[23]

With reengineering, the firm is really trying to rethink the entire way a product or service is produced. For example, to reduce cycle time (the time it takes to complete a given business process), the management of a firm must look for time delays and bottlenecks. The time it takes for products to progress from one area to another should be monitored, and places where products are stacked up, waiting to be worked on, should be eliminated. There should be a continuous flow of operations at all times, which may even require the development of a totally new production process.

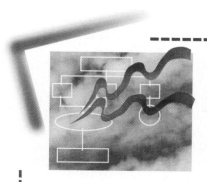

REMEMBER TO COMMUNICATE

Quality Control through Quality Communication

One of the true success stories in American business has to be the turnaround that Cadillac Motor Division made between 1986 and 1990. In 1986, Cadillac ranked very low in quality polls and its image was suffering badly. One of the main reasons for Cadillac's problems was the way in which the division handled customer complaints. In the old system, customer complaints went from the dealer to Cadillac's customer-service department. From there, a complaint went through six other departments before reaching someone who could do something about it. The process took months and obviously produced a huge communication gap between Cadillac and its customers.

To remedy this situation, Rosetta Riley, Director of Continental Improvement Processes for General Motors, instituted a whole new communication system between Cadillac and its customers. The plan consisted of the following points.

- A Listening Post Program was set up with 30 dealers, who agreed to listen very carefully to all of their customers' comments when they brought their cars in for service. The listeners then immediately called these comments into Cadillac's technical services and quality engineering departments.

- Technical assistance hot lines were set up so that dealer mechanics could call the technical operations department in the Cadillac factory if they found unusual engine problems.

- A Gold Key Survey was set up to survey all Cadillac owners within six months of a new purchase.

- Cadillac executives were asked to call five randomly chosen buyers a week and to spend some time fielding calls in the customer-service center.

- New car designs are literally customer-driven. For example, nearly 8700 customers and noncustomers participated in the design of the 1992 Cadillac Seville, which drew rave reviews.

The results of this program have been extremely beneficial. The management of Cadillac learned, for instance, that customers thought the newer Cadillac cars were too short and should be more like the older, more traditional Cadillac. Management also learned that customers felt the Cadillac Cimmaron, a compact car, was just a "dressed up Chevy"—a finding that caused Cadillac to stop production of the car. And management responded to customer comments that the Cadillac Eldorado needed a complete redesign and watched Eldorado sales jump 43 percent in the following year.

ADAPTED FROM: Carolyn Brown, "Quality Pays Off," *Black Enterprise* (June 1992), p. 292; Rosetta Riley, "How I Did It—Getting Faster Feedback from Your Customers," *Working Woman* 54 (November 1991), pp. 55–58.

Once this analysis has been completed, the next step is to repeat the problem-solving cycle over and over again. This technique is called the **Deming circle.** To really get the full benefits of this technique, both managers and workers must be trained thoroughly to work in teams. Incentive programs for quality improvement must be in place, and workers must be given the decision making power to try new methods.

The proof of how well these procedures can work is exemplified by firms such as Solectron Corporation, a California manufacturer of computer disks. Solectron, a 1991 Malcolm Baldrige National Quality Award winner, reduced both its production-cycle time and inventory costs by 80 percent. The corporation

A PERSPECTIVE ON QUALITY

ISO 9000—Doing Business with the EC

The European Community (EC) has a new set of quality standards called ISO 9000. The International Division of the U.S. Chamber of Commerce gives a good definition of what ISO 9000 really means: the purpose of the ISO 9000 is "to ensure that a manufacturer's product is exactly the same today as it was yesterday as it will be tomorrow."

Due to the need for an overall standard of quality, the ISO 9000 certification is quickly becoming more important to achieve than the Malcolm Baldrige National Quality Award. Europeans are demanding product quality, and more and more of Europe's customers are buying only from businesses with ISO 9000 certification.

How does a business obtain this certification? The firm's managers begin with a 100-page, five-part, ISO guidebook that directs them to document how workers perform every function that affects product quality and helps them to install mechanisms to make sure they follow through in all areas. Internal teams verify that procedures are being followed in 20 areas—from purchasing to design to training. Once the applicant feels ready, independent auditors inspect the company to award a certificate of compliance. The bad news is that this procedure can take up to 18 months to complete and may cost more than $200,000.

In the future, U.S. companies may be forced to obtain ISO 9000 certification to do business with the European Community. More than 20,000 facilities in Europe held certificates in 1992, compared to 900 U.S. businesses and 1000 businesses in Japan and Singapore. The United States is the country with the most to lose: 30 percent of all American exports go to Europe. To retain this export rate, U.S. companies had better take a close look at ISO 9000 in the near future.

ADAPTED FROM: Anne Fitzgerald, "Kansas Lags in Quality Standards," *The Wichita Eagle* (June 7, 1993): 1D; Todd Leeuwenburgh, "Quality Standards That Can Open Doors," *Nation's Business* 80 (November 1992): 32–33; Jonathan B. Levine, "Want EC Business? You Have Two Choices," *Business Week* (October 19, 1992), pp. 58–59.

also lowered its defective parts rate from 100 parts per million (ppm) to 2 ppm, which obviously translates into real financial rewards for everyone in the firm.[24]

Another form of total quality management that is being implemented in Europe by the European Community (EC) is called **ISO 9000.** This series of comprehensive, international quality standards applies to both products and services and supersedes the domestic standards of any individual country. Many firms worldwide are going to have to meet this set of standards if they plan on doing business with the EC.

The **quality circle**—a management technique that has been used very successfully in both the product and service industries—is really a form of participative management that encourages employee involvement and improves employee-management communications. A quality circle normally consists of a group of six to ten employees from the same department.

The members of a quality circle usually select a problem, identify its causes, collect and analyze data, and make recommendations to management regarding potential solutions to the problem. Only specific, job-related problems are addressed; the circle does not handle such managerial problems as collective bargaining violations.

Employee involvement in quality circles may be a firm's best way to solve its problems. This quality circle examines and tries to anticipate some of the problems inherent to entering a foreign market.

For many firms, the results have been amazing. The Miller Brewing Company, for example, credits the following successes directly to their quality circles.

■ Miller's Georgia brewery was named the "safest brewery in America."

■ Several Miller plants have set new production records.

■ Since the inception of quality circles, the number of "corrective actions" has dropped 71 percent and the number of employee grievances has dropped 86 percent.

■ Recently, a new line of work teams experienced the smoothest start-up ever.[25]

Quality circles may not always be cost-effective, but the resulting increase in overall communications and the improvement in management-labor relations alone more than justify their use.[26] When they are done right, the rewards can be large.

■ *Productivity Control*

The second tactical question a firm must answer is how to increase productivity. **Productivity** can be defined as the total output of goods and/or services divided by the total inputs needed to produce those goods and services.

Productivity affects every American.

Low productivity rates in and of themselves may not seem important to workers. But lower productivity translates into lower real wages, a lower standard of living, and the loss of many markets to more productive foreign competitors. In American industry, productivity is something that affects everyone.

When we ask why U.S. productivity has not grown faster, there are very few clear answers. One is that the productivity rate in service industries is running at less than one-half the productivity rate in the manufacturing industries. In the past, productivity in the service field has been increased mainly through the addition of more and more people rather than through innovation and automation.

A PERSPECTIVE ON QUALITY

Managers and Employees Learn from Quality-Improvement Program

There once was a time when if you were an employee of the Florida Power and Light Utility Company (FPL), you tried to keep it to yourself. Admitting it to someone often set off a conversation about the terrible service, constant rate increases, and frequent power outages that FPL customers sometimes faced on a day-to-day basis. Today, all that has changed—thanks to a new quality-improvement program.

The program was not exactly a smashing success at the start. Senior managers thought they could force this quality program on FPL employees. One employee stated, "I received a memo saying that I was now a member of a quality-improvement team. They did not even ask me if I wanted to be a member, and I resented that a lot." Middle managers and supervisors were not thrilled with the idea of a quality-improvement program either. They felt that the program took employees away from their jobs for part of the time while they still had to meet the same production quotas.

To rectify these errors, top management set up training programs designed to help middle managers see themselves as facilitators who were there to help employees look for problems and to help them solve them. Employees were trained to see each other as internal customers and to give each other what their "customers wanted." By working closely with employees in other areas, they began to see that only by working together could company-wide problems be solved.

Finally, W. Edwards Demings' teachings were introduced. Both managers and employees have taken a five-week course in advanced statistical process control. Over 8000 employees have studied basic statistics, and every one of FPL's employees has learned how to interpret data.

FPL made it clear that this program was truly an important part of the firm and stressed it repeatedly in all company communications. Management responded, and morale soared. "The real breakthroughs have come from thousands of small ideas for improvements and years of training" [Dusky, p. 63], according to Wayne Brunetti, an executive vice president.

The results are truly amazing. Customer power outages, which used to average 100 minutes per customer per year, are now down to 43 minutes. The industry average nationwide is 90 minutes. Customer complaints, which used to average one for every 1000 customers, now average one for every 4000 customers. Cost savings run as high as $300 million per year, and profits are growing rapidly.

In the spring of 1990, FPL won Japan's prestigious Deming Award for Quality—the only American firm to win this award so far. What did winning this award mean to the FPL employees? As Geisha Williams, a construction services manager, put it, "We felt a tremendous national pride. The impossible had happened." [Dusky, p. 63] Since then, FPL has continued to improve its quality programs even more by stressing cost reduction as well as product quality. The results were a 23-percent increase in profits in 1993.

ADAPTED FROM: Lorraine Dusky, "Bright Ideas," *Working Woman* **138** (July 1990): 58–63; David Greising, "Quality: How to Make It Pay," *Business Week* (August 8, 1994), pp. 54–59.

Now that foreign competitors are entering virtually every U.S. product and service industry, the need to increase productivity rates through the use of better management techniques and automation has never been greater. When we consider the question of how a manufacturing firm or a service organization can increase its productivity, several effective methods are available that have proven successful in many business firms.

PARTICIPATIVE MANAGEMENT A more participative management style has boosted productivity in a large number of firms. Two recent research studies seem to confirm this fact. Masanori Hashimoto has analyzed the Japanese system of industrial relations, and David Levine and Laura Tyson have examined the evidence on participative management in a number of countries. Both studies indicate a substantial link between productivity and "correct" employee participation.[27]

There is a clear link between participative management and productivity.

What is the correct way to engage in participative management? The answer seems to be by improving employee communication through consultation and the use of work teams. The Nucor Steel Corporation provides a good example of autonomous work-team effectiveness. At Nucor Steel, work teams composed of eight or nine employees are put together after training. They are then furnished equipment and, in a real sense, given complete freedom to get the job done as they see fit.

Production bonuses are given to all employees who exceed the standard; a bonus can be as high as 150 percent of an employee's base pay. Workers are encouraged to increase upward communications by submitting opinions and suggestions, as well as complaints, to managers who walk the floor and communicate with workers on a regular basis. Workers are given a voice in the decision-making process, and group meetings are held to air problems and complaints.

Communication is critical to the success of the team-oriented approach. Both managers and employees must understand the goals and standards, where to get help if needed, and the feedback on how they are doing. What results has Nucor realized from this approach? Nucor's production of 980 tons of steel per year per employee is more than double the industry average of 420 tons, and its cost of $60 per ton is less than one-half of the $135-per-ton industry average.[28]

PROFIT SHARING A second method that has proven to increase productivity is profit sharing. Rutger's economist Douglas Kruse has tracked the performance of 500 industrial and service companies for periods of time ranging up to 20 years and arrived at the following conclusions.

- Productivity increases from 3.5 to 5 percent on average after a company adopts a profit-sharing plan.
- Cash payment plans work twice as well as deferred payment plans.
- Profit sharing is a more effective employee incentive than a salary raise.
- Profit sharing works better in small firms than in larger ones.

Managers at these firms also noted that the best productivity results occurred when profit sharing and worker involvement were combined.[29]

Flexible manufacturing systems turn out a variety of products.

TECHNOLOGICAL IMPROVEMENTS Technological improvements are the third basic way to improve productivity. At the forefront are the flexible manufacturing systems (FMS), which can turn out a wide range of products on the same line very quickly. Firms that use this system have doubled or tripled the efficiency rates of both their labor and machinery. They have cut defects and the time it takes to introduce a new product by as much as 90 percent.[30]

GLOBAL VIEW

Motorola "Tours the World"—at Home and Abroad

In the 1980s, Motorola literally toured the world looking for ideas and new ways to produce products because of the severe pressure from the Japanese on its pagers, semiconductors, and cellular phones. What the company found were truly impressive ways to improve product quality and productivity, and top managers have implemented many of these ideas with great success. In fact, they even refer to their new, totally automated, pager assembly line in Florida as their "Bandit Line," since they have literally "stolen" so many of the ideas for it.

But the thing that stood out the most occurred when they toured the Hitachi plant just north of Tokyo. Outside the plant, a flag was flying that had "P200" printed on it. When the Motorola executives asked what that flag meant, they were told that Hitachi had set a goal of increasing productivity by 200 percent by the end of 1992. However, they had only increased productivity to a "disappointing" 160 percent by then.

What does this say to American businesspeople? With most U.S. companies hoping for productivity increases in the 10–20 percent range, it is clear that they may have to raise their sights to stay competitive in the future.

ADAPTED FROM: "Demystifying What Quality Means," *Black Enterprise* **22** (June 1992): 284–92; Ronald Henkoff, "What Motorola Learns from Japan," *Fortune* (April 24, 1989): 159–68; Thane Peterson and others, "Top Products for Less Than Top Dollar," *Business Week* (Quality 1991): 66–68; Otis Port, "Moving Past the Assembly Line," *Business Week* (Reinventing America 1992): 177–80.

The physical work environment can have a positive or a negative effect on productivity.

IMPROVING THE WORK ENVIRONMENT One final way to increase productivity that is receiving increasing attention is the careful examination and improvement of the work environment. Negative environmental effects, such as poor lighting, noise, stale air, and extreme temperatures should be eliminated from the workplace. Robert A. Baron at Rensselaer Polytechnic Institute has found that anything that can be done to make employees experience a positive shift in mood will lead to a more productive and efficient workplace. In particular, proper lighting, the right fragrance in the air supply, and a cool fresh exchange of air all have been found to increase worker productivity and reduce errors.[31]

■ *Inventory Control*

What areas do we have to manage in inventory control?

Inventory control is an area within production management that has received a lot of attention recently. Since both foreign and domestic competitors have been significantly reducing their inventory levels without affecting their production rates or delivery of services, firms that are holding even moderate inventories today are at a significant financial disadvantage. All production firms are going to have to "manage" inventory levels at minimal levels or lose their competitive edge. Inventory costs, including storage; loss due to theft, damage, or obsolescence; and costs of capital tied up in inventory can be substantial.

Basically, three different types of goods are inventoried: raw materials, work-in-progress, and finished goods. Today's firms need to keep all three of these inventoried goods at their lowest possible levels, without causing any delays in production or in delivery of services, while maintaining a level of service that is well within the customers' range of acceptance. To do this, of course, management must have an effective customer communication system in place. **Stock-outs,** or orders that cannot be immediately filled, must be kept to a minimum.

Some of the more common methods of inventory control are fixed point, fixed internal, ABC classification, materials requirement planning (MRP and MRPII), and just-in-time (JIT).

There are five common methods of inventory control.

FIXED-POINT AND FIXED-INTERVAL INVENTORY CONTROLS   Fixed-point and fixed-interval inventory-control systems both add a set amount of inventory, when designated. The **fixed-point inventory system** adds a predetermined amount of inventory when the inventory reaches a given level or point. The **fixed-interval inventory system** adds a predetermined amount of inventory at pre-set times. Both of these systems are designed to provide a sufficient minimum amount of **safety stock,** so that the company will not totally run out of inventory.

THE ABC CLASSIFICATION INVENTORY SYSTEM   The **ABC classification inventory system** attempts to classify all inventory items on the basis of how critical each type is to the firm in the production or delivery of its products or services. This system works particularly well for finished goods, since the marketing **80/20 rule** applies to them. According to this rule, 80 percent of a firm's sales come from 20 percent of its products. Thus

ABC works very well as a finished-goods inventory control.

- The 20 percent of a firm's products that produces 80 percent of its sales would be its "A" inventory products.

- The approximate 60 percent of the firm's goods that produces the next 10–15 percent of its sales would be its "B" goods.

- The last 20 percent of the firm's goods that produces 5–10 percent of its sales would be its "C" goods.

The ABC classification inventory system allows a firm to invest its inventory dollars in proportion to the value management places on each inventory item. The proper amount of safety stock can be kept on hand at all times to assure minimum problems and stockouts.

MATERIALS REQUIREMENT PLANNING (MRP AND MRPII)   **Materials requirement planning (MRP)** utilizes a computer program to ensure that proper inventory levels are maintained. This form of inventory control works very well for raw materials and for component parts that are to be used in the manufacture of products. Once products are designed, the necessary components and all necessary raw materials can be ascertained. After this is done, management can determine a firm's current inventory level for each of these items. After looking at the production schedule and the delivery lead times of suppliers, both initial orders and periodic reorders can be automatically set up so that the proper amount of inventory is available at the time it is needed.

A newer version of MRP, called **MRPII,** is now out. This computer program coordinates *every* aspect of the firm with the production process. Now the finance, marketing, human-resource, and production departments are all tied together in the production schedule.

MMPII ties all departments into the production schedule.

JUST-IN-TIME (JIT) INVENTORY SYSTEM   The **just-in-time (JIT) inventory system** is the newest method of controlling inventories. Initially developed by Toyota,

JIT is the newest inventory control system, but it is not for everyone.

this inventory control system keeps very minimal levels of inventory; the parts or raw materials arrive literally just hours before they are needed. Needless to say, this system must work to perfection or the entire plant could be shut down. This inventory control system has been credited with providing a number of benefits to producers who utilize it properly.

1. An obvious cost savings is derived by not having large sums of money tied up in storing inventory.

2. Quality and productivity increase because suppliers are required to deliver very high-quality parts or raw materials on a very precise delivery schedule.

3. Employee morale increases, since the JIT system is part of the employee-involvement program that many employers have in place.

4. Supplier relations improve; long-term contracts are normally established, and manufacturers work with suppliers to assure proper specifications and quality levels.

To work properly, however, a very extensive and clear communications system must be in place so that suppliers know exactly what to deliver and when to deliver it.

Firms like Toyota, Hewlett-Packard, and Xerox have all implemented the JIT system with a good deal of success. The JIT inventory control system can work effectively if it fits a firm and if management follows the proper steps, as noted in Figure 13–5.[32]

OPERATIONAL-LEVEL DECISIONS IN OPERATIONS MANAGEMENT

At this point, refer back to the operational-level decisions in Figure 13–2. Once management has completed the tactical operations decisions, then only the daily operational-level decisions need to be made to complete the firm's operations management master plan. Scheduling, purchasing, and cost control are the main decisional areas in this section of the plan.

■ Scheduling

Scheduling must start with a **master production schedule,** which is derived from current and/or projected orders for the various products or services being produced. This schedule provides a general framework authorizing various quantities of a given product or service to be produced during a given time period (for example, a one-month period). The master schedule then, in essence, initiates the whole scheduling process for materials, equipment, and personnel, each of which must be carefully scheduled to avoid delays and overloads. This requires extensive communication between everyone involved in the production of the products or services being delivered.

Some scheduling techniques have proved to be very useful. The **program evaluation and review technique (PERT)** is a very useful system when large, complex projects are being planned. This system was originally developed by the U.S. Navy and its main contractors when building the Polaris Missile System. It has since been used in a number of large government and industry projects that have a high degree of uncertainty. The PERT system breaks a project down into every single activity that must be done from the very start to the very end of the project. The activities are then laid out in sequence, and any activities that can be done at the same time are overlapped on the PERT chart.

PERT is useful for scheduling large, new projects.

■ **FIGURE 13–5** The JIT
Inventory Control System

ADAPTED FROM: Paul H. Zipkin,
"Does Manufacturing Need a JIT
Revolution?" *Harvard Business
Review* **69** (January/February 1991):
40–50.

To utilize the JIT inventory control system successfully, the management of a firm must follow these steps.

1. Be sure your firm's products and demand levels are appropriate. The system works best for products that have a relatively stable demand most of the time.

2. Realize that it is going to be a slow and gradual process before significantly low levels of inventory are reached. It took Toyota 20 years to refine its inventory system.

3. The JIT system forces the management of a firm to simplify its production procedures as much as possible, so that other delays are eliminated.

4. Inventories can only be lowered in small increments as the firm's production line becomes more and more reliable and consistent. In fact, reducing all inventories to zero should never happen.

5. Fairly expensive capital expenditures may have to be made to improve consistency, quality, and dependability on the assembly line.

6. Initially, JIT will increase a firm's costs, at least in training, maintenance, and establishing long-term supplier commitments.

7. Suppliers will have to be treated like "partners," and long-term contracts will be necessary.

8. Workers will have to be slowly eased into the JIT system. Employee participation must be promoted, or high levels of stress may occur.

Finally, three time estimates are made for each activity: the most optimistic time frame, the most probable time frame, and the most pessimistic time frame. From these three time frames, a mathematical matrix of expected outcomes can be produced.

CPM is used to schedule familiar projects.

A variation of PERT, called the **critical path method (CPM)**, lays a project out exactly like PERT, except that only one time frame is allotted to each activity. The critical path method is used to schedule projects with which the management of a firm has a high degree of experience, which explains why only one time frame is used. These are instructions for developing a critical path schedule:

Step 1. Every single activity for completing the project is identified, numbered, and circled at the top of the activity.

Step 2. The sequence in which the activities must be completed is determined and laid out in a line. If two or more activities can be done simultaneously, then duplicate "paths" are established. (For example, the plumbing and the wiring of the house can be done at the same time.)

Step 3. A single time estimate in days is made for completing each activity and is placed on the line leading to the next activity.

Step 4. The critical (longest) path timewise is determined. This is the earliest that the project can be completed.

Step 5. The schedule paths are studied to locate any possible bottlenecks and to determine if any changes can be made to shorten the critical path.

Step 6. The schedule is changed as time estimates become a reality and vary from the original time estimates.

Figure 13–6 shows an example of a critical path schedule.

■ **FIGURE 13–6** Critical Path Schedule for Building a New Home*

1
Secure home plans
1 day
2
Do excavation work
3 days
3
Pour foundation
1 day
4
Frame house
5 days
5 days
5
Install plumbing
5
Install wiring
4 days
6 days
6
Put up drywall
4 days
4 days
4 days
7
Put on roofing
7
Finish interior
7
Finish exterior
3 days
4 days
2 days
8
Do landscaping
2 days
9
Receive certficate of occupancy
1 day
10
Move in

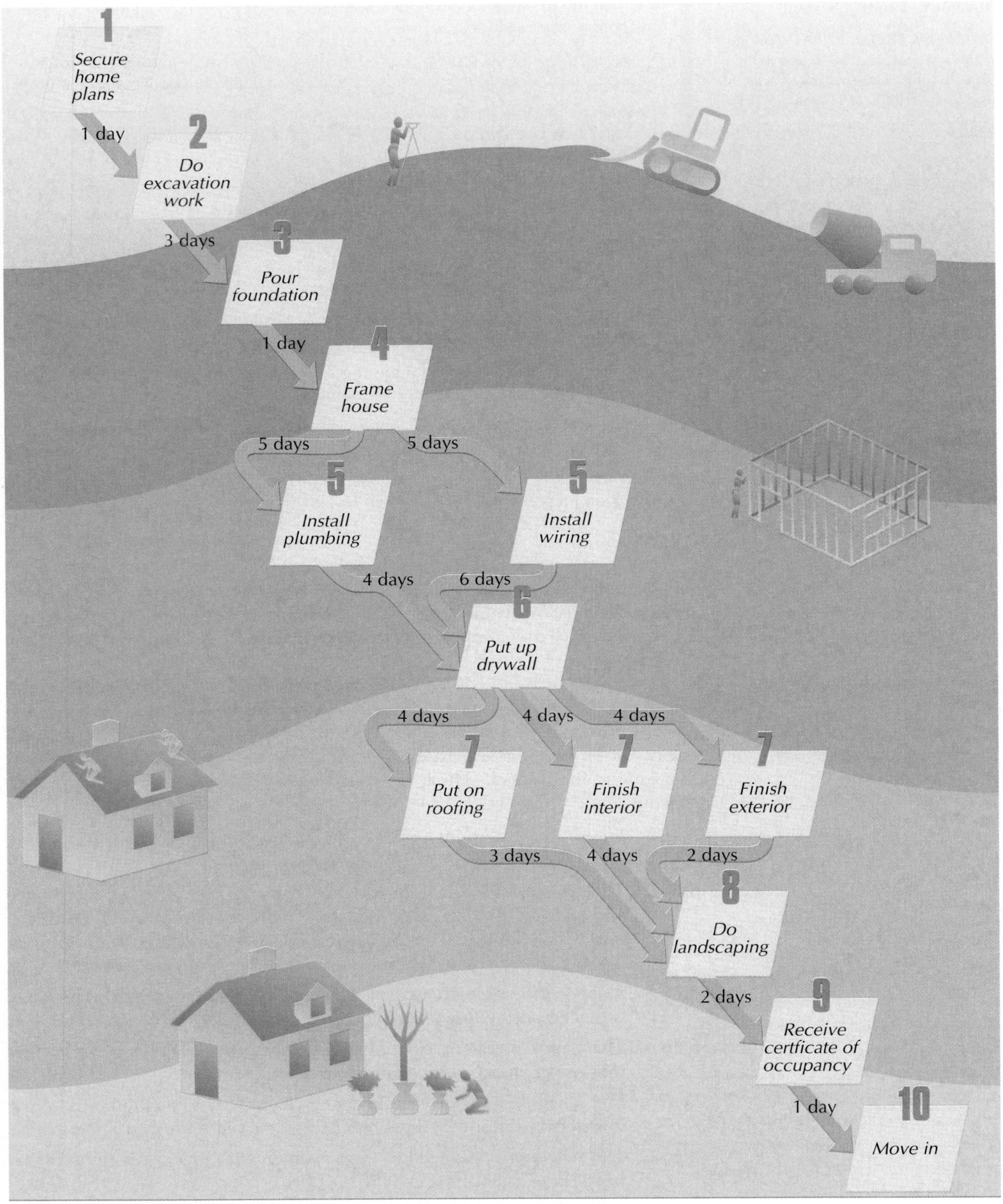

*Estimated number of days for completion listed after each activity.

Sequencing, scheduling, and completion time can all be estimated with a reasonable degree of accuracy using either PERT or CPM. If something happens that is going to cause the schedule to change, the new information is simply put into the computerized version. Then a whole new schedule can be quickly printed and communicated to all parties involved. As illustrated in Figure 13–6, these types of networking schedules can clearly illustrate what and when various activities need to be done.

Finally, scheduling employees can be a difficult and sometimes frustrating job for managers on occasion. To create a workable schedule, a manager must make sure that all of the variables fit together. These variables include the following.

When scheduling employees, all variables must fit together.

- What are the needs of the business in terms of the number of employees required on an hourly basis?
- What skills are needed during each business hour?
- What are the legal requirements (people who must have proper licenses, etc.)?
- What preferences do the employees have in terms of working hours, shift preferences, vacations, and holiday periods?
- What are the overtime requirements?

Fortunately, several mathematical models and some computerized programs are available to help firms develop a schedule that integrates all of these factors.

■ Purchasing

The purchase of various raw materials and component parts obviously must be a careful and systematic process if the quality of the product or service is to remain high and the cost of producing it is to remain low. Although the materials requirement planning (MRP) approach will tell a manager what materials are needed and when they are needed, this may not be the most cost-effective way to purchase them.

Purchasing costs can be broken down into two general categories.

1. *Order costs* are expenses necessary to place the order, follow up on delivery, and inspect and process the order when it arrives.

2. *Holding costs* include monies tied up in inventory; the storage costs of warehousing the inventory; and the costs incurred due to loss from theft, deterioration, or obsolescence.

Managers must also look at the savings that can be derived from purchases having significant quantity discounts.

To balance all of these factors and determine the optimum order size and frequency, the **economic order quantity (EOQ)** must be determined. The EOQ model allows a manager to find the point at which holding costs and carrying costs are minimized. This point is illustrated graphically in Figure 13–7.

To find the EOQ point, we use the formula

The EOQ tells a manager how often to place an order and what size it should be.

$$EOQ = \sqrt{\frac{2 \times \text{Order costs} \times \text{Annual demand in units}}{\text{Cost of items} \times \text{Carrying cost percentage}}}$$

For example, if a retail marine dealer is trying to determine how many VHF marine radios to purchase, the EOQ quantity can be found as follows. If total

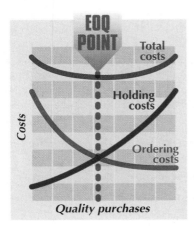

To ensure that a firm receives high-
quality parts and materials,
management should implement
effective communication practices.

annual demand for the radios, including both the units sold directly to customers and the units installed in new boats, is 500 units; if order costs are estimated at $30 per order; if the cost of each radio is $300; and if storage and carrying costs are estimated at 16 percent, then we can see that the EOQ is

$$EOQ = \sqrt{\frac{2 \times 30 \times 500}{300 \times 0.16}}$$

$$= \sqrt{\frac{30,000}{48}}$$

$$= \sqrt{625.0}$$

$$= 25$$

The marine dealer in this case should order 25 radios per purchase order. He
will need to place 20 orders during the year to receive the required 500 units.
The times at which the dealer should place these orders depends on the anticipated monthly demand, the type of inventory control system being used, and
the minimum level of safety stock that must be on hand to avoid stockouts.
This model does assume a fairly stable and constant demand for the items being
ordered. If demand fluctuates extensively and/or is very difficult to predict
annually, then the model only has a limited value.

One other aspect of purchasing that needs to be addressed is the new relationship that many firms now have with their suppliers. In the past, most firms
utilized an extremely large number of suppliers to get them the lowest possible
prices on the items to be purchased. Today, many large manufacturers are taking the opposite approach; they obtain a particular item from only two or three
suppliers, rather than 20 or 30 vendors, to ensure that the quality of the part
or material received is consistently high. Thus, managers must improve their
communications with suppliers so that they truly understand what is needed.

Another reason for a firm to deal with only a few suppliers is the ever-
increasing use of JIT inventory systems. Today, many firms like IBM in
Rochester, Minnesota, actually train, audit, and certify suppliers and even
require them to submit a quality plan. IBM treats its suppliers like partners.
This new type of relationship helped IBM be one of the four winners of the
1990 Malcolm Baldrige Award for Excellence in Quality.[33]

■ *Cost Control*

Cost control is an area that every business must monitor constantly if it is going
to remain competitive. Both foreign and domestic firms are continually looking
for ways to trim costs. Communicating regularly with employees regarding
ways to reduce organizational costs is important and can be quite effective.

Most firms have very accurate figures on direct costs, such as labor and
materials used. The real cost-control challenge is to get a much better grasp of
the firm's indirect costs, including the allocation of all overhead costs (design
costs, public relations outlays, office expenses, maintenance fees, etc.). Management must also figure in such indirect costs as reworking defective products
and down times due to bottlenecks. Indirect costs have soared; they currently
account for 55 percent or more of total manufacturing costs across all products. Conversely, direct labor costs have dropped to 15 percent of manufacturing costs, and they are closer to 5 percent in high-tech industries.[34]

Firms like Tektronix, Hewlett-Packard, IBM, Weyerhauser, and many others are utilizing a new cost-control procedure called "Activity Based Cost Management" (ABC). This computerized form of cost control stresses measuring costs at each step of the manufacturing process, beginning with the design stage and ending with product shipment. By measuring costs at each stage of the process, the costs of delays and defective products can be assessed quite accurately. This method also accounts for all overhead costs, as well as direct labor and material costs. By using this method of cost control, a firm can pinpoint operations that add value as well as those that do not. In this way, firms can work to eliminate hidden costs.[35]

CONSIDER THIS

1. What are the four main questions that management must answer before a new facility can be built?

2. Explain the core concept of Deming's statistical process control approach to quality control.

3. How can a typical firm improve productivity?

THINK ABOUT IT

1. American firms are under competitive attack from foreign firms in virtually every product and service area. In order to survive in its own markets, the United States must do a better "management" job.

2. The American business manager must realize that only by establishing a true, unified team effort that involves all employees will a firm ever be truly successful.

3. The construction of a new facility must be carefully planned; its location, size, production process, and physical layout all must be taken into account.

4. True quality can only be achieved by getting everyone involved who is in the chain from suppliers to customers.

5. Communication must flow freely between suppliers, management, employees, and customers.

6. A firm must have effective inventory-control and cost-control systems in place if it is to remain competitive in today's marketplace.

7. Effective scheduling involves every area of the firm.

8. The service industry needs to adopt a new model that stresses employee training and support by management.

LOOKING BACK

In this chapter, we have examined the planning process in operations management and considered operations decisions at the strategic, tactical, and operational levels. Now let's review the chapter objectives and briefly summarize several highlights for each of them.

Define the role and importance of operations management.

Remember that the term "operations management" is broader than the term "production management." Operations management includes both products and services.

Examine the pros and cons of applying production/operations management principles to the service industry.

The service industry relies much more heavily on people because they perform the services. However, automation is becoming established for some specific uses in service organizations.

The service industry, like the production industry, needs to design a new model that totally integrates everyone in the firm into a united team effort.

Describe how strategic decisions in operations management have changed due to increased competition.

Basically, we see new-product development times growing shorter and shorter. Effective new-product development requires a *total* team effort that includes the firm's suppliers.

Outline the basic steps involved in establishing a new product or service facility.

Once the decision has been made that a new facility is needed, four main questions must be answered:

1. Where will the facility be located?
2. What will be the size or capacity of the facility?
3. What type of production process will be utilized?
4. What will be the physical layout of the facility?

Describe how to control production/productivity, quality, and inventories.

Productivity has been found to be influenced primarily by employee involvement through various forms of participative management, profit sharing, technology, and improvements in the working environment.

Quality control requires a total commitment from everyone in the firm. Constant customer follow-up and a sense of pride, which must be instilled by inspired leadership, are also crucial.

Inventory control starts with an identified level of customer service. Then the most cost-efficient method must be found that minimizes stockouts without driving costs up.

Explain how scheduling, purchasing, and cost management are accomplished.

In scheduling, a number of new, computerized programs are available, such as Manufacturing Resource Planning II (MRPII), the Program Evaluation and Review Technique (PERT), and the Critical Path Method (CPM).

Purchasing needs to be done in a way that costs are minimized and customer-service levels are maintained. The economic order quantity (EOQ) balances both holding and carrying costs.

Finally, cost controls must be established for both direct and indirect costs.

KEY TERMS

ABC classification inventory system
benchmarking
cellular (group-technology) layout

computer-aided design (CAD)
computer-aided manufacturing (CAM)

computer-integrated manufacturing (CIM)
critical path method (CPM)
Deming circle
Deming's chain reaction
economic order quantity (EOQ)
80/20 rule
fixed-interval inventory system
fixed-point inventory system
fixed-position layout
flexible manufacturing system (FMS)
ISO 9000
just-in-time (JIT) inventory system
master production schedule
materials requirement planning (MRP)
materials requirement planning II (MRPII)
operations management
program evaluation and review technique (PERT)
process layout
process planning
product layout
production layout
production management
productivity
qualitative method
quality circle
quantitative method
reengineering
return-on-quality (ROQ)
robotics
safety stock
statistical process control
stockout
total quality management (TQM)

REVIEW AND DISCUSSION QUESTIONS

1. Why is so much emphasis placed on constantly increasing quality and lowering costs in both product- and service-oriented firms?

2. Why is it so important to develop new products or services fast and get them to the marketplace first?

3. What are the four basic layout designs for a new facility? Briefly explain what type of product or service appears to fit each design the best.

4. How has the role of robotics in the service industry changed over time?

5. Define ISO 9000 quality controls and their impact on U.S. firms.

6. Briefly describe some of the benefits of utilizing quality circles.

7. How can a firm lower costs and increase product or service quality at the same time?

8. Why isn't a just-in-time (JIT) inventory control system suitable for use in all firms?

9. In which areas do firms tend to have the most cost-control problems? What, if anything, can be done about them?

10. What does the new service model for the service industry stress?

CRITICAL THINKING INCIDENT 13.1

John Casey's Dilemma

John Casey, president of Casey Manufacturing, recently returned from a seminar on Dr. Deming's 14 points for successful management. Mr. Casey feels that some of Dr. Deming's points are quite controversial. One in particular is to "eliminate individual pay for performance compensation." Dr. Deming states that you cannot accurately measure performance because of differences in the total system. He also states that the size of the bonus or merit pay can never be fairly determined. Dr. Deming flatly states, "Ranking people (for merit pay or bonuses) is one of the evils destroying American companies." Mr. Casey disagrees with this point, stating that incentive pay and stock ownership are appropriate and have been well received by his employees.

According to Mr. Casey, another controversial point is Dr. Deming's statement that management by objectives (MBO) sabotages the company by directing employee efforts toward a few narrow goals. In this same light, Deming states that the top salesperson, for instance, may actually be ruining the company by only concentrating on sales, sometimes even at the expense of the customer. Casey Manufacturing, however, has used MBO for some time now with basically good results.

In Mr. Casey's mind, Dr. Deming's third controversial point is that people are not chiefly motivated by money. He states that pay is not a motivator and cites examples of numerous low-paying professions, such as the clergy and the United States Marine Corps, to show that people who receive very low wages can be highly motivated. Mr. Casey believes that money is a motivator and points to the successful bonus program at Casey Manufacturing as proof.

Finally, few executives are willing to give up final inspections of their products. Dr. Deming feels that if statistical process control is properly utilized, a final inspection of every item that is manufactured is not necessary. Although some executives agree that this "should be true," they still hesitate to eliminate the last checkpoint before a product goes out to a customer. Mr. Casey firmly believes that every product should be checked before shipment to ensure the good quality of all products.

Discussion Questions

1. What does Dr. Deming mean when he states that pay for performance is bad because of "differences in the system"? Give an example.

2. Why doesn't Dr. Deming like management by objectives?

3. Do you agree with Dr. Deming that pay is not a primary motivator? Why or why not?

4. Why does Dr. Deming feel that mass final inspections are no longer needed? Do you agree or disagree? Why?

CRITICAL THINKING INCIDENT 13.2

Con-Tech Encounters Foreign Competition

Con-Tech, Inc., is located in Eau Claire, Wisconsin, and specializes in industrial controls and switches. With annual sales of $1.2 billion, Con-Tech is one of the largest manufacturers of industrial controls in the world.

Con-Tech has tended to concentrate on industrial controls for U.S. markets. The company has one totally automated assembly line for producing industrial motor controls. This assembly line is truly state-of-the-art. It consists of a main control computer, a master scheduling computer, and a very advanced assembly line. As orders are received, they are placed in the main control computer, which tells the master scheduling computer what to produce. This computer in turn prints a bar code, which is placed on the plastic casing by a mechanical arm. The casing then proceeds through the automated assembly-line substations, where parts are automatically added as prescribed by the bar code. At the end of the line, the part is custom-made to a particular customer's specifications.

Recently, Con-Tech has encountered new competition from Japanese and European manufacturers who produce industrial controls for use in the manufacture of electric motors. These foreign controls are designed primarily for Japanese- and European-designed motors and are about one-third the size and one-third the cost of the Con-Tech controls. Current demand for these smaller controls is approximately 10 million units in the U.S. market, but demand is close to 70 million units worldwide, and growing, as more and more U.S. manufacturers purchase these foreign motors. Con-Tech currently receives approximately 70 percent of its total sales from U.S.-designed controls.

Con-Tech is now considering whether to ignore these new competitors and continue to strictly serve its existing product market or to actively challenge them by manufacturing the smaller control units. The challenge would entail going after the manufacturers who utilize the smaller foreign motors in their production process.

If Con-Tech does decide to become an active producer of these new, smaller units, the company faces three choices. First, Con-Tech could set up a conventional assembly line in its current plant. Since the U.S. market for these smaller control units is only 10 million units per year, the manufacturer could probably find enough space to produce its estimated share of this market. If the management of Con-Tech decides to try to market the smaller units globally, then new facilities would have to be constructed. Some advantages of producing the smaller control units in Con-Tech's current facilities would be that the company would be able to oversee product quality and that only minimal investment would be required. However, Con-Tech would only be able to service the U.S. market. Some disadvantages of using the present facilities to assemble the smaller control units are the high cost of labor (averaging $16 per hour) and the problems associated with a conventional assembly line: boredom, high turnover, and absenteeism.

A second alternative would be to go to a country like Mexico and produce the units there. Labor costs in Mexico average $1 per hour, and the cost of new facilities there would be cheaper than they would be in the United States. Disadvantages, however, include questionable consistency in product quality and a number of increased costs due to the need to set up new warehouses and distribution systems. In the final analysis, this probably would be found to be approximately $1–$3 per hour cheaper than utilizing U.S. workers.

The third alternative is to build a totally automated assembly line specifically to produce these products. The cost of this line would be $15 million, but it would produce the smaller controls at the lowest cost per unit. One great disadvantage to this arrangement is that the investment does not look too good based on traditional short-term return on investment (ROI) calculations. It does, however, look good in the long run (8–10 years).

Discussion Questions

1. List the advantages and disadvantages of Con-Tech entering this new market. Based on your analysis, what do you recommend?

2. Assuming that Con-Tech does decide to enter this market, do you recommend responding solely to the U.S. market demand for these products or adopting a global approach? Justify your decision.

3. Which of the three production alternatives do you think Con-Tech should select? Again, justify your answer.

 # CRITICAL THINKING INCIDENT 13.3

Should Waterworks "Hire" the Robot Welder?

Waterworks, Inc., has been manufacturing, installing, and repairing water towers for municipalities for over 50 years. Since this type of business is so specialized, the company has had very little competition in the past. However, this situation is now changing as both new domestic and foreign competitors are entering the field.

Waterworks has traditionally utilized a fixed-position production process due to the size of most water towers. Components are manufactured in the plant, but final assembly, including the welding of all sections of the actual water tank, is done at the site. All seams in the tank must be manually welded on both sides of the panels—a time-consuming process during which a great deal of grinding is required to "clean up" the welds.

With new competition entering the industry, the need to drive down costs is becoming critical. Waterworks has already been underbid on over 40 percent of the new projects available this year. With this thought in mind, the company's top management is now considering buying a new robot welder that can weld the seams in both sides of the tank panels in less than one-half the time a human welder takes—and the weld would require almost no clean up, as the weld is virtually perfect 98 percent of the time. This robot welder could also be reprogrammed to weld the tower struts and even the water pipe that connects the tank to the municipal water system. Again, in each of these cases, the robot is able to do the welding in less than half the time it takes a human to do the job.

There are some problems, however. First, no one at Waterworks has ever worked with robots of any type. Second, this robot, with all the accessories, costs approximately $500,000; financing is available from the robot manufacturer, but the debt service would be substantial. Third, purchasing the robot would mean laying off almost 70 percent of the workers at Waterworks. Many of these men are well into their 50s and have worked for the firm 20–30 years. Finally, this new robot welder has only been on the market for one year, and there have been some "technical" problems which the manufacturer claims have now all been worked out.

Discussion Questions

1. Describe the types of applications that robots can perform better than people.

2. What kinds of applications can people perform better than robots?

3. Determine the pros and cons of purchasing the robot welder in this case. Based on your analysis, should Waterworks purchase the robot welder?

NOTES

1. Edmund Faltermayer, "Is 'Made in U.S.A.' Fading Away?" *Fortune* (September 24, 1990): 62–73.
2. Ibid.
3. William J. Abernathy and others, "The New Industrial Competition," *Harvard Business Review* **59** (September/October 1981).
4. Jerry Flint, "Banzai with a Georgia Accent," *Forbes* (February 4, 1991): 58–62.
5. Leonard A. Schlesinger and James L. Heskett, "The Service-Driven Service Company," *Harvard Business Review* **69** (September/October 1991): 71–81.
6. Weston H. Agor, "Intuition and Strategic Planning," *The Futurist* **23** (November/December 1989): 20–23.
7. John Bussey and Douglas P. Sease, "Manufacturers Strive to Slice Time Needed to Develop Products," *The Wall Street Journal*, 1988. Reprinted in *Applications in Basic Marketing* (Homewood, IL: Richard D. Irwin, 1991).
8. Ibid., p. 25.
9. Ibid.
10. Charles P. Alexander, "GM Picks the Winner," *Time* (August 5, 1985): 42–43.
11. Ira Sager, "The Great Equalizer," *Business Week* (The Information Revolution 1994): 106.
12. David Reed, "Robots March on U.S. Industry," *Reader's Digest* **126** (April 1985): 188–92.
13. "The Advent of the 'Steel-Collar' Worker," *World Press Review* (February 1991): 30–31.
14. Gregory L. Miles, "It's a Dirty Job, But Something's Gotta Do It?" *Business Week* (August 20, 1990): 92–97.
15. "When GM's Robots Ran Amok," *The Economist* (August 10, 1991): 64–65.
16. Ted Marchese, "TQM Reaches the Academy," *AAHE Bulletin* **44** (1991): 3–9.
17. Andrea Gabor, "The Front Lines of Quality," *U.S. News & World Report* (November 27, 1989): 57–58.
18. "Frank V. Murphy III—Emphasizing Total Quality Management at Morton Plant Hospital," *Hospital News Gulf Coast* (1991).
19. Otis Port and others, "Quality," *Business Week* (November 30, 1992): 66.
20. David Greising, "Quality: How to Make It Pay," *Business Week* (August 8, 1994): 54–59.
21. Howard Rothman, "You Need Not Be Big to Benchmark," *Nations Business* (December 1992): 64–65.
22. Greising, "Quality: How to Make it Pay," pp. 54–59.
23. Otis Port and others, "Quality," p. 65.
24. Ibid., p. 71.
25. Allen A. Schumer, "Employee Involvement—The Quality Circle Process," *Vital Speeches of the Day*, delivered at the Association for Quality and Participation (AQP), 10th Annual Spring Conference, Indianapolis, IN (April 11–14, 1988).
26. Ibid.
27. Alan S. Blinder, "Want to Boost Productivity? Try Giving Workers a Say," *Business Week* (April 17, 1989): 10.
28. Thomas M. Rohan, "Maverick Remakes," *Industry Week* (January 21, 1991): 26–30.
29. Alan S. Blender, "Want to Boost Productivity? Try Giving Workers a Say," *Business Week* **3101** (April 17, 1989): 10.
30. John Labate, "Fortune Forecast," *Fortune* (April 19, 1993): 26.
31. Louis S. Richmond, "How America Can Triumph," *Fortune* (December 18, 1989): 52–66.
32. Paul H. Zipkin, "Does Manufacturing Need a JIT Revolution?," *Harvard Business Review* (January/February 1991): 40–50.
33. Brad Stratton, "Four to Receive 1990 Baldrige Awards," *Quality Progress* (December 1990): 19–21.
34. Alex Taylor III, "The U.S. Gets Back in Fighting Shape," *Fortune* (April 24, 1989).
35. Kevin Kelly, "A Bean-Counter's Best Friend," *Business Week* (Quality 1991): 42–43.

SUGGESTED READINGS

Austin, Nancy K. "Dr. Deming and the 'Q' Factor." *Working Women* **14** (September 1991): 31.

Barrett, Mary Jean. "Continuous Quality Improvement as an Organizational Strategy." *Healthcare Financial Management* **47** (September 1993): 20.

Brown, Carolyn. "Quality Pays Off." *Black Enterprise* (June 1992): 281.

Deal, Terrence E., and William A. Jenkins. "Getting Maximum Performance Out of Minimum-Wage Employees." *Success* (March 1994): 45.

"Demystifying What Quality Means," *Black Enterprise* (June 1992): 284–85.

Foreman, Janet T. "Continuous Quality Improvement in Home Care." *Caring Magazine* **22** (October 1993): 32–37.

Hammer, Michael, and James Champy. "The Promise of Reengineering." *Fortune* (May 3, 1993): 94–97.

Juran, Joseph M. "Made in U.S.A.: A Renaissance in Quality." *Harvard Business Review* (July/August 1993): 42–50.

Knapton, Jim. "Without Quality, Profits Disappear." *USA Today* **118** (January 1990): 71–72.

Lerine, Jonathan B. "Want EC Business? You Have Two Choices." *Business Week* (October 19, 1992): 58–59.

Lewyn, Mark. "The Information Age Isn't Just for the Elite." *Business Week* (January 10, 1994): 43.

Perlman, Stephen L. "Employees Redesign Their Jobs." *Personnel Journal* (November 1990): 37–40.

Rothman, Howard. "Quality's Link to Productivity." *Nation's Business* (February 1994): 33–34.

Salvo, Paul V. "People Strategies to Produce Worldclass Quality." *MetalForming* **28** (January 1994): 44–45.

Sherer, Jill L. "Hospitals Question the Return on Their TQM Investment." *Hospitals & Health Networks* (April 5, 1994): 63.

Sonnenberg, Frank K. "If I Had Only One Client." *Sales & Marketing Management* (November 1993): 104–07.

Glossary

ABC classification inventory system A method of inventory control that attempts to classify all inventory items on the basis of how critical each type is to the firm in the production or delivery of its products or services.

Acid test ratio A **liquidity ratio** that indicates how well the company can pay for its operating expenses without selling any of its products.

Adaptation model A model that matches business strategies with environmental conditions.

Administrative management Classical management school of thought that centers on how a business should be organized and what practices an effective manager should follow.

Adverse impact The application of an employment practice that unjustly affects the members of one or more protected groups.

Advocacy promotion A firm's attempt to build customer goodwill and develop a better public image by promoting causes that are not naturally tied in to its products.

Affirmative action program (AAP) A program in an organization that attempts to correct prior workplace discrimination against women and minorities.

Analyzer strategy Positioned between the **defender strategy** and the **prospector strategy,** a business strategy that balances stability with conditions involving some risk and uncertainty.

Assessment center An employee selection method that involves a comprehensive evaluation of prospective employees and of current employees being considered for promotion or career-development programs.

Audiovisual (AV) training An employee training method that involves the use of videotapes, slides, and audio cassettes.

Authority The right delegated to individuals in an organization to make job-related decisions, to perform duties, and to direct others to complete certain tasks.

Balance sheet A document that indicates the overall financial condition of a firm at a given date.

BCG matrix An element of portfolio corporate strategy that compares high and low growth rates with high and low market shares for different business units.

Behavioral approach Research that focuses on behaviors that differentiate effective leaders from ineffective leaders.

Behavioral management A school of thought that emphasizes the role that group social pressure plays in productivity rates.

Benchmarking The continuous process of measuring products, services, and practices against the companies recognized as the industry leaders.

Bona fide occupational qualifications (BFOQ) Employer-determined job requirements which state that only a member of a certain group can perform a particular task.

Brainstorming In the **ordinary group technique** of decision making, a period of time set aside for group members to express as many ideas as possible.

Breakeven analysis A financial control that determines what level of sales or revenues a business must generate to cover all of its total costs.

Breakeven point (BEP) The point at which a firm's total costs are covered by revenues.

Budget A financial estimate developed by management in order to effectively plan, communicate, and control the future activities of an organization.

Bureaucracy A model organizational structure developed by Max Weber in which every worker has specific tasks and areas of responsibility that are clearly defined.

Business strategy A **strategic management** strategy that specifies how each business unit or cluster of subunits should operate.

Capital expenditure budget A financial budget that is used in conjunction with a firm's major capital purchases.

Case-study method An employee training method in which trainees are given information that describes certain decision-making circumstances and asked to recommend solutions.

Cash-flow budget A budget that is used to indicate whether a firm is generating enough revenues to cover its expenditures.

Cause-related marketing The linking of a firm's promotions with charitable organizations or social problems that are in need of financial support.

Cellular (group-technology) layout A layout design that groups clusters of machines and workers into small cells, which feed each other products after completing various processes.

Centralization An organizational condition in which most important decisions are made by top managers.

Certainty A decision-making criterion which implies that the decision maker knows the events that will occur and can choose the one with the largest payoff value.

Chain of command The vertical line of authority that identifies the reporting functions of managers and employees throughout an organization.

Challenge One of the four Cs of motivation, the desire to work toward the completion of assignments or goals.

Classical management Encompasses two schools of thought called **scientific management** and **administrative management.**

Closed system A form of systems management in which an organization does not communicate with or react to its environment.

Code of business ethics A code that tells employees how to act in various situations and makes clear that employees will be expected to recognize the ethical dimensions of corporate policies and actions.

Combination strategy A corporate **grand strategy** in which management combines two or more strategies.

Commitment One of the four Cs of motivation, the persistence needed to take a task to completion.

Communication The sharing of meaning between senders and receivers of messages.

Communication channel The path of a message and the means by which the message is transmitted.

Communication process The sending and receiving of messages for the purpose of sharing meaning.

Communication skills Managerial skills that stress the sharing of meaning.

Communicator role An informational managerial role in which a manager selects information and transmits it to persons who are not direct subordinates.

Community support The volunteering of the time and talents of managers and employees for local community projects.

Competence One of the four Cs of motivation, the know-how needed for a person to complete a task.

Comprehensive listening Listening for the purpose of understanding and remembering the information contained in a verbal message.

Computer-aided design (CAD) A sophisticated computer program that is used extensively in new-product design and development.

Computer-aided manufacturing (CAM) Sophisticated computer programs that are used to actually manufacture a product.

Computer-integrated manufacturing (CIM) Utilizing computers at various stages of product development and during the manufacturing process.

Conceptual skills Managerial skills that involve the ability to consider abstract relationships.

Concurrent controls A control system that assesses progress as a product or service is developing.

Confidence One of the four Cs of motivation, a sense of sureness about a person's ability to do something.

Consideration Leader behavior that demonstrates friendship, warmth, respect, and mutual trust in the relationship with employees.

Content theories of motivation Motivation theories concerned with identifying specific internal needs that motivate individuals.

Contingency management A management theory which states that the proper way to manage any area of an organization depends on a number of different situational variables.

Contingency model of leadership effectiveness A model suggesting that the appropriate leadership style depends on the leader's personality and on how favorable the leadership situation is to the leader.

Contingency plan A type of business plan that provides managers with alternative courses of action to follow.

Continuous reinforcement In the reinforcement theory of motivation, every correct response is reinforced.

Control function The fifth basic management function that "monitors" the other four management functions—**planning, organizing, staffing,** and **leading**—to ensure their effectiveness.

Control standard—A component of the control process based on top management's strategic objectives.

Controlling A management function that focuses on determining if actions conform to expectations.

Corporate strategy A strategic management strategy that identifies the major thrust of an organization.

Cottage industry A form of production in which people work in their homes to produce goods for sale or trade.

Creative process The mental manipulation of information in new and meaningful combinations.

Creativity The bringing together of ideas, concepts, or information in new and different ways.

Critical path method (CPM) A scheduling plan that represents a project as a network with one time frame allotted to each activity.

Cs of motivation Components of motivation that provide insight into behaviors—**confidence, competence, commitment,** and **challenge.**

Current ratio A **liquidity ratio** that indicates how many times larger the value of a firm's current assets are than the amount of its current liabilities.

Customer focus Looking at a firm's products or services from the customer's point of view and striving to give customers innovative features and added value.

Data Numbers and facts, which (by themselves) are meaningless.

Decentralization An organizational condition in which lower-level employees engage in decision making.

Decision making The process of choosing among various courses of action.

Decision support system (DSS) A business information system that assists managers who need specialized types of information.

Decisional role A managerial role involving decision making.

Decoding Interpreting a message.

Defender strategy A business strategy that is feasible in a stable environment and emphasizes competition in a relatively narrow market.

Delegation The practice of empowering employees with the authority and responsibility to use organizational resources for accomplishing assigned tasks.

Delphi Technique A group decision technique in which questionnaires are mailed to collect responses and develop a consensus of opinions from experts who do not meet each other on a personal basis.

Deming circle An illustration of a continuous problem-solving cycle, in which a firm constantly analyzes its production process to maximize productivity and quality.

Deming's chain reaction Developed by W. E. Deming, an illustration of how a firm achieves success by improving the quality of its products.

Departmentalization The technique of grouping jobs and resources into departments to complete assigned goals.

Departmentalization by customer The grouping of jobs according to the customers who purchase the company's goods and services.

Departmentalization by function The grouping of employees with similar jobs into the same department.

Departmentalization by geographic location The grouping of an organization's activities based on geographic location.

Departmentalization by product The grouping of jobs according to the product being produced.

Deviation from the standard The difference between standards set by management and actual company performance.

Diagonal communication The flow of information among people at different levels and involved in different functions of an organization.

Discrimination A favorable or unfavorable action toward a person or group in the workplace.

Disparate impact An aspect of **adverse impact** that implies discrimination against a group.

Disparate treatment An aspect of **adverse impact** that is discrimination against an individual.

Dissatisfiers Part of Herzberg's theory of motivation, factors that represent potential sources of job dissatisfaction. Also called **hygiene factors.**

Disseminator An informational managerial role in which a manager tells some or all of what he or she learns from filtering information.

Disturbance handler A decisional managerial role in which a manager responds to pressures he or she does not voluntarily initiate.

Domestic-market management approach An approach to entering the international market in which a firm exports its current products to a **foreign agent** or broker.

Downward communication The flow of messages from managers to employees.

Economic forces Environmental forces that influence a firm's operating capability.

Economic order quantity (EOQ) A purchasing model that allows a manager to find the point at which holding costs and carrying costs are minimized.

Economic responsibility The responsibility of a business manager to maximize a firm's profits within the "rules of the game."

Effectiveness A management concern that refers to the initial selection of an appropriate task.

Efficiency A management concern that implies proper performance of a task.

80/20 rule An inventory rule stating that 80 percent of a firm's sales come from 20 percent of its products.

Employee orientation Leader behavior that involves the belief that the quality of the manager-employee relationship is of paramount importance and that employees should be treated with respect and encouraged to be involved in decision-making activities.

Empowerment A motivation technique that involves giving workers the knowledge, confidence, and authority to use their judgment to make decisions.

Encoding Putting an idea or thought into message form.

Energy concerns   Social responsibility issues that consist of everything from developing conservation programs to actively engaging in research to find alternative forms of energy.

Entrepreneur   A decisional managerial role in which a manager responds to changes and seeks new ways of doing things.

Environmental issues   Social responsibility issues that deal primarily with pollution of the air, water, or land.

Environmental noise   Surrounding sights and sounds that distract people who are attempting to communicate with each other.

Equal employment opportunities   Responsibility of a business to ensure that all hiring, promotional, and dismissal practices are nondiscriminatory.

Equal employment opportunity (EEO) legislation   Laws that prevent discrimination in job selection or in the performance of job duties after employees are hired.

Equity theory   A motivation theory that involves an individual's perception of fairness.

ERG theory   Clayton Alderfer's theory of human needs involving existence, relatedness, and growth needs.

Esteem needs   One category of **Maslow's human needs**, involving the improvement of self esteem and gaining of recognition from other people.

Ethics   The rules of conduct, moral principles, and values that define how individuals and organizations conduct business.

European Community (EC)   An alliance of the 12 common-market European nations as one large international market.

European Economic Community Agreement (EEC)   The agreement that eliminated all trade barriers, customs delays, and differences in national standards for products and services of the 12 common-market European nations.

Excess thought time   The gap between thinking speed and speaking rate, which gives a person time to think about various things while listening.

Existence needs   Part of the **ERG theory** of human needs, those categorized as basic necessities.

Expectancy theory   A motivation theory that involves the relationship between the desire for preferred outcomes (value) and the likelihood of attaining them (expectancy).

Expected values   In the decision-making criterion of **risk**, the sums of products of each probability multiplied by its respective value.

Expert system   A business information system which uses information to reason like knowledgeable human experts.

Extinction   In the reinforcement theory of motivation, the result of nonrecognition of previously rewarded behaviors.

Fayol's 14 principles of management   An application of **administrative management** developed by Henri Fayol that stresses principles very similar to today's management functions.

Feedback   Any type of response to a message.

Feed-forward (preliminary) controls   A control system that makes sure that necessary resources are of acceptable quality and that potential problems with the production process are anticipated.

Figurehead role   An interpersonal managerial role in which a manager represents the firm, division, or work unit at ceremonial functions.

Financial controls   A control system based on a firm's finances, including budgets and ratio analysis.

First-line manager   A person in the lowest level of management who has direct contact with nonmanagerial personnel. Also called a **supervisor.**

Fixed-interval inventory system   A method of inventory control that adds a predetermined amount of inventory at preset times.

Fixed-interval schedule   Intermittent reinforcement that occurs after a specified amount of time has expired.

Fixed-point inventory system   A method of inventory control that adds a predetermined amount of inventory when the inventory reaches a given level or point.

Fixed-position layout   A layout design that brings people, equipment, and materials to the product being manufactured or serviced because it is too large or cumbersome to move.

Fixed-ratio schedule   Intermittent reinforcement that occurs after a preselected number of correct responses.

Flat organizational structure   An organizational structure with few levels of hierarchy and many employees reporting to one manager.

Flexible manufacturing system (FMS)   A small group of computer-controlled machines that has the flexibility to produce a variety of products in small, medium, or large production runs.

Foreign agent (broker)   The recipient of products from a firm entering the international market on an export basis.

Foreign exchange rate   The value of the home country's currency in terms of another country's currency.

Formal communication   Communication between individuals in an organization about formal, work-related matters.

Formal organizational structure   An organizational structure based on the positions and functions in a company.

Functional strategy   In **strategic management,** involves courses of action for specific areas (such as, marketing or finance).

Gantt chart   Developed by Henry Gantt, a graphically illustrated bar chart showing schedules of specific activities.

Glass ceiling   Invisible, artificial barriers that limit career advancement for women and members of minority groups.

Global firm   A firm that markets its product(s) worldwide.

Global management approach   An approach to entering the international marketplace that uses wholly-owned subsidiaries and global strategic partnerships as basic methods of operations.

Global strategic partnership   A partnership that stresses worldwide leadership by developing a single-product marketing strategy that is designed to dominate its product or service area.

Goal   A result that the managers of a firm hope to achieve.

Goal setting   A motivation technique that involves making a conscious effort to achieve specified goals.

Grand strategies   Corporate strategies that identify the goals sought by a firm.

Grapevine   The informal communication system or the unofficial flow of information about people and events.

Groupthink   A reluctance on the part of group members to offer dissenting opinions.

Growth needs   An individual's needs for personal accomplishment, for learning, and for improvement. Also, part of the **ERG theory** of human needs, those that involve efforts to make creative work contributions and to develop professionally to the fullest extent possible.

Growth strategy   A corporate **grand strategy** in which a firm's management focuses on acquiring additional market shares, opening more outlets, and introducing new products.

Hawthorne Effect   Changes that result from some factor other than the factors being manipulated in a research study.

Hawthorne studies   A scientific analysis by Western Electric industrial engineers of the effects of lighting on productivity.

Horizontal communication   The lateral exchange of messages among people on the same level of authority.

Human resource controls   A control system that monitors the performance and professional development of personnel.

Hygiene factors   Part of Herzberg's theory of motivation, factors that represent potential sources of job dissatisfaction. Also called **dissatisfiers.**

Income statement   A document that indicates the amount of profit or loss that a firm has achieved over a stated period of time.

Inference   The act or process of drawing a conclusion about something unknown based on facts or indications.

Informal organizational structure   An organizational structure based on the relationship patterns that develop as a result of the interests and informal activities of members of an organization.

Information   A meaningful interpretation of **data** by decision makers.

Information-based organizations (IBOs)   A trend of innovative management that bases all pertinent decisions on massive amounts of information collected.

Information controls   A control system that monitors an employee's access to a firm's information resources.

Informational role   A managerial role involving the transmission of information.

Initiating structure   Leader behavior that involves actions taken by a leader to set goals, to structure how a job is to be performed, and to closely monitor the performance of employees.

Innovative management   A theory of management that involves employee participation and emphasizes an organization's flexibility in reacting to constant changes.

Intermediate plan   A type of business plan that covers a time frame between several months and two years.

Intermittent reinforcement   In the reinforcement theory of motivation, a schedule of partial reinforcement.

Internal forces   Environmental forces within departments or subunits of a firm that need to be coordinated with organizational objectives.

Internal motivation   An employee's feelings about a job, positive or negative, that are influenced by how meaningful the job is, the degree of accountability involved, and the amount of feedback received.

International business firm   A firm that has established any type of business relationship with entities in a foreign country.

Interpersonal role   A managerial role involving interaction with people.

Inventory turnover ratio   An **operating ratio** that indicates how many times during a given year a firm turned over or sold its average inventory.

ISO 9000   A series of comprehensive, international quality standards applied to both products and services.

Japanese management   A theory of management that uses mathematically defined flow processes and check sheets, teamwork, and participative decision making.

Job analysis   The process of identifying and recording job tasks and the human qualifications required to do them.

Job characteristics model   A model which suggests that job design should take into consideration workers' competency, their need for personal growth, and their level of satisfaction with work.

Job description A written statement that outlines the duties and responsibilities involved in performing a job.

Job design The determination of tasks to be performed; how they are to be completed; and the expectations, responsibilities, and authority associated with a particular job.

Job enlargement An increase in the number of tasks to be performed in a job.

Job enrichment An increase in the responsibility, scope, and challenge of the work performed in a way that gives workers more control over how they do their jobs.

Job instruction training (JIT) An employee training method that involves preparation of the learner, presentation of knowledge and operations, performance of the job, and follow-up by the teacher.

Job rotation The systematic movement of employees among various jobs in an organization in order to broaden their experiences. It can involve training in which a new employee is moved among a series of jobs to gain an understanding of a firm's operations.

Job satisfaction A term that refers to an employee's feeling of enjoyment or contentment toward a job.

Job specification A detailed statement of the qualifications a person must have to perform certain job duties.

Joint venture (partnership) As an international alliance, a form of ownership in which one firm purchases a minority, a majority, or an equal portion of a foreign firm.

Just-in-time (JIT) inventory system A method of inventory control that keeps minimal levels of inventory.

Key word A specific word that aids a listener in remembering parts of what a speaker says.

Law The first of three levels of **ethics** that attempts to prevent the worst known types of unethical behavior.

Leader-member relations The amount of support and loyalty a manager receives from members of a work group.

Leader position power The amount of formal authority a manager has to make decisions and give orders to employees.

Leadership The process of directing and influencing the activities and behaviors of others through communication to attain goals.

Leadership continuum A leadership model indicating several different leadership behaviors that are available to managers, ranging from a manager making decisions to a manager delegating important responsibilities to subordinates.

Leadership Grid A leadership model stating that the most effective managers have a high concern for both people and production.

Leadership role An interpersonal managerial role in which a manager is responsible for the operations of the firm, selection of personnel, training and development activities, and motivation of employees.

Leading A management function that involves providing instructions and guidance to employees.

Lecture method An employee training method that emphasizes spoken presentations.

Leverage (debt) ratio A measure of the percentage of debt financing that a firm uses to purchase its assets.

Liaison An interpersonal managerial role in which a manager initiates and maintains contacts with many persons inside and outside the firm.

Licensure agreement The granting by one firm of certain brand name rights to another firm for the purpose of entering the international market.

Line department A department that contributes directly to the accomplishment of an organization's goals.

Line organization A direct chain of command from top to bottom of an organization.

Liquidity ratio An indication of a firm's ability to pay its current debts from its current assets.

Listening Paying attention to what a speaker says and giving meaning to what is heard.

Management The effective use of human, equipment, and information resources to achieve objectives, which include making a profit, meeting customer needs, and expanding the firm's market share.

Management by walking around (MBWA) Maintenance of **organizational morale** by becoming better acquainted with employee job responsibilities and problems.

Management information system (MIS) A business information system that gives managers the necessary information for them to do their jobs.

Management science (quantitative) approach The utilization of mathematical models, simulations, statistical trend analysis, linear programming, and a whole series of computer programs for inventory control, production schedules, and "what-if" analysis.

Manager A person who guides the activities of others in order to reach organizational goals.

Manufacturing contract An agreement between a domestic company and a foreign manufacturer that allows the domestic firm to establish a local presence in the foreign country.

Maquiladora program A program that encourages U.S. firms to establish plants just across the border in Mexico for final assembly of products.

Marketing controls A control system that monitors all aspects of a firm's marketing procedures.

Maslow's hierarchy of human needs Five levels of human needs arranged in a hierarchical order; lower-order needs are fulfilled before motivation is directed toward the satisfaction of higher-order needs.

Master production schedule A scheduling plan that is derived from current and/or projected orders for the various products or services being produced.

Materials requirement planning (MRP) A method of inventory control that utilizes a computer program to ensure that proper inventory levels are maintained.

Materials requirement planning II (MRPII) A new version of **materials requirement planning (MRP)** that coordinates every aspect of the firm—including the finance, marketing, and human-resource departments—with the production process.

Matrix design The grouping of jobs in a company based on a dual focus (such as, function and product).

Mechanistic structure An organizational structure in which employees specialize; job descriptions are precise; authority and power are centralized at the top; many formal rules and policies exist; and downward communication dominates.

Middle manager A person who converts policies and strategies set forth by top management into specific operational guidelines for implementation by **first-line managers.**

Mission statement A definition of an organization's purpose, customers, products or services, markets, philosophy, and basic technology.

Modular approach An organizational structure that concentrates a company's efforts and resources on core activities in which it has special expertise and contracts required services to others.

Monitor An informational managerial role in which a manager filters information to glean pertinent facts.

Moral stance The third of three levels of **ethics** that attempts to explain how an individual responds to situations that are not covered by the **law** or by **policies, procedures,** or **rules.**

Motivation An internal process through which human wants, needs, and desires are satisfied.

Motivator factors Part of Herzberg's theory of motivation, factors that contribute to job satisfaction.

Multinational firm A firm that has made significant commitments in the international marketplace in the form of investments—either in fixed assets or in contractual agreements—that produce a significant amount of its revenues and profits.

Multinational management approach A strong commitment to the international marketplace by a firm that moves away from producing its original domestic products and starts to modify them to meet the cultural demands of foreign markets.

Nationalism Consumer support of a country's own products over competitive foreign products, even if the foreign product is better or less expensive.

Needs Unsatisfied psychological, physiological, or social deficiencies.

Negative reinforcement In the reinforcement theory of motivation, adverse consequences used to inhibit undesirable behavior.

Negotiator A decisional managerial role in which a manager strives to attain outcomes that are advantageous for the firm.

Noise Any interference with a message that hinders the sharing of meaning.

Nominal Group Technique (NGT) A decision technique in which people meet as a group to develop solutions to problems.

Nonmonetary budget A firm's allocation of resources other than cash.

Nonprogrammed decision A decision that is nonrepetitive in nature and includes nonroutine choices.

Nonverbal communication Communication made in ways other than through spoken words.

North American Free Trade Agreement (NAFTA) The agreement that eliminates all trade barriers among the United States, Canada, and Mexico over a period of time.

Off-the-job training Employee training methods that include lectures, case studies, role playing, and audiovisual techniques.

On-the-job training Employee training methods that include **job instruction training (JIT)**, job rotation, and special assignments.

Open-door policy Maintenance of **organizational morale** by inviting employees to discuss topics of interest at any time.

Open system A form of **systems management** in which an organization communicates with and reacts to outside environmental forces and adjusts accordingly.

Operating (activity) ratio A measure of how well a firm is utilizing its assets, includes inventory turnover ratio and total asset turnover ratio.

Operating budget An estimate of all the revenues and expenses that will be incurred by an organization during the up-coming year.

Operational controls A control system that assesses performances of individuals or work groups against predetermined standards.

Operational plan A type of business plan that is developed at the lowest organizational level, focuses on short-term time periods, and is narrowly defined.

Operations management A description of management techniques used during the process of producing tangible products and intangible services.

Ordinary group technique A group decision technique that involves interpersonal dialogue among group members in an unstructured setting.

Organic structure An organizational structure in which employees assume responsibility for a wide array of tasks; job descriptions are informal and general; authority is decentralized; minimal formal rules exist; and communication is encouraged both vertically and horizontally.

Organizational morale Generalized attitude of an employee group toward the company, management, or job-related factors.

Organizing A management function that involves grouping tasks, assigning authority, and allocating resources.

Overcontrol A resistance to control that occurs when management attempts to rigidly monitor business areas of relatively minor importance or when control procedures are overly detailed.

Path-goal theory of leadership A leadership theory suggesting that a manager's leadership style will motivate employees to the extent that they believe it will help them to achieve things that are valued.

People skills Managerial skills that involve the abilities to lead, motivate, and understand the feelings and behaviors of others.

Planning A management function that relates to setting goals, formulating policies, and establishing procedures.

Policies (procedures, rules, guidelines) As related to ethics, the second of three levels of **ethics** that indicates proper behavior in a large variety of circumstances.

Policy A planning component that specifies general guidelines for managerial actions.

Political forces Environmental forces that stipulate what actions are deemed legally appropriate or unacceptable.

Portfolio strategy A corporate strategy in which a corporation is viewed as consisting of multiple businesses with units that are dissimilar in nature.

Positive reinforcement In the reinforcement theory of motivation, rewards that recognize desired behaviors.

Post-action controls A control system that assesses the results after a product or service has been completed.

Prejudice An attitude toward a person or group that is based on incomplete information.

Preventive corrective action Actions taken by management to avoid negative deviations from control standards. Routine maintenance programs are examples of such actions.

Probability assessment In the expectancy theory of motivation, a measure based on perceptions of anticipated results.

Procedure A planning component that is a step-by-step sequence of events needed to implement a **policy.**

Process layout A layout design that works best for manufacturing products or offering services that require a lot of flexibility and variations.

Process management In a horizontal organization, a type of management that looks at how well the various integrated functions are working together, groups employees who possess different skills to work together as a team, and provides information directly to where it is needed.

Process planning Determining exactly how a product or service is going to be produced.

Process theories of motivation Motivation theories designed to describe and analyze how internal personal factors interact and influence each other to produce certain kinds of behavior.

Product layout A layout design that works best when standardized products are to be mass produced.

Production controls A control system that attempts to maximize efficiency and quality in the production process.

Production layout The actual physical positioning of equipment, personnel, materials, finished goods, and other organizational elements.

Production management Management techniques utilized by firms that make tangible products.

Production orientation Leader behavior that focuses attention on the tasks to be completed, develops detailed steps for performing the tasks, and closely supervises employees who are viewed primarily as tools of production.

Productivity A measure of output per worker, defined as the total output of goods and/or services divided by the total inputs needed to produce those goods and services.

Profitability ratio A measure of how efficiently a firm utilizes its assets to generate a profit.

Program evaluation and review technique (PERT) A scheduling plan that divides a project into activities and involves calculation of time estimates for its completion.

Programmed decision A decision that is routine and repetitive in nature.

Prospector strategy A business strategy that advocates an active thrust to introduce new products and seek new customers.

Protectionism A government's action to grant domestic firms a more favorable competitive position.

Psychological noise Thoughts and feelings that hinder communication while people attempt to interact.

Public responsibility The responsibility of a business manager to support public policies on major social issues.

Punishment In the reinforcement theory of motivation, penalties that tend to minimize undesirable behaviors.

Qualitative method A method of estimating product demand that is based on the judgment of people who have considerable knowledge in a particular area.

Quality A management concern that implies an anticipated level of excellence or superiority.

Quality circle A voluntary group of workers who recommend solutions to job-related problems.

Quality of the work environment A social responsibility issue that refers to how managers and employees are treated in a number of different areas, including wages and benefits, job security, and promotion opportunities.

Quantitative method A method of estimating product demand that is based on numerical data.

Quota A form of **protectionism** that limits the number of foreign products that a firm may import.

Ratio analysis In terms of financial condition, a tool that tells management how the firm compares to similar firms in the same industry.

Reactor strategy An unstable business strategy that cannot be maintained.

Recruitment The process of building a "pool" of applicants from which to choose persons for employment.

Reengineering The design and implementation of wide-ranging changes in business processes to produce breakthrough results.

Regional trading area Geographic areas without trade barriers.

Reinforcement theory A motivation theory that involves examination of the consequences of past experiences on subsequent behaviors.

Relatedness needs Part of the **ERG theory** of human needs, those that focus on interpersonal relationships.

Relationship behavior A leader's efforts to maintain open communication with employees through listening, facilitating, and being supportive.

Reliability A condition of employment testing that ensures consistency over a span of time.

Resource allocation A decisional managerial role in which a manager decides how resources are distributed.

Responsibility An obligation by an employee to perform certain duties or to make sure they are completed.

Retrenchment strategy A corporate **grand strategy** in which management reduces a firm's activities.

Return-on-investment (ROI) A profitability ratio that is derived by dividing a firm's net income or net profit (after taxes) by its total assets.

Return-on-quality (ROQ) A measure of how a new quality control program will increase a firm's return on investment.

Risk A decision-making criterion which implies that the decision maker does not know which events will occur but can determine the probabilities that these events will occur.

Robotics The use of computer-controlled robots to produce goods and perform services.

Role playing An employee training method that involves acting out roles for various types of decision-making circumstances.

Rule A planning component that is more restrictive than a **policy** or a **procedure**.

Rumor An unofficial piece of information that travels through the **grapevine** without evidence to confirm it.

Safety and security needs One category of **Maslow's human needs**; those needs concerned with an employee's right to be free of physical and economic dangers.

Safety stock The minimum amount of inventory that a firm should maintain so that it never totally runs out of products.

Scalar principle An organizational principle that suggests that a clear, step-by-step line of authority should connect every person from the top to the bottom of a company.

Scientific management Classical management school of thought that attempts to apply scientific principles to job tasks in order to make workers as efficient as possible.

Selection The process of choosing a successful job candidate from the potential employees being considered by a firm.

Self-actualization needs One category of **Maslow's human needs**; those needs that involve reaching the maximum potential for growth and fulfillment.

Self-managing work team A group of well-trained and cross-trained employees who have the specified responsibility and authority to complete a well-defined task.

Self contract A motivation technique that involves a written agreement with oneself to do certain tasks.

Semantic noise Alternative meanings for a message that hinder communication because they are different from the meaning intended by the sender.

Semantics The study of meaning.

Situational (contingency) approach Research which states that a leader should analyze a particular situation to determine the appropriate leadership style to employ.

Situational control The extent to which a leadership situation provides a manager with control and influence.

Situational leadership model A leadership model that considers the readiness level of an employee to be the critical factor in determining an appropriate leadership style for most leadership situations.

Smoke screen communication (SSC) Any message designed to obscure rather than to inform.

Social audit A way to measure the end results of a business ethics program.

Social investment Charitable donations to or the sponsorship of programs to help alleviate social problems.

Social issues in management The responsibility of business managers to scan a firm's internal and external environments so they can identify changes in social issues as early as possible.

Social needs One category of **Maslow's human needs;** the desire for affiliation with other people.

Social responsibility Actions and decisions that consider the legal, economic, and societal factors as well as organizational interests.

Social responsiveness The response of a business to public pressure by implementing social programs that can make an impact on society.

Societal forces Environmental forces that affect customer buying patterns and lifestyles.

Span of control The number of employees a manager is responsible for supervising. Also called **span of management.**

Span of management The number of employees a manager is responsible for supervising. Also called **span of control.**

Special-assignment method An employee training method in which employees are assigned nonroutine work responsibilities to gain experience and develop job/career skills.

Stability strategy A corporate **grand strategy** in which management makes an effort to preserve the status quo.

Staff department A department that provides specialized advice and assistance to members of **line departments.**

Staffing A management function that is concerned with the recruitment, selection, and training of personnel.

Stakeholder Anyone who is affected by the decisions and activities of an organization.

Statistical process control An approach to quality control that involves commitment to provision of quality goods and services and uses statistical calculations to examine variation.

Stockout Product orders that cannot be immediately filled.

Strategic business unit (SBU) In business strategy, separate operating units designed to sell distinctive products or services to identifiable consumer groups.

Strategic controls A control system that assesses the long-range plans and strategies that top management has developed and implemented.

Strategic management The process of defining an organization's mission, identifying long-term objectives, developing and implementing strategies, and monitoring results.

Strategic objective In **strategic management,** a precise objective that emphasizes outcomes to be attained.

Strategic plan A type of business plan that provides a firm with a long-term sense of direction.

Subsidy A form of **protectionism** that consists of government payments to domestic firms that are under intense foreign pressure.

Supervisor A person in the lowest level of management who has direct contact with nonmanagerial personnel. Also called a **first-line manager.**

Supporting detail A detail that confirms a speaker's main idea.

Survival needs One category of **Maslow's human needs;** those needs considered essential to life.

SWOT analysis A consideration of a company's strengths, weaknesses, opportunities, and threats that allows management to assess the firm's competitive position.

Synergy effect A result of **systems management** in which the outcomes from all subsystems working together are greater than the outcome would have been if each subsystem had worked separately.

Systems management An approach to management that attempts to look at an organization as a set of independent but interrelated subsystems that must operate in harmony.

Tactical controls A control system that monitors the performance of individual stores, divisions, or products to be sure that objectives and strategies are progressing as planned.

Tall organizational structure An organizational structure with several hierarchical levels and many managers overseeing the completion of a variety of tasks.

Tariff A form of **protectionism** in which stated fees or taxes must be paid on all imported products brought into the country.

Task behavior A leader's efforts to specifically indicate the duties and responsibilities of employees.

Task structure The extent to which a job is clearly defined and contains step-by-step procedures for success.

Taylor's principles of scientific management An application of **scientific management** developed by Frederick W. Taylor, who tried to find the "one best way" to perform each one of a worker's tasks.

Technical skills Managerial skills that relate to knowledge about the actual jobs that subordinates do.

Technological forces Environmental forces that have altered the way in which people do things in the workplace.

Theory X A theory of management that emphasizes control to ensure compliance.

Theory Y A theory of management that emphasizes employee input and delegation of authority.

Theory Z A theory of management that combines the best

management styles and techniques from successful U.S. firms with Japanese management.

Therbligs The basic hand motions of workers identified by Frank and Lillian Gilbreth.

Top management A level of management that has the overall responsibility for a firm's activities.

Total asset turnover ratio An **operating ratio** that includes how efficiently a firm is using its assets to generate a given level of sales.

Total quality management (TQM) A management approach in which managers constantly communicate with organizational stakeholders to emphasize the importance of continuous quality improvement.

Training The process of acquiring the knowledge, skills, and abilities needed to do job tasks.

Trait approach An attempt to identify key characteristics found in all successful leaders.

Transformational leadership Leader behavior in which a leader inspires and motivates followers to put aside their individual self-interests and work diligently to accomplish organizational goals.

Uncertainty A decision-making criterion which implies that the events that influence decisions and the accompanying probabilities are not known.

Upward communication The flow of messages from employees to managers.

U.S./Canadian Free Trade Agreement (FTA) The agreement that eliminated trade barriers between the United States and Canada.

Validity A condition of employment testing that ensures that tests actually measure what they say they measure.

Variable-interval schedule Intermittent reinforcement that randomly varies the amount of time that elapses between reinforcement of behaviors.

Variable-ratio schedule Intermittent reinforcement that randomly reinforces behaviors according to an average number of responses.

Vertical integration The actions of a firm to own or control a product's manufacturers, distributors, retailers, and/or marketers.

Virtual corporation A temporary combination of independent companies that are linked by information technology to allow them to share skills, reduce costs, and enter new markets.

Wholly-owned subsidiary (multinational and global) Ownership of a firm located in a foreign country.

World Trade Organization (formerly known as General Agreement on Tariffs and Trade or GATT) A set of trading rules cosigned by 117 nations (over 90% of the world's trade) that lowers trade barriers of all types.

Zero-based budgeting A budget that forces every manager to justify the necessity for and the cost of every line item.

Name Index

Company Index

The Wall Street Journal, 7–8
Wal-Mart, 4, 109, 117, 144, 163, 342
Warnaco, 250
Wedel, 395
Weinig, 169
Western Electric, 48
Weyerhauser, 145, 451
Whirlpool Corporation, 325, 392,
408, 409
Whistle blowing, 370
Will-burt Company, 236

X

Xerox Corporation, 20, 296, 369, 436,
438, 446

Y

Yamazaki Mazak Corporation, 389
YKK Zipper Plant, 58

Subject Index

A

ABC classification inventory system, 445
Accountability, 183
Accounting, 160
Achievement-oriented leadership, 261
Acid test ratio, 298
Acquired immune deficiency syndrome (AIDS), 357, 363
Activity Based Cost Management (ABC), 451
Activity ratios, 298–299
Adaptation model, 165–166
Administrative management, 43–45
Adverse impact, 216
Advocacy promotions, 367–368
Affirmative action programs (AAPS), 217, 363
African-Americans, in labor force, 25
Age discrimination, 216
Age Discrimination in Employment Act of 1967, 215
Airline industry
    competition within, 168
    deregulation and, 145
    international air traffic policy and, 117
Americans with Disabilities Act, 216
Analyzer strategies, 166
Assessment centers, 227
Audiovisual (AV) training, 236–237
Authority
    explanation of, 183
    traditional view of, 50
    types of, 45
Automobile manufacturing
    automation in, 434
    Japanese, 36–37, 325
    Saturn and, 422–423
Availability analysis, 217

B

Balance sheets, 296–297
BCG matrix, 163–164
Behavioral approach to leadership
    explanation of, 251
    Leadership Grid and, 254–256
    Ohio State leadership studies and, 251–252
    University of Michigan leadership studies and, 252

Behavioral management
    background of, 47
    conclusions about, 50
    contributors to, 48–50
Benchmarking, 437–38
Bona fide occupational qualifications (BFOQ), 216
Brainstorming, 124
Brazilians, 404
Breakeven analysis, 299–301
Breakeven point (BEP), 299–300
Bribes, 403
Budgets
    advantages and disadvantages of, 295
    explanation of, 294
    types of, 294–295
    zero-based, 295–296
Business environment, 161–162
Business strategies, 157

C

Canada, U.S. trade with, 392, 393
Canadians, cultural differences and, 404
Capital expenditure budgets, 295
Case-study method, 235
Cash-flow budgets, 294–295
Cause-related marketing, 366–368
Cellular layout, 435
Centralization, 179
Chain of command, 179–180
Challenge, 322
Chief executive officers (CEOs), 226
Child labor, 39
Civil Rights Act of 1964, 214, 215
Classical management
    administrative branch of, 43–45
    benefits and drawbacks of, 45–46
    description of, 39–40
    scientific branch of, 40–43
Closed systems, 52, 53
Combination strategies, 163
Commitment, 322
Communication. See also Miscommunication
    control process and, 288, 290–291
    cultural differences and, 56, 110, 403–405
    diagonal, 93
    downward, 86–88, 180

effective, 96–97
explanation of, 11, 71
with foreign-born employees, 81
formal, 85–86
guidelines for, 12
horizontal, 92
importance of, 12, 39, 53–54
informal, 94–96
in international marketplace, 56, 89
motivation and, 324–325, 332
nonverbal, 79–82
office design enhancing, 182
planning and, 147, 151
quality control and, 439
quality in, 93–94
smoke screen, 202
upward, 88–92, 180
Communication distortion, 187
Communication overload, 186
Communication process
    channels in, 74
    description of, 71–73
    feedback in, 75
    noise impeding, 74–75
    role of messages in, 73–74
    role of participants in, 73
Communication skills
    of CEOs, 226
    description of, 15
    of managers, 70–71
Communication styles, 259
Communicators, 14
Community support, 363
Comparative statistics, 216
Competence, 322
Comprehensive listening, 84
Computer-aided design (CAD), 430, 433
Computer-aided manufacturing (CAM), 433
Computer-integrated manufacturing (CIM), 433
Concentration statistics, 216
Conceptual skills, 16
Concurrent controls, 302
Confidence, 322
Consideration, 251–252
Contingency management, 54–55
Contingency model of leadership effectiveness, 262–265
Contingency plans, 154–155

Resource allocators, managers as, 14
Responsibility
  economic, 356–357
  explanation of, 183
  public, 357
Retrenchment strategies, 163
Return on investment (ROI), 299
Return on quality (ROQ), 438
Rewards, 334–336
Risk, as decision making condition, 119
Robotics, 433–434
Role playing, 236
Rules, 145, 368
Rumors, 95–96
Russia
  entry into international marketplace by, 394–395
  implementation of western-style management techniques in, 116
  McDonald's Restaurants in, 386

S

Safety and security needs, 327–328
Safety stock, 445
Salary, as motivational tool, 323
Savings and loan crisis, 284–285
Scalar principle, 179–181
Scheduling, 446–448
Scientific management
  principles of, 40–41
  studies in, 41–43
Security needs, 327–328
Selection
  explanation of, 223
  techniques used for, 223–227
Self-actualization needs, 329
Self-managing work teams, 272–274
Self-motivation, 338. See also Motivation
Semantic noise, 74–75
Semantics, 75
Service industry
  global competition in, 399–401
  operations management in, 426–428
  robots in, 433–434
Situational approach to leadership
  contingency model of leadership effectiveness and, 262–265
  explanation of, 256
  leadership continuum and, 256–260
  path-goal theory and, 260–262
  situational leadership model and, 265–268
Situational control, 263
Situational leadership model, 265–268
"60" Minutes, 119–120
Smoke screen communication, 202
Social audits, 375
Social investments, 363
Social needs, 328
Social responsibility
  benefits and costs of, 359–361
  explanation of, 352–353

implementation of, 367
measurement of, 361–364
opposing views on, 356–358
public opinion regarding, 353–354
types of violations related to, 354–356
Social responsiveness
  explanation of, 358
  methods to improve, 364–368
Societal forces, 22
South Africa, 146
South Koreans, cultural differences and, 404
Span of control, 186
Span of management
  explanation of, 186–187
  factors influencing, 188
Special assignment method, 235
Stability strategies, 163
Staff departments
  explanation of, 181
  human resources as, 182
  role of, 182–183
Staffing
  affirmative action and, 217
  description of, 6
  equal employment opportunity legislation and, 214–216
  explanation of, 213
  human-resource planning and, 217–219
  in international marketplace, 409–410
  in international organizations, 222
  recruitment aspects of, 219–223
  selection techniques used for, 223–227
  steps involved in, 7
Staffing model, 213–214
Stakeholders, 361–362
Statistical process control, 436–437
Strategic business units (SBUs), 164–165
Strategic controls, 303–304
Strategic management, 155
Strategic objectives, 156
Strategies
  analyzer, 166
  business, 157, 164–166, 168–170
  combination, 163
  corporate, 157, 162–164
  defender, 165–166
  development and implementation of, 157–158
  functional, 157, 170
  grand, 162–163
  growth, 163, 167
  portfolio, 163–164
  prospector, 166
  reactor, 166
  retrenchment, 163
  stability, 163
Subsidies, 402
Supervisors, 10
Suppliers
  economic strength of, 169
  social responsibility and, 364
Supporting details, 85

Supportive leadership, 260
Survival needs, 327–328
SWOT analysis
  application of, 156–157
  explanation of, 159
  identifying strengths and weaknesses for, 159–161
  recognizing opportunities and threats for, 161–162
Synergy effect, 54
System management, 51–54
System-structure view of quality, 185

T

Tactical controls, 304
Tall organizational structure, 187
Tariffs, 402
Task behavior, 266
Task structure, 263
Tax structure, 407
Technical skills, 16
Technological forces, 21
Theory X, 326–327
Theory Y, 326–327
Theory Z, 57–58
Therbligs, 41
Time and motion studies, 41
Top management, 9
Total asset turnover ratio, 299
Total quality management (TQM)
  commitment to, 265
  explanation of, 435–436
  implementation of, 437–441
  making shift to, 78
Trade agreements, 390–394
Trainers, 231
Training
  as aspect of empowerment, 339
  benefits of, 230
  to compensate for educational shortfall, 212
  cost of, 228
  diversity, 232
  evaluation of, 237–238
  explanation of, 227
  of international employees, 229–230
  off-the-job, 235–237
  on-the-job, 233–235
  as quality-improvement strategy, 236
  recognition of need for, 230–233
  types of employees receiving, 228–229
Trait approach to leadership, 250–251
Transformational leadership, 269–270
Two-factor theory of motivation (Herzberg), 331, 336

U

Uncertainty
  decision making and, 119–120
  planning for, 150
University of Michigan leadership studies, 252

Upward communication
  explanation of, 88–89
  suggestions for, 89–92
U.S./Canadian Free Trade Agreement
  (FTA), 392
Utilization analysis, 217

V

Validity, 225
Variable-interval schedules, 335, 336
Variable-ratio schedules, 335, 336
Vertical integration, 399

Virtual corporations, 200–201
Virtual factories, 433
Vision systems, 293

W

Wholly-owned subsidiary, 398–399
Women
  in labor force, 24, 25
  leadership style of, 270–271
  workplace discrimination against, 216
Workplace
  diversity in, 24–25

economic forces affecting, 21–22
internal forces affecting, 22–23
political forces affecting, 22
productivity increases by improvements
  in, 444
societal forces affecting, 22
technological forces affecting, 20–21
World Trade Association, 390

Z

Zero-based budgets, 295–296

Photo Credits